FATEFUL DECISIONS

FATEFUL DECISIONS

INSIDE THE NATIONAL SECURITY COUNCIL

EDITED, WITH INTRODUCTIONS, BY

Karl F. Inderfurth

Loch K. Johnson

New York   Oxford
OXFORD UNIVERSITY PRESS
2004

Oxford University Press

Oxford   New York
Auckland   Bangkok   Buenos Aires   Cape Town   Chennai
Dar es Salaam   Delhi   Hong Kong   Istanbul   Karachi   Kolkata
Kuala Lumpur   Madrid   Melbourne   Mexico City   Mumbai
Nairobi   São Paulo   Shanghai   Taipei   Tokyo   Toronto

Published by Oxford University Press, Inc.
198 Madison Avenue, New York, New York, 10016
http://www.oup-usa.org

Oxford is a registered trademark of Oxford University Press

Library of Congress Cataloging-in-Publication Data
Fateful decisions : inside the National Security Council / edited. with introductions, by
  Karl F. Inderfurth, Loch K. Johnson.
      p. cm.
  Includes bibliographical references and index.
  ISBN 978-0-19-515966-0
    1. National Security Council (U.S.)—History—Sources. I. Inderfurth, Karl F., 1946– II. Johnson,
Loch K., 1942–

UA23.15.F38 2003
355′.033073—dc21

                                                                        2003053585

Printed in the United States of America
on acid-free paper

FOR THOSE WHO WILL SERVE AT THE NSC,
AND FOR OUR NEXT GENERATION:
JEAN, KRISTIN, ASHLEY, AND ALISON

CONTENTS

IV THE MODERN NSC

V NATIONAL SECURITY ADVISERS: ROLES

VI NATIONAL SECURITY ADVISERS: PROFILES

VII PERFORMANCE

VIII CONTROVERSIES

IX   REFORMS

FIGURES

PREFACE

In this book, we present a selection of insightful articles, commentaries, and documents drawn from a variety of sources that shed light on the creation, evolution, and current practice of the National Security Council (NSC). Established in 1947, the NSC is the most important formal institution in the U.S. government for the making of foreign and security policy. It is to the NSC that presidents have turned in times of crisis that involve America's national security, from President Harry S. Truman during the Korean War to President George W. Bush immediately after terrorists attacked the United States on September 11, 2001.

Since the Kennedy Administration, the Council has been led by a series of national security advisers, many of whom have been prominent—and sometimes dominant—in the making of U.S. security policy. These advisers have included such well-known public figures as McGeorge Bundy under President John F. Kennedy, Henry Kissinger under President Richard M. Nixon, Brent Scowcroft under presidents Gerald R. Ford and George H.W. Bush, Zbigniew Brzezinski under President Jimmy Carter, Colin L. Powell under President Ronald Reagan, Samuel R. ("Sandy") Berger under President William J. Clinton, and Condoleezza Rice under President George W. Bush.

The centrality of the NSC to the U.S. national security decision-making process was captured in a statement made by Sandy Berger on the occasion of the Council's 50th anniversary. "As you turn to the pages of the last fifty years of American foreign policy," he observed, "from the Korean War to the Cuban missile crisis, from the opening to China to Camp David, the Helsinki Final Act to the Madrid NATO enlargement summit, Desert Storm to the Dayton Accords, the NSC has been at the heart of debate, decision and action" (White House Press Release, October 31, 1997). Moreover, with the end of the Cold War in 1991, the responsibilities of the NSC have broadened into less traditional national security realms, reflecting the more complicated, and in some ways more dangerous, world in which we live. Not only has there been far greater attention given to the global economy, but to new kinds of national security issues as well, among them the risks of international pandemics like HIV/AIDS; worldwide environmental threats; the proliferation of weapons of mass destruction, and the technologies that allow their production; transnational criminal activities; and—most poignantly since the tragic attacks against the World Trade Center and the Pentagon—international terrorism.

It is said that imitation is the highest form of flattery. On that score, the National Security Council as an institution should feel very flattered indeed. When President Clinton took office in 1993, he was determined (in his words) "to elevate economics in foreign policy." This was to be the international equivalent of his presidential campaign mantra, "It's the economy, stupid." During the first week of his administration, Clinton signed an executive order creating a National Economic Council. The NSC was the model. In his initial organizational response to the September 11 attacks, President George W. Bush established a new Homeland Security Council "responsible for advising and assisting the President with respect to all aspects of homeland security." Again, the NSC was the model. Overseas, several nations have drawn on the American experience, establishing their own version of an NSC or the position of national security adviser. These nations include Russia, India, Georgia, and Afghanistan in the post-Taliban era.

Yet, despite its significance and increasing prominence over the years, the National Security Council has been subject only to limited scholarly scrutiny, in part because its deliberations are largely concealed from outside observers. There are signs, however, that this relative lack of attention is beginning to change. In recent years, several books and articles have appeared on the NSC and, most importantly, the Center for International Security Studies at the University of Maryland and the Brookings Institution in Washington have undertaken "The National Security Council Project" (see the For Further Reading section at the end of this volume). Alongside these efforts, we hope this collection of readings and our interpretive introductions will lead to a greater understanding and appreciation of the Council's role in America's government and in world affairs.

ORIGINS AND DEVELOPMENT OF THE NSC

"There is hereby established a council to be known as the National Security Council," the National Security Act of 1947 states simply enough. The statute continues: "The function of the Council shall be to advise the President with respect to the integration of domestic, foreign, and military policies relating to the national security so as to enable the military services and the other departments and agencies of the government to cooperate more effectively in matters involving the national security. The Council shall have a staff to be headed by a civilian executive secretary who shall be appointed by the President . . ."

The NSC would soon come to deal with the most critical threats facing the United States from abroad. Over the years, its members and staff would find on their agenda such topics as how to handle the existence of Soviet nuclear missiles in Cuba (1962); how to resist the collapse of South Vietnam to communism (1964–73); whether, and in what manner, to support the so-called "freedom fighters" (*contras*) in Nicaragua (1982–87); how to respond to the fall of the Soviet empire (1989–91); whether to enter into conflict in the Balkans (1992–99); and how to fight against a rising tide of international terrorism and, with the September 11, 2001, attacks, the most deadly assault on America since Pearl Harbor. These are just a few of the challenges to come before the Council, not to mention a myriad of other considerations in the wake of the Cold War's end. The NSC as a group does not make decisions; that is the lonely responsibility of its top member, the president. Nevertheless, it is a place where fateful decisions are deliberated and where key advisers are expected to offer their guidance to the chief executive.

The National Security Council has had a select and powerful membership. Only four individuals are statutory members: the president, the vice president, the secretary of state, and the secretary of defense. Augmenting this small group are two statutory advisers—the director of central intelligence (DCI, who also serves as the director of the Central Intelligence Agency, or CIA) and the chair of the Joint Chiefs of Staff (JCS)—as well as the assistant for national security affairs, who serves as the day-to-day coordinator of the NSC. Obviously, these individuals are significant players in the creation and management of American foreign policy. Any serious student of government must understand the workings of this exclusive institution to comprehend how the United States decides the great questions of war and peace.

From the sparse language of the National Security Act, few could have anticipated in 1947 how important its executive secretary—known officially since 1953 as the assistant to the president for national security affairs, or, less formally since the Kennedy Administration, the national security adviser—would become in the high decision councils of America's government. The evolution of the NSC adviser to a position of great influence, the policies and personalities of the individuals who have left a mark on the Council, and the consequences of the adviser's prominence are among the subjects addressed in this book.

CONTROVERSY OVER THE NSC

The NSC has had its share of controversies over the years, especially during the Reagan Administration when legislative investigators on the Inouye–Hamilton Committee (chaired by Senator Daniel Inouye [D–Hawaii] and Representative Lee H. Hamilton [D–Indiana]), as well as a special prosecutor, probed allegations that surfaced in 1986 that the Council's staff had entered into covert operations abroad, straying far beyond its original mandate to "advise" and "coordinate." Specifically, the Congress discovered that the NSC staff had participated—more, played a leading role—in the covert sale of arms to Iran in exchange for U.S. hostages, followed by the siphoning of these profits through a secret Swiss bank account to support the *contras* in Nicaragua. All of these events transpired without the knowledge of lawmakers. The secret operations violated statutory prohibitions regarding the sale of weapons to terrorist groups and the shipment of funds to the *contras*. Statutes that required advance reports to Congress before the implementation of covert actions were also ignored. This book helps illuminate how the NSC staff became an operations group deeply involved in the *conduct* of foreign policy, not simply its coordination.

Well before the Iran-*contra* scandal, the NSC had attracted strong criticism from time to time. The office of the national security adviser created a new rival to the secretaries of state and defense—the traditional chieftains of foreign and security policy. Since the days of the Kennedy Administration, critics have contended that the adviser and the NSC staff have gone far beyond their intended role of coordinator and facilitator of the foreign policy process to that of policy initiator and advocate. This emphasis on policy entrepreneurship, argue the critics, has undermined the ability of the security adviser to serve as an "honest broker" among competing department interests and has led to the neglect of the adviser's managerial responsibilities. Further (so runs the argument), a prominent, public role for the adviser—Kissinger and Brzezinski come to mind—can seriously damage American foreign policy by creating confusion at home and abroad about who speaks for the United States on behalf of the president: the secretary of state or the national security adviser.

During the Carter years, this confusion was often manifest. The president was inexperienced in foreign affairs. Brzezinski proved to be outspoken and aggressive as a policy advocate, while Secretary of State Cyrus Vance took a more reticent, low-key approach devoid of salesmanship. Brzezinski's hardline attitude toward the Soviet Union and Vance's interest in renewed *détente* placed further strains on the ties between the NSC staff and the Department of State. In recent years, the tension between the two offices has flared again, albeit not as publicly as between Brzezinski and Vance, as was the case between President Reagan's secretary of state, George Shultz, and national security advisers Robert McFarlane and Admiral John Poindexter. During President Clinton's second term, reports of friction surfaced between Secretary of State

Madeleine Albright and national security adviser Sandy Berger. One report indicated that Albright had been "effectively eclipsed in foreign affairs" by Berger (Perlez 1999: A1). Not so recalled Albright in her memoirs (Albright 2003, see For Further Reading):

> Notwithstanding the occasional gripes, Sandy and I knew that, whatever happened, we were going to sink or swim together. Neither of us would emerge a hero if our foreign policy flopped. We both felt an obligation to submerge any personal irritations and work together.

The media also raised similar questions about the relationship between national security adviser Condoleezza Rice and Secretary of State Colin L. Powell during the early months of the second Bush Administration. A September 10, 2001, cover of *Time* magazine pictured the secretary of state above the caption: "Where Have You Gone, Colin Powell?" The implication was that, once again, a secretary of state was being edged out as the president's top foreign policy counselor. Was Rice or perhaps Secretary of Defense Donald H. Rumsfeld displacing the secretary of state? Probably not, given the stature that Powell brought to the Bush Administration and the Department of State. Without doubt, though, the national security adviser enjoyed strong ties to the president. "She is clearly a person with a close personal relationship with the president—that's not always the case with national security advisers," Zbigniew Brzezinski observed to the *New York Times* (Perlez, 2001: 6). "Some have had close relations with the president, but even more have not." The terrorist attacks against the United States—the day after the *Time* magazine cover appeared—rallied the Bush national security leaders into more of a cohesive team, and the reports of Powell losing influence to Rice or others in the administration disappeared, at least for a while.

In light of these and other important issues surrounding the NSC, this book seeks to provide insights into a series of vital questions:

- How effectively has the National Security Council fulfilled its original mandate to "advise the President with respect to the integration of domestic, foreign and military policies"?
- What has led to the rise in prominence of the national security adviser, including McGeorge Bundy, Henry Kissinger, Zbigniew Brzezinski, Sandy Berger, and Condoleezza Rice?
- What have been the consequences of this rise for the management of U.S. national security policy?
- How did the NSC staff come to be engaged in operational activities during the Iran-*contra* affair in the 1980s, and what steps have been instituted to prevent a reoccurrence of this misuse of power?
- How well has the NSC faced such challenges to the security of the United States and its allies as the Cuban missile crisis, war in the Persian Gulf, conflict in the Balkans, and the struggle against global terrorism?
- How has the end of the Cold War and the fall of the Soviet Union affected the role of the National Security Council in the making of foreign and security policy?
- What changes have taken place (or should) in the NSC as a result of the transformation of world affairs from bipolarity to U.S. preeminence?
- What is the proper role today for the NSC, its adviser, and the staff in meeting the new challenges and threats facing the United States in the twenty-first century, such as the war against global terrorism?

ORGANIZATION OF THE BOOK

This book is organized into nine parts. Each is preceded by an editors' introduction to provide context and continuity throughout the volume. In Part I, entitled "Origins," we begin with a scholarly article that provides background for understanding why the Truman Administration established a National Security Council. Written by Professor Ernest R. May, this opening piece is accompanied by the Eberstadt Report—the basic document from which the Council evolved. We include, too, excerpts from the legislative debate over the National Security Act of 1947 and the key passages from that relating to the NSC. The legislative floor debate clearly reveals that most participants viewed the Council as a strictly limited coordinating or advisory committee. Some lawmakers were prescient enough to warn that the panel could become a danger to democracy if its functions strayed beyond a limited advisory capacity—proven true during the Iran-*contra* scandal of 1987. This portion of the book traces how the idea for an NSC arose from the nation's wartime experience, during which it became clear that a forum was needed in which U.S. military and foreign policies could be connected.

Part II, entitled "Early Years," provides a sense of how the NSC carried out its assignments during the Truman and Eisenhower administrations. As America's involvement in world affairs deepened, so did the responsibilities of the national security adviser. By the time John F. Kennedy came into White House in 1961, conditions were ripe for a much more expansive interpretation of the NSC's role than had been foreshadowed by the narrow language of the 1947 Act.

Parts III and IV of the book, "Transformation" and "The Modern NSC," trace this growing reliance on the NSC from Kennedy through George W. Bush. Taken together, these sections offer a review of over half a century of experience with the Council. The articles suggest that it has performed several major functions. Among the most important has been its use, in various configurations, as a forum at the highest level of government for the discussion of foreign and security challenges. With the rise to prominence of the national security adviser and the NSC staff, it has had even greater value as a source of in-house foreign policy counsel for the president. The selections also illustrate how a president's personality and style of decision making mold the ways in which the NSC is used. The Council is a creature of the president, reflecting the desires and needs of the chief executive. A central point emerges from these readings: The transformation of the NSC into the vital institution it is today is an evolution that must be traced not so much in law, but rather in the preferences and practices of the individuals elected to the presidency.

Parts V and VI examine the "Roles" and "Profiles" of national security advisers. The intention is to illustrate the different "hats" worn by the advisers since 1961, including staff aide, protector of the president's interests, planner, negotiator, neutral policy manager or "honest broker," entrepreneur, and policy advocate. The profiles include sketches of six of the most prominent individuals who have held the adviser position since the Kennedy years (from the total of fourteen who served in this capacity during this time period).

As these selections disclose, a wide variety of personalities have served as NSC adviser: Harvard University dean McGeorge Bundy, with his "mini-State Department" operation inside the Council; former Harvard professor Henry Kissinger, the master of secret diplomatic negotiations who, along with President Nixon, took the NSC to a new pinnacle of power, only to reduce it later (when Kissinger gave up the office to focus exclusively on his secretary of state duties); Zbigniew Brzezinski, another prominent academic and, like Kissinger, a policy advocate and dazzling—if contentious—global strategist; Air Force General Brent Scowcroft, who stayed well in the background as the Council's adviser when Kissinger was secretary of state but who became substantially more active in the same job (and the only person to hold the office under two presidents) a dozen years later in the service of President George H.W. Bush; Sandy Berger, a Washington, D.C.-based international trade lawyer, former government official, and political activist, with longstanding ties to President Clinton; and the current adviser, Condoleezza Rice, yet another academic (with credentials in Russian studies) and practitioner (on the NSC staff under the first President Bush) and the only woman—so far—to serve in this capacity.

The first six parts of this volume examine the sources of power and authority for the NSC, along with its evolution since 1947 and key personalities who have shaped its history. With Part VII, entitled "Performance," we look at the Council at work during different administrations. What kinds of decisions has it addressed? How has it operated and who has participated in its deliberations? How influential has it been? Above all, what have been the consequences of having a National Security Council? The case studies we present include selections about the Cuban missile crisis during the Kennedy Administration; the efforts of the first Bush Administration to cope with the fragmented world that arose in the aftermath of the Cold War, including the threat of outlaw nations like Iraq to international peace; America's response to fighting in the Balkans during the Clinton Administration; and the initial responses of the second Bush Administration to the September 11, 2001, attacks on the United States—the beginning of a dramatic new chapter in the war against terrorism.

Critics of the NSC have been wary of its central, and largely secret, role in foreign policy. They argue that the institution has become too prominent and powerful, and often at odds with other departments and agencies within the executive branch responsible for foreign and defense policies—especially the Department of State. Part VIII, "Controversies," explores the tensions that have developed between the national security adviser and other parts of the government. Some of the criticisms are rooted in policy disagreements, some in bureaucratic politics. At times critics have simply distrusted or disliked the adviser. Two concerns are given special attention in this section: first, the institutional tension between the Council and the Department of State, which, critics contend, has often resulted in State being reduced to a Department of Routine Affairs while the White House shaped and often ran foreign policy; and, second, the entry of the NSC during the Reagan years into foreign policy operations of questionable legality and propriety, with little or no consultation with cabinet officers or the Congress—the NSC staff as rogue elephant, out of control.

The purpose of the last section, "Reforms," is to present a range of proposals offered by leading scholars, practitioners, and blue-ribbon commissions to improve the NSC system (which includes the Council itself, the various committees and subcommittees that support the Council, the national security adviser, and the NSC staff). Here is a normative finale meant to stimulate thought about how to bring the NSC closer to fulfilling its original mandate of providing timely and unbiased advice to the president and other policymakers as they make the fateful decisions that determine the safety and well-being of the American people in a dangerous world.

ACKNOWLEDGMENTS

We are grateful to the authors and publishers of the selections presented in this book for allowing us to reprint their work, and for the encouragement, support, and guidance of Peter M.

Labella, Celeste Alexander, Terry Deal Michelet, and Sean Mahoney at Oxford University Press. For outstanding copyediting, we thank Natalie Goldstein. For their research assistance, we also thank Joshua Caster and Emily Waechter, students at the Elliott School of International Affairs at George Washington University; Ashley Inderfurth, a student at Bowdoin College; and Stacey Gibson-Mitchell, Sophia Qureshi, and Eamon Walsh, students in the new School of Public and International Affairs at the University of Georgia. We are pleased to thank as well Dr. Gordhan H. Patel, Vice President for Research at the University of Georgia, for his indispensable support. Finally, we offer our professional and personal appreciation to Leena Johnson for her editorial guidance and to Merrie Inderfurth for introducing one of the editors to the benefits and pleasures of "logging on."

Karl F. Inderfurth
Loch K. Johnson

PART I

ORIGINS

One of the most compelling lessons of the recent war is that there are imperfections and gaps in the relationships between the military and foreign policies of this country.

—Senator Wayne Morse (D–Oregon)
July 9, 1947

EDITORS' INTRODUCTION

By 1947, the National Security Council (NSC), the first high-level committee to coordinate U.S. military and foreign policies, was an idea whose time had come. It had arrived at glacial speed. Calls for the creation of an NSC came, in part, as a result of complaints about President Franklin D. Roosevelt's sometimes chaotic, ad hoc management style for guiding the war effort. Ironically, Roosevelt, as acting secretary of the navy twenty-six years earlier, had written a letter to then Secretary of State Charles Evans Hughes proposing a "Joint Plan Making Body" to better coordinate political and military affairs. That proposal never reached the secretary's desk; it was misdirected to another office within the State Department and filed away, unanswered.

In the first article included in this reader, Ernest R. May traces the long and somewhat tortured path of "The Development of Political-Military Consultation in the United States," a path that eventually led to the creation of the NSC. At the turn of the century, according to May, the United States had no effective coordination of the nation's foreign and military policies and certainly no high-level body to advise the president on these matters. That job was up to the president. As May relates:

> As a rule, in fact, diplomatic and military recommendations reached the White House separately, and the relationships between political aims and military capabilities had to be gauged, if at all, by the President. Although this rule-of-thumb system would work for a strategy-minded President like Theodore Roosevelt, it displayed its failings even in his time.

At the beginning of the First World War, the first tentative steps were taken to address this deficiency, and an advisory interdepartmental committee—the Joint State-Navy Neutrality Board—was established in 1919. High officials displayed minimal interest, however, in the creation of a formal coordinating entity and, according to May, "long years of isolated safety [for the United States] smothered the idea of political-military collaboration."

The concept of improved coordination was revived, though, as a second world war began to threaten. Secretary of State Cordell Hull took the lead in proposing a coordinating committee made up of representatives from the state, war, and navy departments, and President Roosevelt approved. "Thus was formed," writes May, "the first American agency for regular political-

1

military consultation on foreign policy." Still, that agency, known as the Standing Liaison Committee, was only what its name implied, a means for liaison. It facilitated the flow of information among the departments but had little policy influence and certainly no direct impact—or even contact—with the president. The committee was disbanded in 1943. Two years later, however, another committee was established, and this one set the stage for the NSC.

The State–War–Navy Coordinating Committee (SWNCC) was set up in 1945 at the instigation of War Department Secretary Henry L. Stimson and Navy Secretary James F. Forrestal. It achieved what no other committee had before, providing a forum in which important policy issues could be thrashed out, albeit just among officials of the assistant secretary rank. "This Coordinating Committee," writes May, "prepared the plans for occupying Germany, Austria, and Japan, and pondered in addition, many other questions of post-war policy." But preparing plans and pondering high policy, to use May's alliteration, is distinct from *making* that policy. This authority went well beyond the reach of the SWNCC.

For all intents and purposes, America's war effort was coordinated by one man, President Roosevelt, whose administrative style can best be described as competitive chaos. Rather than relying on formal committees to wed foreign policy and military considerations, he did that himself, with the assistance of a few key advisers like Harry Hopkins and James F. Byrnes. He used the military service chiefs, organized into the Joint Chiefs of Staff, to convey and implement his policies, usually after close consultation in person or by letter with British Prime Minister Winston S. Churchill. Despite these ad hoc arrangements, which usually excluded not only the Department of State but even the secretary of state, the United States achieved its wartime objective: the Axis powers were defeated. But the president's operating style brought complaints from those who had been excluded from policy considerations, or from those, like many members of Congress, who felt that the president's approach was designed—at least in part—to keep them in the dark. So, as the war came to an end, recognition grew that a more formally structured process for the consideration of foreign and military policies was needed. If the United States were to fulfill its new-found responsibilities as a leading world power, changes would have to be made in the way decisions were made at the highest levels of government.

A chief proponent of this view was the new president, Harry S. Truman, who assumed office following Roosevelt's death in April 1945. Truman would later write in his memoirs that he was influenced in this view by his experience working at the Potsdam Conference with the NSC's immediate predecessor, the SWNCC. "At Potsdam I had been impressed with the cooperation between our State, Army and Navy Departments," remembered Truman (*Memoirs* 1956: 49). "Through a coordinating committee they had worked out a way of tackling common practices without the usual jurisdictional conflicts."

So, at war's end, the stage was set for the creation of the National Security Council. The establishment of the NSC took a backseat, however, to a larger bureaucratic battle in Washington: the effort to join the powerful Departments of War (Army) and Navy into a single, civilian-led Department of Defense. President Truman was determined that this fight should not interfere with his decision to see a political-military advisory committee established. "As plans were being drawn up for the unification of the military services, I insisted that policy unification be provided at the same time," Truman later recalled (*Memoirs* 1956: 50). "I wanted one top level permanent setup in the Government to concern itself with advising the president on high policy decisions concerning the security of the nation."

Truman, though, was of two minds about the establishment of the NSC. He favored a panel to advise him on the integration of foreign and military policies, but he was strongly opposed to the creation of any formal entity that might undercut his authority as president. As one means of protecting his presidential prerogatives, Truman initially recommended that the Council exclude the president as one of its members. This would avoid the trap, according to Alfred D. Sander (1972: 377; see For Further Reading), "of setting up an advisory committee whose advice could not be refused by the President because he had been part of the decision-making process." Truman later reconsidered and approved the president's inclusion on the Council as its chair; but, once the NSC was set up, he made it abundantly cleat that the Council was there to advise him, not make policy.

Another key player in the Council's birth was the Secretary of the Navy James F. Forrestal, often described as a consummate operator in the bureaucratic mazes of Washington. Forrestal was one of the chief, and most vociferous, opponents of military unification, believing that in a combined Department of Defense, the army would dominate and the interests of the navy would suffer. Navy supporters in Congress, notably the powerful Chairman of the Senate Naval Affairs Committee, Senator David Walsh (D–Massachusetts), urged Forrestal, though, to temper his opposition with an alternative plan of his own. They suggested he consider backing a high-level planning and coordination agency as a substitute for the consolidation of the War and Navy departments. This suggestion set in motion a study, prepared for Forrestal by his close friend and associate, Ferdinand Eberstadt, that would become the blueprint for the NSC.

Excerpts from the Eberstadt Report, entitled "Unification of the War and Navy Departments and Postwar Organization for National Security," are included as the second article in this section. Forrestal initiated the study in a letter to Eberstadt dated July 19, 1945. He asked the former wartime official to respond to three questions, the third of which presaged the NSC: "What form of postwar organization should be established to enable the military services and other Government departments and agencies most effectively to provide for and protect our national security?"

Eberstadt's reply—a three-volume, 250-page report—arrived three months later. He first addressed the issue of military unification: "We do not believe that under present conditions unification of the Army and Navy under a single head would improve our national security." Then, Eberstadt responded to Forrestal's third question: "To afford a permanent vehicle for maintaining active, close and continuous contact between the departments and agencies of our Government responsible, respectively, for our foreign and military policies and their implementation, we recommend the establishment of a National Security Council."

The NSC, Eberstadt continued, "would be the keystone of our organizational structure for national security," and it should be designed to serve as "a policy forming and advisory, not executive, body." Its membership would include the secretaries of state, war, navy, and air (another of Eberstadt's recommendations was the creation of an independent Department of the Air Force), with the president as Council chair. The NSC would be assisted by a permanent staff and headed by a full-time executive secretary (later to emerge as the president's national security adviser), who would prepare the Council agenda, provide information for its deliberations, and distribute its conclusions to the various departments and agencies. Eberstadt further urged the establishment by law, for the first time in the nation's history, of a Central Intelligence Agency (CIA), to be subordinate to the NSC and responsible to it. "[The CIA's] product," said Eberstadt, "is an important part of the grist of the Council's mill."

Not surprisingly, given that Eberstadt's recommendations were consistent with his own views, Forrestal endorsed the Eberstadt Report. Indeed, its recommendations concerning the NSC soon became known as "Forrestal's revenge." Although the navy secretary was ultimately unsuccessful in blocking the unification of the military services, many of Eberstadt's proposals for the NSC were enacted into law in 1947. This represented at least a modest victory for Forrestal, who wanted to ensure that in the postwar era, the military services—in this case, the navy—were represented in the premier policy councils of the government. He was less successful, however, in his major tactic, which, according to Sander, was "to try to capture the president to get decisions made collectively in his presence." Harry Truman had other ideas about how the Council would be run and, just three months after Eberstadt's Report was completed, the president sent Congress a message containing his own proposals for coordinating national security.

The president's message was sent to Capitol Hill on December 19, 1945, and much to the distress of those opposing unification, Truman called for the establishment of a single department of national defense. But he did not recommend the creation of a National Security Council, apparently believing that the Eberstadt Report failed to make it sufficiently clear that the NSC was to be an advisory body with no policy-formulating or decision-making authority independent of the president. Later, Truman would reverse his position on the need for an NSC, and he reverted to his stated intention of establishing such a panel—but only after Forrestal and Secretary of War Robert Patterson worked out many of their differences concerning military unification and together endorsed an *advisory* NSC (they called it a "Council on Common Defense") to "integrate out foreign and military policies and . . . enable the military services and other agencies of the government to cooperate more effectively in matters involving our national security."

Throughout this embryonic period, an important institutional player remained conspicuously absent in the various attempts to influence the future direction and composition of the NSC, namely, the State Department. This is particularly curious in light of the subsequent history of NSC–State rivalry (see Part VIII) and the battles that would later be fought between the president's national security adviser and the secretary of state. Sander noted (1972, 380) how the then secretary of state, George C. Marshall, was largely disengaged from the NSC debate:

> In view of Secretary Marshall's realization that the Council would be primarily concerned with foreign policy, the State Department's failure to participate more actively in the negotiations leading to its establishment is surprising . . . Nor does it seem they gave any real thought as to how the State Department would function in relation to it, or the scope of the problems it would consider. The most logical explanation may be that they considered the whole unification bill an interservice squabble which did not really concern them.

Disengagement was not, however, the stance of another participant in the establishment of the NSC, the Congress. Excerpts from the congressional debate are included in this section to reveal legislative views on the National Security Act as it wended its way toward final passage. Some congressional initiatives were clearly unpopular with both the executive branch and many members of Congress, as was the case with one proposal offered by Representative Thomas Owens (R–Illinois) on July 19, 1947.

MR. OWENS   Inasmuch as this is a new law which might require action by Congress at some future date, would there be any objection to a provision therein which would require that the Council immediately give a copy of its recommendations and reports to the Speaker of the House and the President [of the Senate] as well as the President?

MR. JAMES WADSWORTH   (R–New York): Does the gentleman refer to the Security Council?

MR. OWENS   Yes.

MR. WADSWORTH   Does the gentleman mean that the Security Council shall report upon all its findings and recommendations directly to the Congress?

MR. OWENS   Yes.

MR. WADSWORTH   If you do that, then you will be reporting to the entire world.

Another and related proposal with little support, which would have fundamentally altered the role of the Council and executive-legislative relations, was suggested not by a member of Congress but Navy Secretary Forrestal. In testimony prepared for his appearance before the Senate Armed Services Committee on the bill establishing the NSC, Forrestal included this recommendation: that "the Chairman of the Foreign Affairs Committees or of other Congressional Committees . . . . might, at appropriate times, sit with the National Security Council." According to Sander (1972, 381), "Navy strategists apparently began to feel that if they could get Congress involved in the Council they could better ensure adequate financial support and provide a counterbalance to presidential attempts to enforce a ceiling on their budgets." The White House strenuously objected to this portion of Forrestal's prepared statement, and it was deleted.

Several portions of the bill, however, reveal that Congress did have a significant influence on the shaping of the NSC. The Senate, for example, was insistent that the president be a member of the Council and chair its meetings when he attended. The upper chamber also overcame House objections that would have stripped the president of the power to appoint additional members to the Council. The House, meanwhile, got its way on some provisions. It was responsible for ensuring that the Council's staff would be directed by an executive secretary and not, as the Senate had wanted, by the soon-to-be established secretary of defense. Throughout their consideration of the National Security Act, many members of Congress expressed concern about the possible excessive influence of the military on the NSC.

At one point, the Senate even considered making the secretary of defense the chairman of the Council. This idea was eventually dropped, but the final membership of the NSC as approved by Congress did include four members—of a total of seven—with defense affiliations: the secretary of defense, along with the secretaries of the army, navy, and air force. This arrangement was subsequently changed by amendments to the National Security Act approved by law in 1949. These changes eliminated the three military service secretaries, added the vice-president, and made the chairman of the Joint Chiefs of Staff "the principal military adviser to the President." The actual statutory *members* of the NSC thus stood at four: the president, the vice-president, and secretaries of state and defense, with the chairman of the Joint Chiefs as the key military adviser. Later, the director of Central Intelligence (DCI) would join as a second statutory adviser.

The excerpts of the congressional debate included in this section make it clear that both the House and the Senate saw the NSC as a coordinating committee that was long overdue and whose job it would be to advise and assist the president in the integration of the nation's foreign and military policies. During the debate, some members touched on issues that would receive much more attention when the NSC reached maturity in later years. A prescient Senator Leverett Saltonstall (R–Massachusetts) worried about the potential power of the NSC.

MR. SALTONSTALL   The Senator was discussing the national Security Council and its importance. Does the Senator agree with me when I say that the purpose of creating the National Security Council is not to set up a new function of government with extraordinary powers, but solely to provide an organization to give advice to the President?

MR. RAYMOND BALDWIN   (R–Connecticut): I agree wholeheartedly.

The role of the official who would have the responsibility for directing the Council's work also drew the attention of legislators. "The National Executive [Security] Council is to have but one executive officer, the Executive Director," offered Senator Wadsworth, who went on to describe the position as "office manager"—not exactly what comes to mind when one thinks of such latter-day holders of this position as Henry Kissinger, Zbigniew Brzezinski, Sandy Berger, or Condoleezza Rice.

On July 26, 1947, the Republican-controlled Congress passed the National Security Act, and President Truman, a Democrat, signed it into law. Those portions of the act relating to the NSC are included as the final selection in this part. After eighteen months of executive-legislative maneuvering, and many more years of fitful starts, a high-level coordinating committee for the integration of the nation's security policies had been realized.

THE DEVELOPMENT OF POLITICAL-MILITARY CONSULTATION IN THE UNITED STATES

Ernest R. May

This selection traces the origins of the National Security Council as a cabinet-level coordinating agency for security policy.

In the Cabinet room of the White House, every Thursday morning, the National Security Council gathers around a long, massive table. On the table are printed briefs reviewing some problem of national policy. Prepared by the Council staff, these briefs blend the views of many departments and agencies, but in Council discussions the members and advisers rehearse these views once again. The Secretary of State and others suggest desirable solutions to the policy problem, while the Secretary of Defense and the Chairman of the Joint Chiefs of Staff describe the military risks entailed in each alternative course of action. The President then reaches his decision, and the United States may acquire a new foreign policy or perhaps a new shading for an old policy.

Nearly all Americans agree on the need for this National Security Council. Everyone realizes that American policy has outgrown the Cabinet, just as the atom has outgrown the college laboratory. Where, fifty years ago, Secretary of State Elihu Root could disregard reports of a crisis in the Middle East, cabling the American envoy, "Continue quarrels with missionaries as usual,"[1] a similar crisis today would call out instructions to diplomats all over the world, orders to military and naval commanders, anxious discussions in Washington, and an earnest session of the National Security Council. Living in a world as sensitive as a can of nitroglycerin, Americans accept the need for exact

weighing of political and military factors before each policy decision.

The nation has acknowledged this need, however, for only a short time. Not before the 1940's would the majority of Americans have endorsed the rationale that underlies the National Security Council. Yet this rationale now seems self-evident: military forces are the rooks and bishops behind the knights and pawns of diplomacy; although the rooks and bishops move less frequently, their role in the game is no less decisive. Before the executors of foreign policy can decide what the nation ought to do, they must learn from political and military experts what the nation is able to do. They must lay objectives alongside capabilities, in the same way that business men compare the blueprints of design engineers with the estimates of cost accountants. In making foreign policy, in other words, ends must be measured against means.

Although this rationale won acceptance only recently, it is not new, even in the United States. Nowhere, in fact, is it more vigorously summarized than in Number 23 of the *Federalist Papers,* written by Alexander Hamilton. But long years of isolated safety smothered the idea of political-military collaboration. It found no new spokesman until Captain Mahan began to preach, late in the nineteenth century. Even then, the idea was not translated into action until after the conquest of the Philippines, when a few Americans, look-

---

Reprinted with permission from Ernest R. May, "The Development of Political-Military Consultation in the United States," *Political Science Quarterly* 70 (June 1955): 161–180.

Ernest R. May is professor of history, John F. Kennedy School of Government, Harvard University.

ing across six thousand miles of water at their new colony, began to believe that the United States had grafted to itself an Achilles heel. They perceived that the safety of this faraway member could not, like the safety of the homeland, be entrusted to Providence.

Realizing the need for hard, far-sighted planning, this handful of Americans also realized their lack of any planning instruments. The State Department, as Tyler Dennett characterizes it in his life of John Hay, was an "antiquated, feeble organization, enslaved by precedents and routine inherited from another century, remote from the public gaze and indifferent to it. The typewriter was viewed as a necessary evil and the telephone as an instrument of last resort."[2] Although the Army and Navy had professionals, while the State Department had none, the armed services were still no better outfitted for strategy-planning than the State Department for policy-planning. Before the Army and Navy could produce coherent advice, they had to nurture brains or general staff organizations, and such brains developed slowly. The Army's General Staff, for instance, was "only just growing to man's estate" fifteen years after its founding, according to the 1918 report of its Chief of Staff.[3] This General Staff and the Navy General Board faced, in addition, the problem of welding Army and Navy differences, so that military advice on policy could be based on estimates of the total military power of the United States. Until a Joint Board of the Army and Navy and the State Department, too, perfected their internal workings, the coordination of strategy and policy could only be haphazard.

During the first two decades after the War with Spain, as a result, consultation among the State, War, and Navy Departments took the antique form of correspondence among the three secretaries. The Navy Secretary, advised by his General Board, would write to the Secretary of State, proposing acquisition of a certain naval base on foreign soil. After referring the proposal to such experts as he could collect, the Secretary of State would return his judgment, either killing the idea or pushing it up for final decision by the President.[4]

Like sophomore letters home, these begging communications from the Secretary of the Navy sometimes hinted casually at subjects under study. The Navy revealed its concern with Panama, for instance, by requesting bases across all the sea approaches to the Isthmus—on the coast of Peru, off the Pacific coast of Panama, on Fonseca Bay, and in Cuba.[5] Never, before completion of the canal, did the Navy General Board say that the Isthmus was of vital importance to the military security of the United States. Alert eyes in the State Department might have detected this thought in the Board's selections of naval bases. And eyes even less alert might have perceived the concept in two bolder letters, reminding the State Department that no great Power should be allowed to perch on Ecuador's Galápagos Islands or on Haiti's Môle St. Nicholas.[6] But the Navy and Army rarely let fall such clues to their strategic thinking.

Neither did the State Department share its political thinking with the services. In the archives of the McKinley, Roosevelt and Taft Administrations, I have yet to find a letter from a Secretary of State, asking for a military cost accounting before some diplomatic stroke. Although Taft's Secretary of State did occasionally ask the fleet to back up his diplomacy, he never inquired ahead of time about the fleet's location and make-up. Thus, in May 1912, when unrest was sweeping Cuba, the Secretary asked for "a considerable naval force . . . in the vicinity of Havana." Only by chance, or as a result of naval clairvoyance, did nine warships happen to be handy at Key West.[7]

Letter writing in the State, War, and Navy Departments failed to bring about effective coordination of policies. As a rule, in fact, diplomatic and military recommendations reached the White House separately, and the relationship between political aims and military capabilities had to be gauged, if at all, by the President. Although this rule-of-thumb system could work for a strategy-minded President like Theodore Roosevelt, it displayed its failings even in his time.

In the summer of 1907, for example, the budding American high command, the Joint Board of the Army and the Navy, discussed the hostility growing between the United States and Japan. Realizing that war, if it came, would find most of the American fleet in the Atlantic, the Board proposed a precautionary shift of battleships to the Pacific, then asked the Secretaries of War and the Navy to suggest such a shift to the President. The Secretaries did so, writing to Roosevelt at Oyster Bay, and Roosevelt agreed, choosing, however, to disguise the movement as a good will cruise. Although he seems to have reached this decision without delay, Roosevelt waited from late June until mid-

July before notifying his Secretary of State, who was still in Washington. For several weeks, therefore, the Secretary of State duelled with Japanese diplomats, wholly unaware, so far as the records show, of the Navy's preparations for a warlike gesture![8]

The first advances from haphazard coordination-by-letter to coordination-by-conference were made, paradoxically, under an administration that would never have endorsed the rationale of political-military collaboration. President Woodrow Wilson may even have denied the need for long-range military planning. At any rate, two generals swore after World War I that Wilson had given verbal orders forbidding the Army and Navy to construct hypothetical war plans.[9] During his Administration, furthermore, a pacifist sat for two years as Secretary of State, a near-pacifist ruled the Navy Department, and a Quaker became Secretary of War.

Perhaps a prevailing attitude of the Administration was expressed on one occasion by this pacifist Secretary of State, William Jennings Bryan. Renewed tension with Japan had brought before the Cabinet another Joint Board recommendation for a fleet movement to anticipate the possibility of war. According to one member of the Cabinet, David F. Houston, this recommendation angered Bryan, who "flared up . . . got red in the face and was very emphatic. He thundered out that army and navy officers could not be trusted to say what we should or should not do, till we actually got into war; that we were discussing not how to wage war, but how not to get into war."[10]

Yet the Wilson Administration, with Bryan as Secretary of State, saw uniformed officers and black-tied diplomats sit down together to discuss questions of foreign policy. Tension with Mexico, during the first year of the Administration, brought Bryan himself to the White House for a conference with the War and Navy Secretaries, the Army chief of Staff, and the head of the Navy General Board.[11] After war exploded over Europe, Bryan and his subordinates found a recurring need for special consultations with representatives of the Army and Navy. The uncertain character of neutral rights and duties brought into being a permanent Joint State and Navy Neutrality Board, an advisory body on diplomacy and international law. The amount of correspondence among assistant secretaries of the three departments increased three times over the pre-war

average. And Bryan's successor, Robert Lansing, met almost daily, according to his desk diary, with officers from the Navy General Board and the Army General Staff.[12] Thus conferences, letters and committee meetings began to knit the three departments together.

But American policy failed to benefit from this increasing teamwork, for Wilson reached his decisions with little assistance from any of the three departments. Lansing had come into office, in Colonel House's words, as a man "to do the details intelligently,"[13] and his Department's share in policy-making was never large. Meanwhile, the military planning agencies lacked not only the Administration's trust but also the ability to justify such trust if it were handed them. The Joint Board of the Army and Navy had virtually disbanded, because one of its recommendations had piqued the President.[14] The Army General Staff had slipped into torpor, while the Navy General Board languished as a casualty of Josephus Daniels' perpetual feud with his admirals. Collaboration among these powerless agencies could result, at best, in a coordination of futilities.

The idea of political-military collaboration nevertheless survived. Since the war had revealed defects in the State Department and in the Army and Navy, the post-war years saw reforms in all three: the Rogers Act for the State Department, reorganization of the Army General Staff, progressive change in the new Office of Naval Operations, and creation of a new and stronger Joint Board of the Army and Navy. To some men in the War and Navy Departments experience had also proved the need for regular, official consultation with the State Department. And these men put forward two successive proposals for consultative organizations.

The first and most ambitious of these proposals came from Franklin D. Roosevelt, then acting as Secretary of the Navy. On May 1, 1919, Roosevelt wrote to the Secretary of State:

> It is a fundamental principle that the foreign policy of our government is in the hands of the State Department. It is also an accepted fact that the foreign policy of a government depends for its acceptance by other nations upon the naval and military force that is behind it. . . .
>
> It is probable that certain policies are of such importance to our national interests that they must be defended at all cost.

On the other hand certain policies are not, by the expense they would entail, justified if they lead to war.

Hence it is submitted that in the framing of our policies, it is necessary for the State Department to know how much they will cost to maintain by force, in order to assign them their relative importance.

Conversely, it is necessary for the Navy Department to know what policies it may be called upon to uphold by force, in order to formulate plans and building programs.[15]

Enclosed with this letter was a giant sheet of blueprint paper, charting with boxes and arrows an organization for planning against all possible wars. Prepared by the Naval War College, this neat chart outlined duties for a State Department planning agency, for the Army General Staff, for a naval general staff, and for a Joint Plan Making Body, composed of officers from all three staffs. To this Joint Body was to go responsibility for estimating national resources, both American and foreign, and the key role of defining American objectives for each possible war and assessing the force needed for success.

Although this grandiose scheme was probably unworkable, hard-headed discussion of the Navy's proposal might have engineered some practical organization for national defense. No such discussion ever took place, and, in fact, Roosevelt's letter was not even acknowledged. The letter and its enclosure went, by mistake, to the State Department's Division of Latin American Affairs. After some misspent months in that Division's filing cabinets, the document was interred in the general records, never opened by the Secretary of State.[16] Indeed, when I found the original of Roosevelt's letter in the State Department archives, the blueprint was stapled to it, closed, and, as far as I could tell, the staple had never been removed, the blueprint never unfolded. Such was the fate of the first proposal for a National Security Council.

The second proposal came on December 7, 1921, this time sponsored jointly by the Secretary of the Navy and the Secretary of War. Considerably less pretentious than the original Navy blueprint, this joint proposal offered only the idea of collaboration between the State Department and the Joint Board of the Army and the Navy. But the reasoning in the service secretaries' letter closely resembled Roosevelt's.

They put forward three proposals. The State Department should designate "a responsible official" to sit in with the Joint Board when "questions involving national policy are under consideration." For similar discussions, one or more State Department people should sit in with the Joint Board's Planning Committee. Finally, the State Department should "refer to the Joint Board those national policies which may require the potential or dynamic support of the Army and Navy" and find out "whether the Army and Navy as at that time constituted and disposed are capable of supporting the policy in question . . . All such opinions and recommendations of the Joint Board," the Secretaries added, "will be referred to the Secretaries of State, War, and Navy for approval."[17]

This letter at least reached the desk of Secretary of State Charles Evans Hughes, but Hughes brushed it into his "Out" basket, noting: "This appears to me to be in substance a suggestion that at least provisionally matters of foreign policy be submitted to the Joint Board. I question the advisability of this." Taking their lead from Hughes, the undersecretary and the assistant secretaries questioned its advisability even more seriously. Consequently, Hughes suavely replied: "The only officials of the State Department who can speak for it with authority on questions of national policy are the Secretary and Undersecretary of State, and it is impossible, in the existing circumstances, for either of them to undertake this additional duty."[18]

Since War and Navy Department officials believed their proposal to be of great importance, they refused to accept the Secretary of State's negative reply. They countered with a new suggestion: the Joint Board should inform the State Department "whenever a subject comes before them for consideration which in their opinion is interwoven with the international policies of the United States." The Secretary of State or his representative could then attend the Joint Board's meeting. To this proposal the Secretary of State gave perfunctory agreement, thus providing the Army and Navy with a valve for starting a flow of military-political discussion.[19] But the military leaders did not open this valve for over thirteen years.

Perhaps this long delay resulted from the series of slights administered to the military departments by the Secretary of State during the Washington Conference on Naval Limitation. Preparing for that conference, Secretary Hughes "worked closely with the Navy," his biographer says, and "was scrupulous in exploring the Navy's point of view while insisting that civilian statesmanship rather than naval strategy should guide the conference."[20] The General Board, anxious to push the Navy's ideas, presented Hughes with long, hard-thought essays on the questions apt to come up for negotiation. The Board advised that the United States fleet should equal the combined fleets of Britain and Japan, cautioned against any let-up in the naval building program, and portrayed the vital importance of fortifying Oahu, Guam and Manila Bay. But Hughes rejected each item of the Board's advice. In his opening speech to the conference, he not only proposed a 5:5:3 ration among the three naval Powers but also offered to scrap thirty American capital ships. Later he proposed a general agreement not to fortify islands in the Pacific.[21] Undoubtedly, Hughes based these stands on careful reasoning and broad advice, but the Navy's feelings were badly hurt, and a sense of resentment over the Washington Conference colored the writings of Navy and Army officers for decades.

As a result, these officers became even more circumspect than before in dealing with political questions. Furthermore, they fell altogether from public favor, as, during the twenties, newspapers and magazines drummed disillusionment, isolationism, and new forms of pacifism and anti-militarism. Whereas to Secretary Hughes a suggestion for political-military collaboration had seemed only imprudent, to either of his successors a similar suggestion would have seemed rash and startling. When Hoover's Secretary of State was preparing for the new naval conference of 1930, for instance, he rejected out of hand suggestions from the General Board and took with him to the conference only one uniformed adviser, an admiral "carefully selected . . . by the administration's civilian leaders," one who "took a different position . . . from most of his colleagues."[22]

During these years, nevertheless, the general staffs were improving their minds by cloistered study of possible wars, and junior officers in the armed services were building friendly ties with their counterparts in the Foreign Service. They were exchanging intelligence data, a practice started soon after World War I,

and they were meeting on various interdepartmental boards, like the Radio Advisory Committee and the committee on strategic raw materials. Early in the twenties, too, Foreign Service officers began to attend the Army and Navy War Colleges and to give lectures before War College classes.[23] Thus the future heads of divisions and branches within the three departments laid a foundation for later cooperation on questions of policy.

Over this foundation a structure began to rise shortly after Franklin D. Roosevelt became President. His Secretary of State, Cordell Hull, found himself dealing with a newly barbarous Germany, an emboldened Italy, and a hostile Japan. As Hull stated to the Pearl Harbor investigators:

> . . . soon after I came into the State Department, when I would be talking with the representatives of the thugs at the head of governments abroad . . . they would look at me in the face but I soon discovered that they were looking over my shoulder at our Navy and our Army and that our diplomatic strength . . . goes up or down with their estimate of what that amounts to.[24]

Consequently, Hull took more interest than his predecessors in military plans and opinions. Preparing for yet another naval conference, he asked the Navy to detail its wishes, and he sent to London, not just a "carefully selected" admiral, but the Chief of Naval Operations and a sizable band of naval officers. In the same year, too, he named a high State Department officer to sit in with the Joint Board's Planning Committee for a reexamination of America's military position in the Far East.[25] Early in his term, thus, Hull began to seat military and political thinkers at the same tables.

As Europe's war drums beat more insistently, Hull drew the State, War, and Navy Departments closer together. After suggesting special conferences on Axis infiltration of Latin America, he proposed a standing interdepartmental committee to consider, among other things, "matters of national policy affecting the three departments." He nominated Undersecretary Sumner Welles to represent the State Department. The President chose the Chief of Naval Operations and the Army Chief of Staff to be the committee's other members, and this three-man group took the name, Standing Liaison Committee. Thus was formed the first

American agency for regular political-military consultation on foreign policy.[26]

The Standing Liaison Committee lasted until 1943. Though it handled chiefly questions of hemisphere defense and Good Neighbor relations, it still gave the military chiefs an opportunity to learn the trends of policy thinking in the State Department. Later, too, it gave the State Department's second officer a chance to learn highly secret Army-Navy plans for possible war, plans formerly withheld from State Department eyes.[27]

Rarely, however, did questions of policy come up for the Committee's discussion, perhaps because the members had little time for talk. The military chiefs were busy, fabricating fleets, armies and air forces out of raw metal and rawer men, while the undersecretary and his department were swirling through diplomatic crises that absorbed their time and powers. So the Liaison Committee failed to march with the perilous times.

In only one instance did the Liaison Committee handle an important issue of policy, and then it patched together a compromise instead of building a solution. The issue came before the Committee in the summer of 1940, when Hitler was looking acquisitively at the Vichy fleet. The Army and Navy, fearing that Germany might seize control of the Mediterranean, proposed a shift of the American battle fleet from the Pacific to the Atlantic. But the State Department disagreed. More fearful of a Japanese attack on Southeast Asia than of German naval expansion and aware that Britain held the same fear, the State Department believed the fleet more effective, stationed at Pearl Harbor, where it might deter Japan from rash aggression. Since the undersecretary and the military members all stood fast behind their differing views, the Liaison Committee's decision solved nothing. The fleet, they agreed, "should be withdrawn from Hawaii only if the Germans actually secured control of the French fleet." If that happened, of course, the issue would still exist and would simply be more urgent.[28]

Other than this decision, the Liaison Committee accomplished little that touched the great issues drawing the United States toward double war. After November 1940, furthermore, its functions shifted to other committee and council tables. A new Secretary of War started weekly conferences with his State and Navy counterparts.[29] The President began to deal directly with his chiefs of staff, by-passing not only the State Department but also the civilian Secretaries of War and the Navy. By the autumn of 1941, in the tempestuous twilight before Pearl Harbor, the President was convening a War Council, made up of his State, War, and Navy Secretaries, and his chiefs of staff.[30]

Despite the resemblance of this War Council to the present-day National Security Council, it hardly served as a palette for the mixing of military and political views. Rather, it provided the President with a platform from which to announce decisions already reached with the help of the chiefs of staff. After November 5, 1941, the War Council spent its time devising ways to carry out the strategic concept long ago devised by the Joint Board and now ratified by the President: "War between the United States and Japan should be avoided while building up the defensive forces in the Far East, until such time as Japan attacks or directly threatens territories whose security to the United States is of very great importance."[31] Then, when war broke out, the President stopped inviting Hull to the War Council's meetings, and the Council, while it lasted, became nothing more than a board of strategy.

The idea of coordinating strategy and policy seemed, indeed, to die out with the onset of war. The President began to consult only with his chiefs of staff and with a few para-military officials like Harry Hopkins. Not only was the Secretary of State excluded from meetings of the War Council, but he was left at home when the President went abroad to meet British and Russian leaders and even left outside when Roosevelt met with Churchill in Washington and Quebec.[32] During most of the war, as a result, the State Department became almost an auxiliary arm of the military services.

Uniformed officers meanwhile filled the chairs left vacant by diplomats. Eisenhower, Stilwell and Wedemeyer negotiated with allied governments. The service chieftains, reorganized as the Joint Chiefs of Staff, met face to face with their allied counterparts and negotiated agreements that were, in effect, military treaties, requiring for ratification only the countersignature of the President. Although the Joint Chiefs continually disclaimed any authority in political affairs, their decisions, in fact, directed American policy. When they concluded, for example, that Russian aid was essential to victory in the Far East, they said, in effect, that American diplomacy should subordinate other aims in order to bring about a Russian declaration of war on Japan. Had professional diplomats desired to challenge this ruling, they would have been unable to do so. In 1944, as a matter of fact, when the State Department wanted the Dumbarton Oaks conferees to begin discussions of post-war boundaries, the Joint Chiefs checked any such discussions.[33] Quarrels among the Allies might result, the chiefs asserted, and Russia might find cause for delaying her entry into the Pacific war. Thus, during World War II, the strategists took command, and the military-State Department relation was reversed. No longer were the military leaders seeking parity with diplomats; on the contrary, the diplomats were looking for space alongside the chiefs of staff.

Not until the last year of World War II did the State Department begin to regain its lost status. Then the need for military government directives and surrender terms caused the creation of the State-War-Navy Coordinating Committee, the National Security Council's immediate ancestor.[34]

This Coordinating Committee, composed of assistant secretaries, prepared the plans for occupying Germany, Austria and Japan, and pondered, in addition, many other questions of post-war policy. Since most or all of these questions involved fleets and forces in the theaters of war, the Coordinating Committee had to clear its decisions with the Joint Chiefs of Staff, and officers representing the Joint Chiefs sat in with the Coordinating Committee's staff groups. Before the Committee's recommendations went to the Secretary of State and the President, therefore, any differences with the Joint Chiefs had already been discovered and explored.

Such a process brought forth, as an example, the Committee's recommendations on post-war aid to China. Had these recommendations been compounded by the State Department alone, Herbert Feis tells us in his recent book, *The China Tangle*, they "would have subordinated the program of military aid to the satisfaction of . . . political ideas"—democratic government and political unity for China.[35] Recommendations drafted by the Army, Navy, and Air Forces, on the other hand, would have fixed on two different objec-

tives—territorial unity for China and military strength for the Chinese government. Thus, while the State Department thought of aid for China as a means of exerting pressure on the Kuomintang, to force a political strengthening of the Nationalist government, the armed forces tended to think of this aid solely as a means for strengthening the battle capabilities of the Nationalist forces.

Since the choice between these points of view depended at all times upon detailed, expert information, the State Department and the military had to reconcile, or at least define, their differences before going to the White House with a program for immediate post-war aid for China. The State-War-Navy Coordinating Committee was an obvious arena where these views might be tested against each other.

The State Department drew up a statement of China policy, emphasizing the political objectives of unity and democratic government. Although this statement of policy has not been printed, an earlier model of it is visible in the MacArthur hearings, and the views of the State Department's chief Far Eastern planner, John Carter Vincent, have been published at length in the records of the McCarran committee.[36] In the final proposals of the State-War-Navy Coordinating Committee, quoted in Feis's book, one can therefore detect phrases written in with stubby blue pencils by the War and Navy Departments and the Joint Chiefs of Staff:

> The achievement of [American] objectives in China requires a friendly, unified, independent nation with a stable government resting, *insofar as practicable*, on the freely expressed support of the Chinese people. . . . The following should be established as policies of the United States: . . .
>
> (b) *To assist and advise China in the development of modern armed forces, ground, sea and air, for the*
> . . .
>
> (1) *Maintenance of internal peace and security in China including the liberated areas of Manchuria and Formosa. . . .*[37]

One can see also the unaltered will of the State Department in such a sentence as: "The extent to which political stability is being achieved in China under a unified, fully representative government is regarded by the U.S. as a basic consideration which will at all times govern the furnishing of economic, military, or other assistance to that nation. . . ."

Thus were political and military views brought into line, through the agency of the State-War-Navy Coordinating Committee. That line admittedly jogged and wavered. And one can argue that events in the Far East would have followed a different course had the opinions of one department or the other prevailed. It remains true, nevertheless, that the State Department and the military departments disagreed, and this disagreement was due, not to a personal difference between John Carter Vincent and some general or admiral, but to a real difference between political and military perspectives. General Marshall, while Chief of Staff, opposed the State Department's idea of using aid to promote reforms in the Chinese government. Then, when he became Secretary of State, he defended this very idea against challenges voiced by the new chiefs of staff.[38] Such real disagreements between the State and military departments had to be reconciled in some place like the State-War-Navy Coordinating Committee, or such a committee had to define the points at issue for the President's adjudication.

But the Committee had its limitations. It suffered, in the first place, from its inability to make policy. Although the Committee was capable of rapid staff work, as evidenced in its eight-day fabrication of a workable surrender instrument for Japan,[39] its mill of subcommittees hummed uselessly in the spring of 1945 when Marshal Tito threatened to march against Allied forces in Trieste. The question of American action simply fell beyond the powers of the assistant secretaries who made up the Coordinating Committee; and the Trieste decision had to be made by the President and his Cabinet Secretaries with little or no preliminary staff study.[40]

In the second place, the Committee went to work only when a question was referred to it by one of the departments. As a result, it failed to handle some questions well within its purview. The four-Power arrangements for occupation of Berlin were worked out hastily by soldiers and diplomats in the European Theater and approved by a nod from President Truman.[41] The Coordinating Committee never had a chance to examine these arrangements, and no provision was made for guaranteeing access to the city.

The nation needed the Coordinating Committee, but it also needed a policy-making agency with the power to review all questions. President Truman fully realized this need, and so did his Cabinet Secretaries, particularly Secretary of the Navy James Forrestal. Within two years after World War II, consequently, Mr. Truman, Mr. Forrestal, and a staff of experts had worked out a plan for a National Security Council. Bedded in the unification act of 1947, this plan received the approval of Congress, and the United States acquired a regular, legally established, cabinet-level agency for the coordination of political and military views on foreign policy. . . .

A committee that effects some political-military coordination has come into existence. Fifty years ago such a committee could not openly have existed in Washington. Had it existed in secret, it would very likely have been ineffective. During World War I, when a need for coordination was recognized, actual coordination was at best haphazard, and the new crises attending World War II saw one experiment tumble after another. The National Security Council is thus the product of a long and painful history. Whatever its present inadequacies and whatever the trials that lie ahead, it is still an institution. It answers an enduring need, and it is likely to be a permanent feature of American government.

NOTES

1. Phillip C. Jessup, *Elihu Root* (New York, 1938), II, 109.

2. *John Hay* (New York, 1934), p. 198.

3. *Annual Report of the War Department, 1918: Report of the Chief of Staff*, p. 3.

4. See Seward W. Livermore, "American Strategy Diplomacy in the South Pacific, 1890–1914," *Pacific Historical Review,* XII (March 1943): 33–51, and "American Naval Base Policy in the Far East," ibid., XIII (June 1944): 113–135.

5. Livermore, "American Strategy Diplomacy in the South Pacific, 1890–1914"; Jessup, *op. cit.,* I, 326. The following from Record Group 80, the General Records of the Navy Department, in the National Archives (hereinafter cited as Navy Dept. Arch., RG 80): C. Darling (Acting Sec. of Navy) to J. Hay, Mar. 5, 1903 (carbon), 8480–8; G. v. L. Meyer to P. C. Knox, Feb. 23, 1910 (carbon), 8480–9; J. Daniels to R. Lansing, Feb. 28, 1920 (carbon), "Spindle File"—State Department. The following from Record Group 45, Naval Records Collection of the Office of Naval Records and Library (hereinafter cited as Navy Dept.

Arch., RG 45): J. D. Long to McKinley, Dec. 13, 1901 (carbon), Confidential Correspondence, vol. III.

6. Livermore, "American Strategy Diplomacy in the South Pacific, 1890–1914." Rear Adm. H. C. Taylor to W. H. Moody, Nov. 10, 1902 (original), Confidential Corr., vol. III, Navy Dept. Arch., RG 45. Jessup, *Elihu Root*, I, 562–563; and the following from the General Records of the Department of State, National Archives (hereinafter cited as State Dept. Arch.): Daniels to Lansing, Jan. 2, 1920 (orig.), 822.014 0/287.

7. Knox to Meyer, May 25, 1912 (orig.); B. Winthrop to Knox, May 25, 1912 (carbon)—both in 27868-4, Navy Dept. Arch., RG 80.

8. Hermann Hagedorn, *Leonard Wood: A Biography* (New York, 1931), II, 79–81; Thomas A. Bailey, *Theodore Roosevelt and the Japanese-American Crises* (Stanford, 1934), pp. 211–227; Taft to Roosevelt, June 22, 1907, Private Papers of Theodore Roosevelt, Manuscripts Division, Library of Congress. Roosevelt to H. C. Lodge, July 10, 1907, in Elting E. Morison, et al (eds.), *The Letters of Theodore Roosevelt* (Cambridge, Mass., 1951–1954), V, 709–710; Roosevelt to Root, July 13, 1907, ibid., pp. 717–719.

9. Frederick Palmer, *Newton D. Baker* (New York, 1931), I, 40–41; Hagedorn, *Leonard Wood,* II, 205.

10. *Eight Years with Wilson's Cabinet* (Garden City, 1926), I, 66.

11. Ray Stannard Baker, *Woodrow Wilson* (New York, 1926–1937), IX, 328–329.

12. Private Papers of Robert Lansing, MS Div., Library of Congress.

13. E. M. House to Wilson, June 16, 1915 (orig.), Private Papers of Woodrow Wilson, MS Div., Library of Congress.

14. Diary of Josephus Daniels, entry for May 16, 1913, Private Papers of Josephus Daniels, MS Div., Library of Congress.

15. (Orig.), 110.7/56, State Dept. Arch. The copy in the Franklin D. Roosevelt library is described in Frank Freidel, *Franklin D. Roosevelt: The Ordeal* (Boston, 1954), pp. 19–20.

16. Memo, Division of Latin American Affairs to Index Bureau, July 21, 1919, 110.7/56, State Dept. Arch.

17. (Orig.) 110.7/123, State Dept. Arch.

18. Hughes to Fletcher, Dec. 12, 1921 (orig.); F. M. Dearing to Fletcher, Dec. 13, 1921 (orig.); W. J. Carr to Fletcher, Dec. 22, 1921 (orig.); Dearing to Fletcher, Jan. 4, 1922 (orig.), noted "(Mr. Fletcher concurs: JBS)"; Hughes to E. Denby and J. W. Weeks, Jan. 17, 1922 (certified carbon)—all in 110.7/123, State Dept. Arch.

19. Denby and Weeks to Hughes, Jan. 25, 1923 (orig.); Memo, Fletcher to Hughes, Feb. 20, 1922 (orig.); Hughes to Weeks and Denby, Mar. 14, 1922 (certified carbon)—all in 110.7/124, State Dept. Arch.

20. Merlo J. Pusey, *Charles Evans Hughes* (New York, 1950), II, 460.

21. Ibid., pp. 460, 462, 477.

22. Henry L. Stimson and McGeorge Bundy, *On Active Service in Peace and War* (New York, 1947), p. 168.

23. Memo, A. Dulles to "Mr. Merle-Smith," Sept. 21, 1920 (orig.), 110.72/8, State Dept. Arch. J. C. Grew to E. Young, Oct. 18, 1924 (orig.); Davis (Asst. Sec. of War) to Grew, Oct. 20, 1924 (orig.); Grew to Davis, Oct. 23, 1924 (certified carbon)—all in 110.72/29, State Dept. Arch. J. M. Wainwright (Acting Sec. of War) to Hughes, July 8, 1922 (orig.); W. Phillips to Weeks, Sept. 1, 1922 (certified carbon)—both in 110.72/13, State Dept. Arch. Rear Adm. W. V. Pratt to Grew, Feb. 25, 1926 (orig.); Grew to Pratt, Mar. 11, 1926 (carbon); T. Dennett to Grew, Mar. 8, 1926 (orig.)—all in 110.75/20–21, State Dept. Arch.

24. *Hearings before the Joint Committee on the Investigation of the Pearl Harbor Attack,* 79 Cong., 1 sess. (hereinafter cited as *Pearl Harbor Hearings*), Pt. II, p. 455.

25. George H. Dern and Claude A. Swanson to Cordell Hull, Nov. 26, 1935 (carbon); Hull to Dern, Nov. 27, 1935 (orig.)—both in WPD 3887, General Records of the War Department, National Archives.

26. Mark S. Watson, *Chief of Staff: Prewar Plans and Preparations* (Washington, 1950), pp. 89–92.

27. Ibid., p. 90.

28. William L. Langer and S. Everett Gleason, *The Challenge to Isolation, 1937–1940* (New York, 1952), pp. 596–597.

29. Ibid., p. 10; Watson, *Chief of Staff,* p. 91; Stimson in *Pearl Harbor Hearings,* Pt. XXIX, p. 2065.

30. *Pearl Harbor Hearings,* Pt. XXIX, p. 2066.

31. Ibid., Pt. XIV, p. 1062; William L. Langer and S. Everett Gleason, *The Undeclared War, 1940–1941* (New York, 1953), p. 846, and chapters xxvi–xxviii.

32. *The Memoirs of Cordell Hull* (New York, 1948), II, 1109–1111.

33. See Department of State, *Post-War Foreign Policy Preparation, 1939–1945* (1949), pp. 276, 660–661.

34. Howard W. Moseley, Charles W. McCarthy, and Alvin F. Richardson, "The State-War-Navy Coordinating Committee," *Bulletin* of the U.S. Department of State, XIII (Nov. 11, 1945), 745–747. Ray S. Cline, *Washington Command Post: The Operations Division* (Washington, 1951), pp. 326–330. John Carter Vincent, "The Post-War Period in the Far East," State Dept. *Bulletin,* XIII (Oct. 21, 1945), 644–648; "Germany and the Occupation," ibid., XIV (May 26, 1946), 910–914; John H. Hilldring, Velma H. Cassidy, "American Policy in Occupied Areas," ibid., XV (July 14, 1946), 47–48, (Aug. 18, 1946), 291–296.

35. Princeton, 1953, p. 374.

36. *Hearings before Committee on Armed Services,* Committee on Foreign Relations, U.S. Senate, 82 Cong., 1 sess., "Military Situation in the Far East," Pt. IV, pp. 2929–2930. *Hearings before Subcommittee on Internal Security,* Committee on Judiciary, U.S. Senate, 82 Cong., 1 sess., "Institute of Pacific Relations."

37. Feis, *China Tangle,* p. 375 (italics [are May's]).

38. U.S. State Dept., *United States Relations with China with Special Reference to the Period 1944–1949* (1949), pp. 251–252, 255–256, 269–273.

39. *Hearings,* "Institute of Pacific Relations," *passim* (see index under "E. H. Dooman," "J. C. Vincent").

40. Joseph C. Grew, *Turbulent Era* (New York, 1952), II, 1474–1485.

41. Speech by Mr. Truman, *New York Times,* Oct. 5, 1952, p. 82. Speech by Mr. Eisenhower, ibid., Oct. 8, 1952, p. 23.

2

POSTWAR ORGANIZATION FOR NATIONAL SECURITY

Ferdinand Eberstadt

This selection is drawn from the 250-page report prepared for the Secretary of the Navy, James Forrestal, who requested a recommendation on what form of postwar organization should be established to "provide for and protect our national security."

INTRODUCTION
Request of Secretary of Navy for This Report

The Secretary of the Navy.
Washington, June 19, 1945.

Mr. F. Eberstadt,
New York City, N.Y.

Dear Mr. Eberstadt:
I would appreciate your making a study of and preparing a report to me with recommendations on the following matters:
1. Would unification of the War and Navy Departments under a single head improve our national security?
2. If not, what changes in the present relationships of the military services and departments has our war experience indicated as desirable to improve our national security?
3. What form of postwar organization should be established and maintained to enable the military services and other Government departments and agencies most effectively to provide for and protect our national security?

Sincerely yours,
James Forrestal.

Reprinted from "Unification of the War and Navy Departments and Postwar Organization for National Security," *Report to Hon. James Forrestal,* Committee on Naval Affairs (Washington, D.C.: Government Printing Office, 1945).

Ferdinand Eberstadt was former chairman of the Army-Navy Munitions Board and vice-chairman of the War Productions Board.

Letter to Secretary of the Navy Transmitting Report

Department of the Navy,
Office of the Secretary.
Washington, September 25, 1945.

The Honorable James Forrestal,
Secretary of the Navy, *Washington, D.C.*

Sir:

Military efficiency is not the only condition which should influence the form of our postwar military organization. To be acceptable, any such organization must fall within the framework of our traditions and customs. It must be of such size and nature as to command public support. It must be aimed at curing the weaknesses disclosed in the late wars. And finally, it must be conducive to fostering those policies and objectives which contribute to the service and protection of our national security.

Since it seemed unlikely that any one form of military organization would equally meet all of these requirements, our ultimate choice fell on that form which promised to advance what appeared to us to be the more essential ones. Within its framework, we undertook to suggest organizational machinery and procedures for the attainment of other important but less vital goals.

The military services are but a part of the national machinery of peace or war. An effective national security policy calls for active, intimate, and continuous relationships not alone between the military services themselves but also between the military services and many other departments and agencies of Government.

This consideration guided our answer to your last and broadest question. Here we have attempted to sketch the major organizations and relationships which are involved in promoting the maintenance of peace or, in default of this, in marshalling our national resources fully, promptly, and effectively in our defense.

We have suggested new organizational forms responsible to our new world position, our new international obligations, and the new technological developments emerging from the war. . . .

Respectfully yours,
F. Eberstadt.

CONCLUSIONS AND RECOMMENDATIONS
Summary of Conclusions

We sum up our conclusions with respect to the three questions contained in your letter of June 19 as follows: . . .

3. *What form of postwar organization should be established and maintained to enable the military services and other Government departments and agencies most effectively to provide for and protect our national security?*

The question of the form of organization of our military forces must be viewed in its proper perspective as only one part of a much larger picture encompassing many elements, military and civilian, governmental and private, which contribute to our national

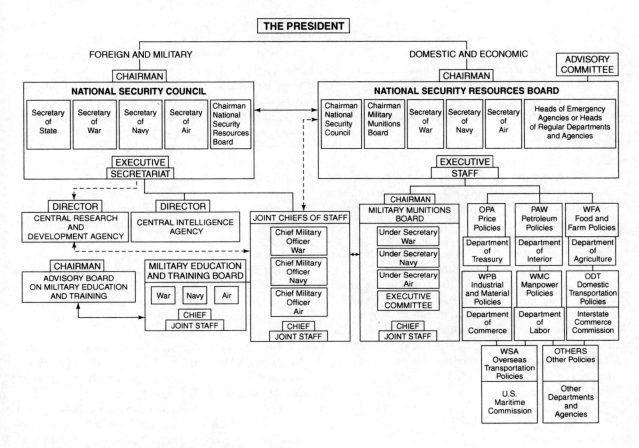

Figure 2.1 Proposed organization for national security

security and defense. It is obviously impossible to unify all these elements under one command, short of the President.

Our goal should be to bind them together in such a way as to achieve the most productive and harmonious whole. This calls for coordination as well as command, for parallel as well as subordinated effort. Where to use one and where to use the other are questions of balanced judgment and adjustment to be determined by the principles and traditions of our form of government, the lessons of experience, and the basic policies and objectives to be achieved.

The necessity of integrating all these elements into an alert, smoothly working and efficient machine is more important now than ever before. Such integration is compelled by our present world commitments and risks, by the tremendously increased scope and tempo of modern warfare, and by the epochal scientific discoveries culminating in the atomic bomb.

This will involve, among others, organizational ties between the Department of State and the military departments, ties between the military departments in strategy and logistics, ties between the military departments and the agencies responsible for planning and carrying out mobilization of our industrial and human resources, between the gathering of information and intelligence and its dissemination and use, between scientific advances and their military application.

The next war will probably break out with little or no warning and will almost immediately achieve its maximum tempo of violence and destruction. Contrasting with the shortened opportunity for defensive preparation is the increased length of time necessary to prepare the complicated offensive and defensive weapons and organizational structure essential to modern warfare.

The nation not fully prepared will be at a greater disadvantage than ever before.

The great need, therefore, is that we be prepared always and all along the line, not simply to defend ourselves after an attack, but through all available political, military, and economic means to forestall any such attack. The knowledge that we are so prepared and alert will in itself be a great influence for world peace.

Much has been said about the importance of waging peace, as well as war. We have tried to suggest an organizational structure adapted to both purposes.

There is attached, marked "Exhibit 1," an organization chart depicting our recommendations for tying together on the one hand the political and military organizations and on the other the economic and civilian ones, with provision for linking the two.

Our specific recommendations follow.

Specific Recommendations

We recommend: . . .

2. *Creation of a National Security Council*

To afford a permanent vehicle for maintaining active, close, and continuous contact between the departments and agencies of our Government responsible, respectively, for our foreign and military policies and their implementation, we recommend the establishment of a National Security Council.

The National Security Council would be the keystone of our organizational structure for national security.

It should be charged with the duty (1) of formulating and coordinating over-all policies in the political and military fields, (2) of assessing and appraising our foreign objectives, commitments and risks, and (3) of keeping these in balance with our military power, in being and potential.

It would be a policy-forming and advisory, not an executive, body.

Its membership should consist of the Secretaries of State, War, Navy, and Air, and the Chairman of the National Security Resources Board (recommendation No. 4 below). Provision should be made for such additions to its membership as the President may from time to time deem proper.

The President should be its Chairman. In his absence, the Vice President, being next in Presidential succession, or the senior member of the Cabinet, the Secretary of State, would act in this capacity.

The National Security Council should have a permanent secretariat, headed by a full-time executive, charged with preparing its agenda, providing data essential to its deliberations, and distributing its conclusions to the departments and agencies concerned for information and appropriate action.

The Joint Chiefs of Staff should be a part of, and meet with, the Council.

The National Security Council should take over the functions at present performed by the State-War-Navy Coordinating Committee.

The Central Intelligence Agency (recommendation No. 9 below) should be a part of, and report to, the National Security Council. Its product is an important part of the grist of the Council's mill.

The Council should also control the policies and activities of the organizations responsible for the conduct of psychological and economic warfare and should maintain close relations with the civilian agency set up to coordinate military and civilian scientific research and development (recommendation No. 7 below).

It should review, and advise the President on, the combined military budget.

The Council should render annual reports to the President and to Congress. To the extent that national security does not absolutely require secrecy, its reports should be published. Thus the public would be kept posted on these vital matters by an authoritative and dependable source. In this way, the Council could aid in building up public support for clear-cut, consistent, and effective foreign and military policies.

In time of war, combination of the National Security Council with appropriate elements of the National Security Resources Board (recommendation No. 4 below) would constitute the basis of a war cabinet. . . .

3

LEGISLATIVE DEBATE ON THE NATIONAL SECURITY ACT OF 1947

U.S. Congress

Though most of the debate on the 1947 National Security Act focused on the issue of military unification, legislators did raise issues about the future of the proposed National Security Council.

CONGRESSIONAL RECORD—SENATE

MR. BALDWIN   ... Briefly, what does this unification accomplish? First, it provides a National Security Council to advise with the President and the Congress on the integration of our domestic, foreign, and military policies. That is a very important consideration. It is something which we did not achieve in World War II until we had had a long and bitter experience with a different situation. We tried to establish it in Washington in a way that would provide the greatest coordination, but we found from experience that there was much delay, much uncertainty, and a lack of a sound integration of policy and program, and it was not until along toward the end of the war that we approached in our organization an establishment which is similar to that provided for in this bill—the National Security Council. True, the personnel are different, but our experience demonstrated conclusively that we needed something of that kind. So this bill creates a National Security Council.

I might point out, Mr. President, that the National Security Council is entirely, as I recall it, a civilian organization. It is made up of the President, the Secretaries, and such other persons as the President may designate. Of course, that Council could bring to its service any officer it might desire. Consequently, it is the main coordinating factor, I think, in all our preparations for national security and for our defense. God grant that we shall not have to prepare for war, but merely for the possibility that it may come, and thus be prepared to defend ourselves.

Under the Council there is established a central intelligence agency to provide coordinated, adequate intelligence for all Government agencies concerned with national security. When one reads the record of the past war in regard to that field it is found that there was much to be desired in the way intelligence was covered, and there was great conflict about it. I say nothing here in depreciation of the men who were engaged in the intelligence service, because some remarkable and extremely courageous things were done. Nevertheless, we demonstrated from our experience the need of a central intelligence agency; and this bill provides such an agency. Neither a National Security Council nor an intelligence agency now exists.

MR. SALTONSTALL   Mr. President, will the Senator yield to me once more?

MR. BALDWIN   I yield.

MR. SALTONSTALL   The Senator was discussing the National Security Council and its importance. Does the Senator agree with me when I say that the purpose of creating the National Security Council is not to set up a new function of government with extraordinary powers, but solely to provide an organization to give advice to the President, not on general affairs of state, but through civilian groups, on affairs of state affecting the national security and tending to make the military forces more efficient? Is not that correct?

MR. BALDWIN   I agree wholeheartedly, Mr. President. In other words, it is not essentially an administrative agency. It is an advisory council.

Reprinted from the *Congressional Record,* July 9 and July 19, 1945, pp. 8496–8497 and p. 9397, respectively.

MR. SALTONSTALL   And it is advisory on security matters alone.

MR. BALDWIN   That is correct.

CONGRESSIONAL RECORD—HOUSE

MR. WADSWORTH   Mr. Chairman, at last we have come to the consideration of the bill known generally as the unification bill, H. R. 4214. It may not be a matter of surprise to many members of this committee that I rise in support of the measure. Having been concerned about the problems of our national defense for something like 25 or 30 years, I welcome this opportunity to support a measure which I am convinced will make this Nation stronger, that will achieve its strength with efficiency, and ultimately with marked economy. It is not my purpose at this time to engage in a general discussion, much less to attempt any oratory, with respect to the defense of our country and the present condition of the world, but rather I thought I would impose upon your patience in an attempt to describe to you as best I may the organizational set-up proposed by this so-called unification bill. It is for that reason I have had this chart prepared. [Not presented here]. Unfortunately, some of the print will be difficult for you to read, but I hope, in an informal fashion, to describe just what this whole is thing is.

We all know that under the Constitution of the United States the President, in addition to his duty to execute the laws, performs two other very, very important functions. One, he conducts the foreign relations of the United States; and, two, he is Commander in Chief of the armed forces.

In this bill we attempt to set up an organization which will assist the President in the performance of those two special functions, the conduct of foreign relations, and his function as Commander in Chief of the armed forces. I, therefore, call your attention to the fact that at the top of this chart there is depicted the organization which is to assist the President in the performance of those functions. He is Commander in Chief, as the chart indicates, of course; and there is organized under the provisions of this bill a National Security Council which is to consist of the Secretary of State, the Secretary of National Defense, whose position and functions I will come to later, the Secretary of the Army, the Secretary of the Navy, the Secretary of the Air Force, and the Chairman of the National Resources Board. That is the National Security Council, and the President is a member of it and, if he so desires, may preside over it.

The National Executive Council is to have but one executive officer, the Executive Director, who might be described as office manager, and he must be a civilian. It is to be noted that all of the members of the Executive Council are civilians, and by reason of their respective offices each one of them must be confirmed by the Senate.

The Executive Council cannot do its work effectively unless it has assistance, and one source of assistance must be a study to be made of the resources of this country. The President must have the advantage of a continued study of the resources of the country as well as a complete understanding of its military strength in order that he may conduct the foreign relations of the United States in a proper fashion.

The presence of the Secretary of State upon the Council is significant. For the first time in our history we propose that the statutes shall provide that the conduct of foreign relations shall be recognized as an exceedingly important part of our general behavior before the world; and the Resources Board is to make continuous study of the resources of America, its natural resources, its manpower, anything of importance which relates to the strength of this country or its potential strength: Oil, iron ore, electric power, food, coal, any number of things that are part of the natural resources of the United States. The Resources Board is to make a continuous study of that part of the problem and make recommendations to the Council, of which the President is the head.

In addition, under the Council there would be another element which is to advise the Council, in the field of intelligence, in the foreign field; and there is established a central intelligence agency subject to the Council, headed by a director.

The function of that agency is to constitute itself as a gathering point for information coming from all over the world through all kinds of channels concerning the potential strength of other nations and their political intentions. There is nothing secret about that. Every nation in the world is doing the same thing. But it must be remembered that the Central Intelligence Agency is subject to the Council and does not act independently. It is the agency for the collecting and disseminating of information which will help the President and the Council to adopt wise and effective policies.

So with information of that sort concerning other nations and information coming in with respect to our own resources, both of which are available to the Council and President, we will have for the first time in our history a piece of machinery that should work and it is high time that we have it. We have never had it before. During this last war all sorts of devices were resorted to, obviously in great haste, to accomplish a thing like this. You may remember the huge number of special committees, organizations and agencies set up by Executive order in an attempt to catch up with the target. We have learned as a result of the war that we should have some permanent organization, and that is the one proposed in this bill.

4

The National Security Act of 1947

U.S. Congress

Included here are excerpts from the National Security Act, signed on July 26, 1947, that deal with the NSC.

Declaration of Policy

Sec. 2. In enacting this legislation, it is the intent of Congress to provide a comprehensive program for the future security of the United States; to provide for the establishment of integrated policies and procedures for the departments, agencies, and functions of the Government relating to the national security; to provide a Department of Defense, including the three military Departments of the Army, the Navy (including naval aviation and the United States Marine Corps), and the Air Force under the direction, authority, and control of the Secretary of Defense; to provide that each military department shall be separately organized under its own Secretary and shall function under the direction, authority, and control of the Secretary of Defense; to provide for their unified direction under civilian control of the Secretary of Defense but not to merge these departments or services; to provide for the establishment of unified or specified combatant commands, and a clear and direct line of command to such commands; to eliminate unnecessary duplication in the Department of Defense, and particularly in the field of research and engineering by vesting its overall direction and control in the Secretary of Defense; to provide more effective and economical administration in the Department of Defense; to provide for the unified strategic direction of the combatant forces, for their operation under unified command, and for their integration into an efficient team of land, naval, and air forces but not to establish a single Chief of Staff over the armed forces nor an overall armed forces general staff.

Title I—Coordination for National Security

National Security Council

Sec. 101. (a) There is hereby established a council to be known as the National Security Council (hereinafter in this section referred to as the "Council").

The President of the United States shall preside over meetings of the Council: Provided, That in his absence he may designate a member of the Council to preside in his place.

The function of the Council shall be to advise the President with respect to the integration of domestic, foreign, and military policies relating to the national security so as to enable the military services and the other departments and agencies of the Government to cooperate more effectively in matters involving the national security.

The Council shall be composed of—

(1) the President;
(2) the Vice President;
(3) the Secretary of State;
(4) the Secretary of Defense;
(5) [1]
(6) [2]
(7) the Secretaries and Under Secretaries of other executive departments and of the military departments, when appointed by the President by and with the advice and consent of the Senate, to serve at his pleasure.

(b) In addition to performing such other functions

Reprinted from 50 U.S.C. 401.

as the President may direct, for the purpose of more effectively coordinating the policies and functions of the departments and agencies of the Government relating to the national security, it shall, subject to the direction of the President, be the duty of Council—

(1) to assess and appraise the objectives, commitments, and risks of the United States in relation to our actual and potential military power, in the interest of national security, for the purpose of making recommendations to the President in connection therewith; and

(2) to consider policies on matters of common interest to the departments and agencies of the Government concerned with the national security, and to make recommendations to the President in connection therewith.

(c) The Council shall have a staff to be headed by a civilian executive secretary who shall be appointed by the President. . . .

(d) The Council shall, from time to time, make such recommendations, and such other reports to the President as it deems appropriate or as the President may require.

(e) The Chairman (or in his absence the Vice Chairman) of the Joint Chiefs of Staff may, in his role as principal military adviser to the National Security Council and subject to the direction of the President, attend and participate in meetings of the National Security Council.[3]

(f) The President shall establish within the National Security Council a board to be known as the "Board for Low Intensity Conflict." The principal function of the board shall be to coordinate the policies of the United States for low intensity conflict.

Central Intelligence Agency

SEC. 102. (a) There is hereby established under the National Security Council a Central Intelligence Agency with a Director of Central Intelligence who shall be the head thereof, and with a Deputy Director of Central Intelligence who shall act for, and exercise the powers of, the Director during his absence or disability. The Director and the Deputy Director shall be appointed by the President, by and with the advice and consent of the Senate, from among the commissioned officers of the armed services, whether in an active or retired status, or from among individuals in civilian life: *Provided, however,* That at no time shall the two positions of the Director and Deputy Director be occupied simultaneously by commissioned officers of the armed services, whether in an active or retired status. . . .

(d) For the purpose of coordinating the intelligence activities of the several Government departments and agencies in the interest of national security, it shall be the duty of the Agency, under the direction of the National Security Council—

(1) to advise the National Security Council in matters concerning such intelligence activities of the Government departments and agencies as relate to national security;

(2) to make recommendations to the National Security Council for the coordination of such intelligence activities of the departments and agencies of the Government as relate to the national security;

(3) to correlate and evaluate intelligence relating to the national security, and provide for the appropriate dissemination of such intelligence within the Government using where appropriate, existing agencies and facilities: *Provided,* That the Agency shall have no police, subpoena, law-enforcement powers, or internal-security functions: *Provided further,* That the departments and other agencies of the Government shall continue to collect, evaluate, correlate, and disseminate departmental intelligence: *And provided further,* That the Director of Central Intelligence shall be responsible for protecting intelligence sources and methods from unauthorized disclosure;

(4) to perform, for the benefit of the existing intelligence agencies, such additional ser-

vices of common concern as the National Security Council determines can be more efficiently accomplished centrally;

(5) to perform such other functions and duties related to intelligence affecting the national security as the National Security Council may from time to time direct.

NOTES

1. The original designee is no longer a member.

2. The original designee is no longer a member.

3. Other advisers to the National Security Council—contained in separate legislation—include the Director, Arms Control and Disarmament Agency, and the Director, U.S. Information Agency (USIA).

PART II

EARLY YEARS

.... each President may use the Council as he finds most suitable at a given time.

—*Robert Cutler, 1956*

Editors' Introduction

The first meeting of the National Security Council took place on Friday, September 26, 1947—two months to the day after President Truman signed the National Security Act into law. The session convened in the Cabinet Room, establishing a precedent for the location of formal NSC meetings that every administration would follow. President Truman presided and was joined by other statutory members of the Council. Also in attendance was the NSC's first executive secretary, Sidney W. Souers. At that point, in addition to Souers, the NSC staff numbered just three employees.

That first meeting was devoted to organizing the work of the Council, and it was decided that there would be no regular meetings; sessions would be called as needed. Further, attendance would be restricted to those officials specifically mentioned in the National Security Act; others could, however, be invited to attend by the presiding officer, depending on the subjects under consideration. The president made it clear that when he was not in the presiding officer's chair, his secretary of state would be—a reflection of his determination to see the State Department, not the newly created Department of Defense, take the lead institutional role in Council deliberations.

With that inaugural session, the work of the NSC was set into motion. But President Truman made another early decision about the NSC that did not come up at the first meeting, namely, that he would rarely attend future sessions. Still concerned about protecting his prerogatives as chief executive and eager to demonstrate from the outset the advisory—not policy-making—role of the Council, Truman kept the NSC at arms length for the next two-and-a-half years, until the outbreak of the Korean War. Between September 1947 and June 1950, he attended only twelve of the NSC's fifty-seven sessions.

Still, during this initial phase of the NSC—and before President Truman turned to this committee in 1950 as a means of coping with the overwhelming problem of coordination during the Korean conflict—the Council was functioning and growing as an institution. That start-up period for the NSC was the subject of an article written by Sidney Souers while he was serving as executive secretary (1949; see For Further Reading).

Souers's credentials for that job were impressive: a rear admiral in the navy, a successful insurance executive from the president's home state of Missouri, the deputy chief of Naval Intelligence during World War II, and the first director of the postwar Central Intelligence Group (the immediate forerunner of the CIA). The article makes clear, though, that Souers envisioned his role on the NSC as a limited one: "an anonymous servant of the Council," as he put it (1949: 537), who must be willing "to subordinate his personal views on policy to the task of coordinating the views of responsible officials." He was almost as circumspect in describing the role of the Council. Not surprisingly he echoed the president's views that the Council itself does not determine policy, but only prepares advice for the president. Moreover, Souers stated (1949: 536), "the Council has no responsibility for implementing policies which the President approves on the basis of its advice. The respective departments traditionally have carried, and continue to carry, this operating responsibility."

The NSC described by Souers after its first two years in existence was a modest one, a Model T compared with the high-performance policy engine it would later become. Still, in that space of time, Truman had demonstrated the underlying truth about the NSC, namely that ". . . . it is a creature of the president, reflecting his desires and needs." Souers also pinpointed the basic lesson to be drawn from those first two years: "While much remains to be done, at least there is now a place for coordinated consideration of our security problems" (1949: 543). Truman knew that as well, and quickly turned to the NSC for assistance at the outset of the Korean War.

The outbreak of hostilities on the Korean peninsula caused Truman to reconsider his arms length relationship with the Council, and he took several steps to make greater use of it. He directed that regular meetings of the NSC would be held henceforth and he would be there to preside, doing so at sixty-two of the seventy-one Council meetings convened between June 1950 and the end of his term. He also directed that attendance at Council sessions would be restricted to its statutory members, the secretary of the treasury, the chairman of the Joint Chiefs of Staff, the director of Central Intelligence, the executive secretary, and one special assistant, thus cutting back on the size of Council meetings that had grown in his absence.

On July 19, 1950, Truman issued a directive that underscored his decision to make the NSC *the* coordinating committee during the Korean crisis. From now on, the directive stated, all major national security policies were to be recommended to him through the medium of the Council. Truman's greater reliance on the NSC, however, represented neither a reversal of his view regarding the advisory role of the Council nor his determination to avoid sharing decision-making responsibilities with it. "I used the National Security Council only as a place for recommendations to be worked out," he later stated in his memoirs (1956). "The policy itself has to come from the President, as all final decisions have to be made by him." At the end of Harry Truman's term in office, that principle had been firmly established, and it has resisted serious challenge ever since. The Council had established several other precedents, mainly procedural, that future NCSs would honor.

Under Truman, the Council never did become a central vehicle for national security policy making, however, and it fell well short of the high-level authority many had envisioned in 1947 when the National Security Act was passed. Instead, Truman used the Council to supplement other entities and individuals he had chosen to give advice and coordinate policy, including a heavy reliance on the State Department, led in turn by George C. Marshall and Dean Acheson, both of whom Truman relied on to play key roles in the conduct of his foreign policy.

While Truman's limited use of the NSC apparently served his needs, this style failed to fit President Dwight D. Eisenhower's conception of what the NSC should be. As other presidential candidates would do in later years, General Eisenhower made the NSC a campaign issue. In a campaign address, he said: "The failure of this agency to do the job for which it was set up—to make the right plans in time—produces waste on a grand scale. . . . *The National Security Council as presently constituted is more a shadow agency than a really effective policymaker*" [emphasis added].

The former five-star commander of the Allied forces during World War II was intent on changing that. On January 21, 1953, the day after taking office, the new president directed his administrative assistant, Boston banker Robert Cutler, to undertake a study of the Council's organization. On March 16, Cutler reported back with a plan that would give the NSC a major policy-making role. The president approved Cutler's proposal the next day.

The Cutler plan "institutionalized" the NSC, taking the basic structure of the Council under Truman and expanding it into a formal "NSC system" with an elaborate network of committees and staff arrangements. The new NSC was designed to match Eisenhower's decision-making style, which placed a premium on organization and clear lines of authority and command—a preference the president had acquired during his long career in military service. In his memoirs (1963: 121), Eisenhower later stated his views on the value of organization:

> Its purpose is to simplify, clarify, expedite and coordinate; it is a bulwark against chaos, confusion, delay and failure. . . . Organization cannot make a successful leader out of a dunce, any more than it should make a decision for its chief. But it is effective in minimizing the chances of failure and in insuring that the right hand does, indeed, know what the left hand is doing.

As approved by the president, the Cutler blueprint placed the Council at the apex of national security policy making in the Eisenhower Administration. Meetings were to take place on a regular basis—an average of one a week during the administration's first two years, somewhat less frequently after that. And the president would attend; Eisenhower presided at 90 percent of the 366 Council meetings held during his eight years in office. In his absence, the vice-president, not the secretary of state, sat in the presiding officer's chair.

President Eisenhower approved other departures from past NSC practice as well. He created the position of "special assistant for national security affairs" to run the Council's day-to-day affairs, and appointed Robert Cutler to that office. The position of executive secretary was retained but downgraded, put in charge of overseeing the Council's staff (which was greatly expanded to meet the increased workload of the NSC). The president used a third staff officer, his staff secretary General Andrew Goodpaster, to keep him informed of daily operations and intelligence matters.

But Eisenhower's most fundamental departure from the NSC's conduct under Truman was the creation of a highly structured network of committees to assist the Council in its work. A chart of the Eisenhower "NSC system" is presented in Figure IIa. The two principal committees reporting to the Council were the Planning Board and the Operations Coordinating Board (OCB). Together with the Council, they became known as "policy hill." Policy recommendations and advice from the various departments and agencies were coordinated by the Planning Board and forwarded "up the hill" to the NSC for its consideration. Once the Council had met and the president had made his decision, policy flowed "down the hill" to the OCB. The OCB then translated that policy into specific guidance and monitored its implementation.

In 1956, soon after he left his position as special assistant for national security affairs (he would return a year later to serve again), Robert Cutler wrote an insider's view of Eisenhower's NSC (1956; see For Further Reading). Not surprisingly, since he was the author of the study that created the Eisenhower NSC, Cutler is enthusiastic in his support for the Council, arguing that during the Eisenhower Administration, the NSC emerged as an executive body equal in impor-

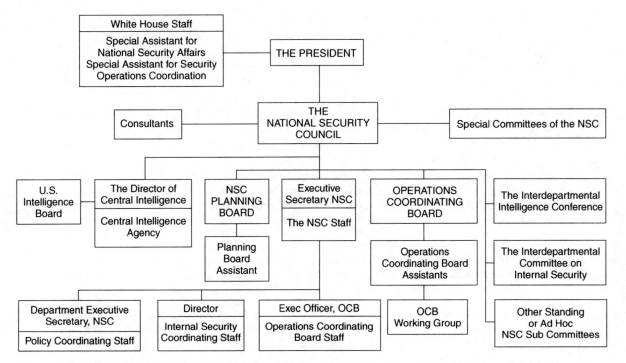

Figure II.A The Eisenhower NSC, 1953–1961 (organization as of 1959) *(Source: U.S. Congress. Senate. Organizing for National Security. Selected Materials. Prepared for the Committee on Government Operations and its Subcommittee on National Policy Machinery (Pursuant to S. Res. 248, 86ᵗʰ Congress). Washington, U.S. Govt. Print. Off., 1960, p. 8)*

tance to the cabinet. His description of Council meetings under Eisenhower is no less an example of NSC boosterism: "Out of the grinding of these minds comes a refinement of the raw material into valuable metal, out of the frank assertion of differing views, backed up by preparation that searches every nook and cranny, emerges a resolution that reasonable men can support" (1956: 443).

Despite this flowery language, Cutler's article provides valuable insights into Eisenhower's perspective on the Council ("a corporate body") and his strong desire for a structured, highly organized Council. "[H]e is at home in this kind of operation," Cutler states (1956: 444). "The old soldier is accustomed to well-staffed work." Cutler also takes into account the incipient criticism directed toward the Eisenhower NSC which, in three years, would assume the formal status of a congressional inquiry. "Of course, disadvantages attend the method of continuous presentation through carefully staffed papers," he admits (1956: 447). "There is a tendency toward formality and stylization. There is eliminated the informal 'kicking out' of a problem at the Council meeting."

Cutler also addressed the roles of the special assistant and the NSC staff. A proposal made by a member of the 1955 Hoover Commission that the staff be increased to "evolve policy ideas for consideration of the Special Assistant and the NSC" was "alien" to him: "An increased permanent staff . . . would, by reason of its location at the apex of government, drift into becoming itself a policy maker . . . an NSC staff operation of the kind suggested would tend to intervene between the President and his Cabinet members . . . Grave damage could be done to our form of government were there an interruption in the line of responsibility from the President to his Cabinet" (1956: 457). Nor did Cutler believe that the role of the national security adviser should be upgraded beyond the administrative tasks of managing the business of the Council and keeping the president informed about its activities.

The first article in this section provides a further look at the Truman and Eisenhower NSCs. Written by Stanley Falk, this essay is a critical analysis of the NSC under its first two presidents. Falk points to lessons learned and precedents set from the experience of both a Democratic and a Republican administration.

Chief among the lessons is one that would remain a constant for future NSCs: the controlling influence would always be the president. According to Falk, "In the final analysis, the personality and individual desires of each president would determine the role and scope of activity of the National Security Council." As Falk emphasizes, President Truman's ambivalence about the Council—stemming from his concern that it might intrude on his decision-making authority—resulted in its limited use during his administration, even after Truman became more directly involved in the NSC with the outbreak of the Korean War. Indeed, at that point, in June 1950, Falk found that: ". . . . the NSC could hardly be regarded as the top policy-formulating agency in government, or even as the primary presidential adviser on national security." And when Falk examined the end of Truman's administration two years later, he found little reason to upgrade his description of the NSC: " . . . during the Korean War phase of the Truman Administration, the NSC played a somewhat larger role in helping to formulate national policy. Yet as a body it was still not dominant."

That conclusion could also be applied to the roles of the Council's executive secretary and the NSC staff. Although they were situated in close proximity to the White House, just across the street in the Executive Office Building (EOB), where all future NSC staffs would reside (the special assistant and his top deputies would move to the White House in the Kennedy Administration), neither the executive secretary nor the NSC staff progressed much beyond their limited administrative functions during the Truman years. At one point, the president even rejected a proposal that his executive secretary be given the additional responsibility of monitoring the presidential decisions that flowed out of NSC deliberations. Truman considered that a departmental, not an NSC, function.

Certain precedents were set, nonetheless, for the Council during this formative stage under Truman. One of the most important, as Falk points out, was Truman's occasional use of the Council as "an intimate forum where the President's top-level advisers could thrash out questions requiring immediate action." Future presidents would make similar use of the NSC as an "intimate forum" during times of crisis. Truman also recognized the occasional need to expand attendance at NSC meetings beyond the Council's statutory membership, as he did in January 1949, when he directed the secretary of the treasury to attend all meetings. President Eisenhower followed suit, arguing that the secretary of the treasury's attendance was necessary "to recognize the relationship between military and economic strength." Truman's NSC set another precedent by establishing certain standing committees to handle particularly sensitive matters, such as intelligence and internal security. These committees were much less formal than the ones established during the Eisenhower Administration, but they set the stage for an "NSC system"—even if in embryonic form.

As for Eisenhower's contribution to the Council, Falk rightly focuses on his principal legacy: the "institutionalized" NSC. With but two exceptions—presidents Kennedy and Johnson—all future presidents would establish formal "NSC systems," albeit suited to their own decision-making style and purposes. Falk notes that supporters of the Eisenhower NSC praised it for its efficient manner of handling the heavy load of Council business, by imposing order and predictability on the process. And during emergencies (including Eisenhower's two extended absences from the White House because of illness), the broad policy guidance that had been approved by the president as a result of Council deliberations "enabled agency and department heads," in Falk's words, "to continue functioning with the full knowledge that they were following approved guidelines."

The centralized NSC system under Eisenhower did not result in the dominance of the special assistant or the NSC staff over the departments and agencies engaged in national security policy. Departmental authority and responsibility for the proposal and implementation of policy was a cardinal tenet of the NSC system throughout the Eisenhower years, reflecting in part the president's reliance on the dominant personality of John Foster Dulles, the secretary of state. Neither was the president himself a captive of the NSC system he had created. Eisenhower sometimes went outside the system, convening different sets of advisers to address issues demanding immediate resolution.

Despite these positive aspects, toward the end of Eisenhower's term in office criticism of the NSC mounted. The NSC had become a "paper mill," said some critics, which presented the Council and the president with overcompromised and watered-down position papers. The highly structured process tended to stifle policy innovation, observed others. Critics charged too, that (in Falk's words) . . . "the Council was incapable of dealing with large, basic problems, that it was over-staffed, excessively rigid, and unable to bring any real focus to bear on major aspects of national security policy."

Not so, says a more recent assessment of the Eisenhower NSC prepared by Fred I. Greenstein and Richard H. Immerman. Their article, entitled "Effective National Security Advising: Recovering the Eisenhower Legacy," appears as the second selection in this section. The two scholars argue that, under President Eisenhower, "the NSC meetings and the process leading up to them made for a well-informed, rigorously analytical national security team, which contributed to the coherence of the administration's policies." Former national security adviser Zbigniew Brzezinski has also lamented the demise of the NSC Planning Board after Eisenhower left office in 1961. "The only place in the government where there can be a long-range planning of a coherent strategy type is," he has suggested, "in some fashion the White House, presumably related to the NSC" (see "Forum on the Role of the National Security Adviser"—the first selection in Part V). Overall, according to Greenstein and Immerman, the depiction of Eisenhower's NSC system by its critics as a bureaucratic machine that spewed piles of useless paper "is a caricature of its operation."

Still, it was that concern (among others) that prompted a member of Congress, Senator Henry Jackson (D–Washington) to call for a major congressional inquiry into the operation of Eisenhower's National Security Council. In a speech to the National War College in April 1959—excerpts of which are included as the third article in this section—Jackson offered a scathing critique of the Council's structure and procedures. "As it now functions," he said, "the NSC is a dangerously misleading facade."

At the heart of Jackson's argument was his view that the most important function of the NSC is to present the president with policy choices, not "ambiguous compromises," which, he maintained, was exactly what the elaborate NSC machinery under Eisenhower was serving up to the chief executive. The result, Jackson summarized succinctly, of this and other organizational ills is that: ". . . . our present NSC system actually stultifies true creative effort in the executive branch."

Three months after this speech, Jackson's congressional inquiry was underway, with him at the helm as chairman of the Senate Government Operations Subcommittee on National Policy Machinery. The Jackson Subcommittee represented the most extensive look at the NSC's operation since the Council's birth twelve years earlier. Not until 1987, the year of the Iran-*contra* scandal, did the NSC again receive such a detailed examination.

The work of the Jackson Subcommittee took more than two years to complete. Over thirty key witnesses were called to testify, and some 2,000 pages of testimony and reports were compiled, bound into three volumes. In December 1960, in advance of the Kennedy inauguration, the subcommittee released a preliminary report "intended to make available to the incoming Administration certain findings about the role of the Council in assisting the President in developing and carrying out national security policy."

Portions of this landmark study are included as the final selection in this part. The next two administrations would largely follow its recommendations; all future administrations would be influenced by it. The report concluded that: "The real worth of the Council to a President lies in being an accustomed forum where he and a small number of his top advisers can gain that intellectual intimacy and mutual understanding on which true coordination depends."

The report recommended "de-institutionalizing" the NSC process, making it more "humanized," with fewer "ritualistic" agendas and meetings; restricting attendance to ensure a more intimate forum; and placing greater emphasis on informal working groups, rather than formal committees, to prepare policy papers and options for Council deliberations. The report also underscored the importance of the secretary of state to the successful operation of the Council, stating that the president must rely on the secretary "for the initial synthesis of the political, military, economic and other elements which go into making a coherent national strategy." Moreover, the secretary "must be mainly responsible for bringing to the President proposals for major new departures in national policy."

At the same time, however, the report emphasized the importance of the NSC staff, and offered a description of the staff's responsibilities that laid the groundwork for more assertive and aggressive NSC staffs—and national security advisers—in the future: "The President should at all times have the help and protection of a small personal staff whose members work 'outside the system,' who are sensitive to the president's own informational needs, and who can assist him in asking relevant questions of his departmental chiefs, in making suggestions for policy initiatives not emerging from the operating departments and agencies, and in spotting gaps in policy execution."

In the introduction to its report, the Jackson Subcommittee noted that an important question facing the new incoming president was "how he will use the Council to suit his own style of decision and action." The early years of the Truman and Eisenhower NCSs had offered contrasting models of how the Council could be used. The recommendations of the Jackson Subcommittee would contribute to yet another institutional change for the Council—indeed, nothing less than a transformation in the role and responsibilities of the national security adviser and the NSC staff.

5

THE NSC UNDER TRUMAN AND EISENHOWER

Stanley L. Falk

The NSC is a creature of the president. This article illustrates how the Council assumed different permutations from 1947–1961, according to the management style for foreign affairs adopted by each president.

I

President Truman's use of the National Security Council,[1] especially in the three years prior to the outbreak of the Korean War, reflected his strong concern for the authority, responsibility, and prerogatives of the chief executive. Congress had declared that the NSC would consist of certain officials whose function it would be to "advise the President . . . in matters involving the national security."[2] But Truman, among others, seriously questioned whether Congress had the constitutional power to require the President to seek advice from specific individuals before reaching decisions on certain subjects.[3] Truman also recognized that the wording of the National Security Act might be construed to establish the Council as an imitation of the British Cabinet, with similar powers and responsibilities, and a subsequent diminution of presidential authority.[4] Indeed, he recalls "There were times during the early days of the National Security Council when one or two of its members tried to change it into an operating super-cabinet on the British model." This he strenuously opposed, as he did all ideas of adopting any aspects of the cabinet system. Under the British system, he wrote later, "there is a group responsibility of the Cabinet. Under our system the responsibility rests on one man—the President. To change it, we would have to change the Constitution. . . ."

As a means of emphasizing the advisory role of the NSC, Truman did not regularly attend Council meetings. After presiding at the first session of the Council on September 26, 1947, he sat in on only eleven of the fifty-six other meetings held before the start of the Korean War. In his absence, in conformity with Truman's view that the Secretary of State was the second ranking member of the Council and that the Department of State would play the major role in policy development, Secretary Marshall (and later Acheson) presided. Beginning in August 1949, when the Vice-President was added to the NSC, that officer took the chair in the President's absence.

Truman's lack of participation in NSC proceedings has often been explained as a means of permitting a free exchange of views that might otherwise have been inhibited by his presence. Some observers have also suggested that the President was simply too busy to attend. It is quite evident, however, that his absence was aimed at clearly establishing the Council's position with respect to the President and at preventing any apparent dilution of his role as chief executive.

This is not to say that Truman regarded the NSC as unnecessary or undesirable. On the contrary, he viewed it as "a badly needed new facility" in the government. "This was now the place . . . where military, diplomatic, and resources problems could be studied and

Reprinted with permission from Stanley L. Falk, "The National Security Council Under Truman, Eisenhower, and Kennedy," *Political Science Quarterly,* 79 (September 1964): 403–434 (the portion dealing with the Kennedy Administration is omitted here).

This study was originally prepared in slightly different form for use by students of the Industrial College of the Armed Forces, Washington, D.C.

Stanley L. Falk is a military historian and lives in Alexandria, Virginia.

continually appraised. This new organization gave us a running balance and a perpetual inventory of where we stood and where we were going on all strategic questions affecting the national security." But the Council was only "a place for recommendations to be worked out." Like the President's Cabinet, it did not make decisions or policy. A vote was "merely a procedural step." Only the President could determine policy and reach decisions, and these were functions he could not delegate to any committee or individual. Even when he sat as chairman of the Council and indicated his agreement with a specific recommendation, this did not become final until the NSC submitted a formal document to the President and secured his written approval. "When the President signs this document, the recommendation then becomes a part of the policy of the government." Here was Truman's understanding of the role of the President, and this firm belief determined his relationship with the National Security Council during the five years that it operated under his direction.

For the first ten months of its existence, the NSC met irregularly in the Cabinet Room of the White House. Beginning in May 1948 meetings were scheduled twice a month, although not necessarily held, and special meetings were sometimes called. Only those officials specified by the National Security Act attended initially, with others invited to participate in discussions of particular interest to their agencies. The Director, CIA, also sat in as an adviser and observer. In January 1949 Truman directed the Secretary of the Treasury to attend all meetings, and, that summer, amendments to the National Security Act eliminated the Service Secretaries from Council membership, added the Vice-President, and, by designating the Joint Chiefs of Staff as the "principal military advisers" to the Council, opened the way for regular attendance by the Chairman, JCS, beginning in 1950.

Reorganization Plan No. 4 of 1949, effective in August of that year, placed the NSC in the Executive Office of the President, where it remains today. This move not only formalized a *de facto* situation, but was dramatic evidence of the position of the Council as an advisory arm of the President rather than as any sort of policy-making "politburo."

To assist the NSC in dealing with specific problems, the Council began to establish certain standing committees, normally representing agencies already participating in its activities but occasionally including members of non-Council agencies as well. These groups were usually created to handle some particularly sensitive matter or one of direct interest to only some agencies on the Council. Among the first of these were two committees concerned with internal security, the Interdepartmental Intelligence Conference and the Interdepartmental Committee on Internal Security, which reported to the NSC through the Council's newly appointed Representative on Internal Security.

The NSC staff, a small body of permanent Council employees and officers detailed temporarily from the participating agencies, was headed by a nonpolitical civilian executive secretary appointed by the President. An "anonymous servant of the Council," in the words of the first executive secretary, "a broker of ideas in criss-crossing proposals among a team of responsible officials."[5] He carried NSC recommendations to the President, briefed the chief executive daily on NSC and intelligence matters and maintained his NSC files, and served, in effect, as his administrative assistant for national security affairs.

The organization of the NSC staff[6] was flexible and, as the Council developed, changed to meet new needs. In general, during the pre-Korean period, it consisted of three groups. First was the Office of the Executive Secretary and the Secretariat, composed of permanent NSC employees, which performed the necessary basic functions of preparing agenda, circulating papers, and recording actions. Next was the Staff, consisting almost entirely of officials detailed on a full-time basis by departments and agencies represented on the Council, and headed by a coordinator detailed from the State Department who was supported, in turn, by a permanent assistant. This body developed studies and policy recommendations for NSC consideration. The third group consisted of consultants to the executive secretary, the chief policy and operational planners for each Council agency. Thus, the head of the Policy Planning Staff represented the State Department, the Director, Joint Staff, represented the Department of Defense, and so forth.

While President Truman, in Walter Millis' phrase, had a "disinclination to make full use" of the NSC,[7] the Council was extremely active in its first years both as a discussion forum and as a medium for drawing up formal statements of national policy on a wide range of subjects. This latter effort was extremely significant. It represented the first attempt in the nation's history to formalize and set down specific national objectives and methods of achieving them in a series of carefully constructed policy papers intended to serve as guides to action for all government agencies. That in practice this attempt turned out to be less successful than many would have hoped is perhaps not as important as the fact that such an ambitious task was ever undertaken in the first place.

Policy papers developed by the NSC fell into four categories. First and most important were the basic comprehensive statements of overall policy, concerned with a broad range of national security problems and the political, economic, and military strategy to be pursued in meeting them. Next were papers bearing on large geographical areas of the world or specific countries. A third category dealt with functional matters such as mobilization, arms control, atomic energy, and trade policies. The final group of papers covered organizational questions, including NSC organization, the organization of foreign intelligence activities, and internal security organization. All of these documents would theoretically dovetail with each other to "form a basis for a balanced and consistent conduct of foreign, domestic, and military affairs related to our national security."[8]

Papers originated in a variety of ways. Some projects grew out of recommendations by the executive secretary, but most developed from suggestions by one or more members of the Council or by the NSC staff. For a while studies or reports prepared by the State-Army-Navy-Air Force Coordinating Committee served as a basis for NSC papers.[9] Initially the State Department was the most important single source of project requests, with the Defense Department a close second.

Most of the early papers developed were of the geographical type, with a basic overall policy document a continuing study under way concurrently. It was not until November 1948 that enough other work had been completed to allow NSC adoption of the first comprehensive basic national security paper. Because this was a formative period for the Council, organizational policies drew next consideration, while few policies of a functional nature were considered. In the spring of 1949, shortly after the beginning of the second Truman administration, the Staff took on the dual job of preparing periodic general reviews of existing policies to determine what revisions were necessary and of drawing up papers on major problems that would discuss policy alternatives without making specific recommendations.

The first step in the development of a paper was usually a meeting of the Staff to consider the problem and define its scope. After each Staff member had obtained the views of his own agency on these questions, one individual would normally be given responsibility for preparation of a draft. The drafts of most of the early NSC papers were written by the State Department Policy Planning Staff, and a few were the products of a number of individual agency contributions integrated into a single report. Whatever its origin, the policy draft was then gone over by the Staff as a whole, which made necessary or desirable changes and attempted to reconcile or spell out any differences of opinion. The paper then went to the consultants who, without formally committing their respective departments, indicated their objections or general concurrences. On occasion, other agencies might also be asked to comment. With this accomplished, the draft, including any unresolved divergencies of view, was forwarded for formal Council consideration. If the subject had military implications, JCS views were also included.

Some papers were submitted to the Council merely for information, others solely as a basis for discussion. Those embodying policy recommendations, however, were forwarded to the President, together with any JCS views, by the executive secretary. The President would then reconcile whatever differences of opinion were still outstanding and, if he agreed, place his approval on the "Conclusions" section of the paper. The appropriate departments and agencies, as notified by the executive secretary, would then implement the new policy. President Truman developed the practice of designating one department head, normally the Secretary of State, as coordinator of all implementation, and periodic reports were also required by the Council.

Once the President had signed an NSC paper and directed that it be carried out, a new policy had, to all intents and purposes, been established and put into effect. But this did not necessarily make it policy in practice. What gave it reality was the President's "will and capability to get it executed."[10] This might mean a hard campaign on the part of the chief executive to educate or arouse public opinion, a long and arduous legislative battle, or a host of other problems to be met before the policy could truly take effect.

In addition to the formal development of policy papers, the NSC during this period also met a number of times to discuss current problems of vital importance to national security. On these occasions, the Council convened without the formality of elaborate preparations or preliminary briefings. Some of these discussions, of course, served as the basis for policy papers, but in other cases the NSC was simply an intimate forum where the President's top-level advisers could thrash out questions requiring immediate action. The Berlin crisis and blockade of 1948 is a good example of this. With President Truman in the chair and General Lucius D. Clay, American commander in Germany, present to report, the Council met several times to discuss developments and make recommendations that the President could act on immediately.[11]

By the beginning of the Korean War, two years and nine months after the establishment of the NSC, the Council had become a well-integrated, functioning organization. It had held more than fifty meetings and taken over three hundred "actions" in the form of approvals, recommendations, and other deliberations. But the Council was still a long way from being the type of body that its creators had envisioned, and many problems, both functional and organizational in nature, were becoming evident.

In the first place, for all of its activities, the NSC could hardly be regarded as the top policy-formulating agency of the government, or even as the primary presidential adviser on national security. President Truman, jealous of his powers and unwilling to rely on the NSC simply because Congress had said he should, did not hesitate to turn to other advisers, in the Cabinet or executive office, or to solicit the advice of members of the Council as individuals in preference to the corporate recommendations of the entire group. The Secretaries of State and Defense were two officials whose counsel the President sought with increasing readi-

ness. Especially important was the role of the Bureau of the Budget in establishing ceilings on defense spending, which gave that agency an impressive fiscal veto on any program recommended by the NSC.

Even the hundreds of policy papers produced by the Council failed to carry overriding weight. These, more often than not, avoided coming to grips with major issues, or when they did so, "lacked the precision and decisiveness necessary if they were to serve as guides to action."[12] Composed less as specific policy directives than as broad statements of principle, they were frequently too general for practical implementation.

In the field of policy-making, as Walter Millis put it, "The effect of NSC is not prominent; NSC no doubt considered the staff papers, debated policy and arrived at recommendations, but every glimpse we have been given of the actual policy-making process in this period shows Defense, State, the Budget Bureau, the White House, making the independent determinations—usually on a hasty if not extemporaneous basis—which really counted."[13] Before the Korean War, noted another observer, NSC actions, with or without presidential approval, "did not play a decisive or a particularly significant role in the defense policy-making or the administration of the military establishment."[14]

If this situation was the result of Truman's unwillingness to use the NSC as Eberstadt had envisioned its use, there were other weaknesses in the system, a few reflecting the President's attitude but others probably the standard organizational growing pains to be expected in such a new and completely different agency.

In the first place, attendance at Council meetings, originally limited to the statutory members, had gradually broadened to include the consultants and other departmental advisers. This not only made for too large a group for free discussion, but also encouraged NSC members to look to their departmental advisers and to present their departmental rather than individual views of problems. In the absence of the President, moreover, discussion was more rambling and diffuse than if he had been present, and important actions were sometimes delayed or taken later outside the Council. Then too, while the executive secretary briefed the President on the meeting, Truman could neither hear the direct expression of individual viewpoints nor, more important, could he discuss these with Council members. This sometimes led members to seek out the President after an NSC meeting and give him their ideas separately, a procedure that downgraded even further the relative importance of the Council as a corporate body.

There were also problems in the functioning of the NSC staff. Other agencies that detailed individuals to the Staff tended increasingly to look upon these people as "foreigners," out of touch with problems and attitudes of their parent organizations. The NSC consultants, on the other hand, heavily engaged in responsibilities within their own departments, were less and less able to devote attention to NSC matters. As a result, Council members began to by-pass the Staff, submitting their policy recommendations directly to the Council, and, at the same time, the Council tended to refer many of its problems not to the consultants but rather to *ad hoc* NSC committees. The absence of sound preliminary staff work frequently led to confusion and delay, as did the necessity for relying on *ad hoc* committees, unfamiliar with the overall national security picture and hampered by difficulties of coordination and perspective. An additional problem was the absence of JCS representation on the Staff, which made it hard to anticipate and allow for probable JCS views on papers before they reached the Council table.

And finally there was the growing anomaly of the Staff representative of the State Department holding the position of Staff Coordinator at a time when the bulk of matters coming before the Council was no longer concerned primarily with foreign affairs. With problems of atomic energy, internal security, defense mobilization, and military strategy becoming increasingly important, and with the consequent growth of the role and responsibilities of other departments and agencies, the Staff Coordinator found himself torn between his duties as an impartial chairman and his function of advocating the State Department position. What was needed, clearly, was a Staff Coordinator without department ties and one, moreover, in close and constant contact with the President and thus personally familiar with his views and requirements.

Recognition of all of these problems led, in late 1949 and early 1950, to considerable study of the role and procedures of the NSC. As a result of recommen-

dations by the executive secretary, deliberations by the Council itself, further investigation by an *ad hoc* committee, the outbreak of the Korean War, and President Truman's own thoughts on the NSC, a number of functional and structural changes took place.

Within a few days after the beginning of the war in Korea, Truman directed that the NSC would meet regularly each Thursday and that all major national security recommendations would be coordinated through the Council and its staff. He himself began presiding regularly at these sessions, missing only nine out of seventy-one NSC meetings held from June 28, 1950, through the end of his administration in January 1953.

In late July 1950, in a directive again underlining the role of the Council in policy formulation, Truman ordered a reorganization and strengthening of the NSC. He limited attendance at NSC meetings to statutory members[15] plus the Secretary of the Treasury, the Chairman, JCS, the Director, CIA, the Special Assistant to the President (W. Averell Harriman), Sidney W. Souers (former Executive Secretary and at this time a Special Consultant to the President), and the Executive Secretary. No one else would be present without Truman's specific approval. The President also directed a reshuffling of the NSC staff. The permanent Secretariat remained, but the Staff and consultants were replaced by a Senior Staff and Staff Assistants. The Senior Staff was composed of representatives of State, Defense, NSRB, Treasury, JCS, and CIA, and shortly thereafter of Harriman's office, and headed by the Executive Secretary, an official without departmental ties. Members were generally of Assistant Secretary level or higher and in turn designated their Staff Assistants.

The Senior Staff participated closely and actively in the work of the Council. Not only did it continue the functions of the Staff, but it also took over responsibility for projects formerly assigned to *ad hoc* NSC committees. It thus provided the Council with continuous support by a high-level interdepartmental staff group. The Staff Assistants, who did most of the basic work for the Senior Staff, spent a large part of their time in their respective agencies, where they could better absorb agency views and bring them to the fore during the developmental phase of NSC papers. The position of the executive secretary, moreover, as chairman of the Senior Staff and also head of the permanent NSC staff in the White House, gave that official an intimate view of the President's opinions and desires that he could bring to bear quite early in the planning process. And finally, JCS and Treasury representation on the NSC staff filled needs that had been long felt.

Other changes also took place on the heels of the 1950 reorganization. At the end of 1950, the President directed the head of the newly created Office of Defense Mobilization to attend Council meetings, and a few months later the ODM Director nominated a Senior Staff member. The Mutual Security Act of 1951, establishing a new foreign aid organization, made the Director for Mutual Security a statutory member of the Council, and he too nominated a member for the Senior Staff.[16] Also, at about the same time, a representative of the Bureau of the Budget began sitting in at certain meetings of the Senior Staff to provide fiscal advice and liaison. And finally, to coordinate the implementation of national security policy and ensure that the NSC was provided with current information, Truman directed the establishment of a unit within the NSC staff to receive and channel to the Council agency reports on the status of approved national security programs.

One other addition to the NSC system came into being in the spring of 1951. This was the Psychological Strategy Board, consisting of the Under Secretary of State, the Deputy Secretary of Defense, and the Director, CIA, with a full-time director and staff. The PSB would develop and coordinate psychological strategy and, as one writer put it, "was to be a sort of a general staff to plan and supervise the cold war."[17] While not actually a part of the NSC, it reported to the Council and its director attended NSC meetings as an observer and was represented by an adviser on the Senior Staff. It marked the first attempt to pull together the nation's psychological planning and operations amidst a growing recognition of the need to counter Soviet use of psychological and other unorthodox methods in the heightening cold war.

The 1950 reorganization did not change substantially the procedure of preparing NSC papers, although it did somewhat tighten up the process. Aside from policy matters concerning the Korean War and related security areas, most Council papers were of the regional policy type and these continued to be pre-pared in initial draft by the State Department. Depending upon the subject, of course, other agencies, the Staff Assistants, and the Senior Staff also contributed to or initiated the draft process. Although President Truman now presided at Council meetings, he did not make an immediate decision on NSC recommendations. This he reserved until after the executive secretary had formally presented him with the Council recommendations and actions.

In the first year after the beginning of the Korean War, the NSC and its Senior Staff were quite active, with the Council meeting about three times each month and the Senior Staff getting together at least twice weekly. By the end of 1951, however, the Council was meeting on an average of a little less than twice a month, the Senior Staff about once a week, and NSC activity was generally lighter. For the most part, during the Korean War phase of the Truman administration, the NSC played a somewhat larger role in helping to formulate national policy. Yet as a body it was still not dominant, since the President continued to look to individuals or other agencies for advice and recommendations in the national security field. The NSC "provided a convenient mechanism" for staffing and coordinating interdepartmental views, but "its position was still somewhat casual."[18]

As summed up by the executive secretary near the close of President Truman's term of office:

> . . . the National Security Council provides the President a readily available means of ensuring that a policy decision he has to make for the security of the nation has been carefully considered from all points of view and by all of the responsible officials in the Executive Branch who are directly concerned. . . . The existence of the Council gives the President a permanent staff agency in his Executive Office which can . . . bring to bear on each grave issue of national security all the talents, resources, and considerations which will help him find the best possible solution.[19]

The NSC was there if the President wanted to use it. But it was no more nor less than he wished to make it.

II

If Harry S. Truman to a large extent limited the role of the National Security Council in policy formulation and integration, Dwight D. Eisenhower may be said to have institutionalized it. President Eisenhower "reactivated" NSC and infused into it a greater responsibility than it had enjoyed under Truman."[20] He did this by formalizing, developing, and expanding the structure and procedures of the NSC and in effect creating an NSC *system* of which the Council was itself the primary but by no means the most significant portion. The NSC system consisted of the central Council supported by a grid of highly standardized procedures and staff relationships and a complex interdepartmental committee substructure. In its final form, this machinery was geared to support the executive decision-making process not as Truman or Kennedy would conceive of it, but, properly, as Eisenhower practiced it. Not surprisingly, the Eisenhower NSC reflected the Eisenhower view of government and specifically of the role of the President.[21]

During the 1952 election campaign, presidential candidate Eisenhower criticized Truman's use of the NSC. He promised that if elected he would elevate the Council to the position originally planned for it under the National Security Act and use it as his principal arm in formulating policy on military, international, and internal security affairs. Accordingly, he asked Robert Cutler, the Boston banker who was soon to become the new President's Special Assistant for National Security Affairs, to make a study of the NSC and recommend ways and means of improving it. Cutler's report, submitted to Eisenhower in mid-March 1953, became the basis of an immediate structural and functional reorganization aimed at systematizing the NSC. Subsequently, these initial changes, and other studies, led to further adjustments during the eight years of the Eisenhower administration.

By 1960, the NSC had developed into a highly complicated but nonetheless smoothly operating machine, with clear lines of authority and responsibility and elaborate yet systematized staff work.[22] The heart of the machine was, of course, the Council itself, with its five statutory members: the President, Vice-President, Secretaries of State and Defense, and Director, Office of Civil and Defense Mobilization.[23] The Council met regularly on Thursday mornings. In addition to the statutory members, as many as a score of others might be present. Normally, the Secretary of the Treasury and the Budget Director attended NSC meetings and, when items pertinent to their responsibilities were being discussed, so did the Attorney General, Chairman, Atomic Energy Commission, and Administrator, National Aeronautics and Space Administration. At the determination of the President, officials such as the Secretary of Commerce or the Chairman of the Council of Economic Advisers might also be present for specific items. Occasionally private citizens, appointed by the President as informal advisers to the Council, might appear to present and discuss their reports. And a large number of others, not formal participants, also attended regularly in various capacities. The JCS Chairman and CIA Director were there as advisers. The Assistant and Deputy Assistant to the President, the Director, USIA, the Under Secretary of State for Economic Affairs, the Special Assistants to the President for Foreign Economic Policy and for Science and Technology, and the White House staff secretary all attended as observers. Staff representation was provided by the President's Special Assistants for National Security Affairs and for Security Operations Coordination and by the NSC Executive and Deputy Executive Secretaries.

As Chairman of the Council, the President was directly supported by two White House Staff members, the Special Assistants for National Security Affairs and Security Operations Coordination. The former was by far the more important. The principal supervisory officer of the NSC, he advised the President on the Council agenda and briefed him before each meeting, presented matter for consideration at the meetings, appointed (with the President's approval) special committees and consultants, and supervised the executive secretary in the direction of the NSC staff. He also had the major responsibility of chairing the Council's two major subsidiary organizations, the Planning Board and the Operations Coordinating Board.

The NSC Planning Board had essentially the same functions as the old Senior Staff and a similar, somewhat expanded, membership. It met regularly on Tuesday and Friday afternoons. Those agencies with permanent or standing representation on the Council itself were represented on the Planning Board by officials at the assistant secretary level, nominated by the department heads and approved by the President. Advisers from JCS and CIA as well as the Special Presidential Assistant for Security Operations Coordination also attended meetings, as did observers from other interested agencies. Staff representation consisted of the NSC Executive and Deputy Executive Secretary and the Director of the Planning Board Secretariat. Planning Board activities were supported by a staff of Board Assistants, the old Staff Assistants under a new name.

The second major staff agency of the NSC was the Operations Coordinating Board. "The OCB," wrote Robert Cutler, "arose like a phoenix out of the ashes of the old Psychological Strategy Board." The PSB "had been premised on the fallacious concept of an independently existing psychological strategy," whereas the members of the Eisenhower administration believed that psychological strategy was an integral part of an overall national security program and could not practically be separated.[24] The purpose of the newly established OCB was not only to coordinate and integrate psychological with national strategy, but also, and more importantly, to act as the coordinating and integrating arm of the NSC for all aspects of the implementation of national security policy.

The OCB met regularly on Wednesday afternoons at the State Department. Permanent membership included the Under Secretary of State for Political Affairs, Deputy Secretary of Defense, Directors, CIA, USIA, and ICA, and the Special Assistants to the President for National Security Affairs and Security Operations Coordination (who served as Chairman and Vice-Chairman respectively). The Chairman, AEC, Under Secretary of the Treasury, and Deputy Director of the Budget attended on a standing basis and other agencies participated on an *ad hoc* basis. An elaborate staff supported the Board, and several of its members normally attended OCB meetings. Despite the strong military representation in other parts of the NSC, no representatives of the JCS participated in the activities of either the OCB or its staff.

Completing the organizational structure of the NSC were the Interdepartmental Intelligence Conference, the Interdepartmental Committee on Internal Security, and other special and *ad hoc* committees, and the NSC staff, which included the Planning Board, OCB, and Internal Security Coordinating staffs.

President Eisenhower's concept of the NSC, as stated by him, was that

> The Council is a corporate body, composed of individuals advising the President in their own right, rather than as representatives of their respective departments and agencies. Their function should be to seek, with their background of experience, the most statesmanlike solution to the problems of national security, rather than to reach solutions which represent merely a compromise of departmental positions. This same concept is equally applicable to advisory and subordinate groups, such as the Joint Chiefs of Staff, the NSC Planning Board, and the Operations Coordinating Board; although the members of the latter two Boards are responsible also for stating the views of their respective departments and agencies.[25]

Within this concept, policy formulation followed a somewhat formalized pattern. A subject for consideration or action might be raised by any part of the NSC system, from the President on down. It might deal with a new problem area, the result of some particular development in world events; it might merely be a suggestion that a standing policy be reviewed; it might be a combination of these or other factors. Discussion or preparation of a preliminary staff study would then begin within the Planning Board. A first draft, prepared by the agency of primary interest, would next be considered, gone over by the Board Assistants working with others within their own departments, and then restudied by the entire Board. This procedure might be repeated several times, frequently in smaller subgroups and often in conjunction with outside consultants, and the whole process would constantly be monitored by the Special Assistant for National Security Affairs and the Executive Secretary. Before formal Council consideration, finally, each member would receive an advance copy of the paper, with JCS comments, and be individually briefed by his Planning Board representative.

Under the Eisenhower administration, NSC papers included a Financial Appendix, something they had not previously contained. This document, specifically called for by the President as a regular part of most NSC papers, was intended to indicate the fiscal implications of the proposed policy and was to be carefully considered by the Council in determining its recommendations.

President Eisenhower sometimes made his decision on these recommendations at the NSC meeting itself, but in most cases a formal record of actions was circulated for comment by the members before it was submitted for final presidential approval. Once the President had made his decision, it was the OCB's function to coordinate and integrate the activities of those departments and agencies responsible for executing the new policy.

The OCB had no authority to direct or control these activities, but it provided a means by which the responsible agencies could consult and cooperate with each other. The Board's own operations were limited to advising, expediting, and following up, although since OCB members were on the Under Secretary level they each had enough authority within their own agencies to see that agreements reached within the Board were carried out. Also, while it did not make policy, the OCB developed or initiated new proposals for action within the existing framework of national security policies. In practice, all of the Board's activities were limited to policies affecting international affairs, since other coordinating mechanisms already existed for the fields of internal security and defense mobilization.

The whole process of policy formulation and implementation has been described by Robert Cutler with a simple and arresting metaphor. The NSC was at the top of "policy hill." Policy recommendations moved up one side of the hill, through the Planning Board to the Council, where they were "thrashed out and submitted to the President." Approved by the chief executive, the new policy traveled "down the other side of policy hill to the departments and agencies responsible for its execution." A short distance down the slope was the OCB, to which the President referred the new policy for coordination and operational planning with the relevant departments and agencies.[26]

The neatness and mechanical order of this process was praised by its supporters as the most efficient means of transacting the heavy load of business with which the National Security Council concerned itself under President Eisenhower. During his first three years in office, for example, the Council met 145 times and took 829 policy actions, as opposed to 128 meetings and 699 policy actions in its more than five years

under Truman. Critics, however, labeled this "mass production, packaging and distribution," and questioned whether truly effective policy could be developed by a form of standardized bulk processing.[27] In reply, supporters of the system pointed out that in times of emergency—President Eisenhower's two illnesses, for example—it had provided a "reservoir of accumulated policy guidance" that enabled agency and department heads to continue functioning with the full knowledge that they were following approved guidelines within "the broad policy concept established by the President."[28]

This sort of exchange was typical of the growing controversy over the NSC that had developed by the late nineteen-fifties. Critics admitted that the Eisenhower NSC had "infused a new order and system into decisions which were once more various and chaotic," that it had "assisted in bringing the departments together in more orderly and cooperative effort" in areas of "comparatively minor importance,"[29] and that its theoretical potentialities were great. But they also charged that the Council was incapable of dealing with large, basic problems, that it was overstaffed, excessively rigid, and unable to bring any real focus to bear on major aspects of national security policy.

Basically, they argued, the NSC was a huge committee, and suffered from all the weaknesses of committees. Composed of representatives of many agencies, its members were not free to adopt the broad, statesmanlike attitude desired by the President, but, rather, were ambassadors of their own departments, clinging to departmental rather than national views. Moreover, the normal interagency exchanges and cross-fertilization that should have taken place outside the NSC were cut off in favor of action within the Council system, where members engaged in negotiation and horse-trading in a process essentially legislative rather than deliberative and rational. The result, as former Secretary of State Dean Acheson charged, was "agreement by exhaustion,"[30] with the ponderous NSC machinery straining mightily to produce not clear-cut analyses of alternate courses, but rather compromise and a carefully staffed "plastering over" of differences.

The Presidential decision, therefore, was based on no deliberate measuring of opposing views against each other, but on a blurred generalization in which the opportunity for choice had been submerged by the desire for compromise. Approved national policy statements, it was argued, were thus not only imprecise, but were also far too broad and sweeping to be applied to specific problems. They were, consequently, all things to all men, with each protagonist of a different line of action finding justification for his own view in the vague or general wording of an approved paper. Even with the best of intentions, an agency or department head often could not divine the precise meaning of an approved policy—with consequent and obvious difficulties in implementing it.[31]

Nor was the OCB of much use in solving the problem. An interdepartmental committee with no authority, it engaged in the same sort of bargaining and negotiation in interpreting and implementing policy as had the Planning Board and Council in creating it. Frequently by-passed or ignored, also, the OCB in the final analysis had little effect on the actual coordination of policy execution.

To make matters worse, the critics went on, the NSC system by its very nature was restricted to continuing and developing already established policies and was incapable of originating new ideas and major innovations. Council members were either too busy in their own agencies or too intent on promoting departmental viewpoints to take the free and unfettered approach to their work on the NSC that was necessary to initiate fresh and imaginative policies. NSC members were well aware, also, that much of national security policy was in fact developed and coordinated outside of the Council, through the Budget Bureau, the Cabinet, or separate policy groups that dealt with matters like disarmament, manpower and reserve policy, or executive organization, or through individuals like the Secretaries of State or the Treasury who exercised personal influence with the President. Frequently departments or agencies purposely by-passed the NSC system in order to ensure the success of critical proposals. Indeed, the whole question of whether national policy was best developed by an NSC consisting of the officials who would implement this policy, and could thus best understand the attendant problems, or by independent bodies of thinkers not limited by operational restrictions was sharply underlined by President Eisenhower's increasing use of outside committees of private citizens to study important problems in the national security field.

To all of these criticisms, the supporters of the NSC system replied vigorously, either denying the accuracy of the critics' premises or the validity of their conclusions or arguing forcefully that if the Council machinery were less than perfect, it was nevertheless an extremely effective means of developing national security policy and the one best suited to the ideas and methods of President Eisenhower.

Some critics, in disparaging the Eisenhower NSC system, had admitted that the policies it developed would probably have been the policies of the Eisenhower administration in any event. Gordon Gray, Special Assistant to the President for National Security Affairs during most of Eisenhower's second term, implied strong agreement with this view. "I suspect," he said, "that the unhappiness of any knowledgeable person with respect to the NSC and its procedures really derives, not from a concern about how the machinery works, but what it produces. This, then, is substantive disagreement. For those, the only solution would seem to be to elect a different President."[32] . . .

V

"Fundamentally," as Robert Cutler observed in 1956, "the Council is a vehicle for the President to use in accordance with its suitability to his plan for conducting his great office." A "peculiar virtue of the National Security Act is its flexibility . . . each President may use the Council as *he* finds most suitable at a given time."[33]

The history of the NSC under [two] chief executives amply bears this out. As a means of assisting the President in the difficult task of forming and implementing national security policy, the Council has played a varied role since its inception. Its role under future presidents may be equally changed, but the need for an NSC or for something similar would appear to be self-evident.

NOTES

1. For this section, see also Sidney W. Souers, "Policy Formulation for National Security," *American Political Science Review,* XLIII (1949), 334–343; James S. Lay, Jr., "National

Security Council's Role in the U.S. Security and Peace Program," *World Affairs*, CXV (1952), 37–39. These and some of the other articles cited below are also reproduced in *Organizing for National Security*, II.

2. National Security Act of 1947, Sec. 101 (a).

3. On this point, see Robert Cutler, "The Development of the National Security Council," *Foreign Affairs*, XXXIV (1950), 442–443; Hammond, "The National Security Council as a Device for Interdepartmental Coordination: An Interpretation and Appraisal." *American Political Science Review*. (Dec. 1960) LIV: 903. President Truman's views on his relations with the NSC are described in his *Memoirs, II, Years of Trial and Hope* (Garden City, N.Y., 1950), 59–60, and the quotations in the following paragraphs are taken from this source.

4. For a fuller discussion of this question, see Hammond, "The National Security Council," 899–901.

5. Souers, 537.

6. In this article, the word "staff" refers to the entire NSC staff organization. The "Staff" and later "Senior Staff" and "Staff Assistants" refer to parts of the "staff."

7. Walter Millis, with Harvey C. Mansfield and Harold Stein, *Arms and the State: Civil-Military Elements in National Policy* (New York, 1958), 182.

8. Souers, 539.

9. The State-Army-Navy-Air Force Coordinating Committee had replaced the wartime State-War-Navy Coordinating Committee. Since its functions closely paralleled or even duplicated those of the NSC staff, the Coordinating Committee was dissolved in 1949.

10. Hammond, "The National Security Council," 907.

11. Truman, *II*, 124–129.

12. Millis, 192.

13. Ibid., 223.

14. Paul Y. Hammond, *Organizing for Defense: The American Military Establishment in the Twentieth Century* (Princeton, 1961), 233.

15. The President, Vice-President, Secretaries of State and Defense, and Chairman, National Security Resources Board.

16. The new Director was Harriman, already a member of the NSC as Special Assistant to the President and already represented on the Senior Staff. He and his representative simply remained at their respective Council assignments, although with different titles.

17. Colonel Wendell E. Little, White House Strategy-Making Machinery, 1952, 1954, Air War College Studies, No. 2 (Maxwell Air Force Base, Alabama, 1951), 20.

18. Millis, 255, 388.

19. Lay, 37.

20. Millis, 182.

21. The literature on the Eisenhower NSC is more extensive than for the Council under Truman. Three NSC officials have written or spoken publicly on the Eisenhower NSC, as have many knowledgeable writers and critics, and extensive testimony was heard by the Jackson subcommittee. A considerable amount of the literature has been reproduced with the testimony in *Organizing for National Security*.

22. For a step-by-step account of organizational developments, see Lay, Jr., James S., and Johnson, Robert H. "An Organizational History of the National Security Council." A paper prepared for the Jackson Subcommittee on National Policy Machinery, 30 April 1960, 23–52.

23. With the abolition of NSRB in 1953, the Director, ODM, replaced the NSRB chairman on the NSC and in 1958 this NSC membership was assumed by the Director, OCDM. Membership in the NSC of the Director for Mutual Security (subsequently the Director, Foreign Operations Administration) was dropped in 1955.

24. Cutler, 448.

25. Quoted in *Organizing for National Security*, II, 129. See also Lay and Johnson, 32–38.

26. Cutler, 448. For case histories of two hypothetical policy decisions, see Cutler's testimony, *Organizing for National Security*, I, 579–583, and Timothy W. Stanley and Harry H. Ransom, "The National Security Council," a study prepared for the Harvard University defense policy seminar, January 1957, in ibid., II, 199–200.

27. Millis, 390.

28. Cutler, 445; Dillon Anderson, "The President and National Security," *Atlantic Monthly*, CXCVII (1958), 46.

29. Millis, 391. Critics and defenders of the NSC under Eisenhower, especially the former, are amply represented in *Organizing for National Security*. See also Hammond, "The National Security Council," 903–910.

30. Dean Acheson, "Thoughts About Thought in High Places," *The New York Times Magazine*, October 11, 1959, reproduced in *Organizing for National Security*, II, 292. The theme of the legislation of strategy is developed at length in Samuel P. Huntington, *The Common Defense: Strategic Problems in National Politics* (New York, 1961), 146–166.

31. The implications of this for military commanders and especially for the JCS were explained by former Army Chief of Staff General Maxwell D. Taylor before the Jackson subcommittee and in his own book: *Organizing for National Security*, I, 787–799; Taylor, *The Uncertain Trumpet* (New York, 1960), 82–83 and *passim*.

32. Gordon Gray, "Role of the National Security Council in the Formulation of National Policy," prepared for delivery to the American Political Science Association, September 1959, in *Organizing for National Security*, II, 189.

33. Cutler, 442–443.

6

Effective National Security Advising
Recovering the Eisenhower Legacy

Fred I. Greenstein
Richard H. Immerman

President Eisenhower "institutionalized" the National Security Council by formalizing and expanding the structure and procedures of the NSC and, in effect, creating an NSC *system*. Critics have said the NSC was overinstitutionalized during this period, with negative consequences for the national security advisory process. This article takes issue with that view.

As the new president and his national security team ready themselves to address the global demands of a new century, they have two broad options. They can follow the precedent of the Clinton administration and take it for granted that the post-cold war international environment does not lend itself to overall planning, responding to international contingencies as they arise. Or they can conclude that precisely because international affairs are no longer defined by the extended confrontation between the United States and the Soviet Union, it is crucial to establish priorities and minimize the danger of being caught flat-footed by emerging developments.

To the extent that it opts for the latter, the new administration would be advised to take note of a national security advisory system that was devised and operated by a chief executive who had devoted much of his adult life to the organization of collective endeavors—Dwight D. Eisenhower, the architect of the Normandy invasion and the Allied campaign in Europe in World War II. During his time in the White House, Eisenhower was beloved by the American people, but widely perceived by political cognoscenti to have been a mere presidential figurehead. We now

know, however, that the former supreme commander was an astute and informed political leader who advanced his purposes by playing down the political side of his leadership and playing up his role as a head of state whose public appeal transcended partisan divisions.[1]

This article is an exercise in the recovery of institutional memory. By outlining the features of the highly systematic Eisenhower national security policy process and analyzing its performance, we seek to enhance the ability of the new administration to structure its operations in a productive manner. The procedures that lead to the selection of American presidents place no premium on choosing candidates with organization competence, particularly in the period since winning the presidential nomination has been a function of a candidate's ability to vie successfully in a marathon of state primary elections. For this reason it is vital that new presidents and their advisers make themselves aware of the rich array of positive and negative models available in the record of the modern presidency. The Eisenhower system has distinctly positive implications for the future of national security policy advising.

Fred I. Greenstein is professor emeritus of politics at Princeton University. Richard H. Immerman is professor and chair of history at Temple University.

A DISCARDED LEGACY

Just as Eisenhower's contemporary critics belittled his political skills, they also deprecated the organizational machinery he instituted for making national security policy. In the aftermath of the Soviet success in launching of a pair of Earth satellites in October 1957, there was an eruption of criticism of the Eisenhower administration for its apparent failure to keep up with the Soviets in intercontinental ballistic missile development.[2] Rather than attack the immensely popular Ike over what they perceived to be a missile gap, many of his critics leveled their fire on the organization of his presidency. They argued that Eisenhower was a misplaced military man who relied on a hierarchy of subordinates, cutting himself off from the diversity of advice and information necessary for a president to engage in effective leadership. One of their principal targets was the institutional machinery he employed to systematize his administration's national security deliberations. Eisenhower's National Security Council (NSC), his critics maintained, was an excessively bureaucratized body out of which emerged "least-common-denominator" policies. Eisenhower's reliance on formal organization, the critique continued, had contributed to unimaginative policies that failed to meet the challenge of global competition with the Soviet Union and its allies.[3]

Upon taking office, John F. Kennedy unceremoniously jettisoned the staff arrangements of the Eisenhower presidency, substituting for it his own famously ad hoc operating methods. Since 1961, there has been an alternating pattern of highly informal and somewhat more formal national security advising, concluding with the notoriously disorganized Clinton advisory process. Meanwhile, the most comprehensively structured of all presidential national security advisory systems—that of Eisenhower—has receded from institutional memory, without receiving an adequate assessment.

Before laying out the principal features of that system, a strong caveat is in order. What we are about to outline is a policy-planning process, not a decision-making process. Eisenhower made the operational decisions of his presidency in informal meetings with small groups of advisers in the Oval Office, not in the

NSC. Nevertheless, the formal and informal national security processes of the Eisenhower presidency complemented one another. Moreover, the formal process was as important for informing Eisenhower's principal national security aides and welding them into a cohesive team as for the written enunciations of national security policy that were its formal product.

Eisenhower's national security system had the following elements, each of which requires elaboration:[4]

- A chief executive with a keen interest in national security policy and the process by which it is made.
- A presidential assistant for national security who was a process manager and not a policy advocate.
- A mechanism for framing the debates of the National Security Council by presenting the participants with draft statements of administration policy and highlighting the points of disagreement among the entities represented in the council.
- Regular NSC meetings in which the policy proposals drafted by the agenda-setting committee were vigorously debated in the presence of the president, who then personally established his administration's policies, providing the council with written reports of his conclusions.
- A body that attended to implementing the policies thus established.

A POLICY-ORIENTED, ORGANIZATION-MINDED PRESIDENT

Dwight Eisenhower entered the presidency with extensive experience in the realms of national security policy and its organization. Before World War II, he had served in responsible staff positions in the War Department and the Philippines, beginning in the late 1920s. Within days after Pearl Harbor, Eisenhower was summoned to the Pentagon to become the army's top strategic planner. In less than a half year later, his base of operations moved to England, where as supreme commander of the Allied military campaign in Europe, he was a significant actor on the international scene, a status that continued in the postwar years.[5]

Eisenhower served as chief of staff of the army from 1945 to 1948. He then retired from active duty to become president of Columbia University, but he regularly commuted to Washington to serve as an unofficial national security adviser to President Harry S. Truman. In 1950, Truman called on Eisenhower as the first military commander of the North Atlantic Treaty Alliance Organization, a capacity in which he played a key part in forging the alliance that waged the cold war. It was only when he reached the conclusion that the almost certain Republican nominee, Senator Robert A. Taft of Ohio, was unprepared to commit the United States to take an active part in the Western alliance that Eisenhower entered the 1952 presidential race. Upon being elected, he embarked on a dual effort to frame an enduring national security strategy and create sound procedures for carrying it out.

No president had a stronger commitment to the effective organization of policy making than Eisenhower. "Organization cannot make a genius out of an incompetent" or "make the decisions which are required to trigger necessary action," he commented in his memoirs. However, "disorganization can scarcely fail to result in inefficiency and can easily lead to disaster."[6] On another occasion Eisenhower observed that the president has a particular need for a "well-developed staff organization" in the sphere of national security, because the international area is fraught with "situations of actual or probable conflict," and "the weaponry of modern military establishments increase their destructiveness" with "bewildering speed."[7]

A NEUTRAL PROCESS MANAGER

The position that has since been occupied by such high profile policy entrepreneurs as McGeorge Bundy, Henry Kissinger, and Zbigniew Brezinski was created by Eisenhower, who stipulated that its incumbent was to be a process manager, not a policy advocate. The importance Eisenhower assigned to that position is evinced by the priority he gave to introducing the first occupant of that role to his colleagues at a 12 January 1953, preinauguration meeting he convened with the future members of his administration. The meeting opened with a review of Inauguration Day events, following which Eisenhower introduced the man he was

appointing to the new position of assistant to the president for national security affairs. He was Robert Cutler, a Boston banker who had been a wartime aide to General George C. Marshall and a foreign policy aide in the Truman administration. Noting that Cutler's position was one of several he had filled with men who were equal in stature to members of the Cabinet, Eisenhower indicated that he planned to transform the NSC into a body that would wrestle constructively with issues bearing on the nation's security.

Cutler then took the floor and outlined his responsibilities. Stressing that he would be exercising his responsibilities with a "passion for anonymity," Cutler remarked that the meetings of the NSC in the Truman administration had been "rather pro-forma."[8] Things would be different in the system he had been instructed by Eisenhower to design. Over the next two months, Cutler consulted with such veteran national security figures as Ferdinand Eberstadt, Robert Lovett, and General George C. Marshall. Marshall set the tone, commenting that Truman's NSC was too "evanescent." The Truman administration NSC meetings were "of busy men who had no time to pay to the business before them, and not being prepared, therefore took refuge in nonparticipation or in protecting their own departments." Marshall identified an additional pair of shortcomings in the Truman NSC: its policy papers "never presented alternatives to decide upon," and Truman himself was not "a force at the table to bring out discussion."[9]

The old hands consulted by Cutler also stressed the need for better coordination of military, diplomatic, and domestic policy; urged that there be greater attention to the financial implications of national security policy; and emphasized the desirability of providing the NSC with a backup staff. Drawing on such advice, Cutler devised a scheme for systematizing the national security advisory process, which Eisenhower instituted by executive order in March 1953.

FRAMING NSC DELIBERATION

The most distinctive component of the newly constituted national security advisory process was the body that set the agenda of the NSC and prepared the documents that framed its debates—the Planning Board.

The board consisted of the assistant secretaries for planning of each of the governmental bodies represented in the NSC, officials who because of their high positions in their departments had full access to their chiefs and could draw on all of the expertise available in their agencies.[10]

The importance of the Planning Board was highlighted by Eisenhower in an early NSC meeting, when he remarked to the council members that they themselves simply did not have the time to think out "the best decisions regarding the national security. Someone must therefore do much of this thinking for you." So that the planning process received the undivided attention of its participants, Eisenhower instructed the board members to avoid accompanying their principals on trips out of the country, remaining on the job in order to "supply a continuity of planning and thought."[11]

The Planning Board, which normally met twice a week, was charged with flushing out the policy views of each of the NSC's member bodies on major national security issues. The board subjected those positions to what Cutler called an "acid bath," sharply delineating them and identifying and specifying points of disagreement. The board was strictly instructed not to water down disagreements or cover them up. Instead, "policy splits" were to be spelled out (often in parallel columns) so that they might be debated in the NSC and resolved by the president.[12]

Before the documents hammered out by the Planning Board were discussed by the NSC, the board members briefed their chiefs on them, explaining their own positions and reviewing the splits. Cutler himself briefed Eisenhower. The superiors of the Planning Board members were not obliged to support the policy recommendations of their department's representatives on the board. Instead, Eisenhower instructed everyone involved in the national security process to view himself as a general presidential adviser rather than a departmental delegate. The Planning Board was the engine of the Eisenhower national security process. While Eisenhower's critics dismissed it as a mere "paper mill," they did so without direct knowledge of its workings. Those who did observe it told a very different story. As one prominent outside observer of the process put it, "Never have I seen a group of men keener, more sensitive in their instinct to understand what was said, more sympathetic to a presentation, or more penetrating in their questions."[13]

THE NSC AS A FORUM FOR RIGOROUS DEBATE

The NSC met 366 times over the eight years of the Eisenhower presidency, an average of forty-four meetings a year. It had a regular meeting time (Thursday mornings) and meeting place (the Cabinet room). Eisenhower presided over 329 of these sessions; the others were held with the vice president or secretary of state in the chair.[14] The council met at a table just large enough to seat the NSC members and a handful of special attendees. Eisenhower sat at the head, flanked by the secretaries of state and defense. Cutler and the men who followed him in his position (Dillon Anderson and Gordon Gray) sat at the foot of the table, presenting the agenda topics and summarizing the points of disagreement in the discussion papers.

Normally the meetings began with an intelligence summary by the director of the Central Intelligence Agency. Eisenhower then typically turned to the secretary of state to open the discussion. Other vocal participants included the secretary of defense, the secretary of the Treasury, the chairman of the Joint Chiefs of Staff, and the vice president. Eisenhower took an active part in the discussions, injecting comments, asking questions, and sometimes taking a devil's advocate stance to probe the implication of a proposal or bring out policy options. In order to make certain that his comments were not mistaken for decisions, Eisenhower and the assistant for national security prepared a record of action after the meeting and distributed it to the council.

Excellent, though not verbatim, records exist of the Eisenhower NSC meetings. These have been extensively studied by historians and political scientists, but largely in analyses of particular episodes, such as the 1954 Indochina crisis and the 1956 Suez crisis. The NSC itself awaits comprehensive examination, but a number of its characteristics are clearly evident. The meetings were notable for their sharpness of focus, which derived from discussion of policy papers prepared by the Planning Board. They were marked by genuine debate, mainly over policies but also over the more general aspects of current operational issues. Early in the 1954 Indochina crisis, for example, there was a pointed disagreement between Joint Chiefs of Staff Chairman Admiral Arthur W. Radford and Treasury Secretary George Humphrey. Radford favored the use of American air power to relieve the French garrison at Dien Bien Phu, but Humphrey warned against squandering the nation's resources on military conflicts in peripheral areas of the world. The final decision, which was made by Eisenhower outside of the NSC, was not to launch an air strike.[15]

Despite the intensity of many of the exchanges, the meetings were conspicuous for their good-humored camaraderie. They also were striking for the openness of the debate. The participants expressed themselves freely, not hesitating to express disagreement with Eisenhower, although it was always evident that he was the ultimate decision maker. The assistant for national security affairs played an active, but largely procedural part in the deliberations. He kept the debate on track, directed the council's attention to disagreements and ambiguities, and watched for signs of policy slippage. Thus on an occasion during the Indochina crisis when Eisenhower remarked that if American troops were deployed in the jungles of Southeast Asia they should be provided with a particular weapon. Cutler pointed out that existing policies made no provision for the use of American troops in Indochina.[16]

Eisenhower never intended the statements of policy produced by the NSC to serve as blueprints for specific operations. When the NSC members did discuss ongoing episodes, they did so in terms of their general implications. In one meeting during the 1956 Suez crisis, for example, Eisenhower redirected a discussion when it strayed into operational matters, reminding the members that they were there to discuss general policy issues. Still, the NSC process informed his operational decisions. Eisenhower stated his view of the relationship between planning and operations in a 1967 volume on national security problems: "To my mind." he wrote, "the secret of a sound, satisfactory decision made on an emergency basis has always been that the responsible official has been 'living with the problem' before it becomes acute." For this reason, he advised President-elect John Kennedy that the NSC was "the most important weekly meeting of the government," an assertion Kennedy did not take to heart.[17]

IMPLEMENTING NSC ACTION

Even before Eisenhower adopted the new process of policy formulation, work had begun on improving the procedure for implementing NSC actions. What emerged was a body called the Operations Coordinating Board (OCB). Like the Planning Board, the OCB was a product of Cutler's consultations with veterans of the postwar national security process. One group of consultants advised Cutler that "there exists a serious gap between the formulation of general objectives and the detailed actions required to give effect to them." The consultants recommended that there be created "within the National Security Council structure, a group capable of assuring the coordinated execution of national security policies"—an organ like the Planning Board that represented the agencies and departments with input into foreign policy. Eisenhower swiftly endorsed the recommendation.[18]

Like the Planning Board, the OCB consisted of top second-level officials in the agencies responsible for national security. It was chaired by the undersecretary of state, and its members included such officials as the deputy secretaries of defense and mutual security. Its executive officer also attended Planning Board meetings. Just as the Planning Board drafted the policy papers deliberated on by the NSC, the OCB made plans for carrying out the policies that emerged from the NSC process. To that end, the OCB transmitted regular reports to the NSC, summarizing the actions it had taken to execute policies, and evaluated the policies' "effectiveness, timeliness, and applicability."[19] Cutler and his successors included discussions of these reports on the NSC agenda. The performance of the OCB never achieved Eisenhower's expectations. Still, he and his associates never doubted that it made an important contribution to America's national security, if only because it fostered regular give and take on the part of officials who needed to cooperate with one another in order to execute the nation's foreign and national security policies.

A BOTTOM LINE

Eisenhower's NSC system was depicted by its critics as a bureaucratic machine that spewed piles of useless paper. That is a caricature of its operation. It did produce numerous policy documents, but a high proportion of them proved to be of enduring value in the nation's foreign policy. It also had major informal consequences. The NSC meetings and the processes leading up to them made for a well-informed, rigorously analytical national security team, which contributed to the coherence of the administration's policies. Eisenhower's aides knew where he stood on particular issues and what his overall policies were. Aware that they had had their say, Eisenhower's associates displayed impressive public cohesion. There was a general absence of the public and semipublic feuds and cleavages that have marked a number of later presidencies, as well as of the tension that existed in many later presidencies between the secretary of state and the national security adviser. Eisenhower's national security process was also unlike that of a number of later presidents in that it made full use of the expertise of the departments and agencies represented in the NSC.

Because Eisenhower was a national security professional with long-established and well-grounded views of national security, he was better equipped than most chief executives have been to operate without an elaborate foreign affairs advisory system. He nevertheless held that the NSC enhanced and enriched his thinking. Even when he chose to take a different course of action from that favored by his subordinates, he once wrote, "the NSC debates never failed to give me a deeper understanding of questions. In several instances, I might add, such deliberations persuaded me to reverse some of my preconceived notions."[20]

The spirit of Eisenhower's national security advisory process anticipated one of the most thoughtful proposals that has been offered for improving national security advising—the Stanford University political scientist Alexander L. George's 1972 proposal for an organizational arrangement in which the president is exposed to vigorous multiple advocacy of a wide range of policies in a process that is supervised by an assistant for national security who is a "custodian-manager" rather than a policy advocate.[21] In an oral history interview that preceded George's proposal by a number of years, Eisenhower presaged that proposal with the following observation about his philosophy of decision making, which is applicable both to the policy planning process he instituted and to his operational decisions:

I have been forced to make decisions, many of them of a critical character, for a good many years, and I know of only one way in which you can be sure you have done your best to make a wise decision. That is to get all of the [responsible policy makers] with their different viewpoints in front of you, and listen to them debate. I do not believe in bringing them in one at a time, and therefore being more impressed by the most recent one you hear than the earlier ones. You must get courageous men of strong views, and let them debate and argue with each other. You listen, and see if there's anything been brought up, any idea, that changes your own view, or enriches your view or adds to it. Then you start studying. Sometimes the case becomes so simple that you can make a decision right then. Or you might wait if time is not of the essence. But you make it.[22]

Eisenhower's NSC process did not guarantee the success of his administration's national security actions. However, it increased the likelihood that those actions would be grounded in sound information and rigorous analysis. Eisenhower's two terms were notable for the absence of the kinds of flawed consultations that led to such fiascoes as Kennedy's abortive effort to land anti-Castro guerrillas at Cuba's Bay of Pigs in 1961 and Jimmy Carter's failed hostage rescue mission in Iran in 1980.[23]

One size does not fit all in presidential organization: advisory processes must be tailored to the individual they serve. Still, even if the next and future presidents do not adopt the Eisenhower system in toto, they may want to adapt features of it to their own needs. Whatever they chose to do, they would be wise to emulate Eisenhower in melding policy planning with political operations.

NOTES

1. Fred I. Greenstein, *The Hidden-Hand Presidency: Eisenhower as Leader* (Baltimore: Johns Hopkins University Press, 1994); and most recently, Greenstein, *The Presidential Difference: Leadership Style from FDR to Clinton* (New York: Free Press, 2000), esp. chap. 4. See also Richard H. Immerman, "Confessions of an Eisenhower Revisionist: An Agonizing Reappraisal," *Diplomatic History* 14 (Summer 1990): 319–342.

2. Peter Roman, *Eisenhower and the Missile Gap* (Ithaca, NY: Cornell University Press, 1995).

3. This critique was reflected throughout the hearings conducted by the U.S. Senate Committee on Government Operations' Subcommittee on National Policy Machinery. The hear-

ings began in 1959 under the chairmanship of Senator Henry M. Jackson (D–WA). See Henry M. Jackson, ed., *The National Security Council: Jackson Subcommittee Papers on Policy-Making at the Presidential Level* (New York: Praeger, 1965).

4. On the organization and fundamental components of Eisenhower's national security process, see Robert R. Bowie and Richard H. Immerman, *Waging Peace: How Eisenhower Shaped an Enduring Cold War Strategy* (New York: Oxford University Press, 1998), esp. chap. 5.

5. Biographies of Eisenhower are numerous. For an explicit discussion of Eisenhower's pre-presidential career as preparation for his management of security after 1953, see Bowie and Immerman, *Waging Peace: How Eisenhower Shaped an Enduring Cold War Strategy*, esp. chap. 2.

6. Dwight D. Eisenhower, *The White House Years: Mandate for Change, 1953–1956* (Garden City, NY: Doubleday, 1963), 114.

7. Dwight D. Eisenhower, "The Central Role of the President in the Conduct of Security Affairs" in Amos A. Jordon, ed., *Issues of National Security in the 1970s: Essays Presented to Colonel George A. Lincoln on his Sixtieth Birthday* (New York: Praeger, 1967), 207.

8. Proceedings of the Cabinet Meetings, 12–13 January 1953, "Cabinet Meeting January 12–13, 1953," Cabinet series, Dwight D. Eisenhower Papers as President of the United States, 1953–1961 (Ann Whitman File), Dwight D. Eisenhower Library, Abilene, KA (hereafter cited as AWF).

9. George Marshall testimony, NSC Study, 19 February 1953, "NSC—Organization and Functions [1949–1953] (5)," NSC series, Administrative subseries, Records of the White House Office of the Special Assistant for National Security Affairs, Eisenhower Library.

10. Unlike the cabinet, the NSC has a statutory basis. It was instituted in the National Security Act of 1947. During the period of the Eisenhower presidency, its statutory members were the president, vice president, secretary of state, secretary of defense, and director of the office of defense mobilization. Because of the importance of economic solvency in his national security policy, Eisenhower added the secretary of the Treasury and the director of the Bureau of Budget to this group. The director of the Central Intelligence Agency and the chairman of the Joint Chiefs of Staff attended NSC meetings in an advisory capacity. Critics of the process had the mistaken impression that the Eisenhower NSC was a huge and unwieldy body, an impression that may have been fostered by the attendance when appropriate of a variety of staff aides, who sat along the wall but did not take part in the discussions.

11. Memorandum of NSC meeting, March 19, 1953, "137th meeting of the NSC," NSC series, AWF; Brief Notes on Planning Board Meeting, May 6, 1953, CJCS 334 (NSC) 1953, U.S.

Department of Defense, Records of the Joint Chiefs of Staff, Record Group 218, National Archives II, College Park, MD.

12. Greenstein, *Hidden-Hand Presidency*, 128–29.

13. Entry for 1 March 1954, Clarence Randall Journals, volume 1, "Washington After the Commission," Princeton University, Clarence Randall Papers, Princeton, New Jersey.

14. Gordon Gray to Eisenhower, 13 January 1961, "Gray, Gordon," Name Series, AWF.

15. John P. Burke, Fred I. Greenstein, with the collaboration of Larry Berman and Richard Immerman, *How Presidents Test Reality: Decisions on Vietnam, 1954 and 1965* (New York: Russell Sage, 1989), 72–73.

16. Cutler's statement may seem to have been an expression of opposition to American military involvement in Indochina, but on other occasions he warned against departures from the existing policy that would have increased the likelihood of a communist victory in Indochina.

17. Dwight D. Eisenhower, "The Central Role of the President in the Conduct of Security Affairs" in Jordon, ed., *Issues in National Security in the 1970s*, 214; entry for December 6, 1960, in Robert F. Ferrell, ed., *The Eisenhower Diaries* (New York: Norton, 1981), 379–80.

18. Report to the President by The President's Committee on Informational Activities [Jackson Committee], 30 June 1953, *Foreign Relations of the United States, 1952–54*, 2:1854–55.

19. Informal note of Jackson Committee meeting, 28 March 1953, "Special Assistant (Cutler) memoranda, 1953 (1)," Executive Secretary's subject file series, Papers of the White House Office of the National Security Council Staff, Eisenhower Library.

20. "As early as 1954," he went on to say, "I had concluded that the American contingent in NATO should immediately be substantially reduced. After long discussions with the state and defense departments and the CIA, however, I had to change my mind." Eisenhower, "The Central Role of the President in the Conduct of Security Affairs," 215.

21. George L. Alexander, "The Case for Multiple Advocacy in Making Foreign Policy," *American Political Science Review* 66 (September 1972): 751–85.

22. Dwight D. Eisenhower, Columbia Oral History Interview, 20 July 1967. Our citation comes from the original draft transcript of the oral history that is available at the Eisenhower Library. The transcript released to the public omits the passage that we quote.

23. The greatest contretemps of the Eisenhower presidency was the Soviets' downing of a U.S. U-2 plane in the spring of 1960, an event that doomed a planned summit conference between Eisenhower and Nikita Khrushchev. The plane in question was overflying the Soviet Union as part of a highly classified program that had not been brought to the attention of the NSC.

7

FORGING A STRATEGY FOR SURVIVAL

Henry M. Jackson

Calling the NSC a "dangerously misleading facade," Senator Jackson urged a reorganization of the Council in a speech before the National War College. He was soon thereafter named chairman of a subcommittee on national policy machinery to study the NSC further and recommend improvements.

General Harrold, faculty, members of the National War College and Industrial College of the Armed Forces, I am honored to have this opportunity to talk to you again. I thoroughly enjoy these occasions—above all the question period which follows this opening statement. So I will immediately get down to the presentation of my theme.

The central issue of our time is this: Can a free society so organize its human and material resources as to outperform totalitarianism? Can a free people continue to identify new problems in the world and in space—and respond, in time, with new ideas? I think you would agree with me that the answer to these two questions is now in doubt. . . .

One thing I am sure would help—better machinery for policy-making.

Organization by itself cannot assure a strategy for victory in the cold war. But good organization can help, and poor organization can and does hurt. Let's face it: we are poorly organized.

Also, unlike some problems that confront us, that of organization is within the power of the Congress to tackle.

We now have an enormous executive branch and elaborate policy mechanisms: The Office of the President, the Cabinet, the National Security Council, and its two subsidiaries, the Operations Coordinating Board and the Planning Board. We have the Joint Chiefs of Staff, the Office of the Secretary of Defense, the Office of the Secretary of State—departmental planning staffs, and hundreds of advisory boards, steering groups, interdepartmental committees, and special presidential committees like the Draper Committee.

Yet this modern Hydra, with nine times nine heads, fails to produce what we need.

According to the chart it does the job:

The Planning Board of the National Security Council plans and proposes new policies and programs. These go for consideration to the heads of Departments who are members of the National Security Council. An agreed paper is approved by the National Security Council—which serves as an advisory board for the President. The President decides. The policy is then implemented under the watchful eye of the Operations Coordinating Board. And the President has a clear and consistent policy to spell out for the American people.

The procedure is pretty as a picture—and that is what it is, a pretty picture on an organization chart. It has little or nothing to do with reality.

First, the NSC is not and by its nature cannot be an effective planning agency, except in the most Olympian sense.

The President may and should make the most basic strategic decisions—such as the decision in 1941 to

---

Reprinted from Senator Henry M. Jackson, "How Shall We Forge a Strategy for Survival?" Address before the National War College, Washington, D.C., April 16, 1959.

Henry M. Jackson served as a Democratic senator from the state of Washington, 1952–1983.

defeat Germany first and Japan second. In making such decisions the President no doubt needs the advice and counsel of an agency like the NSC. But neither the President nor the NSC and its Planning Board can make the detailed plans necessary to give effect to the basic strategic decisions. Planning of this sort requires the knowledge and experience of the experts, and also the resources and the environment of the Department having the main responsibility for the operations being planned. It is only in the Department concerned that the necessary conditions for extended creative planning work can be provided. And of course there must be cross-contacts and cross-stimuli between experts in the several Departments, at the level where planning is done.

The proper role of the NSC is to criticize and evaluate Departmental planning and proposals in light of the knowledge, interests, and possibly conflicting policies of other Departments. In this way what we call a coordinated view may be developed, and such a view may be very helpful to the President in making a clear determination of the executive will.

If, however, the official views of other Departments are expressed at the planning stage, as they will be if planning is undertaken at the NSC level, compromise and Departmental jockeying begin too early. The result is that clear and purposeful planning becomes almost impossible. The effort to make the NSC a planning agency, therefore, has been a serious mistake in my view.

Second, and again in the nature of things, top-level officers cannot thoroughly consider or think deeply about plans. They need to be confronted with the specific issues which grow out of an effort to harmonize a new policy with other policies. The so-called Planning Board can be very helpful by identifying such conflicts, defining them sharply, and presenting the distilled issues to the top level for decision. This is an essential function—but it is not the first step in policy planning and should not be mixed up with the first step.

You know the typical week in the life of a Cabinet officer—7 formal speeches, 7 informal speeches, 7 hearings on the Hill, 7 official cocktail parties, 7 command dinner engagements. It is a schedule which leaves no time for the kind of reflection essential to creative planning. What they can do, should do, must do—and all that they should be asked to do—is to pass judgment on sharply defined policy issues.

Of course Cabinet members have the obligation to encourage and back the officers in their Department who are charged with policy planning. The responsibility of the policy planner should run clearly to his Departmental head. In this way staff planning can be geared into line decisions—and the authority of the Departmental head can support and strengthen the hand of the planner.

But I am convinced that we will never get the kind of policy planning we need if we expect the top-level officers to participate actively in the planning process. They simply do not have the time, and in any event they rarely have the outlook or the talents of the good planner. They cannot explore issues deeply and systematically. They cannot argue the advantages and disadvantages at length in the kind of give-and-take essential if one is to reach a solid understanding with others on points of agreement and disagreement.

Third, and largely for these reasons, a plan originating in the NSC will almost inevitably possess a fatal flaw; namely, a lack of internal consistency.

Good plans must be coherent; they must have sharp edges, for their purpose is to cut through a problem; their various elements must be harmonious and self-supporting. They must have the kind of logic, or, if you prefer, the kind of thematic unity which grows out of the uncompromising and uncompromised efforts of a creative mind. Compromise must come, but it should come *after* the planning process has been completed and as an adjustment of conflicts between a coherent plan and other coherent plans.

As you well know, NSC papers are in the end the result of compromises between different Departments. That is as it must be. The question is: What should the NSC seek to compromise? My answer is that the NSC should be presented with the most sharply defined policy issues and choices, not with papers which have already lost their cutting edge by a process of compromise at lower levels. When compromise begins at the planning stage, the issues which come to the NSC have already lost their sharpness, clarity, and bite. The paper which is already inoffensive to every Department may be easily approved, but it is also useless.

In short, plans which do not lead to sharp disputes at the NSC level are not good plans; they do not present the kind of issues which the top level ought to be called upon to decide in this hard-slugging contest between the Sino-Soviet bloc and ourselves.

There is, I submit, a role for both Chiefs and Indians, and only confusion can result when the Indians try to do the work of compromise which is the job of Chiefs.

As it now functions, the NSC is a dangerously misleading facade. The American people and even the Congress get the impression that when the Council meets, fresh and unambiguous strategies are decided upon. This is not the case, though it ought to be the case. The NSC spends most of its time readying papers that mean all things to all men.

An NSC paper is commonly so ambiguous and so general that the issues must all be renegotiated when the situation to which it was supposed to apply actually arises. By that time it is too late to take anything but emergency action.

Fourth, national decision-making, as a result, becomes in fact a series of ad hoc, spur of the moment, crash actions.

Because the NSC does not really produce strategy, the handling of day-to-day problems is necessarily left to the Departments concerned. Each goes its own way because purposeful, hard-driving, goal-directed strategy, which alone can give a cutting edge to day-to-day tactical operations, is lacking.

Henry Kissinger has well described the kind of strategy which is the product of this process: "It is as if in commissioning a painting, a patron would ask one artist to draw the face, another the body, another the hands, and still another the feet, simply because each artist is particularly good in one category." It is small wonder that the meaning of the whole is obscured both to the participants and to the public.

Indeed, and this is perhaps the most serious criticism, our present NSC system actually stultifies true creative effort in the executive branch.

Because planning is supposed to take place at the NSC level, the Departments are relieved of responsibility for identifying upcoming problems and for generating new ideas and are even discouraged from trying. The Indians are supposed merely to carry out existing policy, not to propose new policy. The result is that a vast reservoir of talent goes largely untapped.

Creative thought generally springs from daily concern with real problems, from the efforts of operators to operate. The new idea seldom comes from the man who turns his mind to a problem now and then; it comes from the man who is trying to lick a problem and finds that he can't lick it with the tools he has.

The present NSC process, furthermore, has reduced the cross-contacts and cross-stimuli between the Departments and services at the level where planning and operating take place or should take place.

One reason for this is that, in principle, no contacts are needed if policy planning is reserved to higher levels, and the lower levels are supposed to restrict themselves to carrying out instructions. Another reason may be that when planning is reserved to the highest levels, each Department considers that it must prepare to fight a battle in the NSC for its special point of view. It, therefore, mobilizes itself for making its case in a manner that will support and show off the Departmental viewpoint to the best advantage. Contacts with other Departments are discouraged because they might provide them with arguments with which to rebut the views of one's own Department.

The bankruptcy of the present NSC technique is dramatized by the administration's increasing reliance on "distinguished citizens committees" both to review past policies and also to recommend future action—the Gaither Committee, the Draper Committee, the Boechenstein Committee—and so on. These committees may come up with excellent ideas—though this is probably the exception, not the rule. But few of the ideas are used.

Once such a temporary committee has presented its report, it is obviously in a poor position to fight its suggestions through to a decision. And the fresher its ideas, the greater the need for a hard fight to overcome vested interests in current policy. The fate of the Gaither Report is a classic case in point.

The sum of the matter is this: Our governmental processes do not produce clearly defined and purposeful strategy for the cold war. Rather they typically issue in endless debate as to whether a given set of circumstances is in fact a problem—until a crisis removes all doubt, and at the same time removes the possibility of effective action.

I grant that the cold war challenges our organizational ability to the limit. Yet think back to what we accomplished in World War II. With the stimulus of war, we put together a clearly defined national program of requirements and priorities. Then we set national goals to meet them. And we exerted the needed effort. Between 1940 and 1944 we increased the real value of our gross national product by 55 percent, and while putting 11 million men into uniform and sending them all over the world, we were still able to increase the real consumption of goods and services by about 11 percent during that period.

Or think back to Korea. Between 1950 and 1953 we increased the real value of our gross national product by 16 percent and while multiplying defense expenditures threefold, we increased the real consumption of goods and services by about 8 percent.

Can we organize such an effort without the stimulus of war? This is the heart problem of our time. Can a free society successfully organize itself to plan and carry out a national strategy for victory in the cold war?

I recently proposed to my colleagues in Congress that we make a full-dress study of this problem, with public hearings and a formal report. This would be the first congressional review of Government methods for formulating national policy in the cold war. The study would be conducted in a nonpartisan manner. We would not be interested in destructive criticism but in constructive help.

The general questions that need consideration run something like this:

1. What is the present structure for formulating national policy?
2. What is it supposed to accomplish?
3. Is it doing it?
4. In what areas are there grave shortcomings?
5. Why is this the case?
6. What improvements should be made?

8

ORGANIZING FOR NATIONAL SECURITY

Jackson Subcommittee

The Jackson Subcommittee presented an important critique of the NSC, faulting it for growing too large and too bureaucratic.

By law and practice, the President has the prime role in guarding the Nation's safety. He is responsible for the conduct of foreign relations. He commands the Armed Forces. He has the initiative in budgetmaking. He, and he alone, must finally weigh all the factors—domestic, foreign, military—which affect our position in the world and by which we seek to influence the world environment.

The National Security Council was created by statute in 1947 to assist the President in fulfilling his responsibilities. The Council is charged with advising the President—

> with respect to the integration of domestic, foreign, and military policies relating to the national security so as to enable the military services and the other departments and agencies of the Government to coop- erate more effectively in matters involving the national security.

The NSC was one of the answers to the frustrations met by World War II policymakers in trying to coordi- nate military and foreign policy. It is a descendant of such wartime groups as the State-War-Navy Coordi- nating Committee (SWNCC).

The Council is not a decisionmaking body; it does not itself make policy. It serves only in an *advisory* capacity to the President, helping him arrive at deci- sions which he alone can make.

Although the NSC was created by statute, each successive President has great latitude in deciding how he will employ the Council to meet his particular

needs. He can use the Council as little, or as much, as he wishes. He is solely responsible for determining what policy matters will be handled within the Coun- cil framework, and how they will be handled.

An important question facing the new President, therefore, is how he will use the Council to suit his own style of decision and action.

This study, drawing upon the experience of the past 13 years, places at the service of the incoming admin- istration certain observations concerning the role of the Council in the formulation and execution of national security policy.

THE COUNCIL AND THE SYSTEM

When he takes office in January, the new President will find in being a *National Security Council* and an *NSC system.*

The Council itself is a forum where the President and his chief lieutenants can discuss and resolve prob- lems of national security. It brings together as statutory members the President, the Vice President, the Secre- taries of State and Defense, the Director of the Office of Civil and Defense Mobilization, and as statutory advisers the Director of Central Intelligence and the chairman of the Joint Chiefs of Staff. The President can also ask other key aides to take part in Council deliberations. The Secretary of the Treasury, for exam- ple, has attended regularly by Presidential invitation.

But there is also in being today an NSC system, which has evolved since 1947. This system consists of

Reprinted from "Organizing for National Security," *Staff Reports and Recommendations,* Vol. 3, Subcommittee on National Policy Machinery, Committee on Government Operations, U.S. Senate (Washington, D.C.: Government Printing Office, 1961).

highly institutionalized procedures and staff arrangements, and a complex interdepartmental committee substructure. These are intended to undergird the activities of the Council. Two interagency committees—the Planning Board and the Operations Coordinating Board—comprise the major pieces of this substructure. The former prepares so-called "policy papers" for consideration by the Council; the latter is expected to help follow through on the execution of presidentially approved NSC papers.

The new President will have to decide how he wishes to use the Council and the NSC system. His approach to the first meetings of the Council under his administration will be important. These early sessions will set precedents. Action taken or not taken, assignments given or not given, invitations to attend extended or not extended, will make it subsequently easier or harder for the President to shape the Council and the system to his needs and habits of work.

He faces questions like these: What principals and advisers should be invited to attend the first Council meetings? What part should Presidential staff assistants play? What should the participants be told about the planned role and use of the NSC system? Who will prepare the agenda? What items will be placed on the agenda? Should the Council meet regularly or as need arises?

THE NEW PRESIDENT'S CHOICE

The New President has two broad choices in his approach to the National Security Council.

First: He can use the Council as an intimate forum where he joins with his chief advisers in searching discussion and debate of a limited number of critical problems involving major long-term strategic choices or demanding immediate action.

Mr. Robert Lovett has described this concept of the Council in terms of "a kind of 'Court of Domestic and Foreign Relations'":

The National Security Council process, as originally envisaged—perhaps "dreamed of" is more accurate—contemplated the devotion of whatever number of hours were necessary in order to exhaust a subject and not just exhaust the listeners.

The purpose was to insure that the President was in possession of all the available facts, that he got first-hand a chance to evaluate an alternative course of action disclosed by the dissenting views, and that all implications in either course of action were explored before he was asked to take the heavy responsibility of the final decision.

Second: The President can look upon the Council differently. He can view it as the apex of a comprehensive and highly institutionalized system for generating policy proposals and following through on presidentially approved decisions.

Seen in this light, the Council itself sits at the top of what has been called "policy hill." Policy papers are supposed to travel through interdepartmental committees up one side of the hill. They are considered in the Council. If approved by the President, they travel down the opposite side of the hill, through other interdepartmental mechanisms, to the operating departments and agencies.

THE COUNCIL'S SPAN OF CONCERN

The voluminous record of meetings held, and papers produced, makes it clear that the Council and its subordinate machinery are now very busy and active. A long list of questions always awaits entry on the NSC agenda.

Presidential orders now in force provide that all decisions on national security policy, except for special emergencies, will be made within the Council framework. In theory, the embrace of the NSC over such matters is total.

Yet many of the most critical questions affecting national security are not really handled within the NSC framework.

The main work of the NSC has centered largely around the consideration of *foreign policy* questions, rather than *national security* problems in their full contemporary sense. A high proportion of the Council's time has been devoted to the production and study of so-called "country papers"—statements of our national position toward this or that foreign nation.

The Council, indeed, appears to be only marginally involved in helping resolve many of the most important problems which affect the future course of national security policy. For example, the Council seems to have only a peripheral or *pro forma* concern with such matters as the key decision on the size and composition of the total national security budget, the strength and makeup of the armed services, the scale and scope of many major agency programs in such fields as foreign economic policy and atomic energy, the translation of policy goals into concrete plans and programs through the budgetary process, and many critical operational decisions with great long-term policy consequences.

The fact is that the departments and agencies often work actively and successfully to keep critical policy issues outside the NSC system. When policy stakes are high and departmental differences deep, agency heads are loath to submit problems to the scrutiny of coordinating committees or councils. They aim in such cases to bypass the committees while keeping them occupied with less important matters. They try to settle important questions in dispute through "out of court" informal interagency negotiations, when they are doubtful of the President's position. Or else they try "end runs" to the President himself when they think this might be advantageous.

Despite the vigorous activity of the NSC system, it is not at all clear that the system now concerns itself with many of the most important questions determining our long-term national strategy or with many of the critical operational decisions which have fateful and enduring impact on future policy. . . .

THE COUNCIL ITSELF

The National Security Council now holds regular weekly meetings. The meetings vary in size. Sometimes the President meets with only a handful of principals in conducting important business. On other occasions, 30 or 40 people may attend. A typical session, however, may have two dozen people present. Some 15 people may sit at the Council table, with perhaps another 10 looking on as observers and aides.

Mr. James Perkins has made this comment on the size of Council meetings:

I think that the more one uses the NSC as a system of interagency coordination and the legitimatizing of decisions already arrived at, the growth in numbers is inevitable, because people left out of it and not at the meetings whose concurrence is required have a prima facie case for attending.

But if one views the Council primarily as a Presidential advisory body, the point quickly comes when the sheer numbers of participants and observers at a meeting limits the depth and dilutes the quality of the discussion. The present size of most Council meetings appears to have reached and passed this point.

There are different kinds of Council meetings. Some are briefing sessions designed to acquaint the participants with, for example, an important advance in weapons technology. Other meetings center around so-called "discussion papers," which aim not at proposing a solution to some policy problem but at clarifying its nature and outlining possible alternative courses of action.

The more typical Council session, however, follows a precise agenda and focuses upon the consideration of Planning Board policy papers. These papers have a routine format. As Robert Cutler has described them:

For convenience, a routine format for policy statements was developed. Thus, the busy reader would always know where to find the covering letter, the general considerations, the objectives, the courses of action to carry out the objectives, the financial appendixes, the supporting staff study; for they invariably appeared in this sequence in the final document.

The standardization of these techniques made it possible for the Council to transact, week in and week out, an enormously heavy load of work.

The main work of the Council, thus, now consists of discussion and a search for consensus, centering around Planning Board papers.

The normal end product of Council discussion is a presidentially approved paper setting forth the recommendations of the Planning Board paper, with such amendments, if any, as are adopted after Council deliberations. This paper is transmitted through the Operations Coordinating Board to the operating departments and agencies.

But one point is fundamental: Policy *papers* and actual *policy* are not necessarily the same.

Pieces of paper are important only as steps in a process leading to action—as minutes of decisions to do or not do certain things.

Papers which do not affect the course of governmental action are not policy: they are mere statements of aspiration. NSC papers are policy only if they result in *action*. They are policy only if they cause the Government to adopt one course of conduct and to reject another, with one group of advocates "winning" and the other "losing."

It appears that many of the papers now emerging from the Council do not meet the test of policy in this sense. . . .

NEW DIRECTIONS

Two main conclusions about the National Security Council emerge:

First: The real worth of the Council to a President lies in being an accustomed forum where he and a small number of his top advisers can gain that intellectual intimacy and mutual understanding on which true coordination depends. Viewed thus, the Council is a place where the President can receive from his department and agency heads a full exposition of policy alternatives available to him, and, in turn, give them clear-cut guidance for action.

Second: The effectiveness of the Council in this primary role has been diminished by the working of the NSC system. The root causes of difficulty are found in overly crowded agenda, overly elaborate and stylized procedures, excessive reliance on subordinate interdepartmental mechanisms, and the use of the NSC system for comprehensive coordinating and follow-through responsibilities it is ill suited to discharge.

The philosophy of the suggestions which follow can be summed up in this way—to "deinstitutionalize" and to "humanize" the NSC process.

The President's Instrument

The Council exists only to serve the President. It should meet when he wishes advice on some matter, or when his chief foreign and defense policy advisers require Presidential guidance on an issue which cannot be resolved without his intervention.

There are disadvantages in regularly scheduled meetings. The necessity of having to present and to discuss something at such meetings may generate business not really demanding Presidential consideration. Council meetings and the Council agenda should never become ritualistic.

The Purpose of Council Discussion

The true goal of "completed staff work" is not to spare the President the necessity of choice. It is to make his choices more meaningful by defining the essential issues which he alone must decide and by sharpening the precise positions on the opposing sides.

Meetings of the Council should be regarded as vehicles for clarifying differences of view on major policy departures or new courses of action advocated by department heads or contemplated by the President himself.

The aim of the discussion should be a full airing of divergent views, so that all implications of possible courses of action stand out in bold relief. Even a major issue may not belong on the Council agenda if not yet ripe for sharp and informed discussion.

Attendance at Council Meetings

The Secretaries of State and Defense share the main responsibility of advising the President on national security problems. They are the key members of the Council. Whom the President invites to Council sessions will, of course, depend on the issue under discussion. However, mere "need to know," or marginal involvement with the matter at hand, should not justify attendance.

Council meetings should be kept small. When the President turns for advice to his top foreign policy and defense officials, he is concerned with what *they themselves* think.

The meetings should, therefore, be considered gatherings of principals, not staff aides. Staff attendance should be tightly controlled.

As a corollary to the strict limitation of attendance, a written record of decisions should be maintained and given necessary distribution.

The Planning Board

The NSC Planning Board now tends to overshadow in importance, though not in prestige, the Council itself. However, some group akin to the present Board, playing a rather different role than it now does, can be of continuing help to the Council in the future.

Such a Board would be used mainly to criticize and comment upon policy initiatives developed by the departments or stimulated by the President. It would not be used as an instrument for negotiating "agreed positions" and securing departmental concurrences.

More reliance could also be placed on informal working groups. They could be profitably employed both to prepare matters for Council discussion and to study problems which the Council decides need further examination. The make-up and life of these groups would depend on the problem involved.

So, too, intermittent outside consultants or "distinguished citizens committees," such as the Gaither Committee, could on occasion be highly useful in introducing fresh perspectives on critical problems.

The Role of the Secretary of State

The Secretary of State is crucial to the successful operation of the Council. Other officials, particularly the Secretary of Defense, play important parts. But the President must rely mainly upon the Secretary of State for the initial synthesis of the political, military, economic, and other elements which go into the making of a coherent national strategy. He must also be mainly responsible for bringing to the President proposals for major new departures in national policy.

To do his job properly the Secretary must draw upon the resources of a Department of State staffed broadly and competently enough with generalists, economists, and military and scientific experts to assist him in all areas falling within his full concern. He and the President need unhurried opportunities to consider the basic directions of American policy.

The Operations Coordinating Board

The case for abolishing the OCB is strong. An interdepartmental committee like the OCB has inherent limitations as an instrument for assisting with the problem of policy followthrough. If formal interagency machinery is subsequently found to be needed, it can be established later.

Responsibility for implementation of policies cutting across departmental lines should, wherever possible, be assigned to a particular department or to a particular action officer, possibly assisted by an informal interdepartmental group.

In addition, the President must continue to rely heavily on the budgetary process, and on his own personal assistants in performance auditing.

Problems of Staff

The President should at all times have the help and protection of a small personal staff whose members work "outside the system," who are sensitive to the President's own information needs, and who can assist him in asking relevant questions of his departmental chiefs, in making suggestions for policy initiatives not emerging from the operating departments and agencies, and in spotting gaps in policy execution.

The Council will continue to require a staff of its own, including a key official in charge. This staff should consist of a limited number of highly able aides who can help prepare the work of the Council, record its decisions, and troubleshoot on spot assignments. . . .

PART III

TRANSFORMATION

Damn it, Bundy and I get more done in one day at the White House than they do in six months at the State Department.

—*President John F. Kennedy*

EDITORS' INTRODUCTION

Kennedy

John F. Kennedy entered the White House promising a new, more vigorous style of leadership. "Let the word go forth," said the new president in his inaugural address on January 20, 1961, "that the torch has been passed to a new generation of Americans." That change in leadership was immediately reflected in Kennedy's style of presidential decision making, marking a radical departure from former President Eisenhower's approach to national security. According to Theodore Sorensen, who served as the president's special counsel: ". . . . from the outset he abandoned the notion of a collective, institutionalized Presidency. . . . he paid little attention to organization charts and chains of command which diluted and distributed his authority. He was not interested in unanimous committee recommendations which stifled alternatives to find the lowest common denominator of compromise" (Sorensen, 1965:281; see For Further Reading).

Responding favorably to the recommendations of the Jackson Subcommittee report on "Organizing for National Security," the new president proceeded to abolish the elaborate "NSC system" established by his predecessor. First to go was the preeminence of the Council as *the* forum for national security decision making in the new administration. Kennedy made it clear that he viewed the NSC as but one of several groups he would use for receiving advice and making decisions. A greater premium was placed on more flexible, informal arrangements, including meetings with his secretary of state, Dean Rusk; his secretary of defense, Robert S. McNamara; and his special assistant for national security affairs, McGeorge Bundy. Although formal NSC meetings were held—sixteen, for example, in the first six months of the new administration—their importance was unmistakably downgraded, as reflected in this comment, again by Sorensen:

> At times [Kennedy] made minor decisions in full NSC meetings or pretended to make major ones actually settled earlier. Attendance was generally kept well below the level of previous administrations, but still well above the statutory requirements. He strongly preferred to make all major decisions with far fewer people present, often only with the officer to whom he was communicating the decision. "We have averaged three or four meetings a week with the Secretaries of Defense and State, McGeorge Bundy, the head of the CIA and the Vice President," he said in 1961. "But formal meetings of the Security Council which include a much wider group are not as effective.

It is more difficult to decide matters involving high national security if there is a wider group present." (1965: 284)

Next to go was the highly structured network of NSC committees and staffing arrangements instituted under Eisenhower. Kennedy embarked on what has been described as a "committee-killing" exercise. One month after taking office, he signed an executive order terminating the Operations Coordinating Board and assigned many of its responsibilities to the Department of State. He also abolished the NSC Planning Board. In the place of these committees came a variety of ad hoc arrangements, including a plethora of interagency task forces to deal with special problems like Berlin, Cuba, Laos, and counterinsurgency. Even during the gravest emergency of the Kennedy Administration—the Cuban missile crisis in October 1962—the president established a special group to deal with it: an Executive Committee, or "ExComm," of the National Security Council.

All of these new arrangements were, of course, designed to suit Kennedy's style of decision making. So, too, was his administration's determined effort to rub out what it saw as the Eisenhower Administration's artificial distinction between planning and operations, institutionalized in the structure of the Planning Board–Operations Coordinating Board. Indeed, the past administration's emphasis on planning and long-term policy guidance received short shrift from the new, more activist Kennedy officials in Washington, and was replaced by a greater attentiveness to day-to-day operations and crisis management. Symbolizing this shift was the establishment in April 1961—soon after the Bay of Pigs debacle—of a "Situation Room" in the basement of the West Wing of the White House. Teletype machines carrying the overseas cable traffic of the departments of State and Defense and the CIA were installed, allowing the president and his top aides to monitor fast-breaking developments more directly. In the past, such information had been routinely, but selectively, forwarded to the White House by the various departments and agencies.

Many of these changes in the way of conducting NSC-related business were contained in a letter from McGeorge Bundy (who had been serving as a Harvard dean when Kennedy recruited him to become his national security adviser) to Senator Henry Jackson eight months into the new administration. Jackson had written Bundy in July 1961, stating that his subcommittee was winding up its study of national policy machinery. The senator asked Bundy to provide the subcommittee with whatever official memorandum the administration had "describing the functions, organization and procedures of the National Security Council and its supporting mechanisms." Bundy responded in September, and his letter—included along with Jackson's request as the first article in this section—summarized the changes Kennedy had wrought, all of which were designed, said Bundy, "to fit the needs of a new President."

First among these was the downgrading of the Council itself: " . . . the National Security Council has never been and should never become the only instrument of counsel and decision available to the President in dealing with the problems of national security. . . . The National Security Council is one instrument among many; it must never be made an end in itself." Bundy went on to explain the rationale for abolishing the Operations Coordinating Board and President Kennedy's desire to see the State Department, and his secretary of state, assume many of its responsibilities:

> . . . . the President has made it clear that he does not want a large separate organization between him and his Secretary of State. Neither does he wish any questions to arise as to the clear authority and responsibility of the Secretary of State, not only in his own department. . . . but also as the agent of coordination in all our major policies toward other nations.

But Kennedy's effort to establish the primacy of the State Department in the administration's planning and direction of foreign policy soon soured. The department was, according to Sorensen in his account of the Kennedy years, either unwilling or incapable of assuming its new responsibilities:

> The President was discouraged with the Sate Department almost as soon as he took office. He felt it too often seemed to have a built-in inertia which deadened initiative and that its tendency toward excessive delay obscured determination. It spoke with too many voices and too little vigor. It was never clear to the President (and this continued to be true, even after the personnel changes) who was in charge, who was clearly delegated to do what, and why his own policy line seemed consistently to be altered or evaded. (1965: 287)

Another Kennedy adviser, Arthur M. Schlesinger, Jr., echoed this observation. "It was a constant puzzle to Kennedy," wrote Schlesinger (1965: 406; see For Further Reading), "that the State Department remained so formless and impenetrable. He would say, "Damn it, Bundy and I get more done in one day at the White House than they do in six months at the State Department." It was this presidential impression of State Department sluggishness—and Bundy's responsiveness—that brought about a fundamental transformation in the NSC and the rise to prominence of the national security adviser.

The recommendations of the Jackson Subcommittee had foreshadowed a more active and aggressive policy role for the national security adviser and the NSC staff. "The President should at all times have the help and protection of a small personal staff whose members work 'outside the system,'" the subcommittee report had stated, "who are sensitive to the President's own information needs, and who can assist him. . . . in making suggestions for policy initiatives. . . . and in spotting gaps in policy execution."

Kennedy and Bundy agreed, and Bundy's mandate as national security adviser was broadened. He retained the adviser's traditional responsibility as the overall director of Council-related activities and became a key participant in interagency meetings and deliberations. Moreover, he assumed the task of managing President Kennedy's day-to-day national security business, a role performed under President Eisenhower not by his national security adviser but by General Andrew Goodpaster, his staff secretary. As a symbol of this more direct and influential position with the president, Bundy's office was moved from the Executive Office Building across the street from the White House into an office adjacent to the Situation Room. There was another departure from the practice of past national security advisers: on occasion, Bundy would assume the role of administration spokesman, giving speeches and appearing on radio and television explaining and defending the president's policies.

Combined with Bundy's expanded mandate as national security adviser was a more direct policy role for the NSC staff. In his letter to Jackson, Bundy noted that "the business of the National Security staff goes well beyond what is treated in formal meetings of the National Security Council." While he was careful to note that the NSC staff was "not to supersede or supplement any of the high officials who hold line responsibilities in the executive departments and agencies," he emphasized: "Their job is to help the President. . . . to extend the range and enlarge the direct effectiveness of the man they serve."

Operationally, that meant that Bundy's staff of fifteen officers, made up of foreign and defense policy experts from the government and academe, became President Kennedy's "eyes and ears" for national security affairs, prodding the bureaucracy to come up with more and better information and analysis, providing additional policy options to the president when those forwarded by the departments and agencies were deemed inadequate, and keeping a close watch on the implementation of the president's decisions. As one indication of this greater degree of intrusion by the NSC staff into departmental affairs, a procedure known as "cross-hatching" was adopted, requiring White House clearance for important outgoing State Department cables. It proved to be a valuable tool for furthering White House control over foreign policy, a practice future administrations would also follow.

The increased scope of activity and influence enjoyed by Bundy and the NSC staff did not, of course, go unnoticed in bureaucratic Washington. Some critics charged that the national security adviser had created a "mini-State Department" within the White House. Still, Bundy's emergence as a key presidential adviser and operator did not become a matter of serious internal dispute within the administration, in large part because that was the way President Kennedy wanted his national security adviser to perform and because Bundy was able to manage NSC-related business in a neutral fashion—despite his strong policy views in certain areas. Neither Rusk nor McNamara complained, for example, that Bundy used his influence and proximity to the president to undue advantage. (Bundy made a point of regularly sending Rusk and McNamara copies of his communications to the president, which helped allay their misgivings.) At the same time, however, a transformation in the role of the national security adviser had taken place. Indeed, the reference to an "NSC staff" was now something of a misnomer; better stated under Kennedy and Bundy, the NSC staff had been transformed into a "presidential staff," becoming the agent of the president's decision to exert greater control and direction over national security policy from the White House.

Johnson

Vice-president Lyndon Baines Johnson inherited Kennedy's "presidential staff" when he assumed office in November 1963, following the president's assassination. While he continued the ad hoc management style that characterized Kennedy's term in office, the new president made some important changes. First among these was an increased reliance by Johnson on advice and counsel from McNamara (later Clark Clifford) and Rusk, whom he retained as secretaries of defense and state, respectively. Johnson also made it clear that he wanted the State Department to become more directly involved in the planning and coordination of his administration's foreign policy. Over time, this would lead to a certain atrophy of the NSC staff, as well as a slight diminution in the role and influence of the national security adviser.

Another change was Johnson's so-called "Tuesday lunch," described by Walt W. Rostow, who succeeded Bundy as national security adviser in 1966, as "the heart of the many-sided NSC process" during the Johnson years (1972; see For Further Reading). The Tuesday lunch became the principal forum for directing the strategy and tactics associated with the war effort.

According to Rostow, the value of the Tuesday lunch group—compared with the formal NSC meetings held infrequently during Johnson's term—could be summarized this way (1972: 360): "The only men present were those whose advice the President wanted most to hear. Also, the group was small, which minimized the possibility of leaks (I can recall none)." Others would later criticize the Tuesday lunch, however, as a procedural nightmare. Because of its restricted membership and informal methods, several government officials complained that they received less than a full account of what had transpired at the meetings, complicating their task of implementing the president's decisions.

The role of the national security adviser also changed somewhat during Johnson's term in office. Initially, the new president relied less heavily on McGeorge Bundy than his predecessor had; but soon Bundy became part of Johnson's "inner circle." He continued to function as a key adviser to the president (increasingly so as the Vietnam War escalated) and as an occasional public spokesman for the administration, but he added yet another line to the national security adviser's growing job description: that of diplomatic trouble-shooter, with a fact-finding visit to Vietnam and a mission to the Dominican Republic following the U.S. intervention there in 1965. In early 1966, Bundy left the White House, however, to become president of Ford Foundation, and Johnson again seemed intent on downgrading the role of the Council's adviser.

The administration brought Rostow, who had served for a time as Bundy's former deputy at the NSC, over from the State Department (where he was then in charge of the Policy Planning Staff) to take the adviser's job. But President Johnson gave him only a part of Bundy's official title of "Special Assistant to the President for National Security Affairs." Instead, Rostow became simply "Special Assistant to the President." Moreover, Rostow's arrival at the White House coincided with the completion of a report prepared for the president by General Maxwell Taylor on the role of the State Department and the NSC in interagency policy coordination. As a result of that report, President Johnson signed a directive in March 1996 assigning the secretary of state "authority and responsibility. . . . for the overall direction, coordination and supervision of interdepartmental activities of the United States Government overseas." The directive also established an interagency panel—the Senior Interdepartmental Group (or SIG)—to oversee the implementation of the administration's foreign policy initiatives, chaired by a senior official from the State Department.

The Taylor report had the effect of significantly reducing the role of the NSC staff, although in practice the SIG framework never became a very effective method for interagency coordination. Nor did it have much of an impact on the increasingly influential role Rostow played as President Johnson's national security adviser. In *The Diffusion of Power,* Rostow describes the four major roles he performed. They included laying before the president "the widest possible range of options"; helping to ensure that the president's decisions were executed; helping the president with his "in-house" foreign policy business, such as speeches, meetings with the press, visits of foreign officials; and offering advice (1972: 364–66). While never attaining the degree of influence Bundy had, the role of the national security adviser clearly was not downgraded very far. Moreover, in one area Rostow went even beyond the boundaries established by Bundy; as a public spokesman, he became an outspoken and frequent defender of the president's policies—especially on Vietnam.

So, by the end of President Johnson's term in office, the rise to prominence of the national security adviser begun under Kennedy continued. And so, too, did the downgrading of the NSC as a forum for high-level policy decisions. At best, the NSC was used by Kennedy and Johnson for educational, ratification, and ceremonial purposes. Richard Nixon promised to change that.

Nixon

During his campaign for the presidency, Richard Nixon pledged to "restore the National Security Council to its prominent role in national security planning." He went on to attribute "most of our serious reverses abroad to the inability or disinclination of President Eisenhower's successors to make use of this important Council." Neither Nixon's pledge nor his charge were particularly surprising, coming from a man who had served as Vice-president for eight years under Eisenhower and who, as a statutory NSC member (and occasional presiding officer), had regularly attended NSC meetings. Nor was Nixon alone in his view about restoring the Council. Many had come to believe at the end of the Kennedy–Johnson years that the NSC process was now too informal and idiosyncratic and a detriment to systematic long-range planning (just as eight years earlier the opposite view was widely shared, among Senator Jackson and others, that the NSC system had become too structured and rigid, stifling creative policy initiatives).

After his election, Nixon moved quickly to bring the NSC back to life. On December 2, 1969, he appointed Henry A. Kissinger, a Harvard professor and frequent government adviser, as his assistant for national security affairs. He directed Kissinger to come up with a plan for revitalizing the NSC and, by the end of the month, the professor had a blueprint for change. Kissinger described his proposed plan in his memoirs:

> On December 27, I sent him a memorandum discussing the strengths and weaknesses of the previous systems as I saw them: the flexibility and occasional disarray of the informal Johnson procedure; the formality but also rigidity of the Eisenhower structure, which faced the President with a bureaucratic consensus but no real choices. Our task, I argued, was to combine the best features of the two systems: the regularity and efficiency of the National Security Council, coupled with procedures that ensured that the President and his top advisers considered all the realistic alternatives, the costs and benefits of each, and the separate views and recommendations of all interested agencies. (Kissinger, 1979: 41–42)

Assembling all the "realistic alternatives," or policy options, for presidential consideration was the stated objective of the elaborate "NSC system" devised by Kissinger and approved by President Nixon. An organizational chart showing the Council as it evolved, along with the various subcommittees, their chairmen, and members, is presented in Figure III.A. At the same time, however, this "NSC system" had another purpose, never stated publicly, namely, to centralize control over foreign policy in the White House. As Kissinger learned in one of his first meetings with the president-elect, Nixon was disinclined to let the State Department assume the leading role in foreign policy formulation and implementation during his administration. "His subject was the task of setting up his new government," recalls Kissinger. "He had very little confidence in the State Department. Its personnel had no loyalty to him; the Foreign Service had disdained him as Vice President and ignored him the moment he was out of office. He was determined to run foreign policy from the White House" (1979: 11).

Running foreign policy from the White House is exactly what Nixon and Kissinger did. In the second article included in this section, Washington journalist John P. Leacacos describes "Kissinger's Apparat" from the perspective of three years into the new administration. By that time, according to Leacacos, there was no question about who was running things ("By being so close to the President and keeping his fingers on all aspects of the NSC process personally, Kissinger without question is the prime mover in the NSC system"), or how the national security adviser accomplished this ("Crucial national security issues have been maneuvered to committees chaired by Kissinger, thence directly to the President"). Another instrument for exerting control was the high-powered NSC staff Kissinger had assembled. With some fifty professional and eighty support personnel, it was the largest staff in the Council's history. Moreover, it was aggressive in carrying out Nixon's mandate. "White House NSC staffers . . . exuberant at their top-dog status, express a degree of condescension for the work of the traditional departments," notes Leacacos.

Leacacos also goes into some detail describing the NSC machinery created by Kissinger, including the various interdepartmental committees and the subject matter they handled, and the instrument Kissinger used to obtain policy analysis and recommendations from the bureaucracy: the National Security Study Memorandum (NSSM). As Leacacos points out, Kissinger assigned fifty-five such study memoranda in his first 100 days, on topics ranging from Vietnam and military posture to East–West relations.

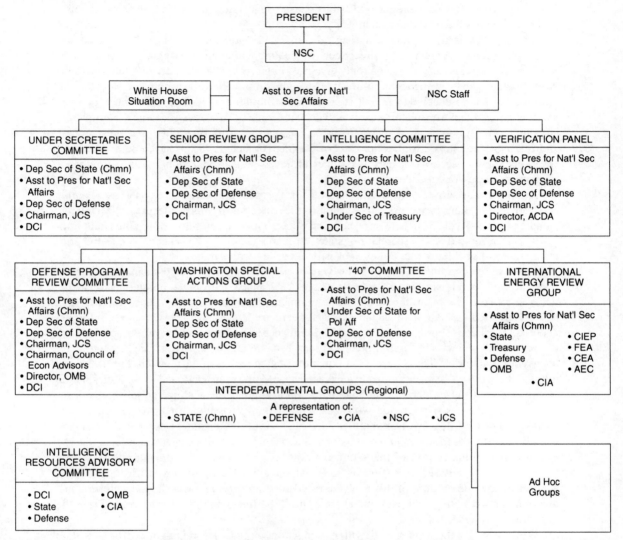

Figure III.A The Nixon NSC, 1969–1974 *(Source: Prepared by the Congressional Research Service, Library of Congress, 1975)*

At least initially, the NSSMs proved to be a valuable tool for engaging the bureaucracy in the interagency process and providing a continuous flow of policy options to the president. The NSSM process was, according to Leacacos, "a way of making the bureaucracy think harder." At the same time, however, there were complaints: "From time to time, gears have clashed within the system. The State Department has complained bitterly of the 'Procrustean bed' fashioned by the Kissinger staff. Meeting excessive White House demands, allege bureaucrats, robs State and Defense of manpower hours needed for day-to-day operations." Some critics charged that another purpose served by the NSSMs was to tie down the departments and agencies responding to studies, while Kissinger and the NSC staff focused on the more immediate and crucial policy issues, as determined by the president.

Those policy issues included, among others, China, Vietnam, and U.S.–Soviet relations. Kissinger became the president's direct agent for dealing with them, serving as his secret envoy to China to prepare the way for Nixon's historic trip there in 1972, conducting talks with the North Vietnamese to arrange a cease-fire, and engaging in so-called "back channel" negotiations with the Soviets to conclude the first strategic arms limitation (SALT) agreement. Moreover, given Nixon's reclusive style of presidential decision making, Kissinger became the primary—sometimes the sole—channel of NSC-related business and information to the president. In short, as NSC watchers I. M. Destler and Ivo Daalder (Center, 1998: iii) have noted, during his tenure as national security adviser, Kissinger achieved greater operational policy dominance than any predecessor or successor.

Kissinger also greatly expanded the role of the national security adviser as a public spokesman, building on the first steps taken in that direction by his predecessors, McGeorge Bundy and Walt Rostow. Kissinger became, in effect, a media star. Short of the president himself—and far more than the secretary of state, William P. Rogers—Kissinger stood as the principal and most visible foreign policy spokesman for the administration.

There were costs involved in this new way of conducting NSC-related business, which the national security adviser himself acknowledged. "Kissinger realizes his unique personal role tends to weaken the institutional role of the permanent bureaucracy," reports Leacacos. Most directly affected was the State Department and Secretary Rogers, who was often not informed about key decisions. Further, as Kissinger's dominance increased, and his preoccupation with the president's immediate foreign policy agenda became almost total, the NSC system itself received less attention. There were less frequent formal meetings of the Council; the NSC committees chaired by Kissinger, with a few exceptions, became moribund; and those issues not on Nixon's policy front-burner, like international economic concerns, were given scant attention.

Secretary Rogers's frustration with the Nixon–Kissinger method of operation came to a head in August 1973, when he submitted his resignation. The president appointed Kissinger, already operating as the *de facto* secretary of state, to replace him. Kissinger was reluctant, however, to give up his control of the White House–NSC machinery; so he sought to retain his national security adviser's position as well. Nixon agreed and, somewhat disingenuously, announced that the purpose of this new, unprecedented arrangement was "to have closer coordination" between the White House and the State Department and "to get the work out in the departments where it belongs."

Which is where the work stayed, with Kissinger directing U.S. foreign policy from the State Department for the remainder of Richard Nixon's term in office—until the president's resignation over the Watergate scandal—and during the subsequent presidency of Gerald R. Ford. One change had occurred, however. Responding to increasing criticism of Kissinger's control of policy, President Ford removed one of Kissinger's two official hats in 1975, naming Kissinger's deputy at the NSC, Air Force Lieut. General Brent Scowcroft, as national security adviser. The chairmanships of several of the NSC committees formerly held by Kissinger were transferred to other officials. Moreover, as the new director of NSC activities, Scowcroft returned the adviser's role to a closer approximation of its original description as a neutral manager and coordinator of the Council's business. Still, despite the loss of one of his hats, Henry Kissinger remained the dominant player within the NSC system—a "one-man show" according to many critics. One of the critics became the next president of the United States, Jimmy Carter.

Carter

At first glance, it appeared that Jimmy Carter knew exactly what he wanted to accomplish in restructuring the NSC to fit his own style of presidential decision making. His first objective was to avoid what he considered the excessive centralization of power and secretiveness within the White House that existed under President Nixon, and what critics called the "Lone Ranger" style of diplomacy as practiced by Henry Kissinger. Carter's second objective, and one that flowed from his first, was a renewed emphasis on cabinet government; he wanted to give his cabinet officers, including his secretary of state, more responsibility and greater authority. As his third objective, Carter wanted to make certain that, in the final analysis, the national security process he established would be responsive to his personal control, that he would be "president of this country" for foreign policy. He made this point when he appeared before the Senate Foreign Relations Committee as president-elect in November of 1976:

> I intend to appoint a strong and competent Secretary of State, but I intend to remember what your Chairman [Senator Frank Church, D, Idaho] said a few minutes ago, that the responsibility [for the conduct of foreign policy] lies in the White House with the President. I will be the President and I will represent the country in foreign affairs.

And, finally, Carter's fourth objective—and the glue that would hold his NSC system and its members together—was "collegiality." As his new secretary of state, Cyrus Vance, would later explain in his account of the Carter years, entitled *Hard Choices* (1983: 35): "In the Carter foreign policy apparatus, the personal dimension would be unusually important. . . . The president made it clear he did not want a repetition of the morbid backbiting and struggling over real or imagined bureaucratic prerogatives that often prevailed. 'Collegiality' was to be the rule among his principal advisers."

On his first day in office, January 10, 1977, President Carter issued a directive to incorporate these management principles into a restructured NSC system. Entitled "Presidential Directive/NCS–2," the directive is included as the third selection in this chapter. The directive stated: "The reorganization is intended to place more authority in the departments and agencies while insuring that the NSC, with my Assistant for National Security Affairs, continues to integrate and facilitate foreign and defense policy decisions."

To accomplish this, Carter mandated the creation of two NSC committees. One, the Policy Review Committee (PRC), would coordinate policy reviews on issues where one department had the major responsibility and would be chaired by that department's head, usually the secretary of state. The other, the Special Coordination Committee (SCC), would deal with crosscutting issues requiring interdepartmental coordination, like arms control and crisis management, and would be chaired from the White House by the national security adviser. This organization arrangement is displayed in the chart in Figure III.B.

Presidential Directive/NSC–2 thus reestablished a central role for the departments and agencies within the NSC system. But it also gave the newly appointed national security adviser, international affairs expert and Columbia University professor Zbigniew Brzezinski, enormous influence within that system, not only to coordinate NSC activities ("coordination is predominance") but to take a leading policy role in its deliberations. Although Brzezinski was not given the near total domination of the NSC process that Nixon had accorded to Kissinger, Carter's decision to appoint him chairman of the SCC (which included the secretaries of state and defense) was unprecedented. Even Kissinger had been restricted to chairing meetings of sub-cabinet level officials. Over time, that decision conferred upon Brzezinski an increasingly dominant policy-making role, as he pointed out in *Power and Principle* (1983: 66):

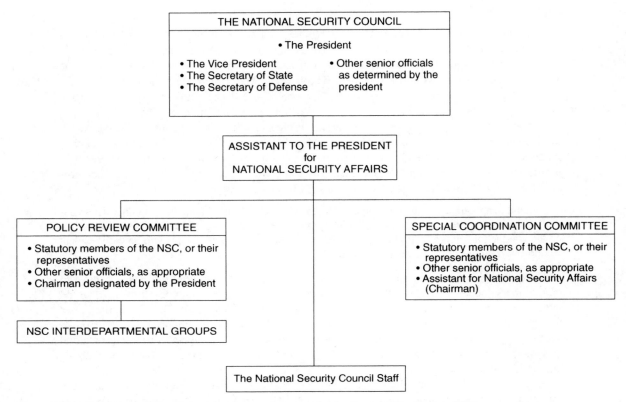

Figure III.B The Carter NSC, 1977–1981 *(Source: Prepared by the Carter White House, 1977)*

During the early phases of the Carter Administration, the PRC met more frequently, usually under Vance's chairmanship. In time, however, the SCC became more active. I used the SCC to try to shape our policy toward the Persian Gulf, on European security issues, on strategic matters, as well as in determining our response to Soviet aggression.

During the first eighteen months of the Carter Administration, this NSC system seemed to operate smoothly. The Council itself was used by Carter to address major policy issues, and a procedure similar to the NSSM process under Nixon and Kissinger was initiated (renamed Presidential Review Memorandum, or PRM) to elicit policy analysis and recommendations from the bureaucracy. Also, several informal coordinating procedures were established, with an emphasis on furthering "collegiality."

The most important of these procedures was President Carter's "Friday breakfast." At first, it included only the president, Vice-president Walter Mondale, Vance, and Brzezinski, but soon it expanded to include Secretary of Defense Harold Brown, White House Chief of Staff Hamilton Jordan, and Press Secretary Jody Powell. Carter would later describe the "Friday breakfast" in his memoirs, *Keeping Faith* (1982: 56): "For about an hour and a half we covered the range of questions involving international and defense matters, to allow me to reach decisions and to minimize misunderstandings among this high-level group. This became my favorite meeting of the week, even when the subjects discussed were disagreeable."

A second informal procedure was a weekly luncheon meeting involving Vance, Brown, and Brzezinski (known in shorthand as the "V-B-B lunch"). According to Brzezinski, who initiated the practice, the luncheon was designed as a forum to resolve issues that did not require the attention of a formal PRC or SCC meeting. And, according to Vance, the gatherings proved useful: "It permitted us to have a free-ranging discussion of current and forthcoming issues without the constraint of formal agendas, agency positions and bureaucratic infighting" (1983: 39).

Yet even these methods proved unable to resolve the tensions that soon became evident within an NSC system that included an activist, policy-oriented national security adviser and his staff (including some thirty-five professionals—slightly smaller than the Kissinger NSC staff) and a competing Department of State. Part of the tension sprang from President Carter's attitude toward the State Department. In a statement reminiscent of President Kennedy's dissatisfaction with the department, Carter described this home of the diplomatic corps in his memoirs (1982: 53) as "a sprawling Washington and worldwide bureaucracy." He complained: "I rarely received innovative ideas from its staff members about how to modify existing policy in order to meet changing conditions." This was in contrast to his more favorable portrayal of the national security adviser and his staff:

> Zbigniew Brzezinski and his relatively small group of experts were not handicapped by the inertia of a tenured bureaucracy or the responsibility for implementing policies after they evolved. They were particularly adept at the incisive analysis of strategic concepts, and they were prolific in the production of new ideas, which they were eager to present to me. (1982: 53)

Other tensions related to the question of who would serve as the administration's chief spokesman for foreign policy, short of the president himself. Continuing a trend established by McGeorge Bundy, Brzezinski emerged as a highly visible policy spokesman. Vance considered that a breach of an understanding he said he had reached with Carter, namely, that "only the president and his secretary of state were to have the responsibility for defining the administration's foreign policy publicly" (Vance, 1983: 35). Carter saw it otherwise: "Almost without exception, Zbig had been speaking with my approval and in consonance with my established and known policy. The underlying State Department objection was that Brzezinski had spoken at all" (Carter, 1982: 53).

A third source of tension that developed within the Carter Administration, and the most divisive of all, related to the strong policy disputes that came to the surface between the president's secretary of state and his national security adviser. "By the beginning of 1978," according to Vance, "the first serious disagreements had broken out within the Administration." On this point, he and Brzezinski were in complete agreement, as the national security adviser would later relate in his memoirs:

> .... by the spring and summer of 1978, some substantial differences on policy had arisen. Though Cy and I both tried to confine them to our in-house discussions, the varying viewpoints filtered down to the bureaucracy, became increasingly the object of interagency conflicts and of gossip, and then started to leak out. This was the case, first over the issue of the Soviet-Cuban role in the African Horn and the likely impact of that on SALT, then came the China question, and in the final year and a half we differed on how to respond to the Iranian crisis. (Brzezinski, 1983: 38)

The Soviet–Cuban role in the Horn of Africa was only the first of several major policy disagreements related to the U.S.–Soviet relationship to emerge within the administration. The disagreements reflected a fundamental policy difference: a more cooperative approach advocated by Vance and a more competitive (critics said, confrontational) approach advanced by Brzezinski.

The epic conflict between Vance and Brzezinski has been the subject of intense scrutiny by scholars over the years, including Louisiana State University political science professor Kevin V. Mulcahy. He makes the point, which has been borne out in past administrations, that "a certain amount of rivalry, even friction, among institutional actors is largely inevitable and may be constructively channeled to produce more effective policy" (Mulcahy, 1986: 285). But, Mulcahy adds: " . . . it is no less true that what a president needs to avoid is an institutionalized conflict between the State Department and the NSC staff that produces nothing more than fragmented policy proposals and leaves the decision making process in disarray." In Mulcahy's view, that was the result in the Carter administration, because the president never settled the differences between Vance (and his successor, Edmund Muskie) and Brzezinski. The president was unable to impose teamwork on his most senior advisers or make a consistent choice between the fundamental policy approaches and alternatives they offered.

By the end of the Carter presidency, those differences—combined with the president's failure to resolve them—were aggravated by a series of foreign policy crises ranging from the Soviet invasion of Afghanistan to the taking of American diplomatic hostages in Iran. The Carter Administration was seen to be in disarray. According to Vance, "A question troubling the Congress, the allies and the American public in the spring of 1980 was whether the Carter Administration had a coherent view of the international situation, a sense of global strategy and consistent policies and objectives" (1983: 395). It was a question American voters, in the 1980 presidential election, answered in the negative.

Reagan

The disarray within the Carter Administration over foreign policy, including the sharp and highly publicized disagreements between Vance and Brzezinski, did not go unnoticed by Republican presidential candidate, Ronald Reagan. Like Dwight Eisenhower in 1952 and Richard Nixon in 1968, he made the Democratic incumbent's handling of national security a campaign issue. "The present Administration has been unable to speak with one voice in foreign policy," said Reagan in a nationwide televised address in October 1980, one month before the election. "This must change. My Administration will restore leadership to U.S. foreign policy by organizing it in a more coherent way."

Once in office, President Reagan moved quickly to implement that campaign promise. The NSC was in for yet another major restructuring. Reagan implemented his pledge to organize his administration's conduct of foreign policy in "a more coherent way" in two concrete steps. First, the administration placed an emphasis on cabinet government, with his secretaries of state and defense (and the head of the CIA) being given vast authority for the formulation and direction of policy within their respective departments and agencies; and, second, it radically downgraded the role and responsibilities of the national security adviser and NSC staff—in effect reversing what had been a twenty-year rise to prominence of both. Brzezinski has referred to this recent phase in the NSC's history as one of "degradation" (1987–1988).

President Reagan appointed Richard V. Allen, a campaign foreign policy adviser who had served briefly on Henry Kissinger's NSC staff, as his NSC adviser, and the signs indicating his lowered status were evident immediately. Allen himself said that he, and the NSC staff, would focus on interagency coordination and long-range planning, not on the kind of day-to-day operational matters that had provided the Bundy, Kissinger, and Brzezinski NSC staffs with a means of exercising direct White House control over the bureaucracy.

Moreover, the administration stripped Allen of the cabinet-level rank that President Carter had accorded Brzezinski. Instead, he was made subordinate to White House Counselor Edwin

Meese, reporting to the president through him. In short, the national security adviser's job under Allen reverted to a staff function, with no mandate to engage in policy advocacy or formulation, as his predecessors had done before him. That suited Allen just fine, since he believed that the policy formulation function of the national security adviser should be passed off to the secretary of state. That also suited President Reagan's newly appointed head of the State Department, retired General Alexander M. Haig, Jr., a former deputy to Kissinger at the NSC, White House chief of staff under Nixon, and Supreme Allied Commander of NATO.

Haig took President Reagan at his word when he said that he wanted to restore cabinet government. In his confirmation hearings for secretary of state, he told the Senate Foreign Relations Committee how he and Reagan envisioned the role he would play. "The President needs a single individual to serve as the general manager of American diplomacy," he testified. "President-elect Reagan believes that the Secretary of State should play this role. As Secretary of State, I would function as a member of the President's team, but with one clear responsibility for formulating and conducting foreign policy, and for explaining it to the Congress, the public, and the world at large."

To put that role into effect (to become, as Haig phrased it, President Reagan's "vicar" for foreign policy), Haig moved quickly—indeed too quickly for Reagan's White House advisers. Haig prepared a "talking paper" for his meeting with the president-elect on January 6, 1981. It found its way into the *Washington Post* in July 1982 (see For Further Reading), the month following Haig's resignation from office. The talking paper shows, as the *Post* put it, that Haig sought in the meeting with Reagan to ensure "that he controlled everything from food policy to crisis contingency planning to all contact with foreign officials and with the press."

Haig's reach for policy influence and power ultimately exceeded his grasp. As Professor Mulcahy has observed (1986: 241), the secretary of state "forgot the fundamental tenet of successful secretarial-presidential relations in foreign policy making: it is the president who makes policy and he is free to consult whomever he wishes and to establish what structural processes he deems necessary." The rise and fall of Alexander Haig can thus be seen as yet another variation of the struggle between the State Department and the White House for control over foreign policy. In this case, Haig's "turf and temperament" fights exaggerated the more traditional institutional conflict and proved to be his undoing. With President Reagan increasingly uneasy in his presence and key White House aides believing he was not a team player, Haig's departure from the administration was inevitable.

Still, during Haig's embattled months in office, the basic structure of the Reagan NSC system was put into place. The PRC-SCC structure established by President Carter was abolished and replaced by a series of Senior Interdepartmental Groups, "SIGs" in bureaucratic lingo, an organizational concept revived from past administrations. Reflecting the president's determination to return authority to the departments and agencies, individual SIGs were set up for state, defense, treasury, and the CIA. Consistent with the president's decision to downgrade the role of the national security adviser, Richard Allen was not made the chairman of any of these new interagency groups. Moreover, a new committee, the Special Situation Group, was formed to handle crisis management with Vice-president George Bush made chairman (after a highly publicized battle with Haig, who wanted this responsibility as well). During Reagan's term in office, this group rarely met.

As for the National Security Council itself, the president stated that it would be his major forum for considering national security issues, and he appointed several members to participate in its deliberations. In an effort to conduct more restrictive and "leakproof" meetings of his key advisers, Reagan established the National Security Planning Group (NSPG), a more informal forum somewhat like President Carter's "Friday breakfast" and President Johnson's "Tuesday lunch" groups. The NSPG became the principal forum within the Reagan Administration for national security decision making.

The president's new NSC machinery got off to a rocky start, and a majority of the complaints were leveled at the president's downgraded national security adviser. Critics said that Allen and the NSC staff had become mere conveyor belts for policy papers from the departments of State and Defense, with no attempt to provide independent analysis or policy options for the president's consideration. Even more damaging, said the critics, Allen was an ineffectual coordinator and failed to play the traditional adviser's role of adjudicating different department views or trying to iron out policy differences. Moreover, the SIGs were not operating in the fashion the organization chart suggested they would. In fact, they rarely, if ever, met, because bureaucratic rivalries among competing agencies made them unwilling to accept the primacy of any one agency.

The problems went even deeper than that. Earlier administrations had witnessed strong rivalries between the national security adviser and the secretary of state. The Reagan Administration was different. The focus of conflict had shifted to struggles between cabinet officers, principally Secretary of State Haig (and later his replacement George P. Shultz) and the Secretary of Defense Caspar E. Weinberger. This struggle centered on major policy issues—the direction of U.S.–Soviet relations and arms control, for example—and, as in past administrations, on who would speak for the administration. As Haig related in his account of his tenure as secretary of state (1984: 87): ". . . . [Weinberger's] tendency to blurt out locker-room opinions in the guise of policy was one that I prayed he might overcome. If God heard, He did not answer in any way understandable to me." Policy gridlock within the administration was often the result of the Haig–Weinberger struggle, with a downgraded NSC adviser too weak to do anything about it. Further, President Reagan's own management style, including his reluctance to resolve policy disagreements among his cabinet officers and his lack of interest in the details associated with running foreign policy, was seen by some critics as adding to the problem. The latter criticism would later come home to haunt the president when the Iran-*contra* scandal erupted in November 1986.

President Reagan was provided an opportunity to remedy at least some of these problems at the end of his first year in office, when Richard Allen resigned because of alleged improprieties (for which he was later exonerated). In January 1982, Reagan appointed a political confidant and former California Supreme Court Justice, William P. Clark, Jr., to replace Allen, the first of five changes he would make in the position of national security adviser—the most ever in an administration. Clark's position was immediately upgraded, reflecting the view of the president and his senior advisers in the White House that the Chief Executive was being ill-served by a weak director for NSC activities. In his new role, Clark would no longer be subordinate to White House Counselor Meese, and he would have direct access to the president. Clark, with his expanded authority and close personal ties to Reagan, was expected to mediate the policy disagreements within the administration. The frictions between Haig (then Shultz) and Weinberger continued, however.

The same problem plagued Clark's successor, Robert C. McFarlane, a former Marine officer with experience on the NSC staff under Kissinger and Scowcroft. McFarlane recognized the need to serve as a manager and minimizer of these policy disputes. His record in this regard was somewhat better than that of his predecessors in the Reagan Administration, but it was a tough assignment. As McFarlane would later say about the differences between Reagan's secretaries of state and defense: "George Shultz and Cap (Weinberger) were always at odds. . . . they almost never agreed" (Center, 1999: 40; see For Further Reading).

McFarlane also played an increasingly influential role in presenting and defending the president's policies in private meetings with members of Congress and with the press. But in late 1985, he ran afoul of a new White House chief of staff, Donald Regan, who wanted to restrict and control access to the president. McFarlane resigned.

That set the stage for yet another national security adviser, McFarlane's deputy on the NSC staff: Navy Vice Admiral John M. Poindexter. Poindexter was seen as a low-key administrator, skillful in handling operational matters (especially those related to military activities or computers), but certainly not a policymaker. Nor did he have the independent stature or influence with the president to play a role in mediating interdepartmental disputes.

It was during Poindexter's tenure as national security adviser that members of the NSC staff (principally Lieut. Col. Oliver L. North) became increasingly involved in the conduct of covert operations, including secret arms sales to Iran and support for the Nicaraguan *contras*. The uncovering of these activities led to Poindexter's abrupt resignation in early 1987—after only eleven months on the job—and touched off extensive executive branch and congressional investigations of President Reagan's involvement in these matters, as well as his overall management of the NSC process.

The president next selected Frank C. Carlucci III, a seasoned former government official with high-level experience in the departments of State and Defense and the CIA, as his fifth NSC adviser. Carlucci tells the story that he assumed Reagan had chosen him because of this experience. But when offering the position, the president said: "Frank, I would like you to be my national security adviser because you're the only person that George and Cap can agree upon." (Center, Oct. 1999: 21)

Once again, President Reagan elevated the national security adviser's position. The adviser was given direct access to the president and was no longer subject to control by the White House chief of staff, Donald Regan. Regan also resigned during the Iran-*contra* affair and was replaced by the former Republican senator and Majority Leader from Tennessee, Howard Baker. Carlucci's mandate was to revitalize the NSC process (an aide said Carlucci saw his job as "coordinating and forcing decisions") and so restore the credibility of the NSC staff. Both would be formidable assignments.

"The table of organization for NSC policy coordination had become a veritable nightmare," observes Zbigniew Brzezinski in the *Foreign Policy* article referred to earlier. In place of Carter's two NSC committees, twenty-five committees mushroomed under Reagan, and the size of the staff almost doubled. "The result," continues Brzezinski, "was a loss of control and increasing absorption in bureaucratic minutiae, at the cost of providing strategic direction and imposing policy coordination." To sort out this organizational mess, Carlucci obtained the president's approval for several changes in the NSC system, which were codified in a National Security Decision Directive (NSDD 276). He established a Senior Review Group, chaired by the national security adviser with cabinet-level attendance. Below the Senior Review Group, Carlucci set up several Policy Review Groups (PRGs) to be chaired by his new deputy, Lieut. Gen. Colin L. Powell. The general had served with Carlucci as a military assistant in the Weinberger Pentagon and was seen as a "rising star" within the military establishment. Powell's PRGs were to do what one NSC official said "the SIGs were supposed to do but didn't," namely, review and coordinate interagency policy positions for the president's consideration.

But even these organizational adjustments proved contentious. In his memoirs, entitled *Turmoil and Triumph* (see For Further Reading), George Shultz described this latest episode of rivalry between the secretary of state and national security adviser:

. . . I confronted Carlucci directly about NSDD 276. I told him that I had no problem with informal meetings of the National Security Council being coordinated by the national security adviser. In fact, I had created the Family Group with the idea that the meetings would be managed by the NSC adviser. But it would be a grave mistake, I said, for the NSC adviser, a non-statutory member of the National Security Council, someone *not* in the cabinet and *not* subject to confirmation by the Senate or to the accountability of appearances before congressional committees, to be designated in an NSDD as the chairman of NSC meetings. "Frank Carlucci is not a member of the NSC," I said. "You are the staff of the NSC. You serve the principals of the NSC, especially but not exclusively the president." (Shultz, 1993: 903)

To make clear his view of where the NSC staff "should be placed in the chain of command," the secretary sent a formal memorandum to Carlucci detailing his objections to the directive. However, as Shultz recounts, the national security adviser "did not yield. 'Forgive my annoyance,' Carlucci told me, 'but I did not return to government in order to be an executive secretary'" (Shultz, 1993: 903).

Other changes made by Carlucci, especially those to restore the credibility of the NSC staff, received widespread support, including from Shultz. Carlucci replaced many of the staff he had inherited from Poindexter with more experienced foreign policy professionals, and he placed NSC staff involvement in covert activities off limits. He also appointed a general counsel to monitor NSC activities and ensure their legality and propriety. In many of these changes, Carlucci was implementing the recommendations of the Tower Commission, the executive branch panel of inquiry into the Iran-*contra* scandal. As Colin Powell would later comment in his autobiography, *My American Journey* (see For Further Reading): "The Tower Report became our owner's manual. We did what it recommended. Carlucci issued an order that the NSC was not to become involved in operations. We advised Presidents; we did not run wars or covert strategies. We had a Defense Department and a CIA for those roles" (Powell, 1995: 335).

Carlucci's tenure brought a degree of stability back to the operation of the NSC, although there were times, according to Powell, that President Reagan's "big picture–hands off" style of governing left them both feeling a little adrift. Recalls Powell in his memoirs:

The President's passive management style placed a tremendous burden on us. Until we got used to it, we felt uneasy implementing recommendations without a clear decision. Would the decision hold if criticized later by one of the losers? Would the President recall it? One morning after we had gotten another decision by default on a key arms control issue, Frank moaned as we left, "My God, we didn't sign on to run this country!" (Powell, 1995: 334)

Also of concern was the rancor that persisted between secretaries Shultz and Weinberger. Their differences were finally laid to rest with Weinberger's resignation in 1987. President Reagan nominated Carlucci to succeed him and asked Powell to become his sixth, and final, national security adviser.

Once in office, the new team of Shultz, Carlucci, and Powell were determined not to repeat the departmental (and personality) struggles of the past several years. At Shultz's suggestion, the three began meeting every morning at seven o'clock in Powell's West Wing office. They came with no set agenda or aides. They did bring their schedules so they could lay out the day's events and see if they could reach agreement on how to proceed on the various issues they would be facing.

By the end of Ronald Reagan's second term in office, national security advisers Carlucci and Powell had done much to repair the damage done to the president's NSC system by the Iran-*contra* affair, by battles between departmental heads and several national security advisers, and by years of radical shifts in NSC practices and personnel. It had been a tumultuous eight-year period, later described by James A. Baker III in *The Politics of Diplomacy* (see For Further Reading) as often "a witches' brew of intrigue, elbows, egos, and separate agendas." (Baker, 1995: 26) Several of those who would assume high-level national security positions with the incoming administration were veterans of the Reagan years and had witnessed the often dysfunctional NSC at close range. They were determined not to repeat the experience. Among those were the incoming secretary of state (James Baker), the soon to be Chairman of the Joint Chiefs of Staff (Colin Powell) and the new president himself, George H. W. Bush. They would be further assisted by Brent Scowcroft, who would become the national security adviser for a second time.

Scowcroft's return was especially important. The Tower Commission had made numerous recommendations for changes in the organization and procedures of the NSC. As a principal member of that Commission, Scowcroft wrote most of that portion of the report. Carlucci and Powell implemented virtually all of these recommendations during their tenure; Scowcroft made certain they were continued into the next administration.

With hindsight, it can be said that the adoption of the Tower Commission's recommendations (to be discussed in greater detail in Part IX of this book) marked another milestone in the history of the National Security Council. The transformation of the NSC begun under President Kennedy was now complete. The preeminence of the NSC system was established, as was the key role of the president's national security adviser and staff. The NSC had survived the difficulties presented during the Reagan years; new procedures were in place to prevent their reoccurrence. The NSC was entering a new era, one marked more by continuity than change.

9

LETTER TO JACKSON SUBCOMMITTEE

McGeorge Bundy

In his written response to the Jackson panel, Mr. Bundy emphasized the changes President Kennedy had made to the NSC he had inherited from President Eisenhower. It was now smaller, and the line between planning and operations had been dissolved so that NSC staff officers were involved in the follow-up as well as the formulation of policy. He also stressed the importance of the secretary of state as the president's top foreign policy adviser.

U.S. Senate,
Subcommittee on National Policy Machinery,
July 13, 1961

Mr. McGeorge Bundy,
Special Assistant to the President for National Security Affairs,
The White House, Washington, D.C.

Dear Mr. Bundy:

As you know, our subcommittee will shortly hold hearings bringing to a close its nonpartisan study of how our Government can best staff and organize itself to develop and carry out the kind of national security policies required to meet the challenge of world communism.

As you also know, we have been deeply concerned from the outset with the organization and procedures of the National Security Council, its subordinate organs, and related planning and follow-through mechanisms in the area of national security.

Early in our study, the previous administration was kind enough to make available to the subcommittee a series of official memorandums describing the functions, organization, and procedures of the National Security Council and its supporting mechanisms. These memorandums, which were printed by the subcommittee in our Selected Materials, proved of great interest and value to our members, to students and interpreters of the policy process, and to the wide general audience which has been following our inquiry.

The purpose of this letter is to ask whether the present administration could now furnish us with official memorandums which would be the current equivalent of the above documents given us by the Eisenhower administration.

Reprinted from "Exchange of Letters Concerning the National Security Council Between Henry M. Jackson and Mr. McGeorge Bundy, Special Assistant to the President for National Security Affairs." Subcommittee on National Policy Machinery, U.S. Senate Committee on Government Operations.

McGeorge Bundy served as special assistant for national security affairs from 1961–1966.

I presume that this material is readily at hand, and that it could be made available to us by August 4, so that we could profit from its study during the final phase of our hearings and make it a part of our permanent record.

Sincerely yours,
Henry M. Jackson,
Chairman, Subcommittee on National Policy Machinery

The White House,
Washington, September 4, 1961

Hon. Henry M. Jackson:
U.S. Senate, Washington, D.C.

Dear Senator Jackson:
I have thought hard about your letter of July 13, which asks for official memorandums that would be the current equivalent of memorandums submitted by the previous administration. I find that this is not easy to do, but let me try. The previous administration wrote out of many years of experience in which it had gradually developed a large and complex series of processes. This administration has been revising these arrangements to fit the needs of a new President, but the work of revision is far from done, and it is too soon for me to report with any finality upon the matters about which you ask. It seems to me preferable, at this early stage in our work; to give you an informal interim account in this letter.

Much of what you have been told in the reports of the previous administration about the legal framework and concept of the Council remains true today. There has been no recent change in the National Security Act of 1947. Nor has there been any change in the basic and decisive fact that the Council is advisory only. Decisions are made by the President. Finally, there has been no change in the basic proposition that, in the language of Robert Cutler, "the Council is a vehicle for a President to use in accordance with its suitability to his plans for conducting his great office." As Mr. Cutler further remarked, "a peculiar virtue of the National Security Act is its flexibility," and "each President may use the Council as he finds most suitable at a given time."[1] It is within the spirit of this doctrine that a new process of using the NSC is developing.

The specific changes which have occurred are three. First, the NSC meets less often than it did. There were 16 meetings in the first 6 months of the Kennedy administration. Much that used to flow routinely to the weekly meetings of the Council is now settled in other ways—by separate meetings with the President, by letters, by written memorandums, and at levels below that of the President. President Kennedy has preferred to call meetings of the NSC only after determining that a particular issue is ready for discussion in this particular forum.

I know you share my understanding that the National Security Council has never been and should never become the only instrument of counsel and decision available to the President in dealing with the problems of our national security. I believe this fact cannot be overemphasized. It is not easy for me to be sure of the procedures of earlier administrations, but I have the impression that many of the great episodes of the Truman and Eisenhower administrations were not dealt with, in their most vital aspects, through the machinery of the NSC. It was not in an NSC meeting that we got into the Korean war, or made the Korean truce. The NSC was not, characteristically, the place of decision on specific major budgetary issues, which so often affect both policy and strategy. It was not the usual forum of diplomatic decision; it was not, for example, a major center of work on Berlin at any time before 1961. The National Security Council is one instrument among many; it must never be made an end in itself.

But for certain issues of great moment, the NSC is indeed valuable. President Kennedy has used it for discussion of basic national policy toward a number of countries. He has used it both for advice on particular pressing decisions and for recommendations on long-term policy. As new attitudes develop within the administration, and as new issues arise in the world, the NSC is likely to continue as a major channel through which broad issues of national security policy come forward for Presidential decision.

Meanwhile, the President continues to meet at very frequent intervals with the Secretary of State, the Secretary of Defense, and other officials closely concerned with problems of national security. Such meetings may be as large as an NSC meeting or as small as a face-to-face discussion with a single Cabinet officer. What they have in common is that a careful record is kept, in the appropriate way, whenever a decision is reached. Where primary responsibility falls clearly to a single Department, the primary record of such decisions will usually be made through that Department. Where the issue is broader, or where the action requires continued White House attention, the decision will be recorded through the process of the National Security Council. Thus the business of the National Security staff goes well beyond what is treated in formal meetings of the National Security Council. It is our purpose, in cooperation with other Presidential staff officers, to meet the President's staff needs throughout the national security area.

The second and more significant change in the administration of the National Security Council and its subordinate agencies is the abolition by Executive Order 10920 of the Operations Coordinating Board. This change needs to be understood both for what it is and for what it is not. It is not in any sense a downgrading of the tasks of coordination and followup; neither is it an abandonment of Presidential responsibility for these tasks. It is rather a move to eliminate an instrument that does not match the style of operation and coordination of the current administration.

From the point of view of the new administration, the decisive difficulty in the OCB was that without unanimity it had no authority. No one of its eight members had authority over any other. It was never a truly Presidential instrument, and its practices were those of a group of able men attempting, at the second and third levels of Government, to keep large departments in reasonable harmony with each other. Because of good will among its members, and unusual administrative skill in its secretariat, it did much useful work; it also had weaknesses. But its most serious weakness, for the new administration, was simply that neither the President himself nor the present administration as a whole conceives of operational coordination as a task for a large committee in which no one man has authority. It was and is our belief that there is much to be done that the OCB could not do, and that the things it did do can be done as well or better in other ways.

The most important of these other ways is an increased reliance on the leadership of the Department of State. It would not be appropriate for me to describe in detail the changes which the Department of State has begun to execute in meeting the large responsibilities which fall to it under this concept of administration. It is enough if I say that the President has made it very clear that he does not want a large separate organization between him and his Secretary of State.

Neither does he wish any question to arise as to the clear authority and responsibility of the Secretary of State, not only in his own Department, and not only in such large-scale related areas as foreign aid and information policy, but also as the agent of coordination in all our major policies toward other nations.

The third change in the affairs of the NSC grows out of the first two and has a similar purpose. We have deliberately rubbed out the distinction between planning and operation which governed the administrative structure of the NSC staff in the last administration. This distinction, real enough at the extremes of the daily cable traffic and long-range assessment of future possibilities, breaks down in most of the business of decision and action. This is especially true at the level of Presidential action. Thus it seems to us best that the NSC staff, which is essentially a Presidential instrument, should be composed of men who can serve equally well in the process of planning and in that of operational followup. Already it has been made plain, in a number of cases, that the President's interests and purposes can be better served if the staff officer who keeps in daily touch with operations in a given area is also the officer who acts for the White House staff in related planning activities.

Let me turn briefly, in closing, to the role of the Presidential staff as a whole, in national security affairs. This staff is smaller than it was in the last administration, and it is more closely knit. The President uses in these areas a number of officers holding White House appointment, and a number of others holding appointments in the National Security Council staff. He also uses extensively the staff of the Bureau of the Budget. These men are all staff officers. Their job is to help the President, not to supersede or supplement any of the high officials who hold line responsibilities in the executive departments and agencies. Their task is that of all staff officers: to extend the range and enlarge the direct effectiveness of the man they serve. Heavy responsibilities for operation, for coordination, and for diplomatic relations can be and are delegated to the Department of State. Full use of all the powers of leadership can be and is expected in other departments and agencies. There remains a crushing burden of responsibility, and of sheer work, on the President himself; there remains also the steady flow of questions, of ideas, of executive energy which a strong President will give off like sparks. If his Cabinet officers are to be free to do their own work, the President's work must be done—to the extent that he cannot do it himself—by staff officers under his direct oversight. But this is, I repeat, something entirely different from the interposition of such a staff between the President and his Cabinet officers.

I hope this rather general exposition may be helpful to you. I have been conscious, in writing it, of the limits which are imposed upon me by the need to avoid classified questions, and still more by the requirement that the President's own business be treated in confidence. Within those limits I have tried to tell you clearly how we are trying to do our job.

Sincerely,
McGeorge Bundy

NOTE

1. Robert Cutler, "The Development of the National Security Council," Foreign Affairs, April 1956 ("Organizing for National Security," reprinted in "Selected Materials," committee print of the Committee on Government Operations of the Senate, GPO, 1960).

10

KISSINGER'S APPARAT

John P. Leacacos

The selection below evaluates the strengths and weaknesses of the NSC under the direction of Dr. Henry A. Kissinger. During this era, the NSC adviser and staff achieved unparalleled influence over the conduct of U.S. foreign policy. Appended to this study is a list of 138 "National Security Study Memoranda" commissioned by the NSC between 1969–1971, providing a sense of the principal topics addressed by the Council.

Atop Washington's complex foreign affairs bureaucracy sits the National Security Council, a 24-year-old body given new status in 1969, when President Nixon moved to make it a kind of command and control center for his foreign policy. The new Nixon NSC system, run from the White House by Henry A. Kissinger, has now existed for nearly three years, producing 138 numbered study memoranda, reaching 127 formal decisions, and employing a permanent staff of about 120 personnel (more than double the pre-Nixon figure). Though the substance of its operations is necessarily secret, interviews with officials permit tentative evaluation of the strengths and weaknesses of the Kissinger NSC. There is broad agreement on the following seven points:

• The NSC has served President Nixon more or less as he desired, that is, in the ordered style of formal answers to detailed questionnaires. The volume of this paperwork has at times been staggering, but it has sharpened focus on the search for policy choices.

• The answers and alternatives for action "coming up through the NSC" have produced few panaceas, but have contributed greater coherence of outlook in foreign affairs management. NSC recommendations are more pragmatic than academic, reflecting Kissinger's view: "We don't make foreign policy by logical syllogism."

• Explicit insistence on the "limited" nature of U.S. power and the need for greater restraint and cautious deliberation about its exercise have been reinforced at the highest level by Nixon's habit of withdrawing to make final decisions in solitude and of frequently deciding on no action rather than accepting advice to initiate new action.

• By being close to the President and keeping his fingers on all aspects of the NSC process personally, Kissinger without question is the prime mover in the NSC system. The question arises whether the NSC would function as effectively without Kissinger, and whether it can bequeath a heritage of accomplishment to be absorbed by the permanent machinery of government.

• Secretary of State William P. Rogers operates within the NSC system and also utilizes it as a forum to establish whatever policy position is preferred by his State Department; but he side-steps the NSC on occasion to carry his demurrer, dissent or alternate position to the President privately.

• Defense Secretary Melvin R. Laird is less personally involved in the NSC process, having apparent indifference to what he believes is unnecessary NSC paperwork, which he leaves to his deputy, David Packard. Laird's main day-to-day operational preoccupation is with the exit of U.S. forces from Vietnam. His International Security Affairs Bureau in the

Reprinted with permission from John P. Leacacos, "Kissinger's Apparat," *Foreign Policy*. (Winter 1971–72), pp. 3–27. Copyright 1971 by the Carnegie Endowment for International Peace.

John P. Leacacos served as the Washington bureau chief for the *Cleveland Plain Dealer*.

Pentagon performs poorly by Washington bureaucratic standards.

- The influence on foreign policy of the military, including the Joint Chiefs of Staff, who are usually represented in the NSC process, is at the lowest point in several years. This has been attributed to the anticlimactic winding-down atmosphere of the Vietnam war, and to the fact that the Chiefs' once diehard views and abstract argumentation on strategic nuclear superiority over the Soviet Union have been successfully emulsified into the Nixon-Kissinger basic principles for SALT negotiations with Russia. Kissinger has commented: "In my experience with the military, they are more likely to accept decisions they do not like than any other group."

From time to time, gears have clashed within the system. The State Department has complained bitterly of the "Procrustean bed" fashioned by the Kissinger staff. Meeting excessive White House demands, bureaucrats allege, robs State and Defense of manpower hours needed for day-to-day operations. After his first year, Kissinger conceded: "Making foreign policy is easy; what is difficult is its coordination and implementation."

White House NSC staffers, on the other hand, exuberant at their top-dog status, express a degree of condescension for the work of the traditional departments. In 1969 Kissinger staffers rated State-chaired studies and recommendations only "50 to 70 percent acceptable" and based on mediocre reporting which failed to sift wheat from chaff in the political cables constantly arriving from 117 U.S. embassies overseas. The Kissinger staff say that they have to hammer out the real choices on the hard issues, since a cynical and sometimes bored bureaucracy offers up too many "straw options." State's planners, for their part, criticize the NSC staff for overdoing the options game. As senior Foreign Service officers say, "After all, what needs to be done is usually fairly obvious common sense. The crux is *how*, and *when* to do it."

Cogito Ergo IG

The NSC system today is not the tidy blueprint of January, 1969. The older it has gotten, the more informal and overlapping its procedures have become. The amounts of analysis manufactured sometimes threaten to outrun the capacity of the decision-makers to absorb. Crucial issues have been maneuvered to committees chaired by Kissinger, thence directly to the President. The frequency of full NSC meetings has diminished: 37 in 1969, 21 in 1970 and 10 in 1971 (through September).

Normally, an NSC study is jointly prepared through the "IG's" (Inter-departmental Groups) by all concerned agencies (State, Defense, CIA, etc.). There are six IG's for Europe, the Far East, the Middle East, Africa, Latin America and politico-military affairs, all headed by Assistant Secretaries of State. The spread of the 138 NSC study assignments through the first 33 months of the Nixon Administration was: Middle East-14; Far East-12; Latin America-9; Africa-4; Europe-11; Verification Panel-2; Under Secretaries Committee-1; individual departments and agencies-13; *ad hoc* groups-67. Due to overlapping, it is estimated that at least 30 percent of the studies contained contributions from State's Bureau of European Affairs, more than 40 percent from its Bureau of East Asian and Pacific Affairs, as high as 80 percent from its Bureau of Politico-Military Affairs, and close to 90 percent from its Bureau of Intelligence and Research, which had a finger in practically every pie.

The Middle East shop is one of the few to have a high degree of autonomy from "normal" procedures. Assistant Secretary Joseph J. Sisco works directly with the President, Secretary Rogers and Kissinger, although a Kissinger staff man, Harold Saunders, monitors the paper flow.

Vietnam policy has been under close White House NSC supervision. Subsidiary NSC units at State, Defense and CIA serve as operational checkpoints for coordination, and update and verify information required for decision via the NSC Vietnam Special Studies Group. The quality of that group's analysis is rated high by Kissinger—on a par with the exhaustive SALT inquiries. It is chaired by Wayne Smith, Kissinger's systems analysis specialist, to guarantee that no White House doubt is left unanswered. Smith's staff aims at precise intelligence on current Vietnam operations, but also tries to make projections five years ahead. A second, separate NSC *ad hoc* group on Vietnam, chaired by Deputy Assistant Secretary of State William H. Sullivan, who also works directly with the

President, Rogers and Kissinger, concentrates on the Paris negotiations.

Kissinger keeps a close eye on SALT via the NSC Verification Panel, Washington's "action center" for the Helsinki and Vienna talks with the Soviets. Wayne Smith monitors daily operations while Philip J. Farley, deputy director of the Arms Control and Disarmament Agency, acts as a coordinator within the larger bureaucracy.

What the Nixon Administration sees as its five principal areas of foreign affairs initiative—Vietnam, the Middle East, arms control, Berlin, China—have all been under more or less tight NSC White House grip, that is, direct Nixon-Kissinger overview. The NSC took special satisfaction in the August 1971 four-power Berlin accord because *there,* it felt, it had prevented the bureaucracy from rushing into a premature agreement. Progress on SALT and dramatic changes in China policy are also cited as achievements of the new NSC system, although Vietnam remains a more ambiguous test-case and most Middle East peace moves have come directly from the State Department, not the NSC.

WSAG TO THE RESCUE

Between the interdepartmental groups at the base and himself and his personal staff at the apex of the NSC pyramid, Kissinger has created several special units for unique tasks. One is the Under Secretaries Committee, now chaired by Under Secretary of State John N. Irwin and originally designed as the chief implementing body to carry out many (but not all) Presidential NSC directives. Its actual importance (never very great) continues to lapse.

Another is the Senior Review Group, now at an Under Secretary level and chaired by Kissinger, which usually gives final approval to the NSC study memoranda after making sure that "all realistic alternatives are presented." Kissinger also chairs the Defense Programs Review Committee, whose purpose is to keep the annual defense budget in line with foreign policy objectives. A further group, again chaired by Kissinger, though not formally part of the NSC structure, is the "40 committee" which supervises covert intelligence operations (though CIA and green beret commando missions in Laos and Cambodia have been transferred to a separate NSC committee, the Washington Special Actions Group).

This last-named unit, the WSAG, is the top-level operations center for sudden crises and emergencies. It watches developing situations which could gravely affect U.S. interests, such as the apparent imminence of hostilities on the Ussuri River in 1969 between the Russians and Chinese. WSAG kept tabs on Soviet submarines in Cuba in 1969, the Jordan crisis in 1970 and the East Pakistan revolt in 1971, as well as acting as the watchdog during the Cambodian sweep and the Laos incursion. It was created in April, 1969, after Nixon's surprise and embarrassment when the North Koreans shot down an American EC-121 aircraft and the normal bureaucratic mechanisms "muffed" the incident through over-caution. WSAG's chairman is Kissinger, naturally.

Regarding WSAG's work on the Jordan crisis, Kissinger recalled: "We deliberately kept options open to do enough to discourage irresponsibility, but not so much as to give a sense of irreversibility to what was going on; to restrain outside forces (Syrian) that had intervened, but not to the point where we'd trigger a whole set of other forces (Israeli), and to make sure that Soviet power would not be used." The WSAG command-and-control function in this and other crises appeared to work more smoothly than did White House controls on Vietnam in the Johnson Administration. A classic pre-WSAG snafu occurred in 1966–67, when air power advocates made detailed arrangements for the rendezvous of 13 aircraft carriers, practically all those in service, to immobilize the port of Haiphong before North Vietnam's air defenses could be organized—only to be turned down at the last minute by President Johnson.

Temporary White House NSC groups have been formed from time to time for special projects such as post-mortems over Cambodia (pre-invasion intelligence had failed to pinpoint North Vietnamese supply capabilities) and Chile (the narrow election win of Socialist President Allende was a bit of a surprise, and its implications for future U.S. policy were at first unclear).

The WSAG and the Verification Panel have emerged as the President's innermost councils of war, the closest Nixon approximation to John F. Kennedy's "ExCom" which handled the Cuban missile crisis in

1962. Highlighting the importance of these two groups is the occasional attendance at their meetings of Attorney General John N. Mitchell, who plays a role with Nixon not unlike Robert Kennedy's position as chief back-stair adviser for his brother, President Kennedy. Mitchell, who once sardonically described Kissinger to a society reporter as an "egocentric maniac, but brilliant and indispensable," is pictured by senior Nixon aides as a man of "soundness" and sensitivity, a hard loser at giving up U.S. interests and a counselor valued for "good, tough, hard" judgments in complicated situations, particularly in intelligence evaluations affecting the Soviets. Mitchell says relatively little at the meetings he attends, but gives his private assessments directly to the President.

Other WSAG members are CIA Director Richard C. Helms, Deputy Defense Secretary Packard, Joint Chiefs Chairman Admiral Thomas H. Moorer and Under Secretary of State for Political Affairs U. Alexis Johnson. The WSAG likes to work with as few aides as possible. As one of its members says, this eliminates kibitzers and guards against leaks.

THIRTY KEY OFFICIALS

In all this elaborate series of NSC channels and committees, only some 30 key officials are estimated to be involved in making critical decisions. Another 300, at maximum, including officials of State, Defense, and CIA, have a partial role in contributing to the decision-making process and in carrying out Presidential directives.

Despite his perfectionist impatience with the State Department, Kissinger realizes that his unique personal role tends to weaken the institutional role of the permanent bureaucracy. He has frequently said that he would consider it a signal achievement if his NSC system goaded the State Department into "better and better" performance. The more effective State became, the less the White House staff would have to do.

In mid-1971 State began to take up the Kissinger challenge. At Secretary Rogers' urging, a new system of evaluating, country by country, programs, costs and resources, especially those controlled overseas by other agencies, is being installed within State. The goal is to give State more weight bureaucratically vis-à-vis

other agencies in the implementation of foreign policy, thus compensating in part for the ineffectiveness of the moribund NSC Under Secretaries Committee. The long-term objective is to "institutionalize" within State the procedural patterns of the Nixon NSC, thus assuring that they survive beyond the Nixon Presidency. The State Department, after all, starts out with a huge advantage in manpower and trained expertise—over a thousand Foreign Service officers in Washington, compared with the White House staff of a hundred-odd, of which only 10 are currently Foreign Service officers. But if State is to get more of the action in this Administration, it will have to revise the trade-shop slogan of its professionals who say, "Policy is made in the cables," that is, that the actual pattern of U.S. foreign policy in the field is literally made by the spot-instructions drafted in Washington. The White House NSC's more intellectualized approach is that policy is made in Washington *after* all the incoming cables from the field have been sifted, weighed and related to *a priori* grand strategy. Kissinger aides finally got a handle on significant outgoing cables when new LDX (Limited Distribution Xerox) communications equipment was installed in the White House basement. This gave the NSC Presidential assistants enhanced technological means to enforce White House "clearance" of all important outgoing cables.

Much of Kissinger's time is spent writing memoranda to the President, compressing the summaries of lengthy NSC studies to six pages or less. Beyond these formal tasks, he has spent countless hours with the President discussing specific problems and also responding to Nixon's contrapuntal remarks and queries concerning philosophy, history, student restlessness, foreign personalities, public opinion. Presumably Kissinger finds in Nixon a sympathetic audience for observations like this one, made after Cambodia in May 1970: "The unrest on the campus has very deep ... maybe even metaphysical, causes, in that it is the result of the seeming purposelessness of the modern bureaucratic state, of the sense of impotence that is produced in the individual in relation to decisions that far transcend him, and that he does not know how to influence—the result of 30 years of debunking by my colleagues and myself in which now the academic community has managed to take the clock apart and doesn't know how to put it together again." To young staff members, who have sometimes argued with him about the generation gap, Kissinger has asserted that today's youth need fathers, *not* brothers.

FROM VIGOR TO RIGOR

Behind the Nixon-Kissinger table of organization lies a philosophy that is not easily articulated in public, but seems nonetheless real. What began in mid-1969 to be called "the Nixon Doctrine" is intended, for all its ambiguity, to symbolize a fundamental shift of foreign policy. The doctrine looks to the beginnings of a more multipolar, less bipolar balance of world power, greater emphasis on military reserves at home rather than troops abroad, and a phasing-out of U.S. experiments in unilateral "social engineering" in developing nations. It is a conscious attempt to liquidate some of the vestiges (such as Vietnam) of an outworn global containment policy, but to do so in a way that does not leave gaping power vacuums in wake of U.S. "limited disengagement" and also does not provoke a domestic backslide into isolationism.

From the start Kissinger has sought to make the operating bureaucracy tie specific objectives to these broader purposes. There had, he felt, been far too much instant diplomacy in the past, crisis-reactions and concentration on tactical rather than long-term strategic interests. A new bureaucratic methodology based on probing questions followed by searching and systematic analysis of every major U.S. policy was designed to provide Washington officialdom with "a new intellectual grid." To the catchword of the Kennedy Administration—"vigor"—Kissinger added "rigor." The desired end-product of a massive re-analysis of foreign policy within the NSC was to be a series of logical options, alternatives or choices consistent with long-range U.S. goals.

In the first weeks of the Nixon Administration in 1969, Kissinger installed the framework of the new NSC system, arguing that it would help stimulate "conceptualized foreign policy germination." But the structured NSC system made for an orderliness which the bureaucracy could also translate as routine, prompting Kissinger to say later: "Process itself is a boring subject. You can make awfully stupid decisions

with a brilliant process. The basic question the President has asked me to produce from the bureaucracy is: where are we going, and how are we to get there? It is the question he keeps constantly before us."

Kissinger felt that the McGeorge Bundy and Walt Rostow NSC systems of 1961–69 were too loose, had too many prima donnas, and lacked sufficient "checks and balances" to prevent factual error or premature judgments based on false assumptions. Hence, Kissinger's passion for elaborate filters, safety valves, controls. At a background briefing he once said rather sadly:

"Anybody who has seen high officials in Washington will recognize that one of the nightmarish aspects about it is that, contrary to what I knew in academic life where, when one is identified with a problem, one could work on it as long as necessary, [here] one is forced to develop a hierarchy of priorities. . . . There are many issues that senior officials may know are coming. They may even know how they will deal with these issues—if they only had the time to get around to them. So one of the arts of policy-making is to order your issues in such a way that the most urgent ones get solved before some that appear less urgent hit you. . . . The greater number of issues that a country takes on, the more it taxes the psychological resilience of its leadership group. It is not possible to act wisely at every moment of time in every part of the world. It isn't possible for domestic opinion to understand long-range policy in every part of the world at every moment of time."

THE 138 MEMORANDA

Now, nearly three years after the effort began, it is increasingly clear that the Kissinger method has succeeded in shifting a number of American foreign policy assumptions. This has occurred not through any revolution-by-*Diktat*, but instead through a subtler process of evolution-by-memorandum. It is in part by forcing his staff and the larger bureaucracy to answer searching questions in detailed written memoranda, and by refusing to "accept" those memos if they are not sufficiently "rigorous," that Kissinger has churned out the beginnings of new policies toward China, arms control, and European security. His cumbersome method is at its simplest a way of making the bureaucracy think harder.

The process began in January, 1969, when he asked for a study that would answer 26 questions on Vietnam. Ten more study assignments were given out in the next 10 days. The subjects were: the Middle East, U.S. military posture, foreign aid, Japan, NATO, international monetary policy, "review of the international situation," East-West relations, Nigeria, and contingency planning.

In his first 100 days, Kissinger assigned 55 such study memoranda, or "term papers," as they are sometimes called. A total of 85 were assigned in 1969, 26 in 1970, and 27 during the first nine months of 1971. Most of the studies and many of the early efforts were returned to their bureaucratic authors for further work on further questions, before winning Kissinger's approval. Some studies, complete with annexes and tables, were a foot high. These contributed to the overkill of planning by not being read by the principal NSC officials because they were simply too long to digest. But shorter studies, prepared in a careful format to outline proposed choices, costs and consequences did succeed in widening the horizons of policy-makers. NSC aides felt the sharpness of Kissinger's displeasure whenever they let a major policy consideration "fall between the cracks," as occurred when the issue of toxins was not mentioned in a chemical-biological warfare study assigned in May, 1969. The entire study had to be reassigned and re-done in December.

TITO, KHORAT, AND THE PERSIAN GULF

The contents of the 138 NSC study memoranda are classified, but a look at their subject-titles discloses a fascinating variety of topics covered. Thus, a 1970 North African study explored the merit of improving U.S. relations with Algeria and Libya. Another study presented "options" as to what might happen in Yugoslavia after Tito's death. Three times in 1969, twice in 1970, and twice in 1971 there were studies of growing Soviet naval capabilities in the Persian Gulf and the Indian Ocean. The Middle East and the Arab-Israeli conflict rated six studies in 1969, four in 1970, with the trigger that prompted orders for each new study usually some change in the military balance or a new Israeli weapons request.

Among the most prescient of Nixon decisions was the President's request of February 1, 1969 for an NSC study on China (which was followed by two more China studies in 1970 and one in 1971, along with a Japan study still underway). One problem identified and analyzed early in China studies was the place of Thailand in any future, "neutralized" Southeast Asia, and, in particular, whether to demilitarize the $30 million U.S. command and communications complex at Khorat. This U.S. base on Thai territory, constructed in the mid-1960's with reinforced concrete for defense against nuclear attack, was conceived by the Joint Chiefs of Staff as the site of U.S. theater headquarters in event of general war with China. A few short years later, the Khorat base looks like a very white elephant.

Among the most vital of all the studies are those relating to nuclear weapons, done in preparation for the Strategic Arms Limitation Talks (SALT) with the Soviet Union. There have been four basic and exhaustive SALT studies and at least 25 further collateral studies (21 in 1969, four in 1970 and four in 1971), including the first review of U.S. civil defense requirements in two decades. They are Kissinger's pride. He has asserted that the SALT studies, centered in the Verification Panel, have been the most thorough and meticulous analyses ever made of the politics of nuclear strategy. He also asserts that they have virtually eliminated the narrow adversary approach to arms limitation hitherto practiced within the U.S. government, which used to provoke bitter intramural controversies leading to stultified international negotiations. Half the time used to be spent negotiating among ourselves, Kissinger says, one-quarter with our allies, and one-quarter with the Russians. . . .

TWO WEAK SPOTS

The Achilles' heel of the NSC system has been international economics; and its Albatross has been foreign intelligence. As Kissinger is the first to admit, his reputation in diplomacy and nuclear strategy does not extend to economics, a field largely beyond his knowledge or competence. Thus the NSC has had only marginal, if not minimal, impact on economic policy.

Early efforts in 1969 to secure the staff services of a national authority in the foreign economic field lapsed under the pressure of more immediate problems. During the first year about 70 percent of the bureaucracy's contributions to NSC economic studies came from the Treasury Department, and only 30 percent from State. No senior interdepartmental group for economics was organized. Receiving little attention from Kissinger, the NSC's own economic specialists carried no bureaucratic clout. Kissinger's remedy in 1970 was to suggest formation of a Council of International Economic Policy, which was finally created in early 1971. The new body, however, has yet to get off the ground, for it is not comparable in prestige, influence, or expertise to the regular Kissinger NSC staff. The State Department, which argues that half of its work is normally economic, continues to oppose the rationale for a foreign economic council, because, professional Foreign Service officers argue, economics and politics cannot be separated. Thus it was the Treasury and the President's domestic advisers, not State or the NSC, that formulated Nixon's new economic policies of last August 15.

The NSC's second weak spot, intelligence, is probably Kissinger's greatest personal disappointment. He had once said that the test of statesmanship was the ability to anticipate and evaluate threats before they occurred. His passion for objectivity and commitment to rigorous analysis appear in this case to have fallen afoul of the disorganized chaos of the multiple intelligence agencies in the U.S. government. . . .

THE OPTIONS GAME

How realistic are the famous "options"? Judging by the results thus far, Nixon has been better served by his more formalized national security advisory system than either Lyndon Johnson or John F. Kennedy were served by their informal systems, even though it was Robert McNamara, as Defense Secretary to the two predecessor Presidents, who first made the options concept fashionable. The idea was simple enough: serve up the President a bundle of alternatives. But one sometimes wonders, while prowling the White House basement, whether often-repeated phrases like "keeping the options open" and "the President's spread of options" don't have more a liturgical than an intellectual significance. The options mystique has even inspired some critics to accuse Kissinger of cynically circumventing the bureaucracy by hogtieing it to meaningless NSC studies while he and his staff focus on the essential issues. The charge would have more

plausibility if Kissinger were indeed the Nietzschean superman his critics assume—and commanded a sufficient number of junior supermen to perform the whole job in the White House.

The path from Kissinger wish to NSC consummation has been by no means easy. President Nixon, recalling the recommendations of the Eisenhower Administration NSC, felt they had been too homogenized. In the Johnson regime, the NSC did not act as a functioning process binding agencies together; by contrast with the Nixon system, the Johnson NSC was practically nonexistent. And Johnson staffers only infrequently and informally presented the President with options. After all, it was felt, "There were only one or two sensible things to do."

So Kissinger upon entering the White House basement found little rough and ready argumentation among bureaucrats over alternative policy courses. He inherited, instead, the bureaucracy's time-tested habit of elaborate, negotiated "consensus" among subordinate officials and agencies (with an occasional dissenting view included as a footnote) *prior* to their submission of advice to the President. He shook this system up by passing out new kinds of study-assignments. Harvard professor that he is, he made the bureaucrats write theses, and proved to be a tough grader. He rated many of the early NSC studies no better than "C"— barely passing. He also came to recognize that the options game could frequently be a disguised form of special advocacy: two or three obviously untenable "straw options" served up alongside only one clearly realistic choice.

What is less clear is whether the NSC options game shades analysis toward competition within the bureaucracy for discovery of the most striking plausibility that can appeal to the holders of political power. By stimulating foreign affairs officials to engage in an adversary process, does one perhaps change the whole focus of the system toward scoring bureaucratic points on opponents, rather than defining national objectives and deciding how best to attain them?

And there may be a final dilemma, evident in the unhappiness of the Nixon NSC with the intelligence it is getting. Intelligence evaluators, by the very nature of their function, restrict options; their role is to determine likely, "reliable" outcomes, probable and feasible patterns of events. The role of the President's men, on the other hand, is to avoid being squeezed into one course, and to maintain and expand the options.

The product of all the memos and meetings, questionnaires and options is the refined raw material of Presidential decision-making, the identification of what opportunities and escape-hatches are open to the nation's leadership. To date, Nixon's foreign policy record has indicated the seizure of opportunities, and so the NSC process that made those opportunities apparent must be judged a success.

Table 3.1 National Security Study Memoranda 1969

1: January 21	Vietnam
2: January 21	Middle East
3: January 21	Military Posture
4: January 21	Foreign Aid
5: January 21	Japan
6: January 21	NATO
7: January 21	International Monetary Policy
8: February 3	U.S. Military Forces
9: January 23	Review of International Situations
10: January 28	East-West Relations
11: January 28	Nigeria
12: January 30	Contingency Planning
13: February 5	Non-Proliferation Treaty
14: February 5	China
15: February 3	Latin America
16: February 5	Trade Policy
17: February 6	Middle East
18: February 7	Peru
19: February 11	Vietnam
20: February 12	Disarmament
21: February 13	Vietnam
22: February 13	Vietnam
23: February 20	Defense Budget
24: February 20	Military Posture
25: February 20	Nuclear Test Ban Treaty
26: February 21	South Asia
27: February 22	Korea
28: March 13	SALT
29: March 12	Vietnam
30: March 19	Middle East
31: March 19	Malaysia and Singapore
32: March 21	Cuba
33: March 21	Middle East
34: March 21	Korea
35: March 28	Trade with Communist China
36: April 10	Vietnam
37: April 10	Vietnam
38: April 10	Asian Policy
39: April 10	Southern Africa
40: April 11	Israel Arms
41: April 11	Seabeds Treaty
42: April 11	Peru
43: April 15	NATO
44: April 19	NATO
45: April 21	Foreign Aid
46: April 21	Spain
47: April 21	France
48: April 24	Tariff Preferences
49: April 24	Trade Policy
50: April 26	Naval Forces
51: April 26	Thailand
52: April 26	Greece
53: April 26	Korea
54: April 29	Naval Shipbuilding
55: April 30	France
56: May 14	Uranium Enrichment
57: May 23	Civil Defense
58: May 26	Civil Defense
59: May 28	Chemical-Biological Agents
60: May 29	France
61: June 23	Indonesia
62: July 2	SALT
63: July 3	Sino-Soviet Relations
64: July 8	Military Capabilities
65: July 8	NATO
66: July 12	Persian Gulf
67: July 12	Brazil
68: July 12	Latin America
69: July 14	Asia Nuclear Policy
70: July 22	Haiti
71: August 14	Advanced Nat'l. Security Technology
72: September 4	Space Cooperation
73: September 16	Philippines
74: September 17	Laos
75: September 23	Turkey
76: September 27	Laos
77: October 8	Program Budgets
78: October 8	Deferment Policy
79: October 13	European Community
80: October 27	President's Annual Review
81: November 6	Israel
82: November 6	Israel
83: November 21	European Security
84: November 21	U.S. Forces in Europe
85: December 31	Toxins
1970	
86: January 2	Panama Canal
87: January 22	North Africa
88: February 12	Italy and North Mediterranean
89: February 12	Southwest Africa
90: February 26	Mediterranean
91: March 27	Preferential Trade Arrangements
92: April 13	Mutual Balanced Force Reductions
93: April 13	Middle East

94: May 25	Indochina		116: January 26	Greece
95: June 6	Indochina		117: February 16	Caribbean
96: July 23	Laos Peace Initiatives		118: February 16	Pakistan
97: July 24	Chile		119: February 20	Soviet Navy
98: August 10	Israel Arms		120: February 19	Peaceful Uses Atomic Energy
99: August 17	Southeast Asia Strategy		121: April 13	NATO
100: September 1	French Military Cooperation		122: April 15	Japan
101: September 14	Uranium Enrichment Defense Needs		123: April 17	U.S.-U.K. Relations
102: September 21	President's Annual Review		124: April 19	Communist China
103: September 26	Middle East		125: April 21	Oceans Policy
104: November 9	Indian Ocean Navies		126: April 22	Civil Defense
105: November 13	Middle East Future		127: May 27	Australia-New Zealand
106: November 19	China		128: June 4	Arms Control
107: November 19	U.N. China Admission		129: June 15	Yugoslavia
108: December 10	Latin America		130: June 18	Cyprus
109: December 19	South Asia		131: June 23	U.S. Foreign Investment
110: December 22	Indian Ocean		132: June 28	Nuclear Arms Control
111: December 29	Germany and Berlin		133: July 2	Southeast Asia
1971			134: July 15	Iceland
112: January 7	Vietnam Riot Control		135: July 17	Malta
113: January 15	Declassification Official Documents		136: July 30	Berlin
114: January 15	Oil		137: September 22	President's Annual Review of Foreign Policy
115: January 25	Africa		138: October 2	European Security Conference

11

PRESIDENTIAL DIRECTIVE/NSC–2

Jimmy Carter

Printed below is President Carter's directive, dated January 20, 1977, reorganizing the NSC. Two key entities were established within the existing framework of the Council: the Policy Review Committee (PRC) and the Special Coordination Committee (SCC).

TO: The Vice President
     The Secretary of State
     The Secretary of Defense

ALSO: The Secretary of the Treasury
       The Attorney General
       The United States Representative to the
         United Nations
       The Director, Office of Management
         and Budget
       The Assistant to the President for
         National Security Affairs
       The Chairman, Council of Economic
         Advisers
       The Administrator, Agency for International Development
       The Director, Arms Control and Disarmament Agency
       The Director, United States Information Agency
       The Chairman, Joint Chiefs of Staff
       The Director of Central Intelligence
       The Administrator, Energy Research
         and Development Administration
SUBJECT: The National Security Council System

To assist me in carrying out my responsibilities for the conduct of national security affairs, I hereby direct the reorganization of the National Security Council system. The reorganization is intended to place more responsibility in the departments and agencies while insuring that the NSC, with my Assistant for National Security Affairs, continues to integrate and facilitate foreign and defense policy decisions.

A. THE NATIONAL SECURITY COUNCIL (NSC)

The functions, membership, and responsibilities of the National Security Council shall be as set forth in the National Security Act of 1947, as amended. In addition, other senior officials, including the Secretary of the Treasury, the Attorney General, the United States Representative to the United Nations, the Director of the Office of Management and Budget, the Assistant to the President for National Security Affairs, the Chairman of the Council of Economic Advisers, the Director of the Arms Control and Disarmament Agency, the Chairman of the Joint Chiefs of Staff, the Director of Central Intelligence, and the Administrator of the Energy Research and Development Administration, shall attend appropriate NSC meetings.

The National Security Council shall be the principal forum for international security issues requiring Presidential consideration. The NSC shall assist me in analyzing, integrating and facilitating foreign, defense, and intelligence policy decisions. International economic and other interdependence issues which are pertinent to national security shall also be considered by the NSC.

Declassified on April 22, 1977.

Jimmy Carter of Georgia served as president of the United States from 1977–1981.

The Council shall meet regularly. The Assistant to the President for National Security Affairs, at my direction and in consultation with the Secretaries of State and Defense and, when appropriate, the Secretary of the Treasury and the Chairman, Council of Economic Advisers, shall be responsible for determining the agenda and insuring that the necessary papers are prepared. Other members of the NSC may propose items for inclusion on the agenda. The Assistant to the President shall be assisted by a National Security Council staff, as provided by law.

B. NSC Policy Review Committee

An NSC Policy Review Committee is hereby established to develop national security policy for Presidential decision in those cases where the basic responsibilities fall primarily within a given department but where the subject also has important implications for other departments and agencies. This Committee shall deal with such matters as:

• foreign policy issues that contain significant military or other interagency aspects;
• defense policy issues having international implications and the coordination of the annual Defense budget with foreign policy objectives;
• the preparation of a consolidated national intelligence budget and resource allocation for the Intelligence Community (thus assuming under the chairmanship of the Director of Central Intelligence the functions and responsibilities of the Committee on Foreign Intelligence); and
• those international economic issues pertinent to U.S. foreign policy and security, with staffing of the underlying economic issues through the Economic Policy Group.

I shall designate for each meeting the appropriate Chairman of the Policy Review Committee and attendance, depending on the subject matter being considered. Membership, in addition to the statutory members of the NSC and the Assistant for National Security Affairs, shall include, as appropriate, other senior officials.

C. The NSC Special Coordination Committee

A second NSC Committee, the Special Coordination Committee, is hereby established to deal with specific cross-cutting issues requiring coordination in the development of options and the implementation of Presidential decisions. The Committee shall deal with such matters as: the oversight of sensitive intelligence activities, such as covert operations, which are undertaken on Presidential authority; arms control evaluation; and it will assist me in crisis management.

The Special Coordination Committee shall be chaired by the Assistant for National Security Affairs. Membership shall include the statutory members of the NSC, or their representatives, and other senior officials, as appropriate.

D. NSC Interdepartmental Groups

Existing NSC Interdepartmental Groups, chaired by a designated senior departmental official, are to continue as needed under the direction of the NSC Policy Review Committee.

The membership of the Interdepartmental Groups shall include the agencies represented on the NSC Policy Review Committee. Depending on the issue under consideration, other agencies shall be represented at the discretion of the Policy Review Committee.

E. National Security Council Ad Hoc Groups

When appropriate, I intend to appoint NSC Ad Hoc Groups to deal with particular problems, including those which transcend departmental boundaries.

Jimmy Carter

PART IV

THE MODERN NSC

At a time when the world's increasing inter-dependence challenges
us all to new patterns of thought and action, the NSC's role is more
important than ever.

—Message of President Bill Clinton on the 50th Anniversary
of the National Security Council
September 18, 1997

EDITORS' INTRODUCTION

George H. W. Bush

The four-year tenure of the first President Bush could appropriately be labeled a "foreign policy presidency." Monumental events took place during his watch, including the collapse of the
Soviet empire, the unification of Germany, Tiananmen Square and its impact on U.S.–China
relations, and the Persian Gulf War. The Bush NSC—specifically the president, the principal
members of his national security team, and the Council's staff—was the key institution for
responding to each of these crises.

Upon taking office, President Bush was intent on establishing a coherent and sound
approach to national security policy making. He selected people he had confidence in and who
he believed could work together. James Baker, Bush's secretary of state and longtime friend and
adviser, believes the president accomplished his objective. In his account of the Bush years,
Baker writes:

> I had the additional good fortune to be part of a Bush national security team that consisted of a
> group of experienced, collegial peers who liked and respected one another. We not only enjoyed
> one another's company, we trusted one another. That's not to suggest we didn't disagree. . . . But
> our differences never took the form of the backbiting of the Kissinger-Rogers, Vance-Brzezinski
> eras, or the slugfests of our national security teams during the Reagan years . . . As a result, I
> firmly believe that one of the foremost accomplishments of the Bush presidency was that we made
> the national security apparatus work the way it was supposed to. (Baker, 1995: 21–22)

People and their relationships made the Bush NSC a model of collegiality, but this was
enhanced by the organizational structure put into place by the incoming administration. On January 30, 1989, President Bush issued National Security Directive 1 (NSD-1), establishing his
new NSC system. Compared with past arrangements, it was streamlined. The formal Council
would be supported by two key NSC subgroups—a Principals Committee and a Deputies Committee. The former would include the secretaries of state and defense, the director of central
intelligence, the chairman of the Joint Chiefs of Staff, the president's chief of staff, and the

national security adviser, who would serve as chairman. Other officials, such as the secretary of the treasury and the attorney general, would be invited as needed. This Committee, according to Brent Scowcroft, was the major organization change he wanted to make in the operation of the NSC, based on his past experience as national security adviser. In *A World Transformed* (see For Further Reading), which he co-authored with President Bush, Scowcroft says, "I was eager to add a 'principals' committee' which would be the NSC without the President and Vice President. I thought this could help clarify issues and positions among the principals before the issues were taken to the President. It could save him considerable time, and time, I believed, was his most valuable commodity" (Bush and Scowcroft, 1998: 31).

The Deputies Committee would be chaired by the deputy national security adviser and would include the second- or third-ranking official from each of the departments or agencies represented on the Principals Committee. According to NSD-1, its task was to "ensure that all papers to be discussed by the NSC . . . fully analyze the issues, fairly and adequately set out the facts, consider a full range of views and options, and satisfactorily assess the prospects, risks and implications of each." As a result of a supplement to the directive, signed by Scowcroft in October 1989, the Deputies Committee took on another formal assignment: crisis management. The "DC," as the Committee was called, would spend a great deal of its time during the Bush Administration fulfilling this responsibility.

As with many administrations, the formal structure of the NSC was one thing on paper, another in actual practice. In this regard, the Bush NSC was no different. After four years, observers could detect certain distinguishing characteristics that best defined its operation and set it apart from its predecessors.

To begin with, the Bush NSC system was largely personality driven, a reflection of President Bush's operating style. A close-knit constellation of individuals gathered around the president to direct the system—Scowcroft, Baker, Powell, Cheney, Robert Gates (the deputy national security adviser who would later become the CIA director), sometimes one or two others. Moreover, as President Bush points out in *A World Transformed*, the institutional tension between his NSC adviser and his secretary of state was practically nonexistent:

> Brent and Jim did get moderately crosswise, but very rarely. Jim worried that he might be excluded from a decision that affected his department. As a former chief of staff, he knew how a strong-willed presidential advisor, if backed by the president, can easily isolate a cabinet member. It is probably accurate to say that the NSC staff and Brent were also concerned about what State might be up to. We tried very hard, and I think successfully, to keep all the participants informed and eliminate personality clashes which could undermine policy-making as well as effective diplomacy. (Bush and Scowcroft, 1998: 36)

Not only was the Bush NSC highly personalized, it was also characterized by informality at the top, its second distinguishing characteristic. Formal structure (with the important exception of the Deputies Committee) was less important than informal arrangements. While the NSC convened more frequently in 1989 and 1990, it met only four times in 1991 and three times in 1992. By mid-term, formal Council sessions had given way to informally called meetings of the president and others selected for the issue at hand. During the Persian Gulf War, there were meetings of the "Big Eight"—Bush, Scowcroft, Baker, Cheney, Powell, Vice-president Dan Quayle, CIA director William Webster, and White House chief of staff John Sununu—held more often than not in the Oval Office.

Nor did the Principals Committee meet that often in formal session. Indeed during the first two years of the Bush Administration it hardly met at all. The reason was President Bush. Robert Kimmit, who served as undersecretary of state, explains: "When the president learned his senior advisors were meeting just down the hall without him, he made clear to Brent Scowcroft that he wanted to be involved in such discussions" (Center, April, 1999: 7).

This informality did not extend, however, to the Deputies Committee, which was seen by Scowcroft and others as the indispensable part of the system. The "DC" convened often—almost 160 times in 1990 alone. Remember, this Committee doubled as a policy review group and as a crisis manager. By most accounts, the Deputies Committee was able to be effective for two reasons: first, it included a small group of people senior enough to get things done; and, second, participants in the meetings had immediate and direct access to their principals, so they could either commit to their views at the table or be able to get back quickly to say yes or no. Still, the operation of the "DC" did receive some criticism, especially from those with the view that it became too operational, functioning well in crises but not focusing enough attention on long-range policy development.

The third, and final, distinguishing characteristic of the Bush NSC was the stress it placed on the role of the NSC as "honest broker." This was not surprising, given that Brent Scowcroft had become the model for the "honest broker" under President Ford. He made it into something of an art form under Bush.

In an operational sense, the "honest broker" role meant that cabinet secretaries felt comfortable with Scowcroft in the chair at Principals Committee meetings, and with the deputy national security adviser chairing the Deputies Committee. Because top NSC officials were not perceived as pushing their own policy agenda, they were considered the natural chair for senior policy meetings. Moreover, the NSC's "honest broker" reputation led other departments and agencies to try to push their issues into the NSC process, believing they would be handled impartially and that decisions would actually be made (a premium in bureaucratic Washington, where debate can drag on for months without coming to closure). The NSC's reputation for "impartiality" did not mean, however, that the national security adviser and his staff were without opinions. It did mean that it was believed that these views would not "tilt" the process, but allow the departments and agencies a chance to be fairly heard.

With President Bush's defeat in the 1992 election to Arkansas Governor Bill Clinton, changes were again in store for the operation of the National Security Council. The Bush NSC would, however, leave behind a legacy of collegiality and simple organizational structure that future administrations would seek to emulate. It also left behind a number of vexing and unresolved foreign policy issues for the incoming Democratic administration—ranging from the containment of Saddam Hussein in Iraq, to a major humanitarian relief operation in Somalia, to an increasingly vicious ethnic conflict raging in the Balkans.

All of these issues would be passed to a new president—the nation's first post-Cold War chief executive—who made it clear during the presidential campaign that his priority upon entering office would be his domestic agenda and the economy, not foreign policy. As I. M. Destler points out in *The National Economic Council: A Work in Progress* (see For Further Reading), the president-elect underscored his declared priority by announcing his economic team first, in the second week of December, before his national security advisers, who included Anthony Lake to head the NSC, his deputy Samuel (Sandy) Berger, incoming Secretary of State Warren Christopher, and UN Ambassador Madeleine Albright. Clinton's national security team was acutely conscious of his need to focus on his domestic and economic agenda in the early months of his administration.

Clinton

On Inauguration Day, January 20, 1993, Clinton issued Presidential Decision Directive/NSC–2 (PDD/NSC–2), establishing his new NSC framework. In his directive, Clinton sent a number of important signals about how he intended to conduct national security decision making during his term in office.

The most important of these signals was, in the words of White House spokesman George Stephanopoulos, the new president's resolve to make certain that economic dimensions are at "the center of our national security policy." The directive underscored this determination in several ways. First, it expanded the original language of the 1947 National Security Act to cite economic policy explicitly as part of the Council's mandate to integrate "all aspects of national security policy as it affects the United States." Second, in addition to its permanent members prescribed by statute, the Council was enlarged to include the secretary of the treasury and the president's new Assistant for Economic Policy. Third, these officials or their deputies would be integrated into the work of the NSC subgroups established by the directive.

The PDD/NSC–2 document sent other important signals as well. Operating on the principle 'if it ain't broke, don't fix it' (or rename it), the directive adopted the Bush Administration's structure of a Council supported by a Principals Committee and Deputies Committee. This was the first time in the NSC's history that an incoming administration adopted the main organizational features of its predecessor. The directive also continued the practice of the national security adviser or his deputy chairing the two committees, thus signaling agreement with a conclusion of the 1987 Tower Commission that the NSC generally operates better when the key committees are chaired by the individual with the greatest stake in making the NSC system work, namely the national security adviser. At the same time, the administration made it clear that while policy coordination would be centered in the White House, policy action would be the responsibility of the departments. Finally, the directive made a statement about the president's commitment to multilateralism and the United Nations by placing the U.S. Ambassador to the UN on the Council and the Principals Committee.

While the steps Clinton announced on January 20 were important, the principal institutional innovation of his administration followed five days later, when the president signed an Executive Order establishing the National Economic Council (NEC). Using the NSC as the model, a formal Council was established to include the president and vice president; the secretaries of state, treasury, commerce, and energy; the director of the office of management and budget; the U.S. trade representative, and other officials within the government with economic responsibilities, for a total of eighteen members. The president created a position of Assistant to the President for Economic Policy to direct an NEC staff. The Executive Order spelled out the functions of the NEC, beginning with the responsibility "to coordinate the economic policy-making process with respect to domestic and international economic issues." Over time, the NEC would consider trade policy, international monetary and fiscal policy, economic sanctions and export controls, economic negotiations with key countries, such as Japan and Germany, foreign economic assistance, and assistance to nations or economics in transition, like Russia. The Executive Order also attempted to head off institutional tensions between the national economic adviser and the secretary of the treasury, like those that had often troubled the NSC. "The Secretary of the Treasury," reads the president's order, "will continue to be the senior economic official in the executive branch and the President's chief economic spokesperson." To head up treasury, Clinton chose Senator Lloyd Bentsen of Texas; for his first national economic adviser, he brought into government New York investment banker Robert Rubin.

Administrations dating back to President Nixon had established a staff unit within the White House to coordinate economic policy, with President's Ford's Economic Policy Board being the most prominent example. Still, it had always been an uphill battle to see international economic policy receive equal footing with traditional national security issues. Part of the problem was the NSC; throughout its history neither the Council nor its national security advisers were particularly interested in giving priority to economic issues. But under President Clinton this would change, so the challenge facing the incoming administration was to ensure that the NSC and the NEC would work together. Integration of the work of the two Councils—not separation—was the goal. As Destler points out in his book on the NEC:

> With each staff seeing international economic issues as an important part of its domain and with both working for a president who wanted collegiality among his aides, they needed to talk. And they did: Cutter [Bowman Cutter, Rubin's deputy] with Berger, and as a foursome with Lake and Rubin. Before the transition was over, they had settled on an unusual power sharing arrangement. Rather than recruiting separate international economic staffs, they would share one. Aides in this sphere would wear two hats . . . Each reported up two chains of command: Rubin/Cutter and Lake/Berger. Both Cutter and Berger, moreover, would attend and chair meetings of the interagency "deputies committee" on international economic issues. (Destler, 1996: 11)

This arrangement proved successful, and it allowed the NEC to establish itself as an important institutional player alongside the longstanding NSC. By all accounts the president's national security and economic advisers—Lake and Rubin—had a good working relationship. Moreover, Rubin's clout, both inside and outside the administration, was a major factor in the effective functioning of the NEC during his two-and-a-half year tenure. The NEC's influence diminished, however, when Rubin departed to become treasury secretary after Lloyd Bentsen stepped down in December 1994. While the NEC stayed active and engaged through the end of President Clinton's second term, Rubin—like Henry Kissinger years before—took much of his clout with him when he left the White House to head an executive department.

The broader mandate of the Clinton NSC was reflected not only in its attention to international economics, but to other issues of increasing importance in the post-Cold War era. In 1993, new offices were created at the NSC to deal with the danger of the proliferation of weapons of mass destruction—nuclear, chemical, and biological—and threats to the world's environment. By Clinton's second term, other issues moved higher on the national security agenda, with international terrorism at the forefront. In May 1998, Clinton signed Presidential Decision Directive/NSC–62, establishing within the NSC the Office of the National Coordinator for Security, Infrastructure Protection and Counter Terrorism. Finally, in April 2001, the administration took the unprecedented step of declaring the worldwide HIV/AIDs pandemic a national security threat, placing it on the NSC policy agenda.

The next selection in this chapter, Vincent A. Auger's "The National Security Council System After the Cold War," takes a close look at the operation of the Clinton NSC during the president's first term. Auger focuses on four issues that "analysts or administration officials themselves have identified as central to the functioning of that system: the NSA [national security adviser]/NSC role as 'honest broker' and coordinator among the foreign policy bureaucracies; the management of the interagency process; the coordination and integration of the economic and noneconomic aspects of the administration's foreign policy; and the role of the president in leading and overseeing the system."

Of these issues, Auger gives highest marks to Clinton's first NSC adviser, Anthony Lake, in performing the "honest broker" role. "By all accounts," Auger writes, "Lake was remarkably even-handed in representing other agencies and principals fairly to the president, in ceding the spotlight to the secretary of state, and in minimizing the open disharmony and competition that characterized NSC relations with the line agencies in previous administrations." That said, Auger is less complimentary about how the NSC was actually run, especially its management of the interagency process. He cites several problems in this regard, but draws greatest attention to one—what a NSC staffer called a "fetish for consensus building." Writes Auger:

> In his attempt to ensure a collegial relationship among administration officials, Lake (who advised Clinton in this matter during the transition) created a policy-making environment in which there were few major differences among the top officials. When differences on policy did exist, the first priority was to find a solution that every principal could support. Lake himself seemed to recognize that this could lead to problems when he remarked in October 1993: "I think there is a danger that when people work well together, you can take the edge off the options."

The perils of "consensus building" notwithstanding, Auger's most pointed criticism of the Clinton NSC during the first term was what he described as inconsistent presidential leadership:

> A striking aspect of the Clinton administration's foreign policy process, given the advisory and staff structures it selected, has been what one State Department official termed the president's "selective interest" in foreign policy. On certain topics, such as Russia or trade ("economic security"), the president evinced enthusiasm, sustained interest, and a certain consistency in policy pronouncements. On most foreign policy issues, however, Clinton has taken an active role only when confronted by a crisis.

Underscoring the lesson of past NSCs, Auger states that while the formal structure and process of the NSC system are important, "it is crucial to remember that, ultimately, that system is an extension of the president's own concerns and interests."

As President Clinton moved into his second term—with his domestic and economic priorities now in place and a greater degree of experience and confidence in handling international affairs—his "selective interest" in foreign policy became more continuous, including a major commitment of his time to Middle East diplomacy. Moreover, several of the interagency management problems identified with his first NSC were addressed by his second national security adviser, Sandy Berger, who ran, by all accounts, a tighter ship.

At the same time, as the presidential election of 2000 approached, criticism of a different sort was being heard about the NSC: that the national security adviser had, again, become too dominant in the policy-making process. Observers pointed out that the NSC staff had almost doubled in size since 1993 and that it had taken on too many assignments and responsibilities, from issues like international health to adding new offices for NSC speechwriting and communications. A chart, Figure IV.A, depicting the Clinton NSC staff organization in 2000 follows.

George W. Bush

The presidential election of 2000 proved to be one of the closest and most controversial in American history. After the American people and the United States Supreme Court had spoken, Texas Governor George W. Bush was declared the winner. In line to become his national security adviser was Condoleezza Rice, who had served as a Soviet specialist on the NSC staff under

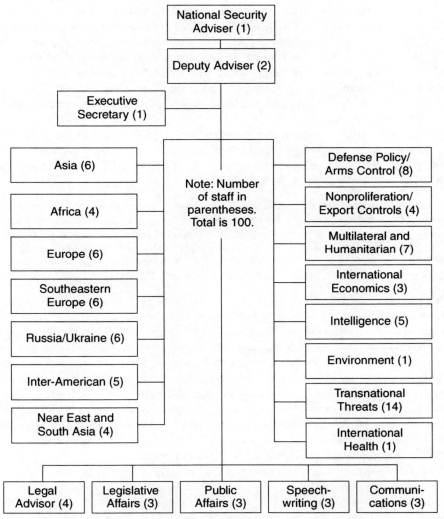

National Security Adviser (1)

Deputy Adviser (2)

Executive Secretary (1)

Note: Number of staff in parentheses. Total is 100.

Asia (6)

Africa (4)

Europe (6)

Southeastern Europe (6)

Russia/Ukraine (6)

Inter-American (5)

Near East and South Asia (4)

Defense Policy/ Arms Control (8)

Nonproliferation/ Export Controls (4)

Multilateral and Humanitarian (7)

International Economics (3)

Intelligence (5)

Environment (1)

Transnational Threats (14)

International Health (1)

Legal Advisor (4)

Legislative Affairs (3)

Public Affairs (3)

Speech-writing (3)

Communi-cations (3)

Figure IV.A The Clinton NSC, 2000 *(Source: "A New NSC for a New Administration," Brookings Policy Brief No. 68, November 2000.)*

Brent Scowcroft during the administration of the first President Bush. Days before the Inauguration, she appeared at an event sponsored by the U.S. Institute of Peace and spoke about the national security challenges facing the new administration (see For Further Reading). In her opening remarks, Rice said she was looking forward "to joining the fraternity of national security advisers," then added: "I don't know if they're going to have to change the rules of admission or not" (Rice, 2001: 57)—a clear and humorous reference to the fact that she would be the first woman to hold that high office. While no such changes were required, the president-elect and his new national security adviser did have some changes in store for the NSC system.

With the new Bush administration settling into place, the *Washington Post* ran a front page article on: "A Leaner and Less Visible NSC" (see For Further Reading). According to the *Post*, the NSC had been substantially restructured during the president's first three weeks in office. National security adviser Rice had cut the NSC staff by a third and reorganized it to emphasize the administration's priorities, including national missile defense and international economics. Offices handling international environmental and health issues were eliminated, as were those responsible for communications and legislative affairs (these functions were returned to the main White House staff).

Moreover, the *Post* reported, the reorganization of the NSC revealed how Rice envisioned her relationship with other powerful and high-profile members of Bush's national security team, including Vice-president (and former defense secretary) Richard Cheney, Secretary of State Colin Powell, and Defense Secretary Donald Rumsfeld. According to the *Post*:

> Rice has made it clear she will not be a policy initiator or implementer, and that she expects to be seen and heard far less than her predecessor, Samuel "Sandy" Berger. Several administration offi- cials said she sees her task as making sure Bush is briefed and staffed to play his role in foreign and security matters, advancing his strategic agenda while thinking though big issues such as guidelines for foreign intervention, and serving as an honest broker of differences among the major policy players. (De Young and Mufson, February 9, 2001: A1)

President Bush took nearly a month after entering office before issuing his formal directive for the organization of his NSC system. There was speculation that the delay was caused, in part, by an internal debate about the role Vice-president Cheney would play, perhaps chairing impor- tant meetings of the Council. But enhanced responsibilities for the vice president could come at the expense of the authority of the national security adviser. When the president's directive was finally signed and issued on February 13, 2001, that speculation was laid to rest, although Cheney and his staff would come to play an unprecedented role in the Bush administration, weighing in on every major foreign policy question. The directive—formally known as National Security Presidential Directive (NSPD) 1 and included as the next selection—affirmed Rice's primacy for directing the work of the Council and, along with her deputy, chairing the two prin- cipal NSC subgroups—the Principals and Deputies committees.

A further sign of continuity with the previous administration was the directive's emphasis on international economics. "National security also depends on America's opportunity to pros- per in the world economy," states NSDP-1. To ensure the coordination of security and economic concerns, the secretary of the treasury was not only named as a member of the formal NSC, but was added as a regular attendee of the Principals Committee.

At the same time, NSPD 1 signaled certain changes in approach. The directive was addressed to forty-one officials of the U.S. government—almost twice the number (twenty one) that had received Clinton's directive. On the list were the traditional heads of the departments and agencies dealing with foreign, defense, economic, and energy policy; but also included on the list were the secretaries of agriculture, health and human services, and transportation; the directors of the Peace Corps and the Federal Emergency Management Agency; and the admin- istrator for drug enforcement. This inclusion of those traditionally outside the national security realm was foreshadowed in the remarks Condoleezza Rice made to the U.S. Institute of Peace just before taking office:

> In 1947 the challenge was to tame the clashing interests of the State, War, and Navy Departments. In 2001 the challenge is to unite the far-flung concerns of all the agencies that are working across

our real and virtual borders. . . . The National Security Council system with the president at its top is the instrument we use. Now, it's not my job to make people "toe the line." Instead, the challenges and the great opportunity is to sense the possibilities of this new era and to make connections, to work as a team toward an American foreign policy that is coherent and successful. We can no longer afford stovepipes . . . (Rice, 2001: 61)

Despite this inclusiveness, one official who would be dropped from the directive establishing the president's NSC system was the U.S. ambassador to the United Nations. Here, too, the new administration was sending a signal—that multilateralism and the UN would have a lower priority than they did under the Clinton presidency.

A contrast between the incoming and outgoing administrations was also seen in the second President Bush's use of the NSC itself. President Clinton had rarely called formal meetings of the Council, and never in his second term. Reflecting his corporate style of decision making—with a premium on an orderly, deliberative process with clear lines of authority and responsibility—President Bush reinstituted formal sessions of the NSC, and held them on a regular basis. This practice would continue when, on September 11, 2001, America was attacked by terrorists in New York and Washington, D.C., and George W. Bush would face the gravest crisis of his new presidency.

Immediately upon his return to Washington on the evening of 9/11, the president convened his NSC. In the days that followed, he would attend a Council meeting in the morning and sometimes join his national security team again in the afternoon by secure video teleconference. As the first President Bush turned to his "Big Eight" advisers during the Persian Gulf War, a "War Cabinet"—composed of top national security officials from the White House, CIA, State Department, and Pentagon—formed around the second President Bush. Most important among them were Cheney, Powell, Rumsfeld, Rice and George Tenet (the director of Central Intelligence)

The demands of the "war on terrorism" forged a united front among Bush's top national security advisers. Prior to September 11, there was increasing speculation that his team was split among those advocating a hawkish, "go-it-alone" unilateralist approach to world affairs (most often associated with Defense Secretary Rumsfeld) versus a more cautious, multilateralist approach (seen to be championed by Secretary of State Powell). Moreover, there were reports that institutional tensions between State and the NSC were beginning to resurface, with Condoleezza Rice's profile and influence with the president on the rise. After 9/11, such speculation stopped, although within a year questions were again being raised about divisions within the administration over such issues as Iraq.

The "war on terrorism" had another institutional impact on the NSC. In a speech to a joint meeting of Congress on September 15, 2001, the president announced that Pennsylvania Governor Thomas Ridge would head a new Homeland Security Council (HSC), housed in the White House. The model for the new organization would be the National Security Council. The president followed the speech with an Executive Order later in the month. Similar to the NSC, the new Homeland Security Council would be "responsible for advising and assisting the President with respect to all aspects of homeland security." Like the NSC, the HSC would be supported by an office of Homeland Security staff and an interagency process to include a Principals Committee (chaired by Ridge) and a Deputies Committee. The White House also decided to establish two new NSC offices in response to 9/11, one focused on counterterrorism and the other on cyberspace security. Drawing on the experience of NSC and National Economic Council coordination, the directors of these offices would report to both National Security Adviser Rice and

Homeland Security Adviser Ridge. Subsequently the Bush Administration established a Department of Homeland Security with Ridge as its first secretary.

Again in times of national crisis (the gravest since the Cuban missile crisis in 1962), the NSC was proving to be a very flexible instrument, reflecting the president's operating style and responding to his most urgent needs.

The Modern NSC

In her book *Flawed by Design* (see For Further Reading), Amy B. Zegart traced the evolution of the NSC (along with that of the CIA and the Joint Chiefs of Staff). As Zegart relates, the evolution of the modern NSC has transpired under nine presidents, of liberal and conservative persuasions, Democrats and Republicans. She has identified three major hallmarks that distinguish today's NSC system from the one that operated during the Truman and Eisenhower administrations. Writes Zegart:

- First, the national security adviser has evolved from a purely administrative executive secretary servicing the Council's needs to a powerful political presidential adviser.
- A second feature of the modern National Security Council system follows from the first. The rise of the national security adviser has increased the power, jurisdiction, and capabilities of the NSC staff.
- Third, the modern NSC system is marked by a pronounced decline in the role of the formal National Security Council . . . Presidents have instead turned to the NSC staff and to a host of informal meetings with relevant Cabinet members to solicit information, analysis, and advice. (Zegart, 1999: 85–87)

The consequences of these changes? In Zegart's view, "these hallmarks reveal a modern NSC system that has steadily drawn foreign policy-making power away from the Cabinet departments and into the White House . . . The palace guard has, indeed, eclipsed the king's ministers" (Zegart, 1999: 87).

In addition to Zegart's hallmarks, the experiences of the first Bush Administration, the two terms of President Clinton, and the second Bush Administration suggest a further maturing and strengthening of the NSC as an institution. While there have been variations in the decision-making style of each president, there has also been unprecedented continuity in the formal structure of the NSC system, reflected best in the continuation of the Principals and Deputies committees. A general consensus seems to have emerged on the appropriate role of the national security adviser, including public appearances to explain and defend the president's policies. Finally, general rules, or "do's and don'ts," for the day-to-day activities of the NSC staff appear to be in place, derived in large part from lessons learned from the Iran-*contra* affair and the recommendations of the Tower Commission which followed.

On September 15, 1997, President Clinton observed the 50th anniversary of the NSC with a Proclamation. "In creating the National Security Council," he stated, "the National Security Act of 1947 provided the President with an invaluable forum for the consideration and coordination of domestic, foreign, and military policies related to America's security." The president did not elaborate on the evolution of this "invaluable forum" since the days of Harry Truman. Indeed Truman himself would barely recognize it. There will be more discussion about the implications of the modern NSC later in this book, but first we turn in the next introduction to a closer examination to the many roles played by the national security advisers.

12

THE NATIONAL SECURITY COUNCIL SYSTEM AFTER THE COLD WAR

Vincent A. Auger

This selection examines the structure and operation of the National Security Council system during the first term of President Clinton, and its effectiveness in coping with the myriad international challenges facing the United States in the post–Cold War era.

The Clinton administration came to office in January 1993 proclaiming "the challenge of shaping an entirely new foreign policy for a world that has fundamentally changed" and the need to "adapt our foreign policy goals and institutions" to meet those changes (Christopher 1993, 45–46). The end of the cold war demanded a reformulation of American priorities, with economic issues singled out as having paramount importance. Bill Clinton declared during the 1992 campaign that "the currency of national strength in this new era will be denominated not only in ships, tanks and planes, but also in diplomas, patents and pay-checks" (quoted in Wessel 1992). He promised to create an "economic security council," modeled after the National Security Council, to ensure sufficient attention to U.S. economic interests in his administration's foreign policy.

Clinton's choice of the template for his new economic council was understandable but ironic, since the National Security Council (NSC) is the quintessential cold war institution in the U.S. foreign policy structure. By 1992, however, some experts were questioning the adequacy of the NSC system (comprised of the council and its interagency committee process, the assistant to the president for national security affairs—also called the national security adviser, or NSA—and the NSC staff of foreign policy analysts, which reports to the NSA) for formulating a post-cold war U.S. foreign policy. Those questions were prompted by two related developments: The dominant threat to U.S. security, which justified the centralization of foreign policy making in a council that emphasized the military component of national security concerns, no longer existed. The second development was the increasing salience of "new issues" on the foreign policy agenda, especially economic and ecological interdependence, which the NSC as traditionally constituted was poorly suited to manage (Shoemaker 1991, 82–83).[1]

It was somewhat surprising, therefore, when Presidential Decision Directive 2 (PDD 2) was issued on January 20, 1993, outlining an NSC structure and process extremely similar to that the Bush administration had used since January 1989 (see Clinton 1993b). While several factors influenced this choice, the most important were the incoming administration's own evaluation of the Bush NSC system and the expectation that foreign policy would not be among the president's highest priorities. Clinton and several of his top advisers were impressed with the efficient operation of their predecessor's NSC system; they hoped to achieve the same results by simply plugging their own personnel into the existing structure and process. Several administration officials also mentioned in interviews that the president and his political advisers saw such continuity

From Randall B. Ripley and James M. Lindsay, eds., *U.S. Foreign Policy After the Cold War* (Pittsburgh: University of Pittsburgh Press, 1997), 42–73. Some notes and text have been excised.

Vincent A. Auger is a political scientist at Hamilton College.

as attractive because they intended to devote relatively little time to foreign policy issues. According to one former NSC staffer, "This administration wanted to put foreign policy on autopilot, and the Clinton people consciously chose the Bush model to do that."[2]

In doing so, the incoming administration fell into the trap of believing that choosing the "correct" NSC organization and process was the key to producing a successful foreign policy. This belief is only partially correct, however. Rational organization and coherent processes in the NSC system can reduce the number of mistakes an administration will make in foreign policy, but those structures and procedures ensure neither consistency in policy making nor successful policy outcomes. The level of criticism concerning the consistency and coherence of the Clinton foreign policy is evidence that the Bush NSC system had no talismanic qualities.

I argue that the interests and abilities of the individuals who serve in the NSC system, and the level and nature of presidential involvement in that system, are the crucial variables in explaining NSC behavior. That is, the *people* filling the organizational slots and their skill in making the process work are the key to understanding both the strengths and weaknesses of the NSC system and its role in shaping Clinton's foreign policy. This insight is especially relevant in the case of the National Security Council, because of the unique nature of the NSC system, when compared to typical bureaucracies involved in making foreign policy. . . .

THE CLINTON SYSTEM: STRUCTURE AND PROCESS

Within a week of the 1992 election, it became clear which models the new administration planned to use. The Clinton transition office announced that the new president would create an "economic security council" (later changed to the National Economic Council, or NEC), following the model presented by the Commission on Government Renewal (Wessel 1992). Several of the commission's members had been foreign policy advisers to the Clinton campaign, and they were subsequently selected to fill policy positions in the new administration. Clinton himself was favorably impressed by the operation of the Bush NSC system, and wished to create a similar structure that would produce

powerful initiatives in the area of economic policy (Ifill 1993).

Clinton's directive establishing his NSC system did expand the formal scope of NSC activities, compared to the language of the National Security Act of 1947:

> The NSC shall advise and assist me in integrating all aspects of national security policy as it affects the United States—domestic, foreign, military, *intelligence and economic (in conjunction with the National Economic Council)*. (Clinton 1993a, emphasis added)

This clearly indicated that the NSC was to be the forum where the integration of the economic and noneconomic aspects of foreign policy would occur.

The basic structure of the NSC itself and the interagency committee system, as well as the role of the national security adviser and the NSC staff, all remained very similar to the Bush NSC system, even though some changes were made to accommodate the incoming administration's new priorities. In addition to the reasons already mentioned, Clinton's national security adviser, Anthony Lake, had a conception of the NSA's role that was close to that held by Brent Scowcroft. Lake had also warned previously (Destler, Gelb, and Lake 1984, 279) that a new administration should not precipitously dismantle the policy process inherited from its predecessor, however strong the political temptation to do so: "Just take the existing mechanism, use it for a while, see how things really work, and then formalize the relationships [the president] finds effective." Under these conditions, substantial continuity rather than dramatic change was to be expected in the Clinton NSC system, despite the end of the cold war.

Advisory System Organization: The NSC

The Clinton administration made only minor changes in the composition of the NSC itself and no significant changes in the interagency committee structure. The membership of the National Security Council proper was expanded by presidential order to include the secretary of the treasury; the U.S. representative to the United Nations; the assistants to the president for national security affairs and for economic policy; and the White House chief of staff. This change was intended to facilitate the consideration of economic policy concerns in the discussion of traditional national security issues, and to reflect the increased importance of multi-lateralism in the administration's approach to foreign policy.

Subordinate to the NSC is a hierarchy of committees. The Principals Committee (NSC/PC) is "the senior interagency forum . . . available for Cabinet-level officials to meet to discuss and resolve issues not requiring the President's participation" (Clinton 1993b, 2). The members of the NSC/PC are the secretaries of state and defense (or their designated representatives), the U.S. representative to the UN, the chairman of the Joint Chiefs of Staff (JCS), the director of central intelligence, and the national security adviser (who serves as chair).

One rung below the NSC/PC is the Deputies Committee (NSC/DC). It is at this level that the great bulk of the NSC's work is done. The primary functions of the NSC/DC are to monitor the NSC interagency process and to resolve policy disputes that resisted resolution at earlier stages in the process, especially in the interagency working groups (to be discussed later). The Deputies Committee is expected to "focus significant attention on policy implementation," including reviews of existing policy directives. The NSC/DC is also charged with ensuring the adequacy of issue papers to be considered by the NSC/PC or the NSC. Finally, the Deputies Committee is responsible for "day-to-day crisis management" as well as crisis prevention and contingency planning (Clinton 1993b, 2–3).

Mirroring the membership of the NSC/PC, the Deputies Committee is composed of the deputy national security adviser (chair), the deputy secretary of defense, the deputy secretary of state, the deputy director of central intelligence, the vice chairman of the JCS, and the deputy U.S. representative to the United Nations. The vice president's assistant for national security affairs is also a member of this body.

The Deputies Committee is also authorized to establish and oversee a system of interagency working groups (IWGs, pronounced "I-wigs"), to prepare preliminary studies of foreign policy options, and to coordinate the implementation of presidential decisions. These IWGs are chaired by an assistant secretary of state, defense, or treasury, or by NEC or NSC staff, as appropriate to the policy area under consideration and as determined by the Deputies Committee. Several IWGs are specifically earmarked as the NSC staff's

responsibility: intelligence, nonproliferation, arms control, and crisis management (Clinton 1993b, 4).

The IWGs are supplemented and backstopped by a large number of ad hoc working alliances among officials, alliances that cut across agencies. According to NSC and State Department staffers, these informal groups of four to six officials are very useful for generating ideas, building consensus across organizations, and hashing out some policy differences before a formal IWG or NSC/DC meeting on an issue.

Several aspects of this system are worth noting. One of the most striking, in light of the administration's rhetoric, is the relatively small role for economic officials in the formal structure of the NSC system. While both the assistant to the president for economic policy and the secretary of the treasury are members of the full NSC, their agencies are not automatically represented on either the Principals or Deputies Committees. NEC and Treasury officials are to be invited to meetings of those committees "as appropriate" or "as needed" (Clinton 1993a, 2–3). There is a stipulation that the assistant to the president for economic policy "shall be informed of [NSC/PC] meetings and be invited to attend all those with international economic considerations" (Clinton 1993a, 2), but this still leaves considerable discretion for the national security adviser in defining when those "considerations" warrant an invitation to his counterpart at the NEC. Interviews with NSC and NEC officials indicate there have been relatively few instances where this power of invitation has been manipulated in an attempt to exclude NEC people from NSC-sponsored meetings, but all agree that this is due primarily to the cordial and scrupulous working relationship established by Lake and Robert Rubin, when he was the assistant to the president for economic policy and director of the NEC staff. As an example, early in the administration, Rubin and some of his staff complained to Lake that they felt they were out of the policy loop on some issues the NSC was handling; Lake responded by instructing the NSC staff to route their memos to the NEC to ensure their inclusion in the process.

Another noteworthy feature of this organization is the dominance of the national security adviser and his deputy in the process. The NSA chairs the Principals Committee, the deputy NSA chairs the Deputies Committee: in each instance, the chair is responsible for

calling meetings of the committee, inviting participants in addition to those who are core members of the
committee, setting the agenda, and preparing the necessary paperwork. Only at the level of the interagency
working groups do representatives of other agencies
chair meetings, and even here (as noted previously)
several of the most important IWGs are chaired by
NSC staffers. This central role for the NSA is highly
consistent with the prescriptions of the Tower Commission Report, and it is extremely similar to the system the Bush administration used (Snow and Brown
1994, 149–52).

Organization of the NSC Staff

The administration did modify the NSC staff structure
it inherited from the Bush administration somewhat
(U.S. Congress, House Committee on Appropriations
1993, 759–60). Initially, three new offices were created to account for the new political geography of the
post-cold war era (the Office of European Affairs was
divided into an Office for Western European Affairs
and an Office for Russia, Ukraine and Eurasian
Affairs) or to focus attention on issues whose relative
importance has increased since the end of the cold war
(the offices for Non-Proliferation Policy and for Environmental Affairs). The Office of Global Issues and
Multilateral Affairs (formerly International Programs)
was expanded and reorganized in recognition of the
"increasing emphasis on multilateral approaches to
regional problems" (U.S. Congress, House Committee
on Appropriations 1993, 779). A new position of staff
director, who was supposed to serve as a "policy coordinator," was created (U.S. Congress, House Committee on Appropriations 1993, 779). Two additional
offices were created in 1994: the Office of Democracy
Affairs and (through a new division of the Office for
Western European Affairs) the Office for Central and
Eastern European Affairs.[3] Additional staff were also
assigned to the Office of Legislative Affairs and the
Press Office.

Even while the administration increased the number of offices within the NSC staff, however, the overall size of the staff was reduced significantly. As a
result of Clinton's pledge to reduce White House staff
by 25 percent, the NSC staff was cut in 1993 from 179
to 147 positions (60 of these are professional and staff

slots funded directly through the NSC staff budget; the
remainder are detailees from executive branch departments). Finding they had cut too deeply, administration officials restored four positions in 1994, bringing
the authorized staff to 151, but budget pressures forced
the number back down to 145 by January 1995.

This meant that some NSC offices shrank considerably from their size during the Bush administration.
The Defense Policy and Arms Control Office, for
example, was reduced by 50 percent after the Clinton
administration took office. Other offices were asked to
handle more issues without any additional resources or
staff.

In an attempt to ensure policy coordination between
the parallel advisory structures of the NSC and NEC,
two levels of interaction were built into the policy-making system. The national security adviser is a member
of the NEC, and the economic policy adviser sits on the
NSC. At the staff level, "the management, direction and
coordination" of U.S. foreign economic policy was
institutionalized in the form of the Office of Trade and
International Economic Policy, jointly funded and
staffed by the NSC and NEC (according to administration officials, this arrangement resulted from a conversation between Lake and Rubin during the transition, as
they discussed how to coordinate their operations and
cope with anticipated staff shortages). The "Sherpa
function" of preparing for the annual G-7 economic
summits was moved from the State Department's
Office of the Undersecretary for Economic Affairs
(which had performed this task during the Reagan and
Bush administrations) to this joint NSC/NEC office
(U.S. Congress, House Committee on Appropriations
1993, 768–69).

Advisory System Organization: The NEC

Although the structure and function of the National
Economic Council is not a primary concern of this
study, a brief examination is in order, given the role the
NEC was expected to play in shaping administration
policy and in elevating the level and quality of attention devoted to economic issues in foreign policy.

The NEC was established by executive order in
January 1993 (Clinton 1993a); two years later, Clinton
proclaimed it was "one of the most significant organizational changes we . . . have made, and one that I pre-

dict all future administrations will follow" (quoted in Harris and Pearlstein 1995). Given the fact that the NSC supposedly provided the inspiration for its economic counterpart, the contrasts between the NEC and the NSC are as notable as the similarities. The council itself has eighteen members, six of whom (the president, vice president, secretaries of state and treasury, and the assistants to the president for national security affairs and for economic policy) also sit on the NSC (interviews and press reports indicated that it was Lake's deputy, Samuel R. Berger, who usually attended NEC meetings: see Ifill 1993). This makes the formal NEC twice as large as the NSC, encompassing a much broader array of agencies and interests. Provisions were made for the creation of committees and working groups; unlike the very detailed hierarchy of NSC committees, these were left unspecified in the executive order creating the NEC.

Like the NSA, the assistant for economic policy is charged with managing the interagency coordination process and is provided with a staff. Due to tight budget restrictions and Clinton's pledge concerning staff cuts, however, the NEC staff remained extremely small. In 1994, there were twenty-two professional staff at the NEC, seven of whom had international policies or programs as their primary responsibility (this number included those "dual-hatters" who serve both the NSC and NEC).

The NEC was given several specific functions, the first of which was "to coordinate the economic policy-making process with respect to domestic and international economic issues" (Clinton 1993a, 95). Other functions involved ensuring the implementation and consistency of the administration's economic policies. Notably absent from the description of functions was any responsibility for integrating economic with noneconomic facets of foreign policy decisions.

There is a final characteristic of the NSC/NEC advisory and staff system created by Clinton and his aides that must be mentioned. In opting for an NSC system modeled on the Tower Commission's recommendations, and in embracing the Commission for Government Renewal's preference for a parallel advisory and staff system for economic policy, Clinton chose two models which (in the eyes of their proponents) demanded sustained and forceful presidential involve-

ment in the foreign policy process. The adoption of both placed an enormous burden on the incoming president and his White House chief of staff to ensure that the various pieces of the foreign policy machinery meshed smoothly. However, given Clinton's clear desire to focus on domestic issues and to relegate foreign policy to the "back burner" as much as possible (Drew 1994, 138), the responsibility for the successful operation of the system was delegated primarily to the national security adviser and his top aides. The ability of these officials to manage this system, especially absent any sustained presidential interest, was therefore crucial to the effectiveness of the interagency process.

THE CLINTON NSC SYSTEM: OPERATION

In evaluating the strengths and weaknesses of the Clinton NSC system, I will examine four salient issues that analysts or administration officials themselves have identified as central to the functioning of that system: the NSA/NSC role as "honest broker" and coordinator among the foreign policy bureaucracies; the management of the interagency process; the coordination and integration of the economic and noneconomic aspects of the administration's foreign policy; and the role of the president in leading and overseeing the system.

The NSA/NSC as "Honest Broker"

By all accounts, Lake was remarkably evenhanded in representing other agencies and principals fairly to the president, in ceding the spotlight to the secretary of state, and in minimizing the open disharmony and competition that characterized NSC relations with the line agencies in previous administrations. Officials interviewed at the NSC, NEC, and State Department were unanimous in their view that the relatively smooth working relationship among those agencies was primarily due to the commitment by all the principals—but especially Lake—to the idea that differences over policy would not be permitted to erupt into "bloodletting" among administration officials. Even when such sniping occurred—for example, concerning the U.S. military intervention in Haiti in September 1994—Lake and Christopher were quick to rebuke their subordinates and they swiftly brought an end to the public recriminations (Kirschten 1994b).

Lake's desire to maintain a low profile as NSA was also increasingly seen as a source of difficulties, however. The president's unwillingness to articulate a clear foreign policy strategy, and the inability of Secretary of State Warren Christopher to do so effectively, left a glaring gap in the domestic support for the administration's foreign policy initiatives. Indeed, Lake argued near the end of his first year as NSA that this was the main foreign policy failure of the administration: "Tell me of another Administration that has gotten so much done on so many issues in its first 10 months. The failure has been in explaining our policy adequately to the public" (quoted in Sciolino 1993). Lake vowed to play a more public role in educating Congress and the American people about the administration's foreign policy.

His first notable attempt at public explication came in September 1993, when he outlined the "strategy of enlargement" as "the successor to a doctrine of containment" (Lake 1993, 659). This and a handful of subsequent forays by Lake into the public arena during the next nine months were not very well received, however; in June 1994 Lake conceded he was still not playing a very visible role in building support for administration policy, admitting, "I may have made a mistake in how I conceived of my own job" (quoted on C-SPAN 1994). The administration's continuing concern over this issue was demonstrated by the attendance of communications adviser David Gergen at meetings of the NSC/PC during the last half of 1994, in an effort to ensure that the public presentation of policy be considered during the decision-making process (Kirschten 1994a).

Lake did take a more public role beginning in 1995, largely in reaction to the new political difficulties the administration was encountering as a result of the 1994 elections, when the Republicans gained control of Congress. His speeches emphasized the dangers of "backdoor isolationism" and outlined the parameters for using U.S. military forces in the post–cold war era (Lake 1996), and Lake led a delegation to Europe in August 1995 in an attempt to make progress in negotiating a solution to the war in Bosnia. Lake's more prominent public role and forceful assertion of his own policy preferences raised questions, however, about his ability to play the "honest broker role" effec-

tively, especially in the State Department (DeParle 1995).

Management of the Interagency Process

Discussions with administration officials clearly indicate that poor management has seriously hampered the Clinton NSC committee system and interagency process. Participants identify several reasons why this was the case.

The NSC staff structure, and the division of labor among the staff, constituted one set of factors. The expansion of the number of offices within the NSC staff, combined with constraints on staff hiring, reduced the size of many individual NSC offices and produced a situation where the workload sometimes overwhelmed the staff. Attention to many issues was sporadic, and the paper flow slowed to a crawl; one State Department official remarked that an important cable to U.S. embassies in Europe, providing instructions for consultations and negotiations in the wake of the G-7 summit in June 1994, took two weeks to receive routine clearance from the NSC staff.

Contrary to the initial guidelines of PDD-2, reports from both State and NSC officials indicated that NSC staffers chaired the vast majority of IWGs. Veteran officials attributed this to what they viewed as the mistaken belief by new NSC staffers that the only way they could stay on top of policy was to chair as many working groups as possible.[4] This was an enormous administrative burden for the small NSC staff and further slowed the decision process on many issues.

This problem was also compounded by the fact that several individual "shops" in the NSC were forced to confront multiple crises during the first eighteen months of the administration. The Office for Global Issues and Multilateral Affairs, for example, had primary responsibility for policy coordination on Somalia, Haiti, and Rwanda during this period. According to several NSC sources, the tendency of beleaguered offices was to "circle the wagons" rather than ask for help from other NSC offices. Several staffers criticized the staff director, who could have assisted in a redistribution of staff/workload, for her inattention to this problem and unwillingness to take corrective action.[5]

A related problem administration officials identified was the apparent lack of interest of the national security adviser and his deputy in managing the NSC staff and the interagency process. Unlike the Bush NSC system, in which Scowcroft primarily advised the president on foreign policy substance and Gates managed and oversaw the process, Lake and Berger divided the substantive issues between them. Berger, for example, was said by NSC staffers to take the lead on Haiti and economic issues; one staffer, when discussing Haiti policy (in early July 1994), said: "Lake doesn't touch it" (see also Kirschten 1994b, 2973). Neither Lake nor Berger took primary responsibility for oversight of the process.

This resulted in the ineffective coordination of interagency working groups and the often poor quality of their recommendations to the Deputies Committee. The IWGs quickly became very large and unwieldy; different IWGs with overlapping responsibilities disagreed on policy options, and senior NSC officials were reluctant "to butt heads" to resolve the differences. As a result, in many cases the problem was merely bucked up the organizational hierarchy to the NSC/DC, where the issue would be reworked almost from scratch. This also slowed the decision process enormously, creating a backlog of issues that needed resolution and a pattern of postponed and rescheduled NSC/DC meetings.

One public glimpse of this difficulty occurred regarding the administration's policy in Somalia. Secretary of State Christopher publicly criticized the Deputies Committee, which Berger chaired, for failing to conduct a review of Somalia policy after several American troops were killed in June 1993. Lake defended the work of the NSC/DC, arguing that the committee's schedule was overloaded and that the interagency working group the State Department chaired should have done more preparatory work for a high-level review (Sciolino 1993). NSC staffers said that the performance of the Deputies Committee in this instance was not unusual and that the problem continued well into 1994.

Another example of this problem of interagency coordination was the delay in the completion of the administration's National Security Strategy paper. This document, a report to Congress required by law, has usually been a bland statement of an administration's general national security policy goals. In 1993, however, the drafting of the document was compli-cated by questions concerning U.S. foreign policy priorities after the cold war and the budget implications of those choices. Initially, the NSC staff—viewing this as a routine reporting requirement—delegated responsibility for drafting the document to the Defense Department. The DOD draft focused primarily on military strategy, with little comment about economic or other "global issues," and the IWG led by Defense Department officials cleared the document and passed it up the staff ladder to the NSC/DC level. However, at the State Department, officials from the Office of Policy Planning complained that the narrow definition of national security was "totally inadequate," and they pushed within the department for a much broader definition of foreign policy and national security. Secretary Christopher refused to concur with the Defense Department draft, and the Policy Planning staff wrote their own version, which Christopher sent to Lake at the NSC. Lake preferred the State draft and, after insisting that the concept of "enlargement" be worked into the document, sent the State-based draft back through the interagency process for approval. The document was finally issued in July 1994 (Clinton 1994).

Defense Department officials and some NSC staffers were very upset by what they viewed as the State Department's ability to hijack the process and be rewarded for it. These officials implied that State's actions were motivated primarily by a desire to raid the Defense Department's budget by expanding the definition of national security to include issues in which the State Department would take the lead (see also Holmes 1993). State Department officials insist that the budget issue was separate and coincidental to the debate over the national security strategy document, and they were disturbed that the White House did little to curb press leaks from the Pentagon that attacked State's actions on this issue. Congress and the press criticized the administration for its seeming inability to accomplish even routine tasks in foreign policy making (see also Lancaster and Gellman 1994).

Finally, a major management and leadership difficulty that almost every NSC, NEC, and State official interviewed identified was what one NSC staffer called a "fetish for consensus building" among the administration's foreign policy principals. In his attempt to ensure a collegial relationship among administration officials, Lake (who advised Clinton in this matter during the transition) created a policy-making environment in which there were few major differences among the top officials. When differences on policy did exist, the first priority was to find a solution that every principal could support. Lake himself seemed to recognize that this could lead to problems when he remarked in October 1993: "I think there is a danger that when people work well together, you can take the edge off the options" (quoted in Friedman 1993b; also see Sciolino 1993).

According to some administration officials, however, the consequences of this attitude went beyond a lack of creative tension among the foreign policy leadership. They identified two additional problems: a failure to maintain discipline within the decision process and a failure to "sharpen the options" available to the president.

The failure to maintain discipline within the decision process had two components. The desire by top NSC officials to maintain cordial relations among the agencies paradoxically encouraged individuals in those agencies to attempt "end runs" around the NSC-based policy coordinating mechanisms. Few penalties or sanctions were imposed on those who deviated from agreed policy or circumvented the prescribed channels for policy coordination. On many issues, according to several clearly frustrated NSC staffers, Lake and Berger were obviously unwilling to confront State or Defense Department officials in order to resolve such problems.

The second failure of discipline within the process was the absence of a clear mechanism for forcing decisions on issues. Several NSC staff members related tales of lengthy meetings, especially at the working group and Deputies Committee levels, where no decisions were taken. Several days later, the participants would reconvene and rehash the issue. This sequence was sometimes repeated for months; two NSC staffers specifically mentioned the IWG on Bosnia as a case where this occurred, and Elizabeth Drew (1994, 150) reports that one administration official commented that policy discussions of Bosnia during 1993 were "group therapy—an existential debate over what is the role of America, etc."

This indecisiveness was also directly linked to the second facet of the pursuit of consensus: the failure to

"sharpen the options" presented to the president. Indeed, Lake and Berger preferred to reach an agreed *recommendation* among the foreign policy principals for presentation to the president. When a consensus was not found, they tended to "walk the issue back" to a point where everyone could agree. This was not only a very time-consuming process, it tended to produce a "least common denominator" solution to policy problems. One veteran government official likened the process to that of the Eisenhower NSC system, which emphasized compromise recommendations and "agreement by exhaustion," as Dean Acheson once remarked (in Falk 1988, 75; for a different view of the Eisenhower NSC, see Henderson 1988, chap. 4). Eventually, Lake seemed to recognize that this was a problem, and he began to assert his own preferences more forcefully "because it helps to move issues to a resolution" (quoted in DeParle 1995, 37).

Most officials who discussed this problem saw it as a reflection of the personalities of the foreign policy principals and their goal of smoothing over internal administration disputes.[6] One former NSC official also suggested that this reflected a broader "cultural" context in the Democratic Party, which emphasized consensus building and increased the reluctance of administration officials to take decisions in the face of open dissent (for a related argument, see Ignatius 1994). However, this desire to smooth differences and present a consensus recommendation may have also reflected their recognition that the president preferred to rely on the advice of his "wise men" as a way of limiting his own direct involvement in foreign policy. One of Lake's jobs was to "keep foreign policy submerged" and to prevent foreign policy concerns from interfering with domestic policy (Drew 1994, 138). In this case, the search for an elusive consensus may have been an appropriate response to the president's own preference to be told what needed to be done on foreign policy issues, rather than devoting the energy and time to decide this himself.

Integration of Political-Military and Economic Issues

A major question about the advisory structure Clinton chose was whether it would provide an effective method of integrating political-military and economic facets of a post-cold war foreign policy. In two areas where both these factors were very important, China and Japan, the answer would have to be no, though for different reasons.

In the case of China, the problem was the administration's inability to maintain a clear set of priorities concerning diverse U.S. goals regarding human rights, security issues, and economic interests (see Auger 1995). Policy toward China was initially dominated by Assistant Secretary of State Winston Lord and guided by Clinton's own campaign statements. Human rights considerations were given a very high priority, especially in declaratory policy, despite growing concern among the business community and the members of the NEC that economic interests were being slighted.

Clinton did renew China's most-favored nation (MFN) trade status in May 1993, but with a list of specific human rights conditions that the Chinese government would have to meet before that status could be renewed in 1994. Lord and Deputy NSA Berger wrote the executive order that announced this shift in U.S. policy, in close consultation with Democratic leaders in the Congress (Greenberger 1994). The economic agencies in the executive branch had virtually no role in drafting that initial policy statement, despite the rapidly expanding trade and investment relationship between the United States and China.

Within weeks of the May 1993 announcement, however, the administration's official policy was challenged from within. An interagency review completed in September recommended a policy of engagement rather than confrontation with China. Treasury and Commerce Department officials visited China, stressing the U.S. desire to expand trade and investment, even as officials from State were threatening to revoke MFN status because of Beijing's continuing human rights violations. One State Department official complained, "It's irritating. We seem to do the Chinese work for them. If they need someone to argue against revoking MFN, they only have to get hold of some guy from the economic branch of [the U.S.] government" (quoted in Williams 1994).

This tension within the administration came to a head with the perceived failure of Secretary of State Christopher's visit to China in March 1994, when the Chinese government brusquely rejected his message about human rights. Officials in the Treasury and Commerce Departments began to call publicly for eliminating the linkage between China's human rights policies and U.S.–China economic relations. At a joint meeting of the NSC and NEC principals (which the president did not attend) after Christopher's return to Washington, the State Department and the NSC staff regained control over the debate by reaffirming MFN conditionality as administration policy, with one State Department official arguing, "It's not tenable to have the economic agencies in open revolt against the policy" (quoted in Sciolino 1994b). However, in return for their agreement to support the official policy, the NEC officials insisted that the policy-making process regarding China be changed to give greater weight to the economic aspect of U.S.–China relations. Ultimately, in May 1994, Clinton sided with his economic advisers, declaring that China had done the bare minimum to meet his May 1993 conditions and was therefore eligible for MFN status. He also eliminated any further linkage between the Chinese government's human rights practices and its trade status with the United States.

After May 1994, the administration's China policy continued to be hampered by an inability to integrate the economic and noneconomic components of policy, though the officials from the economic agencies were now playing a much larger role in shaping that policy. In early 1996, for example, Clinton's trade officials began to push for economic sanctions against China for violation of intellectual property rights, even as the State Department and White House attempted to persuade China to relax its pressure on Taiwan in the period before Taiwan's presidential elections (Sanger and Erlanger 1996). In May, on the advice of his economic advisers, Clinton announced sharp increases on the tariffs for more than $2 billion in Chinese exports to the United States as punishment for those violations, just five days after the State Department had declined to impose sanctions on China for the export of nuclear weapons-related equipment to Pakistan. During all the administration discussions leading up to these decisions, the focus was on the tactical details of the sanctions. Despite growing recognition and concern within the administration that the various components of its policy toward China were at odds, in the words of one report, "There was little discussion of a grander plan for dealing with China" (Sanger 1996).

A very different problem characterized the administration's Japan policy. Many officials and analysts have argued that during the cold war, American foreign economic policy was subordinated to the political and military concerns of the Defense and State Departments, especially in Asia (Fallows 1989; Harrison and Prestowitz 1990). From the start of the Clinton administration, that balance was almost completely reversed, with concerns about the stability of the broader U.S.–Japanese relationship receiving much less attention than U.S. economic interests. This was a deliberate decision, fully consistent with Clinton's emphasis during the campaign on "economic security" and with statements by Secretary Christopher that foreign economic policy would no longer be the poor relation of traditional foreign policy issues.

According to NSC and NEC staffers, the NEC and officials from Treasury, Commerce, and the U.S. Trade Representative's office (USTR) dominated policy concerning Japan from the outset. These officials emphasized confrontation with Japan, in the belief that only sustained and substantial pressure would produce acceptable changes in Japanese economic policy. The political consequences of that pressure were dismissed as irrelevant or of secondary importance. One American official stated that "the politics are obviously delicate. . . . Our business is with Japan, and their political problems are their problem" (quoted in Bradsher 1993). U.S. officials also appeared willing to hold the broader political relationship hostage until Japanese economic policies met American demands. Deputy U.S. Trade Representative Charlene Barshefsky declared: "The political climate between the United States and Japan will be determined by economics. If the economics aren't right, the political climate isn't going to be right. To the extent the Japanese are concerned about the political climate, they have it in their power to ensure that the political climate is positive". Even the collapse of what U.S. officials considered a "reformist" Japanese government in April 1994 elicited no immediate signs that the administration was reconsidering its strident approach (Davis 1994). By May 1995, U.S. Trade Representative Mickey Kantor had convinced the president to levy heavy sanctions on Japanese luxury auto exports to the United States in retaliation for what Clinton administration officials declared were restrictive Japanese trade practices. Six weeks of brinkmanship followed, and the imposition

of sanctions was avoided by a last-minute compromise in which the Clinton administration settled for considerably fewer, and less specific, Japanese concessions than it had originally sought.

This close call did have the effect of beginning the process of rethinking the balance between economic and political-strategic issues in U.S. policy toward Japan. In explaining why the administration ultimately settled for a vague compromise, one senior official said, "We all looked over the precipice and discovered we couldn't see the bottom. The sanctions were a big risk. So we took what we had in hand" (quoted in Sanger 1995a). Shortly after this, Undersecretary of Commerce Garten suggested that the United States and Japan needed to place their trade disputes in a larger political context, saying that the constant conflict "seems as anachronistic as the old gunboat diplomacy" (quoted in Pollack 1995). Although the administration quickly repudiated Garten's statement, other forces at work in the U.S.–Japanese relationship during the next nine months (including the outrage in Japan over the rape of an Okinawan girl by American military personnel based there, the growing aggressiveness of China, and a drop in Japan's trade surplus with the United States) did lead to more attention to the political-strategic aspects of the U.S.–Japan relationship. By the time Clinton visited Japan in April 1996, trade issues had lost their priority on the bilateral agenda and the economic agencies were no longer so dominant in shaping U.S. policy toward Japan (WuDunn 1996). This was due primarily to the changing international context, however, and was not attributable to the NSC/NEC system's ability to integrate and coordinate the various components of the administration's policy toward Japan.

One of Clinton's senior economic advisers said in July 1995: "Everyone acknowledges that economics now plays a central role in foreign policy—that battle is over. What no one has really grappled with is what happens when commercial interests push out other concerns" (quoted in Sanger 1995b). The trade-offs and coordination of policy with political-strategic goals are inherently difficult when economic priorities clash, but this is *exactly* the area in which the NSC/NEC arrangement should have a comparative advantage over alternative organizational arrangements, according to its proponents. The fact that the economic and noneconomic components of foreign policy toward China and Japan remained uncoordinated or in open competition for so long suggests that the NSC/NEC system has failed a crucial test as an effective mechanism for integrating those aspects of policy.

Inconsistent Presidential Leadership

For all the attention justifiably devoted to understanding the formal structure and process of the NSC system, it is crucial to remember that, ultimately, that system is an extension of the president's own concerns and interests. Robert Hunter (1982, 92) has argued that while a well-ordered NSC system can facilitate coherent policy making, "the president's own behavior in operating the system will speak more loudly than formal structures."

A striking aspect of the Clinton administration's foreign policy process, given the advisory and staff structures it selected, has been what one State Department official termed the president's "selective interest" in foreign policy. On certain topics, such as Russia or trade ("economic security"), the president has evinced enthusiasm, sustained interest, and a certain consistency in policy pronouncements. On most foreign policy issues, however, Clinton has taken an active role only when confronted by a crisis. In these cases, the president became intensely engaged for a brief period, and officials who attended NSC meetings where Clinton was present attested to his ability to assimilate information and quickly identify the crux of the matter. However, as the immediate crisis faded, the president would return to a general lack of interest in the subject, rarely following up the decisions made or the general line of policy established.

This pattern was established beginning in January 1993. Clinton reportedly did not hold a meeting of the NSC during his first three weeks in office; one foreign policy official commented, concerning Clinton's participation in foreign policy discussions early in his term, "He is there to do things when asked. But that is the extent of it" (quoted in Friedman 1993a).

According to several NSC officials, this reduced the effectiveness and morale of the NSC staff, and produced puzzlement among the executive branch agencies concerning the direction of policy. For example, in mid-May 1993—less than three weeks before the initial deadline on MFN status—the president had yet to look over an interdepartment review of options on China policy prepared weeks earlier (Kristof 1993). The disengagement of the president from policy discussions on Bosnia and Somalia in 1993 produced uncertainty and inaction among foreign policy officials, who had no clear lead to follow. This distance also meant that at times, it was clear that the president was unaware of activities his officials were undertaking in his name (Sciolino 1993).

Clinton rarely attended meetings of his top NSC officials, even when China's MFN status or (until mid-1995) policy concerning Bosnia was the subject (on Bosnia, see Engelberg 1995). This in itself is not unusual; most presidents have relied more heavily on informal advisory systems for information and options rather than attend formal NSC meetings (see Rosati 1993, 90–103). In Clinton's case, however, he also rarely participated in the informal advisory process during his first two years in office. Persistent efforts by Lake and Christopher to get the president to commit to weekly meetings with his foreign policy advisers were repeatedly rebuffed. Even Lake's daily morning briefing of the president was often shortened or canceled (Drew 1994, 144; Sciolino 1994a).

Lake's expressed wish to draw the president into "larger contemplative discussions" (quoted in Friedman 1993b) with his advisers about foreign policy goals and strategies was rarely fulfilled, according to NSC and State Department officials. As with every president, there was great competition between the domestic and foreign policy staffs for Clinton's time and attention. Given Clinton's professed priorities, the domestic aides had a clear advantage; Lake constantly had to fight to get foreign policy issues on the president's agenda.

The selective and crisis-driven nature of presidential attention to foreign policy was compounded by a chaotic White House staff operation, in part the result of the president's personal style and in part due to the managerial weakness of Clinton's first chief of staff, Thomas McLarty. As one official complained, the president encouraged "deliberate disorganization" within the White House and easy access to the Oval Office for the staff. While this allowed Lake access to the president for brief discussions, there was rarely the follow-up by Clinton or his aides that might have been expected from lengthier, more structured meetings.

By late 1993, it was clear to some administration officials that the coordination across policy arenas needed improvement; as one White House aide complained, "Policy decisions aren't getting closed and don't necessarily hang together" (quoted in Drew 1994, 188). An attempt was made to move Deputy NSA Berger to a broader policy coordination role within the White House, but he successfully resisted the change. In early December, a new deputy chief of staff was appointed with the explicit responsibility of coordinating the work of the NSC, the NEC, and the Domestic Policy Council (Devroy 1993). Finally, in June 1994, the overall inadequacy of White House management was acknowledged, with the appointment of Leon Panetta as chief of staff. One of Panetta's first moves was to limit access to the Oval Office by most senior officials, including Lake (Solomon 1994). Panetta's arrival eventually improved policy coordination and discipline somewhat, but it still could not substitute for sustained and consistent presidential attention to foreign policy substance and process. Warren Christopher noted this in early 1996, in a comment that could be read as a veiled criticism of most of the first three years of Clinton's administration: "One of the lessons of my three years is how essential presidential leadership is. . . . You can't do without presidential leadership."

It is instructive on this point to note that those few areas of foreign policy where Clinton has evidenced sustained attention and commitment are those that reflect what Berman and Goldman call Clinton's "domestic national-purpose orientation," which "locates the chief threats to U.S. interests in the domestic and social condition of the nation" (1996, 297). For example, Clinton's commitment to free trade principles, born of his conviction that U.S. economic prosperity can only be maintained in a liberal global economic system, was responsible for the sustained efforts on NAFTA and GATT (though even in these cases the president was accused by his allies in Congress of waiting until the hour was very late before throwing his personal political capital into the ratification fights).

Similarly, the remarkable turnabout in presidential attention to, and administration policy concerning, Bosnia after June 1995 can be attributed largely to domestic political concerns. After the failure of NATO attacks in May (when the Bosnian Serbs seized hundreds of UN peacekeepers as hostages) and the embarrassing confusion of early June (when Clinton first stated that U.S. troops might be sent to Bosnia shortly and then quickly backed away from that position), the president pressed his advisers to develop a much more active and forceful U.S. approach to the problem. Given the likelihood that the U.S. would have to send troops to Bosnia to help with the withdrawal of the UN peacekeepers if the war in Bosnia continued to escalate, Clinton told his advisers that "the status quo is not acceptable." Administration officials clearly understood the president's concerns; according to one senior aide, "I don't think the President relishes going into the 1996 election hostage to fortune in the Balkans, with the Bosnian Serbs able to bring us deeper into a war" (quoted in Engelberg 1995). The president was also faced with the embarrassing possibility that the Republican Congress might override his veto of a bill ending U.S. participation in the UN-sponsored arms embargo on Bosnia if the prospects for peace did not improve.

The dramatic U.S. diplomatic effort that eventually led to the Dayton Peace Accords and the deployment of U.S. troops to Bosnia under very controlled conditions did result from sustained presidential attention (and from the changed conditions on the ground, where a joint Croatian-Bosnian offensive in August and September succeeded in retaking much of the territory held by the Bosnian Serbs). However, it was a turnaround driven more by the lurking danger to Clinton's reelection prospects than by a broader commitment to remain involved in foreign policy.

CONCLUSION

I have analyzed the structure and operations of the Clinton NSC system, but two tasks remain: to evaluate the effects of the end of the cold war on the organization and functioning of that system, and to weigh the relative importance of structure and process versus personnel in understanding NSC behavior and performance.

In thinking about how the end of the cold war affected the National Security Council system, we should distinguish between two types of effects: *direct* (where the NSC structure or process was deliberately changed to conform to the "new realities" of the post-cold war era), and *indirect* (where new political and economic pressures, constraints, and incentives influenced the environment in which the NSC operates). We can then identify the influence of each of these effects, first, on the structure of the NSC/NEC advisory system and, second, on the interagency process.

At the structural level, the direct effect of the end of the cold war was the creation of several new offices within the NSC staff and (in combination with the domestically motivated pledge to cut the White House staff) a "thinning out" of the available staff across a larger number of offices. This resulted in high-level attention to a larger variety of issues, at the risk of straining the very limited resources of the NSC staff.

The indirect structural effects were much more significant. The cold war's conclusion was clearly instrumental in the sharp shift of national priorities toward domestic rather than foreign policy, and within foreign policy toward economic rather than political-military issues. As Bert Rockman has noted, presidents take an interest in organizational matters only to the extent that those issues affect their core political agenda. Since the NSC was much more closely identified with the traditional foreign policy agenda than with economic issues, the creation of the NEC as a parallel—and potentially competing—advisory system reflected Clinton's priorities and his feeling that the NSC system alone would be substantively and politically inadequate to address those priorities. The unusual sharing of staff by the NEC and NSC was also an innovative (and generally successful) structural adaptation to coordinate this parallel advisory system.

Ironically, these indirect effects also played a role in the incoming administration's willingness to adopt much of the Bush/Scowcroft NSC model. Since Clinton did not wish to devote very much time to most traditional foreign policy issues, the lure of using a proven structure and process to handle those issues in a low-profile manner was very powerful.

The direct effects of the end of the cold war on the NSC process are more subtle. In some ways, the process was characterized by a significant degree of continuity with the last cold war variant of the NSC system. The formal system of interagency committees, and

the role of the national security adviser and NSC staff at the center of the policy-making process, were very similar to both the Bush administration's approach and to the recommendations of the Tower Commission.

Yet officials at the NSC and the State Department pointed to other ways in which the demise of the cold war directly altered the process. Most frequently mentioned was the absence of a clear focus and sense of priorities among the staff. One State Department official who had previously served on the NSC staff said he had been able to devote most of his attention to two or three crucial issues related to the U.S.-Soviet competition; he would periodically check on other issues in his area of responsibility, but felt no need to monitor them constantly. The loss of "the Soviet prism," through which events were interpreted and priorities established, left the NSC staff working on a larger number of issues of seemingly equal importance. This diffusion of effort has slowed the policy process and has left the staff scrambling to catch up with events even more than had normally been the case for previous NSC staffs.

The indirect effect of the conclusion of the cold war on the NSC process is closely related to this point. The collapse of the Soviet Union left the United States without a clear foreign policy "doctrine" to replace the idea of containment. It is widely recognized that such doctrines play a useful function in declaring U.S. intentions to allies and adversaries abroad, and in explaining (however simplistically) the rationale for U.S. involvement overseas to a skeptical American public. What is not so often recognized is that such doctrines—clear statements of general foreign policy goals and purposes—also play a crucial role in focusing internal planning and providing guidance to foreign policy officials throughout the government. Despite the need for such guidance from the top, the Clinton administration has not clearly articulated such a purpose. The president rarely tries to do so, and Lake and Christopher were not effective in this role.

In the absence of such a statement, it is more difficult for the NSC to define and guide policy and get cooperation from the agencies; as one administration official put it, "The NSC doesn't control the strands of policy as much as they used to." Not only does this produce less coherent policy, it also increases the level of frustration and dissatisfaction among NSC staffers.

The direct effects of the end of the cold war on the structure and process of the NSC system have therefore been fairly modest. Given the nature of the NSC system, even those structural changes the Clinton administration has made could be reversed or modified easily by subsequent presidents. The indirect effects are likely to be much longer lasting and pervasive; a new administration will not be able to sweep away the different priorities, expectations, and constraints that the end of the cold war has generated. These effects will therefore continue to pose considerable challenges to any NSC system operating in the post-cold war environment.

Analysts who have served on the NSC have long warned against overemphasizing the impact of NSC structure on the effectiveness of that system. Morton Halperin (1974, 105) cautions that "the attention focused on alternate NSC systems because they are visible tends to obscure the fact that most business is conducted outside of those systems." Robert Hunter adds that "procedure is only as good as the people administering it and the quality of their relationships. This is at the heart of foreign policymaking, once the formal lines of authority and action are established" (1982, 39). Christopher Shoemaker suggests that "more than any other organization in Washington, the NSC staff depends on its people. There are no insulating layers to screen the system [from poor personnel performance]" (1991, 130–31; see also Odeen 1985, 38).

These insights certainly find validation in the history of the Clinton NSC system. The very fact that the Clinton NSC system is so similar to that of its predecessor in design, but is seen by most analysts *and* a significant number of Clinton NSC and State Department officials as so different in its effectiveness, would support the conclusion that the *people* in the process constitute the crucial variable in explaining that result.[7] Both the strengths (the degree of coordination between the NSC and NEC, the success of the NSC's role as an "honest broker" among the executive branch foreign policy agencies) and the weaknesses (mismanagement both at the NSC staff and White House levels, confused policy pronouncements, the inability to expedite decision making or to discipline those who undermine established procedures) of the Clinton NSC system

can be traced primarily to the personnel who lead and manage that system.

This is particularly true concerning those at the apex of the decision process: the president and his top advisers. As Colin Campbell has noted (1996, 53–54), weaknesses in the relationship among these principals—which Campbell calls the second "gearbox" of the institutional presidency—have been a major problem for several recent administrations, not just Clinton's (though the foreign policy consequences may be more severe than in any administration since Carter). The president must play an active role in giving what Rockman calls "directional clarity" and in overseeing his subordinates' management of the NSC system and the larger foreign policy process, *especially* if a White House-centered system is chosen. The value that the Tower Commission and others saw in having the NSA and NSC staff at the center of the process declines immensely if it becomes clear that the national security adviser does not have the ear or the confidence of the president, or if the NSA and the NSC staff are unable to use that central position effectively.

Many of the foreign policy problems the Clinton administration has faced would be difficult to solve even with a well-organized and efficiently managed NSC process (after all, the Bush administration had made little progress on Haiti or Bosnia when it handed those issues to the incoming administration). Conceptual lacunae, tactical errors, or plain bad luck may also explain many of the administration's foreign policy difficulties. No process ensures correct decisions; however, a well-organized and carefully staffed NSC system, adequately supported by the president, can help an administration avoid the perception of confusion or incompetence which is so damaging politically, both at home and abroad. It can also provide high-quality options and information for decision makers and help to ensure that decisions are made in a timely manner. The difficult nature of the foreign policy problems facing the United States after the cold war is precisely the strongest argument for getting the NSC process—and the personnel who lead and manage that process—right. Only then will any administration have at least a fighting chance of coping successfully with the myriad international challenges facing the United States in the years ahead.

NOTES

I would like to thank the following individuals for their valuable comments about this analysis: Jim Lindsay, Rip Ripley, Paul Stockton, Pietro Nivola, Loch Johnson, Samuel Lewis, and Duncan Clarke, and the two reviewers for the University of Pittsburgh Press. Two former NSC officials who wish to remain anonymous also read the entire manuscript and offered valuable criticisms, and I thank them for their efforts. I also thank those current and former officials from the NSC, NEC, and State Department who so generously allowed me to interview them and who shared their knowledge and insights about the foreign policy-making process with me.

1. These issues are not "new" with the end of the cold war, of course; they have been staples of both academic analysis and political rhetoric for two decades. Rather, the end of the cold war eliminated the issue that dominated the U.S. foreign policy agenda since the late 1940s, thereby creating room for other issues to rise in priority and for debate about the very nature of the agenda itself.

2. In addition to published sources, my analysis draws on interviews with current and former officials of the National Security Council staff, National Economic Council staff, and State Department, conducted during 1994 and 1995. For obvious reasons, all interviewees requested anonymity, and I have honored those requests.

3. Some NSC staff indicated that these offices were not created primarily for substantive policy reasons, but to pave over personnel problems and create positions for individuals whose original appointments were not working out.

4. One Bush NSC staffer said he usually let an official from one of the agencies chair working groups in his area of policy. While that official was busy coordinating the paperwork for a meeting involving as many as thirty to thirty-five participants, the NSC aide would meet with a small group of trusted allies to plan their strategy for the meeting. He said this allowed him more time and flexibility both to shape the substantive agenda and to oversee the entire process.

5. Several NSC staffers were highly critical of the staff director. They viewed her as a gatekeeper whose job was to review their work for possible domestic political ramifications, and they believed she knew or cared very little about the substance of foreign policy issues. These staffers saw her office as a paperwork bottleneck, and attempted to circumvent her review of their work at every opportunity—which was apparently the source of some tension within the staff.

6. Several NSC staffers suggested that Lake had a strong personal distaste for conflict and confrontation. As an example, they discussed his reluctance to dismiss one senior director even though it was widely known among the staff that Lake had lost all confidence in that individual. More than six months passed before he finally asked the person to leave.

7. Especially striking was the conclusion offered by each of the NSC, NEC, and State Department officials interviewed that,

except for the decision-making bottleneck at the NSC/DC level and the potential for conflict between the NEC and NSC principals, the basic structure and process of the Clinton NSC system was sound. They all suggested that the crucial issues were *who* was running the system and *how* they were running it. One individual who had served in the Bush NSC pointed out that that system had functioned much less effectively after Deputy NSA Robert Gates left the staff to go to the CIA.

REFERENCES

Alison, Graham, and Peter Szanton. 1976. *Remaking Foreign Policy: The Organizational Connection.* New York: Basic Books.

Auger, Vincent A. 1995. *Human Rights and Trade: The Clinton Administration and China.* Washington, D.C.: Institute for the Study of Diplomacy, Georgetown University, Press.

Berman, Larry, and Emily O. Goldman. 1996. "Clinton's Foreign Policy at Midterm." In *The Clinton Presidency: First Appraisals,* edited by Colin Campbell and Bert A. Rockman. Chatham, NJ: Chatham House.

Bradsher, Keith. 1993. "U.S.–Japan Chip Rift Deepens," *New York Times,* December 28: A6.

Brzezinski, Zbigniew. 1987–1988. "NSC's Midlife Crisis." *Foreign Policy* 69: 80–99.

Callahan, David. 1992. "The Honest Broker: Brent Scowcroft in the Bush White House." *Foreign Service Journal* 69: 27–32.

Campbell, Colin. 1996. "Management in a Sandbox: Why the Clinton White House Failed to Cope with Gridlock." In *The Clinton Presidency: First Appraisals,* edited by Colin Campbell and Bert A. Rickman. Chatham, N.J.: Chatham House.

Carnegie Endowment for International Peace and the Institute for International Economics. 1992–1993. "Special Report: Policymaking for a New Era." *Foreign Affairs* 72: 175–89.

Christopher, Warren. 1993. "Statement at Senate Confirmation Hearing." *U.S. Department of State Dispatch* 4: 45–49.

Clarke, Duncan L. 1989. *American Defense and Foreign Policy Institutions: Toward a Sound Foundation.* Cambridge, MA: Ballinger.

Clinton, Bill. 1992. Address at Georgetown University, excerpted in "Secretary Aspin Announces Bottom Up Review Results." *DOD News Release.* Washington, D.C.: Department of Defense, September 1.

———. 1993a. "Executive Order 12835—Establishment of the National Economic Council." *Weekly Compilation of Presidential Documents* 29: 95–96.

———. 1993b. "Organization of the National Security Council." Presidential Decision Document 2, January 20.

———. 1994. *A National Security Strategy of Engagement and Enlargement.* Washington, D.C.: U.S. Government Printing Office.

Commission on Government Renewal. 1992. *Report of the*

Commission on Government Renewal. Carnegie Endowment for International Peace.

C-SPAN. 1994. "American Profile: Anthony Lake," June 26.

Davis, Bob. 1994. "White House Maintains Its Hard-Line Approach to Japan, Despite Ongoing Political Turmoil," *Wall Street Journal,* April 14: A1.

DeParle, Jason. 1995. "The Man Inside Bill Clinton's Foreign Policy," *New York Times Magazine,* August 20: 28–33.

Destler, I.M. 1980. "A Job That Doesn't Work." *Foreign Policy* 39: 80–88.

———. 1994. "A Government Divided: The Security Complex and the Economic Complex." In *The New Politics of American Foreign Policy,* edited by David A. Deese. New York: St. Martin's Press.

Destler, I.M., Leslie H. Gelb, and Anthony Lake. 1984. *Our Own Worst Enemy.* New York: Simon and Schuster.

Devroy, Ann. 1993. "Latest White House Reorganization Plan Leaves Some Insiders Skeptical," *Washington Post,* December 12.

Drew, Elizabeth. 1994. *On the Edge: The Clinton Presidency.* New York: Simon and Schuster.

Engelberg, Stephen. 1995. "How Events Drew U.S. Into Balkans," *New York Times,* August 19, p. A1.

———. 1996a. "For Christopher, It's Foreign Policy, Not Politics," *New York Times,* January 8: A6.

———. 1996b. "U.S. Won't Punish China Over Sale of Nuclear Gear," *New York Times,* May 11: A1.

Falk, Stanley L. 1964. "The National Security Council Under Truman, Eisenhower, and Kennedy," *Political Science Quarterly* 79 (September): 403–434.

Fallows, James. 1989. "Containing Japan." *Atlantic Monthly* 263: 40–54.

Friedman, Thomas L. 1993a. "Clinton Keeping Foreign Policy on a Back Burner," *New York Times,* February 8: A12.

———. 1993b. "Clinton's Foreign Policy: Top Adviser Speaks Up," *New York Times,* October 31: A14.

Frisby, Michael K. 1993. "At the White House, Titles Offer Few Clues About Real Influence," *Wall Street Journal,* March 26: A1.

Garten, Jeffrey. 1992. "White House Renovation." *International Economy* 6: 45–47.

Gordon, Michael R. 1986. "Reagan, the Joint Chiefs of Staff, and Arms Control." *New York Times,* November 3: A8.

———. 1994. "U.S. and Bosnia: How a Policy Changed," *New York Times,* December 4: A6.

Greenberger, Robert S. 1994 "Cacophony of Voices Drowns Out Message From U.S. to China," *Wall Street Journal,* March 22: A1.

Halperin, Morton H. 1974. *Bureaucratic Politics and Foreign Policy.* Washington, D.C.: Brookings Institution.

Harris, John F., and Steven Pearlstein. 1995. "Clinton Chooses Adviser Tyson to Chair National Economic Council," *Washington Post,* February 22: A1.

Harrison, Selig S., and Clyde V. Prestowitz, Jr. 1990. "Pacific Agenda: Defense or Economics." *Foreign Policy* 79: 56–76.

Henderson, David C. 1988. *Reforming Defense: The State of American Civil-Military Relations.* Baltimore, MD: Johns Hopkins University Press.

Holmes, Steven A. 1993. "State Department Seeks Funds of Other Agencies," *New York Times,* November 11: A8.

Hunter, Robert E. 1982. *Presidential Control of Foreign Policy.* The Washington Papers, 91. New York: Praeger.

Ifill, Gwen. 1992. "Clinton to Summon Economic Leaders to Set Priorities," *New York Times,* November 9: A1.

———. 1993. "The Economic Czar Behind the Economic Czars," *New York Times,* March 7: A6.

Ignatius, David. 1994. "The Curse of the Merit Class," *Washington Post,* February 27: A12.

Inderfurth, Karl F., and Loch K. Johnson. 1988. *Decisions of the Highest Order: Perspectives on the National Security Council.* Pacific Grove, CA: Brooks Cole.

Kamen, Al, and Thomas Lippmann. 1993. "Task Force Favors Restructuring and Refocusing Troubled AID," *Washington Post,* July 3: A8.

Kirschten, Dick. 1994a. "Martyr or Misfit." *National Journal* 26: 2502–06.

———. 1994b. "Mensch on the Move." *National Journal* 26: 2971–73.

Kristof, Nicholas D. 1993. "Clinton Aide Ends China Trip With No Sign of Accord," *New York Times,* May 13: A1.

Lake, Anthony. 1993. "From Containment to Enlargement." *U.S. State Department Dispatch* 4: 658–64.

———. 1995. "The Price of Leadership." *U.S. State Department Dispatch* 6: 388–91.

———. 1996. "Defining Missions, Setting Deadlines: Meeting New Security Challenges in the Post-Cold War World." *U.S. State Department Dispatch* 7: 127–30.

Lancaster, John, and Barton Gellman. 1994. "National Security Strategy Paper Arouses Pentagon, State Dept. Debate," *Washington Post,* March 3: A8.

Odeen, Philip A. 1985. "The Role of the National Security Council in Coordinating and Integrating U.S. Defense and Foreign Policy." In *Public Policy and Political Institutions: United States Defense and Foreign Policy—Policy Coordination and Integration,* edited by Duncan L. Clarke. Greenwich, CT: Jai Press.

Pine, Art. 1994. "Clinton Unveils Long-awaited Security Strategy," *Los Angeles Times,* July 22: A1.

Pollack, Andrew. 1995. "U.S. Trade Negotiator Urges Shift in Approach on Japan," *New York Times,* August 1: A4.

Robbins, Carla Anne. 1993. "Gore's Success in Foreign Policy Role Depends on Commitment from Clinton," *Wall Street Journal,* December 13: A1.

Rosati, Jerel A. 1993. *The Politics of U.S. Foreign Policy.* New York: Harcourt Brace.

Sanger, David E. 1995a. "At the End, U.S. Blunted Its Big Stick," *New York Times,* June 30: A9.

———. 1995b. "Trade's Bottom Line: Business Over Politics," *New York Times,* July 30: A5.

———. 1996. "Clinton Approves Plan for Sanctions Against China Over Piracy," *New York Times,* May 9: A1.

Sanger, David E., with Steven Erlanger. 1996. "U.S. Warns China Over Violations of Trade Accord," *New York Times,* February 4: A1.

Sciolino, Elaine. 1993. "3 Players Seek a Director For Foreign Policy Story." *New York Times,* November 8: A4.

———. 1994a. "NATO Rebuffs the Russians on Role in Decision-Making," *New York Times,* June 10: A1.

———. 1994b. "U.S. to Try a Conciliatory Tack with China," *New York Times,* March 23: A1.

Shoemaker, Christopher C. 1991. *The NSC Staff.* Boulder, CO: Westview Press.

Snow, Donald M. and Eugene Brown. 1994. *Puzzle Palaces and Foggy Bottom.* New York: St Martin's.

Solomon, Burt. 1994. "Despite A Take-Charge Conductor. . . . the Orchestra Is Still Off Key." *National Journal* 26: 2298–99.

Stokes, Bruce. 1992–1993. "Organizing to Trade." *Foreign Policy* 89: 36–52.

Tower Commission. 1987. *The Tower Commission Report.* New York: Bantam/Times Books.

"Tower Report Assumes Biblical Status at NSC," 1987. *Washington Times,* March 10: A1.

U.S. Congress, House Committee on Appropriations. 1993. *Treasury, Postal Service and General Government Appropriations for Fiscal Year 1994, Part 3.* 103d Cong., 1st sess.

U.S. Department of State. 1992. *State 2000: A New Model for Managing Foreign Affairs.* Report of the U.S. Department of State Management Task Force. Washington, D.C.: U.S. Department of State Publication 10029.

Walker, Martin. 1992–1993. "The Establishment Reports." *Foreign Policy* 89: 82–95.

Wessel, David. 1992. "Economic Security Council Stirs Debate," *Wall Street Journal,* November 10: A1.

Williams, Daniel. 1994. "China's Hard-Nosed Rights Stance Working Against Trade Status," *Washington Post,* March 12: A1.

WuDunn, Sheryl. 1996. "In Summit Silences, a Truce in U.S.–Japanese Trade Wars," *New York Times,* April 18: A4.

13

NATIONAL SECURITY PRESIDENTIAL DIRECTIVE 1

George W. Bush

Printed below is President Bush's directive, dated February 13, 2001, organizing the National Security Council system for his administration. The key features of the NSC since 1989—a Council supported by a Principals Committee and a Deputies Committee—were continued.

The White House
Washington

February 13, 2001

MEMORANDUM FOR THE VICE PRESIDENT
THE SECRETARY OF STATE
THE SECRETARY OF THE TREASURY
THE SECRETARY OF DEFENSE
THE ATTORNEY GENERAL
THE SECRETARY OF AGRICULTURE
THE SECRETARY OF COMMERCE
THE SECRETARY OF HEALTH AND HUMAN SERVICES
THE SECRETARY OF TRANSPORTATION
THE SECRETARY OF ENERGY
ADMINISTRATOR, ENVIRONMENTAL PROTECTION AGENCY
DIRECTOR OF THE OFFICE OF MANAGEMENT AND BUDGET
UNITED STATES TRADE REPRESENTATIVE
CHAIRMAN, COUNCIL OF ECONOMIC ADVISERS
DIRECTOR, NATIONAL DRUG CONTROL POLICY
CHIEF OF STAFF TO THE PRESIDENT
DIRECTOR OF CENTRAL INTELLIGENCE
DIRECTOR, FEDERAL EMERGENCY MANAGEMENT AGENCY
ASSISTANT TO THE PRESIDENT FOR NATIONAL SECURITY AFFAIRS
ASSISTANT TO THE PRESIDENT FOR ECONOMIC POLICY
COUNSEL TO THE PRESIDENT

Reprinted from Federation of American Scientists web site: http://www.fas.org/irp/offdocs/nspd/nspd-1.htm
George W. Bush of Texas was inaugurated as the nation's 43rd president on January 20, 2001.

CHIEF OF STAFF AND ASSISTANT TO THE VICE PRESIDENT FOR NATIONAL SECU-
RITY AFFAIRS
DIRECTOR, OFFICE OF SCIENCE AND TECHNOLOGY POLICY
CHAIRMAN, BOARD OF GOVERNORS OF THE FEDERAL RESERVE
CHAIRMAN, COUNCIL ON ENVIRONMENTAL QUALITY
CHAIRMAN, EXPORT-IMPORT BANK
CHAIRMAN OF THE JOINT CHIEFS OF STAFF
COMMANDANT, U.S. COAST GUARD
ADMINISTRATOR, NATIONAL AERONAUTICS AND SPACE ADMINISTRATION
CHAIRMAN, NUCLEAR REGULATORY COMMISSION
DIRECTOR, PEACE CORPS
DIRECTOR, FEDERAL BUREAU OF INVESTIGATION
DIRECTOR, NATIONAL SECURITY AGENCY
DIRECTOR, DEFENSE INTELLIGENCE AGENCY
PRESIDENT, OVERSEAS PRIVATE INVESTMENT CORPORATION
CHAIRMAN, FEDERAL COMMUNICATIONS COMMISSION
COMMISSIONER, U.S. CUSTOMS SERVICE
ADMINISTRATOR, DRUG ENFORCEMENT ADMINISTRATION
PRESIDENT'S FOREIGN INTELLIGENCE ADVISORY BOARD
ARCHIVIST OF THE UNITED STATES
DIRECTOR, INFORMATION SECURITY OVERSIGHT OFFICE

SUBJECT: Organization of the National Security Council System

This document is the first in a series of National Security Presidential Directives. National Security Presidential Directives shall replace both Presidential Decision Directives and Presidential Review Directives as an instrument for communicating presidential decisions about the national security policies of the United States.

National security includes the defense of the United States of America, protection of our constitutional system of government, and the advancement of United States interests around the globe. National security also depends on America's opportunity to prosper in the world economy. The National Security Act of 1947, as amended, established the National Security Council to advise the President with respect to the integration of domestic, foreign, and military policies relating to national security. That remains its purpose. The NSC shall advise and assist me in integrating all aspects of national security policy as it affects the United States—domestic, foreign, military, intelligence, and economics (in conjunction with the National Economic Council (NEC)). The National Security Council system is a process to coordinate executive departments and agencies in the effective development and implementation of those national security policies.

The National Security Council (NSC) shall have as its regular attendees (both statutory and non-statutory) the President, the Vice President, the Secretary of State, the Secretary of the Treasury, the Secretary of Defense, and the Assistant to the President for National Security Affairs. The Director of Central Intelligence and the Chairman of the Joint Chiefs of Staff, as statutory advisors to the NSC, shall also attend NSC meetings. The Chief of Staff to the President and the Assistant to the President for Economic Policy are invited to attend any NSC meeting. The Counsel to the President shall be consulted regarding the agenda of NSC meetings, and shall attend any meeting when, in consultation with the Assistant to the President for National Security Affairs, he deems it appropriate. The Attorney General and the Director of the Office of Management and

Budget shall be invited to attend meetings pertaining to their responsibilities. For the Attorney General, this includes both those matters within the Justice Department's jurisdiction and those matters implicating the Attorney General's responsibility under 28 U.S.C. 511 to give his advice and opinion on questions of law when required by the President. The heads of other executive departments and agencies, as well as other senior officials, shall be invited to attend meetings of the NSC when appropriate.

The NSC shall meet at my direction. When I am absent from a meeting of the NSC, at my direction the Vice President may preside. The Assistant to the President for National Security Affairs shall be responsible, at my direction and in consultation with the other regular attendees of the NSC, for determining the agenda, ensuring that necessary papers are prepared, and recording NSC actions and Presidential decisions. When international economic issues are on the agenda of the NSC, the Assistant to the President for National Security Affairs and the Assistant to the President for Economic Policy shall perform these tasks in concert.

The NSC Principals Committee (NSC/PC) will continue to be the senior interagency forum for consideration of policy issues affecting national security, as it has since 1989. The NSC/PC shall have as its regular attendees the Secretary of State, the Secretary of the Treasury, the Secretary of Defense, the Chief of Staff to the President, and the Assistant to the President for National Security Affairs (who shall serve as chair). The Director of Central Intelligence and the Chairman of the Joint Chiefs of Staff shall attend where issues pertaining to their responsibilities and expertise are to be discussed. The Attorney General and the Director of the Office of Management and Budget shall be invited to attend meetings pertaining to their responsibilities. For the Attorney General, this includes both those matters within the Justice Department's jurisdiction and those matters implicating the Attorney General's responsibility under 28 U.S.C. 511 to give his advice and opinion on questions of law when required by the President. The Counsel to the President shall be consulted regarding the agenda of NSC/PC meetings, and shall attend any meeting when, in consultation with the Assistant to the President for National Security Affairs, he deems it appropriate. When international economic issues are on the agenda of the NSC/PC, the Committee's regular attendees will include the Secretary of Commerce, the United States Trade Representative, the Assistant to the President for Economic Policy (who shall serve as chair for agenda items that principally pertain to international economics), and, when the issues pertain to her responsibilities, the Secretary of Agriculture. The Chief of Staff and National Security Adviser to the Vice President shall attend all meetings of the NSC/PC, as shall the Assistant to the President and Deputy National Security Advisor (who shall serve as Executive Secretary of the NSC/PC). Other heads of departments and agencies, along with additional senior officials, shall be invited where appropriate.

The NSC/PC shall meet at the call of the Assistant to the President for National Security Affairs, in consultation with the regular attendees of the NSC/PC. The Assistant to the President for National Security Affairs shall determine the agenda in consultation with the foregoing, and ensure that necessary papers are prepared. When international economic issues are on the agenda of the NSC/PC, the Assistant to the President for National Security Affairs and the Assistant to the President for Economic Policy shall perform these tasks in concert.

The NSC Deputies Committee (NSC/DC) will also continue to serve as the senior sub-Cabinet interagency forum for consideration of policy issues affecting national security. The NSC/DC can prescribe and review the work of the NSC interagency groups discussed later in this directive. The NSC/DC shall also help ensure that issues being brought before the NSC/PC or the NSC have been properly analyzed and prepared for decision. The NSC/DC shall have as its regular members the Deputy Secretary of State or Under Secretary of the Treasury or Under Secretary of the Treasury for International Affairs, the Deputy Secretary of Defense or Under Secretary of Defense for Policy, the Deputy Attorney General, the Deputy Director of the Office of Management and Budget, the Deputy Director of Central Intelligence, the Vice Chairman of the Joint Chiefs of Staff, the Deputy Chief of Staff to the President for Policy, the Chief of Staff and National Security Adviser to the Vice President, the Deputy Assistant to the President for International Economic Affairs, and the Assistant to the President and Deputy National Security Advisor (who shall serve as chair). When international economic issues are on the agenda, the NSC/DC's regular membership will include the Deputy Secretary of Commerce, a Deputy United States Trade Representative, and, when the issues pertain to his responsibilities, the Deputy Secretary of Agriculture, and the NSC/DC shall be chaired by the Deputy Assistant to the President for International Economic Affairs for agenda items that principally pertain to international economics. Other senior officials shall be invited where appropriate.

The NSC/DC shall meet at the call of its chair, in consultation with the other regular members of the NSC/DC. Any regular member of the NSC/DC may also request a meeting of the Committee for prompt crisis management. For all meetings the chair shall determine the agenda in consultation with the foregoing, and ensure that necessary papers are prepared.

The Vice President and I may attend any and all meetings of any entity established by or under this directive.

Management of the development and implementation of national security policies by multiple agencies of the United States Government shall usually be accomplished by the NSC Policy Coordination Committees (NSC/PCCs). The NSC/PCCs shall be the main day-to-day fora for interagency coordination of national security policy. They shall provide policy analysis for consideration by the more senior committees of the NSC system and ensure timely responses to decisions made by the President. Each NSC/PCC shall include representatives from the executive departments, offices, and agencies represented in the NSC/DC.

Six NSC/PCCs are hereby established for the following regions: Europe and Eurasia, Western Hemisphere, East Asia, South Asia, Near East and North Africa, and Africa. Each of the NSC/PCCs shall be chaired by an official of Under Secretary or Assistant Secretary rank to be designated by the Secretary of State.

Eleven NSC/PCCs are hereby also established for the following functional topics, each to be chaired by a person of Under Secretary or Assistant Secretary rank designated by the indicated authority:

Democracy, Human Rights, and International Operations (by the Assistant to the President for National Security Affairs);

International Development and Humanitarian Assistance (by the Secretary of State);

Global Environment (by the Assistant to the President for National Security Affairs and the Assistant to the President for Economic Policy in concert);

International Finance (by the Secretary of the Treasury);

Transnational Economic Issues (by the Assistant to the President for Economic Policy);

Counter-Terrorism and National Preparedness (by the Assistant to the President for National Security Affairs);

Defense Strategy, Force Structure, and Planning (by the Secretary of Defense);

Arms Control (by the Assistant to the President for National Security Affairs);

Proliferation, Counterproliferation, and Homeland Defense (by the Assistant to the President for National Security Affairs);

Intelligence and Counterintelligence (by the Assistant to the President for National Security Affairs); and

Records Access and Information Security (by the Assistant to the President for National Security Affairs).

The Trade Policy Review Group (TPRG) will continue to function as an interagency coordinator of trade policy. Issues considered within the TPRG, as with the PCCs, will flow through the NSC and/or NEC process, as appropriate.

Each NSC/PCC shall also have an Executive Secretary from the staff of the NSC, to be designated by the Assistant to the President for National Security Affairs. The Executive Secretary shall assist the Chairman in scheduling the meetings of the NSC/PCC, determining the agenda, recording the actions taken and tasks assigned, and ensuring timely responses to the central policymaking committees of the NSC system. The Chairman of each NSC/PCC, in consultation with the Executive Secretary, may invite representatives of other executive departments and agencies to attend meetings of the NSC/PCC where appropriate.

The Assistant to the President for National Security Affairs, at my direction and in consultation with the Vice President and the Secretaries of State, Treasury, and Defense, may establish additional NSC/PCCs as appropriate.

The Chairman of each NSC/PCC, with the agreement of the Executive Secretary, may establish subordinate working groups to assist the PCC in the performance of its duties.

The existing system of Interagency Working Groups is abolished.

- The oversight of ongoing operations assigned in PDD/NSC-56 to Executive Committees of the Deputies Committee will be performed by the appropriate regional NSC/PCCs, which may create subordinate working groups to provide coordination for ongoing operations.
- The Counter-Terrorism Security Group, Critical Infrastructure Coordination Group, Weapons of Mass Destruction Preparedness, Consequences Management and Protection Group, and the Interagency Working Group on Enduring Constitutional Government are reconstituted as various forms of the NSC/PCC on Counter-Terrorism and National Preparedness.
- The duties assigned in *PDD/NSC-75* to the National Counterintelligence Policy Group will be performed in the NSC/PCC on Intelligence and Counterintelligence, meeting with appropriate attendees.
- The duties assigned to the Security Policy Board and other entities established in *PDD/NSC-29* will be transferred to various NSC/PCCs, depending on the particular security problem being addressed.
- The duties assigned in *PDD/NSC-41* to the Standing Committee on Nonproliferation will be transferred to the PCC on Proliferation, Counterproliferation, and Homeland Defense.
- The duties assigned in *PDD/NSC-35* to the Interagency Working Group for Intelligence Priorities will be transferred to the PCC on Intelligence and Counterintelligence.
- The duties of the Human Rights Treaties Interagency Working Group established in *E.O. 13107* are transferred to the PCC on Democracy, Human Rights, and International Operations.

- The Nazi War Criminal Records Interagency Working Group established in *E.O. 13110* shall be reconstituted, under the terms of that order and until its work ends in January 2002, as a Working Group of the NSC/PCC for Records Access and Information Security.

Except for those established by statute, other existing NSC interagency groups, ad hoc bodies, and executive committees are also abolished as of March 1, 2001, unless they are specifically reestablished as subordinate working groups within the new NSC system as of that date. Cabinet officers, the heads of other executive agencies, and the directors of offices within the Executive Office of the President shall advise the Assistant to the President for National Security Affairs of those specific NSC interagency groups chaired by their respective departments or agencies that are either mandated by statute or are otherwise of sufficient importance and vitality as to warrant being reestablished. In each case the Cabinet officer, agency head, or office director should describe the scope of the activities proposed for or now carried out by the interagency group, the relevant statutory mandate if any, and the particular NSC/PCC that should coordinate this work. The Trade Promotion Coordinating Committee established in E.O. 12870 shall continue its work, however, in the manner specified in that order. As to those committees expressly established in the National Security Act, the NSC/PC and/or NSC/DC shall serve as those committees and perform the functions assigned to those committees by the Act.

To further clarify responsibilities and effective accountability within the NSC system, those positions relating to foreign policy that are designated as special presidential emissaries, special envoys for the President, senior advisors to the President and the Secretary of State, and special advisors to the President and the Secretary of State are also abolished as of March 1, 2001, unless they are specifically redesignated or reestablished by the Secretary of State as positions in that Department.

This Directive shall supersede all other existing presidential guidance on the organization of the National Security Council system. With regard to application of this document to economic matters, this document shall be interpreted in concert with any Executive Order governing the National Economic Council and with presidential decision documents signed hereafter that implement either this directive or that Executive Order.

[signed: George W. Bush]
cc: The Executive Clerk

PART V

NATIONAL SECURITY ADVISERS
Roles

We at the National Security Council are going to try to work the seams, stitching the connections together tightly. If we can do that, if we can provide glue for the many, many agencies and the many, many instruments the United States is now deploying around the world, I think we will have done our job on behalf of the President of the United States.

—Condoleezza Rice
Remarks, U.S. Institute of Peace
January 17, 2001

EDITORS' INTRODUCTION

The National Security Council system consists of three key groups of people: the statutory principals (the president, the vice president, the secretary of state, and the secretary of defense), the statutory advisers (the director of Central Intelligence and the chair of the Joint Chiefs of Staff), and the Council staff. The professional (nonclerical or support) staff has ranged in size from only a few people in the early days, to around fifty during the Nixon years, down to forty in the administration of George H.W. Bush (Bush I), and upwards of 100 during the Clinton years (in each case, all but a handful on loan from various executive agencies). According to one recent study, "the NSC has become the largest policy group in the White House" (Patterson, 2000: 72; see For Further Reading). In Figure V.A (p. 132), Daalder and Destler trace the rise in the number of professional staff on the NSC from 1960 to 2000, which reveals a steep rise during the Clinton years.

The bridge that joins all three groups is the "special assistant to the president for national security affairs," a job title established in the Eisenhower Administration to designate that individual who would be the overall director of the NSC's activities. During the Truman Administration, this position was known as the NSC executive secretary; but early in the Eisenhower Administration that title became the designation for a lower office reporting to the new special assistant. The executive secretary was expected to handle administrative and other routine tasks, freeing the special assistant to devote more time to NSC committee affairs and policy coordination. (During the Eisenhower years, General Andrew J. Goodpaster also served as security aide to the president with the title "staff secretary and assistant for national security activities.") The cumbersome formal title of "special assistant to the president for national security affairs"

NSC Policy Staff 1961–2000

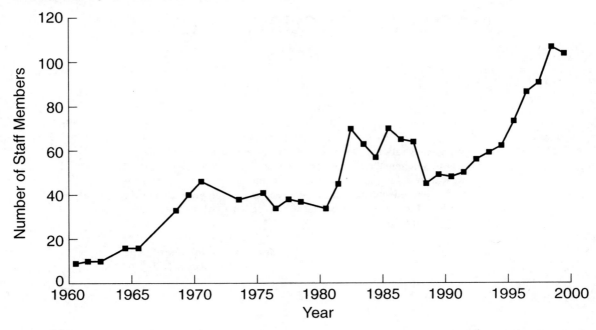

Figure V.A NSC Policy Staff 1961–2000 (*Source: Ivo H. Daalder and I.M. Destler, "A NSC for a New Administration,"* Policy Brief No. 68. *Washington, D.C.: The Brookings Institution, November 2000.*)

was shortened under President Nixon to "the assistant for national security affairs" or, in everyday parlance, "the national security adviser"—today's common usage.

From Executive Secretary to NSC Adviser

Whatever title one prefers, this conclusion is certain: the position has become one of great importance in the government of the United States. Initially, with the passage of the National Security Act of 1947, officials in Washington, D.C., viewed the post of executive secretary as little more than a neutral coordinator of information prepared for the president by those government departments and agencies with foreign policy responsibilities. Now, as journalist Elizabeth Drew has accurately noted (*New Yorker,* 1978: 90), the national security adviser resides "at the center of the system for making foreign and defense policy."

Clark M. Clifford, a former top White House aide to President Truman and one of the principal drafters of the 1947 National Security Act, once recalled in congressional testimony:

Senator, your first question had to do with whether or not those of us who drafted the Act contemplated the creation of a position like the national security adviser and did we have in mind that it would become as important as it did.

We had no such thought in mind. It was not even conceived that there would be such a position. After the Act was passed in 1947, an assistant and I for the balance of the time I was there performed that function. We performed it mainly because of relationships that already had been established with State, with Dean Acheson in State, and with Jim Forrestal in Defense.

It worked well. The government was not quite as complicated then as it is now. But I think it worked well. As time went on, apparently a need was felt for such a position. . . . each of the presidents felt that they needed this role. (Senate Foreign Relations Committee, *Hearings,* 1980)

By the 1960s, the renamed position had evolved into a number of complicated—and sometimes contradictory—roles. As Colin Powell, who served as national security adviser under Ronald Reagan, once put it: "I was to perform as judge, traffic cop, truant officer, arbitrator, fireman, chaplain, psychiatrist, and occasional hit man" (Powell, *My American Journey,* 1995: 352). The job stretched from the original task of paper coordinator all the way to one of policy advocacy on behalf of the president.

While much has been written about the statutory principals on the NSC, less attention has been directed toward the national security adviser. The purpose of this section on "Roles" is to provide the reader with a sense of the range of duties carried out by individuals selected by presidents to fill this vital office. Since the establishment of the NSC in July 1947, twenty-one men and one woman have served as either executive secretary during the Truman and Eisenhower years (three) or—beginning with Robert Cutler—as national security adviser during and since the Eisenhower years (nineteen). Their names and years of service follow:

Table V.A. Executive Secretaries and National Security Advisers Since 1947

THE NSC EXECUTIVE SECRETARIES

Truman Administration

Sidney W. Souers	1947–1950
James S. Lay	1950–1953

Eisenhower Administration

Robert Cutler	1953

THE ASSISTANTS TO THE PRESIDENT FOR NATIONAL SECURITY AFFAIRS

Eisenhower Administration

Robert Cutler	1953–1955
Dillon Anderson	1955–1956
William Jackson	1956–1957
Robert Cutler	1957–1958
Gordon Gray	1958–1961

Kennedy and Johnson Administrations

McGeorge Bundy	1961–1966
Walt W. Rostow	1966–1969

Nixon and Ford Administrations

Henry A. Kissinger	1969–1975 (while also Secretary of State in 1973–1975)
Brent Scowcroft	1975–1977

Carter Administration

Zbigniew Brzezinski	1977–1981

Reagan Administration

Richard V. Allen	1981–1982
William P. Clark	1982–1983
Robert C. McFarlane	1983–1985
John M. Poindexter	1985–1986

| Frank C. Carlucci | 1986–1987 |
| Colin Powell | 1987–1989 |

George H. W. Bush Administration

| Brent Scowcroft | 1989–1993 |

Clinton Administration

| W. Anthony Lake | 1993–1997 |
| Samuel R. Berger | 1997–2001 |

George W. Bush Administration

| Condoleezza Rice | 2001– |

The individuals who have served as either executive secretary or adviser have displayed a range of approaches to the job. Some have engaged only minimally, if at all, in policy advocacy (the executive secretaries and early advisers); others have been active policy entrepreneurs and advocates (Kissinger, Brzezinski, and most recent advisers). Two advisers succumbed to the temptation of involvement in questionable foreign policy and intelligence operations (McFarlane and Poindexter). Some have become internationally known as a result of serving as national security adviser (none more than Kissinger who, in 1973, combined the job with his position as secretary of state); others have been as hidden to history as a museum curator.

A Panoply of Roles for the NSC Adviser

Crowding the NSC's agenda are a constant flow of committee and subcommittee meetings, covering everything from budget reviews and crisis management to policy evaluations of specific topics (like arms control) or regions of the world. The adviser is steadily on the telephone with other top officials, or meeting with them, and occasionally will host foreign representatives in the adviser's West Wing office. In addition, the activist national security adviser faces many managerial tasks: assigning studies for the NSC staff or other experts to prepare for the president; reading and commenting on completed studies, then distilling the findings and recommendations into a report for the president; serving as traffic cop for the constant flow of paper to the Oval Office on security and foreign policy matters from cabinet officers and other officials; monitoring the implementation of decisions made by the president to ensure they are properly interpreted and carried out by the bureaucracy; and occasionally meeting with newspaper, magazine, and television reporters.

The first selection in this portion of the book is entitled "A Forum on the Role of the National Security Adviser." Sponsored by the Woodrow Wilson International Center in Washington, D.C., and the Baker Institute at Rice University, this oral history offers insights into the views held about the NSC by a number of former national security advisers, plus General Goodpaster, (as mentioned earlier) a security aide to President Eisenhower. According to the roundtable remarks by Samuel ("Sandy") R. Berger of the Clinton Administration, the adviser's principal role is to provide the president with information that "he needs to know in addition to what he wants to know. . . . and to keep the process moving in a direction that he wants it to move." Later in this selection, Berger stresses that the objective of the NSC (and, therefore, its adviser) is "trying to have a coherent decision-making process" and "determining what [the] priorities are and what is important for the rest of the government to focus on."

Another former adviser, Walt W. Rostow of the Johnson Administration, lays out these five basic duties for the man or woman who holds the office:

- gathering information;
- presenting, sympathetically, the point of view of each relevant cabinet member;
- stating his or her own opinion, without becoming domineering;
- helping to hold together the president's foreign policy team;
- implementing the president's decision.

Of these duties, the "biggest job" (according to Rostow) is the gathering or "mobilization" of information.

In another forum with NSC advisers, sponsored in 1999 by the Center for International and Security Studies at the University of Maryland and The Brookings Institution in Washington, D.C. (under "Center" in For Further Reading), Rostow emphasized again that the adviser's "number one duty [is] to give the president the facts." The role of fact-presenter is not the adviser's alone. This responsibility is also considered the first duty of the director of Central Intelligence (DCI), although the NSC adviser is expected as well to give policy advice while the DCI is traditionally supposed to stick to the facts. Not every DCI has honored this distinction, however—notably, John McCone during the Kennedy years and William Casey under President Reagan, both of whom routinely weighed in with policy recommendations (Johnson, 1989).

In still another forum on the NSC, held at the U.S. Institute of Peace in Washington, D.C., advisers Brent Scowcroft and Anthony Lake also addressed the question of roles. Scowcroft offered ten "axioms" on the subject. The adviser had to be a policy integrator and an honest broker. He or she also had to be willing to concentrate mainly on advising the president, not making public pronouncements, and to be prepared to defer to the secretary of state as the chief "explicator" of foreign and security policy. The adviser had to be prepared to eschew the temptation of running foreign policy from the White House, to carefully husband the president's time, and sharply limit the operational role of the NSC staff. The adviser had to engage only sparingly in diplomacy with foreign nations—and only in tandem with the secretary of state, and be able to organize the NSC staff to suit the president's "habits, needs, and proclivities." Finally, the national security adviser had to work in a close partnership with the director of the Office of Management and Budget (OMB), "instead of allowing OMB to make policy by default by dint of its control over money" (summarized by Cronin, 2001: 24).

Lake offers his list less in the form of axioms than "challenges" about the new world in which advisers must carry out their duties. According to Lake (again, as summarized by Cronin 2001: 24), the national security adviser should perform these roles:

- agenda setter, defining priorities;
- arbiter, adjudicating conflicting interagency recommendations ("the referee of internal bureaucratic scrimmages");
- diplomat, selectively using the White House venue to engage foreign officials;
- intelligence officer, helping to identify emergent threats and provide early warning;
- media source, feeding media demand for explanation with background interviews [Lake now wishes he had done more of this; see Lake, 2000: 262];
- congressional liaison, building trust with leaders on Capitol Hill; and,
- national security professional, preserving a firewall between national security and U.S. domestic politics.

Anthony Lake also participated in the University of Maryland and Brookings Institution roundtable mentioned earlier, at which he succinctly stated his notion of the three essential duties of any NSC adviser. They were to make sure that others in the foreign policy hierarchy—

not only the president—know the adviser's views, so there are no surprises; to drive the foreign policy decision-making process forward; and to engage in selected diplomatic activities, as the president sees fit. While the NSC staff was widely criticized for its involvement in dubious operations during the Iran-*contra* affair, Lake's advocacy of an operational role in the world of diplomacy is less extreme. It stems from the complexity of modern relations among nations and Lake's sense that the secretary of state needs help from other key administration officials in the presentation and implementation of foreign policy.

Clearly, a primary obligation of the national security adviser is to help ensure that the president hears a range of opinions before making a decision, serving as a kind of "Special Assistant for Multiple Advocacy" in the domain of national security. Political scientist Alexander George once proposed the creation of a new White House Office of Special Assistant for Multiple Advocacy for policy issues across the board (George, 1980: 153–54). The NSC adviser, if performing properly, already has this responsibility as a part of his or her job description. The adviser is expected to keep the channels of communication open between the White House and the departments and agencies; to make sure that weaker advocates are heard; to dredge new channels, if necessary, in the persistent search for information and policy options to assist the president; and to be alert constantly for malfunctions in the flow of information to and orders from the White House. This may have been what President George W. Bush had in mind when he described the role of Condoleezza Rice as the "un-sticker" in an October 28, 2003 press conference: ". . . her job is also to deal interagency and to help unstick things that may get stuck."

An Office of Growing Influence and Visibility
The early NSC executive secretaries served largely as neutral conveyer belts, carrying along information to the president that came to the White House from executive branch agencies and departments. But as David K. Hall has noted (1975: 100), when Cutler became Eisenhower's NSC adviser, the position took on new vigor "in identifying issues, in pressing for information, in suggesting alternatives, in seeking compromises, in *occasionally* [Hall's emphasis] advocating a view."

With the exception of Brent Scowcroft when he labored for President Ford under the shadow of Secretary of State Kissinger, the national security advisers from the Kennedy Administration until the Reagan Administration eschewed the passive executive secretary model in favor of a steadily more expansive interpretation of their responsibilities. The adviser position evolved rapidly into an office of considerable authority during the Kennedy years. Lake believes the watershed break in the adviser's job description came with the Bay of Pigs fiasco (Center, 1999: 4). Whatever the initial impetus, the exceptional energy and intellectual abilities of McGeorge Bundy and his successors (well-regarded scholars like Rostow, Kissinger, and Brzezinski), along with the backing of presidents Kennedy, Johnson, Nixon, and Carter, allowed these advisers to expand the traditional boundaries of the office. Kissinger and Brzezinski took the office public, becoming leading spokesmen for foreign policy and appearing frequently on television talk shows. Brzezinski brought a press secretary on board—a first for the NSC.

Drs. Kissinger and Brzezinski may have gone too far in their public appearances as advisers. At least this was the view of some critics, including some officials who served under secretaries of state William P. Rogers in the Nixon years and Cyrus Vance in the Carter years. These officials viewed Kissinger and Brzezinski, respectively, as overly aggressive competitors for the title of chief foreign policy adviser and spokesman for the president. When Gerald R. Ford replaced Nixon as president in 1974, he kept Kissinger on as both his secretary of state and NSC adviser.

In November 1975, though, the president decided to split these offices again into the hands of two individuals, with Kissinger continuing as secretary and Lt. Gen. Brent Scowcroft (who had been Kissinger's deputy national security adviser) becoming the national security adviser. At the time, Kissinger "resented the decision bitterly" (Kissinger, 1982: 435), but he came to view the split as wise, realizing that a determined secretary of state "cannot fail to have his view heard"— regardless of who is chairing interdepartmental security committees, the secretary or the adviser.

Both by personality and philosophy, Scowcroft settled into a less dominant role than the one Kissinger had displayed as adviser. "I bent over backwards," Scowcroft recalls (Center, 1999: 9), "not to appear to be repeating, frankly, what Henry Kissinger did." Given Kissinger's wile and great stature as secretary of state, it would have been difficult anyway for Scowcroft or any-one else to rise above the secretary as the president's chief foreign policy official.

In hopes of toning down the tensions between the national security adviser and the secretary of state, which occurred most prominently during the Nixon and Carter years, the Reagan Administration vowed to carry on in the style of Scowcroft, not Kissinger or Brzezinski. Messrs. Allen, Clark, and McFarlane—the first three Reagan NSC advisers—assumed a more behind-the-scenes supportive role focused on the president's needs, allowing Reagan's secretaries of state, Alexander M. Haig, Jr., and George Shultz, to be the point men for foreign policy. During these years, the secretaries's major rivals were less the national security adviser than other pow-erful cabinet and White House officials, especially Secretary of Defense Caspar W. Weinberger and White House Chief of Staff Donald T. Regan.

The fourth Reagan NSC adviser, Adm. John Poindexter, seemed by all accounts destined to fit well into the new, low-key style of his immediate predecessors. The Iran-*contra* scandal of 1986 (involving shady arms deals with Iran and the improper funneling of monies to the *contra* rebellion in Nicaragua) would reveal, however, that behind Poindexter's spit-and-polish, by-the-book countenance hid an adviser prepared to push the boundaries of the office beyond the break-ing point and into a region of questionable propriety, if not downright illegality—although to this day Poindexter continues to believe that the NSC staff never violated the law during the Iran-*contra* affair (Center, October 25, 1999: 61–74). This interpretation put him at odds with a number of lawmakers and legal scholars (e.g., Cohen and Mitchell, 1989; Tribe, 1987: A31). Poindexter joined the government again in the second Bush Administration, leading an effort in the Pentagon to develop better surveillance techniques against suspected terrorists and improved methods for predicting terrorist attacks. He became embroiled in controversy over his perceived insensitivities to civil liberties and resigned in 2003.

The Iran-*contra* scandal dealt the office a serious blow, and the Reagan Administration brought in Frank Carlucci, a seasoned government official, to help repair the damage. He moved quickly to take the NSC out of operations and return it to its managing and coordinating respon-sibilities. "We had to back the NSC out of that role," he recalls, "because once you became oper-ational you couldn't be the honest broker" (Center, 1999: 3).

Carlucci also took steps to shift the focus back to the Department of State. In dealing with the media, he adds: "The national security adviser should not be out front, but should be part of a coordinated public relations strategy." McFarlane and Lake, however, continued to advocate a media role for the adviser, since (in McFarlane's words) "it takes a lot of resources"—not just the president and the secretary of state alone—to explain the nation's foreign policy initiatives to the American people and the rest of the world. Lake agrees: "With the increasing range of talk shows, news channels, and so on, you especially need all the voices you can get when you're trying to explain a policy." He is critical of himself for not spending more time on such public activities, though he acknowledges that Secretary of State Warren Christopher "didn't like it very much when I did public work" (Center, October 25, 1999: 14).

As a further means for limiting conflict between the State Department and the NSC staff, Berger of the Clinton Administration emphasized the need for the secretary of state and the national security adviser to stay in close contact. He and Secretary of State Madeleine Albright worked out a rule whereby they agreed "never to believe anything that we read about each other in the newspaper, or that [is] said about each other by people who work for us without picking up the phone and talking to each other."

The NSC Adviser as Honest Broker

In the second selection of Part V, entitled "The NSC Advisor: Process Manager and More," Colin Powell discusses his views of how the adviser's office should function. The adviser exists, he writes, "to help the president manage foreign policy," especially by ensuring that the chief executive receives "full, objective, coherent, and balanced recommendations on issues he must decide" and that decisions are forced forward ("not allowing the bureaucracy to sit and spin its wheels and fail to move issues forward for decision"). The president must hear "the strongest views as well as the weakest views." Moreover, Powell adds, it is imperative for the adviser to make the secretaries of state and defense "look good"—not exactly Henry Kissinger's prime motivation when he served as adviser! "It is in the best interest of the United States," underscores Powell, "for the secretary of state and the secretary of defense to be seen as the principal players in the executive of the president's foreign policy."

Further, the adviser is often called upon to be a crisis manager. Powell writes: "When something happens in the world—a military action in the Persian Gulf, a crisis in a foreign land, any kind of crisis that is going to be a major international event—there is only one place that crisis can be managed from, and that is the West Wing of the White House, and it immediately flows into the National Security Council staff and the national security adviser."

Perhaps above all else, the NSC adviser has evolved into an important "honest broker" to mediate disputes among the cabinet departments—and especially to mollify as much as possible the institutional tensions between State and Defense, serving as a bridge between the two. Elsewhere, Powell has referred to the adviser as "the conflict resolver" (Daalder, 1999: 51).

Brent Scowcroft, considered by many the quintessential honest broker during the two times he served as adviser (to Ford and the first President Bush), has said: ". . . . if you are not the honest broker, you don't have the confidence of the other members of the NSC. If you don't have their confidence, then the system doesn't work, because they will go around you to get to the president and then you fracture the system" (Center, 1999: 2).

An Adviser Typology

The final selection in Part V, entitled "The Lessons of the Iran-Contra Affair for National Security Policy Making," presents a fourfold classification of adviser roles: the administrator, the coordinator, the counselor, and the agent (see Figure V.B). As explained by the creators of the typology, Cecil V. Crabb and Kevin V. Mulcahy, the adviser *qua* administrator is highly deferential to the secretary of state, unwilling to enter into policy advocacy, and devoted to the day-to-day chores of moving national security papers in and out of the Oval Office—the conveyor-belt role. The executive secretaries—Souers and Lay—are classic examples, according to the authors (to which we would add early Cutler as well, before he became adviser). So are some later advisers, they suggest, including most assuredly Allen, but also Carlucci and Powell. We

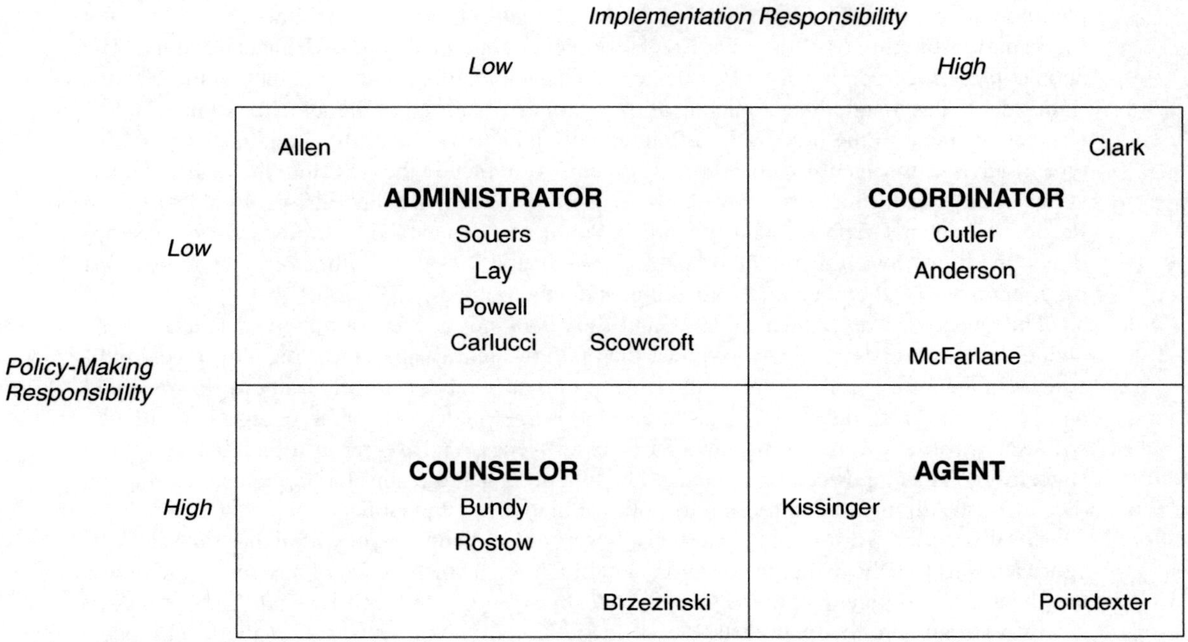

Implementation Responsibility

	Low	High
Low *Policy-Making Responsibility*	Allen **ADMINISTRATOR** Souers Lay Powell Carlucci Scowcroft	Clark **COORDINATOR** Cutler Anderson McFarlane
High	**COUNSELOR** Bundy Rostow Brzezinski	**AGENT** Kissinger Poindexter

Figure V.B Styles of leadership among NSC advisers *(Source: Cecil V. Crabb and Kevin V. Mulcahy,* American National Security: A Presidential Perspective *(Pacific Grove, CA: Brooks/Cole, 1991), p. 177.)*

agree with the Allen judgment, but feel that Carlucci and Powell played a more expanded role (see below). The authors place Scowcroft in this category, with respect to his posture during the Ford Administration, but not (and the authors concur) when he became adviser to the first President Bush.

Crabb and Mulcahy's second category is the NSC adviser as "coordinator," whereby the job takes on the added dimension of taking greater policy initiative by defining policy options for the president. Into this cell of the typology, according to the authors, fall officeholders like Cutler (as adviser, not as executive secretary), Anderson, Clark, and McFarlane—though we would place McFarlane into a more assertive category (discussed further in Part VI), based on his involvement in the Iran-*contra* affair and the bypassing of the secretary of state. The third category of "counselor" refers to an adviser's entry into the world of policy advocacy, presenting his or her own views to the president and helping the administration project its policy initiatives to the public. Here the authors appropriately place Bundy, Rostow, and Brzezinski.

The fourth category is "agent." In this guise, the adviser "combines the duties of a coordinator (directing the planning process) with those of a counselor (serving as a personal presidential adviser)." The adviser-cum-agent dominates the national security process and acts as the chief spokesperson for the president on foreign affairs. Henry Kissinger is the only pure example of an agent in the Crabb–Mulcahy schema, although the authors maintain that it "was not for want of aspiration or effort" that Brzezinski never quite made it into the agent domain. The authors place Vice-admiral John Poindexter in the agent cell in Figure 16.2, but on the extreme right side. In this manner they indicate (as they explain in the text of the selection) that Poindexter's involvement in the Iran-*contra* affair actually brands him as a fifth—and unacceptable—type of adviser: the agent-extremist or "insurgent," who moved the NSC into the realm of operations of dubious legality and propriety. As a result of inadequate supervision or guidance from President Reagan, Crabb and Mulcahy argue, Poindexter pushed the NSC adviser's job description to the limit "by acting on the basis of his personal assessment of the president's *intentions* [their emphasis] rather than on expressed presidential policies."

The selection was written in 1991 and thus does not account for more recent advisers, including Scowcroft's performance under the first President Bush or the three most recent individuals in that office: Lake, Berger, and Rice. Using the Crabb–Mulcahy framework, we would designate Scowcroft under Bush I, and Lake and Berger under Clinton, as counselors—though with Scowcroft and Lake at the low end of assertiveness and Berger at the higher end (with Brzezinski). Thus far, Rice also appears to be functioning as a counselor, to include helping the second Bush Administration present its policy initiatives to the public.

The distinction we draw between such advisers as Lake and Berger within the counselor category leads us to believe that the development of a more nuanced scale of adviser assertiveness may be a useful supplement to the Crabb–Mulcahy typology. In Part VI we take up that task. It is worth noting here that many students of the NSC look upon Scowcroft as the ideal type of adviser. Beginning with his earlier posting as a policy coordinator under President Ford and continuing his service in the first Bush Administration, he has a deserved reputation as an honest broker. But his roles in the Ford and first Bush administrations must be differentiated. As Scowcroft himself has put it, ". . . in the Ford Administration, I stayed much more behind the scenes than I did later on" (Center, 1999: 11). In his second incarnation in this office under George H.W. Bush, he was a counselor who firmly clarified policy alternatives and forcefully presented his own views—though not to the point of trying to dominate policy making at the expense of agencies and departments with alternative perspectives.

As we will explain further in Part VI, this more assertive "Scowcroft II" model appears to suit the office better in the era following the end of the Cold War. As Scowcroft demonstrated under President George H.W. Bush and as Berger showed under President Clinton, an adviser can be an honest broker and at the same time have strong personal opinions. The key is to bend over backwards in the careful and accurate presentation of the positions of others, then explicitly and separately add into the mix one's own policy views and recommendations.

14

A FORUM ON THE ROLE OF NATIONAL SECURITY ADVISER

Cosponsored by the Woodrow Wilson International Center for Scholars and the James A. Baker III Institute For Public Policy of Rice University

This selection provides an oral history roundtable with five former national security advisers (Samuel R. Berger, Zbigniew Brzezinski, Frank C. Carlucci, Robert C. McFarlane, and Walt W. Rostow) and a top-level security aide from the Eisenhower Administration (Andrew J. Goodpaster). It is moderated by Wolf Blitzer of CNN. Covering a wide range of subjects related to the National Security Council and its staff, the participants offer first-hand insights into the roles played by the NSC adviser from the 1950s to the present.

APRIL 12, 2001

SPEAKERS:

WOLF BLITZER, CNN, MODERATOR

EDWARD P. DJEREJIAN, DIRECTOR, JAMES A. BAKER III INSTITUTE FOR PUBLIC POLICY, RICE UNIVERSITY

SAMUEL R. BERGER, FORMER NATIONAL SECURITY ADVISER UNDER PRESIDENT CLINTON

ZBIGNIEW BRZEZINSKI, FORMER NATIONAL SECURITY ADVISER UNDER PRESIDENT CARTER

FRANK C. CARLUCCI, FORMER NATIONAL SECURITY ADVISER UNDER PRESIDENT REAGAN

ANDREW J. GOODPASTER, FORMER STAFF SECRETARY AND ASSISTANT FOR NATIONAL SECURITY ACTIVITIES UNDER PRESIDENT EISENHOWER

ROBERT C. MCFARLANE, FORMER NATIONAL SECURITY ADVISER UNDER PRESIDENT REAGAN

WALT W. ROSTOW, FORMER DEPUTY SPECIAL ASSISTANT FOR NATIONAL SECURITY AFFAIRS TO PRESIDENT KENNEDY AND SPECIAL ASSISTANT FOR NATIONAL SECURITY AFFAIRS TO PRESIDENT JOHNSON

LEE H. HAMILTON, DIRECTOR, WOODROW WILSON INTERNATIONAL CENTER FOR SCHOLARS

INTRODUCTION

DJEREJIAN   Ladies and gentlemen, good afternoon. Thank you very much for coming to this forum on the role of the national security advisor.

I'm Ed Djerejian, the director of the Baker Institute of Rice University. And this is really a distinct pleasure for me. . . .

. . . And as you can see, we have a very distinguished panel of former national security advisors. . . .

Our moderator is a person who really does not need an introduction Wolf Blitzer, the anchor of CNN's Wolf Blitzer Reports. . . .

So, please join me in welcoming Wolf Blitzer to the podium.

Reprinted from "A Forum on the Role of the National Security Advisor," Cosponsored by the Woodrow Wilson International Center for Scholars in Washington, D.C., and the James A. Baker III Institute for Public Policy of Rice University in Houston, Texas, held on April 12, 2001, with permission from the Center and the Institute.

(APPLAUSE)

BLITZER   Thank you very much, Ed.

Thank you very much, ladies and gentlemen, for coming over this afternoon. This is an exciting time to be discussing this issue of the national security advisor to the president of the United States. I think there's a lot of international issues right now on the agenda, and you'll probably have some opportunity later this afternoon to get into some of those.

Let me briefly introduce our panel, and then we can begin right away with the questioning. And I think that, just as I didn't need much of an introduction, I don't think our panel needs much of an introduction. These are former national security advisors to different presidents, all of whom probably see the roles that they played in slightly different ways, perhaps even in considerably different ways.

We'll begin with Sandy Berger, Samuel Berger, or as I called him last night on the air, Sam Berger.

I don't know why I called you Sam Berger, I never heard any—anybody ever call you Sam Berger?

BERGER   Yes, my mother used to call me that.

(LAUGHTER)

BLITZER   Sandy Berger, of course the most recent national security advisor, serving the past four years as the national security advisor for President Clinton, before that, the deputy national security advisor.

Dr. Zbigniew Brzezinski, also someone who needs no introduction, served as national security advisor for four years to President Jimmy Carter.

Frank Carlucci served a more brief period of time as national security advisor under President Reagan, later of course becoming the secretary of defense.

Andrew Goodpaster, who's right over there, goes further back, to President Eisenhower, when that job was less, I guess, clearly defined than it subsequently became.

Bud McFarlane was national security advisor to President Reagan.

And Walt Rostow was national security advisor to President Johnson.

All of whom went on to have distinguished careers and saw their roles, as I said, in slightly different ways.

And why don't we begin with the most recent national security advisor, Sandy Berger, and then just simply go down the panel and ask the simple question—and if you can give us a relatively brief answer, I think it would help all of us.

I said that the other day when I interviewed Dr. Henry Kissinger. Before the program, I said, "Dr. Kissinger, this is a limited program, it's only a half-hour program, we don't have a lot of time. So if you can keep your answers relatively short, we can get through a lot of issues." And he said to me, "Mr. Blitzer, the art of diplomacy is the possible, not the impossible."

(LAUGHTER)

But he did very well, I must say.

Sandy Berger, how did you come to see your role as the president's national security advisor?

THE ROLE OF NATIONAL SECURITY ADVISER

BERGER   Well, first of all, I want to thank you, Wolf, for congratulating me on my distinguished career, since I left my job two months ago.

(LAUGHTER)

I think if I had to say it in a phrase, I would say, to paraphrase the phrase from the Clinton campaign, "It's the president, stupid." I think the national security advisor's principal role, focus, is in assuring that the president is well-served in his decision-making, that his decisions are executed by the government in some kind of coherent way.

It is one of the only jobs I know of that is both a line job and a staff job. You're both a principal, you're both an advisor, but you're also, in a sense, the foreign policy chief of staff. You have to make sure the speech is ready.

But I suspect for most of us, the unique focus is to, in a way that the other Cabinet secretaries can't, look at how the president would be best served in his decision-making, what he needs to know in addition to what he wants to know and how to keep the process moving in a direction that he wants it to move.

BLITZER   Dr. Brzezinski?

BRZEZINSKI   I would agree with what Sandy said, but I would add to it the following: The role of the national security advisor to the president is not defined by the national security advisor to the president; it is defined by the president. That is to say, if you have a president who comes to office intent on making foreign policy himself, in the literal and even kind of on a daily basis, you have a different role than if the president comes to office, let's say, more interested in domestic affairs and more inclined to delegate authority to his principal advisors, in which case the role is also different.

In the first instance, the national security advisor is the inevitable bureaucratic beneficiary of deep presidential involvement. In the second case, the secretary of state, who has a constitutional responsibility, tends to be more important.

And I would say that historically, since President Truman, we have had these two kinds of systems. I call one the presidential, the other one the secretarial. Some have worked well. Some have worked badly. But neither system is superior to the other. Some of each have worked well, and some of each have worked badly.

BLITZER   Frank Carlucci?

CARLUCCI   Well, I would agree with my two colleagues here. Essentially, they're to serve the president, and president's styles vary from president to president. As Zbig said, some want to focus the foreign policy decision-making process in the White House, and others prefer to delegate it, and the national security advisor has to play it by ear.

I think it's important to note that the national security advisor job, while it does have line aspects, Sandy, is essentially a staff job. A lot of Americans get the National Security Council confused with the national security advisor. The national security advisor serves the National Security Council, and he has to serve many masters as he or she does that.

BLITZER   General Goodpaster?

GOODPASTER   In Eisenhower's time, you have to think of this in two parts. He set up a well-structured National Security Council with a planning board at the assistant secretary level which really carried out the preparation that he wanted of carefully thought through plans, long-range plans and policies.

In addition, he had, in my service, not a national security advisor, but a national security assistant. And this was to differentiate, as he wished to do, between policies and long-range plans on the one hand and action decisions on the other. He quoted to us often Von Multke's dictum that, at the time of decision, plans are nothing, but plans are everything. The preparatory work that went into that preparation pays off, because people understand the issues thoroughly but can adapt to the particular circumstances on which decisions are needed.

I would add, just to the euphemisms that you've heard, what we came to call "empirical rule number one" during Eisenhower's presidency, very simple: The president is right.

(LAUGHTER)

BLITZER   Bud McFarlane?

MCFARLANE   The reference to serving the president is foremost, I think, in determining the role of the advisor. The president is a steward of our national interest, and he or she will face different circumstances and, therefore, different limits to what he or she can accomplish. So when President Reagan came to office, the body politic of our country was willing once more, with enough distance from Vietnam, to play a more activist role.

The resources, they were more willing to support congressional enactment of larger appropriations. And the president, to his credit, was able to take that political support and fiscal support and to bring down Marxism in the Soviet Union, to end the Cold War, and to reduce nuclear weapons and so forth. It would not have been possible to do that 10 years beforehand.

The advisor, in short, and the president, are defined in what they can do, in part, by the resources that are available. And these are not something of their own making. But what my colleagues have said about taking those resources and doing as much as you can, as both a staff officer and as an advisor, is what you must figure out.

BLITZER   Professor Rostow?

ROSTOW   Despite the uniformity of our judgment that the president's style determines what the national security advisor does, these are the five elements that I have written down.

The first is, mobilizing of the information. It's not generally realized that the president steps off into the dark with almost every decision. Therefore, the mobilization of this information—because the gap may be between what he ought to know and what he knows—is very moving, and it's the biggest job faced by the national security advisor. And it underlines the difference between responsibility, which goes with the decision-making, black as the future may look, and advice.

Advice is cheap. The president has to live with the consequences of his decisions, whatever the information on which he must act.

Secondly, the national security advisor ought to be able to state the point of view of each member the president consults, with sympathy. He may disagree with it, but if it's ever looked at by a Cabinet member, what is in the summary paper, nothing is more gratifying to a national security advisor than to have him say, "The State Department couldn't have done any better itself."

(LAUGHTER)

Then the national security advisor is called upon to state his own opinion. He may state it temperately, but I remember the first few memos that I forwarded to President Johnson, he gently said, "Never send me one without your own opinion at the end." And I did, but I kept it in language tempered enough so that it was part of the team effort.

Then the national security advisor has an opportunity, which is a very serious one, which is to hold the small team around the president together. This is not always possible. It may be a matter of personality that makes it difficult. But at least he sees and talks with the individual members around the president, he has their point of view, and he can quite often be of some use in being an intermediate between a member of the Security Council in a technical sense.

And then the president decides, surrounded by a small team. And then comes the final act, which is to help in the execution.

And let me tell you that many times in a bureaucracy, the bureaucracy says, "He doesn't mean it," and goes on doing what it's doing. And the president has to say it three times.

(LAUGHTER)

BLITZER   Let me at this point also encourage our panelists to, if they want to comment on each other's remarks or want to add or elaborate or disagree, whatever, please feel free to just signal that you'd like to do so.

But I want to go back to Sandy Berger now, and maybe we'll go down the panel again, but once again, feel free to interrupt each other, if you want.

You spent four years as the national security advisor to President Clinton, a lot of major issues of course were on the agenda. I'm sure there were times when the secretary of state had one strongly held position, the secretary of defense had another strongly held position. You probably agreed with one or the other, but you wanted to give the president all of the options honestly, fairly. Could you do that, though, if you really felt strongly, for example, the secretary of defense was right, the secretary of state was wrong?

BERGER   Well, I think Professor Rostow, what he said probably would be echoed by most of us. I think you have to be perceived by your colleagues as an honest representative of their viewpoint, or the system breaks down. And you would want in any given situation, if the secretary of defense or secretary of state read the memo, that they would feel that their opposition had been stated fairly.

That doesn't mean that you don't express your own view, because I think that's important. In fact, I guess I would say one thing that plays off what Bud McFarlane said, not only the president is right, but I think the national security advisor has to be the one often that says the president's wrong.

I always felt it was my particular obligation and responsibility to give the president the downsides of a particular step he was about to take or to simply state to him, not as my own, but as something—there may be a consensus among his decision-makers, but maybe consensus does not reflect another serious point of view.

BLITZER   Can you give us one specific example when you said to President Clinton, "You're wrong."

(LAUGHTER)

BERGER   Don't you know about executive privilege, Wolf?

(LAUGHTER)

No, I don't think I said, "You're wrong," I think I said, "I disagree," many times. Some of my former colleagues are in this audience and have been there when I've done that.

But I think, you know, your advice obviously is an important input. But I think, to go back to the original question, I think if your colleagues do not believe that you are fairly representing their point of view when they're not there—often they will be there—in the decision-making process, you've failed.

BLITZER   Dr. Brzezinski, you were well-known and still are, of course, as a strategic thinker. As a national security advisor, you had to balance all the other positions, but you obviously came to the table with strongly held views. How did you do that? How did you accurately, fairly, represent the views of various Cabinet members on key international issues while at the same time aggressively putting forward your view?

BRZEZINSKI   Well, I hope not aggressively, I hope persuasively.

I think that one would have to be awfully stupid to misrepresent the views of your colleagues to the president, because you know that if the issue is important, there will be a discussion. The president will go back and discuss it, in your presence or even the absence of your presence, with his principal advisers, be they secretary of state or secretary of defense. And it would very quickly be evident that you distorted their views if you did. So you have to be absolutely precise and use as persuasive as you can the arguments that they have mustered in favor of their position.

But it is true, as it has already been said, that the president usually wants also his national security advisor's opinion. And then you state your own, and you give the reasons for it. And if you do both, then you may have disagreement with your colleagues, but the president then has the options clearly stated. And over time, your colleagues, even if they disagree with you, learn as to how reliable is your transmission of their views.

And I repeat, if the issue is important, it's likely to be discussed. And at some point, the president may pull out the paper and read from it. So you would have to be awfully dumb to distort your colleagues' point of view.

But I think the presidents do want advice. And there is a relationship, a synergistic relationship, between the president and the national security advisor. You wouldn't be in that job, fundamentally, if you didn't get along with the president and if you didn't see him a few times a day. So you do have a relationship.

And while I do agree that the president's always right in public—whenever there's a group, he's right, because the national security advisor is helping him—in private, you have the obligation to tell him that he's wrong. And I did that repeatedly, and the president wanted me to. There was only one time that he finally sent me a little note saying, "Zbig, don't you know when to stop?" when I went back several times, trying to argue that this was not right.

(LAUGHTER)

BLITZER   Even after that note?

BRZEZINSKI   I think I waited a day.

(LAUGHTER)

BLITZER   You want to tell us what that issue was?

BRZEZINSKI   Well, yes, it involved the question of the shah and Iran and the question of what kind of an obligation did we have to admit him to the United States, given the previous relationship that we had.

BLITZER   And your position was?

BRZEZINSKI   That we had an obligation.

BLITZER   You went, Frank Carlucci, from being the national security advisor to becoming the secretary of defense, so you saw that role from within and also outside as a secretary of defense. Did President Reagan always say to you, "Well, Frank, what do you think?" when he got conflicting advice?

FRANK CARLUCCI   He expected me to. He didn't always say it.

But let me tell you a story. When he first asked me to be national security advisor, I was looking for a bit of flattery, like maybe, "You know something about foreign policy; you've had a certain amount of experience." He didn't say that at all, he said, "Frank, I'd like you to be my national security advisor, because you're the only person that George and Cap can agree upon."

(LAUGHTER)

And I had to mediate any number of disputes between George and Cap. Fortunately, I had worked for both of them and knew them both quite well.

But I would go through an exhaustive process to try and get them together, lunch after lunch, reducing their positions if need be to the written word. Then when I thought we had the differences defined, would present both their sides to the president. The president would ask my recommendations, and I'd give them to him, always in the knowledge that either George or Cap could appeal to the president if they so desired. And I made that absolutely clear to them. And it did happen on any number of occasions.

Did I tell the president I thought he was wrong? I can remember Colin Powell, who was my deputy at the time, coming out of one meeting—and I can't remember the subject, Wolf, at this point, so don't ask me—saying, "Frank, you were pretty rough on the president," because I certainly didn't hesitate to tell him that he was wrong.

But that is done, as Zbig said, in private. In public, you support the president.

BLITZER   But you do remember that President Reagan always used to say at the end, "Well, what do you think?"

CARLUCCI   No, he didn't always say that; he expected me to do it. I thought I had an obligation to do it.

BLITZER   What about . . .

BRZEZINSKI   Can I add to that?

BLITZER   Yes, go ahead.

BRZEZINSKI   Just the converse of that. There's one issue that is an example on which I disagreed with the president, but he had a view on it. So at the National Security Council, I supported his point of view, even though he knew that I disagreed with him. But I felt my obligation was to support him.

BERGER   And sometimes, it's even a little more subtle. You know the president's thinking on a particular issue before he's made a formal decision, by virtue of the discussion you've had with him.

And particularly if you think that, you know, he's headed in the right direction, you can try to tee up a decision for him in a way that does not put him in a box. There's sort of a process by which you can try to bring the secretary of defense, the secretary of state and others to what I used to call the highest common denominator. If there was not a consensus at a fairly high level, it was better to bring the president two starkly different points of view. But some of this is a function of trying to clear the underbrush of decisions before they get to the president.

CARLUCCI   Can I add a point there?

BLITZER   Please, go ahead.

CARLUCCI   Towards the end of the Reagan administration, when Colin Powell became national security advisor, to get to your point, when I was secretary of defense, at George Shultz's suggestion, Colin, George Shultz and I met—no substitutes—every morning at seven o'clock in Colin's office, no agenda, no substitutes, just to lay out the day's events and see if we could reach agreement. And invariably, we reached agreement. And a number of decisions that had to go to the president was greatly reduced by that process.

BLITZER   President Eisenhower, General Goodpaster, came at the presidency from his obvious military background. You had a military background as well. Was that kind of role, as a staff assistant to the president, the forum that you adhered to?

GOODPASTER   He put great stress on looking down the road anticipating the problems that might arise and having preparatory work done and done very carefully. That being focused primarily in this structure of the National Security Council.

To quote from him, he said, speaking of a president, he said, "He will always need the vital studies, advice and counsel that only a capable and well-developed staff organization can give him."

Now, many times, things came up that had not been anticipated. And you were likely to receive the ire of Dwight D. Eisenhower if he thought they should have been anticipated. But he wanted these things thought through. He wanted them analyzed. And then, he wanted to deal directly with what he called his principal lieutenants, the secretary of state, the secretary of defense, the chairman of the Joint Chiefs, the director of Central Intelligence, bring them around a table. And if a recommendation had not been worked out and agreed upon, he wanted to hear what each one said.

There was not as much, I think, of conveying the thinking of his lieutenants. On occasion, he would tell us, "Now wait a minute, boys. That's not a staff matter, that's a policy matter. I want the secretary of state in here." And that's what happened.

So we had there the practice, the conviction on his part, that these things needed to be anticipated. They needed to be thought through. They needed to be worked through in the planning board of the National Security Council. And then he wanted to meet eyeball-to-eyeball with his principal associates. They would not always agree.

He required that every policy study have a financial annex. Well, the financial annex meant he wanted to hear from George Humphrey. And what George Humphrey had to say was often not what other senior members of the administration had to say.

But he would hear that out and resolve it and then make his own decision. He made the point, also, "Organization cannot make a genius out of a dunce, neither can it make decisions for its head." But that was the modus operandi that he had: careful preparation and then direct discussion with his principal subordinates.

BLITZER   Bud McFarlane, did you see yourself when you were President Reagan's national security advisor more as the honest broker or as a policy adviser?

MCFARLANE   You can't escape being both. I think your role as a staff person and to present fairly the views of the Cabinet officers is helped by having the opportunity that Andy just described for frequent discussion with the Cabinet officers and the president.

I don't know, I've never tabulated it, but I imagine we had more National Security Council meetings in which the secretary of state and defense and their colleagues could present their own point of view than, say, at Dr. Kissinger's NSC, when NSC meetings were very rarely held at all.

At the end of the day, it's what the president prefers, as to where the center, the locus, of decision-making and discourse ought to be.

I think that the time in which you may find yourself as a counselor or an adviser being more important is when you're trying to take the country in a fundamentally new direction, where you may have concerns or the president may have concerns about a very novel idea being undermined if it is bureaucratized to the point of pre-emptive destruction.

Here, I suppose, I would cite—Henry's not here to defend himself—but the very timely reopening to China, an idea whose time really had come might well have been undermined and criticized. After all, this is a time where China was supplying weapons that were killing Americans in Vietnam. It was a time when, from a human rights point of view, China was going through a cultural revolution, killing literally hundreds of thousands of its own people, in short, a lot of reasons to criticize China from the right or the left had that been put out for popular discussion. And so the national security advisor and the president conceived an idea which I think most would say today has served the national interest well, but it was not heavily bureaucratized.

Similarly, moving away from offensive deterrents and toward strategic defense, Star Wars, here was an idea that President Reagan believed would have been pre-emptively destroyed, or strangled in the crib, as Cap used to say, had it been bureaucratized and open to the criticism of a very well-informed Congress and body politic.

BLITZER   Professor Rostow, how visible should the national security advisor be to the American public?

THE ADVISER AS A PUBLIC ADVOCATE

ROSTOW   I think it's important that he be the president's own property, as it were. But I think it does this group, who's assembled and knows a great deal about these things, a disservice not to dramatize and make clear that a national security advisor can differ markedly on a major issue with the president and still function and still have his confidence.

On the question of Vietnam, I happen to have taken a view different from the general view, which is that we ought to cut the Ho Chi Minh trail thoroughly on the ground and break their supply system. The

president knew I held this view, and I stated it in the presence of the Cabinet and Joint Chiefs on a day in the spring of 1967.

The fact that I took this position, and the fact that it was turned down by President Johnson and Secretary Rusk, didn't for one moment keep me from doing my job or keep the president from knowing that I would continue to hold my view and see him through to the end as his man, if he wanted it.

That was . . .

BLITZER   But once you expressed that view and it was rejected by the president, didn't you, yourself, question your credibility with the president? Wouldn't that be normal?

ROSTOW   Well, that's what I wanted to tell these people, that by that time he knew enough of me, that I knew that he, not I, had made the decision as to the disposition of our forces. He had accepted these terms of engagement, which held our troops inside Vietnam, and we could not cut the Ho Chi Minh trail. And he had very deep feelings—in which, I believe, he was wrong—that, on analogy with the war in Korea, the Chinese might come in, they were nuclear; the Russians might come in, they were nuclear; and he would not subject the United States to a larger war and possibly a nuclear war. That was the nature of the decision.

And he and Rusk were very much affected by the entrance of the Chinese into the Korean War. And as I say, this was a decision which only a president could make. The president should know and my colleagues should know that I took a different view. And that I did take that view. But also he knew that I approved greatly of what he was doing at home and the rest of his foreign policy. And unless he wanted me to take another job, which I would have been delighted to do, but I would stay with him to the end.

Now, that was the element of trust, that's what I'm really dramatizing, that grew up between President Johnson and myself, was very considerable. This was a major issue, and I took one view and he took another. But that didn't affect, really, my ability to do my job. And I was quite ready, of course, to resign.

BLITZER   General Goodpaster?

GOODPASTER   I might add an instance during Eisenhower's time as president. One day, he called me in by punching the buzzer on my desk. And I always knew that was not good news in prospect when that happened. And he said, "We're not doing anything about reducing our forces in Europe. And that's our policy." And he felt committed to try to do that, going all the way back to his time when he took the command there and persuaded our Congress and our government to send four additional U.S. divisions there. He always felt that those should be reduced as soon as possible. And he felt, or he said, that that was our policy.

I said, "Well, Mr. President, it's not quite complete, because in your policy paper, NSC paper, it says that that's to be done when the Europeans are prepared to assume that additional responsibility for their defense."

"No," he said, "our policy is very clear, it's a reduction."

I said, "Well, sir, there is that qualification."

He said, "Foster Dulles is coming over today, and I'm going to have him straighten you out on this."

(LAUGHTER)

I went in with Secretary Dulles. I hadn't said a word to him in advance. The president had this on his mind. He went through this litany. And Foster Dulles, bless his heart, pursed his lips as he always did, blinked his eyes, looked up to the ceiling, and said, "Well, Mr. President, it's not quite as simple as that. We do have this qualification."

He looked at the secretary, and he said, "Foster, I've lost my last friend."

(LAUGHTER)

But that's the way we would try to talk through the issue and, in a way, make sure that, as Eisenhower himself was wont to say, "We didn't make any mistakes in a hurry."

THE NSC STAFF

BLITZER   As far as the organization of the National Security Council—Sandy Berger, why don't we begin with you—some have said it's like, sort of, a mini-State Department, others have said it's a sort of mini-Defense Department, a lot of duplication among staffers at the NSC, what others are doing at the State Department or other agencies of the U.S. government. Was that a problem, the overlap? Or was it something that you could easily deal with?

BERGER   No, I don't think it's overlap. I think that one of the important functions of the National Security Council staff is to coordinate decision-making, particularly at the working level, between the various agencies.

And I suspect as you look over the historical period here, the number of those agencies has grown. The Treasury Department is now more often involved if there's a financial crisis in Asia. The Justice Department may be more often involved if it's a terrorism and law enforcement issue.

And the best the senior director at the National Security Council is able to bring people around a table and run an interagency process in a way that often the State Department or Defense Department could not do.

BLITZER   For example, the senior official at the NSC on the Middle East, let's say. There would be senior officials on the Middle East at the State Department who are doing almost exactly the same thing that your adviser on the Middle East was doing at the NSC.

BERGER   No, I don't think so. I mean, every issue is different. Let's take the Middle East. The Middle East, obviously the senior working-level diplomat was Dennis Ross, just as in Russia it was Strobe Talbott at the State Department. Dennis was our principal negotiator below the secretary, but someone had to do the briefing memo for the president when King Hussein was coming, when he was going into a meeting with Prime Minister Netanyahu or Prime Minister Rabin or Prime Minister Barak.

So I think there was a complementarity and a team that worked very well together.

The Middle East actually is a very good example—Ed Djerejian is quite familiar with it—where there has been a very good blending of tasks between the State Department and the NSC and often the Defense Department.

So it depends very much on the area and the personalities. That is, there will be a particular area where clearly the dominant working-level personality is at the State Department or at the Defense Department and will naturally—the decision-making will cluster around that person. But generally, I don't see what the NSC does as duplicative; I see it as trying to have a coherent decision-making process.

BLITZER   Dr. Brzezinski, was it your experience that there would be rivalries, jealousies, between officials at the NSC and the State Department who were fundamentally working in the same areas?

BRZEZINSKI   Never.

(LAUGHTER)

BERGER   I was at the State Department at a lower level when Dr. Brzezinski was at the National Security Council.

BRZEZINSKI   Let me say this. First of all, you know, everyone thinks that . . .

BLITZER   Very subtle question.

BRZEZINSKI   . . . when they were in charge the system was just great. I mean, let's take that as a given, OK?

It's also a fact that the NSC system has changed over the years. It started with a very small cluster of people. It grew over time, a great deal.

Where I might perhaps differ from Sandy is in defining where NSC coordination should take place. It may be simply a question of terminology, but it may be a little more substantive than that.

Sandy said that the NSC provides coordination at the working level. I would put it differently, and I think it has implications for the size of the staff and what it does. I would say, coordination has to take place at the presidential level. That is to say, when the decisions are of a presidential-level type decisions, then NSC coordination is necessary.

I don't think it should be at the working level, because at the working level, there are a great many decisions which are really not of presidential type. And if you try to make decisions more or less at the desk-officer level, you will end up with a staff on the NSC which, in my view, is too large. It becomes a mini-foreign ministry, and it shouldn't be.

Now, I don't know what the happy medium is. I would suspect it's probably somewhere around, I don't know, 50, 60 or so, given the role the United States plays in the world today.

But I would say, in general, the staff should coordinate only those decisions which really have what might be called a presidential-level character to them.

BERGER   I don't entirely agree with that.

BLITZER   How big was your staff when you were there?

BERGER   Well, in terms of policy people, it was similar, 60, 70 policy people. There were a lot of administrative people and people who run the Situation Room and do other tasks. We're talking here about people who are policy-makers.

Take an example. During the run-up to a period involving Bosnia, our engagement in Bosnia, there were day-to-day decisions that needed to be made, that were not at the presidential level, but were critically important, that are generally made at the assistant secretary level or above, sometimes at the deputy level. And the Deputies Committee has become an extremely important part of the engine of decision-making.

And I think in those issues that are high priority and fast-moving, it is often useful, although I think you can't generalize, for the NSC to be convening the Defense Department, the State Department and others because the institutional tensions between State and Defense often are such that without a third party in the chair, things fall back on bureaucratic instinct.

BLITZER   Picking up on that point—go ahead, General Goodpaster, go ahead.

GOODPASTER   Well, I'd like to add just a bit to that. I worked with President Nixon—President-elect Nixon—while he was organizing his administration for the conduct of foreign policy and security policy.

A very intense and acute disagreement arose involving those of us who had seen the operation in the Eisenhower time, had seen it, especially in the time of President Johnson, as to who should chair the subordinate groups, the ad hoc groups, that are pulled together to deal with some regional set of issues, some functional issue and the like.

And on the one side were those, myself included, who felt that it was absolutely necessary to have those groups chaired by someone at the Security Council level. Otherwise, the issue would be vulnerable to bureaucratic drift pushed by one or the other of the departments which simply was not ready to have the matter decided.

After this argument was thoroughly voiced, President Nixon came down on the side of having the groups chaired in that way. There are those of us who think that when Henry Kissinger took the post, that was perhaps pushed a little more than had been intended to have the energy, the drive, come from the White House.

But for what President Nixon had in mind, which is that he, himself, was going to be very active, directly engaged in the great questions of foreign policy and security policy, a procedure that put the White House representatives in the chair—and they had to be informed representatives who could hold their own in the debates in those groups—that seemed to be absolutely essential.

BLITZER   Is that, Frank Carlucci, always inevitable that there will be a rivalry between the secretary of state, let's say, and the national security advisor to the president?

CARLUCCI   No, I don't think it's inevitable. I think there is a healthy tension between the Department of Defense and the Department of State, which, in many instances, the national security advisor has to mediate.

There was some tension when I came in. You may recall, I came in in the wake of Iran Contra. And George Schultz held a dim view of the National Security Council at that point, and he did not want me to chair meetings. He's got this in his book.

I said, "fine." And I borrowed a leaf from Zbig's book, because I remembered when Zbig was national security advisor, you had deputy secretaries meetings. And I said, "Fine, we'll have a deputy secretary's group, and it'll be chaired by Colin Powell." And that worked very nicely.

Then when the president chaired the meetings, I briefed the president. I kicked off the meetings. The president would say a few words, and then I'd frame the issues for the group. So, George, in his book, ends up saying, "Well, it worked out OK."

So you can find a way to do this. But at least initially in an administration, who chairs the meetings always tends to be a difficult issue.

BLITZER   Bud McFarlane, when you were the national security advisor, there was a lot of that—he raised the issue of the Iran Contra. There was obviously a very active National Security Council team that was involved in Central America, sometimes without the knowledge of the State Department or even the Defense Department. I don't know if that was an aberration, or if that's what had developed over the years leading up to you.

MCFARLANE   Well, it's a very good point. The National Security Council can, and must, restrict its role to staff or advisory and not to operations.

There is one point of disagreement. There was never anything done that the secretary of state and defense were not fully informed about. And that's a matter of public record now.

But it's true that what can happen, and what he security advisor must guard against, is the frustration a president can experience as someone who is there for four years to get something done, to be able to demonstrate leadership in X or Y area, and the frustration of not seeing that the Department of State or others in his administration are apparently moving in that direction.

But that cannot lead the Security Council or the advisor to go beyond the line and take on an operational role. You simply don't have the resources, and you don't have the mandate in law to do that. So that's big mistake.

BLITZER   Is that, Professor Rostow, a mistake for the NSC to get involved operationally in implementing various policy decisions the president might make?

ROSTOW   Before responding to your question, I should introduce from outside this room some testimony which arrived to me as e-mail. This is my wife's diagram out of a book she's using to teach American foreign policy. And what you're listening to is one of the eternal fights of this group. This group very largely takes from the sociological point of view.

This, from George Marshall's move to the State Department to Henry Kissinger's moving back from the White House, all of these moves, up to the present day, when Colin Powell and Donald Rumsfeld and the vice president have moved, are among a group who have wrestled with this problem over the years. And Al Smith wanted this group to be reminded of it, that's why I got this e-mail this morning.

But the point about it is that this is a problem which can be solved, as Frank says, between the secretary of defense and the secretary of state. And my own view and my own experience with Secretary Rusk over the years has been that, with the right characters in place and a mutual deference and mutual trust, it can be solved.

But it is not always solved. I mean, the relations between State and Defense are one thing when Mr. Truman's friend from Missouri was in Department of Defense; quite different when his successor was— what was his name again?—moved over to Defense, who was close to Acheson. And a lot does depend upon the relations between these two parties.

The truth is . . .

GOODPASTER   You're thinking of Louis Johnson and Dean Acheson?

ROSTOW   Yes, Acheson. Then there was, in secretary of defense, there was another man involved who was Acheson's contemporary at Yale.

GOODPASTER   Art Clifford?

ROSTOW   Well, it doesn't matter. The question of personality does matter.

As for the issue involved, my own preference has been to have the State take the role of coordinator as far as possible and leave the National Security Council to concentrate on the issues which the president ought to concern himself with.

The truth about General Eisenhower was that he found the endless meetings of the NSC a great burden to him when he couldn't get out of them exactly what he hoped to get out of them. And as he himself once said to his national security advisor, that he was getting at these meetings what you could get from the *New York Times* if you read it carefully.

(LAUGHTER)

It's very easy to overload the president. He should be able to find the time, like any executive of a big organization, to concentrate on a major issue and not be diverted. And a lot of those issues should be settled beneath him.

And the Eisenhower administration had a very successful committee of undersecretaries. It really saved the president a great deal of work, and it was congenial. We had trouble convincing the successors of the Eisenhower administration that at the undersecretary level, this committee worked well. And the committees that worked well also were headed by strong assistant secretaries, the so-called "aries" worked well.

And we did something at that time which I am very proud of and I had a hand in, which was to reduce the size of the NSC. As you all know from your own experience, the good Lord only produces a certain number of first-rate people.

(LAUGHTER)

And it's much better to have a small, first-rate staff than to load it up with a big bureaucracy. I don't know when that took place. It took place after the Kennedy-Johnson period.

But it's wonderfully clarifying if a man has a responsibility for a certain field and the only person working for him is a secretary. And everyone who works for somebody else takes some of his time, takes some of his energy. And we could have an interdepartment meeting at the NSC level, staff level, very easily by calling three or four people into the room who knew all about the cables which came from Europe and the UN and from Africa and so on, whatever the issue might be.

So I would opt for a small staff. And I would opt for a concentration of effort in the White House on the major issues. And I would opt for putting a great deal of responsibility on the undersecretaries and the assistant secretaries to take the issues off the neck of the president.

TENSIONS BETWEEN THE ADVISOR AND THE SECRETARY OF STATE

BLITZER   Sandy Berger, correct me if I'm wrong, but there were times when the president would want to send you on a diplomatic mission overseas as opposed to someone from the State Department or the Defense Department or someplace else. Was there a time or two when you did that?

BERGER   Very rarely. I mean, I think it is an unusual circumstance when the national security advisor should be the principal negotiator or diplomat.

BLITZER   What were the occasions when you went someplace at the request of the president, as opposed to an assistant secretary of state, or the secretary of state or somebody else?

BERGER   You know, I went to Moscow before a summit between President Clinton and President Yeltsin, at which NMD and the ABM Treaty were to be discussed to try to see whether we could get some closure before the meeting. And because of a configuration authority in the Kremlin, it was appropriate in that circumstance for me to go.

But I think, generally, that the chief diplomat, the chief negotiator, should be the secretary of state. I know that's not always been the case. And there have been some extraordinary initiatives that have been executed by the national security advisor. We talked about Kissinger and China and some of the work that Zbig did in China.

But I think, generally, it is better to have the secretary of state in that role. Otherwise, he or she is often undermined in terms of the credibility that they bring to the important work that they're doing every day.

BLITZER   Isn't that a fact, Dr. Brzezinski, that, especially with foreign leaders who know there is a very active, smart, national security advisor, they'd rather deal—and perhaps there's a weaker secretary of state—they'd rather deal directly with that national security of advisor than the secretary of state?

BRZEZINSKI   Well, sure. But if there is a passive and stupid national security advisor, they'd rather deal with the secretary of state.

(LAUGHTER)

I think it really depends on the circumstances.

In my case, I think, I recall four trips in which I had to play a role. And I think there were reasons in each case. One was China. Sandy alluded to that. The secretary's trip to China didn't work out quite the way the president had hoped. So I was sent to China, and that led to some consequences.

BLITZER   Didn't that undermine the secretary of state, though, once you were sent there?

BRZEZINSKI   It probably did. But it furthered the American-Chinese relationship and furthered what the president wanted, and that's a trade-off.

(LAUGHTER)

Another occasion was the Middle East. And the president wanted me to go to talk to Sadat about an issue that I don't think the secretary of state could have really talked about. And it's the relationship between the prospects for progress and our domestic political scene and the president's own situation.

The third one was INF, when the Soviets posed a challenge in Europe. The Europeans were very alarmed. We had to deploy cruise missiles and Pershings. And we had to negotiate that with the Europeans—rapid deployment of missiles.

And the last one was the Soviet invasion of Afghanistan and the need to organize some sort of response in the region backed by the United States.

BLITZER   And in all four of those cases, the president thought you were the best qualified person as opposed to the secretary of state or somebody else?

BRZEZINSKI   Yes, and in these cases, I agreed with the president.

(LAUGHTER)

(CROSSTALK)

CARLUCCI   At least these cases.

(LAUGHTER)

BRZEZINSKI   Well, to put it in its more defensible light, it can be driven—the decision as to who goes—by what is the perception of the foreign government about the authenticity, the president's commitment to a given decision. That is, especially for authoritarian governments, the Soviet Union, for China. Because they don't put much credence in their own bureaucracy, they assume that they shouldn't attach much to that of the United States. And so, they attach more legitimacy to something that comes from the White House directly.

But George Schultz had a very, I think, sensible understanding of that. And specifically because he wanted it always to be clear that he was speaking for the president, he would usually take me on a trip. And I was in a subordinate role, and I saw it that way. But I saw that I was there as kind of a prop to make it very clear to the Soviet Union and to China that the secretary of state was speaking clearly for the president here.

ROSTOW   The president, from time to time, will choose a special representative to go and engage in a more intimate and a form of dialogue which is recognized as quite authentic in terms of the interests of our country. Normally, in my observation, these have been peo-

ple that have been even nominated to the president, suggested to the president, but it's people in whom the president has special confidence. And that's known at the receiving end and can be very useful.

BERGER   I think there is one other dimension here. And that is that, you know, the secretary of state, when she or he travels, cuts a broader public swath than perhaps the national security advisor. They travel with the press corps from the State Department. They are there in an official capacity. There are certain protocol and ceremonial circumstances that surround it.

And there are times when you want to engage at the highest levels less obtrusively. And the national security advisor can get on a plane with one or two people and fly into Beijing and meet with leadership and fly out, maybe drawing some attention from the local media, but not a lot from the national media here. And that sometimes is useful for trying to make progress on a particularly delicate issue.

BLITZER   Did you want to say something, Bud McFarlane?

MCFARLANE   Well, if you'll indulge a moment of humor that's related to this. In December of '84, President Reagan was promoting a concept, the Star Wars concept, as kind of the centerpiece of a larger policy for engaging the Soviet Union. And Prime Minister Thatcher was being critical, and persuasively critical. And it was undermining the president's case here in the Congress and elsewhere.

And she came to Camp David in December of '84. And in the privacy of that setting said, "Now look here, Ron, this is expensive. It's technologically risky. It is presenting the appearance that you are trying to achieve a first strike capability. It's going to de-couple you from Europe." A very, very penetrating analysis which had some merit to it.

And the president was chagrined. We papered over it in the press conference. But afterward he said, "Bud, would you go to London please and try to talk to the prime minister and at least ask her to be a little bit more subdued." And so I went to London the following month.

And about two paragraphs into the talking points, I could see I was getting nowhere. And before going, Cap Weinberger, to his credit, had said, "Bud, you know there is going to be a need to subcontract a lot of this work, and the UK ought to get some of that."

And well, I could see I was getting nowhere. And the prime minister paused for a moment. And I said,

"Prime Minister, the president believes that up to $300 million, on occasions, ought to be subcontracted to British firms." Long pause.

(LAUGHTER)

And a couple of weeks later—I've forgotten the circumstance—but the president and she met again. And she took me aside and she said, "You know, there may be something to this after all."

BLITZER Professor Rostow, years ago I wrote a book on U.S.-Israeli relations. And I remember the chapter on the Six Day War in 1967. You were intimately involved. Dean Rusk was the secretary of state. And President Johnson had to make some major decisions, obviously, during that war.

And I remember a lot of the Israelis I interviewed during my research saying that they would often find it a lot better from their standpoint to go to the NSC, meaning you and your aides, who they felt had a direct pipeline to President Johnson, than to work through the State Department and Dean Rusk where they found that there was a lot of resistance to what they wanted. Do you remember those days? I'm sure you probably do.

ROSTOW I don't remember them in those terms.

(LAUGHTER)

The president had very strong views and he was on top of that from morning until night, quite literally. And nothing engaged him more personally, I should think, than the Arab-Israeli war because it had rather ominous Soviet connections, especially with Syria.

And so the view of the diplomats from Israel about the relative advantage of working through State or through the White House, referred really to the extent to which the president of the United States was desk officer for that war. And very quickly, you got a decision from him, which was a personal decision.

BLITZER Did you, Frank Carlucci, did you find that that was the case when you were at the NSC as well?

CARLUCCI I don't think there's any doubt that people want to get as close to the president's office as they can. When Hans-Dietrich Genscher was foreign minister of Germany, he was always in our office. He was in Howard Baker's office. He was in my office. He insisted on seeing Ronald Reagan every time he came into town. He was all over the place.

You know, the standard joke, they had an airplane crash over the Atlantic and Genscher met Genscher because he traveled so much.

(LAUGHTER)

And it's very hard for a national security advisor to say, "No, I'm not going to receive the prime minister," of whatever it might be. So you have to just keep tapping it down and handle it skillfully and, above all, keep the secretary of state informed.

BLITZER Dr. Brzezinski, when you were the NSC advisor, a lot of us remember, who covered you, some of the tensions that existed with the secretary of state. Were those overblown, or were those real?

BRZEZINSKI Well, quite honestly, they were overblown, and I'm serious.

(LAUGHTER)

And that is to say, on many issues, we agreed. We disagreed basically just on one issue, fundamentally. And that was how to handle the Soviet Union, how to combine deterrent and cooperation with competition and potential conflict.

But on the Middle East, we agreed. We agreed on China. We agreed on a lot of issues. But once the press determines there is a conflict between two principals, you can't do anything about it. I'll give you an account which pertains to one of your colleagues.

There was a day when the secretary of state and I were supposed to make speeches in the same place, on the same subject, that is U.S.-Chinese relations. And Vance and I sat down and decided how to do it. And we had two speeches drafted. His assistant, Holbrooke, and my assistant, Oxenberg, worked together drafting the two speeches. Then we reread them to make sure they're consistent.

And then at the last minute, I forget whether it was me or Vance, one of us said to the other, "You know, actually, it would be better if you give this speech and I give that speech, because one stresses more the domestic security aspect, the other one is a little more foreign policy. So I'll take this speech and you give that speech." So we both gave those speeches, changing who read which manuscript first.

Next day, the *New York Times* diplomatic correspondent has a front page story says "Vance and Brzezinski disagree again on China."

And then once that mindset is created in the press, nothing can stop it. And I'm sure right now, Rumsfeld and Powell are pretty much condemned to that scenario.

BERGER There's also, Wolf, I think, an institutional dynamic that tries to—that maximizes the potential for conflict . . .

BRZEZINSKI   Oh, yes.

BERGER   . . . because there is really two layers of spin before you get a conflict here. First, you've got something reported in the press. In the morning you read that—the secretary of state reads that—officials at the White House said "da ta da ta da," which maybe is disparaging of the State Department's point of view or vice versa. So that's layer number one.

That gets delivered to the secretary or to the national security advisor by his or her press person, who tends to see their role rather protectively in terms of their principal. That's layer number two.

And by the time you've got the story to the national security advisor and the secretary, it sounds like thermo-nuclear war.

And one of the rules that Secretary Albright and I worked out under these circumstances was never to believe anything that we read about each other in the newspaper or that are said about each other by people who work for us without picking up the phone and talking to each other. And we defused more incipient conflicts by doing that than I can tell you.

BLITZER   Is it wise, General Goodpaster, for the national security advisor from time to time to be, in effect, the principal foreign policy spokesperson for the president?

GOODPASTER   Well, times have changed so drastically since Eisenhower's time that I don't know that his example would have much relevance today. And he himself recognized there will be differences, personal differences, in the characters of the successive presidents.

But his conviction was that the secretary of state should have a major role as the spokesperson for foreign policy. He stayed in very close touch with Eisenhower directly on this. But that system worked out very well.

And whereas Jim Hagerty, who was Eisenhower's press secretary, played a very major role, he really stayed out of foreign policy and security policy to a large extent. So when you heard these issues discussed, they would be discussed in an authoritative way by the secretary of state, or by Eisenhower himself, who felt that he had an obligation on the major issues to take a public stance.

I don't think that can be done today. But to the extent that as much as possible can be pushed out of the White House, I think that the Executive Branch performance will benefit from that.

BLITZER   Frank Carlucci, do you want to . . .

CARLUCCI   Yes. In my judgment, the national security advisor should not be out front, but should be part of a coordinated public relations strategy. I thought the administration last Sunday worked it very well, where you had Colin Powell on there as the principal spokesman. You had Dick Cheney commenting, and you had Condi Rice on, I think, your show.

BLITZER   That's right.

CARLUCCI   And they all were saying the same thing, and that's reassuring.

BLITZER   But invisible was Donald Rumsfeld, the secretary of defense.

CARLUCCI   Well, that's appropriate. It's part of the strategy.

BLITZER   What was the strategy?

CARLUCCI   The strategy was to make sure this was handled in diplomatic channels, not military channels. And that message came through loud and clear. I thought it was very well handled.

BERGER   I agree with Frank on that. I think that it is important for the secretary of state to be the definitive and principal spokesperson below the president.

But one of the things, if you look at the trajectory of time represented on this panel, the media playing field has gotten much larger. And you need a lot of players on the field very often.

There was no CNN when most of these gentlemen served as national security advisor. And the world was, of course, much worse for it, Wolf.

(LAUGHTER)

But now, in both the pace of media scrutiny, the pace of the news cycle is now almost continuous, and the breadth of the media tends to pull the national security advisor out more as part of a team of people who goes out, but always with the secretary of state at the lead.

BLITZER   That's a point, Dr. Brzezinski, that's well made, because there is such an appetite out there now in television. There's all the cable channels and five Sunday morning shows that the White House somehow has to service. You can't just expect the secretary of state to appear on five shows if there's a major foreign policy issue that week.

BRZEZINSKI   Well, that's already been said, and I completely agree with that.

I would merely add the following: Precisely because of these pressures, these competitive pressures, the skills, the communicative skills of a secretary of state have become very different.

Let's say in the '50s, the secretary of state primarily made speeches, formal speeches. Or he would write a ghost-written article for the foreign affairs magazine, and it would be kind of authoritative.

Now, you not only are pulled in many different directions, but you have to be quick on the uptake. You have to be, to some extent, photogenic. You have to be able to communicate in—what are they called, those . . .

BLITZER   Sound bites.

BRZEZINSKI   . . . sound bites.

BLITZER   Something I'm familiar with.

(LAUGHTER)

BRZEZINSKI   These are skills which a secretary of state has to have. And some of them in recent years have had them, currently have them as well. Some in recent years didn't have them quite to the same degree.

So a president and his people have to sort of say, "Well, who else on the team can help here?"

And I think the present administration is doing very well. And I think the previous one did, too, in kind of covering the front and more or less blanketing the programs on Sunday, for example, with leading spokesmen.

GOODPASTER   I would just add . . .

BLITZER   General, you didn't have to worry about CNN in your day.

GOODPASTER   That's right. When I came into the White House as a staff officer and asked for advice on what I should do, it was very brief. It said, do your job the best you know how and stay out of the newspapers. And that was very welcome advice.

Well, the appetite is voracious today, and it will not be denied. And all of this has to be reconstructed to conform to that, in my opinion.

BLITZER   Bud McFarlane, that was a factor when you were the NSC advisor, but certainly not the way it is right now.

MCFARLANE   Well, I guess I'd make a different point. And that is, in my judgment, the Vietnam War is kind of—one of the many lessons learned ought to be that no administration can carry its policy if it can't define

for the American people, what are our interests and how are they engaged and what is our strategy for winning it?

And I think that it was largely the inability to do that—it does go to your point and the question in the sense that, as Frank said, the secretary of state has to be the person who is the spokesperson. But that is buttressed by a strategy that uses the resources you have, because it is, in our Constitution, an obligation to explain what it is you're trying to do. And it takes a lot of resources to do that, as Sandy said.

BLITZER   Let me go around the panel, because we're getting close to taking a break.

But I'm just curious, the national security advisor to the president does not have to be confirmed by the U.S. Senate as opposed to all the members of a Cabinet, senior officials in the Executive Branch. Is that useful nowadays? The downside, of course, is that the national security advisor almost usually is not a member of the Cabinet.

ROSTOW   That's a blessing, judging from the Cabinet meetings that I've attended. I'm sorry to be so flat in my statement, but that's the truth.

If you sit and look at the Cabinet closely and see the number of people along the wall: First, there are very few issues on which all the members of the Cabinet should be present. It is simply not their business to worry about national security items. Just as issues that are very important to the secretary of transport should not engage the secretary of state or the secretary of defense.

Besides, the Cabinet meetings leak. Any meeting in Washington with that many people present will leak. And that is the reason why a great deal of the business with the president is discussed with two or three Cabinet members present.

BLITZER   President Kennedy used to have a lot of formal Cabinet meetings.

ROSTOW   Well, I don't know. I don't recall, it because I was not directly responsible.

I was directly responsible for the national security meetings. And I finally worked out the sort of national security issue which could usefully engage the whole Cabinet. And they were not issues generally in which the president would make a decision. To get where domestic and foreign policy considerations had to be woven with financial considerations, it was a chance to get the issue formulated and then special studies allocated to different departments.

This was a very specific procedure that was worked out. And one of the meetings I remember very well was one in which a decision was made that we better open up quickly some new areas for grain production. The world situation demanded that.

There were also very useful meetings which involved a great many people before the meetings of the UN, which were occasions for a lot of bilateral. There were also occasions in which the ambassador came home to say country X was having a visit to Washington. And the prime minister was interested in getting A, B and C accomplished from his point of view. "Good," said the president. "Now let me tell you what I'm interested in. Now go away and produce a paper on that."

There were a set of meetings which were worthy of bringing together the whole Cabinet and bringing together a president's instruction for the next operational decisions.

BRZEZINSKI   Can I comment on this for a second?

BLITZER   Go ahead, because you're satisfied with the way the structure was done?

BRZEZINSKI   Well, I want to make a distinction, which I don't think was made here which needs to be made. One should not confuse Cabinet status with Senate confirmation. They're not the same thing.

BLITZER   Right.

BRZEZINSKI   Now in my case, I didn't have Senate confirmation, but I had Cabinet status. But it was totally irrelevant. You know, I had to attend the Cabinet meetings. And I think the only difference between me with Cabinet status as a national security advisor and my colleagues who weren't is that I sat at the table instead of sitting against the wall. But most Cabinet meetings are routine, nonsignificant events, especially when it comes to foreign policy.

(LAUGHTER)

Now confirmation is a different issue. Now the national security adviser could be confirmed. And there have been ideas to that effect, just as the head of the Bureau of the Budget is confirmed. I personally preferred that it not be so, because if you get confirmed you also have to testify a lot, you have to go down to the Hill a lot.

The schedule demands on you are so enormous already that that would be an additional burden and would greatly complicate the issue we talked about earlier, namely, who speaks for foreign policy in the government besides the president? And it should be

the secretary of state. And if you are confirmed, that would become fuzzed and confused.

BLITZER   You were a member of the Cabinet. But, Sandy Berger, you were not a member of the Cabinet.

BERGER   Well, I sat at the table. I don't know if I was a member of the Cabinet or not.

BRZEZINSKI   You were a semi-member.

BERGER   No one ever told me whether I was or not.

(LAUGHTER)

I just, I guess, took the chair there.

But I think the point that Zbig just made is a key point here. With confirmation comes an almost legal obligation of accountability to the Congress. The secretary of state, secretary of defense spend enormous amounts of time on the Hill.

The secretary of state, secretary of defense may have to testify six or eight times on the budget of their agency. And each of those testimonies, of course, is an occasion to answer the question of every member of the House Foreign Affairs Committee or the Senate Foreign Relations Committee, which may or may not be related to the budget.

I actually think that this has become too burdensome on the secretary of state, secretary of defense. But perhaps a third of their time is engaged in this.

And so the one benefit of not having confirmation is that you can say no to a congressional committee. In fact, most presidents have taken the view that under executive privilege that the their national security advisor, just like their chief of staff, can't be compelled to go up on the Hill.

GOODPASTER   I'd like to reinforce that. Going back, particularly to the Eisenhower time when he really established in modern years the idea of executive privilege and the idea of confidential advice that the president is entitled to receive that need not be reported in any other place.

Now, so long as it's advice, that works, and there is no confirmation. There is a risk any—moving over into the area of operations, then under the Constitution there is an obligation to report, and a necessity, I think, would come from that for a confirmation.

So if that line between advice and operations can be held, it can be greatly to the advantage of the needs of the president.

BLITZER   Let's take Bud McFarlane and Frank Carlucci, then we're going to take a break.

But correct me if I'm wrong, Mr. McFarlane, you were a member of the Cabinet, right?

MCFARLANE Well, it's a little bit like what Sandy said. Yes, I was at the table, I've got a chair in my office now and so forth. But the Cabinet secretary said I was but, I think I agree what my colleagues have said here. And yet I believe that there has got to be a congressional relations strategy from the White House as there is a public affairs strategy.

And while it relies on your liaison people that are chosen for that job, the—let me take Star Wars. This was something on which the Congress—and Lee Hamilton would remember this—had quite a number of legitimate critics and well-informed people, Sam Nunn, Les Aspin, thoughtful, analytical minds. And so I was spending, certainly, a fourth of my time in meetings with congressional leaders and simply explaining what the president intended here. And I think that that is something that has to continue.

And it never got to the point where they tried to subpoena, because it wasn't necessary. You have to have a working dialogue with members of Congress.

BLITZER Frank Carlucci, we're going to take a break right after, you know, you're final—you've got the last word in this segment.

But you spent a lot more time meeting with members of Congress when you were defense secretary than when you were the national security advisor.

CARLUCCI I was up there forever.

(LAUGHTER)

And there are days when you—weeks when you testified practically every day, morning and afternoon. So I feel even more strongly than my colleagues that if you make the national security advisor subject to Senate confirmation, you're going to degrade the process significantly. The president will have a very difficult time implementing a coherent foreign policy. I think the president would simply name another staff person to do what the national security advisor does and let this confirmed official run around on the Hill.

And I think it would impede the ability to give confidential advice to the president, so I would strongly recommend against it.

BLITZER All right. . . .

I'm going to say good-bye.

I want to thank all of you for coming. . . .

15

THE NSC ADVISOR

Process Manager and More

Colin L. Powell

Having served as national security adviser to President Ronald Reagan, General Colin L. Powell reflects on his experiences and emphasizes the wide variety of roles that the adviser is expected to play in the White House—including crisis management.

The history of the National Security Council and the national security advisor is the story of a wide range of personalities playing a wide variety of roles. This observation illustrates the essential truth that the national security advisor and the NSC system exist to help the president manage foreign policy in the manner that the president desires and in the manner that the president instructs.

ENTER CARLUCCI

As National Security Advisor Frank Carlucci's deputy, I arrived with him at the NSC in January 1987, under circumstances that focused keen attention on the proper role and mission of the NSC advisor and the role and mission of his staff. Shortly after taking over, we had the benefit of the Tower Commission's work, to which my successor Brent Scowcroft contributed so importantly. Frank Carlucci and I also brought our own sense of the job from prior experience in the government.

Frank Carlucci was one of the most experienced professionals to assume the role of the national security advisor. He was a career ambassador who had been deputy director of the CIA, deputy secretary of defense, and deputy director of the Office of Management and Budget. He was a man of maturity and sound

professional judgment. I felt myself privileged to be his deputy. What I brought to the team was experience at OMB, the Department of Defense and, of all places, the Department of Energy.

TWO MODELS OF OPERATION

The general wisdom is that there are two models that apply to the role of the NSC advisor and the operation of the National Security Council staff. Zbigniew Brzezinski describes them as the presidential model and the secretarial model. The presidential model holds that the NSC advisor is a powerful person working with a president who has decided to drive the day-to-day foreign policy of the United States directly from the White House. For that reason he needs a national security advisor with sufficient stature and bureaucratic skill to help him perform that role from the White House. In this model the State Department and other agencies play a distinctly secondary role.

In the secretarial model, the secretary of state is the major foreign policy driver in the administration. Foreign policy remains the responsibility of the president. But in this model he allows the secretary of state and, in turn, the bureaucracy of the State Department to be the principal actors in formulating and executing foreign policy. The president always retains responsibility

Reprinted from "The NSC Advisor: Process Manager and More," *The Bureaucrat* 18 (Summer 1989): 45–47.

When he wrote this piece, Colin L. Powell was General and Commander, U.S. Forces Command, Ft. McPherson, Georgia, and had served as national security adviser to President Ronald Reagan. He went on to serve as secretary of state in the second Bush Administration.

to set strategic direction and to approve the actions of the secretary of state.

When Frank Carlucci and I took over, we found no law which spelled out the duties of the position. There was no job description, there was no directive, and there was no specific guidance from the president. The best we had, which was very good indeed, was the model subsequently recommended by the Tower Commission.

Frank Carlucci and I did not spend a lot of time reflecting on the various models. We were tossed into a difficult situation at a difficult time. The model we adopted, which seems to have worked rather well, was something of a combination between the two extremes. The national security advisor, first and foremost, had to be the manager of the process. It was his job to make sure that the bureaucracy functioned well and the trains ran on time. At the same time he had to be a powerful figure in his own right not only to make that happen, but to use that same power to provide advice to the president on foreign policy issues even when that advice was contrary to that of the secretary of state or other cabinet officials.

FIRST AND LAST

The first mission of the national security advisor is to serve the president, to serve the president, to serve the president. The president alone has the responsibility for deciding the foreign policy of the United States in the name of the American people. The national security advisor must serve the president in that role as must every other official in the national security system.

Beyond that, the national security advisor, as the director of the National Security Council staff, must also serve the other statutory members of the National Security Council, namely the vice president, the secretary of state, and the secretary of defense. In addition to these statutory members, there are a large number of statutory advisors and other cabinet officials who have business before the National Security Council and, therefore, must be served by the NSC staff as well. These include the chairman of the Joint Chiefs of Staff, the director of Central Intelligence, the director of the Arms Control and Disarmament Agency, the director

of the United States Information Agency, and, outside the statutory and cabinet realms, just about anyone else with access to a White House telephone number.

A BUREAUCRAT FIRST CLASS

It can be seen then, that the national security advisor wears two hats. In his first hat, he is a bureaucrat first class. He drives a staff that must be totally dedicated to the process and that must serve all members of the NSC and the others mentioned above. In his other hat the national security advisor is an assistant to the president, accountable and answerable to him and to him only.

I believe that the national security advisor and the National Security Council staff must also act to enhance the role, prestige, power, and influence of the members of the National Security Council and, particularly, that of the secretary of state and the secretary of defense. It is in the best interest of the United States for the secretary of state and the secretary of defense to be seen as the principal players in the execution of the president's foreign policy. These are the two cabinet officers who are appointed by the president and confirmed by the Senate to represent the United States government and oversee the president's national security program. It is in the best interest of the foreign policy of the United States for the world to see a secretary of state and a secretary of defense who are solidly supported by the entire Washington bureaucracy; who are armed with coherent, consistent, well-supported positions.

FULL, OBJECTIVE, COHERENT, AND BALANCED

The NSC exists not to conflict with or work at cross purposes with the two cabinet officials who are charged by the president and by law and by the American people with implementing the president's foreign policy. The NSC advisor and the NSC staff must always be working to make these two officials look good. In his process role the national security advisor must insure that the president gets full, objective, coherent, and balanced recommendations on issues he must decide. The national security advisor cannot allow end runs. He cannot allow unpleasant information to be shunted aside. He cannot allow minority views to be ignored because they do not reflect the consensus view. He cannot allow the decision process to ill-serve the president by keeping from him minority perspectives. The NSC advisor must always ensure that the president gets the full range of objective and subjective information to make his decision. The process must not be allowed to produce papers that reflect a common denominator or that suffer from an absence of tone and tint or the emotional flavor of an issue. The national security advisor must make sure that the president hears the strongest views as well as the weakest views.

The national security advisor must also make sure that the Washington bureaucracy executes the president's decisions in the spirit that he intended. The NSC advisor must be seen as the ever vigilant truant officer of the Washington schoolhouse. The national security advisor must also force decisions. He must not allow the bureaucracy to sit and spin its wheels and fail to move issues forward for decision. A process must exist which focuses issues, assembles relative information, resolves issues, and pushes forward for decision by the president those issues on which agreement cannot be reached.

Crisis Management

Another role of the national security advisor is as crisis manager for the national security interagency process. When something happens in the world—a military action in the Persian Gulf, a crisis in a foreign land, any kind of a crisis that is going to be a major international event—there is only one place that crisis can be managed from, and that is the West Wing of the White House, and it immediately flows into the National Security Council staff and the national security advisor. It can't be managed at the State Department, it can't be managed at Defense, it can't be managed anywhere else for the simple reason that each one of those departments has a separate and distinct role to play and that role has to be coordinated with the West Wing staff, and the NSC advisor is the person who has that responsibility.

The national security advisor must also try to find time to do some strategic thinking, some conceptualiz-

ing of where our international relations should be going. He should have some responsibility for long-range studies and plans and never forget that the principal mission is to serve the president.

If the advisor is doing his job correctly as the process manager and, much more, as an advisor to the president, someone is usually unhappy with him at the end of every day. Every day it may be a different person, but nevertheless, there is no escaping that the exercise of his authority will cause someone to be unhappy. And so it is not a job for anybody with a thin skin or who is not willing to suffer the slings and arrows of outrageous bureaucratic fortune in Washington.

Derived Authority

Where does the national security advisor get the authority to run the process? The authority derives first from the president, from the advisor's position in the West Wing, from his proximity to the president, from his access to the president, and from the confidence that exists between him and the president.

He also derives authority by doing the job competently. If he is seen to be running a competent operation, a fair operation, an honest operation, an operation that stands the test of time, then that, in and of itself, confers authority on the process and on the advisor.

The advisor also derives authority from the cabinet departments. To the extent that the secretaries of state and defense and other senior officers allow his decisions to stand with their departments without going to the president, they confer a level of authority on the national security advisor, the kind of authority that can only be obtained through a high level of trust and confidence among the players. That I submit is the situation that existed in the last two years of the Reagan administration.

The final source of authority is one all public administrators are familiar with—the kind of authority that is captured in the expression, "you never know what you can get away with until you try." You never know what kind of authority you have until you let the White House operator make telephone calls for you. And one of the great treats of being an official in the West Wing is being able to get the White House operator to place calls. Wonderful things happen when the White House is calling.

The Multi-processor

The national security advisor is also a major coordinator of congressional activity and a major spokesman to the Congress, although he is never required to testify before the Congress.

Of course, there's also the direct support of the president on a day-to-day basis in getting him ready for foreign visitors and for foreign trips, such as the Moscow Summit.

As I said earlier, the national security advisor is first and foremost a process manager—a coordinator of the process, an honest broker, and a tiebreaker.

The Tower Commission recommended that the national security advisor keep a relatively low profile. It's the secretary of state who has the responsibility to be the principal spokesman on foreign policy. But at the same time, there will be occasions where the national security advisor needs to speak out to give a very distinct White House perspective. In time of crisis or when there is a very contentious issue, the public wants to hear from the White House, and that has to be either the president himself, a spokesman, or the national security advisor. This is a very legitimate but limited role for the advisor.

However sound the process might be, the national security advisor owes the president his own direct, personal advice on any issue that is before him if he believes that the advice coming in from the principal cabinet officers does not adequately present to the president the pictures he needs to see before making a decision.

The System Is Working

Now, performing this intimate advisory role, while at the same time managing an interagency process which comprises the team objectives, is a tough job. But we can be encouraged by the fact that men like Brent Scowcroft are around and are willing to perform such jobs; our country can be grateful for a Brent Scowcroft and I'm looking forward to watching the contribution that he is going to make. And you can be sure that President Bush will put his own imprint on the NSC and on the NSC system and the interagency process. That is as it should be.

I believe right now we have a good NSC system. It's a system that is working. It ensures an efficient process and ensures that the national security advisor has sufficient authority and access to the president to act as an advisor in a way that serves the president's interests as well as the interests of the American people.

16

The Lessons of the Iran–Contra Affair for National Security Policy Making

Cecil V. Crabb, Jr.
Kevin V. Mulcahy

The authors present a useful classification of roles played by national security advisers: administrator, coordinator, counselor, agent, and, lastly, an extreme form of the agent role: the insurgent.

Events in the last two years of the Reagan administration associated with the Iran-Contra affair dramatized certain problems in the making of national security policy. In particular, the roles of the assistant for national security affairs (ANSA) and the National Security Council staff in the policy-making process have come under close scrutiny. For all the importance of the ANSA and his staff in the conduct of American foreign affairs, the nature of this position and the patterns of presidential management of the policy-making process have received comparatively little attention. For example, how might the president, the secretaries of state and defense, the director of central intelligence, and the assistant for national security affairs structure their institutional relations? What is the appropriate mechanism for managing the policy-making process?

The Iran-Contra hearings suggested a number of lessons to be learned about the conduct of national security affairs. These lessons involved the responsibilities of the president as chief diplomat and commander in chief vis-à-vis the rights of Congress to collaborate in foreign relations, and the claiming of a privileged status with regard to national security concerns in contrast to the expectation that international covenants will be openly arrived at and politically

reviewed. The lessons that concern us are admittedly more limited in scope. Specifically, we focus on the peculiar nature of the NSC as a decision-making body, examine the unique position of the president in the management of national security, and analyze in detail the roles that assistants for national security affairs have come to play in the policy-making process.

The National Security Advisory System: A Typology

The administrative history of the Office of the Assistant for National Security since 1947 suggests the elements of a typology, admittedly one of several that might be constructed, that is useful in better understanding the general problem of policy making with regard to national security. We have used certain designations— administrator, coordinator, counselor, agent—to describe different roles that past national security assistants have played and that constitute a repertory available to future assistants. Of course, the particular role to be played by an ANSA is always a presidential prerogative. The Iran-Contra affair also suggests an aberrant role—the ANSA as insurgent—that serves as a warning as to what can happen when a national security policy-making system gets out of control.

Reprinted from *American National Security: A Presidential Perspective* (Pacific Grove, California: Brooks/Cole, 1991), 175–92.

Professors Cecil V. Crabb, Jr., and Kevin V. Mulcahy teach political science at Louisiana State University in Baton Rouge.

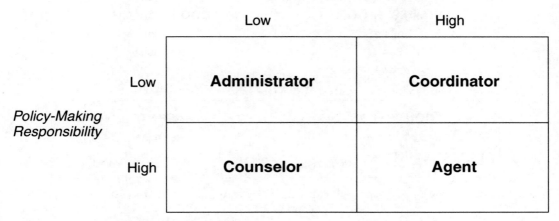

Figure 16.1 A typology of national security assistants' roles

It cannot be emphasized too strongly that the particular role that an ANSA will play is strictly determined by presidential preference. How the assistant for national security affairs is to be cast depends ultimately on what role the president has cast for him- or herself in the management of American foreign affairs. Similarly, an assistant's success will depend on his or her adapting to whatever role best suits the president's managerial preferences. The importance of the president's approach to managing the policy-making process and of clearly defining the role of the national security adviser will become abundantly clear in the course of our discussion.

In Figure 16.1 we present a typology of the roles that national security assistants have played since the late 1940s, classifying them according to their patterns of responsibility. Before elaborating on the patterns represented, two limitations on the usefulness of such a typology should be noted. First, all such summary representations involve some oversimplification. Thus, our identification of a specific assistant with a single role might be more accurately understood as indicative of that assistant's dominant role.

Second, the variables associated with the typology—responsibility for policy making and responsibility for implementation of policy—are very broad measures selected from among the many that might be applied in defining the ANSA's role. Nonetheless, a formal construct such as our typology can call attention to certain identifiable patterns by which ANSAs have performed their duties, patterns that should remain management options. Furthermore, identifying these roles helps to clarify the consequences of each for the policy-making process.

In Figure 16.2, we have categorized the sixteen national security advisers who have served between 1947 and 1988 according to our typology of roles.

We believe that our classifications generally accord with the historical record. The ideal types come quickly to mind: Souers as administrator, Cutler as coordinator, Bundy as counselor, Kissinger as agent. Understandably, however, there may be differences over the classification of particular ANSAs. Accordingly, we have used the placement of the ANSAs within the matrix to suggest ambiguities. For example, Brzezinski was a counselor who aspired to be an agent,

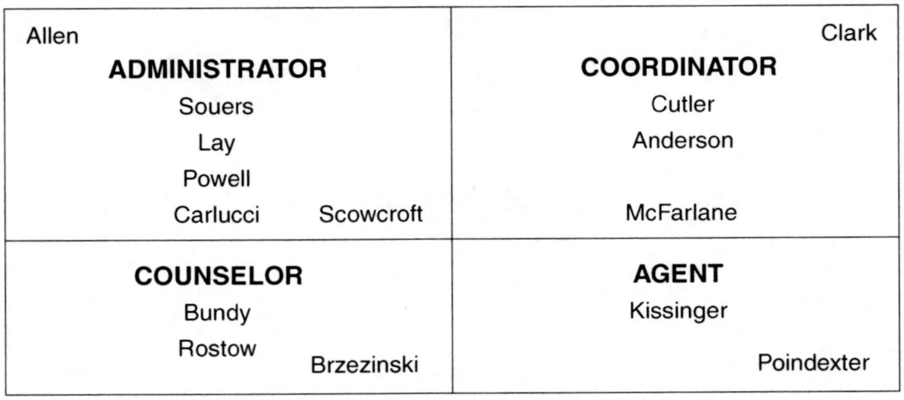

Allen   Clark
ADMINISTRATOR   **COORDINATOR**

Allen	Clark
ADMINISTRATOR	**COORDINATOR**
Souers	Cutler
Lay	Anderson
Powell	
Carlucci Scowcroft	McFarlane
COUNSELOR	**AGENT**
Bundy	Kissinger
Rostow	
Brzezinski	Poindexter

Figure 16.2 National security assistants and their roles in the policy-making process, 1947–1988

but he never acquired Kissinger's mastery over the policy-making process. Allen and Clark were weak representatives of their respective roles. Poindexter is classified as an agent, but he might be better placed outside the typology. We will discuss this deviant case of the ANSA as insurgent in greater detail after the following elaboration of our typology of roles.

THE ROLES PLAYED BY NATIONAL SECURITY ASSISTANTS

The national security adviser as administrator has a low level of responsibility with regard to both implementation and policy making. Such an ANSA is essentially a servant of the NSC as a presidential institution, rather than a personal and political aide. The duties of this type of ANSA include briefing the president on the international situation, representing departmental proposals and viewpoints, scheduling matters for presidential decisions, and monitoring NSC directives. The role of administrator emphasizes the day-to-day business of the foreign policy-making process[1] and represents a pattern of management that radically curtails the stature of the ANSA and his staff. In this model, neither the preeminence of the State Department nor the position of the secretary of state as the "orchestra leader" and "first among equals" in national security policy making[2] is threatened.

The quintessential example of an ANSA who played the role of an administrator was Admiral Sidney W. Souers, President Truman's executive secretary of the NSC. Souers, a model of political rectitude and administrative restraint, was extremely sensitive, even deferential, with regard to the position of the State Department. He must have perceived President Truman's high personal regard for his secretaries of state and defense and realized that Truman preferred the "classical model" of State Department dominance of foreign affairs.[3]

Souers's custodial role over the NSC advisory process was almost as highly circumscribed as his political role, which precluded attending White House staff meetings, despite efforts by some Truman aides to augment his political responsibilities. "The security assistant had little authority, staff capability or (often) desire to monitor the bureaucracy's implementation of the president's decisions; and his ability to coordinate defense and foreign policy was also constrained."[4] Essentially, Souers saw his role as that of a nonpolitical presidential official responsible for facilitating the NSC's advisory function.[5]

Another ANSA who falls into the category of administrator is General Brent Scowcroft under President Gerald Ford. General Scowcroft's operating style under President Bush will be discussed in the concluding section. It should be noted here, regardless, that

THE LESSONS OF THE IRAN

Scowcroft's operating style under Ford was completely opposite to that of the preceding ANSA, Henry Kissinger. Scowcroft, who had served as Kissinger's deputy, saw his position as requiring a more self-effacing style, giving priority to organization and the faithful presentation of the views of NSC members. He did not act independently or negotiate for the president but functioned instead as a senior administrative aide and staff assistant. The qualities attributed to Scowcroft—"cool, hardworking, straightforward, a good administrator"—were precisely the qualities that appealed to Ford.[6]Scowcroft never appeared on a national interview show, and his name was rarely mentioned in the press.[7] Despite a more limited role as ANSA when compared to that of Kissinger, Scowcroft has often been singled out as the ideal type for the ANSA position.[8]

President Ronald Reagan's first ANSA, Richard Allen, was also essentially an administrator. As noted in chapter 8, Allen consistently endorsed a low-profile conception of his job and asserted that he had no interest in making policy. As he put it, "the policy formulation function of the national security adviser should be off-loaded to the Secretary of State."[9] On the other hand, Allen's diminished status as ANSA deprived the White House of an adviser who could compensate for the president's admitted deficiencies in foreign affairs.

The role of the ANSA as coordinator involves recognizing two enduring characteristics of national security policy making: (1) that even with a strong secretary of state, most decisions affecting the nation's security involve more than just diplomacy and cannot therefore remain the exclusive preserve of the State Department and (2) that interdepartmental policies and programs need active management, which will inevitably lead to some conflict among the principals involved. Overall coordination of this management process is necessarily a presidential task, with the ANSA a necessary presidential taskmaster.

As a coordinator, the ANSA facilitates the making of policy but does not initiate it. He is, instead, responsible for defining policy options for the NSC to consider. He also manages the flow of ideas, information, policies, and programs involved in national security. Although the ANSA may exercise considerable influ-

ence, it is as a presidential staff assistant, not as an independent actor. The ANSA's role entails reviewing policy and managing programs, while the principals (particularly the president and the secretary of state) make the final decisions.

Robert Cutler, President Eisenhower's special assistant for national security affairs, typified the ANSA as a coordinator of national security policy. As our earlier discussion emphasized, Eisenhower's national security system could be characterized as a "policy hill." On the up side, the NSC Planning Board considered policy recommendations to be submitted to the council, where they were debated prior to presidential approval. Approved policy went "down the other side of the policy hill to departments and agencies responsible for its execution,"[10] with the Operations Coordinating Board, or OCB, monitoring implementation. The NSC was the apex of this formalized and highly structured system, and Cutler was responsible for its direction.

Even though Cutler chaired the two interdepartmental committees that buttressed the NSC (the Planning Board and the OCB) and initiated discussions at council meetings, his primary responsibilities were to ensure that all points of view were considered and to summarize these findings at NSC meetings, "maintaining the quality and character of advising as a process, not simply . . . expressing those views he and his staff favored."[11] Cutler sought to ensure an orderly policy-making process by relating current and past NSC decisions, seeing that the council's discussion remained on track, and spelling out the implications of all options.[12] Cutler, along with his successors, Dillon Anderson and Gordon Gray, saw himself as a servant of the NSC rather than as an independent actor in the policy-making process, though at the same time, he institutionalized presidential staff involvement in the evolution and evaluation of national security policy.

Two of President Reagan's ANSAs also exemplified the role of coordinator: William P. Clark and Robert McFarlane. McFarlane, in particular, acted as an "honest broker" in the national security policy-making process. His ability to work as a team player allowed Secretary of State George Shultz to become the administration's premier foreign policy maker while maintaining the White House support that was prerequisite to such preeminence. For a two-year period (1983–1985), in fact, the Shultz-McFarlane axis lent coherence to the Reagan administration's foreign policy, in which disarray seemed more the order of the day.

The ANSA as counselor functions in a largely personal relationship to the president: evaluating, rather than simply presenting, policy alternatives; intervening in the departments to get information or other points of view; articulating the presidential perspective on proposed policy—generally seeking "to pinpoint and balance others' biases rather than to press his own."[13] The ANSA as counselor does not preside over a highly structured advisory system and is consequently allowed to spend more time on ad hoc policy making and serving immediate presidential needs.

The more-operational orientation of the NSC staff under a counselor is designed to introduce the widest possible range of alternative actions from which the president may choose. Though the ANSA might respect the secretary of state and his "formal prerogatives,"[14] he and his staff can venture deeply into State Department business—for example, clearing and drafting cables and monitoring the communications system. Moreover, as the NSC staff assumes greater operational responsibilities, the likelihood of conflict between "the president's prime agent of coordination" and the State Department over questions of which policies will meet presidential expectations increases.[15]

President Kennedy's ANSA, McGeorge Bundy, created and typified the role of presidential counselor. Bundy saw his job as clarifying alternatives set before the president, recording decisions, and monitoring follow-through. However, his work was not as without competition with the State Department as he may have thought. As Kennedy's frustrations with the State Department's bureaucratic routine mounted, the role of Bundy—"a crisp, terse intellectual operator"—grew.[16] Most important, Bundy (as well as his successor Walt W. Rostow) was close to "an aggressive, pragmatic President whose style meshed well with his own."[17]

Bundy's service as ANSA points up an aspect of White House staffing that has not been lost on subsequent advisers or secretaries of state: Physical proximity to the president creates special relationships. When Bundy maneuvered his office from the Executive Office Building to the west wing of the White House and established the situation room, he engineered a major administrative coup. He was now "at the end of the buzzer," at the president's immediate call, ensconced among the political staff, capable of access to the Oval Office without necessarily having an appointment or a specific agenda. No other national security policy maker has enjoyed such a potential advantage.

President Carter wanted Secretary of State Cyrus Vance to be his principal foreign policy adviser and ANSA Zbigniew Brzezinski to serve as a personal counselor. To Secretary Vance's disadvantage, Brzezinski proved to be aggressive in gaining both the president's confidence and access to his person. Brzezinski realized that, as the president's assistant, the ANSA was the guardian of the "presidential perspective" in decision making. As time passed, Brzezinski acted more and more as Carter's foreign policy spokesman and became increasingly involved in diplomatic operations. By mid-1978, Brzezinski had transformed his role as presidential counselor into one of vigorous public advocate for important foreign policy decisions.[18] Although Brzezinski never realized the policy-making preeminence of Kissinger—he never succeeded in becoming an *agent*—this was not for want of aspiration or effort.

The ANSA as agent combines the duties of a coordinator (directing the planning process) with those of a counselor (serving as a personal presidential adviser). As an agent, the ANSA dominates the process of formulating national security policy—making many decisions himself and advocating others—and acts as the primary presidential spokesman for foreign affairs. This virtually eliminates any distinction between the duties of the national security adviser and those of the secretary of state. Thus, the ANSA becomes "the key line operator in every important respect."[19] The overall purpose of this type of system is to strengthen the intellectual and bureaucratic resources of the White House to ensure direct presidential control over national security policy making.[20] Administratively, the State Department is displaced to the periphery, and the NSC staff, in effect, becomes a "rival State Department."

Henry Kissinger, ANSA under Richard Nixon, was, like McGeorge Bundy, an intellectual who was disposed to advance his own ideas. However, what distinguished Kissinger from other ANSAs before or since was the degree to which he transformed the scope of his office. Before the end of Nixon's first term, Kissinger was unquestionably the prime presidential adviser on foreign affairs: "If Bundy had intruded on the role of the Secretary of State, Kissinger obliterated it."[21] The actual Secretary of State, William P. Rogers, was eclipsed by Kissinger, who would eventually combine both positions in an unprecedented consolidation of policy-making powers.

As a presidential agent, Kissinger not only briefed Nixon daily on the nation's security but increasingly spoke on behalf of the president, and finally served as the prime negotiator for matters relating to Vietnam, China, and SALT I. These were the principal items on the Nixon foreign policy agenda, and Kissinger was the focal point for both their conception and their realization. The situation room provided the "backchannels" by which foreign policy could be conducted from the White House. Kissinger ultimately acquired decisive control over both the formulation and conduct of foreign affairs. By doing so he acquired de facto powers greater than the de jure authority of the secretaries of state and defense.

After his tenure at the State Department, Kissinger declared his conviction (while admitting that he had not held it when in the White House) that the secretary of state should be every administration's chief foreign policy spokesman. The ANSA, in contrast, he said, should play only a coordinating role in ensuring that all points of view on a proposed policy are heard. "If the security adviser becomes active in the development and articulation of policy, he must inevitably diminish the Secretary of State and reduce his effectiveness."[22] This, of course, was exactly Secretary Rogers's experience. Though successive presidents and national security assistants have announced themselves opposed to a Kissinger-type approach to national security policy making, the allures and successes of the agent role remain undeniable. Indeed, Admiral John Poindexter pushed the agent role one step further by acting on the basis of his personal assessment of the presi-

dent's *intentions* rather than on expressed presidential policies.

THE IRAN-CONTRA AFFAIR: THE ANSA AS INSURGENT

In the last two years of the Reagan administration, great attention was focused on the structure and operation of the National Security Council, as highlighted by the Iran-Contra affair. We have designated the widely publicized activities of Admiral Poindexter and his aide, Lt. Colonel Oliver North, a case of insurgency in the formulation and implementation of national security policy. What principally distinguishes this model from the others we have identified is its status as an aberration that no student of the policy-making process could seriously recommend. The Iran-Contra episode is the clearest example to date of the NSC system out of control. In effect, the ANSA and members of the NSC staff mutinied: They attempted to seize control of the policy-making process to realize their own conception of American national security. Whether this was with the president's tacit consent or without his knowledge remains controversial.

President Reagan believed, with some accuracy, that a preoccupation with the details of foreign policy making had seriously weakened Jimmy Carter's standing and effectiveness as president. Reagan preferred, therefore, to focus on the "big picture," leaving his advisers to fill in the details of policy. Consequently, Reagan was more than ordinarily dependent on his advisers; however, with few exceptions, they were little better informed than he was. When no consensus existed among his advisers (as was the rule during most of his tenure in the White House), President Reagan appeared bewildered and uncertain of what to do about it. More than any president in recent memory, Reagan distanced himself from the policies undertaken in his name. His aides may well have concluded that this distancing was deliberate and then sought to assist him in achieving it.

Internal operating procedures within the NSC under Reagan were poorly defined and loosely supervised. For example, Admiral Poindexter said that Reagan would have approved the proposed sale of missiles to Iran for an exchange of American hostages "if he had been asked." Ronald Reagan said he would not have done so but maintained that he was never asked.[23] As with many NSC decisions President Reagan made, most concerning the Iranian arms deal were never recorded.[24] Reagan appeared not to have been really interested in the details of how the NSC staff was aiding the anti-Sandinista Contra cause in Nicaragua. According to Poindexter, the president knew about it but "in general terms."[25] Testifying to further examples of poorly supervised decision making, Colonel North contended that he sent President Reagan several memos concerning covert aid to the Contras. Admiral Poindexter said that these were never received, and President Reagan denied having seen or approved them.[26]

Under Reagan, there were six national security advisers. Two had prior experience in external policy making (Robert McFarlane and Frank Carlucci). Two others came from the military (Admiral Poindexter and Lt. General Colin Powell). Two had little or no background in the management of national security affairs (Richard Allen and William Clark). The average tenure of a Reagan ANSA was sixteen months. No other administration had such a high turnover in this important position. Lacking adequate preparation and expertise, the ANSAs and their staffs during the Reagan era were understandably uncertain about their proper roles.

This situation was exacerbated by President Reagan's inability or unwillingness to specify their duties. President Reagan was faulted by the Tower Commission for major deficiencies in what was termed his "management style."[27] Reagan was also likened to a modern-day James Buchanan: Faced with conflicts and competitiveness among his principal advisers, he was unable to make a decision. Failure to exercise this presidential responsibility puts the president at risk of losing control over the policy-making process. Ultimately, the Iran-Contra affair was attributable to a lack of presidential decisiveness.

Reagan, as noted, liked to make policy on the basis of staff consensus, approving agreements reached among his principal subordinates. Unfortunately, such consensus rarely existed—and perhaps never could have—on important issues such as arms control, Cen-

tral America, and the Middle East. The long-standing feud between the Departments of State and Defense over intermediate nuclear weapons went largely unarbitrated by the White House. Both Secretaries Shultz and Weinberger also expressed serious reservations about White House initiatives concerning the arms-for-hostages deal with Iran. Adjudicating such disputes is a presidential responsibility. Most presidents since 1945 have had either a forceful secretary of state or a forceful ANSA to assist them in doing so, but most of the time Reagan had neither. The predictable outcome of such a state of affairs was drift and disarray in the policy-making process—conditions encouraging insurgency by members of the White House staff.

In the Reagan White House, the ANSA and other members of the NSC staff came to perform, often on their own initiative, interesting and novel functions. These included protecting the president from certain other advisers whose views they regarded as unwelcome, projecting a tough American image abroad and voicing a willingness to use force when necessary, preventing political damage to the president's reputation, and keeping peace among departmental rivals. As the details of the Iran-Contra affair indicate, some members of the NSC staff also seemed to interpret their responsibilities to include carrying out actions that other executive agencies were legally prohibited from conducting by virtue of the Boland Amendments. Poindexter and North, for example, conducted such activities in accordance with what they maintained was implicit presidential approval.[28] Regardless, directing covert actions involved the NSC staff in a variety of questionable activities: personally negotiating with foreign governments, diverting funds to selected Contra leaders from the sale of arms to Iran, attempting to influence congressional opinion for repeal of the Boland Amendments, and, using the NSC staff as a military strategy board to advise the Contras in their fight against the Sandinista government.

In the Iran-Contra affair Americans thus witnessed a dramatic perversion of the proper role of the NSC staff in the policy-making process as defined both by statute and tradition.[29] It was not just that the arms-for-hostages deal with Iran was "an inept policy, poorly implemented,"[30] or that the NSC system failed; even more damaging, the advisory process was ignored or not used at all.[31] Under Poindexter and North, the NSC became a "shadowy parallel government," operating with little or no supervision and without the limitations on executive actions that are normally assumed in a democratic system.[32] Accountability was further undermined by cabals within the executive branch that acted to keep major public officials (such as the CIA director and the secretaries of state and defense) from knowing the details of the Iran-Contra activities.[33] Admiral Poindexter testified that he deliberately withheld knowledge of the details from President Reagan so as to protect the president with "plausible deniability."[34] Deniability thus replaced constitutional accountability.

Irrespective of the particular national security advisory processes that a president may use, the record on the Iran-Contra affair suggests the need for a series of steps or established procedures to be followed in the decision-making process. These include:

1. clear and accurate identification of the problems confronting the United States in the area of national security,
2. comprehensive and objective intelligence gathering and evaluation,
3. consultation with experts,
4. solicitation of the views of all major participants about proposed policy alternatives,
5. full evaluation of policy proposals at the highest level,
6. clear and objective identification of the consequences of all major policy options,
7. final decision by the president and wide communication of his decision at all levels of government,
8. observance of all legal restraints on the government's proposed action,
9. careful and systematic monitoring of policy implementation, and
10. periodic policy evaluation and program review.

As should be clear from the record on the Iran-Contra affair, few of these guidelines were observed or even acknowledged during the Reagan administration. Though the insurgency of Poindexter and North was an aberration in the history of national security advisory models, there is much to suggest that a precondition for this insurgency was the president's failure to take charge of the national security process. Whatever the ultimate legal judgments on his subordinates, President Reagan must bear the ultimate responsibility for the insurgency within his administration.

Despite the public scandal and breaches of the law involved in the Iran-Contra activities, the machinations of Admiral Poindexter and Colonel North may have had the unanticipated consequence of bringing about a reevaluation of the National Security Council, the NSC staff, and especially the role of the assistant for national security affairs. For example, there have been only two major congressional analyses of the NSC system: the comprehensive, if controversial, Jackson subcommittee report in 1960 and the Zorinsky hearings in 1978. Perhaps another subcommittee on national policy needs to be created to spell out in detail the substantive and structural reforms suggested by the particulars of the Iran-Contra hearings. For so important an agency of American foreign policy making, the NSC has been comparatively under-scrutinized and underlegislated, at least in relation to the Departments of State and Defense. In part, this fact can be explained as due to the traditional deference of Congress to "executive privilege" in the conduct of the presidential office. Of equal importance has been the tradition of deference—by Congress, the press, and the public—to the president's claims to primacy in the conduct of national security affairs. . . .

. . . . Is There a Preferred ANSA Role?

Constitutional provisions, administrative precedents, and electoral promises collectively dictate that a newly elected president approach the organization of government from a personal perspective. Defining the president's perspective is a central responsibility of the White House staff; the management of national security is hardly an exception to this rule. Indeed, given the centrality of presidential decision making in the conduct of foreign affairs, how a president organizes for national security is one of his or her most crucial decisions. Clearly, mandating a particular mode of decision making for the president is also both impossible and inadvisable. Nevertheless, the evidence from

Implementation Responsibility

	Low	High
Low	**Department-Centered** Administrator	**Formalized** Coordinator
High	**Collegial** Counselor	**Palace Guard** Agent

Policy-Making Responsibility

Figure 16.3 Presidential management styles and ANSA roles

this review of the historical record does suggest certain conclusions—and a few recommendations—with regard to the effective management of national security affairs.

The most obvious conclusion is that the ANSA has been institutionalized as part of the national security policy-making process on a level with the secretaries of state and defense and the CIA director. At the same time, we have observed rather dramatic oscillations in the ways in which presidents have used their national security assistants and the NSC staff. Almost as a rule, successive administrations have reactively reorganized, restructuring their national security advisory process to presumably correct the defects of their predecessors.[35] Kennedy, for example, deconstructed the Eisenhower machinery in light of the Jackson subcommittee's criticisms; Nixon reversed the collegiality of the Kennedy administration and reconstructed a hierarchial NSC staff.

To some extent these shifts in organizational structure reflect the conventional political wisdom of the day. As we have observed, the making of national security policy involves the exercise of presidential responsibilities in ways that are largely unfettered by constitutional or institutional constraints.[36] The ANSA's political and administrative role consequently varies, because the nature of this role "is primarily determined by the man [sic] it serves."[37]

Is there a preferred ANSA role? Though answering a question so dependent on personalities and politics is

admittedly difficulty, both future presidents and the concerned public must still ask it. Figure 16.3, "Presidential Management Styles and ANSA Roles," represents an attempt to help answer this question.

Using the same values and variables as in Figure 16.1, we can classify a president with little interest in the hands-on administration of foreign affairs and with few policies initiated by the White House as having a department-centered management style. This is the classical pattern of policy making and implementation, in which the State Department is the lead agency within the executive branch and the secretary of state is the president's chief foreign policy deputy and spokesperson to the international community. In this pattern, the president, though unquestionably in charge of external policy and of making the final decisions, designates the secretary of state his chief of staff for foreign affairs and supports the secretary in this role against bureaucratic rivals and political criticisms. In turn, the secretary of state relies heavily on State Department personnel for analytical and operational support. In this model of presidential management, the ANSA appropriately plays the role of administrator.

A president who looks to the cabinet departments for policy proposals but maintains a high degree of personal control over the administration of foreign affairs is classified as having a formalized management style. With a president bent on considering the fullest range of policy proposals and implementation plans, the NSC becomes an interdepartmental forum for the presentation and elaboration of matters for presidential disposition. With formal briefings by standing committees of the NSC and a careful delineation of the different departmental perspectives, the president can survey the range of options available and evaluate the effectiveness of ongoing operations. In this model, the ANSA serves as a coordinator of the advisory machinery.

In contrast to the formalized management of national security policy making, in the collegial model of presidential management the president eschews direct administrative responsibility for an active part in shaping the content of the policy. Ad hoc working groups rather than a formal hierarchy of interdepartmental committees are typical. Presidents matching this model are presumed to distrust the State Department and the other national security bureaucracies (even if this is not expressed overtly). The president's goal is to shift the locus of decision making to the White House and to use the NSC staff as an independent analysis and review agency. Decision making is based on an open exchange among relative equals in the policy-making process. Without clearly demarcated areas of responsibility, NSC participants (at the council level and below) are encouraged to seek a preferred solution rather than protect bureaucratic turf. In this model, the ANSA, as the guardian of the president's interests, serves as a counselor.

In the "palace guard" pattern of presidential management, administrative and policy-making responsibilities are centralized within the confines of the White House. Virtually excluded from an active role, the State Department and its NSC colleagues are relegated to carrying out policies devised by the president and the national security adviser (within their "rival State Department"). In such a situation, the ANSA tends to be an articulate and ambitious aide with strongly held international views that complement those of the president. As the president's designated alter ego, the ANSA is free to operate as an agent with the authority to represent American security interests traditionally reserved for the secretary of state.

The question still remains: "Is there a preferred ANSA role?" This may be addressed in three ways. First, a president would be advised to define a role for the ANSA that is consistent with his or her preferences regarding the general management of the government. For example, if a president is committed to the principle of cabinet government—that is, the predominance of the State Department—the appointment of an ANSA with strong policy positions and personal ambitions would invite the kind of bureaucratic warfare that debilitated the Carter foreign policy. If President Carter really wished to have Secretary Vance direct the policy process, he should have appointed someone more like Brent Scowcroft instead of Zbigniew Brzezinski as his ANSA.

Second, the history of the NSC over the past forty years does suggest that neither the agent nor the administrator roles of the ANSA are to be recommended. The machinations of Admiral Poindexter, a self-appointed presidential agent, indicate how easily the exigencies of national security can provide a veil for insurgent operations—that is, operations without presidential authorization and uninformed by departmental expertise. On the other hand, the administrator role may easily prove too weak in providing the advice that the president needs to make transdepartmental decisions. For an ANSA who is an administrator to be effective, both the president and the secretary of state must be knowledgeable about foreign affairs and able hands-on administrators. This can prove a rare combination.

Third, whether a president chooses to manage national security policy with a coordinator or counselor is largely a matter of background and temperament. Yet, both of these models have costs as well as benefits. Not every president will be knowledgeable about the international situation, confident in voicing his or her opinion, or comfortable with the give-and-take of collegial decision making. Although a counselor can assist the president in managing the process, he or she will inevitably be tempted to do more than this. On the other hand, the structured character of formalized national security management may prove exasperating to presidents preferring a more flexible and freewheeling approach. Some presidents may perceive the benefits of a formalized approach—procedural regularity, predictability, and accountability—as stultifying wheel spinning.

The worst situation arises when a president vacillates in designating the ANSA's role or chooses a national security assistant with personality traits inconsistent with the demands of the designated role. For example, Carter seemingly could not choose between the roles of counselor and agent for his ANSA; Reagan, with six ANSAs, seemed unable to choose at all. It is hard to disagree with what Alexander George has concluded: "The experience of every president from Truman to Reagan makes one conclusion inescapable: a president must first define his own role in the national security policymaking system before he can design and manage the roles and relationships of the major participants."[38]

NOTES

1. Stanley L. Falk, "The National Security Council under Truman, Eisenhower, and Kennedy," *Political Science Quarterly* 79 (September 1964): 414.

2. U.S. Senate, Committee on Government Operations, Subcommittee on National Policy Machinery, *Organizing for National Security*, vol. 1 (Washington, D.C.: Government Printing Office, 1961), pp. 561 and 564.

3. Cecil V. Crabb, Jr., and Kevin V. Mulcahy, *Presidents and Foreign Policy Making: FDR to Reagan* (Baton Rouge: Louisiana State University Press, 1986), pp. 122–155.

4. Joseph G. Bock and Duncan L. Clarke, "The National Security Assistant and the White House Staff: National Security Policy Decisionmaking and Domestic Political Considerations, 1947–84," *Presidential Studies Quarterly* 16 (Spring 1986): 259.

5. Sidney W. Souers, "Policy Formulation for National Security," *American Political Science Review* 43 (Spring 1986): 537.

6. *New York Times*, November 4, 1975; Gerald Ford, *A Time to Heal* (New York: Harper & Row, 1979), p. 326.

7. I. M. Destler, "A Job That Doesn't Work," *Foreign Policy* 38 (Spring 1980): 89.

8. Ibid., p. 85.

9. *New York Times*, November 19, 1980.

10. Robert Cutler, "The Department of the National Security Council," *Foreign Affairs* 34 (April 1956): 448.

11. Fred I. Greenstein and John P. Burke, "Comparative Models of Presidential Decisionmaking: Eisenhower and Johnson." Paper presented at the annual meeting of the American Political Science Association, August 29–September 1, 1985, pp. 13–14.

12. Ibid., p. 15.

13. I. M. Destler, "National Security II: The Rise of the Assistant," in *The Illusion of Presidential Government*, ed. Hugh

Heclo and Lester M. Salamon (Boulder, Colo.: Westview Press, 1981), p. 268.

14. I. M. Destler, Leslie Gelb, and Anthony Lake, *Our Own Worst Enemy: The Unmaking of American Foreign Policy* (New York: Simon & Schuster, 1984), p. 194.

15. I. M. Destler, *Presidents, Bureaucrats, and Foreign Policy* (Princeton, N.J.: Princeton University Press, 1972), pp. 102–103.

16. Destler, Gelb, and Lake, *Our Own Worst Enemy*, p. 184.

17. Ibid.

18. Alexander George, *Presidential Decision Making in Foreign Policy* (Boulder, Colo.: Westview Press, 1980), p. 200.

19. Destler, "National Security II," p. 271.

20. George, *Presidential Decision Making*, p. 177.

21. Destler, Gelb, and Lake, *Our Own Worst Enemy*, p. 208.

22. Henry Kissinger, *The White House Years* (Boston: Little, Brown, 1979), pp. 11–12.

23. *Report on the Congressional Committee Investigating the Iran-Contra Affair*. Joint Hearings before the Select Committee on Secret Military Assistance to Iran and the Nicaraguan Opposition, U.S. Senate, and the Select Committee to Investigate Covert Arms Transactions with Iran, U.S. House, 100th Cong., 1st sess. (Washington, D.C.: Government Printing Office, 1987), p. 13. Hereafter referred to as *Iran-Contra Report*.

24. *The Tower Commission Report: The Full Text of the President's Special Review Board* (New York: Times Books and Bantam Books, 1987), p. 70. Hereafter referred to as Tower Commission Report.

25. *Iran-Contra Report*, p. 77.

26. Ibid., p. 13; and *Tower Commission Report*, pp. 77–78.

27. *Tower Commission Report*, p. xv.

28. *Iran-Contra Report*, p. 21.

29. Ibid., p. 17.

30. *Tower Commission Report*, p. xv.

31. Ibid., p. 80.

32. Ibid., p. xv.

33. *Iran-Contra Report*, p. 14–16.

34. Ibid., p. 17.

35. Destler, Gelb, and Lake, *Our Own Worst Enemy*, p. 168; Anna Kasten Nelson, "National Security I: Inventing a Process," in *The Illusion of Presidential Government*, ed. Hugh Heclo and Lester M. Salamon, (Boulder, Colo.: Westview Press, 1981), p. 259; and Destler, "National Security II," pp. 263 and 272.

36. Bock and Clarke, "The National Security Assistant and the White House Staff," p. 258.

37. John E. Endicott, "The National Security Council," in *American Defense Policy*, ed. John E. Endicott and Roy W. Strafford, Jr. (Baltimore, Md.: Johns Hopkins University Press, 1981), p. 314.

38. George, *Presidential Decision Making*, p. 146.

PART VI

NATIONAL SECURITY ADVISERS:
Profiles

Political science without biography is a form of taxidermy.
—*Harold D. Lasswell*
Psychopathology and Politics, *1945*

EDITORS' INTRODUCTION

Among the individuals who have served as national security adviser are seven attorneys and businessmen (Lay, Cutler, Anderson, Jackson, Gray, Clark, and Berger); five military men (Rear Adm. Souers, Lieut. Gen. Scowcroft, Lieut. Col. McFarlane, Vice Adm. Poindexter, and Lieut. Gen. Powell); six academicians (Dean Bundy, professors Kissinger, Lake, Rostow, and Brzezinski, and Provost Rice); two men with longstanding government backgrounds (Gray and Carlucci); and a foreign policy consultant-entrepreneur (Allen). Republican administrations have been inclined to select military men for the executive secretary/adviser position more often than Democratic administrations (four, compared to one for the Democrats—Souers), although in both parties most advisers have been from civilian backgrounds (seventeen, compared to five military men).

A Day Filled with Meetings

When the national security adviser plays an activist role (which depends upon the support and encouragement of an activist foreign policy president), the workday is full. The adviser arrives early in the West Wing of the White House, where his or her office is a short walk to the Oval Office (see Figure VI.A), just a few strides down a corridor lined with oil paintings and watercolors of early American leaders and landscapes. The adviser's weekday mornings often start in the Oval Office when he or she briefs the president on those world events of the last twenty-four hours that have, or threaten to have, an effect on U.S. national security interests. Sometimes the director of Central Intelligence (DCI) participates in the briefings as well; and, in response to the terrorist attacks in September 2001, the national security adviser, the DCI, and the director of the Federal Bureau of Investigation (FBI) often joined together as a team to brief the president. This allows each of these presidential aides to hear what all the others are telling the president, which presumably enhances sharing of information between the intelligence and the law enforcement communities (both important players in this age of global terrorism), as well as within the NSC system.

The NSC adviser is normally in attendance at both the CIA and FBI briefings and, under President George W. Bush, so is the vice president, the White House chief of staff, and (less routinely)

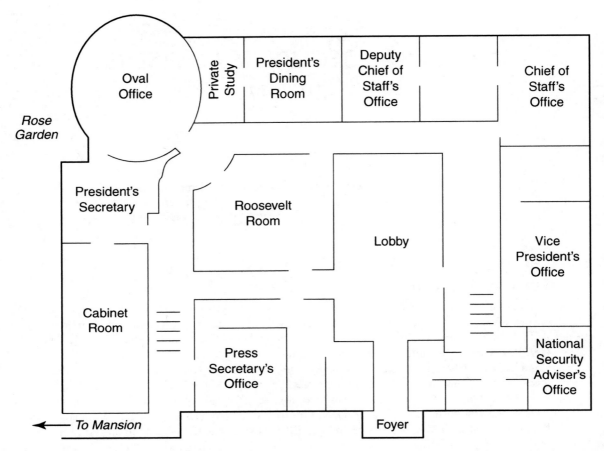

Figure VI.A The physical relationship between the Oval Office and the Office of the Natinal Security Adviser in the West Wing of the White House, 2002 *(Source: Adapted from* The West Wing: A Brief History, 5*)*

the Secretary of Homeland Security and the attorney general. Some NSC advisers have absolutely insisted on being present for any national security briefing, so they can be fully informed and—if necessary—try to help the president make sense out of divergent views. "I took the position," Frank Carlucci remembers (in the first selection of Part V), "that I couldn't be national security adviser if [the DCI] was holding meetings on national security issues where I was not present." In contrast, Richard Allen was content to let DCI William J. Casey, a personal friend of President Reagan, meet in the Oval Office alone with the chief executive as often as he wished (and could not have stopped these meetings anyway, most likely, given Casey's domineering personality).

Despite the greater number of people participating in national security briefings with the president than used to be the case before the second Bush Administration (an effort to achieve what the current NSC adviser Condoleezza Rice often refers to as a greater "fusion of intelligence"), the morning briefings are actually shorter than was often the case in earlier years—at the insistence of President George W. Bush, who demanded a more focused summary of what he needs to know about world affairs and homeland security. During these briefings, further questions may arise from the president or other policymakers in attendance. These questions are converted by the NSC adviser into formal requests for additional information from the relevant agencies and departments, a process known to government officials as "tasking."

While serving as an official in the CIA, Carlucci recalled a veritable "rain" of requests for information from Zbigniew Brzezinski following briefings during the Carter Administration (see selection one of Part V). George H.W. Bush also remembers using CIA briefings to good advantage. "I made a point from day one to read the PDB [President's Daily Brief—the CIA's top intelligence report] in the presence of a CIA briefer and either Brent [Scowcroft] or his deputy," writes the former president. "This way I could task the briefers to bring in more information on a certain matter or, when the reading would bring to mind policy matters, ask Brent to follow up on an item of interest. The CIA officers would write down my questions; in a day or so, I would get an answer or an elaboration" (Bush and Scowcroft, 1998: 30).

Sometimes the tasking of departments and agencies can be driven by an agenda other than the search for good information. It has been asserted that the Nixon Administration would from time to time issue specific tasking instructions to the bureaucracy in an attempt to bog it down and keep it away from more important matters the White House wanted to dominate. An official on Kissinger's NSC staff, Richard V. Allen (who would become President Reagan's first national security adviser), recalls the Nixon Administration "almost immediately swamping the bureaucracy with an impossible series of tasks to keep it immobilized over a period of time so that decisions could be made in the White House" (Center, 1999: 3).

When the morning briefings are over, the national security adviser typically attends a meeting of the White House senior staff. At this staff session (which met three times a week during the Carter years, and sometimes daily in other administrations), the president's political and domestic aides are present. This provides the national security adviser with the opportunity, normally missed by the secretaries of state and defense, to hear about all the other matters on the president's agenda, and to get a direct sense of the pressures that the chief executive and his top domestic aides are feeling from legislators, interest groups, and public opinion polls. While this is a valuable opportunity for the national security adviser to acquire a more comprehensive view of the demands facing the president, Anthony Lake warns that "increasingly in modern Washington you have to make sure that you act as non-politically as possible and keep your distance from the political side of the White House" (Center, 1999: 6). As Lake has added elsewhere: ". . . . in public statements, the national security adviser should avoid taking partisan positions. It can diminish his or her credibility, and only adds to the distrust and divisions between the Executive and Congress" (Lake, 2000: 262).

However valid Lake's advice may be, physical proximity to the Oval Office does give the NSC adviser certain advantages over cabinet members and their deputies, not least of which is observing at close hand what domestic political problems the president confronts daily and being able to discuss security policy regularly with the president, while having a timely awareness of these domestic pressures. Being in the White House every day is, in short, a big plus for the adviser. As Washington insider Undersecretary of State George Ball once wryly observed, "Nothing propinques like propinquity" (Drew, 1978: 95).

The rest of the adviser's day consists of attending a series of meetings between the adviser and his or her staff, as well as NSC committee meetings with top officials in the administration who have responsibility for security and foreign affairs. Who should act as the formal chair of these meetings can sometimes be disputatious. As earlier noted in Part III, Secretary of State George P. Shultz complained when NSC adviser Carlucci sought to preside over key meetings. "It would be a grave mistake," he told Carlucci, "for the NSC adviser, a nonstatutory member of the National Security Council, someone *not* in the cabinet and *not* subject to confirmation by the Senate or to the accountability of appearances before congressional committees, to be designated [in a National Security Decision Directive] as the chairman of NSC meetings." Carlucci refused to yield and replied to Shultz, "Forgive my annoyance, but I did not return to government in order to be an executive secretary" (Shultz, 1993: 903–04). In more recent years, the wrangling has subsided, as a general consensus emerged in favor of the NSC adviser serving as chair—a part of the adviser's "honest broker" role.

The adviser also meets periodically with foreign officials, including ambassadors whom the adviser calls to the White House in order to pass along messages from the president for their respective heads of state. Sometimes foreign dignitaries prefer to meet with the NSC adviser rather than cabinet members, including the secretary of state, because they feel that dealing with someone who is right inside the White House—a stone's throw from the Oval Office—is both more prestigious and more likely to result in quicker action than a visit to Foggy Bottom, the location of the State Department. As Carlucci recalls, for example, the German foreign minister Hans-Dietrich Genscher "was always in our office. . . . [because] people want to get as close to the president's office as they can" (see the first selection in Part V). During the Reagan years, heads of state, such as Margaret Thatcher (the British Prime Minster), Francois Mitterrand (President of France), and Helmut Kohl (Chancellor of Germany), sometimes preferred direct contact with someone in the White House rather than in the State Department.

McFarlane remembers serving as the president's surrogate ear on such occasions, but claims to have always carefully kept the secretary of state (George P. Shultz) informed about the back-channel communications. This secretary, however, disputes how well the adviser tried to keep him informed (see Shultz, 1993: 903–04; and Smith, 1988: 629).

Now and then, the adviser is also called upon to represent the administration abroad—a delicate role, since the secretary of state may cry "encroachment!" on his or her responsibilities as chief diplomat for the United States. During the Reagan years, Secretary Shultz threatened to resign when he discovered that NSC adviser McFarlane had undertaken a mission to the Middle East without his prior approval (Smith, 1988: 629). Brzezinski remembers four trips that President Jimmy Carter called upon him to make: to China, the Middle East, Europe, and Afghanistan (Brzezinski, 1983: 56). When asked if he thought that the trip to China, for example, might have undermined the Secretary of State, Brzezinski replied bluntly: "It probably did. But it furthered the American–Chinese relationship and furthered what the president wanted, and that's a trade-off" (see selection 1, Part V). Recall, too, Sandy Berger's remark that sending the adviser on a mission can be less obtrusive and, therefore, less likely to draw a swarm of reporters than the hullabaloo that accompanies secretaries of state and their entourage of security personnel and aides as they travel abroad (see selection 1, Part V). As the quotes in this introduction suggest, the personalities of the individual advisers are a significant aspect of how the NSC functions. In this part of the book, we examine more closely the backgrounds and individual styles of prominent Council advisers.

Adviser Profiles

BUNDY   The first profile is on McGeorge Bundy of the Kennedy Administration. Bundy has been described as "a one-man replacement" for the Planning Board of the Eisenhower Administration (Wise, 1961:121), and the author of the selection presented here, journalist Kai Bird, seems to agree. By virtue of his keen mind, boundless energy, and close relationship with another Harvard University man, the president, Bundy was able to build the NSC into what has been characterized as "a domain which by the end of the decade would first rival and then surpass the State Department in influence" (Halberstam, 1972). He was the leader in the transition of the NSC staff from a secretariat to a muscular advisory body. In the selection, Bird observes that Bundy dismantled the Eisenhower NSC bureaucracy and introduced a much more fluid organizational structure. The White House would be run "as if it were Harvard, with Bundy as dean and Kennedy as president. . . . intellectuals, not bureaucrats, would make foreign policy."

KISSINGER   With Henry Kissinger, the subject of the next profile, the adviser position achieved the zenith of its influence. After his landslide reelection in 1972, President Nixon appointed Kissinger as secretary of state. Kissinger kept the job as national security adviser as well and, from 1973–1975, he rode astride both positions—one way to avoid the conflict between the two offices that had become increasingly apparent before this convenient solution. As never before or since in the modern era, foreign policy would be run essentially from the White House, as if it were a private game of chess between Kissinger and Nixon on one side of the table and the rest of the world on the other side.

The portrait of Kissinger, written by the brothers Marvin and Bernard Kalb, distinguished journalists and astute Washington watchers, reveals how Kissinger—even before being named secretary of state—already had managed to gather considerable control over key foreign policy issues, moving them into the bailiwick of the adviser. In his persistent battle against the constraints of bureaucracy (an overarching theme of Kissinger's academic writings), he converted the making of American foreign policy into something akin to a cult of his own personality. This achievement was made possible by the extraordinary reliance President Nixon placed on his judgment, and by Kissinger's own considerable skills in nurturing this close relationship with his patron.

The combined job of secretary of state and NSC adviser became too much even for the remarkable Dr. Kissinger. His remedy was to put into the adviser slot a person of unquestioned loyalty to him, someone who would avoid what he himself had done: that is, use the NSC system as a rival department of state. The perfect choice was Lt. Gen. Scowcroft, a trusted Kissinger deputy who was low-key, competent, and possessed by the requisite passion for anonymity that Kissinger sought in his staff assistants. Here was an adviser who seemed willing to act in the tradition of Sidney Souers and James Lay. For a brief interlude, Scowcroft revived the neutral "administrator" style. Foreign policy remained firmly in the hands of Dr. Kissinger, even as the Nixon Administration collapsed when the president was forced to resign over the Watergate scandal. Kissinger moved on to serve in the same capacity (secretary of state) in the succeeding Ford Administration.

Scowcroft would also continue to serve as national security adviser in the Ford Administration, and would later return to this position for a second time during the administration of the first President Bush. Later in this section, we present a profile of the "second Scowcroft" in his more assertive role. Before that, though, we examine the resurgence of an aggressive style of leadership in the NSC adviser's position that arose again during the Carter Administration after the quiet interlude of the "first Scowcroft" under President Ford.

BRZEZINSKI   When Jimmy Carter entered the White House in 1977, he asked Zbigniew Brzezinski (his principal foreign policy adviser from the presidential campaign) to join him.

Journalist Dom Bondafede sketches a picture of the Polish-born academic that suggests yet another intellectually gifted and strong-willed individual in the mold of Bundy and Kissinger.

Although Dr. Kissinger was a difficult act to match in terms of policy dominance, Dr. Brzezinski also enjoyed an excellent relationship with his president, and the White House's next intellectual set out to revive the status of the NSC adviser as more of a counselor than a mere administrator or even coordinator. At times, he seemed to exercise as much sway over American foreign policy as had Kissinger. "I'm a synthesizer, analyzer, coordinator," Brzezinski declared to a journalist. "I might also be alerter, energizer, implementer, mediator, even lightning rod. All of these roles I play at different times, depending on the issues" (Drew, 1978: 96). For his detractors, though, he had become (as Bonafede notes) too much the policy advocate and not enough the policy coordinator.

SCOWCROFT   David Lauter's portrait of Brent Scowcroft depicts him as a principal architect of foreign policy in the first Bush Administration. In contrast to his low-profile stance as adviser during the Ford Administration (in reaction to criticism of Kissinger's usurpation of foreign policy in that role), Scowcroft stepped forward more boldly under the first President Bush's looser rein. Scowcroft was close to the president. Both were former fighter pilots, liked to jog together, and after leaving the White House they would co-author a book (Bush and Scowcroft, 1997). Scowcroft specialized in providing guidance to the chief executive on the mysterious details of nuclear weaponry and arms control and, through camaraderie, helped the president relax from one of the world's most stressful jobs.

As Lauter notes, "Scowcroft's image in Washington's energetic gossip mill is more that of an institution than of a person." Many view Scowcroft as an ideal national security adviser. "People talk about the 'the Scowcroft Model,'" a White House official said to Lauter, "suggesting the way the individual has been able to disappear behind the image of the institution." Yet, as Lauter makes clear, Scowcroft is not without self-confidence and a mind of his own. He took the initiative, for example, during the first Bush Administration to provide leadership for the White House in the domain of strategic planning. *Time* magazine concluded that while Secretary of State James Baker was the "ingenious political quarterback" in the first Bush Administration, Scowcroft set "the overall game plan" (Painton, 1991: 3).

Steadfastness is another of Scowcroft's attributes. An aide told Lauter that Scowcroft "has a turtle-like demeanor. He just keeps moving forward, slow but steady, and he always gets to the end." Scowcroft also has a capacity for honest self-evaluation. "I don't have a quick, innovative mind," he has said (Painton, 1991: 4). "I don't automatically think of good new ideas. What I do better is pick out good ideas from bad ideas." These discerning policy instincts won him the trust of both presidents Gerald R. Ford and George H.W. Bush.

BERGER   When the Clinton Administration came to Washington in 1993, the president first picked Anthony Lake as his NSC adviser. Described by the *New Yorker* magazine as a "Harvard-honed, behind-the-scenes foreign-policy mandarin" (Southgate, 1997: 33), Lake attempted to take the adviser's role out of the limelight, content to remain a policy coordinator and occasional quiet counselor. Samuel ("Sandy") Berger, who had been Lake's deputy and long-time associate, became national security adviser in 1997. Formerly an international trade lawyer in Washington, D.C.—and colleague with Lake at the State Department's Policy Planning office during the Carter Administration—Berger upped the energy level of the adviser position, converting the Council into what one senior official outside the White House referred to as "by far, the most dominant entity in foreign policy making in this administration" (Harris, 1999: A1).

Within the first two weeks of his tenure, Berger had already equaled the number of appearances on Sunday morning television talk shows that Lake had made during his four years in office (*National Journal*, 1997: 1176). The Kissinger–Brzezinski model was back in play—and so was speculation about Berger's increasing preeminence in the administration. As a *New York Times* correspondent reported in 1999, Secretary of State Madeleine K. Albright had been "effectively eclipsed in foreign affairs by Samuel R. Berger, the national security adviser, who has brought his physical proximity to the Oval Office and his personal relationship with President Clinton to bear on every foreign policy issue . . ." (Perlez, 1999: A1). In contrast to other administrations, these principals quickly refuted this line of speculation, although in her account of those years Albright acknowledged her relationship with Berger had not been "trouble-free":

". . . I sometimes became irritated by what I saw as the NSC's attempts to micromanage. At first I blamed it on myself, because my default drive is always to cooperate. Then I blamed it on the male dominance of the system. The real answer is that, when problems arose, it was simply because Sandy and I were trying to occupy each other's space. Although the NSC's job was supposed to be limited to coordinating the actions and policies of the departments, proximity to the President sometimes tempted Sandy and his staff to assume an operational role." (Albright, 2003: 348)

Both Berger and Albright went to some lengths to downplay any tensions between them, saying that they had worked together closely for many years in the past and would continue to do so. According to Albright, they took several practical steps to facilitate this: " . . . we made frequent use of a direct phone link between Sandy's office and mine that, on some days, might be used a dozen times or more. Every Monday when in town, the two of us had lunch with Secretary of Defense Bill Cohen in Sandy's office . . . the sessions were very useful in coordinating policy, breaking logjams and clearing the air" (2003: 349).

The selection on Berger by the seasoned observer of the Washington scene, R.W. "Johnny" Apple, Jr., captures the impressive skills and occasional setbacks experienced by Berger, including Henry Kissinger's early public dismissal of him as a mere trade lawyer unlikely "to be a global strategist." Despite Kissinger's harsh prognosis, in Apple's judgment Berger proved to be "perhaps the most influential national security adviser since Henry A. Kissinger," though he was more of a "political rather than a strategic figure."

RICE President George W. Bush's choice for NSC adviser was Condoleezza Rice, a former provost at Stanford University and an academic specializing in Soviet affairs. As a young professor at Stanford, her talents were soon to impress many people, including someone of special importance. While attending a dinner for arms control experts hosted by Stanford in 1984, Brent Scowcroft recalls being impressed by "this young slip of a girl"—the only woman, the only black, and the youngest person at the dinner—who asked a "brilliant question" about international law and "absolutely captivated me" (Russakoff, 2001: W23). Scowcroft asked Rice to join a foreign policy group at the Aspen Institute.

When George H.W. Bush became president and named Scowcroft as his national security adviser, Scowcroft in turned asked Rice to join the NSC staff. She accepted the offer and served for two years as his director for Soviet and East European affairs during the disintegration of the Soviet empire. She returned to Stanford in 1991 and, at age 38, became the university's youngest provost ever. In 1999, Texas governor George W. Bush asked her to tutor him on foreign policy, which led to her role as senior foreign policy adviser during the governor's bid for the presidency and, with victory in 2000, the job of national security adviser. A *New Yorker* profile observes:

> Rice perhaps most closely resembles McGeorge Bundy, of the Kennedy Administration, who was the first non-invisible national-security adviser: he was a young prodigy, and a protégé of various establishment figures, in international relations, and he came to the White House from a position at Harvard that was similar to Rice's at Stanford, and held at a similarly early age. (Lemann, 2002: 177)

Rice joined an NSC team of well-known former government officials, including Secretary of Defense Donald H. Rumsfeld; former secretary of defense and now Vice-president Dick Cheney; and Secretary of State Colin Powell, who once remarked that he regarded Rice "like a daughter" (Keller, 2001: 65). While often overshadowed by these cabinet principals, Rice has nonetheless been more than an administrator or coordinator. Some see her as a go-between in the administration, attempting to arbitrate difficulties that arise between the policies and approach of the secretary of state, on the one hand, and the vice president and secretary of defense, on the other—on many occasions to little avail.

Counting Zbigniew Brzezinski among her heroes (Heilbrunn, 1999/2000: 51), Rice also weighs in on policy and, with the leverage that comes with close ties to the president and proximity to the Oval Office, she has assumed the role of counselor. Rice's close relationship with President Bush was further evidenced by his decision to designate her as his "personal representative" to peace talks in the Middle East and to head an "Iraq Stabilization Group" to better coordinate post-war U.S. efforts in that country. At the same time, however, her enhanced stature was undercut by the controversy surrounding the administration's use of intelligence during the buildup for the Iraq war. According to one account, "two uncomfortable possibilities" surrounded her role in this regard as the national security adviser: "Either she missed or overlooked numerous warnings from intelligence agencies seeking to put caveats on claims about Iraq's nuclear weapons program, or she made public claims that she knew to be false" (Milbank and Allen, 2003, A1).

In the last section of Part VI, reporter Elaine Sciolino of the *New York Times* looks at Dr. Rice's early life and finds a bookish young woman with strong musical talents. At the University of Denver, Rice abandoned her plans to become a concert pianist and switched to political science. Professor Josef Korbel, the father of Secretary of State Madeleine K. Albright, helped her "fall in love" with Russian history.

Rice explained her major objective in a speech to the U.S. Institute of Peace in Washington, D.C., after her appointment as security adviser. "We at the National Security Council are going to try to work the seams, stitching the connections together tightly," she said. "If we can do that, if we can provide glue for the many, many agencies and the many, many instruments the United States is now deploying around the world, I think we have done our job on behalf of the President of the United States" (Rice, 2001). The goal of "stitching the connections" became all the more important after the terrorist attacks against America in 2001.

The Counselor's Role Prevails

From the passage of the National Security Act in 1947 until today, the history of the NSC adviser's performance has swung between passive and more active roles. As Crabb and Mulcahy observe (in the last selection of Part V), passive advisers can perform as "administrators" and— acting more forcefully as managers of the planning process—as "coordinators," helping to

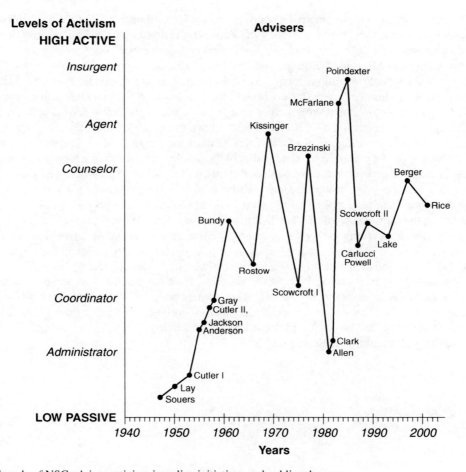

Figure VI.B Levels of NSC adviser activism in policy initiatives and public advocacy

move paper between the bureaucracy and the White House but staying away from policy initiation. When performing as "counselors" and "agents," the advisers become increasingly more assertive in the policy-making process. The counselor is much more involved in the substance of policy than either the administrator or coordinator, serving as the personal adviser to the president on foreign policy issues. The agent goes a big step further, becoming a vigorous public advocate for specific foreign policy positions. Recall that Crabb and Mulcahy point to a fifth role as well: the adviser-as-insurgent, who takes the NSC staff into an aggressive—and inappropriate—operational role based more on the adviser's "assessment of the president's *intentions* rather than on expressed presidential policies."

During the Council's first two decades, the adviser's role moved steadily toward a more assertive stance, as measured by the adviser's internal NSC managerial responsibilities and advocacy of policy (especially in public forums). This trend reached a high point under Dr. Kissinger, as depicted in Figure VI.B. In reaction to Kissinger's dominance of the policy-making process, the level of activity in initiating policy and "going public" fell back toward a more behind-the-scenes approach under Scowcroft during the Ford Administration. The role of adviser began to rise again under the aggressive leadership of Brzezinski, then experienced another decline with the more passive Allen and Clark, followed by a disastrous turn upward on the aggressive scale with the questionable operations carried out under McFarlane and (particularly) Poindexter. The strong personalities of advisers Carlucci and Powell no doubt helped to retard a full plunge back into a mere administrator or coordinator role in the wake of the Iran-*contra* excesses. More recently, the role of adviser has leveled off in the activist "counselor" mode.

This narrowing oscillation of adviser roles between the extremes of administrator and insurgent, settling on the preferred job description of "counselor," is a result of a long and sometimes painful process of trial and error within the office. The wide swings between passive and assertive advisers proved both inadequate (the administrator and coordinator roles failed to assist the president in grappling with policy choices) and dangerous (the insurgents brought to the nation the Iran-*contra* affair). The fact that the counselor role has prevailed reflects a learning experience regarding the dysfunction of extremes, either passive or active. Further, presidents have understood that the complex issues of foreign and security policy in the aftermath of the Cold War and demand an active adviser—but not an independent "insurgent" in the McFarlane–Poindexter sense of the word. The ideal is an adviser who can serve as an honest broker, faithfully representing the views and recommendations of NSC principals while sharing his or her own thoughts with the president; an adviser who keeps the paper flowing into and out of the Oval Office, and assists the administration in explaining its foreign policy initiatives to an increasingly demanding public and media.

17

McGeorge Bundy

Kai Bird

A former dean at Harvard University, McGeorge Bundy became the national security adviser for President John F. Kennedy in 1961. Under Bundy's leadership, the NSC staff became a powerful force in the planning and coordination of America's foreign and security policies.

Mac Bundy returned from his Caribbean vacation in early January 1961 to a bitterly cold New England winter. A few days later, President-elect John F. Kennedy was escorted inside Arthur Schlesinger, Jr.'s Cambridge home to meet with a select group of his Harvard-based advisers. As a team of Secret Service men stood guard outside, Bundy rode his bicycle past a crowd of onlookers, dismounted and, after leaning his bicycle against the gate, strode in to meet with his new boss.[1] Inside were some of the well-known scholars who would be joining Bundy in Washington. Schlesinger himself was already slated to work as one of the president's assistants; Jerome B. Wiesner became White House science adviser, and John Kenneth Galbraith was named ambassador to India.

When Kennedy announced Bundy's appointment on January 1, the president-elect said that his national security adviser would be "helping me to strengthen and to simplify the operations of the National Security Council."[2] What he really meant was that Bundy was going to dismantle much of the NSC's bureaucratic paraphernalia created during the Eisenhower years. Both Kennedy and Bundy had read Richard Neustadt's 1960 book, *Presidential Power,* which contrasted the freewheeling presidential style of Franklin Roosevelt with the rigid, military chain-of-command system Dwight Eisenhower had brought to the White House. A trendy political scientist at Columbia University, Neustadt argued that Roosevelt's disorderly style actually exposed him to more information from a wider range of sources and gave him the flexibility that was the genius of his administration. Neustadt's book gave Kennedy and Bundy the intellectual rationale to do what they were going to do anyway—run the White House as if it were Harvard, with Bundy as dean and Kennedy as president.

They would promote disorder. There would be fewer people, reports and formal meetings of the National Security Council. Bundy himself would take the jobs of five of Ike's NSC aides. The NSC would become more of a mini-State Department and less of a debating society. Within a month the NSC's staff was cut from seventy-one to forty-eight. In place of weighty policy papers, produced at regular intervals, Bundy's staff would produce crisp and timely National Security Action Memoranda (NSAMs). The new name signified the premium that would be placed on "action" over "planning." In effect, foreign policy would no longer be made at cabinet-level meetings. In theory, the men who came to advise the president in these smaller, freewheeling NSC meetings would represent no bureaucratic constituency other than the president, and they would argue the merits of each policy course based on substance. This was how intellectuals, not bureaucrats, would make foreign policy.[3]

Bundy immediately began recruiting his own staff, and many of them were also Cambridge men. Kennedy himself hired Walt W. Rostow to fill one slot in the

From Kai Bird, *The Color of Truth: McGeorge Bundy and William Bundy* (New York: Simon and Schuster, 1998), 185–90.
Kai Bird is an independent scholar and biographer.

NSC. Temperamentally, Bundy's old MIT friend was hardly the kind of man to serve as a deputy. Rostow was voluble, exuberant and full of good and sometimes foolish ideas. Bundy didn't mind. The former Harvard dean would give Rostow all the flexibility of a tenured member of the faculty.

Just ten days after the inauguration Bundy phoned another Cambridge friend, Carl Kaysen, forty, and said, "I need help. I'm having a lot of fun. Come work with me." Kaysen replied, "Mac, have you already forgotten Harvard? I have two courses I am committed to teaching this semester."

"Oh, just come and we'll talk about it," Bundy insisted. Kaysen came, was introduced to Kennedy in the Oval Office and agreed to start work in May.[4]

Bundy was not as eager to recruit Henry Kissinger; he knew from personal experience that Henry was hardly a team player. At Kennedy's invitation Kissinger visited the White House in early February. It is unclear whether Bundy ever offered Kissinger a full-time position; Kissinger later suggested that Bundy did not seem to share "the President's sense of urgency to add to the White House staff another professor of comparable academic competence."[5] Kissinger wanted to be a player in the new administration, but he also wanted to retain his tenured position at Harvard. Bundy was annoyed, but nevertheless arranged a part-time consultancy in which Kissinger would fly down four or five days a month. The arrangement did not last, and when Kissinger created a diplomatic gaffe during a trip to India in early 1962, Bundy quietly dismissed him.[6]

Having recruited quite a few outsiders, Mac called his brother Bill for the names of a few veterans of government service who knew the drill in Washington. Bill gave him the names of two colleagues from the CIA, Bob Komer and Chet Cooper. Cooper would soon spend half his time in the White House under Bundy. Komer soon went to work as Bundy's man on the Middle East and South Asia. (Blunt and abrasive, Komer would later earn the sobriquet "Blowtorch Bob" for his tough stance on the Vietnam War.)[7]

Despite his qualms about Bundy's move to the White House, or perhaps because of them, David Riesman began lobbying his old dean early that year to hire a young man whom he promised would be the "conscience" of his staff. At twenty-six, Marcus Raskin came to Washington with hardly any of the usual establishment credentials expected of an NSC staffer. A concert-level pianist (he once taught the composer Philip Glass), Raskin had abandoned a career in music to study law at the University of Chicago. In 1959, two years after earning a law degree, he became a staff assistant to Congressman Robert W. Kastenmeier (D.-Wis.). Kastenmeier put Raskin to work coordinating an informal caucus that included nine other congressmen interested in developing a new liberal agenda. They called themselves the Liberal Project, and by 1960, Raskin was editing a collection of essays for publication. Together with another Kastenmeier aide, Arthur Waskow, Raskin had drafted for inclusion in the book an essay critical of nuclear deterrence theory called "The Theory and Practice of Deterrence." Riesman was greatly impressed with the essay and the work of the Liberal Project.

Soon after the inauguration, Riesman persuaded Bundy to talk to Raskin about a White House job. The interview took place in Bundy's office, Room 374A of the Old Executive Office Building next door to the White House. "We had a good talk," Raskin recalled. "He was funny and witty; I was also at my best. I remember him asking me, 'Well, Mr. Raskin, do you have a liberal theory of deterrence?' I was all of twenty-six, and I handed him this essay."[8] Bundy was not altogether unfamiliar with the arguments contained in the Raskin-Waskow essay; he had, after all, picked up a healthy skepticism of deterrence theory from his work with Oppenheimer nine years earlier.

Later, as Raskin was about to come on board, Bundy asked him some difficult questions that clearly stemmed from the FBI's security check. Didn't he have a cousin, he asked, who was a communist? Raskin said he really didn't know, and hadn't seen her in years.

"You were on a program with I. F. Stone," the radical journalist, Bundy said. "We know that he is a communist."

"I don't know that," Raskin replied hotly. At this sign of vehemence, Bundy turned crimson, and Raskin later recalled being struck that Bundy was clearly embarrassed. Despite this exchange Raskin was hired.

Bundy knew he was getting a free spirit, a left-of-center, Jewish intellectual who might be troublesome.

Curiously, at one point he asked Raskin, "Would you mind being the Oppenheimer of this administration?"

A few weeks later Bundy wrote Riesman, thanking him for his referral of Raskin: "With any luck, he should be at work here in another few days. In my few conversations with him, I have found just the qualities you describe. . . . He has a remarkably powerful and lively mind, and it is flanked by both moral and physical energy. I think we shall probably have some disagreements, but I shall feel a lot better for knowing that certain problems have passed by his critical eye on their way to resolution."[9]

Informality was the rule in Bundy's shop, which he likened to a think tank. Mac had pulled together a staff of very independent-minded men: Kaysen, Rostow, Komer, Raskin, Bromley K. Smith, Dave Klein, Ralph Dungan and, on occasion, Kissinger. These were all "very high-powered, strong-minded people" and Bundy generally made no attempt to block their access to the president. He and his principal deputy, Kaysen, made a point of taking staff members into the Oval Office and allowing them to brief Kennedy on their area of expertise. "We were few enough," Kaysen recalled, "so that the president had some idea of who we were and what we were doing."[10]

Bundy's daily routine was hectic. Each morning at 7:45 A.M. a government-chauffeured Mercury sedan picked him up at his spacious, white-bricked home in the Spring Valley section of Washington and ferried him down to the White House. Along the way, he dropped off his sons at St. Albans, Washington's elite prep school. After glancing at the early-morning cable traffic—some seven pounds of paper each day— Bundy would preside over a 9 A.M. staff meeting where he peppered his aides with questions. "Mac is brilliant at 9 o'clock in the morning, as very few other people can be," recalled one staffer. Afterwards, Bundy would go up to the president's quarters and brief Kennedy on the overnight intelligence developments from around the globe.[11]

Most evenings he did not return home until eight o'clock at night. Over a bourbon-on-the-rocks or a martini, he would spend a little time in horseplay with his sons before their bedtime. He enjoyed good food and vintage wines, and was known to consume large quantities of ice cream. He and Mary rarely enter-tained in their home, but not infrequently attended dinner parties on the diplomatic circuit or with such old friends as Joe Alsop, Walter Lippmann and Felix Frankfurter. Mary found the change of pace from Cambridge "a little frightening. All those parties—I wasn't used to it, you know. It took a lot out of me."[12]

Kennedy's foreign policy team was ostensibly headed by Secretary of State Dean Rusk (formerly president of the Rockefeller Foundation) and Robert S. McNamara, who had left his new job as president of the Ford Motor Company after only thirty-four days to become secretary of defense. Bundy immediately recognized a soul mate in McNamara, whose persona as a "whiz kid" meshed nicely with his own peppery personality. By contrast, Mac quickly decided that Rusk's bland demeanor masked neither wit nor intelligence. Very early in the new administration it became clear that Bundy's shop was running circles around Rusk's State Department. Bundy had daily access to the president; Rusk did not. With calculated modesty, Bundy would tell the press that his job was only that of a "traffic cop—to see what gets forwarded to the President." It was that and much more. One day, the president told his wife, Jacqueline, "Damn it, Bundy and I get more done in one day in the White House than they do in six months at the State Department." Soon, the *Washington Post* labeled Bundy a "shadow secretary of state." Asked what he would have done if Bundy had been at the NSC when he was secretary of state, Dean Acheson replied, "Resign."[13]

After two months on the job Bundy quipped to a *New York Times* reporter, "Yes, at this point we are like the Harlem Globetrotters, passing forward, behind, side-wise and underneath. But nobody has made a basket yet."[14] About the same time he wrote Stanley Hoffmann, then attending a seminar in Geneva, "Your description of Geneva makes it sound like the opposite of Washington. There you have serious discussions in an atmosphere of unconcern, and here . . ." But then he confided, "I think perhaps we are moving toward a period in which we shall be able to take serious decisions, some of them even based on thought."[15]

Kennedy had a special rapport with his national security adviser. "They think alike," said one colleague. "He knows what the President wants. The President's intensity is perfectly complemented by Bundy's ability to move things."[16] Kennedy hated small talk and quickly cut off those who bored him. Bundy, of course, never bored anyone. It was not long before the *New York Times* was quoting an anonymous official as saying that Bundy was the president's "alter-ego . . . another Harry Hopkins—with hand grenades."[17] The analogy was both apt and inept. Franklin Roosevelt's friend and confidant was a gentle soul, an intensely introspective man who arrived at his judgments after exhaustive consultations. There was nothing abrupt about Hopkins. But perhaps just as Hopkins came to symbolize an archetype for the action-oriented intellectual of the Roosevelt era, so too Mac Bundy would soon become a model for the liberal policy intellectual of the 1960s. He knew he was serving a man impatient with the language of bureaucrats. So he took to summarizing tedious State Department cables with one-liners that amused the president. He once said of a visiting foreign diplomat that the man possessed a "very tactical sense of the truth."[18]

Bundy didn't hesitate to push Kennedy if he thought the president was wrong. When Kennedy kept interrupting Bundy's early-morning intelligence briefing with complaints about press leaks, Bundy calmly cut the president off. "Goddammit, Mac," Kennedy was once overheard exclaiming, "I've been arguing with you about this all week long."[19]

There was no mistaking that they liked each other immensely. Kennedy jokingly told his (and Bundy's) childhood friend, *Newsweek* bureau chief Ben Bradlee, "I only hope he [Bundy] leaves a few residual functions to me. . . . You can't beat brains. . . . He does a tremendous amount of work. And he doesn't fold or get rattled when they're sniping at him."[20] Temperamentally, Bundy and Kennedy were cast from the same impatient mold. A Harvard professor who knew both men said of Bundy, "He pays no attention to what the other fellow may think. He's as cold as ice and snippy about everything. He and Jack Kennedy are two of a kind."[21]

Yet, Bundy sometimes could surprise people with unexpected warmth. Once, after hearing Kennedy give a State Department official a tongue-lashing on the phone that "made the wires sizzle," Bundy called the official fifteen minutes later and said, "I was in the room when the President was . . . er, talking to you,

and I just wanted to say that it has happened to all of us. This little hot spot will quickly cool, and you should realize that the President would not have permitted himself that kind of blow-off if you were not one of those he regards highly and fully trusts." The official in question, Roger Hilsman, would have his differences with Bundy, but he always thought of him as a "man of warmth and thoughtfulness."[22]

Kennedy also found it convenient that his national security adviser was a Republican. When Bundy suggested that he now "felt like a Democrat" and that perhaps he ought to change his party registration in time for the 1962 congressional elections, Kennedy told him that it was "marginally more useful to me to be able to say that you're a Republican."[23]

Jack Kennedy was also a man who felt compelled to complicate his sexual life with a large cast of women—both inside and outside the White House. It helped that Bundy was the kind of Boston Brahmin who was not a prude. Evidently, Kennedy trusted him enough that he felt no need to hide all of his sexual dalliances from his friend. Still, it could be awkward, particularly when the president arranged for one of his lovers—a Radcliffe graduate he had met in 1959—to work on Bundy's staff. "It was very embarrassing," the woman later told Seymour Hersh. "It put McGeorge in a very creepy situation."[24] In any case, Bundy was a paragon of discreetness.

What for some was Bundy's arrogance appeared to Kennedy as simple "balls." Kennedy respected balls. When the president's brother Bobby, the attorney general, resigned his membership in the Metropolitan Club over the club's refusal to admit a black guest, Bundy astonished all of Washington by joining the club just a month later. When reporters queried him about it, Bundy responded, "This is a question each man must decide for himself. . . . If I were Attorney General I might come to a different conclusion. I have no quarrel with those who reached a decision to resign." He did not say so, but among those who had resigned was his own brother Bill, then deputy assistant secretary of defense. "There'd been a recurrent question of blacks coming to the club," Bill Bundy recalled. When the club made it clear that blacks weren't welcome even as guests, "this raised it to the level of outrage," he said, "and I resigned. It wasn't a very great sacrifice. . . ." It was not an issue between the brothers, but the incident spoke volumes about their respective political sensibilities.[25]

NOTES

1. David Wise, "Scholars of the Nuclear Age: McGeorge Bundy, Walt W. Rostow and Jerome B. Wiesner," in Lester Tanzer, ed., *The Kennedy Circle* (Washington, D.C.: Luce, 1961), p. 38.

2. John Prados, *Keepers of the Keys: A History of the National Security Council from Truman to Bush* (New York: Morrow, 1991), p. 97.

3. During Bundy's tenure, "no hard decision was ever taken in the formal National Security Council meetings." Michael V. Forrestal interview transcript by Joseph Kraft, Apr. 8, 1964, Secret, p. 40, MF. This transcript was obtained by the author from the late Averell Harriman.

4. Carl Kaysen interview, June 18, 1993.

5. Walter Isaacson, *Kissinger: A Biography* (New York: Simon and Schuster, 1992), p. 110.

6. MB interview, Nov. 17, 1993; Prados, *Keepers of the Keys,* pp. 114–15; Arthur Schlesinger, Jr., interview, June 6, 1995.

7. Robert Komer interview, Oct. 5, 1993.

8. This was a staff report prepared for Congressman Robert W. Kastenmeier and later published in *The Liberal Papers,* ed. James Roosevelt (New York: Doubleday Anchor, 1962).

9. Marcus Raskin interviews, June 4, Sept. 3, 1993; MB to David Riesman, Apr. 4, 1961, Bundy Papers, Chronological File, Box 398, JFK. There were limits to Bundy's New Frontier openness. Even before recruiting Raskin, he had tried to bring aboard Michael Maccoby, twenty-seven, his former aide from Harvard. But when Maccoby published an article with Erich Fromm in *Commentary* critical of the whole "counter-force" strategy of nuclear deterrence, Bundy sent him a note saying he could better advance the debate while serving outside the government. (Michael Maccoby interview, Dec. 13, 1993.)

10. Forrestal interview by Kraft, p. 58; Prados, *Keepers of the Keys,* p. 114.

11. Forrestal interview by Kraft, pp. 16, 21.

12. *Newsweek,* Mar. 4, 1963, p. 24; Stephen Birmingham, *The Right People: A Portrait of the American Social Establishment* (Boston: Little, Brown, 1968), p. 229.

13. *Newsweek,* Mar. 4, 1963; *WP,* Jan. 18, 1961; Michael R. Beschloss, *The Crisis Years: Kennedy and Khrushchev, 1960–1963* (New York: HarperCollins, 1991), p. 249.

14. *NYT,* Mar. 20, 1961.

15. MB to Stanley Hoffmann, Apr. 3, 1961, Bundy Chronological File, Box 398, JFK.

16. *Newsweek,* Mar. 4, 1963, p. 20.

17. Sidney Hyman, "When Bundy Says, 'The President Wants—'" *NYT Magazine* Dec. 2, 1962. See also Lloyd Gardner, "Harry Hopkins with Hand Grenades? McGeorge Bundy in the Kennedy and Johnson Years," courtesy of Gardner, on file at LBJ.

18. Max Frankel, "The Importance of Being Bundy," *NYT Magazine,* Mar. 28, 1965.

19. Robert Smith Thompson, *The Missiles of October* (New York: Simon & Schuster, 1992), p. 185.

20. Beschloss, *The Crisis Years,* p. 249.

21. *Newsweek,* Mar. 4, 1963, p. 23.

22. Roger Hilsman, *To Move a Nation* (Garden City, N.Y.: Doubleday, 1967), pp. 45–46.

23. Beschloss, *The Crisis Years,* p. 250.

24. Seymour M. Hersh, *The Dark Side of Camelot* (Boston: Little, Brown, 1997), p. 111.

25. *WP,* Oct. 5, 1961, and WPB interview, Nov. 1, 1993. Shortly before his assassination, President Kennedy's "persistent and not always gentle needling" persuaded Mac Bundy to resign his membership from the club in protest against its segregation. Mac regretted that he never got around to telling Kennedy that he had finally resigned. (William Manchester, *The Death of a President* [New York: Harper & Row, 1967], p. 581.)

18

HENRY KISSINGER

Marvin Kalb and Bernard Kalb

Doubtless the most famous of the national security advisers, Henry Kissinger, who served during the Nixon Administration, converted the NSC staff into another—and more important—Department of State within the White House. The Kalbs profile his meteoric career through the 1960s and 1970s, and reveal a few sides of this notable statesman's complex personality.

Henry Alfred Kissinger is an extravaganza—all by himself. At fifty-one, after only five years in Washington, this energetic balancer of power has emerged from the relative obscurity of a Harvard professorship to become the most celebrated and controversial diplomat of our time. He has come to be recognized as the very portrait of American diplomacy, the way George Washington is identified with the dollar bill. A legend in half a decade, he has been described as, among other things, the "second most powerful man in the world," "conscience of the Administration," "official apologist," "compassionate hawk," "vigilant dove," "Dr. Strangelove," "household word," "the playboy of the Western Wing," "Nixon's Metternich," "Nixon's secret agent," "the Professident of the United States," "Jackie Onassis of the Nixon Administration," "Nobel warrior," "Mideast cyclone," "reluctant wiretapper," and "Secretary of the world"—a long list, especially in Washington, where praise of any sort is the only thing that never exceeds its budget.

From the beginning, Kissinger outraged the gray men who guarded the corridors of Richard Nixon's White House. His accent, his brilliance, his flair for self-promotion labeled him a heretic, destined for banishment. Yet it turned out that *they*—the Haldemans, the Ehrlichmans, those caught up in the torrent of Watergate—were to go, and *he* was to go on to even greater heights. From his start in the basement of the West Wing of the White House, as Assistant to the President for National Security Affairs, he would vault to the seventh floor of the State Department as Secretary of State, a position once held by Thomas Jefferson, Daniel Webster, and John Foster Dulles. It was an unprecedented leap for someone of his origins—a refugee from Nazi Germany, a Jew. En route, Kissinger acquired such a formidable reputation that, by the beginning of 1974, he would be viewed by many of Nixon's critics as the sole legitimizer of a President discredited by Watergate. Whereas Kissinger had once needed Nixon as a channel to power, Nixon now needed Kissinger to help him remain in power. Their relationship had become so topsy-turvy that the academic aide at Nixon's side was seen as perhaps the last fortress against the unmaking of a President.

Henry Kissinger arrived in Washington at a ripe moment internationally. The United States and the world, he recognized, were in a fluid, transitional period. For the first time, the nuclear superpowers were beginning to appreciate the limits of their own power and the need to find some way of reducing tensions. And the other fellow's increasingly bigger bomb wasn't the only convincing reason; wherever Kissinger looked, he saw significant changes taking place within countries and among countries.

From Marvin Kalb and Bernard Kalb, *Kissinger* (Boston: Little, Brown, 1974), 3–13.

The brothers Marvin and Bernard Kalb are journalists who have covered U.S. foreign affairs.

The United States no longer regarded itself as the policeman of the world; those long, frustrating years of war in Indochina had altered America's image of itself, but, even more important, the lopsided strategic advantage that America had once enjoyed was lost. The Soviet Union and China were now more hostile to each other than to the United States; what was once thought by many analysts to be pure gospel—a monolithic unity among the Communist countries, with Moscow calling the signals—had proved to be a misreading of history. What is more, the conflict between Moscow and Peking, coupled with their domestic problems, had prodded Russia into softening its policy of blunt confrontation with the West, and China into reexamining its policy of lofty isolation. Europe and Japan had more than regained their economic vitality; they were now capable of playing a greater role in international affairs. Some Arab leaders were beginning to recognize that war with Israel was not the only policy option open to them. The new countries had emerged from their first outbursts of nationalism and now seemed eager for more profitable dealings with the rest of the world. There were tensions, but not all were threatening. The world seemed to be rumbling its way toward new relationships.

To Kissinger, these changing facts of international life added up to a unique moment in history. He regarded timing as critical. "Opportunities can not be hoarded; once past, they are usually irretrievable," he once wrote. *When* to act, not only what to do, became a cardinal feature of his diplomatic style. He shuttled to and from everywhere, tenaciously trying to exploit the moment of opportunity. And, operating in the dangerous but potentially productive area between new hopes for peace and old fears of extinction, he helped promote policies that would be widely regarded as an effort to create a more relaxed, if still well-armed, world.

Foreign policy was the Administration's forte, with Kissinger its peripatetic negotiator. He would sip champagne with Kremlin leaders, humanizing them for a whole generation of Americans raised on the Cold War. He would try to establish a new, more rational and responsible dialogue with them, making détente—still one more try at détente—a worthy goal of American policy and putting limits, if possible, on the production and deployment of deadly nuclear weapons. He would journey to Peking, replacing two decades of hostility with a new effort to communicate with a quarter of the human race. He would fly the Atlantic at least a dozen times secretly, many more times publicly, to negotiate a compromise settlement of the Vietnam war, fighting off the hawks with one hand, the doves with the other, until, finally, in January, 1973, he was able to arrange a deal with Hanoi for the return of American prisoners from North Vietnam and the withdrawal of American troops from South Vietnam. In the Middle East, he would introduce "shuttle diplomacy"—flying back and forth between Jerusalem and Aswan, or Jerusalem and Damascus—in a major effort to substitute a pattern of negotiations for the endless conflicts of the region, achieving at least the start of disengagement by Arab and Israeli armies from the war zone. Altogether, his extraordinary efforts to recruit the nations of the world, big and small, to new rules of behavior became the stuff of international drama. They reached a climax in late 1973 when he was awarded the Nobel Prize for Peace for his role in the Vietnam cease-fire negotiations.

Not that everything he touched turned to gold.

More than one of his heralded agreements, when scrutinized in the cold light of dawn, appeared to lose some of their glow. His penchant for secrecy and surprise kept a number of America's allies out in the cold. His virtuoso style of diplomacy during the first Nixon term left the State Department demoralized and Congress just another spectator. Even his Nobel Prize was challenged by some critics as premature, a bad joke, particularly since Vietnam was still at war.

There were other criticisms, too, more specific in nature.

From the left there was a chorus of indictments accusing him of having failed to justify, in moral or political terms, those extra four years of U.S. war in Vietnam and divisiveness at home. From the right came the accusation that he had given away too much to the Russians during the SALT negotiations, compromising American security in his quest for détente. And from his friends, right and left, there was deep disappointment that he had "tilted" in favor of Pakistan against India in 1971, while the soldiers from Islamabad were conducting what was described as mass murder of the Bengalis of East Pakistan.

Nor was that all.

He came under increasing suspicion as to the exact extent of his involvement in the wiretapping of his own National Security Council staff and of the press. His attempts to explain his relationship with the "plumbers" and to play down reports of military spying within the NSC left many with the uneasy feeling that he was being less than candid. His defense of his role was regarded by his admirers as plain realism and by his critics as plain deception.

Kissinger's route to power was created by the presidential election of 1968: Nixon won, and Kissinger was available. Though he had been anti-Nixon, Kissinger found the invitation to join the White House irresistible; it was a question of opportunity over doubt. He had been shuttling from Cambridge to Washington ever since the Eisenhower Administration, offering his opinions about foreign policy as a consultant on the outskirts of power. The new President-elect wanted to bring him into the center of power. Nixon was seeking a foreign policy specialist who shared his perception of how to manipulate America's dwindling power to achieve a new balance of power—what he would later call "a structure of peace." The fact that Kissinger's crossing over to Nixon was seen as a defection from the skeptical Eastern Establishment only heightened Nixon's conviction that he had made the right choice.

They converged from different starting points: Nixon, via hard-nosed politics, a Californian, chauvinistically conservative; Kissinger, via intellectual achievement, an immigrant, a hard-liner with an international bent. Yet they ended up with reasonably similar views on policy and the uses of power. Moreover, Kissinger would provide a coherent conceptual framework for Nixon's sudden diplomatic maneuvers. In their new role as gravediggers of ideology, both shared a global *realpolitik* that placed a higher priority on pragmatism than on morality. Both, almost as if they saw the planet as an unsafe place to inhabit, shared a compulsion for secrecy, a distrust of bureaucracy, an elitist approach to diplomacy; both preferred to present the world with a fait accompli rather than to reveal their intentions in advance.

True, their personalities are different, and both men are undoubtedly relieved that this is so widely recognized. Kissinger is warm, friendly, sensitive; Nixon's aloofness can never be mistaken. Kissinger can be a connoisseur of nuance, with a talent for subtle explanations and, when necessary, for elegant double-talk; Nixon specializes in the hard hyperbole, the sentence painted in black and white. Indeed, there are times when one catches a glimpse of pained self-control as Kissinger listens to a presidential oration. Both men are loners, at the summit yet still dogged by insecurities; but one prefers to hide away at crowded social gatherings, often with interchangeable celebrities, while the other hides away in more traditional hideaways.

Indeed, they are an odd couple. After more than five years of constant contact, their personal relationship remains more correct than close—even though Kissinger no longer has to worry about proving his loyalty or being undercut by the President's praetorians. For all practical purposes, Kissinger's dealings with Nixon have been business, not social. Occasionally, the President will invite his foreign policy adviser to a private dinner at the White House, but as a companion to the President, Kissinger has always been outdistanced by Charles "Bebe" Rebozo. Formality, the tone set by the President, has always characterized the Nixon-Kissinger relationship. Despite their differences in temperament, the man whom Nixon named as Secretary of State in August, 1973, wholeheartedly supports his chief's foreign policy. "You can assume," Kissinger once said, "that if I could not support a major policy I would resign."

It can be said of Henry Kissinger that the government saves money by paying him at a flat rate instead of by the hour. He puts in one of Washington's longest days. Up early—six hours of uninterrupted sleep means that the world has enjoyed a restful night, too—he's quickly on his way out of his six-room townhouse overlooking Rock Creek Park, often with his laundry in one hand and his attaché case in the other. In his early NSC days, he used to drive a white Mercedes through the two miles of rush-hour traffic to the White House but, both because of the pressures of work and the requirements of security, he soon capitulated to a chauffeur-driven limousine. He usually has breakfast at his office. While the decor in his home has been described as Midwestern Holiday Inn, his office is more a mix of Early American and Contemporary Bureaucratic. Since 1970, his NSC office has been on street level, just down the hallway from the Oval Office. It has tall French windows, and he's often framed in one of them, foot on the sill, while he talks on the phone. He'll wave to reporters passing by on their way to the White House Press Room, just a few yards away.

The walls, shelves, and tabletops are decorated with a variety of paintings, bric-a-brac, and mementos of his world travels. The most striking painting hangs just over a couch; it is a huge canvas in subtle tones of purple undulating out of a central reddish circle. Kissinger finds it relaxing. The painting, on loan from a friend in Cambridge, is the work of Jules Olitski, an abstract colorist of the New York school. "Don't tell Olitski where it is," the friend once said during the days of heavy U.S. involvement in Vietnam. "He's against the war, and he wouldn't like the idea of it hanging in Henry's office in the White House." Other paintings are souvenirs of his journeys to Moscow and Peking. Leonid Brezhnev presented him with a large still life, a bouquet of flowers painted by P. Kongolovsky, a socialist realist artist, in 1952. The Chinese gave him a scroll copy of a horse painted by Hsü Pei-hung, who achieved international fame before his death in 1953. The shelves are filled with books, including some he wrote himself. On a table behind his desk is a framed photograph of the President. "To Henry Kissinger," says the inscription, "for whose wise counsel and dedicated services far beyond the call of duty I shall always remain grateful. From his friend, Richard Nixon." On the desk, a direct telephone to the President.

When he was named Secretary of State, he inherited a second, more commodious suite of offices on the seventh floor of the huge governmental building in Foggy Bottom that he once did his best to avoid. He quickly introduced a more contemporary decor into the main sitting room, with abstract art, including paintings by Rothko and Pousette-Dart, illuminated by floor lights, replacing some of the portraits from the pages of American history that were on display during the tenure of his predecessor, William P. Rogers. A glance through his office window offers a panoramic view of the Washington Monument, the Lincoln Memorial, and, on a clear day, the Lee Mansion on the other side of the Potomac. He now spends more time here than he does at his NSC office, not only because of the requirements of being Secretary but perhaps because he wants to put a bit of distance between himself and the stricken leader in the White House.

Toward dusk, Kissinger will be reminded by his secretary about what's on the calendar for the second half of his working day. It could be a diplomatic reception at one of the embassies on Massachusetts Avenue, a cocktail party in Georgetown, an opening of a new play at the Kennedy Center, or sometimes all three. His very appearance at any affair proclaims it a triumph; most hostesses would rather have, say, twenty-three minutes of Henry than a full evening of all the other members of the Cabinet and Congress combined. Depending on the ambience, he will turn up as either an intellectual besieged by the problems of the world or a swinger tossing off surefire one-liners from his growing repertoire. The party over, Kissinger will begin working again. Often he waves a breezy farewell to his hostess, steps into his limousine, and promptly settles down to study a sheaf of documents handed him by an aide waiting out in the cold.

Yet for all the long hours he puts in, he has never looked better. Since his arrival in Washington, he's been wearing his hair and his waistline a little thicker. His contours seem to change with each overseas trip. In November, 1973, he came back from a ten-country, twenty-five-thousand-mile journey that took him to the Middle East and China looking as though Chou En-lai had fattened him up on shark's fin in three shreds and spongy bamboo shoots with egg-white consommé. "When I negotiate," he confessed, "I get nervous. When I get nervous, I eat. By the time this Arab-Israeli affair is over, I'll probably weigh three hundred twenty pounds." In Washington, he usually can be found lunching at the fashionable and expensive Sans Souci, where other diners will spend more time studying Kissinger than their checks. His fluctuating waistline has been good business for one of the local formal attire rental establishments. Since he can never be sure what he will weigh in at for any White House state dinner, he generally ends up renting white tie and tails at seventeen dollars a night. During Nixon's first term, Kissinger was outfitted no less than thirty-three times. Before dinner, his size is forty-two regular.

Along with the change from campus tweeds at Harvard to diplomatic uniform in Washington came, perhaps surprisingly to Kissinger himself, a new reputation as the nation's reigning "swinger." "I'm baffled and stunned," confessed a professor friend in Cambridge. "It is not the Henry we knew here."

"His swinging?" says another old friend. "Why not? It humanizes him."

Kissinger had his own assessment of his appeal. "They are women attracted only to my power," he used to say. "But what happens when my power is gone? They're not going to sit around and play chess with me." His most celebrated diagnosis of his success: "Power is the ultimate aphrodisiac."

Before he became Secretary of State, he cultivated his swinger image; but many people suspected he was really a swinger by photograph. He would pop up next to one charmer or another at one function or another and a lurking cameraman would film them side by side; the publication of the photo in the morning newspaper would further enhance his image as a swinger. As for Kissinger himself on this subject, he used to play it cool. There's a story that once when Peter Peterson, then Commerce Secretary and one of Kissinger's closer friends in town, asked him, "Tell me, Henry, when you go out with the girls . . ." Kissinger interrupted, grinning broadly. "Eat your heart out, Peterson," he chortled. That implied question might better be answered by the girls themselves, or at least by one who perhaps knows him best. "Henry," she says, definitively, "is very old-fashioned. He has old-fashioned virtues, and a strong belief in family life. He is a very moral man. The 'swinger' is as square as he can be."

After Kissinger became Secretary of State, the "swinger" became a "square." The Hollywood starlets vanished from his side and, on March 30, 1974, he married Nancy Sharon Maginnes, a tall, attractive New Yorker whom he had known since the early 1960s. With the same sort of secrecy that had marked his early trips to Peking and Moscow, he slipped out of the State Department and crossed the Potomac to Arlington, Virginia, where the civil ceremony took place. The newlyweds were already airborne for a ten-day honey-moon in Acapulco, Mexico, when the State Department made the announcement. This was one society note that was front-page news around the world.

The genius of Kissinger, a columnist once remarked, is that he tells you what he is *not* but never what he is. The result has been that the search for Henry's true personality has become an amusing Washington parlor game.

"Are you shy, by any chance?" he was once asked by an Italian journalist.

"Yes, I am rather," he replied, although there is no record of the expression on his face as he spoke. "On the other hand, however," he went on, "I believe I'm fairly well balanced. You see, there are those who describe me as a mysterious, tormented character, and others who see me as a merry guy, smiling, always laughing. Both these images are untrue. I'm neither one nor the other. I'm . . . no, I won't tell you what I am. I'll never tell anyone."

It may be that for a man who reigns wherever he goes, who cannot possibly live up to all the demands on his time, who has had the rare pleasure of discovering that there is a shortage of Kissinger, mystery is more spellbinding than autobiography. It is as if the details of his life, as refugee, immigrant, and professor, were too unexotic for the world of power and glamour in which he now lives. Hence, the gamesmanship, the enhancing of the social image he most exults in: the charming hieroglyphic.

But someone who has been out there in the floodlights as often as he has cannot remain wholly undecipherable. Quite often, in recent years, he has revealed some of the layers beneath surface.

"When you think of my life," he confided early in 1974, "who could possibly have imagined that I'd wind up as Secretary of State of the greatest country in the world? I mean, when I couldn't even go to German schools . . . when I think I was a delivery boy in New York." The feeling of vulnerability that he acquired in his youth has never been totally eradicated. He is forever on the lookout for enemies—much more so than most Washington officials and Harvard professors are as a matter of course. Naturally he has turned this into a joke. "The first question I ask myself just before retiring every night, as I look under my bed: 'Is someone trying to get me?'"

When he catches a glimpse of a potential antagonist, Kissinger's instinct is to win him over with charm
and humor. When he has a difference of opinion with a
friend, someone whose allegiance is beyond question,
he can be blunt and candid. When the friend is also a
subordinate, Kissinger can be brusque and impatient.
He is a demanding taskmaster, expecting, and for the
most part getting, total loyalty and dedication. He
knows he represents action, and he knows that everyone wants a part of it.

The same blend of humor and charm, toughness
and candor, topped by no small amount of guile, characterizes his style with Congressmen and foreign leaders. He has the remarkable ability to convince two people with opposing viewpoints that he agrees with both
of them—without in any way compromising his own
position. One case in point was the reaction of Senators Henry Jackson and J. William Fulbright to separate briefings by Kissinger about the Brezhnev letter
on the Middle East war that led to the U.S. military
alert in October, 1973. Jackson, who is skeptical of
détente, found it encouraging that the letter was
assessed as "brutal." Fulbright, who is for even more
détente, found it reassuring that the letter was assessed
as "reasonable." Kissinger would later deny that he had
spoken to either one of them.

Today, the prominence of Henry Kissinger is a
matter of fact, but when the Nixon Administration first
came to Washington, he was not even permitted to be
"Henry Kissinger." Although he was always the "background" briefer on foreign policy issues, he could
never be identified as anything other than "White
House officials" or "a high Administration source."
There were a couple of reasons for keeping Kissinger
a top secret. For one thing, the Nixon people wanted no
one to compete with the President as *the* voice of the
Administration. For another, because of his accent

Kissinger himself was not keen on having his voice
recorded. "And there was also some concern about
Henry's 'Dr. Strangelove' image," an ex-White House
aide recalls. "Henry was quite sensitive about all this."
But as Kissinger quickly demonstrated that he was the
best briefer in recent Washington history, a virtuoso in
explaining the President's foreign policy, and as his
own confidence grew, he was liberated from the depths
of the White House to appear "on the record" before
the White House press corps. He made his official
debut at the end of October, 1971, after one secret and
one public trip to China.

Though he has been described as everything from
"resident genius" to "con man," Kissinger prefers to
avoid the flamboyant in describing his own role. Once,
in early 1974, while driving along the San Diego Free-
way from San Clemente to Los Angeles, he was asked
to reflect on his hopes and ambitions.

"I'd like to leave behind a world that seemed to be
more peaceful than the one we entered," he said softly.
"More creative in the sense of fulfilling human aspirations. And of course, it's been my dream, which for
many reasons has not been fully realizable, to have contributed in some sense to unity in the American people.
That was my approach in Vietnam. And, you know, we
couldn't foresee Watergate then." He looked out the
window, watching California go by at fifty-five miles an
hour. "No, I have my vanity and ego and everything else
that people allege, and I'm sure it's true. But my policy
is really more geared to what people will think in 1980
than to what the newspapers say tomorrow."

Yet when he is out there on the stage, being
cheered as a global lion-tamer, he cannot resist the
temptation to join in the applause. Once at a large
Washington dinner a man walked up to him and said,
"Dr. Kissinger, I want to thank you for saving the
world." "You're welcome," he replied.

19

ZBIGNIEW BRZEZINSKI

Dom Bonafede

The national security adviser in the Carter Administration, Zbigniew Brzezinski became an active public advocate for a range of foreign policy initiatives, competing at times (a la Kissinger) with the secretary of state for the job of spokesman for the United Nations in its international affairs.

U.S. foreign policy had been dominated so long by Henry A. Kissinger that when President Carter appointed Zbigniew Brzezinski as his assistant for national security affairs last January, it was inevitable that comparisons would be made. And they have been, to the possible disservice of both Kissinger and Brzezinski, who despite their common credentials as foreign-born intellectuals with impressive academic credits, served different Presidents in different times.

Yet the specter of Kissinger, who shuttled across the world stage for eight years on errands of personal diplomacy, was unlikely to vanish quickly and Brzezinski, aware of the savagery of academic, press and political critics, was too smart and cautious, as his tour of duty began, to subject himself to premature analogies. For the most part he stayed in the shadows of the presidency. Furthermore, Carter had set down a commandment that foreign policy would be directed from the Oval Office, albeit with the cooperative assistance of a triumvirate composed of Secretary of State Cyrus R. Vance, Defense Secretary Harold Brown and Brzezinski, director of the National Security Council (NSC).

Now, after nine months, there are signs that Brzezinski is coming out of the shadows and into the light, confident of his position among the architects and executors of Carter's foreign policy and of the role established by the White House-based NSC staff. He has survived the early months of the Administration

without a glove being laid on him by pedagogical combatants who do their verbal brawling in ivy-covered faculty clubs.

During a recent interview, Brzezinski conceded he had been purposely keeping a low profile. "When I first came here, I operated under a cloud of suspicion that I would use this office to undercut either the Secretary of State or the Secretary of Defense," he said. "I have no intention of so doing and I've said so from the very beginning. But I was sensitive to the fact that if I started running around being the object of numerous interviews and television programs, that this impression would be abetted and people would simply thrive on it. . . . Moreover, I do think that [in avoiding this], I can be more effective in influencing what is of central importance, namely the direction of things."

Influencing the direction of things, subtly and discreetly, and not in the flashy style of Kissinger, is indeed Brzezinski's *raison d'etre* as Carter's in-house foreign policy adviser. Notwithstanding his brief spell at the White House, Brzezinski already has revised his notion of what his function should be. Prior to taking over the NSC staff, he said that he would give the President advice only when asked and that he did not visualize himself as a policy maker. He saw his role, he said, as being mainly that of an operational line officer. Possibly, Brzezinski made the remark because he held an innocent view of his forthcoming role, but that seems inconceivable considering his background as a

---

From Dom Bonafede, "Brzezinski—Stepping Out of His Backstage Role," *National Journal* (October 14, 1977): 1596–1601.

Dom Bonafede was a reporter for the *National Journal* in Washington, D.C.

sophisticated student of government and respected specialist in foreign policy affairs. More likely, he believed it would allay any concern that he was bent on wielding more influence than the Secretary of State, as Kissinger did when he was national security assistant to President Nixon and William P. Rogers was Secretary of State from 1969 to 1973. Similarly, the general perception was that McGeorge Bundy and Walt W. Rostow, NSC chiefs during the Kennedy and Johnson years, carried more weight than Secretary of State Dean Rusk.

However, Carter's stress on reviving the Cabinet's authority tends to preclude a repetition of such a relationship in the present Administration. Also, from all accounts, Brzezinski and Vance collaborate as equals. Symbolic of this is the fact that although Brzezinski does not hold Cabinet status, he sits at the principals' table during Cabinet sessions.

More important, while Brzezinski is not technically a policy maker, he does "help in the process of making policy," as he delicately phrases it. The distinction, to many, is exceedingly narrow; to others, it is nonexistent, since high-level executive policy is seldom, if ever, made by a single official, except by the President.

Of his professional association with Carter, Brzezinski said, "I work very closely with the President. I'm his adviser in foreign policy and security matters. And I'm the coordinator for him of all the work that comes for his decision from the State Department, from Defense and from the CIA. Finally, and expressly so, the President wishes me and my staff to help him play an innovative role, that is to say, to try to look beyond the problems of the immediate and help him define a larger and more distant sense of direction."

Certainly, by his own description, and within the limits imposed on all Administration officials, Brzezinski must be classified as a policy maker in the generally accepted and practical meaning of the term.

Brzezinski's first-floor, corner office is one of the most select in the White House, with oil paintings of American frontier Indian guides and old masted schooners and two globes, a silver, modernistic version and a traditional floor model. Indirect lighting provides a pale yellow radiance. Books are piled in one corner and tennis togs in another.

While Brzezinski speaks, he restlessly sketches an elaborate design on a white pad. His words are tinged with the accent of his native Poland and pour forth at a rapid tempo.

Does he give advice only upon presidential request? Brzezinski smiled at the suggestion and said, "I think the President probably concedes the fact he sometimes obtains unsolicited advice—and disagreement—from me."

Later, he recalled that when the NSC was created in 1947, it was expected that the staff director would serve largely in a bureaucratic capacity as a secretarial coordinator. "I don't think I'm that," he said. "I think I'm an adviser also. The President wants me to be an adviser. And I think that both Cy Vance and Harold Brown find it useful for me to be involved, which I am actively, debating our SALT position or determining our Middle East position. I think I have certain talents in the area of synthesis and integration that help me perform a useful role in that respect, which perhaps others would not. Just as they have talents and information and intellect that I don't have."

If Brzezinski possessed any doubts about the breadth of his White House position, it is now evident that, with Carter's assurance, he enjoys a broad mandate and near-equal, if not equal, status with Cabinet-level officials.

THE COUNCIL

The NSC is the rock upon which Brzezinski's authority rests. In a Brookings Institution study, I. M. Destler said, "In form and in public imagery, the National Security Council is the most exalted committee in the federal government."

Created in 1947 as part of an institutional reform in national security policy making, it was intended to counsel the President "with respect to the integration of domestic, foreign and military policies relating to national security."

Statutory members of the NSC are limited to the President, Vice President and Secretaries of State and Defense. Included as statutory advisers are the chairman of the Joint Chiefs of Staff (JCS) and the director of the Central Intelligence Agency (CIA). The President may, and almost always does, invite other aides to join in the deliberations, such as the Secretary of Treasury, the Attorney General, the director of the Office of Management and Budget (OMB), the chairman of the Council of Economic Advisers (CEA), the director of the Arms Control and Disarmament Agency and the assistant for national security affairs.

Serving as a supporting arm is the NSC staff, currently estimated at 39 professional members and 25 detailees on loan from other federal agencies. This represents a substantial reduction; when Kissinger directed the NSC staff during the Nixon Administration, it usually included more than 60 members, with about the same number of detailees.

The NSC process may be used by the President as an intimate forum to discuss and debate long-term national security policy issues or to take action on those issues demanding immediate response; it may further be used as a mechanism to develop policy proposals. In the words of former Eisenhower aide Robert Cutler, "It recommends, the President decides."

It should be kept in mind that the President seeks and receives foreign policy advice from numerous sources in and out of the government, including Members of Congress, federal agency executives, foreign leaders, personal aides, special interest groups, international organizations, independent publications and former government officials.

Increasingly, foreign policy has become too complex to be left solely to diplomats. Almost all issues involve a mix of interdependent considerations—international trade and economics, domestic affairs, national politics, defense policy, mass opinion, intelligence, scientific and technical concerns and, as particularly stressed by Carter, moral values. This has led to a massive network of alliances, multilateral organizations, defense treaties, aid programs, educational and cultural exchanges and information programs.

In dealing with these varied concerns, the President requires an immediate advisory body and personal staff to bring order out of potential chaos, to coordinate interagency activities and to provide him with information from a presidential, rather than a bureaucratic, perspective. Hence, the need for the NSC system.

Since its inception, a succession of Presidents have utilized the NSC in a manner compatible with their individual styles and in keeping with their personal concepts of presidential decision making. Accordingly, the form, standing and usefulness of the NSC has run an uneven course.

Under President Truman, the NSC served as a major advisory forum, particularly in dealing with the Korean War and the Communist challenge abroad. Truman, however, always was conscious of the fact that the final responsibility was his. President Eisenhower, with his penchant for formal organizational structure, relied heavily on the NSC and upgraded its stature. But, even then, its influence was offset by the strong voice of Secretary of State John Foster Dulles. President Kennedy, disillusioned by the advice he received at NSC councils on the Bay of Pigs assault in Cuba, ordered a complete overhaul of the NSC process. Still, he never found it suitable to his style, preferring instead informal consultations with ad hoc groups of advisers. Under Lyndon B. Johnson, the role of the NSC was partially revived. Nevertheless, the main forum of his foreign policy and Vietnam War discussions was his "Tuesday lunch" gatherings in the White House. Richard M. Nixon pledged to give the NSC a central role in the decision-making process, but the agency quickly became a personal vehicle for Kissinger. While Kissinger served as Secretary of State in the Ford Administration, the NSC was virtually a quiescent limb of the presidency.

Over-all, as Destler pointed out, "Postwar experience provides ample reason to conclude that the use of the National Security Council as a regularized, major advisory forum is the exception rather than the rule."

Interestingly, every President has in some way refined or left his mark on the NSC system. Eisenhower created the position of special assistant for national security affairs; Kennedy established the situation room in the White House basement as an information center for the reception of communications from the various departments; Nixon, at Kissinger's suggestion, set up a "Washington Special Actions Group" to deal with immediate, critical situations. Nixon also established the National Security Study Memorandum (NSSM) system, which essentially entailed the drafting of interagency policy papers, complete with analytical data, options and recommendations. This was the forerunner of the Presidential Review Memorandum (PRM) process now being implemented by Carter's NSC staff.

Over the years, the value of the NSC as a formal, deliberative body has declined, and it has played a diminishing role in foreign policy affairs; yet, at the same time, the use of the NSC staff has increased in importance. More often than not, when people refer to the NSC, they mean the NSC staff. As reported by Arthur M. Schlesinger Jr. in *A Thousand Days* (Houghton Mifflin Co., 1965), even among the Kennedy crowd, the NSC staff was "indispensable."

From evidence gathered so far, it appears that Carter has restored the prestige of the NSC staff following a brief eclipse during the Ford years and created a national security operation which, in effect, is an amalgamation selectively drawn from the experiences of his predecessors.

For example, while Carter advocates a formally structured NSC staff and relies on its studies for help in making decisions and issuing directives, he also believes in more flexible procedures, such as informal, yet regularly scheduled luncheon meetings with his top national security advisers.

Like Kennedy, he prefers an open decision-making process with the active participation of the President.

Carter allows relatively liberal access to the Oval Office and has decentralized the advisory system. NSC staff members, for instance, get to meet with the President far more than ever before.

He is briefed each morning by Brzezinski, but also receives daily memoranda from Vance and Brown.

He has held only seven formal NSC meetings in nine months, considerably fewer than any of his predecessors. This may be at least partly attributable to the fact that there have been no major foreign crises since he assumed the presidency. However, precedent indicates that Presidents are inclined to call more NSC sessions early in their Administrations than they are afterwards.

It also appears that Carter has effectively split the roles played by Brzezinski and Vance, with the former managing day-to-day national security affairs for the President and directing policy studies and the latter serving as Carter's personal envoy and negotiator and principal foreign policy adviser. As one White House aide remarked, "It is not mutually exclusive, but Vance is more operational and Brzezinski more conceptual."

That may be an oversimplification, yet it does coincide with a widely held perception.

BRZEZINSKI

Brzezinski, historian and political scientist, is convinced that the U.S. stands at the juncture of a new era in world affairs. "I think we are at the end of a phase of turmoil and disintegration which began in the mid-'60s," he said. "If things work out well, we are on the eve of a new and creative thrust in American foreign policy which will result in the shaping of an international system that is wider and more cooperative. If we do not do as well as we hope and should, then we may confront a world that would be increasingly chaotic and unstable."

While Carter's foreign policy is clearly his own, reflecting his moral concepts and global vision, Brzezinski generally is recognized as its principal architect. Brzezinski's early association with Carter in his capacity as head of the Trilateral Commission, sponsored by David Rockefeller in 1972 to promote the mutual interests of Japan, Western Europe and the United States, is already part of political folklore. From all accounts, Brzezinski, then a Columbia University professor, schooled Carter in the intricacies of foreign policy affairs.

In his autobiography, *Why Not The Best?* (Broadman Press, 1975), Carter paid tribute to the Trilateral Commission: "Membership on this commission has provided me with a splendid learning opportunity and many of the other members have helped me in my study of foreign affairs."

Through his books, lectures, articles and teaching, Brzezinski became known within the academic community as an agile scholar with a passion to succeed and an attraction to power and the men who wield it. Some characterized him as "the Polish Kissinger." Actually, as the son of a diplomat, he left Poland as an infant and spent his early life in Canada, where his father was the Polish consul in Montreal. He received his bachelor's degree from McGill University there and did graduate work at Harvard University. His wife, Mushka, is the grandniece of Eduard Benes, the last non-Communist president of Czechoslovakia.

In the pursuit of his career, Brzezinski became a member of a small, elite group of foreign policy establishment figures who moved with easy grace between Washington, Wall Street, university campuses, prestigious law firms, big-name think tanks and well-heeled foundations. An article written by Leslie H. Gelb and published in *The New York Times Magazine* on May 23, 1976, listed Brzezinski as one of the Big Eight in contention for the post of Secretary of State in the next Administration. Gelb, then a *Times* reporter and now director of the State Department's Bureau of Politico-Military Affairs, wrote, "At one extreme (if one can use that word about any of these mandarins of the political center), there is Brzezinski, the seeker; at the other, there is Vance, the sought-after."

The article described how Brzezinski was one of the first of the establishment group to pay attention to Carter, to take him seriously and to tutor him in the fine points of foreign policy. Gelb reported that Brzezinski courted other potential presidential candidates and added, "His strategy seems to be portraying himself as the Good Kissinger—a man with Kissinger's intellect and maneuverability but with a different world view."

Of the eight men cited by Gelb, five became members of the Carter Administration, Vance, Brzezinski, Energy Secretary James R. Schlesinger, Paul C. Warnke, director of the Arms Control and Disarmament Agency, and Elliot L. Richardson, an ambassador-at-large to the United Nations Conference on the Law of the Sea. The remaining three were prominent officials in previous Administrations, George W. Ball, Melvin R. Laird and Peter G. Peterson.

Today, Brzezinski's theories and idealism are recognizable in some of Carter's foreign policy initiatives: the shift in the focus of U.S. foreign policy from the East-West axis; the concern with human rights (but not as a condition that would harm U.S. national security); a new world order based less on preoccupation with communism, as proposed in Carter's speech at Notre Dame University in May; detente with the Russians but with greater emphasis on reciprocity; a restriction on arms sales; control of the flow of nuclear materials; improved relations with the Third World.

Brzezinski acknowledged that Carter's human rights campaign is in harmony with his own Catholic religion and personal philosophy. Elaborating, he said:

"The President's preoccupation with certain basic moral values happens to be quite congenial to me. I do happen to think politics is not a game to be played just to play it; it is not a game just to play in order to get instant acclaim. It really is an effort to relate organized human activity to the promotion of more enduring and more morally responsible objectives. If one forgets that, then one, I think, is forgetting ultimately why we all exist.

"There is a certain transcendental quality to man and politics which is in the collective expression of man's organized behavior. If our politics do not reflect the inherent transcendental qualities of man, if that doesn't point to some moral goals, if it is not imbued with moral objectives, then I think we have failed as human beings. That is a view I happen to hold very strongly. It is not a view which means that we cannot deal with countries with which we do not agree; it does not mean we have to insist on everyone emulating us. But it does mean that we have to have some central beacon in our lives, whether as individuals or as public servants. On that, I think, the President and I have a rather similar outlook."

Replying to the suggestion that his academic interest in the Third World may have been a factor in Carter's plans for an eight-country trip next month, Brzezinski said, "I developed the trip basically, in close conjunction with the Secretary of State. The President asked me back in March to start thinking about such a trip. It was designed to symbolize the larger and broader historical concerns that he expressed in his Notre Dame speech. . . . It also stresses the fact we are now moving into an age in which the scope of American relationships, worldwide, have to be wider than just the Atlanticists or even the Trilateral worlds."

There is about Brzezinski something of the Man of La Mancha, prompting some of his university colleagues to call him a romantic. "I don't mind being described as such," he commented. "I do not think that in life a little bit of a dream is to be slighted or dismissed. Like a motto I sometimes cite from Browning, 'A man's reach should exceed his grasp, or what's a heaven for?' I don't think that it's bad in politics to have goals which you know you cannot entirely reach but to which you ought to strive to point."

As a planner and activist in foreign policy affairs, Brzezinski might also borrow a quote from Cervantes's Don Quixote, "Patience, and shuffle the cards."

STAFF

Traditionally, NSC staff members comprise a special class within the presidential complex, scholarly, intellectually self-assured—and mainly anonymous. They are as familiar with weapons systems and Keynesian economic theories as they are with Metternich. It could be said that they belong to the second echelon of the establishment foreign policy community. Of the 39 staff members, more than half have earned doctoral degrees, and several have worked at State, Defense and the CIA. Some are holdovers from previous Administrations, such as David L. Aaron, deputy assistant for national security affairs; William Hyland, Soviet affairs expert who will soon be leaving; and Roger C. Molander, specialist in strategic arms negotiations. One staff member, Samuel P. Huntington, is well known as a Harvard professor of government and a founding editor of *Foreign Policy* magazine.

Brzezinski, who proudly maintains his staff "is the best in the history of the NSC in terms of individual quality," made several changes in the organizational structure. He erased the senior-junior differential that had existed in the previous staff setup and abolished titles. ("I didn't abolish my own, though," he remarked, smiling.)

He also created some new slots. Jerrold L. Schecter, former *Time* magazine diplomatic editor and foreign correspondent, was appointed to the new post of associate press secretary and congressional liaison. Likewise, Jessica Tuchman was assigned to a newly created section on global issues, and Huntington was named coordinator of security planning, a new designation.

"I really wanted to have a very creative and collegial staff of people who would span different experiences from within and outside the government and people who spanned generations," said Brzezinski. "I wanted a staff that would be innovative and within

physical limits be accessible to me and me accessible to them. A hierarchy within a staff inhibits that.

"Although there are obviously people who are de facto more senior to others and it works out that way, I didn't want rigid hierarchical staff divisions within a group that ought to work closely together. And I have made a point of doing something that had never been done before—I have tried to get the staff members to see the President. I have tried to get the President to get to know them. The President attended two of my staff meetings, which I don't believe has ever happened. Once a week, I report to the staff in full on my dealings with the President and on presidential business, so that vicariously, if not directly, they have a sense of engagement with a man for whom they are working so hard. In that sense, I have tried to engage them more than used to be the case."

Work responsibility for the staff is little changed from what it always has been—analyzing issues, drafting policy papers, coordinating interagency memoranda and proposing new ideas and initiatives.

Although the staff agrees that the atmosphere is more relaxed than during the tumultuous days of Kissinger and that Brzezinski is almost always accessible, there are complaints that they are overextended in handling daily demands and lack sufficient time to devote to long-range analyses or to prepare new proposals. Said one staff member, "We have too big a plate and can't do justice to all the issues, particularly in view of the role they want us to play. We're supposed to move new ideas and initiatives but there simply isn't the time. . . . Word was, in the beginning, with the smaller staff they would take away some of the routine stuff, but even with that, it is tough to find time for everything.

"There are two ways to do this job; you can put in 70 hours a week and stay on top of your work and do creative things, or you can work 55 hours and simply clean out your in-box. Neither is a satisfactory way to live."

A sampling of some of the staff load, for example, shows that Robert Pastor, a regional specialist, alone deals with issues covering all of Latin America and the Caribbean; Jessica Tuchman, the daughter of historian Barbara Tuchman, author of *The Guns of August,* copes with such priorities as nuclear proliferation, arms sales, human rights, the international environment, law of the sea and the International Labor Organization; Victor Utgoff is compelled to compete with the Defense Department in analyzing such complex issues as the B-1 bomber, the Seafarer communications project, the neutron bomb and the massive defense budget.

One aide felt that although Brzezinski generally is available, neither he nor his deputy, Aaron, is able to give sufficient attention to each staff problem. Another felt that even with the increased accessibility to Carter, the staff members should meet with the President more often.

While the complaints may be valid, they are endemic to the system. Conceding the legitimacy of some of the complaints, Brzezinski said, "There is rarely enough time to sit down and really talk about an issue in depth."

He was less sympathetic, however, to complaints about lack of presidential access. "From a human point of view, naturally everyone would like to see the President more," he said. "If I was on the staff, I would like to see the President more, too, than is possible. On the other hand, the President cannot have a situation in which he deals on these matters with a large number of individuals; there has to be a process of coordination, and that's what I'm here for."

Possibly the major difference in working for Brzezinski, as opposed to Kissinger, is in the nature of their personalities. Those who have had personal experiences with each maintain that Kissinger was more theatrical, tended to deal only with senior staff assistants and was vastly more volatile.

"Kissinger was a tyrant with his staff," an aide said. "Before, you had to be summoned to talk with him— and then with trepidation. . . . Zbig wants people to be personally responsible and deeply involved. He gets the staff people to meet with the President—that was unheard of before. He is not a father figure or an authoritarian. But he demands good work."

Another staff member, however, observed that Kissinger and Brzezinski should be viewed from different vantage points. "Things were more tense then, there was the war in Vietnam, the Mideast flareups and then Watergate. Also, they worked for entirely different Presidents."

For all of that, some of the senior members of the NSC staff confided that they occasionally communicate and informally consult with Kissinger.

Brzezinski's academic contacts have been helpful to him in his NSC post. As a case in point, Huntington originally came to Washington to direct a comprehensive assessment of the global balance of power as a temporary assignment and then return to Harvard. Brzezinski, however, induced him to stay on for another year. Huntington was mainly responsible for the famous PRM 10, which laid out basic U.S. strategy in East-West relations and the nation's proposed military posture in Europe. The interagency project involved 12 task forces and an estimated 175 people.

Huntington is chiefly involved in broad studies that do not require day-to-day responsibilities.

The unprecedented appointment of a press assistant prompted some suspicion that Brzezinski intended to promote himself and NSC activities with the news media. So far, there has been little evidence of that. As Schecter noted, "I work for Brzezinski but I also work with [White House press secretary] Jody Powell." Schecter backs up Powell at press briefings, sometimes conducts briefings himself on foreign policy developments and helps put together the President's briefing book prior to his regular press conferences. Also, each morning, Schecter consults with his counterparts at State and Defense on a three-way telephone hookup to coordinate their flow of information.

OPERATIONS

Always close to Brzezinski are two black, loose-leaf notebooks, one labeled "Presidential Review Memoranda" and the other "Presidential Directives." They constitute Brzezinski's working catechism, the sum of which represents the Administration's approach to every major national security issue from arms to Zaire.

The contents of the two notebooks are the product of the NSC's operational system, which revolves around two working groups—the Policy Review Committee (PRC) and the Special Coordination Committee (SCC). The two committees were created on Jan. 20, the day Carter was inaugurated, replacing seven NSC committees that existed during the Ford Administration.

Basically, the Policy Review Committee deals with specific issues and is headed by a presidentially designated chairman, normally a Cabinet member whose agency is deeply involved with the problem, Vance, for example, on the Mideast negotiations and the Panama Canal treaty, Brown on the neutron bomb. Membership includes other senior agency officials, the statutory members of the NSC and Brzezinski.

The coordinating panel is concerned more with continuing issues that cut across departmental lines, such as SALT and arms control evaluation. It is always headed by Brzezinski and includes members from appropriate agencies.

Brzezinski's leverage hinges on the fact that he and the President decide what issues will be reviewed, which committee will deal with them and who will be in charge if an issue is assigned to the policy committee. Once the decisions are made, a Presidential Review Memorandum is circulated, identifying the issue and directing that policy research be undertaken by the appropriate agencies. A NSC staff member is chosen by Brzezinski as the lead coordinator for the project. Other NSC aides are called on to contribute analyses, serve as liaison with agency counterparts and make suggestions.

Meetings are scheduled to debate the issue. Papers stating each agency's position and recommendation are sent to the NSC coordinator. Often, the reports make up several volumes before being synthesized by the NSC staff. This is forwarded to Rick Inderfurth, who manages the NSC's paper flow. It next goes to Aaron, who sees and checks everything before it is passed to Brzezinski. If the latter decides that the issue has been thoroughly explored and that every participant's view is fairly presented, it then goes to the President, generally in the form of a two- or three-page memorandum.

Carter, again in consultation with Brzezinski and other high officials, must decide what course to take and whether his response should be sent down as a matter of policy or, to add emphasis to the action, as a presidential directive.

Thus far, Brzezinski's notebooks indicate there have been 32 Presidential Review Memorandum responses and 20 presidential directives.

The obvious danger in the system is that the NSC staff, because of its strategic position within the White House, could short-circuit or distort agency arguments. This, however, is considered unlikely because of the frequent access that key department executives, such as Vance and Brown and Treasury Secretary W. Michael Blumenthal, have to the President. Another deterrent is the close communication between NSC staff members and their counterparts in the agencies, principally Gelb and W. Anthony Lake, director of policy planning, at State; David E. McGiffert, assistant Defense secretary for international security affairs; and C. Fred Bergsten, assistant Treasury secretary for international affairs.

Brzezinski and other NSC staff members insist that he and Vance are working in concert with a minimum of friction or back-biting.

"So far, nobody has called us 'the Little State Department,'" remarked Aaron, an allusion to a often-heard label when Kissinger headed the NSC staff.

"Cy Vance and I came here as reasonably good acquaintances," said Brzezinski. "I think I can fairly say we are now good, personal friends—which is not exactly the way people predicted it would be. I think there has developed a good division of labor between us. He does certain things that I could not do as well; I hope I do some things better than he could do.

"Operationally, we see each other face to face at least once a day; we have formal meetings which involve him and the President and me once a week; we have a formal lunch that involves him and Secretary Brown and me once a week. Then, in addition, I would say that Cy and I talk on the phone about 10 times a day. He consults me, I consult him. I try to expedite things. I convey to him what the President wishes to be done. Sometimes, we disagree. But I would say we probably work more closely together than any two people who have been in our positions in the past."

Such bureaucratic camaraderie throughout the executive branch does not exist merely because of a lack of institutional bias or the stifling of personal ambitions or the submersion of policy preferences; tranquility prevails mostly because Carter wants it that way. And it seems to be working.

Hyland, a veteran government official, observed that under the present operation, "Much more goes to the President through the system than in the past.

Before, issues were not brought to him until they were talked out at the Cabinet or sub-Cabinet level. Issues now are ventilated much earlier."

OUTLOOK

Although Carter so far has made little use of the NSC as a formal, sitting body, its place in the Administration probably will not be known until he is faced with a serious foreign crisis requiring immediate action. It is apparent, however, that he depends on Brzezinski and the NSC staff for advice. But that, too, could change if some of his foreign policy initiatives go sour or if a hitch develops in the relationship between Brzezinski, Vance and Brown.

Among the options proposed in a reorganization study of the national security operation is that the White House's domestic and foreign policy components be merged, but that has little or no chance of being adopted.

Brzezinski, meanwhile, is optimistic about the settlement of several international issues, notably SALT and the Mideast strife, prior to the end of Carter's first term.

"I think on SALT we will get an agreement which deals with fundamental concerns, the need for reductions, the need for restraint on those strategic systems which are particularly threatening to us," he said.

"On the Middle East, I think we will be pointed towards a settlement, if we don't have one by the end of his Administration. Hopefully, we will have one before then. But we will certainly be moving towards a comprehensive settlement, and the Geneva Conference will be one of the vehicles."

20

BRENT SCOWCROFT

David Lauter

The only person to serve as national security adviser in two administrations (Ford and the first Bush), Brent Scowcroft is noted for his ability to play the role of an honest broker in presenting the views of the foreign policy bureaucracy to the president. He became particularly close to President George H.W. Bush, for whom he served as a confidant and policy coordinator.

It is Aug. 3, Iraqi troops have invaded Kuwait, and President Bush has flown to the Colorado Rockies for a meeting with British Prime Minister Margaret Thatcher and a speech to the Aspen Institute.

As he begins his address, Bush pauses to thank his national security adviser, Brent Scowcroft. He looks around and finds him standing at the edge of the stage, half-concealed among a collection of potted palms.

In memory, it seems as if Scowcroft has always been there, half-hidden near some President's side.

There he was, two decades ago, the White House military aide, carrying the briefcase containing codes for nuclear war as Richard M. Nixon strode through history. There he was, telling Gerald R. Ford of the helicopter evacuation of the American Embassy in Saigon at the close of a war that Scowcroft still believes the United States could have won.

And here he is now, the short, slender, balding figure at Bush's side—at the golf course, on the speedboat, in the Oval Office, the ever-present adviser, the confidant. The man who wakes the President up in the middle of the night with news of war.

Over the past year and a half, no other Bush adviser has had more influence on the agenda of American national security policy—from the "go-slow" approach toward changes in the Soviet Union to the drastic scaling back of Ronald Reagan's brainchild, the "Star Wars" space-based Strategic Defense Initiative.

And today, as the United States inches toward war in the Persian Gulf, the path it is following is one that has been laid out by Brent Scowcroft, the man in the background.

For a man who has played a key role in national affairs for nearly 20 years, Scowcroft remains almost unknown. A deeply private man—"I've never been to his house," says one longtime friend. "I don't know anyone who has"—Scowcroft has appeared in countless newspaper photographs and television clips. But he is almost always in the shadows.

In a capital full of officials energetically creating larger-than-life public personas, Scowcroft has cultivated anonymity. His spacious White House office, dominated by a score or more of neatly stacked piles of paper, each with the top sheet turned over to avoid prying eyes, contains not a single personal photograph and only one memento—the three-star flag of an Air Force lieutenant general, the rank with which he left active duty.

Others in Washington seek power by publicity. Scowcroft has cultivated a different route—proximity. His thin, reedy voice, which has the timbre of a clarinet without the lower register, does not carry far. But seldom has it had to travel more than a few feet to reach the President's ear.

Scowcroft's image in Washington's energetic gossip mill is more that of an institution than of a person.

From David Lauter, "The Man Behind the President," *Los Angeles Times* (October 14, 1990), A1.

David Lauter is a staff writer for the *Los Angeles Times*.

"People talk about 'the Scowcroft Model,'" says one White House official who has worked closely with him, suggesting the way the individual has been able to disappear behind the image of the institution.

The image is that of the discreet, hard-working, self-effacing coordinator, above all that of a man "who doesn't have ideas or an agenda of his own." And that, says the official, "just ain't true."

Still, parts of the image are correct: hard-working, for example. Scowcroft routinely arrives at his desk in the White House West Wing by 7 in the morning and is nearly always there until 8 or 9 at night.

And discreet, as well. Scowcroft's thin lips are quick to break into a smile. They are also quick to purse tightly shut. Words leave his mouth slowly, with long pauses between phrases, each carefully weighed to ensure that they contain not a gram more of information than their author wishes to convey.

Henry A. Kissinger, a former national security adviser himself, recalled in his memoirs that when he won the Nobel Prize for his role in the Paris peace talks, it was Scowcroft, then his deputy, who passed him the word. In the middle of a meeting, Scowcroft handed Kissinger a copy of a news wire story announcing the award. He did so, Kissinger recalled, without a word of comment.

Even close aides often do not know what he has in mind. When Bush announced his Helsinki summit meeting with Soviet President Mikhail S. Gorbachev, among the many people surprised by the announcement was Condoleezza Rice, the NSC's director for Soviet affairs—and one of Scowcroft's most trusted deputies.

At a press briefing, Scowcroft had unabashedly "stonewalled" reporters asking about rumors of a summit, declining even to hint that something was planned until Bush interrupted the session by calling to say that the announcement was ready.

"I thought I was doing pretty well," Scowcroft quipped when Press Secretary Marlin Fitzwater handed him a note telling him he could stop refusing to comment.

And he is self-effacing, as well. Until recently, Scowcroft almost never spoke to reporters for quotation or appeared on a television interview. In large part because of the long illness of his wife, Marian, who has been an invalid for most of the time that Scowcroft

has been in the public eye, he seldom appears at Washington social events.

The avoidance of publicity is often mistaken for an absence of ego. And the presumed lack of ego caused many to assume—when Scowcroft accepted the job as White House national security adviser—that he would play a sharply restricted role, sandwiched between an energetic President with extensive foreign policy experience and the President's closest friend, James A. Baker III, as secretary of state.

As Ford's national security adviser—following Kissinger, who remained secretary of state—Scowcroft had had a relatively confined role. But this time, he made clear to friends, he had a different concept of the job in mind.

In Bush, Scowcroft told friends, the country had a President with extensive knowledge and experience in foreign affairs, but one who was more comfortable with handling problems one at a time than with developing overall strategy. Nor, he believed, would strategy come from Baker—a master tactician but an impatient one and one with relatively little experience in foreign affairs.

Strategy, Scowcroft made clear, would be his job.

Scowcroft "does not see himself as being only a general or only a policy adviser to presidents," says his friend, John Deutch, a former deputy secretary of energy and now provost of the Massachusetts Institute of Technology. "He sees himself as one of the individuals in this country who really understands three things that are vital: foreign affairs, the military and domestic politics."

Scowcroft's aides delight in telling stories about his ability to fall asleep during meetings, even sessions with Bush. The White House staff has even invented a "Scowcroft Award" for the person who most blatantly falls asleep in public.

But what is often missed among the jokes is what stunning self-confidence such easy dozing reflects: Few people are sure enough in their position to fall asleep on the President of the United States.

"He's 65 years old. He's made his mark. He's at ease with himself," says Scowcroft's deputy, Robert M. Gates.

Bush puts the matter another way. Among his ambitious advisers, the President reportedly has told friends, he trusts Scowcroft because "Brent doesn't want anything."

As a child, Scowcroft recalled in an interview recently, what he did want—from the age of 12 when he read a book about the U.S. Military Academy—was to attend West Point.

Born in 1925, Scowcroft was the only son and youngest child of a prosperous, influential family in Ogden, Utah, a city of 42,000 just north of Salt Lake City, dominated by the rail yards of the Union Pacific and Southern Pacific that made the town the largest freight-switching center between Omaha and the West Coast.

His father ran a wholesale grocery business serving the mostly Mormon communities of northern Utah and southern Idaho. The business succeeded so well that shortly after the birth of his son, James Scowcroft built a new house for his family in the foothills of the Wasatch Mountains.

The young Brent Scowcroft was a bright student. "Brent was a speed reader when we didn't know what speed-reading was," recalls his oldest sister, Janice Hinckley. "In elementary school, the principal wanted to skip him a few grades," she says. Their father rejected that idea, feeling that his slightly built son would be unable to take part in sports if he were thrust among older boys.

Instead, he was put on a special reading program and ran track—100-yard dashes—as he passed through high school.

By then, the nation was at war. When the family traveled east in the fall of 1942 to examine colleges for Brent, they stopped at West Point to allow Janice to visit her fiancé, a cadet at the academy and the son of a high official in the Franklin D. Roosevelt Administration.

One look around the campus and the decision was made. "I don't think there ever was a point when I said, 'I want a career in the military,'" Scowcroft recalls. West Point, he says, "just sounded fantastic."

He enrolled in the class of 1947. And in a move that foreshadowed the sort of roles he would take on later, he quickly became a manager of the Army football team.

"He wasn't big enough to play, but he wanted to make a contribution," recalls his classmate and friend

Air Force Gen. William Y. Smith, now the head of the Pentagon's Institute for Defense Analysis. "He always wanted to do that."

In 1948, Scowcroft earned his wings as a fighter pilot. And then, flying a training exercise in a P-51 Mustang over a forested region of New Hampshire, "I lost the engine," he recalls.

"I thought I was too low to bail out," Scowcroft says, matter-of-factly describing the crash that nearly killed him. He found a small clearing and went in.

The crash—"I prefer to call it a forced landing," he says—broke Scowcroft's back and left him in a military hospital in Boston for two years. When his father died later that year at the age of 57, Scowcroft flew back to Utah in a body cast, stretched out in the aisle of the airplane.

In the hospital, Scowcroft met his future wife, a military nurse who, as a captain, then outranked the young lieutenant. There, too, he began what would become his lifelong career, deciding to earn a graduate degree and become part of a new weapon that the American military was developing—a group of people who would become known as the "defense intellectuals."

World War II had convinced many American leaders that brainpower—in both the hard sciences and the social sciences—could be a major military asset for the United States. In time, the community of defense intellectuals would grow to be enormous, spinning off institutions ranging from the national weapons laboratories to think tanks such as Santa Monica's RAND Corp.

In time, too, many of the young men (and a few women) who devoted their brainpower to the national security apparatus—"the best and the brightest," in writer David Halberstam's phrase—would grow disillusioned by the horrible failure of their strategies and weapons in Vietnam.

But in the early 1950s, when Scowcroft, then married, finished his graduate program at New York's Columbia University and took a teaching post at West Point, the defense intellectual community was still young, idealistic and small.

At West Point, the chief proponent of the role of intellect in war—and a chief recruiter of intellectuals for the Cold War—was the head of the school's social sciences department, Col. George A. (Abe) Lincoln, an adviser to George C. Marshall, the one-time Army chief of staff who later became secretary of state. Lincoln was one of Scowcroft's early mentors.

Scowcroft is not a man whom others recall as ever seeming young. Even as a junior faculty member at West Point, Scowcroft was "a very serious guy," recalls another classmate and friend, Wesley Posvar, now chancellor of the University of Pittsburgh. "I don't think Brent has changed much in the past 40 years, even in appearance," Posvar says.

Nor, as he advanced through a series of choice career posts—air attaché at the American Embassy in Yugoslavia, stints at the Armed Forces Staff College, the National War College and the Air Force Academy, and staff jobs at Air Force Headquarters and the Pentagon—did Scowcroft fundamentally alter the beliefs that had animated his career at the outset.

They are a set of assumptions that once were virtually a consensus among American policy-makers, but which now have become embattled: a belief that America's No. 1 international interest is its relationship with Europe; an emphasis on the strategic competition with the Soviet Union, rather than economic competition with other industrial nations; an insistence that the United States must maintain the role as military and political leader of the Western alliance, and a willingness to use military power as an instrument of policy.

Even the experience of Vietnam, which traumatized so many of his colleagues, seems to have left Scowcroft relatively unscathed. "I was not in the group that became disillusioned," Scowcroft says, "—the ones who were involved in the policy, and then, if you will, became ashamed."

Having spent the war years in military academia and long-range planning posts before moving to the White House as Nixon's military aide in 1972, Scowcroft continues to believe, he said, "that even as late as the Paris peace agreement" in 1972, "(the Vietnam War) could have worked if we had done it differently."

During Ronald Reagan's tenure, Scowcroft's beliefs set him at odds with the Administration's ideological hard-liners. He worked as an executive for the international consulting firm that Kissinger founded, traveling the world meeting with leaders of nations and multinational corporations.

Although Reagan named Scowcroft to head a commission to study U.S. strategic forces—a panel that helped establish his reputation as a policy maker independent of Kissinger—Administration policy makers kept him at arm's length.

And Scowcroft became a sharp critic of the Administration's policies. No overall strategic sense seemed to animate either Reagan's huge military buildup or the Administration's policies toward arms control, he argued. Scowcroft opposed the bombing of Libya, believing that economic sanctions should have been used against Moammar Kadafi. And he criticized the mining of Nicaragua's harbors, saying the operation had been too costly politically, damaging the CIA and harming American ability to use covert actions in the future.

But while he argued that the Administration was too quick to use force against little countries, he was even more critical of then-Secretary of Defense Caspar W. Weinberger's restrictive criteria for when military power should be used. Weinberger's policies, he argued, meant that armed might could be employed only in no-risk adventures such as Grenada or in "crusades" such as World War II.

In Weinberger's reluctance to let the military be used, Scowcroft discerned a hangover from Vietnam—a fear on the part of military leaders that if they once again became involved in a major conflict they would, once again, find themselves without public support.

For him, and for Bush, the current crisis in the gulf has been, in part, a chance to show the world that America's post-Vietnam blues are over.

American goals, he believes, are fundamentally good. And the nation should not be reluctant to threaten the use of force to achieve those goals, not only in cases where absolute national survival is at risk, but also in cases, as in the gulf, where the stakes include the economic health of America's allies and the political strength of international institutions.

Failure to deter Saddam Hussein, he says, would "give a green light to every tinhorn dictator" in the world. At the same time, he has resisted pressure from many outside the Administration—and some within—who argue that the United States should pledge now to use force not only to push Hussein out of Kuwait, but also to destroy Iraq's war machine and end Hussein's rule. Just as the country should not be reluctant to use force when necessary, he argues, it should not overestimate the ability of military power to solve all problems nor underestimate the unpredictability of war.

For a time, Scowcroft thought he might not return to government. Well paid in the consulting business—he earned more than $500,000 in 1988—he told Bush in 1987 that he would advise his campaign, but that he desired no job after the election.

But Scowcroft's personality—co-workers and friends describe him over and over with adjectives such as fair, calm, disciplined, cautious, pragmatic, careful, unflappable—and his experience fit the description of the person Bush wanted to head his National Security Council. The two are old friends who share similar senses of humor. They have known each other since the days when Bush was Ford's CIA director and Scowcroft the national security adviser.

So when the call came, Scowcroft could not say no.

The chance to influence the course of events once more, to be at the center of them, could not be turned away. International affairs, he explains, "are not only my profession, but my hobby."

Or, as one senior Bush aide puts it, Scowcroft "is a man who lives for his work."

The gulf crisis has magnified Scowcroft's influence in the Administration. The need to coordinate both military and diplomatic policy has prevented either Baker or Secretary of Defense Dick Cheney from dominating the stage alone.

And Baker, preferring to concentrate his energies in one or two areas that he can control, has not tried to challenge Scowcroft's lead, instead sticking close to the negotiations with Soviet Foreign Minister Eduard A. Shevardnadze over the future shape of Europe.

Moreover, Bush's own personal day-to-day involvement in the details of the policy have ensured that the crisis is run out of the White House, rather than the Pentagon or the State Department.

Scowcroft serves as Bush's counselor, his sounding board and often, even, as his speech writer. The night before Bush gave his early morning Oval Office speech announcing that he had dispatched troops to Saudi Arabia, Scowcroft and his Middle East deputy, Richard Haas, sat on the couch in Scowcroft's office until 3:30 a.m., revising the speech word by word. After a few hours of rest, they returned before 7 for a final check.

Even before the Iraqi invasion, however, Scowcroft was in a clear ascendancy.

During the Administration's first year, he had crafted an overall foreign policy strategy for Bush that emphasized a cautious approach to the Soviets and focused on maintaining NATO with Germany as a central member of the alliance.

The critics, who were legion, said that Scowcroft's innate caution, reinforcing Bush's own aversion to risk, was itself running the risk of missing the historic opportunities offered by Gorbachev.

Today, however, with the Berlin Wall down, Germany unified, NATO intact and the Warsaw Pact essentially gone, Scowcroft and his aides are understandably feeling vindicated—enough so that the critics' charge of plodding unoriginality has become an in-house joke.

"Brent has a turtle-like demeanor," said one aide. "He just keeps moving forward slow but steady, and he always gets to the end."

21

SAMUEL R. BERGER

R.W. Apple, Jr.

Samuel R. Berger became one of the most active national security advisers in the history of the NSC, almost matching Henry Kissinger and Zbigniew Brzezinski in his assertiveness as a policy counselor and media spokesman. A political activist and international trade lawyer based in Washington, D.C., before he became adviser, "Sandy" Berger proved skillful at relating to Congress as well as working closely with his longtime friend, President Bill Clinton.

A DOMESTIC SORT WITH GLOBAL WORRIES

WASHINGTON—When President Clinton made a televised address to the nation about Kosovo last March 24, he uttered a sentence for which he was belabored that day and every day for the next 10 weeks, until he finally declared victory on June 10: "I do not intend to put our troops in Kosovo to fight a war."

On May 18, with the outcome of the bombing campaign still in serious doubt, the President sharply altered course with the comment, "I don't think we or our allies should take any options off the table, and that has been my position from the beginning," which of course it had not.

It was Mr. Clinton's national security adviser, Samuel R. Berger, known as Sandy, who wrote the initial offending sentence. Both he and his boss saw fairly quickly that it was a mistake, because they realized that having plunged into the conflict with President Slobodan Milosevic of Yugoslavia, there was no acceptable alternative to a NATO victory. If ground troops were needed to get the Serbian tanks out of Kosovo, then ground troops it would have to be.

Mr. Milosevic may well have held out longer than he otherwise would have because he believed that he faced no danger of land combat, and he certainly gained

time to savage ethnic Albanians in Kosovo and drive them out. Mr. Berger told a friend as early as April that he should have put in something about leaving all options on the table.

He did not do so, Mr. Berger said a few days after the bombing had stopped, because "the American people would not have supported the war without European participation, and we never could have gotten all 19 allies on board at the outset if they thought we had any plan to use ground forces." In keeping with that view, Mr. Clinton cut his rhetorical cloth to fit the politics of both NATO and the United States.

The explosion of criticism crossed party and ideological lines. In an op-ed article in The Wall Street Journal, Zbigniew Brzezinski, President Carter's national security adviser, accused the Administration of indulging in "a new technological racism" based on the premise that the life of "one American serviceman was not worth risking in order to save the lives of thousands of Kosovars." The Economist headlined an editorial, "A Bungled War." Michael Kelly, a columnist, suggested that a ham and cheese sandwich could run foreign policy better than Mr. Berger and his colleagues.

Mr. Berger's place at the nexus of Kosovo strategy was no surprise, nor was his concentration on the political aspects of the matter. Widely regarded as the President's closest foreign-policy aide, perhaps the most

---

From R.W. Apple, Jr., "A Domestic Sort With Global Worries," *New York Times* (August 25, 1999), A1.

R.W. "Johnny" Apple, Jr., is an experienced correspondent for the *New York Times*.

influential national security adviser since Henry A. Kissinger, he is at bottom a political rather than strategic figure. Unlike the professors, diplomats and military officers who have for the most part preceded him in his job, he made his way to the White House by way of the salons and back rooms of Democratic politics while pursuing a public career as a trade lawyer.

"He has the lawyer's inherent caution," said John Dyson, a New York investor and political operative who has known Mr. Berger since college. "The craft is a tactical craft. You focus on the downside, always worrying about avoiding negative results."

Beefy and chubby-cheeked at 53, serious and formal in dark suits and white shirts, Mr. Berger makes a sharp contrast to his elfin predecessor, Anthony Lake, whom he served as a deputy during Mr. Clinton's first term. Mr. Lake wore professorial tweeds. He was so seldom seen in public that friends called him "the submarine." But Mr. Berger's is a familiar face on television and on Capitol Hill, where he has built strong links to both parties.

THE STYLE: A 15-HOUR DAY, AND A MODEST EGO

In the first term, Mr. Lake and the other main foreign-policy figures were older than Mr. Clinton. Now they are contemporaries. Mr. Berger, who has known Mr. Clinton since the McGovern Presidential campaign of 1972, helped him in small but important ways at low points in his career.

He has a closer relationship to the President than Secretary of State Madeleine K. Albright, who is better at formulating policies than in selling them to Mr. Clinton, or Defense Secretary William S. Cohen, a Republican who spent the first Clinton term in the Senate.

It is difficult to find anyone who knows him who does not like Mr. Berger personally. You might as well try to find someone who doesn't like Sara Lee. His ego is of normal dimensions. He buys his reading glasses at the drug store. In a city where backbiting is the preferred contact sport, he is widely considered a gentleman. In a culture of 12-hour-days, he regularly puts in Stakhanovite stints of 15 and 16, fueled by endless glasses of iced coffee, which he took to drinking when he gave up smoking. Colleagues worry that he might

fall victim to the same tensions as Leon Fuerth, Vice President Al Gore's foreign-policy counsellor, who suffered a heart attack this year.

But Mr. Berger gets very mixed reviews as a security adviser from those outside his immediate circle. A European ambassador said he lacked "the indispensable ability to see around corners, to anticipate events and to see how one problem relates to another." A friend and sometime Administration colleague said Mr. Berger lacked strategic vision but "wants to be accepted as a kind of Sandy Kissinger."

Mr. Kissinger himself commented rather condescendingly, "you can't expect a trade lawyer to be a global strategist."

Dick Morris, Mr. Clinton's former political guru, wrote recently that "there are hundreds of members of the Council on Foreign Relations who know more about foreign policy than Berger," but he added that Mr. Berger was "just right" for the President's concept of foreign policy which, he said, centers on domestic political and economic considerations, not on strategy.

In his defense Mr. Berger's friends note that Mr. Clinton's attention to events abroad is intermittent. One retired American diplomat blamed "a disastrous Balkan policy in which every aspect has been treated incrementally" mostly on the President. During the Lewinsky matter, a Cabinet member added, "The whole rhythm of the Government was thrown off, because the big guy had something more important on his mind than any foreign-policy crisis—a 900-pound gorilla that was always in the room with him, named impeachment.

Finally, Mr. Berger has to deal with a world seismically remade by the end of the cold war.

"Everyone wants a new framework for American foreign policy," said Harry McPherson, a Texan who worked in the Johnson White House and has closely watched all the White Houses that followed his. "Well, great. But who has produced one? Sandy's a carpenter, not an architect, like everyone else these days. He's a good one, and that may be the best we can hope for now."

As things turned out in Kosovo, Mr. Milosevic buckled under the pressure of bombardment. But it was "an exceptionally close-run thing," a senior Administration official said, with talks about peace terms taking place at the same time as discussions about sending in the troops if no agreement was reached by the end of June. And the allies were unable, in the end, to prevent the slaughter of many of the Kosovo Albanians they acted to protect.

Mr. Berger said "the President truly believed, as I believed and no more than three other people in America did, that air power would prevail."

But it is not yet clear that the war has been won. It is not clear how many ethnic Albanians will ultimately be able to rebuild their lives, or how successful the NATO alliance will be at achieving the multi-ethnic society it says it wants for Kosovo. There is little prospect of stabilizing the Balkans, an important goal of American policy, without a stable Serbia. Yet that land is in ruins, Mr. Milosevic remains in office and Mr. Clinton has vowed to give only minimal rebuilding aid as long as he clings to power.

THE BEGINNINGS: SMALL-TOWN KID, SOLID DEMOCRAT

Mr. Berger grew up in Millerton, a then-isolated rural community of 900 people in the dairy country of Duchess County, N. Y., northeast of Poughkeepsie. His father died when he was only 8, and his mother ran a struggling Army-Navy surplus store. From his mother, he inherited the habit of hard work and a love of order; he still makes lists each Sunday, in his immaculate handwriting, of things to be done the following week.

The Bergers stood apart from the Millerton mainstream, as Democrats in a town where "people gave parties when F.D.R. died," and as Jews in the WASP heartland. Mr. Berger took his religious training from a rabbi in a nearby hospital for the mentally retarded. Young Sandy Berger had another distinguishing feature: he was a fervent Brooklyn Dodger fan in a Yankee town.

"Where I grew up is very important to what I am," he said. "My perspectives are still more Millerton 1960 than Washington 2000. The small-town sense of community and social responsibility—that's the lasting imprint of Millerton on me."

Mr. Berger likes to tell about visiting an aunt in Brooklyn when he was 10 and sleeping fitfully all night because of the fire and police sirens. When he asked her about them, she answered, "Oh, you get used to it." But when a siren sounded in Millerton, he said, "You knew that you'd know the people whose house was on fire, so you never got used to it."

At Cornell University, his good nature and his organizational ability led him into student politics. As head of the interfraternity council, he came under the sway of an assistant dean, Albert Miles, who interested him in questions of social justice. He asked civil rights leaders like Stokely Carmichael to Cornell to speak, he fought discrimination in the fraternities, closing down one that barred blacks from a party, and he persuaded James Perkins, the university president, to fly to Cornell a group of black schoolchildren from Brooklyn who had created a black history project that no one had come to see. The project was displayed at the Student Union.

Also at Cornell, where he met his wife, Susan, with whom he has lived in the same unpretentious house for 26 years, Mr. Berger encountered an important intellectual mentor, George McT. Kahin, a historian of Southeast Asia. He took the course on Vietnam taught by Professor Kahin, whose books became the testaments of the anti-war movement. His opposition to the war derived from that course, he says today, as does his habit of "questioning everything that I read."

But he never marched against the war, preferring, as he put it, to work within the system, first as a summer intern in Washington for Representative Joseph Resnick, a millionaire television-antenna manufacturer from the Catskills. At Harvard Law School, he volunteered first for Eugene McCarthy, then for Robert F. Kennedy, displaying the kind of pragmatism that sometimes gets him in trouble in his present job with more ideologically rigorous types.

Four years later, on the dovish McGovern campaign, he met a man wearing a Colonel Sanders white suit, Bill Clinton, and the two quickly became buddies. Senator McGovern's ignominious defeat is regarded by most politicians as an instructive example of what happens when a candidate totally loses touch with an electorate, but Mr. Berger views him as an "inspiring" leader, describing the 1972 fiasco as the result of tactical errors.

The dovish theme continued at Hogan & Hartson, one of Washington's premier law firms, where Mr.

Berger, who represented Japanese and other clients, talked often with the firm's most eminent figure, former Senator J. William Fulbright, the godfather of the anti-war movement. When he went into the State Department in the Carter Administration, he fought in the trenches alongside the dovish Secretary, Cyrus Vance, against the more hawkish national security adviser, Mr. Brzezinski, and resolved to do all he could to avoid such fights if he ever found himself in a position of real power.

However much he may have hated the Vietnam War, along with most of his peers, Mr. Berger is in essence a consensus-seeker and a deal-cutter, and work as a trade lawyer strengthened those tendencies. His contacts with Asia gave him a profound belief in free trade as a means of knitting the world together—a view that would color his subsequent attitudes toward China, the issue on which he has probably spent more time than any other in the White House.

THE WHITE HOUSE: A FRIEND OF BILL'S WHO NEVER LEFT

Except for the Carter Administration, the years from 1968 to 1992 were Republican years, but Mr. Berger found ways to keep a political oar in. He formed an important alliance with Pamela Harriman, the Washington social doyenne, writing speeches for her to give her the cloak of political gravitas she longed for, and benefiting, in turn, from her wealth and connections.

One button on Mrs. Harriman's telephone in her elegant Georgetown residence was marked "Sandy."

When Mr. Clinton lost a re-election bid in 1980, he persuaded Mrs. Harriman to put the young ex-Governor on the board of her political action committee, which came to be a major fund-raising arm of the Democratic Party. That gave Mr. Clinton a reason to come to Washington to schmooze. Eight years later, when Mr. Clinton muffed a big chance, delivering an agonizingly boring speech at the party convention in Atlanta, the Berger-Harriman team stepped in again, organizing a midnight dinner to pick up the Clintons' spirits.

When Mr. Clinton ran in 1992, Mr. Berger joined him as a senior foreign-policy adviser. When he won, Mr. Berger helped persuade him to send Mrs. Harri-man to Paris as Ambassador. Mr. Berger was offered the national security adviser's job but demurred on the grounds of limited experience, suggesting Mr. Lake instead. Mr. Berger became Mr. Lake's deputy.

But during Mr. Clinton's first term, says a person who held a senior position during that period, "everyone with a problem in the security area went to Sandy—honest, helpful Sandy, who never lied—and he built up a tremendous amount of credibility that helped him enormously once he took over." He has worked hard to maintain his network, talking by telephone as many as a dozen times a day with Ms. Albright, meeting once a week for breakfast with her and other security "principals" like George J. Tenet, the Director of Central Intelligence, and visiting Capitol Hill often.

Senior officials in the State Department and the Defense Department praise Mr. Berger's trustworthiness and his ability to run meetings, though some of the generals and admirals are not entirely comfortable with him or any of the old anti-war crowd and their brand of cautious interventionism.

The bonds of friendship between Mr. Clinton and Mr. Berger—one of the few who has served the entire two terms at the White House under four chiefs of staff—have held, even in bad times, such as the town meeting on Iraq in Columbus, Ohio, in May of last year, conceived in Mr. Berger's office, which ended with Mr. Cohen and Ms. Albright being shouted down. Mr. Berger himself describes the event as "a complete fiasco."

Nor is there any sign that Mr. Berger's standing with the President has slipped because of the Administration's difficulties with China, the country with which he is most closely identified. It is the country whose development, he once said, "will have the biggest impact on our children."

To shape that development, Mr. Berger has championed a policy of engagement, in which the United States has tried to bind China to the United States through economic and security arrangements. But a lot of things have gone wrong lately, from illicit Chinese campaign contributions to the Democrats to the accidental bombing of the Chinese Embassy in Belgrade.

Mr. Berger's biggest setback on the China front came when he was unable to persuade President Clinton in April to sign a trade deal during Prime Minister

Zhu Rongji's visit to the White House. Despite his clout with Mr. Clinton, he was outflanked on this occasion by John S. Podesta, the White House chief of staff. Mr. Podesta had the foresight to win the backing of a man even more influential than Mr. Berger, Treasury Secretary Robert Rubin, and they persuaded the President to hold out for more concessions to placate Congress. Despite efforts to regroup, no treaty has been signed yet.

Even worse for Mr. Berger personally were charges that he reacted too passively when told about the suspected Chinese theft of nuclear secrets. He insists that he acted properly when told of the charges, even though he briefed Mr. Clinton only very tardily, after March of this year, on detailed charges that Mr. Berger had learned of in July, 1997. Asked if he felt that he had dropped the ball in any way, either in terms of substance or in terms of appearances, he replied, cold-eyed, "No."

Mr. Berger's cherished reputation on the Hill has nonetheless taken a hit, with several influential members of Congress calling for his resignation. These calls have subsided, but he remains "very exposed and very vulnerable on this," according to a government China specialist who admires him.

"He is the best link we have with China," the specialist said. "But he is viewed by our critics as someone who cares more about China than the United States, and that limits his ability to take initiatives with China. You need to explain the bombing, but you can't send Sandy to Beijing."

There is also an inescapable sense that the Administration makes policy on the fly.

Michael McCurry, a former White House press secretary, concedes that "we don't have a new definition of the U. S. role in the world yet." In some moods, Mr. Berger sounds as if that's fine with him. In 1991, he said during a panel discussion that most "grand strategies" were after-the-fact rationales developed to explain successful ad hoc decisions.

He said in a recent conversation that he prefers to "worry about today today and tomorrow tomorrow."

22

CONDOLEEZZA RICE

Elaine Sciolino

This selection presents a profile of Dr. Condoleezza Rice, national security adviser in the second Bush Administration. Elaine Sciolino takes a look at Dr. Rice's preparation for the job of NSC adviser, suggesting that she and President George W. Bush share a similar outlook on the world: "a realist, Republican balance-of-power approach that focuses more on the big powers and less on the interests of 'the international community.'"

In 1991, only two years into the Bush administration, Condoleezza Rice suddenly left her powerful job as the top Russia expert on the National Security Council and went back to California—to get a life.

"I like balance in my life," Ms. Rice said in an interview in Palo Alto, Calif., during the presidential campaign earlier this year. "I wanted a life. These jobs are all-consuming. And I have strong reservations about going back to that all-consuming life and leaving what is a blessedly normal life here. I like going to the cleaners and the coffee shop on Saturday morning." But in accepting the offer to become national security adviser in a George W. Bush administration, the 46-year-old former political science professor and provost at Stanford University has decided to return to that all-consuming life.

Perhaps it is not at all surprising. As a child growing up in a segregated bourgeois neighborhood in Birmingham, Ala., Condi, as she is called, was pushed relentlessly to achieve. She started piano lessons at the age of 3, was tutored in French and Spanish as a young girl and entered eighth grade at the age of 11.

As a high school student in Denver, she became both a competitive ice skater (getting up at 4:30 A.M. for lessons) and an accomplished pianist (sometimes staying up until 3 a.m. to practice). She did her senior year of high school and her freshman year in college at the same time. Her parents piled up so many books by her bedside table that she stopped reading for pleasure, and still does not.

"I grew up in a family in which my parents put me into every book club," she recalled. "So I never developed the fine art of recreational reading."

As Mr. Bush's top national security adviser during the campaign, Ms. Rice played a variety of roles. She was his private foreign policy tutor, the person, Mr. Bush once said, who "can explain to me foreign policy matters in a way I can understand." She was his intellectual quarterback, "both a good manager and an honest broker of ideas," he said in an interview. And she was his trusted friend, "a close confidante and a good soul," he added.

At 46, she will not be the youngest national security adviser in American history. McGeorge Bundy was only 41 when he became national security adviser to President John F. Kennedy; Henry A. Kissinger in the Nixon administration and Richard V. Allen in the Reagan administration were only 45. Nor is she the first black national security adviser. Retired Gen. Colin L. Powell, the former chairman of the Joint Chiefs of Staff and Mr. Bush's choice for secretary of state, served as national security adviser in the final year of the Reagan administration.

But Ms. Rice will be the first woman to hold the job.

With her girlish laugh and gushes of Southern charm, Ms. Rice can be utterly captivating—without

From Elaine Sciolino, "Compulsion to Achieve—Condoleezza Rice," *New York Times* (December 18, 2000), A1.

Elaine Sciolino is a reporter for the *New York Times*.

ever appearing confessional or vulnerable—a quality that can mask her spine of steel.

In 1989, in her previous National Security Council stint, for example, she physically blocked Boris N. Yeltsin, then the leader of Russia's reform movement, in the basement of the White House when he balked at seeing the national security adviser, Brent Scowcroft, and demanded to see President George Bush. (After five minutes, Mr. Yeltsin backed down.)

During the campaign, none of the other members of Mr. Bush's foreign-policy team dared to speak to reporters without her permission. "You make me sound like a tyrant!" she exclaimed when asked to explain why, then added with a smile, "We are disciplined, we are disciplined."

She eats either a bagel or cereal every day for breakfast. She is always impeccably dressed, usually in a classic suit with a modest hemline, comfortable pumps and conservative jewelry. She keeps two mirrors on her desk at Stanford, apparently to check the back as well as the front of her hair. ("I do try to make sure everything is in place," she explained.) She has an oil supertanker named after her, a result of being on the Chevron Corporation board.

"Condi was raised first and foremost to be a lady," said General Powell, in an interview during the campaign. "She was raised in a protected environment to be a person of great self-confidence in Birmingham, where there was no reason to have self-confidence because you were a 10th-class citizen and you were black."

Ms. Rice (whose first name is pronounced kahn-dah-LEE-za) was born on Nov. 14, 1954, in Birmingham, a world of colored-only water fountains and segregated swimming pools. She is the only child of the Rev. John W. Rice Jr., who ran the Westminster Presbyterian Church, which her grandfather had founded. Her father once formed a shotgun brigade after a gas bomb was hurled through a neighbor's window.

Ms. Rice's mother, the former Angelena Ray, and father taught at a black Birmingham high school, where her father was also the football coach. Her mother died of breast cancer in 1985; her father, who still calls his daughter "little star," lives close by her in Palo Alto with his second wife.

Ms. Rice's first name is derived from the Italian musical term "con dolcezza," to perform "with sweetness." The family "lore," she said, is that a great-great-grandfather on her mother's side was an Italian who emigrated to the United States and bought slaves. Her great-great-grandparents on her father's side were slaves.

She once planned for a career as a concert pianist until she realized she was not good enough. "Mozart didn't have to practice," she said in an interview during the campaign. "I was going to have to practice and practice and practice and was never going to be extraordinary."

Asked whether that was upsetting for her, she replied: "I don't do life crises. I really don't. Life's too short. Get over it. Move on to the next thing."

Her mentor at the University of Denver, where she earned a bachelor's degree (Phi Beta Kappa) in political science in 1974, was Josef Korbel, the father of Secretary of State Madeleine K. Albright, who helped Ms. Rice "fall in love" with Russian history, she said. From there she earned a master's degree from the University of Notre Dame in 1975 and a doctorate from Denver in 1981, joining the Stanford political science faculty immediately afterward.

Ms. Rice started her political life as a Democrat, switched sides in 1982, and has called herself "an all-over-the-map Republican."

In her two years in the Bush White House, no task was ever beneath her. On the day Iraq invaded Kuwait in August 1990, she typed the president's talking points for his first public message rather than watch her colleague Richard N. Haass hunt and peck on the computer.

In 1993, she became the youngest, the first female and the first nonwhite provost at Stanford. Faced with a $43 million deficit, she cut services and fired staff with only limited faculty consultations. "I don't do committees," she said.

Unlike General Powell, Ms. Rice is not an across-the-board supporter of affirmative action. As provost, Ms. Rice was criticized for not doing enough to promote diversity in the Stanford faculty, prompting her to tell the San Jose Mercury News in May 1998, "I'm the chief academic officer now. I say in principle that I don't believe in and in fact will not apply affirmative action" in promotions. Yet the year before, she was quoted as telling a Stanford faculty meeting, "I myself am the beneficiary of a Stanford strategy that took affirmative action seriously."

Like Mr. Bush, she is a sports and fitness enthusiast, and at Stanford, she trained hard with the football coach. (The reason her dress size is between a 6 and an 8, she said, is because of "muscle mass.")

"Exercise," she said, "is a very high priority for me, especially if you don't have children who are a break on working all the time, you can work all the time." And, Ms. Rice, who is single, added, "I do some of my best thinking on the treadmill."

Ms. Rice and Mr. Bush seem to share a similar view of the world: a realist, Republican balance-of-power approach that focuses more on the big powers and less on the interests of "the international community."

During the campaign, Ms. Rice urged Mr. Bush to avoid making foreign policy statements that he might regret later. She coordinated Mr. Bush's nuclear policy initiative, which called for building a national missile defense system combined with reductions and possibly unilateral cuts in America's nuclear arsenal. Cautious about using American military force, she alarmed America's NATO allies in October when she suggested that if elected president, Mr. Bush planned to tell NATO that the United States should no longer participate in peacekeeping in the Balkans.

That caution runs deep, and in an interview with The San Francisco Chronicle in 1993, she was reluctant to recommend the overthrow of President Saddam Hussein of Iraq. "Saddam is an outlaw but I would be careful about trying to do anything to act to overthrow him," she said.

The co-author of two books, one on the reunification of Germany, the other on the Soviet Union and the Czechoslovak Army, she would be the first to admit that the task of national security adviser will be challenging. At the height of the presidential campaign last spring, she confessed that there were vast areas of the world that were new to her. "I've been pressed to understand parts of the world that have not been part of my scope," she said in an interview. "I'm really a Europeanist."

Now, as President-elect Bush's appointee as national security adviser, Ms. Rice suddenly will have to prove that she can be master of the universe.

PART VII

PERFORMANCE

> History is much more the product of chaos than of conspiracy. The external world's vision of internal decision-making in the Government assumes too much cohesion and expects too much systematic planning. The fact of the matter is that, increasingly, policy makers are overwhelmed by events and information.
>
> —*Zbigniew Brzezinski*
> *New York Times*
> *January 18, 1981*

Editors' Introduction

"Domestic policy . . . can only defeat us," President Kennedy once observed, "foreign policy can kill us." Presidents quickly learn the importance of foreign policy, even if they may have run for election on a domestic policy platform. The world simply refuses to be ignored. In the first two months of his administration, Kennedy was forced to concentrate more on Laos than any other topic. Then came the disaster at the Bay of Pigs in May 1961. For the first President Bush, Iraq soon dominated his every day, leading to the Persian Gulf War. For President Clinton, his tenure was supposed to be about economic prosperity at home; the president said he wanted to focus on the economy "like a laser beam." Instead, the White House was forced to direct that beam toward Somalia, Haiti, the Balkans, the dangerous proliferation of weapons of mass destruction around the world, and the growing threat of international terrorism. The second President Bush started out by concentrating on tax cuts, education, and missile defense—until 9/11, at which point the 'war on terror' and the "axis of evil" (Iraq, Iran, North Korea) took over the White House agenda.

Every international issue of consequence affecting the United States comes to the attention of the NSC principals, whether sitting formally as members of the Council gathered in the Cabinet Room of the White House or in some other less formal configuration, like Kennedy's "ExComm" during the Cuban missile crisis, Johnson's "Tuesday lunch," Carter's "Friday breakfast," or the second Bush's War Cabinet. The president has the responsibility for deciding on the great issues that come before the nation; the purpose of the NSC system is to provide the best information and advice possible to help illuminate the options.

The purpose of this section is to draw back the curtains on a series of NSC meetings, taking the reader inside this hidden domain to see how the Council operates during the making of important foreign policy decisions. These meetings include deliberations over the Cuban missile crisis (1962), the transition from the Cold War to a world of more fragmented state relations

(1989–92), the conflict in the Balkans (1995), and the ongoing struggle against international terrorists (2001–). The intent is to impart a sense of how the National Security Council has functioned in a few critical cases.

Before turning to the first selection on the Cuban missile crisis, we review here two earlier NSC decisions that provide insight into its performance before the Kennedy years. A central issue that came before the NSC during the Truman Administration was the outbreak of war on the Korean Peninsula in 1950, discussed in Dean Acheson's memoirs (entitled *Present at the Creation,* 1969; see For Further Reading). Acheson served as secretary of state during the Truman era and witnessed attempts by the NSC to grapple with an increasingly unsettling situation in Korea, involving a brilliant, but sometimes rebellious and unpredictable U.S. field commander, General Douglas MacArthur, and a great deal of uncertainty about the intentions—or even the whereabouts—of a large and dangerous Chinese army.

In his memoirs, Acheson underscores the strong dependence of the NSC system on good intelligence gathered by the CIA and other agencies around the world. Without reliable, timely information from around the world, the United States is like a giant without eyes. From the days of the Korean War to the modern era of fighting global terrorisms, a fundamental duty of the NSC staff is to make sure that the Council's principals are not blinded by ignorance.

In 2003, a controversy erupted in the United States over whether intelligence on the possible presense of weapons of mass destruction (WMD) in Iraq had been either improperly reported to the NSC or perhaps exaggerated by the Council staff or principals. The issue was important, since the original rationale for going to war against Iraq that year rested at least in part on the fear that Saddam Hussein might have such weapons and might use them against the United States, or provide them to terrorists with the same result. At the heart of the controversy was an intelligence report, passed to the CIA by the British foreign intelligence service (MI6), suggesting that Iraq may have tried to acquire from the African nation of Niger a bomb-making form of uranium known as "yellow cake." Relying on this information, President George W. Bush said in the State of the Union Address of January 2003—in a now celebrated sixteen words—that "the British government has learned that Saddam Hussein recently sought significant quantities of uranium from Africa."

Subsequently, it was determined that the Niger information had been based on forged documents. A hue and cry arose over who was responsible for the intelligence gaffe. Was it MI6 for sharing dubious information with the United States? The CIA for inadequate checking of the allegation when it first arose? The NSC staff for allowing the statement to surface in one of the President's most important speeches, despite the fact that weeks before the address CIA director George Tenet had informed the deputy national security adviser that the information was suspect? Or the president and his top cabinet officers for possibly seeking shock value in the allegation, as a means for buttressing their Iraqi war plans? Wherever the blame rightfully lie, one lesson was clear: Intelligence reports require checking and rechecking, by both the CIA and the NSC staff, before being presented to the American public and the international community by the president and other high officials. Clearly, instances of intelligence officers or policy officials exaggerating or altering factual information to suit their political objectives (the "cooking" of intelligence) should be met with opprobrium.

In 1950, the intelligence on events in Korea had been inadequate. First, the CIA failed to predict the outbreak of war—indeed, its analysts said that war would not come; and then the NSC remained in a fog about what the enemy was doing in the field. The distance of 7,000 miles between the White House and Korean Peninsula left the Council at the mercy of the judgment exercised by General MacArthur, and his judgment proved deeply flawed on this occasion. Surprising the general (and the CIA's best analysts), a massive Chinese army swept across the frozen Yalu River in defense of North Korea and, with great loss of life on both sides, pushed the dispersed American and South Korean forces back across the 38th parallel (a belt of land at the midsection of the peninsula).

President Truman displayed feelings of ambivalence toward the NSC system. He presided over the Council's very first meeting, but ten months elapsed in his presidency before he ever came to another. He believed in the NSC's basic role of policy coordination, having been appalled by the lack of intelligence sharing among U.S. agencies during the Second World War; however, he was reluctant to allow a committee to assume, or even seem to influence unduly, his decision-making authority as president. In his memoirs, Secretary of State Acheson revealed that during the Korean War, he, President Truman, and other key figures would occasionally convene formally as the NSC, although the actual decision to enter into the conflict was made outside the formal NSC framework. Moreover, in addition to formal meetings of the NSC, just as often its principals would gather in informal ad hoc groups of varying composition, such as those who met periodically with the president and Acheson at Blair House (including the secretary of the treasury and a number of generals and admirals).

The full cabinet, in Acheson's view (and most everyone else's), was an especially poor place for the serious discussion of policy. "No wise man asked the President's instruction in Cabinet meetings," the secretary of state recalled in his memoirs. "He would surely find a number of articulate and uninformed colleagues intervening with confused and confusing suggestions. The Cabinet, despite its glamour, is not a major instrument of Government; the National Security Council, properly run, can and should be."

During the Truman Administration, the Department of State was meant to be the lead player in matters of foreign policy. As Acheson recalls, "President Truman looked principally to the Department of State in determining foreign policy and—except where force was necessary—exclusively in executing it; he communicated with the Department and with the foreign nations through the Secretary."

In 1954, only one year after the end of the war in Korea, the NSC faced another key challenge in Asia. According to an account in *The Reporter* by the distinguished journalist Chalmers M. Roberts ("The Day We Didn't Go to War," 1954), the NSC had reached a decision in March of that year to intervene in the war between the French and Vietnamese communist insurgents in Indochina—if assurances were forthcoming that America's allies would be supportive of this intervention. To garner political backing within the United States for the action, President Eisenhower told his secretary of state, John Foster Dulles, to call a meeting with key lawmakers. The secretary was supposed to explain to them the strategic importance of Vietnam and then gauge their willingness to pass a congressional resolution in favor of the military operation.

On April 3, eight legislators representing both political parties met with Dulles and the chairman of the Joint Chiefs of Staff at the Department of State. The response of the legislators to the briefing on Indochina and the desperate military situation faced by the French forces was not what the secretary had anticipated. The members of Congress—an experienced group (including Richard B. Russell of Georgia, a giant in the Senate on issues of national security) who had seen many presidents, secretaries of state, and foreign policy proposals come and go—asked sharp questions about the military plans and insisted that Dulles demonstrate stronger support for the operation among U.S. allies. Dulles flew to London, where he soon discovered that the

British actually opposed immediate military intervention by the United States, a finding unlikely to help his case with the lawmakers. President Eisenhower decided to back away from the idea of intervention. In May, at the battle of Dienbienphu in Vietnam, communist forces surrounded and defeated the French.

This Indochina case involved a rare *advance* consultation with leaders of Congress by an NSC principal before a decision was made and a policy carried out. The merits of the decision not to intervene to rescue the French forces can be debated; but the case does suggest the benefits of the two branches working together, pooling their collective wisdom. The combined experience of the eight legislators with whom Dulles met added up to many years of institutional memory about foreign policy initiatives and the limits of public tolerance. Before rushing pell-mell into the jungles of Vietnam, the lawmakers posed a useful condition: let the United States not go alone. It was a point that, according to Roberts, the NSC staff had also stressed, but one that Secretary Dulles and the chair of the Joint Chiefs seemed unwilling to consider in their anti-communist zeal for taking on the Vietnamese insurgents—until they were pulled up short by the weighty visitors from Capitol Hill.

As with Truman, in making this decision (and several others), President Eisenhower relied more on ad hoc informal consultations with his top aides than he did on the elaborate formal machinery of the NSC that had evolved during his eight years in office. Recall from the earlier Greenstein–Immerman selection (Part II) that "Eisenhower made the operational decisions of his presidency in informal meetings with small groups of advisers in the Oval Office, not in the NSC." For most of the Eisenhower years, the individual responsible for coordinating these various informal meetings (including the one at which the initial NSC decision to aid the French in Vietnam was reversed) was not even the national security adviser, but rather the president's staff secretary. Eisenhower sometimes referred to the staff secretary, a job held by army generals (briefly by General Paul "Pete" Carroll, who suffered a fatal heart attack in 1954, and then by General Andrew Goodpaster), as his White House "sergeant major."

The Cuban Missile Crisis

Turning now to the Kennedy Administration, the first selection in this section presents an account of the Cuban missile crisis of 1962, drawn from the study of President John F. Kennedy's presidency written by historian Arthur M. Schlesinger, Jr., and entitled *A Thousand Days*. The account gives a vivid sense of "you are there" for the days of agonizing by the NSC over what to do about the placement of Soviet missiles on the island of Cuba, just ninety miles from America's shoreline. The CIA and the NSC accurately presumed at the time that these weapons would soon be armed with nuclear warheads; once ready to fire ("operational"), they would be able to obliterate many of this nation's major cities only minutes after their launch. The United States faced what many consider to be its most dangerous crisis ever.

This was not the Kennedy Administration's first run-in with Cuba. In May 1961, just a few months after his inauguration, the young president suffered a humiliating reversal in a covert invasion carried out against Cuba by the CIA. The Cuban exiles who served as the CIA's soldiers in the paramilitary operation were gunned down or quickly rounded up by Cuban forces on the beaches of the Bay of Pigs (see Wyden, 1979). The expected air support from U.S. fighter planes never materialized. The president, in agreement with Secretary of State Dean Rusk, decided to cancel the air cover, for fear that the involvement of American military aircraft in an escalating war against a small nation might cause an international reaction against the United States. The end result was one of the most conspicuous failures in the annals of American foreign policy.

The disaster at the Bay of Pigs had many causes, but among them was the faulty use of the NSC system. Designed to present a president with good intelligence and a range of policy options, the Council during this episode offered little of either. The intelligence in the hands of the president and other NSC principals was abysmal. The operation rested on the assumptions of operatives in the CIA's Operations Directorate that, first, the people of Cuba would rise up against their leader Fidel Castro once an invasion was underway and, second, if this proved incorrect, the invaders could escape to the Escambray Mountains. In reality, Castro's popular base of support in Cuba was strong in 1961. Moreover, escape to the Escambrays was blocked by the imposing Zapata swamp! Analysts in the CIA's Intelligence Directorate or Cuban specialists in the State Department could have provided the president with a better understanding of the situation he faced, yet they were never consulted by the president or the NSC.

Further, few policy options to the planned invasion were ever considered. President Eisenhower, the famous general, had approved the plan, and his imprimatur for a covert paramilitary operation carried great weight in the new Democratic administration, headed by a president inexperienced in foreign policy or intelligence matters. Besides, the CIA seemed so self-assured and certain that the operation would succeed. Its planner, Richard Bissell, the chief of the CIA's covert action branch, was generally recognized as a brilliant individual and, in addition, he enjoyed a close Georgetown social relationship with the president. In light of Eisenhower's and Bissell's standing in the Washington establishment, no one in the inner circle of decision making questioned the plan openly in the presence of President Kennedy, even as devil's advocate. Invited at the eleventh hour by the president to attend an ad hoc meeting in the Department of State on the proposed operation, Senator J. William Fulbright (D–Arkansas) attempted to take on this task of critic—he was the lone naysayer against the invasion, on moral grounds—but he was quickly overruled by a room full of high-ranking military and intelligence officials.

The limited number of formal NSC meetings held on the invasion plan tended to be stilted and infused by a sense of "groupthink," Irving L. Janis's term to describe the tendency among cohesive groups to seek concurrence at the expense of gathering accurate information and engaging in critical debate (Janis, 1972). Even if these meetings had been more open and encouraged broad discussion of the plan, they might have had minimal effect, since the president made his key decisions outside the arena of formal deliberations with NSC principals. Kennedy relied instead on telephone calls and private consultations with a few experts—chiefly his friend, Bissell—and rarely with the secretary of state.

In contrast, the Cuban missile crisis of October 1962 showed that the NSC had learned some lessons from the Bay of Pigs fiasco. This time a premium was placed on openness; the president wanted to hear from a range of experts and trusted "outsiders"—though, once again, lawmakers were excluded from the deliberations. Candor and free debate were encouraged in each of the NSC meetings, of which there were several in the augmented form of a specially created Executive Committee or "ExComm." Wary of the groupthink trap, participants—and the president's brother, Robert Kennedy, in particular—raised hard questions, probed assumptions, weighed alternatives, sought intelligence from various sources (not just the CIA's Operations Directorate), remained skeptical about CIA agent reports from Cuba (most of which proved false), and dropped the usual protocol of deference to the views of senior officials.

The president aided freewheeling discussion by absenting himself from several of the NSC meetings. This encouraged a forthrightness among his advisers that a presidential presence might have stifled. When Kennedy was in attendance, he made sure that he heard from each person in the room, not just the Council's principals. Experts who had never set foot in the White

House before were brought in and listened to. As Janis has observed, the concurrence-seeking behavior of the NSC during the Bay of Pigs crisis was replaced with "vigilant appraisal" during the missile crisis—the antithesis of groupthink. By all accounts, the improvements in the style of NSC decision making in 1962 helped achieve a great foreign policy success.

It should be remembered, however, that even with this successful outcome in October 1962, the decision-making process revealed serious shortcomings. Again, as during the Korean War and the Bay of Pigs operation, the importance of good intelligence for effective NSC deliberations becomes apparent by close analysis of the Cuban missile crisis. Not only did the CIA's analysts fail to anticipate the placement of Soviet nuclear missiles in Cuba (although the director of Central Intelligence, John McCone, expressed a hunch that the Soviets might try this ploy, and he told the president so), but once they were discovered by U–2 surveillance, many other intelligence questions remained unanswered during the tense discussions within the ExComm. How long would it take to operationalize the missiles? What degree of discretion did the local Soviet and Cuban commanders have over their firing? Did the Soviet jet fighters (MIG 21s) and bombers based in Cuba possess a nuclear capability? Only in recent years, with access to Soviet archives, have scholars learned that the situation in Cuba was even more dangerous than they thought at the time (Blight, Allyn, and Welch, 1993; Fursenko and Naftali, 1997; Gaddis, 1997).

Consultations between Congress and the White House during the missile crisis were virtually nonexistent. Just three hours before President Kennedy was to speak to the nation on television about the crisis, thirty lawmakers were called down to the White House and told of the impending naval blockade. They had no time to discuss the alternatives or to reflect on the implications of the military option selected by the president—a far more prudent military approach than the one initially advanced by Pentagon brass, who preferred a full-scale invasion of Cuba (see May and Zelikow, 1997). As the secretary of state at the time, Dean Rusk, later conceded in an unpublished oral history with one of the authors of this volume (Johnson, 1985): "To be frank, the only question before them at that moment was, 'Are you prepared to support your country at this moment of grave danger?' I do not consider that to be effective consultation between the two branches." As a step toward improving the degree of NSC consultation with lawmakers, President Carter's national security adviser, Zbigniew Brzezinski, has recommended the establishment of "an informal monthly NSC meeting with legislative leadership . . . Such discussion could help infuse into the NSC process a domestic political perspective it currently lacks" (Brzezinski, 1987–88).

The War in Vietnam

The next case study presented in this book is about the transition from the Cold War to the fragmented world in which we now find ourselves. But first, we look briefly at another important foreign policy episode during the Cold War: the war in Vietnam.

Many volumes have been written on the subject of the Vietnam War, and scholars will continue for decades to seek an understanding of the fateful decision to send U.S. forces to Indochina. The memoirs of President Lyndon Johnson are a good source of insight into the dynamics of that decision from the vantage point of the White House (Johnson, 1971). As a product of his Capitol Hill background, Johnson may have been more sensitive to the opinions of lawmakers than most presidents. In an early NSC meeting on Vietnam held in 1964, he invited Speaker of the House John McCormick (D–Massachusetts) and Senate Majority Leader Mike Mansfield (D–Montana) to attend. At the meeting, Mansfield provided the single voice of dissent, opposing the option of a military strike against North Vietnam in retaliation for communist attacks against U.S. military advisers in South Vietnam. Mansfield expressed concern about triggering a Chinese entry into the conflict—which was so disastrous during the Korean War. In subsequent meetings, Johnson invited other legislative leaders from both parties and in both chambers of Congress, and he would meet with lawmakers outside the NSC setting as well.

Criticism of "Johnson's War" in Vietnam mounted on Capitol Hill, although Congress as a whole continued to support the president's war plans, perhaps in part because Johnson had been skillful in making them feel they had been part of the decision-making process. Yet, the involvement of the legislative branch in the president's war-making plans should not be overestimated. After all, the most important NSC meetings on the war took place during the "Tuesday lunch" sessions attended by Secretary of State Rusk, Secretary of Defense Robert S. McNamara, and national security adviser Walt W. Rostow. No lawmakers were invited into this inner sanctum, or to any of the frequent weekend meetings between Rusk and McNamara. Moreover, the record seems clear now that the White House misled the Congress at the time of the Gulf of Tonkin Resolution (August 1964) by giving lawmakers the impression that U.S. naval ships had been attacked by North Vietnamese patrol boats in the South China Sea. Only much later did Congress learn that reports on at least some of these attacks had been mistaken. Further, throughout the war the executive branch frequently provided legislators and the public with misleadingly optimistic evaluations of its progress, leading to Johnson's notorious "credibility gap." The invitations to NSC meetings offered to selected lawmakers began to look more like efforts by the Johnson Administration to co-opt the Congress than to permit an open and meaningful exchange of views on the conduct of the war in Indochina.

Similarly, in 2003, critics charged that the Bush Administration had failed to play it straight with lawmakers and the public. The Administration maintained that it had solid evidence regarding the presence of weapons of mass destruction in Iraq; and, moreover, that Saddam Hussein had covert ties to Osama bin Laden and the Qaeda terrorist group responsible for the September 11, 2001, attacks against the United States. Based in part on these assurances, the Congress passed a joint resolution authorizing the conduct of war against Iraq. For critics, this congressional action seemed like the Gulf of Tonkin Resolution all over again, with lawmakers acting too hastily and without solid information. As with President Lyndon Johnson in the aftermath of the Gulf of Tonkin Resolution, cracks began to appear in the credibility of the Bush Administration with the American public.

Comparable to the approach toward Iraq taken by the second President Bush, Lyndon Johnson's approach toward Vietnam was shaped as much by his worldview as by intelligence reports. Johnson's memoirs spell out his thinking on world affairs as he faced events rapidly unfolding in Indochina during the mid-1960s. "If we ran out on Southeast Asia, I could see trouble ahead in every part of the globe—not just in Asia but in the Middle East and in Europe, in Africa and in Latin America," he wrote. "I was convinced that our retreat from this challenge would open the path to World War III."

Also, as a young Rhodes scholar at Oxford University, Rusk was present at the Oxford Union when its members voted overwhelmingly in support of appeasement toward the Nazis. Rusk opposed appeasement at the time, and the world soon learned that Hitler could not be appeased with a few morsels; his appetite was insatiable. Rusk believed that a policy of appeasement in Vietnam would fail, too; America had to take a stand against communism.

It was a view widely held at the time, inside and outside the government, in the White House and on Capitol Hill, and one often reiterated by Rusk and McNamara, and by NSC advisers Bundy and Rostow. Not until the U.S. casualties mounted in Vietnam, with no victory in sight, did the American people and their elected representatives begin seriously to reappraise this argument. Student protests, congressional hearings, television images of a brutal war, a plummeting presidential standing in the polls—these external influences, not deliberations inside the NSC, provided the catalysts for policy changes in the failing Vietnam War.

Kevin V. Mulcahy ("Rethinking Groupthink," 1995; see For Further Reading) has identified two rules of thumb used by President Johnson's national security adviser, Walt W. Rostow, for ensuring that NSC meetings were a success. First, the Council's intelligence briefings had to add value to reports from the *New York Times*, not merely repeat what the NSC principals were already reading in the public domain; and, second, issue presentations had to be designed so as give the principals a "heads up" about decisions likely to come to their desk, along with a sense of the key elements they would have to weigh as they considered the problems. In the Mulcahy article, Rostow concedes that the Tuesday lunches had become "the heart of the NSC process," leaving the Council in its more formal guise to attend to middle-range issues of less importance.

Mulcahy's research also raises questions about the influence of groupthink during the Vietnam War deliberations. Key participants, like Undersecretary of State George Ball, reject the concept, arguing that they believed the president and others listened carefully to their dissents, even if they decided not to follow their counsel. Mulcahy paints a portrait of an NSC reaching out beyond the confines of the White House, the Department of State, and the Department of Defense, to consult widely with former leading government officials (such as former Secretary of State Dean Acheson). Johnson and Rostow listened to others, but what they heard for the most part reinforced the view of NSC principals that the war in Vietnam had to be fought. Mulcahy cites an important study by David Barrett, entitled *Uncertain Warriors* (1993), that demonstrates how President Johnson supplemented NSC meetings and the Tuesday lunches with extensive discussions on the war with old Capitol Hill colleagues like William Fulbright and Richard Russell.

Mulcahy rejects the idea that Rostow discarded the notion of the national security adviser as an "honest broker" and imposed his own philosophy about Vietnam on the president. While it is true that Rostow had "hawkish" views on the need to pursue the war, these views were already widely held by the NSC's principals. Further, "doves" like Ball had access to the president. "The dissidents remained as such for one paramount reason," Mulcahy argues: "Johnson did not agree with them." Mulcahy reaches this summary conclusion about the "constricting and distorting" effects of the Tuesday lunches on the NSC advisory process: the verdict "must be either 'not guilty,' or most certainly 'not proven.'" As memoirs by leading figures of this era continue to be published (see, for example, Robert S. McNamara, *In Retrospect*, 1995), the debate over the openness of the Johnson Administration will continue.

Cold War's End and the War in the Persian Gulf

The next reading in this section takes us inside the NSC system during the administration of the first President Bush. In their co-authored book, entitled *A World Transformed* (1998), the president and his national security adviser, Brent Scowcroft, take turns discussing (in alternating, interwoven presentations) their recollections of how the NSC operated during the four-year period from 1989–92. Scowcroft tells the reader early in the selection that he instituted a major organizational change in the way the NSC conducted its work; he created a "principals' committee"—the NSC without the president and the vice president. In this fashion, he hoped to have issues and positions clarified before they came to the president for a decision, thereby saving much of what Scowcroft considered a president's most valuable commodity: time. To further preserve this commodity, the president says that he "relied heavily on Brent to sort out the flow of national security papers and who should see what." As the first President Bush recalls, "Brent tried to reduce the issues to the point where he and I, and perhaps [Secretary of State] Jim Baker or [Secretary of Defense] Dick Cheney, could sort out any remaining problems."

Scowcroft vowed to improve relations between the NSC and Congress as well, noting that "the Congress is crucial in so many ways to the success of foreign policy. . . ." He appointed a staff member as the Council's liaison to Capitol Hill, and she kept (Scowcroft recalls) "Congress at the forefront of my thoughts." Another innovation during the first Bush Administration was to include the White House press secretary (Marlin Fitzwater) in NSC sessions, so that he could respond intelligently to the media on security issues—while at the same time walking the delicate line of keeping sensitive information out of the newspapers. Another regular "non-expert" in attendance, as in most recent administrations, was the White House chief of staff (John Sununu), to ensure that the president's domestic political stakes were not overlooked by those planning foreign policy on his behalf. The president also wanted in attendance any department or agency head who had responsibilities related to the issue or problem being discussed at the NSC meeting.

One of the important issues facing the NSC during this period was the unraveling of the Soviet Union. Scowcroft played a pivotal role as national security adviser by first posing key questions to the Council about the Soviet leader Mikhail Gorbachev and politics in Moscow: What was the internal situation in the U.S.S.R.? What were Gorbachev's ties with the conservatives, and what was his staying power? He then prodded the national security bureaucracy to come up with reliable intelligence to answer the questions. President Bush wisely sought outside opinion as well, having Scowcroft gather together groups of scholars at the Bush vacation home in Kennebunkport, Maine. The broad national security establishment prepared a strategic review on the Soviet Union, known as the National Security Review or NSR–3 (the administration's label for the National Security Decision Memoranda or NSDMs of earlier administrations). This report proved disappointing to the president because it lacked details and imaginative initiatives designed to bring about cordial U.S.–Soviet relations. The NSC turned instead to a "think piece" on Gorbachev and his likely intentions, generated by an NSC team led by future national security adviser Condoleezza Rice—a trumping of the bureaucracy by the NSC staff. A steady stream of memos from Rice and her associates to Scowcroft and the NSC principals continued to guide the deliberations.

It didn't take long (March 1989) before Scowcroft came to the conclusion "that a full-blown NSC gathering was not always the place for a no-holds-barred discussion among the president's top advisers. Some might be inhibited from expressing themselves frankly with staff present and the constant possibility of leaks." The national security adviser decided to convene a less formal meeting in the Oval Office, with only a few key officials present to appraise U.S. foreign policy goals with respect to Europe. On the roster to meet with the president were the vice president (Dan Quayle), Baker, Cheney, Scowcroft, DCI Robert M. Gates, Sununu, and State Department expert (and later, briefly, secretary of state) Larry Eagleburger. As Scowcroft recollects, "The President liked the suggestion, and it worked. This marked the beginning of a new pattern for top-level meetings (the "core group") during the rest of the Administration. While we continued to hold formal NSC meetings, an informal group became the rule rather than the exception for practical decision-making."

As if managing the end of the Cold War were insufficient challenge, the first Bush Administration also faced a crisis in the Persian Gulf region. The Bush–Scowcroft selection looks at the role of the NSC during the war with Iraq in 1990–91. It imparts the chaotic nature of some

NSC meetings, especially during times of international tension. The Council met only infrequently during the buildup toward the conflict and as the war unfolded but, throughout, the president relied heavily on Secretary of State Baker, Secretary of Defense Cheney, and Scowcroft. Along with the president, this group exhibited a collective management style that Crabb and Mulcahy have described well elsewhere as "consensual decision making by a cohesive group of elites" (*American National Security,* 1991).

Like Truman, George H.W. Bush saw NSC meetings not as decision-making sessions (Scowcroft notes in this selection), but as "a discussion of the situation and options for reacting." The combined recollections of the president and Scowcroft call attention once again to how important intelligence is in the early stages of a crisis. The initial NSC meetings on the Persian Gulf situation were dominated by a search for facts and insights into what the Iraqi invasion into Kuwait really meant and how other countries were reacting to the invasion. The question of America's military capabilities for a response soon came to the forefront. General Norman Schwarzkopf, who later in the war would become known as "Stormin' Norman," laid out the facts about air strike capabilities and how long it would take to move U.S. forces into the area to defend the oil fields of Saudi Arabia.

Scowcroft again assumed the role of asking key questions and prodding the experts for answers—in times of crisis, perhaps the adviser's most important function. When NSC discussions on what the United States should do about the invasion seemed to falter and lack imagination, Scowcroft asked the president in private if he "could depart from custom in NSC meetings and speak first, outlining the absolute intolerability of this invasion to U.S. interests." The president said he agreed, and offered to make the point first. Scowcroft thought this might stifle discussion and the two agreed to begin with a statement from the national security adviser. In between prodding debate, offering his own views, and keeping track of events unfolding in the Persian Gulf, Scowcroft found himself engaged in yet another occasional task of the adviser: speechwriting. Policy often takes form when words must be set down on paper; and while drafting a speech for the president on a new military strategy, it became clear in discussions with President Bush that he would use force to evict Iraq from Kuwait.

In these early stages of the crisis, the NSC staff prepared memos for Scowcroft's use in briefing the president about the implications of the invasion, drawing on expertise from throughout the government. These were read closely, edited, and otherwise amended by Scowcroft and then provided to the president, thus shaping policy in significant ways. During the crisis, Scowcroft dealt directly with Prince Bandar of Saudi Arabia, inviting him to the White House and working with him on policy proposals to protect the Saudi kingdom. While this apparent bypassing of the Department of State would have been sure to cause sparks in some administrations, the collegiality of the first Bush team allowed these kinds of interactions to occur without NSC principals feeling threatened by an invasion of their turf. When Scowcroft indicated that he wanted to lead a delegation to Saudi Arabia to discuss war plans, Secretary of Defense Cheney suggested that he would be more appropriate in that role. Again avoiding sparks, Scowcroft and Cheney discussed the pros and cons, then settled on a Cheney-led delegation.

As Iraq showed no signs of retreating from Kuwait, President Bush warned in a press conference on August 5, 1990, "This will not stand. . . ." Colin Powell felt that the president had declared war on Iraq that day. After the press conference, the NSC moved forward to prepare the nation for the use of force in the Persian Gulf, should that become necessary (as it did) to remove Iraq from Kuwait.

Conflict in Kosovo

The last two selections in Part VII provide insights into the planning for two more recent wars: in the Balkans during the Clinton Administration and against global terrorists during the second Bush Administration. In the first article, scholars Eric Moskowitz and Jeffrey S. Lantis begin by setting the historical stage, then examine America's involvement in efforts to seek an end to Serbian aggression against Kosovo. The NSC's Principals Committee was the chief forum for policy deliberations during this crisis, with Secretary of State Madeleine Albright becoming the chief advocate of coercive diplomacy, including the threat of military action to restore stability in the region.

Other top administration officials disagreed with the secretary of state. As Moskowitz and Lantis write: "National Security Adviser Berger preferred diplomatic options, and Secretary Cohen and General [Henry] Shelton [Chairman of the Joint Chiefs of Staff] argued against the deployment of U.S. troops." Berger believed that the Serbian leader, Slobodan Milosevic, could be coerced into stopping his aggression with the right carrots and sticks of diplomacy. Albright, though, looked upon Milosevic as another Adolf Hitler, bent on territorial expansion and the brutal eradication of ethnic opponents in Kosovo. Only the threat of immediate NATO air strikes against Serb units and facilities in Kosovo would stop the ethnic killing, in her view. *Time* magazine would later feature her on its cover (May 17, 1999), with the caption "Madeleine's War."

The president was reluctant to use a U.S. invasion force to repel the Serbian aggressors— another Persian Gulf War, only this time in the Balkans—for fear that in this rough mountain terrain against well-trained and aggressive Serbian soldiers the end result might be another Vietnam or Somalia. NATO military planners had reported to President Clinton a worst-case scenario: 200,000 troops would be required to stop the killings in Kosovo and to occupy Serbia in the event of a ground war. An air campaign seemed more palatable. Siding with Berger and analysts on the NSC staff, the Joint Chiefs of Staff questioned the wisdom of the use of force at all, asking in Council meetings whether Kosovo really had anything to do with American security interests. The military, joined by Defense Secretary Cohen, recommended instead the use of economic sanctions and indicting Milosevic for war crimes in Bosnia.

The impeachment proceedings against President Clinton prevented a "sustained focus" on the crisis in Kosovo, the authors tell us, and the White House was distracted by brinksmanship with Iraq on U.N. inspections of suspected nuclear, chemical, and biological weapons facilities; but media coverage of the ethnic cleansing in Kosovo (the so-called CNN effect) demanded attention from the government nonetheless. Unlike the Bay of Pigs episode that remained hidden from media view until it had blown up in President Kennedy's face, this growing crisis was on the front pages of the *New York Times* almost every day in 1998.

Recall that in 1954, the Eisenhower Administration checked with leadership opinion on Capitol Hill before supporting the French war effort in Vietnam, then backed away from support in response to the lack of encouragement from lawmakers (and allies). In 1998, the Clinton Administration briefed legislative leaders on the president's intention to participate in a NATO air war against Serbia. Once more, the congressional reaction was swift and negative, with Republicans accusing the president of trying to distract public attention from his own impeachment woes (the so-called "wag the dog" scenario, after a Hollywood film with a plot of that nature).

The administration seemed to be at loggerheads, with sharp disagreement among its leading officials on how to proceed in Kosovo and the president embroiled in an embarrassing domestic fight with GOP lawmakers over his own political survival. But fate intervened. The Serbs massacred forty-five unarmed people in the Kosovo village of Racak. Four days later, on January 19, the Principals Committee convened again and, as Moskowitz and Lantis note, "Racak had changed the decision-making dynamics in the administration." Amid intelligence reports that more massacres could be expected, refugees would be flooding out of Kosovo as the fighting spread, and a major Serbian escalation was planned for the Spring, Berger and then Cohen sided with Albright.

A consensus had finally been reached to take a tougher stance against Milosevic. The administration moved toward an air war to halt Milosevic's aggression. Berger and others saw a number of problems with a U.S.-led ground war in Kosovo: it could split NATO, destroy U.S. relations with Russia, and devastate U.S. public support for efforts to stop Milosevic. The Joint Chiefs soon joined the consensus, concerned about the credibility of NATO as well as the spreading humanitarian crisis in Kosovo. On March 24 President Clinton addressed the nation to announce that NATO air strikes on Yugoslavia had begun. He added: "But I do not intend to put our troops in Kosovo to fight a war."

The Kosovo war lasted seventy-eight days. As Moskowitz and Lantis relate, "Eleven weeks into the campaign, the war abruptly ended after Milosevic agreed to limited provincial autonomy for Kosovo, to remove Serb security forces from the region, and to a 50,000-strong NATO peacekeeping force under UN auspices." Throughout the crisis, the NSC's Principals Committee was the vital forum for the review of intelligence reports, the sifting of options, and the give-and-take of debate among top policymakers. In the Kosovo case, the position of the secretary of state on the use of force prevailed, but only after events on the ground persuaded the other principals—and ultimately the president—to move in her direction.

The NSC and Global Terrorism

In the final selection of Part VII, Dan Balz and Bob Woodward of *The Washington Post* report on President George W. Bush's immediate preparations for war against Osama bin Laden and Al Qaeda terrorists responsible for the attacks against the United States on September 11, 2001. In their article (a precursor to the book by Woodward, *Bush at War,* 2002), the two journalists recount how the first meeting of the NSC took place at nine o'clock in the evening on the day of the attack—an obvious indication of the importance the president gives to the Council as a forum for national security matters. In various permutations, the NSC would remain the central forum for deliberations over America's latest war: against terrorists throughout the world. The key players in the second Bush Administration involved in this unfolding drama included President George W. Bush, Vice-president Dick Cheney, Secretary of State Colin L. Powell, Secretary of Defense Donald H. Rumsfeld, and Chairman of the Joint Chiefs of Staff Gen. Henry H. Shelton. In addition, Secretary of the Treasury Paul H. O'Neill, Attorney General John D. Ashcroft, Director of Central Intelligence George J. Tenet, Director of the Federal Bureau of Investigation (FBI) Robert S. Mueller III, and Chief of Staff Andrew H. Card, Jr. participated, with Condoleezza Rice playing a central role as national security adviser.

As during previous national crises, the starting point for the NSC was to establish a set of facts and insights based on the latest intelligence from the CIA, the FBI, and other intelligence agencies. Tenet briefed the president on capabilities for aggressive paramilitary and other covert actions in Afghanistan, where Al Qaeda terrorists were primarily based (under the protection of the Taliban regime). With the NSC expanding to bring in the FBI, Mueller (the Bureau's newly appointed director) provided another briefing on his organization's efforts to identify the airplane hijackers who carried out the attacks, and where the nation stood on trying to locate other terrorists who might still be hiding within America's borders. The 9/11 attacks had clearly begun to dissolve the traditional boundaries between foreign and domestic policies, as exemplified by the CIA and the FBI working more closely together at this NSC meeting toward the common goal of thwarting further terrorist attacks against the United States.

The day after the attack, the president again met with the NSC, then continued on after that session with a small group of individuals—the Council in yet another permutation. Later in the day, it was back to the full NSC to work on a statement expressing the intended reaction of the United States to the attacks. Around and around the table in the Cabinet Room debate flew about what the goals should be, who the target was—certainly Al Qaeda, but perhaps other terrorist organizations, as well as nations like Iraq suspected of supporting terrorists—and what kind of international coalition would be necessary.

Shifting to the White House Situation Room as a meeting place, the NSC formed again on September 13, 2001 (a Thursday). The president announced his decision to move forward with covert actions in Afghanistan, and Secretary of the Treasury O'Neill briefed the group on how the United States could go after the worldwide financial assets of the terrorists. Needing to separate himself from the ever-present demands on his time in Washington, the president decided to reconvene the NSC over the weekend in the solitude of Camp David, the 125-acre presidential retreat in the Catoctin Mountains of Maryland. "I need options on the table," the president said, ". . . . By the time we get to Camp David, we need a clear timetable for action. . . ."

At Camp David, the government's senior foreign policy officials, dressed informally, were able to discuss America's response to the terrorist attacks not in short meetings interrupted by other duties, but in lengthy sessions. This afforded plenty of opportunities for back-and-forth discussion and probing into details. Intelligence chief George Tenet came armed with a stack of documents on Al Qaeda and its leader, Bin Laden. Relying on a top-secret "Worldwide Attack Matrix," he outlined a clandestine antiterrorist campaign in eighty countries around the globe, asking the president for (in the words of journalists Balz and Woodward) "the broadest and most lethal authority in [the CIA's] history." It was precisely the approach the president sought.

The Tenet plan focused on using CIA paramilitary officers in conjunction with the Pentagon's Special Forces to root out Al Qaeda members hiding in Afghanistan. In an earlier era, the president could have ordered the CIA to carry out such operations without much supervision from the White House or the Congress. Frequently, the NSC would give the CIA broad or "generic" authority to plan and carry out covert actions as the Agency saw fit. All this changed in 1974. Responding to charges that the CIA had been given too much discretion to pursue aggressive secret operations in Chile and elsewhere, Congress decided in the Hughes–Ryan Act of December 31, 1974, to bring at least some semblance of accountability into this hidden side of government. Henceforth, paramilitary operations (as well as more benign political and economic covert actions) would require formal written approval from the president in a document called a "finding," a term drawn from the operative verb in the Hughes–Ryan statute: "The President finds this covert action important to America's national security." A presidential finding is followed by secret briefings presented by the Director of Central Intelligence to the House and Senate Intelligence Committees on the details of the proposed operations (Johnson, 1989).

At Camp David, the Tenet plan sought a generic finding for the CIA to pursue operations against terrorism around the world—including the use of deadly force—without having to return to the president each time for specific findings when the CIA wanted to target a new terrorist group. The tradeoff is between efficiency (not having to get a separate finding for every operation) and accountability (making sure the CIA carefully justifies and explains each of its planned operations). President Bush came down on the side of efficiency. Tenet also wanted, and received, permission to expand the CIA's ties with other intelligence services around the world interested in fighting terrorism, including some in totalitarian regimes with highly questionable reputations. Above all, the Intelligence Director wanted money and flexibility—and, in the crisis mood of 9/11, that is exactly what he got.

In the tradition of effective national security advisers, in an afternoon session at Camp David Rice attempted to bring greater focus to the NSC's deliberations as, that morning, the meeting had wandered all over the place. According to Balz and Woodward, Rice's main role "was to help make the decision-making process orderly, to ensure that Bush had received all the information he needed"—the central theme in this book about what national security advisers do. Toward that end, she and the president agreed that he would go around the table, asking each person to offer views on what should be done. Her job would be to listen; then, according to their accustomed working arrangement, she would give the president her own evaluations later, in private. The polling, of course, would not be binding. An expression of an adviser's views can provide the president with added information, but there is only one vote that matters on the NSC: the president's.

Powell was asked to lead off and he did so, forcefully, arguing that Al Qaeda and Afghanistan should be the targets. Deputy Defense Secretary Paul Wolfowitz maintained that the Iraqi leader, Saddam Hussein, was "the real source of all the trouble and terrorism" (in Balz and Woodward's summary of his remarks). The events of September 11, 2001, provided the opportunity, in Wolfowitz's view, to strike directly at the Iraqi dictator. Since no one had evidence that Iraq was in fact connected to the terrorists attacks, Powell reasoned that the Hussein regime should not be on the response agenda at this time. Joining Powell were Cheney, Tenet, and Card in opposing a retaliatory attack against Iraq. Secretary of Defense Donald Rumsfeld chose to stay neutral on the topic, despite the reported urging of his top deputy to place Iraq on the target list for regime change.

Wolfowitz had lost in this forum and Powell had won. But it was only the beginning of the administration's internal wrangling over what to do about Saddam Hussein and his suspected efforts to develop weapons of mass destruction. Vice-president Cheney made it clear that Iraq might be a target down the road. The president himself remained cautious. As he said to Balz and Woodwood in a subsequent interview (part of the selection presented here): "My theory is you've got to do something and do it well and that . . . if we could prove that we could be successful in this theater [Afghanistan], then the rest of the task would be easier. If we tried to do too many things—two things, for example, or three things—militarily, then . . . the lack of focus would have been a huge risk." A few months later in the summer of 2002, this presidential caution dissolved into full-fledged support for the possible use of force against Iraq. At the time of the Camp David meetings, though, the president said only: "I'm going to think about it and I'll let you know what I've decided."

Assembling again back at the Cabinet Room in the White House the following Monday morning, September 17, the NSC principals awaited the president's decision. Al Qaeda would be the target; Iraq would be tabled for the time being. "It starts today," said George W. Bush, in an echo of his father's remark in response to Iraq's 1990 invasion of Kuwait, "This will not stand."

What emerges from the selections in Part VII is a sense of the NSC in its many forms. Sometimes the Council has been important as a forum for policy planning, with the president subsequently making the actual policy choices in smaller, less formal groups—or even in consultation with only one, two, or three trusted aides. At other times, the NSC has provided a venue for vital debate about planning and the merits of specific operations, from Kennedy's ExComm to the second Bush's meetings in response to the September 11 attack against the United States.

The cases presented in this section point to many of the barriers to clear thinking that presidents and their advisers must confront, including the perils of groupthink, poor intelligence, and inadequate consultation both within the executive branch and with legislators. In Part VIII, we take up two problems in particular that have led to serious disorders in the performance of the National Security Council: institutional tensions between the adviser and the secretary of state (referred to often in this book), and the misuse of the NSC staff in an operational capacity.

23

THE CUBAN MISSILE CRISIS

Arthur M. Schlesinger, Jr.

In October 1962, the Soviet Union placed ballistic missiles in Cuba, ninety miles from the United States, with a range capable of striking most major American cities. In response to this potential danger, President John F. Kennedy convened an Executive Committee of the National Security Council. The superpowers teetered on the brink of a nuclear war. This selection, written by one of America's most prominent historians, reveals the NSC in one of its most difficult—and successful—moments.

THE EXECUTIVE COMMITTEE

About 8:30 that evening [October 14] the CIA informed Bundy of the incredible discovery. Bundy reflected on whether to inform the President immediately, but he knew that Kennedy would demand the photographs and supporting interpretation in order to be sure the report was right and knew also it would take all night to prepare the evidence in proper form. Furthermore, an immediate meeting would collect officials from dinner parties all over town, signal Washington that something was up and end any hope of secrecy. It was better, Bundy thought, to let the President have a night's sleep in preparation for the ordeal ahead.

The President was having breakfast in his dressing gown at eight forty-five on Tuesday morning when Bundy brought the news. Kennedy asked at once about the nature of the evidence. As soon as he was convinced that it was conclusive, he said that the United States must bring the threat to an end: one way or another the missiles would have to be removed. He then directed Bundy to institute low-level photographic flights and to set up a meeting of top officials. Privately he was furious: if Khrushchev could pull this after all his protestations and denials, how could he ever be trusted on anything?

The meeting, beginning at eleven forty-five that morning, went on with intermissions for the rest of the week. The group soon became known as the Executive Committee, presumably of the National Security Council; the press later dubbed it familiarly ExCom, though one never heard that phrase at the time. It carried on its work with the most exacting secrecy: nothing could be worse than to alert the Russians before the United States had decided on its own course. For this reason its members—the President, the Vice-President, Rusk, McNamara, Robert Kennedy, General Taylor, McCone, Dillon, Adlai Stevenson, Bundy, Sorensen, Ball, Gilpatric, Llewellyn Thompson, Alexis Johnson, Edwin Martin, and others brought in on occasion, among them Dean Acheson and Robert Lovett—had to attend their regular meetings, keep as many appointments as possible and preserve the normalities of life. Fortunately the press corps, absorbed in the congressional campaign, was hardly disposed or situated to notice odd comings and goings. And so the President himself went off that night to dinner at Joseph Alsop's as if nothing had happened. After dinner the talk turned to the contingencies of history, the odds for or against any particular event taking place. The President was silent for a time. Then he said, "Of course, if you simply consider mathematical chances,

From Arthur M. Schlesinger, Jr., *A Thousand Days* (Boston: Houghton Mifflin, 1965), 801–806.

Professor Schlesinger is a Pulitzer Prize winner and teaches history at the City University of New York.

the odds are even on an H-bomb war within ten years." Perhaps he added to himself, "or within ten days."

In the Executive Committee consideration was free, intent and continuous. Discussion ranged widely, as it had to in a situation of such exceptional urgency, novelty and difficulty. When the presence of the President seemed by virtue of the solemnity of his office to have a constraining effect, preliminary meetings were held without him. Every alternative was laid on the table for examination, from living with the missiles to taking them out by surprise attack, from making the issue with Castro to making it with Khrushchev. In effect, the members walked around the problem, inspecting it first from this angle, then from that, viewing it in a variety of perspectives. In the course of the long hours of thinking aloud, hearing new arguments, entertaining new considerations, they almost all found themselves moving from one position to another. "If we had had to act on Wednesday in the first twenty-four hours," the President said later, "I don't think probably we would have chosen as prudently as we finally did." They had, it was estimated, about ten days before the missiles would be on pads ready for firing. The deadline defined the strategy. It meant that the response could not, for example, be confided to the United Nations, where the Soviet delegate would have ample opportunity to stall action until the nuclear weapons were in place and on target. It meant that we could not even risk the delay involved in consulting our allies. It meant that the total responsibility had to fall on the United States and its President.

On the first Tuesday morning the choice for a moment seemed to lie between an air strike or acquiescence—and the President had made clear that acquiescence was impossible. Listening to the discussion, the Attorney General scribbled a wry note: "I now know how Tojo felt when he was planning Pearl Harbor." Then he said aloud that the group needed more alternatives: surely there was some course in between bombing and doing nothing; suppose, for example, we were to bring countervailing pressure by placing nuclear missiles in Berlin? The talk continued, and finally the group dispersed for further reflection.

The next step was military preparation for Caribbean contingencies. A Navy-Marine amphibious exercise in the area, long scheduled for this week, provided a con-

venient cover for the build-up of an amphibious task force, soon including 40,000 Marines; there were 5000 more in Guantanamo. The Army's 82nd and 101st Airborne Divisions were made ready for immediate deployment; altogether the Army soon gathered more than 100,000 troops in Florida. SAC bombers left Florida airfields to make room for tactical fighter aircraft flown in from bases all over the country. Air defense facilities were stripped from places outside the range of the Cuban missiles and re-installed in the Southeast. As the days went by, 14,000 reservists were recalled to fly transport planes in the eventuality of airborne operations.

In the meantime, the Pentagon undertook a technical analysis of the requirements for a successful strike. The conclusion, as it evolved during the week, was that a 'surgical' strike confined to the nuclear missile bases alone would leave the airports and IL-28s untouched; moreover, we could not be sure in advance that we had identified or could destroy all the missile sites. A limited strike therefore might expose the United States to nuclear retaliation. Military prudence called for a much larger strike to eliminate all sources of danger; this would require perhaps 500 sorties. Anything less, the military urged, would destroy our credibility before the world and leave our own nation in intolerable peril. Moreover, this was a heaven-sent opportunity to get rid of the Castro regime forever and re-establish the security of the hemisphere.

It was a strong argument, urged by strong men. But there were arguments on the other side. The Soviet experts pointed out that even a limited strike would kill the Russians manning the missile sites and might well provoke the Soviet Union into drastic and unpredictable response, perhaps nuclear war. The Latin American experts added that a massive strike would kill thousands of innocent Cubans and damage the United States permanently in the hemisphere. The Europeanists said the world would regard a surprise strike as an excessive response. Even if it did not produce Soviet retaliation against the United States, it would invite the Russians to move against Berlin in circumstances where the blame would fall, not on them, but on us. It would thereby give Moscow a chance to shift the venue to a place where the stake was greater than Cuba and our position weaker. In the

Caribbean, we had overwhelming superiority in conventional military force; the only recourse for the Soviet Union there would be to threaten the world with nuclear war. But in Berlin, where the Russians had overwhelming conventional superiority, it was the United States which would have to flourish nuclear bombs.

All these considerations encouraged the search for alternatives. When the Executive Committee met on Wednesday, Secretary McNamara advanced an idea which had been briefly mentioned the day before and from which he did not thereafter deviate—the conception of a naval blockade designed to stop the further entry of offensive weapons into Cuba and hopefully to force the removal of the missiles already there. Here was a middle course between inaction and battle, a course which exploited our superiority in local conventional power and would permit subsequent movement either toward war or toward peace.

As the discussion proceeded through Thursday, the supporters of the air strike marshaled their arguments against the blockade. They said that it would not neutralize the weapons already within Cuba, that it could not possibly bring enough pressure on Khrushchev to remove those weapons, that it would permit work to go ahead on the bases and that it would mean another Munich. The act of stopping and searching ships would engage us with Russians instead of Cubans. The obvious retort to our blockade of Cuba would be a Soviet blockade of Berlin. Despite such arguments, however, the majority of the Executive Committee by the end of the day was tending toward a blockade.

That afternoon, in the interests of normality, the President received the Soviet Foreign Minister Andrei Gromyko. It was one of the more extraordinary moments of an extraordinary week. Kennedy knew that there were Soviet nuclear missiles in Cuba.

Gromyko unquestionably knew this too, but did not know that Kennedy knew it. His emphasis was rather grimly on Berlin, almost as if to prepare the ground for demands later in the autumn. When the talk turned to Cuba, Gromyko heavily stressed the Cuban fears of an American invasion and said with due solemnity that the Soviet aid had "solely the purpose of contributing to the defense capabilities of Cuba"; "if it were otherwise," the Russian continued, "the Soviet Government would never become involved in rendering such assistance." To dispel any illusion about possible American reactions, the President read the Foreign Minister the key sentences from his statement of September 13. He went no further because he did not wish to indicate his knowledge until he had decided on his course.

In the evening the President met with the Executive Committee. Listening again to the alternatives over which he had been brooding all week, he said crisply, "Whatever you fellows are recommending today you will be sorry about a week from now." He was evidently attracted by the idea of the blockade. It avoided war, preserved flexibility and offered Khrushchev time to reconsider his actions. It could be carried out within the framework of the Organization of American States and the Rio Treaty. Since it could be extended to nonmilitary items as occasion required, it could become an instrument of steadily intensifying pressure. It would avoid the shock effect of a surprise attack, which would hurt us politically through the world and might provoke Moscow to an insensate response against Berlin or the United States itself. If it worked, the Russians could retreat with dignity. If it did not work, the Americans retained the option of military action. In short, the blockade, by enabling us to proceed one step at a time, gave us control over the future. Kennedy accordingly directed that preparations be made to put the weapons blockade into effect on Monday morning. . . .

24

THE TRANSITION FROM THE COLD WAR

George H.W. Bush and Brent Scowcroft

President George H.W. Bush and his national security adviser Brent Scowcroft vividly recall the activities of the National Security Council during the first Bush Administration—particularly the role of the Council in the buildup to the Persian Gulf War.

GEORGE BUSH

In the days after the inauguration, we immediately began to establish routines and procedures. One important fixture was the 8:00 A.M. national security meeting in the Oval Office, at which the CIA briefed me on the latest developments around the world. It had two parts. The first portion was the intelligence briefing, at which I was joined by Brent, Bob Gates, usually John Sununu, and, once or twice a week, Bill Webster. A CIA officer would bring in the President's Daily Brief (PDB), which was a written rundown of important intelligence reports and analysis put together during the night and small hours of the morning. I made it a point from day one to read the PDB in the presence of a CIA briefer and either Brent or his deputy. This way I could task the briefers to bring in more information on a certain matter or, when the reading would bring to mind policy matters, ask Brent to follow up on an item of interest. The CIA officers would write down my questions; in a day or so, I would get an answer or an elaboration.

Knowing of my interest in the oft-berated but essential clandestine service, Webster would occasionally ask to bring along some individual who had risked his or her life to gather critically important intelligence. I found those sessions fascinating, and I was always impressed with the courage, the patriotism, and the professionalism of those who served in the Directorate of Operations. I have great respect for the people who devote their lives to the intelligence field. They never get recognition and never get to sit at the head table, but they are among the most dedicated Americans I know. There was always a danger that they or any one of their comrades would be killed because of their cover being blown by people I consider traitors; but they continue to serve with honor.

BRENT SCOWCROFT

After the CIA briefing, the second part of the national security meeting would begin. The Vice President, already briefed separately by a different CIA team, would arrive and I would go over pertinent events of the day, items where the President's guidance was needed, and anything else requiring discussion. The President, who by this time usually had scanned at least seven newspapers and the White House News Summary, would frequently have questions or comments from his reading, and would raise issues of current concern or pursue other subjects that might be on his mind.

I was mindful of questions which arose during the Iran-Contra investigations about "process" in these daily meetings, questions implying that this was the venue for secret, irregular decisions "slipped by" the President without the knowledge of others who should have been informed. Therefore, I was careful not to try to use them to seek decisions involving other national security departments or agencies. If the President indi-

From George Bush and Brent Scowcroft, *A World Transformed* (New York: Knopf, 1998), 30–42, 314–33.

George H.W. Bush served as the 41st president of the United States; Brent Scowcroft was national security adviser in the Ford and first Bush administrations.

cated a policy direction he wished to take, I made sure that others concerned were advised so they could provide any comments they might wish to make. In addition, I established the procedure of having Gates attend the meeting as well, to take notes and serve as a check on the proper interpretation of communications which might have taken place, something I extended to formal NSC meetings as well. While I almost invariably met with the President at other times during the day, these early-morning discussions were an invaluable instrument for the shaping of foreign policy.

The Tower Board, which had investigated the Iran-Contra affair, had made numerous recommendations for changes in the organization and procedures of the National Security Council. Most of that portion of the report had been written by me, and I had discussed its findings with Frank Carlucci and Colin Powell when each in turn became national security advisor. As a result, virtually all of the Board's recommendations had already been implemented and the NSC was operating well and with great integrity. The major organizational change I wanted to make in NSC operations had nothing to do with Iran-Contra (which I thought had been largely a function of the people involved). I was eager to add a "principals' committee," which would be the NSC without the President and Vice President. I thought this could help clarify issues and positions among the principals before the issues were taken to the President. It could save him considerable time, and time, I believed, was his most valuable commodity. I included such a committee in the draft directive on NSC structure and practice that I circulated to Baker and Tower shortly after the inauguration. There was no objection from either of them. The committee proved extremely valuable.

There was one area where I wished to make a significant change in my own manner of operating—congressional relations. Since the national security advisor does not testify before the Congress, that relationship is informal. In the Ford Administration, I had tended not to give it top priority. I subsequently decided that was a mistake. The Congress is crucial in so many ways to the success of foreign policy, and, at the other end, the leverage to be gained by involving someone like the national security advisor, with such close proximity to the president, should not be wasted.

Therefore, as I put together the NSC staff, one of my first moves was to ask Virginia Lampley to assume congressional liaison responsibilities. She always knew instinctively when and whom I should call, and kept Congress at the forefront of my thoughts, with constant advice for tailoring what we were doing to enhance its receptivity. Ginny coordinated the interagency legislative process with just the right mix of diplomacy and iron fist and ensured, more often than not, that the Administration spoke on the Hill with one voice on national security issues. Her personality and understanding of my priorities made her a natural hub for other directors in sounding out ideas before they came forward. The result was that I relied on her a great deal in matters far beyond her congressional responsibilities.

GEORGE BUSH

Like any new administration, we went through the drill on access to the president. It was very hard to strike the right balance between what I wanted to know and what I needed to or should know. Working out the procedure was painful. As vice president, I had loved the direct outreach and personal contact possible, but now Sununu understandably wanted to keep me from being inundated or too busy on the wrong things or overwhelmed with details. I missed reading all the materials that had come across my desk as DCI or even as vice president. I envied past presidents of a slower era, who had tons of time to read and write. I did not wish to undermine Sununu's well-crafted system: there had to be some controls. I relied heavily on Brent to sort out the flow of national security papers and who should see what.

BRENT SCOWCROFT

One organizational question was attendance at formal NSC meetings. President Reagan had designated a number of additional individuals beyond its statutory membership and advisors to join discussions. But because this was such a sought-after privilege, any exceptions tended to open the floodgates to additional requests. The President and I both wanted to keep numbers to the minimum necessary to transact the particular business at hand, both to facilitate frank and open dialogue and to reduce the likelihood of leaks. Attendance was not simply a matter of substance, however. There were some who seemed to feel that if they were left out, it would show that they had no clout with the Oval Office.

The President instructed that, at a minimum, whenever important issues of relevance to a particular department or agency head were discussed, he wanted that individual present. He also believed Marlin Fitzwater, his press secretary, in whom he had great confidence, should normally be there. This was more complicated. It was important that Fitzwater be aware of what was happening but, at the same time, not be embarrassed by having to refuse to discuss with the press issues that he would know about but which were too sensitive for disclosure. Marlin said he could handle any such problem, and he did—with great skill. John Sununu also had to know what was going on and was therefore on hand. While there were complaints from time to time, we were able to keep the situation manageable.

GEORGE BUSH

Not that everyone always made it through NSC and cabinet meetings they attended. Often members would be racked with jet lag or had been up half the night struggling with a crisis. Despite valiant efforts to remain awake, they would sometimes fail. Brent worked the longest hours of anyone in the White House. He'd labor into the night, then go home to run, eat a light dinner, and get a few hours' sleep. As a result, from time to time—well, maybe a lot—Brent would doze off in meetings. Perhaps *fall sound asleep* is a better description. He had it down to an art of style and form. He'd sleep solidly for a few seconds, then awaken as though he hadn't missed a beat of the discussion. We marveled at this ability to catnap and at what became known as the "recovery factor." This might consist of waking up and immediately writing something, anything, on a pad, or a vigorous nod of approval as the speaker made what *might* have been a telling point, although Brent hadn't heard a word of the presentation.

Brent's sleep-and-recovery performance was so outstanding that in the first year of the Administration I named an award in his honor. *The Scowcroft Award*

for Somnolent Excellence was presented at an annual festive dinner for the cabinet. Various cabinet members would, during the course of the season, observe the performance of contestants who they felt merited nomination for the prize, although the nominees did not need to be cabinet members themselves.

A secret, one-man "ranking committee" subjectively evaluated the contestants on soundness of sleep-and-recovery techniques, for which competitors developed all kinds of resourceful methods to take attention away from the nap itself, and from the fact that they had no clue as to what was going on around them. While the first award clearly belonged to Brent, who walked—snored—away with it, after that it became slightly more difficult to choose. Some of the contestants earned the respect of the committee for the length of their challenges, or for the diverse nature and originality of their recoveries. Every once in a while a contender, clearly oblivious to the deep and prestigious honor of the award, would protest that he or she had not been asleep—just something caught in the eye, or the effects of a cold. The committee could not be bought off. It kept copious notes of the nominees' performances, which were then secured in a computer file. . . .

CRISIS MANAGEMENT

GEORGE BUSH

. . . Brent and Jim did get moderately crosswise, but very rarely. Jim worried that he might be excluded from a decision that affected his department. As a former chief of staff, he knew how a strong-willed presidential advisor, if backed by the president, can easily isolate a cabinet member. It is probably accurate to say that the NSC staff and Brent were also concerned about what State might be up to. We tried very hard, and I think successfully, to keep all the participants informed and eliminate personality clashes which could undermine policy-making as well as effective diplomacy.

BRENT SCOWCROFT

The first "test" of our "crisis management process" began on the first working day of the Administration, Monday, January 23. The Secret Service quietly informed me that a mysterious large box from the Soviet Union had been delivered to the White House. There was no identifying information whatever on it, and a call to the Soviet embassy drew a complete blank. The Secret Service, exercising every precaution, mobilized its bomb disposal unit, removed the box to a safe place, and carefully opened it. Inside was a colorfully decorated, five-hundred-pound cake, now somewhat the worse for wear. Someone had gone to a great deal of trouble, but who?

I assigned the cake to Gates, who logically made Condoleezza Rice, the NSC Soviet director,* chief detective in tracking down its origin. Diligent sleuthing revealed that the cake had been baked for the President by a collective in a Soviet town (the name of which I forget) in honor of his inauguration. It was a very thoughtful gesture and the President was touched. He suggested that a picture of it be taken, if possible with members of his family standing beside it. He would then send the photograph with a note to the collective, and the cake itself could perhaps be given to a local charity. All this took days, and, by the time the arrangements had been made, the rats in the Secret Service warehouse had had a field day. The donation-to-charity idea had to be abandoned. However, some—by now probably dismantled—bakers' collective has a picture of its cake with a personal note of thanks from the President. This first encounter demonstrated that our crisis-management system needed some improvement.

DEALING WITH THE SOVIETS

BRENT SCOWCROFT

In those opening days we launched our strategic reviews reexamining existing policy and goals by region, with reviews of arms control as well. They

---

*I had chosen Condi because she had extensive knowledge of Soviet history and politics, great objective balance in evaluating what was going on, and a penetrating mind with an affinity for strategy and conceptualization. She also had served as a fellow with the Joint Chiefs of Staff and was therefore conversant and up to date with military affairs. She was charming and affable, but could be tough as nails when the situation required.

would take time to complete, but we wanted quickly to put our own stamp on policy. This was a new and different administration, something the press did not seem to understand. We needed this opportunity to determine what direction we wanted to take, rather than simply accepting what we had inherited. Dealing with Moscow and the changes in the Soviet Union was obviously our first priority, and with it getting ahead of the ferment in Eastern Europe.

Developments and opportunities inside the Warsaw Pact formed the backdrop to our initial thinking about the Soviet Union. Unrest was rising in Central and Eastern Europe, in a kind of two-steps-forward, one-step-back manner (or occasionally vice versa). Over the years, a pattern had emerged in the region: repression, a gradual buildup of resentment, then an explosion, followed by another round of repression. But now there were new twists: Gorbachev had given reformers there new hope. Soviet self-absorption had led to a sort of benign neglect of its European satellites. Perestroika and the easing of Moscow's control were allowing the Central and East Europeans to assert more control over their own affairs and to move away from the authoritarian political systems and centralized economies of the past. The result was a general, if uneven, bubbling up of political challenges to the existing regimes. . . .

. . . . One of the complicating factors in determining what might constitute a sustainable rate of change was Gorbachev's apparent strategy in Eastern Europe. He was encouraging reform there and, in some respects, he could be considered a *de facto* ally. He seemed motivated by an interest in being able to point to progress there as a prod to recalcitrants inside the Soviet Union who were standing in the way of his own reforms. I thought Gorbachev did not understand the true nature of the situation in Eastern Europe. He appeared to be trying to cultivate a number of "little Gorbachevs" who would have popular support and thus represent a positive and permanent improvement in the region. What he apparently failed to realize was that the Communist regimes, whatever their complexion, were an imposition from the outside and would be overthrown as soon as the opportunity presented itself.

Gorbachev's domestic policy also had to be considered. What was the internal situation in the Soviet Union? What were his relations with the conservatives, and what was his staying power? These questions further complicated an already complex calculation, adding to the difficulty of assessing a tolerable pace of reform, and they remained at the forefront of every policy decision related to Eastern Europe.

GEORGE BUSH

While the formal internal NSC review on the Soviet Union was under way, I also sought other expert views. Jack Matlock, our ambassador to Moscow, first appointed by Reagan and a longtime Soviet observer, offered long, detailed, and helpful cables. I also told Brent to organize gatherings with outside scholars, and met with the first group in early February up in Kennebunkport—meeting in our master bedroom, which was about the only heated room in the house. Although the opinions varied, I found their input helpful in thinking more about what might happen next in the Soviet Union. From this point on I asked for similar discussions on every major foreign policy issue.

BRENT SCOWCROFT

The formal report from the strategic review on the Soviet Union (NSR-3) was on the President's desk on March 14. It was disappointing—mainly a "big picture" document, short on detail and substance, without the kind of specific and imaginative initiatives needed to set US-Soviet relations on a productive path. Because of its shortcomings, we worked instead with a "think piece" on Gorbachev's policies and intentions, drafted by an NSC team headed by Condoleezza Rice.

Condi's memo laid out the premises that I believed should guide the development of an overall strategy for US-Soviet relations, and it evolved into a four-part approach for coping with Gorbachev. First, we should work on the domestic side to strengthen the image of America's foreign policy as driven by clear objectives. We could not meet Gorbachev head on if we did not appear confident about our purposes and agenda. Second, we needed to send a clear signal that relations with our allies were our first priority. It would be important to underscore the credibility of NATO's nuclear deterrent through modernization. In addition, the alliance would soon require a political strategy for

the upcoming conventional arms reduction talks and where we wanted them to lead. We also would have to prepare carefully for bilateral arms control, including START, which was closely watched by the world community. If we performed competently in arms control, alliance confidence in our ability to manage the broader relationship would soar.

Third, after our review of policy, we might undertake initiatives with Eastern Europe. Since the Eastern Europeans were taking advantage of Gorbachev's invitation to exercise greater control over their own affairs, the region had become a potential weak link in the solidarity of the Soviet bloc. Our best tool would be the promise of economic assistance. Fourth, and finally, was regional stability. Recent developments in Afghanistan and southern Africa had raised hopes that US-Soviet cooperation would spur agreements in other parts of the world. We had to work aggressively to promote regional stability, aware that the Soviet Union could be an important asset in some but not all places. Central America was one such exception. There the Kremlin had shown no signs of abating its support for communist military activities.

The memo picked up on one intriguing possibility that Matlock, among others, had begun to suggest: that we might have leverage over Moscow because of its need for Western economic resources and know-how. In a supporting memo at the time, Condi reminded us that the Soviet Union was in the midst of domestic turmoil and was looking to the outside world for ideas and resources to rebuild its failing system. It appeared we might be able to take advantage of that situation to make dramatic progress across the entire US-Soviet agenda. This was, as she pointed out, an argument for setting our sights literally on transforming the behavior of the Soviet Union at home and abroad. It was both an ambitious goal and a distinct and positive departure for US policy. This four-part strategy became our blueprint for crafting policy toward the Soviet Union in the early days of the Administration. It would, however, require extensive revision—alongside some improvisation—as changes in Eastern Europe began to unfold rapidly through the coming months.

After what seemed an eternity, but was actually less than six weeks since they had been commissioned, the results of the other strategic reviews on Eastern

Europe (NSR-4) and Western Europe (NSR-5, emphasizing the planned unification of 1992—what became the Maastricht Treaty), were beginning to emerge.* Discussion on Eastern Europe was scheduled for an NSC meeting on March 30. As I started to prepare, however, it became apparent that we should not begin our top-level debates on the direction of policy with only a portion of what was a closely interconnected whole. I asked the President to delay the meeting on Eastern Europe in order that we could first have a session covering all of Europe. I also raised another idea. Even this early in the Administration, it was becoming apparent to me that a full-blown NSC gathering was not always the place for a no-holds-barred discussion among the President's top advisors. Some might be inhibited from expressing themselves frankly with staff present and the constant possibility of leaks. I suggested that this opening session take place informally, in the Oval Office, and with only a select group present, in this case Quayle, Baker, Cheney, myself, Eagleburger, Gates, and Sununu. The President liked the suggestion, and it worked. This marked the beginning of a new pattern for top-level meetings (the "core group") during the rest of the Administration. While we continued to hold formal NSC meetings, an informal group became the rule rather than the exception for practical decision-making. . . .

CRISIS IN THE PERSIAN GULF

GEORGE BUSH

On the morning of August 2. . . . Brent arrived just before 5:00. Visibly exhausted, he filled me in on the emerging details of the invasion and the discussions he'd had the night before. Iraq's official story was that it had moved in on the pretext that there had been a coup and that its "leaders," purporting to be the "legitimate" government in Kuwait, had requested their help. Our immediate options were limited. We had not yet officially been asked for help by the Kuwaitis or Saudis, but it was important to display promptly our support. I ordered our already alerted warships at the island of Diego Garcia in the Indian Ocean to head for the Persian Gulf. Our next requirement was to get air forces into the area. Brent explained that Bob Kimmit was already checking with the Saudis to obtain approval for sending an F-15 squadron. He handed me an Executive Order freezing the assets of Iraq and Kuwait in the United States. I signed it. At least we could take some economic measures.

After I showered, I headed for the Oval Office. At 6:30, Tom Pickering phoned to report on the UN Security Council's actions. Like Brent, he had been up all night working through the details of a resolution with the Kuwaitis and the other Council members. By morning, the Council had voted 14–0 in favor of UNSC Resolution 660, condemning Iraq's aggression, demanding that it withdraw its troops from Kuwait, and demanding that the dispute be resolved by negotiations. I was disappointed and concerned that Saudi Arabia's neighbor Yemen had abstained, probably in an effort to curry favor with Iraq. I knew President Ali Abdullah Saleh and didn't feel he would recklessly side with Saddam. Still, the UN action was good news. The Soviets had supported us, and that was step one in building opposition.

At about 7:00, Brent arrived in the Oval Office and at 7:30 Bill Webster and Hank Applebaum (the CIA briefer) appeared with a bundle of papers to give the daily CIA general briefing. During it, and with Brent on the line, I called Jim Baker, who was in Ulaanbaatar, Mongolia, on a side trip from an arms control meeting with Shevardnadze in Irkutsk. Jim had been warned of the ominous signs in the Gulf and had already spoken with Shevardnadze about the danger of an invasion. Shevardnadze said he believed, as we had earlier, that Saddam was simply "strong-arming" the Kuwaitis. With the news of the invasion, Jim had urged the Soviets to join an arms embargo of Iraq, and Shevardnadze departed for Moscow to consult with Gorbachev.

---

*Heading up my European team at the NSC was Robert Blackwill, a Foreign Service officer who had been in the process of leaving government service for academia. I had known him for nearly twenty years, though not well. He had a reputation for brilliance, laced with irascibility. He was a forward-looking original thinker who reveled in finding ways to take advantage of the rapidly changing European scene to fashion strategies which would advance American interests and move us toward a new international structure.

A little after 8:00, I joined Brent and the rest of the NSC in the Cabinet Room. In the "photo-op" just before our discussion began, I spoke briefly to reporters, who had been speculating wildly about what we were going to do. Among the forest of boom and hand-held microphones, I was careful in my remarks. I condemned the invasion and outlined the steps we had taken, as well as the fact that this was an exploratory meeting concerned with reviewing all options for defending our interests in the Gulf. Right off, Helen Thomas of UPI asked me whether I was considering intervention as one of those options.

I did not want my first public comments to threaten the use of American military might, so I said I was not contemplating intervention, and, even if I knew we were going to use force, I would not announce it in a press conference. The truth is, at that moment I had no idea what our options were. I did know for sure that the aggression had to be stopped, and Kuwait's sovereignty restored. We had a big job ahead of us in shaping opinion at home and abroad and could little afford bellicose mistakes at the start. What I hoped to convey was an open mind about how we might handle the situation until I learned all the facts.

BRENT SCOWCROFT

The President's comment that he was not contemplating intervention has been taken by some to indicate he was passive or indecisive about the notion of doing anything about the Iraqi invasion until Margaret Thatcher "put some stiffening in his spine" at their meeting later that day. Such speculation is wrong, although his choice of words was not felicitous. His language was picked with two thoughts in mind: First, don't say anything at this early point which would telegraph his thinking. Second, make clear that the NSC meeting was not a decision session but a discussion of the situation and options for reacting.

GEORGE BUSH AND BRENT SCOWCROFT

The NSC meeting was a bit chaotic. We really did not yet have a clear picture of what was happening on the ground, and the participants focused mainly on the economic impact of the invasion and what Saddam would do next. Webster outlined the extent of the invasion, and some of the responses from other countries. The Arab League had passed a resolution condemning Iraq, but there was no call for armed action. Moscow had still not said anything officially. NATO and Japan had called for Iraq's withdrawal. "The stock market in Tokyo is down; oil prices are increasing," said Webster. "The British have declared a grave threat to regional peace. It appears there was no military objective but Kuwait."

Bob Kimmit, sitting in for Baker and Eagleburger, spelled out the diplomatic steps we had already taken. State had called in the Iraqi ambassador, who claimed to know nothing more than what Baghdad had told the world. Diplomatic posts had all been briefed, and the Europeans were already working with us. No one was supporting Iraq. We had sent out cables asking others to join our economic measures. The British were in a cabinet meeting debating what to do. We were also asking the Soviets, French, Italians, and Chinese to stop arms shipments to Iraq. There were no reports of harm to any of the 3,800 American civilians and 130 embassy staff in Kuwait, or the 500 Americans and 42 embassy personnel in Baghdad.

Nicholas Brady pointed out that the source of Iraq's power was its oil. Without it, Baghdad would have no money to keep its military going. He proposed that we shut off Iraqi and Kuwaiti oil and ask other countries to make up the difference. Cheney added that if only economic and political sanctions were in effect, Iraq could become a major oil power overnight. "The rest of the world badly needs oil," said Dick. "They have little interest in poor Kuwait. It may be difficult to organize a good package of economic sanctions."

The discussion moved to the effects of cutting off oil, and then Colin Powell introduced our military options. "For several weeks the CINC [General Norman Schwarzkopf] and the [Joint Chiefs of Staff] have prepared military options should the need arise," he said. Schwarzkopf, Commander-in-Chief of Central Command (CENTCOM) and responsible for implementing any military response in the region, had been invited to the meeting as well. He now described what was at hand for air strikes, a naval bombardment of

Iraq, when they could act, and also how quickly we could move forces to defend Saudi Arabia. While we had a few ships in the Gulf that could hit some targets within hours, it would take a few days to get a broader force prepared. We had F-15s and F-16s on standby and they could be deployed to defend Saudi Arabia. However, this would require that they be based there. So far, the Saudis had said no.

Schwarzkopf added that there was also a rehearsed plan for defending the Saudi oil region, using forces in the area, and he was confident we could blunt an Iraqi attack there. If we wanted an air campaign against Iraq itself, however, we would need far more forces and more time. We were facing over a million Iraqi troops. It would take about twenty days to deploy sufficient aircraft and carrier battle groups.

"Let's step back," said Scowcroft. "The most significant option economically is oil. . . . There are some things we can do: shut off the two pipelines [through Turkey and Saudi Arabia], tell tankers going into Kuwait to stop—in theory it's easy, but in practice it will be difficult. . . . We should mount an embargo of Kuwaiti and Iraqi oil purchases." A long debate ensued over the effects of disrupting oil, and which countries would be affected. President Bush asked Brady to get an analysis on the issue and asked about international economic sanctions under Chapter VII of the UN Charter, which provides for mandatory observance by members. Pickering said we were ready to propose the matter at the UN. "International sanctions will give us security cover," said the President. "They will give some spine to Saudi Arabia and others to take difficult actions, like closing the pipeline."

Kimmit reported that State was reviewing the question of evacuating Americans from Kuwait and Baghdad. They had also discussed breaking off diplomatic relations, but decided against recommending it. The safety of American citizens was at stake, and we needed our officials in Baghdad to protect them.

President Bush suggested we ask Congress to pass resolutions imposing unilateral sanctions, commending the UN action, and supporting our responses. But we needed more information, he said. We didn't want to make statements committing us to anything until we understood the situation.

"Saudi Arabia and others will cut and run if we are weak," warned Cheney. Powell asked if we should declare that Saudi Arabia was a vital interest to the United States. "I think there is no choice," he said. "The question is how do you lay it out to the public."

"I agree," said the President, adding that we could not overlook getting the other major powers involved either. So far the reaction of the Soviets had been good. "We can get them to kick in," he said. "That is, no adventurism, but get them to agree to some action. US-Soviet relations are good, but we don't want to overlook the Soviet desire for access to warm water ports. We don't want to resurrect that. Maybe something positive like a joint statement." The next step was at the UN and the Security Council. "In New York we should press to put the heat on Saudi Arabia and the others. . . . Let's get [US] sanctions in place before noon."

BRENT SCOWCROFT

I was frankly appalled at the undertone of the discussion, which suggested resignation to the invasion and even adaptation to a *fait accompli*. There was a huge gap between those who saw what was happening as the major crisis of our time and those who treated it as the crisis *du jour*. The remarks tended to skip over the enormous stake the United States had in the situation, or the ramifications of the aggression on the emerging post-Cold War world. While some statements seemed to reflect the gravity of what had occurred, most tended to focus on the price of oil and the resultant upset in the Middle East. The tone implied that the crisis was halfway around the world and doing anything serious about it would just be too difficult. Later that morning, I spoke to President Bush of my concerns. I asked if, in the next meeting, I could depart from custom in NSC meetings and speak first, outlining the absolute intolerability of this invasion to US interests. He shared my concern and proposed that he himself make such an opening statement. I told him I thought that would stifle discussion, and we agreed I would go first.

Almost immediately after the NSC meeting we left for Colorado and what proved an unforgettable flight. The 707 usually used as Air Force One could not land at Aspen airport and, rather than waste time switching aircraft in Denver, the President decided to fly directly to Aspen on a small C-20 Gulfstream. He, John Sununu, and I crammed together in the small front compartment, knees practically touching, sharing the telephones, with papers strewn everywhere.

The President was scheduled to give a major address at Aspen, setting forth a new military strategy and force structure in response to the winding down of the Cold War. That speech now required a number of revisions. I frantically drafted changes and, in between the President's calls to Congressional and foreign leaders, checked them out with Washington, all the while trying to keep abreast of developments in the Gulf. It was in discussion on the changes in his speech that it became obvious to me that the President was prepared to use force to evict Saddam from Kuwait if it became necessary, although he did not explicitly say so.

GEORGE BUSH

I used the time aboard Air Force One to poll foreign leaders. I called Hosni Mubarak and King Hussein, who happened to be together in Alexandria, Egypt. Both were disturbed by the situation.

King Hussein told me he was just about to go to Saudi Arabia and Iraq. "I really implore you, sir, to keep calm," he said. "We want to deal with this in an Arab context, to find a way that gives us a foundation for a better future." I told the King that the world would not accept the status quo now, and that it was unacceptable to the United States. "I'm sure Saddam Hussein knows this, but you can tell him that from me." The King replied that Iraq was "determined to pull out as soon as possible, maybe in days," and promised to push for it.

Mubarak explained that they were trying hard to find a solution for withdrawal that would not "throw away" the Kuwaiti government. "George, give us two days to find a solution," he asked. I told him about the economic measures we had taken. "The only exception is, of course, if there are threats to Americans—that would be a whole new ballgame." Hosni supported sanctions (even though I had not specifically raised the issue). "I will talk to Saddam Hussein right now," he said. "I am also in contact with the Saudis."

"That is very important," I said. "Please tell Saddam Hussein that the United States is very concerned about this action. We are very concerned that other forces will be released—you know what that means, my friend. Tell Saddam that if you like." Hosni said he would, or this would be an even bigger disaster. "I'll pray for you," I said.

BRENT SCOWCROFT

I was wary of an "Arab solution," fearing that it might end up in a compromise with Saddam. It was a real dilemma. If we refused to give time for a possible Arab settlement, we could alienate our best friends when we needed them badly. But if we acquiesced, and the Arabs came out with a compromise, how could we reject it?

GEORGE BUSH

I got Baker on the line again in Mongolia and we went over our efforts with the Soviets. Simultaneously, Brent was hunched over another phone to the State Department's director of the Policy Planning Staff, Dennis Ross, who, with Bob Zoellick, was in Moscow with Shevardnadze. Jim said he would go back to Moscow to try to work out a joint statement (already being prepared by Ross and Zoellick) that would condemn Iraq's action and call for withdrawal from Kuwait.

I had a chance to talk with Margaret Thatcher in the living room of our ambassador to Great Britain, Henry Catto, who had a home in Aspen. Margaret and I saw the situation in remarkably similar ways, which I think was mutually reassuring. I told her about the US-Soviet statement we were working on, and that I had spoken to Mubarak and King Hussein. "Both were going to talk to Saddam and urged that we go slow—they needed time. I said we couldn't accept the status quo. It had to be withdrawal and the restoration of the Kuwaiti government." I added that I was moving a carrier battle group from Diego Garcia.

"If Iraq wins, no small state is safe," said Margaret. "They won't stop here. They see a chance to take a major share of oil. It's got to be stopped. We must do everything possible." She said she and her cabinet had been talking about trade sanctions, but this was something the whole world had to do. She wondered whether the Arabs would act and if the Saudis would close their pipeline. If they did, what would be the impact on the oil market? "The Saudis are *critical,* we can't do anything without them." She urged that by Monday we should go to the UN to ask for sanctions. "King Hussein was not helpful," she added. "He told me the Kuwaitis had it coming—they are not well liked. But he grudgingly agreed to weigh in with Saddam . . ." She wasn't sure where Syria and Iran stood.

I told her the Saudis could make up the difference for the Kuwaiti and Iraqi oil we cut off, and that Iran had been making some overtures. "One of my fears is that the Israelis might take some action," I said. "That's one thing which could unite the Arabs." Margaret thought it all came back to getting sanctions through the Security Council. "We must win this," she said. "Losing Saudi oil is a blow we couldn't take . . . We cannot give in to dictators. [And] we can't make an oil embargo work without a blockade."

At about two o'clock, Margaret and I stepped out to a patio for a press conference. We condemned Iraq's aggression and called for a peaceful solution, with the withdrawal of Iraqi forces and the restoration of the Kuwaiti leadership. She put her finger on the most important point—whether the nations of the world had the collective and effective will to implement the resolutions of the Security Council and compel withdrawal and restoration. It would be up to American leadership to make that happen.

I called King Fahd from the Cattos' bedroom later that afternoon, the phone perched on the bed and Brent hovering over my shoulder. Saudi Arabia would be indispensable to any military moves we might make, and might itself be in danger. At this point, we did not know whether Iraqi forces would stop at the Saudi border. It was an emotional call. The King was agitated and the interpreter struggled to keep up.

Fahd explained how he had tried to resolve Iraqi-Kuwaiti differences before Iraq struck and that both sides had expressed a willingness to talk. Saddam had even assured the Saudis that he "had no interest in attacking Kuwait." The King angrily added that Saddam had done the opposite "because he is conceited. He doesn't realize that the implications of his actions are upsetting the world order. He seems to think only of himself. He is following Hitler in creating world problems—with a difference: one was conceited and one is both conceited and crazy. I believe nothing will work with Saddam but the use of force."

He had reminded Saddam that during the Arab summit in Baghdad the Iraqi leader had suggested a nonaggression pact among the countries, agreeing not to intervene in one another's affairs. "My conversation with him today was strict and strong," the King said, "and I asked him to withdraw from Kuwait now, and that we would not consider any [imposed] regime representative of Kuwaiti public opinion or Arab public opinion." Saddam had asked to hold talks with the Saudis, and the King speculated that something might be done to find a solution. "I told him that I hold him responsible for the safety of all people in Kuwait—Kuwaiti or not," he declared.

King Fahd said he was willing to meet with Saddam's envoy, who was due to arrive the next day, but Saddam would have to understand that Iraqi troops had to withdraw. "The only other solution is the use of force," he said severely. "Mr. President, this is a matter that is extremely serious and grave. It involves a principle that can't be approved or condoned by any reasonable principle or moral." Mubarak had proposed an Arab summit for the next day, which the King thought an excellent idea. "I hope these matters can be resolved peacefully," he said. "If not, Saddam must be taught a lesson he will not forget for the rest of his life—if he remains alive."

I asked whether the Kuwaiti royal family was safe, which he assured me was the case. (We subsequently learned that the Emir's younger brother had decided to stand and fight. He was shot on the steps of one of the palaces.) The Emir had barely five minutes to escape and the Foreign Minister was nearly captured. I then outlined what we were doing. I offered him an F-15 squadron, but he asked to discuss that option further.

King Fahd's hesitation rang alarm bells in my head. I began to worry that the Saudis might be considering compromise, that they might accept the new status quo on their northern border if there were guarantees from Iraq. There is a historical Arab propensity to try to work out "deals." Even though we knew the Saudis well, and trusted them, we could not be completely certain what course they would take. In these early hours of the crisis, with so much going on, I had to wonder if, under pressure, they might be inclined to strike some kind of behind-the-scenes arrangement with Saddam. I do not know if they even thought about it, but the King's reluctance to accept aircraft had me concerned. We couldn't have a solo US effort in the Middle East. We had to have our Arab allies with us, particularly those who were threatened the most—the Saudis.

Brent Scowcroft

While we were in Colorado, I called Haass and asked him to draft an overview memo from me to the President as background for the next NSC meeting. In it we described a policy to contain Iraq, slow its development of both conventional and unconventional military capabilities, and effect its withdrawal from Kuwait. "The necessary instruments of such a policy," it read, "would be export controls, other economic sanctions, and enhanced military actions, both unilateral and with others." It warned that while it was proper at this point to emphasize diplomacy and sanctions, we had to anticipate that these might fall short and we would be faced with a choice between living with this new status quo or challenging Iraq directly, either with force or with actions (closing their pipelines, etc.) that were almost certain to lead to armed conflict. The memo summed up the stakes:

> I am aware as you are of just how costly and risky such a conflict would prove to be. But so too would be accepting this new status quo. We would be setting a terrible precedent—one that would only accelerate violent centrifugal tendencies—in this emerging "post Cold War" era. We would be encouraging a dangerous adversary in the Gulf at a time when the United States has provided a de facto commitment to Gulf stability—a commitment reinforced by our statements and military movements—that also raises the issue of US reliability in a most serious way. As if this were not enough, we must recognize too that Iraq has the capacity and the desire to complicate the peace process in the Middle East. We don't need to decide where to draw any lines just yet, but we do need to take steps—moving forces, pressing allies and reluctant Arabs, etc.—that would at least give us a real choice if current efforts fall short.

We arrived back in Washington very late that night. The next morning, before the NSC gathered again in the Cabinet Room, President Bush and I confirmed again that, after the intelligence briefing, I should speak first and remind everyone of the stakes. Eagleburger and Cheney would follow to reinforce solidarity for the larger group.

George Bush and Brent Scowcroft

Despite rumors that Saddam had pledged to withdraw from Kuwait in a couple of days, Webster was not optimistic. Our intelligence was still sketchy, but what information we had was grim. Saddam was consolidating his hold on Kuwait. "All the intelligence shows he won't pull out," said Webster. "He will stay if not challenged within the next year. This will fundamentally alter the Persian Gulf region. He would be in an inequitable position, since he would control the second- and third-largest proven oil reserves with the fourth-largest army in the world. He would also have Kuwaiti financial assets, access to the Gulf, and the ability to pour money into his military. There is no apparent internal rival to Saddam. His ego cannot be satisfied; his ambition is to have ever more influence. Jordan and Yemen have tilted toward Iraq. Iran is militarily and economically weak, so it would not be an effective counter. . . . It would not be a pretty picture. We don't expect the Arabs to confront Iraq, but instead to buy their way out."

". . . I detected a note at the end [of the previous NSC meeting] that we might have to acquiesce in an accommodation," said Scowcroft. "My personal judgment is that the stakes in this for the United States are such that to accommodate Iraq should not be a policy option."

Eagleburger added his support. "This is the first test of the postwar system," he said. "As the bipolar world is relaxed, it permits this, giving people more flexibility because they are not worried about the involvement of the superpowers. . . . Saddam Hussein now has greater flexibility because the Soviets are tangled up in domestic issues. If he succeeds, others may try the same thing." He believed that Saudi Arabia would be Saddam's next objective, and that over time he would control OPEC and oil prices. "If he succeeds, then he will target Israel."

Cheney was sober about both the gravity of the situation and the price of confronting it. "Initially, we should sort this out from our strategic interests in Saudi Arabia and oil," he said. "[Saddam] has clearly done what he has to do to dominate OPEC, the Gulf, and the Arab world. He is forty kilometers from Saudi Arabia and its oil production is only a couple of hundred kilometers away. If he doesn't take it physically, with his new wealth he will still have an impact and will be able to acquire new weapons. The problem will get worse, not better. Looking at the military possibilities and options," he added, "we should not underestimate the US military forces we would need to be prepared for a major conflict."

Eagleburger reported that Pickering was circulating a draft resolution on sanctions to the other permanent members of the Security Council. "The Soviets support it, the British and French want to discuss the details, the PRC is now not sure they won't support it." He was optimistic that we would succeed. The President asked about Iran. Eagleburger explained that it had condemned the invasion. The Kuwaitis and Iranians had been meeting. "According to the Kuwaiti ambassador here, Iran said to them, 'You tell us what you want and we will do it.' Kuwait said we want you to persuade Iraq to leave. After some delay Iran is now saying it will be supportive." He added that Syria asked us to push the Arab states. "In twenty-four hours there will be an Arab [League foreign minister meeting] in Cairo," he said. "Maybe they will agree."

Cheney gave an update on the military situation. He was concerned about the Saudi reluctance to agree to stationing our forces on their soil. "We need Saudi Arabia to agree to a presence," he urged. He asked that the President discuss the matter with King Fahd.

Powell briefed us on the forces required for contingencies. "There are two," he said. "The first, to deter further Iraqi action with Saudi Arabia, would require US forces on the ground. This is the most prudent option and we need to push it with Saudi Arabia so Saddam Hussein looks south and sees a US presence." The second was to deploy forces against the Iraqi troops in Kuwait, to defend Saudi Arabia or even strike against Iraq. "Looking at this option," said Powell, "this is harder than Panama and Libya. This would be the NFL, not a scrimmage. It would mean a major con-

frontation. Most US forces would be committed to sustain, not just for one or two days. He is a professional and a megalomaniac. But the ratio is weighted in his favor. They also are experienced after eight years of war."

"If we look at economic pressure, then we need to think how he will respond and look at the costs," Scowcroft pointed out. The question was not only what steps were needed to put sanctions in place, but also how to enforce them. Powell explained that the warships were already in place to interdict merchant vessels.

Scowcroft warned of the possibility that Saddam might use Americans as hostages. Eagleburger said that fourteen or fifteen US citizens were already in Iraqi custody, with reports of others being held in Kuwait. We could try to evacuate our people, but it would have to be done with the cooperation of Iraq. State had been working with other embassies to find a neutral ambassador willing to ask for all to leave. "It probably won't work," he added. They had warned the Iraqi foreign ministry not to harm Americans, and had called in the Iraqi ambassador. "He made no promises. Saddam is a tough son of a bitch. He recognizes this asset."

"We should tell Saddam this would be a new ballgame, and give him our bottom line," the President said. " . . . American deaths and hostages will not be tolerated."

BRENT SCOWCROFT

The tone of the NSC discussion was much better than the day before. We had established our case. Had the President taken his cue from the earlier meeting, our policy would have been vastly different, focusing on controlling the damage rather than reversing it. We wanted to act, but, as the discussions revealed, our immediate options, such as moving forces to the area and international sanctions as the President directed, were for the moment limited for practical and political reasons. Kuwait was so far away that it would take some time before enough troops were in place to do anything more than be a symbolic presence. Even putting those forces in place remained a question. We still had to convince the Saudis. For the moment we had to sit tight as Iraqi units continued to head south toward the Saudi border. All we could do was give Iraq a strong warning not to invade Saudi Arabia, which we did that day.

To help persuade the Saudis to accept US forces, we asked Ambassador Prince Bandar to come to the White House later that morning to discuss the situation. Son of the Saudi defense minister and King Fahd's favorite nephew, Bandar was Western-educated and a fighter pilot who had trained with the US Air Force. Most important, he was a trouble-shooter for King Fahd, with the equivalent rank of minister in the Saudi government. The King frequently turned to him for advice. For these reasons, we knew he was a special conduit from us to Fahd.

Bandar came to my office a little after 11:00. After setting forth the serious military threat which we believed faced his country, I told him we were considering the offer of US forces to the kingdom, to assist in its defense. He seemed ill at ease and did not react with enthusiasm to the suggestion. Somewhat surprised at his equivocal posture, I asked him why he appeared to have a problem with an offer I thought was generous. His answer really set me back. He explained that the Saudis were not at all sure they wanted to be defended by the United States. The US, he said, did not exactly have a reputation in the region for reliability. He cited two examples to make his point.

In 1979, when the Shah was forced to flee Iran, the United States offered a squadron of F-15s to Saudi Arabia as a gesture of support and of warning to the Iranian radicals. The Saudis had immediately accepted. Then, as the aircraft were on their way, Washington had announced that they were unarmed. The second example he described was the US intervention in Lebanon in 1982–84. We sent the Marines into Beirut with great fanfare. Shortly after the terrible terrorist attack on the Marine barracks, the United States quietly loaded the Marines back on their ships and slipped away. Why should the King not be concerned that, if the going got tough, the United States would behave in the same manner once again?

I replied that we could debate the past, but I would prefer to get right to the point. President Bush had thought this issue through carefully, in full recognition of all the consequences. In light of that, I could give him a pledge that, if the troops were offered and accepted, we would stand with them to the end. Bandar said these assurances transformed the situation, but it would help if he was briefed on our defense plans. I consulted Cheney and sent Bandar over to the Pentagon, where he was shown CENTCOM's plan for responding to the Iraqi threat. This seemed to dispel the Prince's doubts about our resolve. The Saudis had previously planned to send a low-level technical team to Washington to discuss the situation and the best form of cooperation. Bandar now agreed that a senior US team should go to Saudi Arabia instead.

GEORGE BUSH

Early in the afternoon of August 3, I spoke with President Turgut Ozal of Turkey, who angrily said Saddam should "get his lesson." He had been on the phone with King Fahd an hour earlier, and was worried that the Saudis might not take action. "I told him that if the solution is that Iraq pulls back and Kuwait pays, that is not a solution but another Munich." I reminded him of Turkey's key geostrategic position and asked if he was willing to close down the pipeline from Iraq. He didn't respond, but said we needed more than an embargo. He suggested we get NATO together to discuss the situation. "We should not repeat the mistakes made at the beginning of World War II," he declared.

I also spoke with François Mitterrand, who concurred that we could not accept the status quo and that to do so would allow Saddam to secure his hegemony over the Arab world. If there was to be an oil blockade, he added, it had to succeed. If not, there would be tremendous loss of face to the West. We also had to be careful not to create solidarity against us in the Arab world. The key would be the Saudis. "If Saudi Arabia takes a courageous stand against the annexation of Kuwait, this would bring along others," he said. Helmut Kohl and Japanese prime minister Toshiki Kaifu, with whom I spoke later that day, agreed that we needed collective action.

BRENT SCOWCROFT

Later that day, Baker and Shevardnadze issued a joint declaration in Moscow condemning the Iraqi invasion. The statement was extremely important and surprised many, since it demonstrated that Iraq's principal backer would not support Saddam's aggression. It dramatically put the two superpowers on the same side of a major crisis for the first time since the Cold War began. While I had felt that a united Germany's membership in NATO marked the end of the Cold War, this was certainly further compelling evidence of it. The declaration translated into essential Soviet help at the UN in forming a solid bloc of support for resolutions against Saddam. We learned later that it masked political divisions within the Kremlin over chastising the Iraqis. While Gorbachev seemed to support the declaration, he steered clear of Shevardnadze's internal political battle to approve it. In the end, Shevardnadze had courageously gone out on a limb, taking personal responsibility for the statement.

GEORGE BUSH AND BRENT SCOWCROFT

At the August 4 NSC meeting at Camp David, we concentrated on military options. "Of course, much depends on what we decide are our goals," Cheney pointed out. Powell outlined the military situation and options. "What we will present is a longstanding plan refined over the last few weeks," he began. It would defend Saudi Arabia and lay the foundation for moving north into Kuwait. "It is difficult but doable," he added. "It will be enormously expensive to project and sustain a force of this size. It will require some reserve call-up."

There were two dimensions to the plan, he continued—deterrence and war fighting. "The sooner we can get an invitation from the Saudis the better," he said. "I believe the Iraqis would think twice before engaging us. We can get our air power in quickly. We can handle the Iraqi Air Force. We also have some naval forces that can be augmented. Ground forces can be introduced over the course of a month. All this would draw down our ability to act anywhere else in the world. The ultimate size of the force would be a hundred thousand men."

Schwarzkopf described what we were up against. "Iraq has over eleven hundred aircraft, but most are antiquated and they have almost no experience with using their airpower offensively," he explained. "Iraq is not ten feet tall, but is formidable. They have an army of nine hundred thousand men, sixty-three divisions, over fifty-seven hundred tanks. Once again we see a pattern of a large number of weapons but only a small number of high quality. They have no self-propelled artillery. One of our advantages is that they would have problems fighting over long distances. They have bigger forces but much lower quality than what we could field. Their aircraft could not reach the lower peninsula. It would be a short amount of time before we would gain air superiority. Their navy is insignificant. Very quickly we would gain control of the Gulf. They have dense SAM [surface-to-air] envelopes around key sites such as Baghdad. Overall, their strengths include numbers, experience, chemical weapons, and some modern arms. Their weaknesses are centralized command and control, a dependence on foreign spare parts, and a lack of offensive experience."

Schwarzkopf told us our major problem was distance. "Within one week, we could get five tactical fighter squadrons and carrier battle groups on the scene," he said. "We could double this over two weeks. We could also have a force slightly larger than a division in after two weeks. The overall plan would take seventeen weeks."

"We can have four hundred aircraft in the area in eleven days," added Lieutenant General Charles Horner, Schwarzkopf's air commander. "Our forces are on alert and ready to go."

What Schwarzkopf and Horner were suggesting relied on air power, at least in the short term. "The history of air campaigns suggests they are not terribly successful," observed Cheney. "Why would this one be different?"

"I am not an advocate of air power alone," replied Schwarzkopf. "But this is a target-rich environment. There is no cover in the desert. Their army has never operated under attack, and we have sophisticated munitions."

"I worry over one thing," said Scowcroft. "The Saudis are concerned about our seriousness. Ground forces are the best symbol of our commitment, but this plan is air-heavy."

"Bandar made a point that they were unhappy with our offer of one tactical fighter squadron, but they have no doubts now after hearing our briefing," put in Cheney.

"My worry is the lack of Saudi will and that they might bug out," said President Bush. "We need to ask them."

After the briefers left the room, the discussion turned to what to do next. Powell said he did not think Saddam wanted to mess with us. He believed we had to get Americans into Saudi Arabia, to show the flag. The President thought Powell was on the right track. "I'm inclined to feel that a small US military presence and an air option will do it," he said. "Iraq did badly versus Iran." Still, he was worried about the implications of attacking Baghdad, as the air option would require.

Baker, now back from Moscow, agreed. "Our using air against Baghdad could turn things against us unless it is done in conjunction with an Iraqi move into Saudi Arabia," he said.

"Our first objective is to keep Saddam out of Saudi Arabia," said the President. "Our second is to protect the Saudis against retaliation when we shut down Iraq's export capability. We have a problem if Saddam does not invade Saudi Arabia but holds on to Kuwait."

Cheney said we should start this only if we were prepared to see it through. "You must be prepared to defend Saudi Arabia and put the [Kuwaiti] royal family back," he said. "The problem is the American people might have a short tolerance for war." He added that it would all cost "one hell of a lot of money." Scowcroft felt that the American people would support intervention. Cheney was doubtful. "The oil mostly goes to Japan," he said. "We'll be seen as helping royal families. Their support may be short-lived." He urged that we must consider what we would do if Saddam did not attack Saudi Arabia. The President thought he might be underestimating world opposition. "Lots of people are calling him Hitler," he said.

"If we got a request from the Saudis, we should do more than simply show the flag," said Powell. "We may be able to do something along the lines of the Korean War model of a US-led multinational force," suggested Haass.

Baker wondered if we might lose international support if we blockaded Iraq. Scowcroft disagreed. "Closing shipping is no more than closing the pipeline," he said. The President suggested we try a blockade.

GEORGE BUSH

Our stakes and options now seemed clearer. I had a better feel for the military situation on the ground and the strategic implications of the invasion for the United States and for stability in the Gulf. I approved the plan, although we couldn't implement it until the Saudis agreed to accept our troops.

It was critical that King Fahd ask us to send forces before Iraq could attack Saudi Arabia. I understood that the Saudis would be under great internal and external pressure if US and Western troops were operating from their soil. Historically, Arab countries did not welcome US air or ground forces in the area. A naval task force such as a carrier was different—it was an accepted stabilizer of Gulf security since it was off-shore and out of sight. But having planes and troops stationed on the ground was problematical.

I spoke with King Fahd on Saturday afternoon from Camp David to press for a decision to accept troops. He evaded the question and thanked me for our interest in Saudi affairs, and he kept referring to the team we were sending. We went back and forth for a few minutes like this, I pressing the King, he implying our team would discuss the matter.

"Good," I said, "but I want to know where you think matters stand on the ground. What are Iraq's statements on withdrawal? Will the Emir return? Are you worried about Iraq moving across your border? We worry about that very much."

"First," Fahd replied carefully, "the only solution must involve the return of the Emir to Kuwait. Second, there are no Iraqi troops near the Saudi border, but Saddam is not to be trusted. That is why it is important for a team to come as soon as possible to coordinate matters to prevent that from happening."

I tried to emphasize the gravity I saw in the situation, and the urgency. We couldn't wait any longer to deter an Iraqi move south and to pressure Saddam to withdraw and permit the return of the Kuwaiti government. "We must now begin taking the actions we described in detail to Bandar. And we can't wait until it is too late." I told Fahd that the Emir had asked us for military intervention, but by that time Iraqi troops had already occupied Kuwait City and there was nothing the United States could do. "It takes a long time to deploy troops," I said. "That is why I am worried about Saudi Arabia. . . ."

"It is probable that Iraq could attack, but then an invasion may not happen," said the King. He wanted the team to work on all contingencies, and thought we still had a few days to coordinate and make a tight, successful plan. "That's all we want."

"We will get the team underway," I said. "Another point I want to make here involves a word of honor. The security of Saudi Arabia is vital—basically fundamental—to US interests and really to the interests of the Western world. And I am determined that Saddam will not get away with all this infamy. When we work out a plan, once we are there, we will stay until we are asked to leave. You have my solemn word on this."

BRENT SCOWCROFT

Not long after President Bush had spoken to Fahd, Bandar entered my office. He had obviously discussed the situation with the King, and he agreed with the need for quick action. He now suggested I lead the team. The President thought that was fine, so I called Cheney and asked him to think about who should be on it from Defense. When Dick phoned back, he told me that he himself wanted to head the group, since the mission was basically Defense. I readily agreed, as did the President. There was one problem, however. If Cheney, a cabinet officer, went, it would inevitably become a high-profile mission; a Saudi rejection could trigger a crisis, in the sense that the inability of our two countries to cooperate would further encourage Saddam's aggression. If I went, I could go there quietly and if the Saudis decided not to cooperate, no one need ever know. I explained to Bandar that if Cheney went, we would have to know in advance that the King would approve and invite the deployment of US troops to the kingdom. Bandar blanched and hesitated, but he saw the logic of our position and the danger. He supported Cheney's heading the mission on the presumption that we were not talking about "if" we were deploying but "how" and what types of units would go, but said he had to clear it with the King. After a slight delay while he called the King, he agreed to the terms.

GEORGE BUSH AND BRENT SCOWCROFT

Saudi Arabia was not alone in its hesitation. Many of the Arab countries were anxious about what Saddam would do next. We were concerned that, out of fear, some of the moderates would accept the puppet regime

Iraq had installed in Kuwait as a way to mollify Saddam. Unfortunately, one of the worst offenders was Jordan's King Hussein, a long-time ally of the United States, who had become almost a spokesman for his neighbor Iraq. We had to keep Baghdad from intimidating the other states. We also knew we had to be extremely sensitive to Arab perceptions of our intent in the Gulf. With our long and close association with Israel, we could not be seen as picking on an Arab country. Our efforts had to be made in coordination and consultation with the Arab world and with their full participation. This would take careful personal diplomacy on the part of the President and our highest officials. The first signs seemed promising, but the radicals who often influenced Arab popular opinion could easily decide to make big trouble, including mass demonstrations and a campaign of terrorism.

Sanctions, and the practical embargo of trade with Iraq, constituted an essential first step of the coordinated international response. Over the weekend of August 4–5, the President called the emir of Kuwait to update him and began to poll the allies to line up support for sanctions. The permanent members of the Security Council met the morning of August 5. Pickering reported that the UK and France strongly favored sanctions, but that the Soviets, though supportive, were still without instructions. China seemed to be leaning toward them, but claimed to be "impressed" by King Hussein's support for Iraq. Nevertheless, the Chinese did announce they would no longer sell arms to Iraq, which was an important show of support. Pickering was to table a resolution and try to get a vote on August 6.

Getting support for the sanctions was one thing, but making them stick—enforcing them—would be another. We were skeptical of them as a means for getting Saddam out of Kuwait. Too often there were "holes," when countries didn't comply with them, and we couldn't be sure what effect they would have on Iraq. We had to make sure nothing would be going in and out by sea—that would mean a naval blockade. Since Iraq is virtually a landlocked country, this posed a different, and more difficult, problem. We could not be sure that all of its neighbors would observe an embargo and, if they did not, its long borders might prove very porous. We were confident Turkey and Saudi Arabia would back sanctions. These were key countries. There were major pipelines for Iraqi oil through both and these had to be closed off. While it appeared that Syria would cooperate as well, Jordan and Iran remained uncertain.

GEORGE BUSH

On August 5, Brian Mulroney told me of a discussion he had with Turgut Ozal. Ozal was prepared to blockade all oil coming out of Iraq, but warned that there was another source through the Jordanian port at Aqaba on the Red Sea. He added that Baghdad had sent an emissary to try to wean Turkey away from the West. The Iraqi had brazenly told Ozal that Baghdad had no intention of pulling out and planned to annex Kuwait. "The West is bluffing," he had said. Ozal believed that without Western action Iraq would probably invade the UAE and Saudi Arabia.

Ozal phoned me a couple of hours later with more details and concerns. The emissary had told him the Iraqis were forming a government in Kuwait, as well as a "people's army" of about 25,000. He had spoken to King Fahd, who would support an oil embargo but was waiting for UN action. Ozal urged that we get started with sanctions as soon as possible, after which he would close the pipeline. He warned that we would have to consider military action. "Saddam is more dangerous than Qaddafi," he said. "He must go. He killed a hundred and twenty officials who refused to fight. If the blockade is very effective, [his people] may over-throw him." The Iraqi emissary had boasted that they could live with a blockade, saying, "We are twenty million, we will fight to the end. . . ." Ozal wanted NATO to give a clear signal that the alliance would back him if Iraq attacked in retaliation for closing the pipeline. We tracked down NATO Secretary General Manfred Wörner, who was fishing in western Canada. He was confident that the alliance would back Ozal, and said he would come to Washington the following day to discuss it.

I flew down to Washington from Camp David on the afternoon of Sunday, August 5. Haass met me as I emerged from the helicopter on the South Lawn and brought me up to date on the latest developments. I walked up to the crowd of waiting reporters for a few informal remarks. Although over the weekend I had been thinking about the need to voice my determination to the American people, I had not decided when I should do it. At the moment, I just planned to fill everybody in on the diplomatic steps we were taking and the international reaction. I explained that none of our allies was willing to accept anything less than total Iraqi withdrawal from Kuwait, nor would they tolerate a puppet government. Then the questions started flying.

What we were willing to do about the puppet regime? Were we going to respond militarily? I simply said, "Just wait. Watch and learn." Everyone, of course, wanted to know what measures we would take ourselves to protect Americans in Kuwait, especially in view of Iraqi threats to close down foreign embassies. To this I answered:

> "I am not going to discuss what we're doing in terms of moving forces, anything of that nature. But I view it very seriously, not just that but any threat to any other countries, as well as I view very seriously our determination to reverse this awful aggression. And please believe me, there are an awful lot of countries that are in total accord with what I've just said, and I salute them. They are staunch friends and allies, and we will be working with them all for collective action. This will not stand, this aggression against Kuwait."

Afterward, Colin Powell remarked that he felt I really had declared war on Iraq that Sunday. It was a widespread reaction. In retrospect, I don't know if I had yet determined that the use of force would be required. After all, the UN was still taking action and I hoped the matter could be ended peacefully with political and economic measures. It was still too early to make that call. On the other hand, I certainly felt that force *could* be necessary. I had decided that it was up to Saddam. I never wavered from the position that I would do whatever it took to remove Iraq from Kuwait.

25

CONFLICT IN THE BALKANS

Eric Moskowitz and Jeffrey S. Lantis

This selection by two political scientists examines the role of the National Security Council in the planning and coordination of America's involvement in the war in Kosovo during the Clinton years.

INTRODUCTION: THE CHALLENGE OF KOSOVO

The crisis in Kosovo represented a major challenge for U.S. foreign policy in the post-cold war era. The Clinton administration was faced with mounting evidence of systematic killings of ethnic Albanians in Kosovo at the hands of Serb paramilitary groups in 1998 and 1999. On the heels of the war in Bosnia, President Clinton and his advisers faced a brewing humanitarian tragedy in which ethnic Albanians sought independence from Serbia while the Serbs struggled to retain control of the province. Clinton administration officials could agree that Kosovo represented a special challenge for the United States and raised important questions about humanitarian intervention, but for almost a year the president's advisers could not agree on what to do.

After months of internal disagreements over the best course of action for the United States and its allies, the Clinton administration first chose to conduct coercive diplomacy in the fall of 1998—pressuring Serbian president Slobodan Milosevic to negotiate a limited autonomy deal for Kosovo while at the same time threatening the use of military force to stop the killings. In the face of Serb resistance to independence for Kosovo, Clinton then chose to pursue a temporary diplomatic solution in October 1998. Sadly, the situation in Kosovo rapidly deteriorated through the winter months that followed, as Serb paramilitary units and

Kosovars stepped up their raids and reprisals against one another.

Media coverage of massacres in Kosovo in early 1999 brought the crisis into stark relief for western governments. The Clinton administration pursued several rounds of new diplomatic overtures, including the Rambouillet conference that began in February 1999, but Milosevic remained steadfast in his refusal to negotiate autonomy for Kosovo. U.S. officials finally felt compelled to act militarily. On March 24, 1999, Clinton announced his decision to launch massive air attacks against Serbia in cooperation with NATO allies. He claimed that ending the tragedy was "a moral imperative" and important to the U.S. national interest. Operation Allied Force was the largest military assault in Europe since World War II and led to the introduction of 50,000 NATO peacekeepers into Kosovo. This case study reviews these significant foreign policy decisions and considers the pressures and constraints faced by the Clinton administration in responding to a humanitarian tragedy.

BACKGROUND: CRISES IN THE BALKANS

The Kosovo crisis of 1998–1999 was an extension of close to a century of upheaval in the Balkans. In 1914, the assassination of Archduke Franz Ferdinand of the Austro-Hungarian Empire by a Serbian nationalist in the streets of Sarajevo effectively ignited the fires of World War I. After the war, the Kingdom of the Serbs,

---

From Eric Moskowitz and Jeffrey S. Lantis, "The War in Kosovo: Coercive Diplomacy," in Ralph G. Carter, ed., *Contemporary Cases in Foreign Policy: From Terrorism to Trade* (Washington, D.C.: CQ, 2002), 59–87.

Professors Moskowitz and Lantis teach political science at The College of Wooster in Ohio.

Croats, and Slovenes was created from the remains of the Ottoman and Habsburg Empires. The first leader of the unified country, King Alexander, changed the name to Yugoslavia but was unable to resolve simmering rivalries among the three nationalities in the region. He, too, was killed by an assassin, in 1934.[1]

In 1945, Josip Broz Tito emerged as the victor of the communist partisan resistance against the Axis occupation in World War II, and he soon became the popular ruler of a liberated Yugoslavia.[2] Under the so-called Tito Constitution of 1974, Yugoslavia was established as a federal state consisting of six republics—Bosnia-Herzegovina, Croatia, Macedonia, Montenegro, Serbia, and Slovenia—and regions with provincial autonomy, including Kosovo and Vojvodina, to be governed by a collective federal presidency with rotating political authority.[3] Tito's approach to dealing with ethnic nationalist differences in the Balkans was heavy-handed; he stifled the expression of differences through determined support for federal unity. Tito's death in 1980 created an opening for a liberalization of the system, which would include free market economics, democratization, and a resurgence of ethnic nationalism.[4]

In 1987 Slobodan Milosevic became president of Serbia, the dominant national component within Yugoslavia. Milosevic interpreted the liberalization of politics in the region as a challenge to the power of the Yugoslav federal government and a threat to Yugoslavia's security.[5] He began to mobilize Serbian nationalist sentiment and stepped up rhetorical attacks against Albanians, Croats, Muslims, and Slovenes, all of whom he believed were threatening the centralization of Yugoslav political authority. At the same time, new leaders in Slovenia and Croatia opposed Milosevic's demands for a return to a centralized system, preferring instead a loose confederation of states.[6]

Yugoslavia dissolved on June 25, 1991, when the regional governments of Slovenia and Croatia declared their national independence. Milosevic declared war on the secessionist republics, demanded a return to federation, and sent the Serb-dominated Yugoslav National Army (JNA) to stop them.[7] The war pitted Slovenia against Yugoslavia. The conflict lasted only ten days, with the Slovenes quickly winning de facto independence. The war between Croatia and Serbia,

however, was much more intense. After six months of fighting that claimed 10,000 lives, Croatian and Serbian negotiators agreed to a cease-fire and the positioning of United Nations peacekeeping troops in a buffer zone in the spring of 1992.

April 1992 marked the beginning of a third conflict: the war in Bosnia, which had declared its independence in March 1992. This war began when Serb soldiers from the JNA crossed the Drina River in eastern Bosnia and joined forces with Bosnian Serb irregulars. The Serbs pressed their attacks against towns and villages in eastern Bosnia and soon surrounded Sarajevo, the Bosnian capital.[8] Experts estimate that 250,000 people were killed during the war and 2 million more became refugees between 1992 and 1995. The conflict ended with a negotiated settlement, the Dayton Peace Accord, on November 21, 1995. Leaders of the warring groups agreed that Bosnia would remain intact and its 1992 international borders legitimized. All parties to the conflict would provide for the safe return of refugees to their home regions, and an international tribunal for the investigation and prosecution of war crimes would be established at The Hague.[9] This arrangement would be supported by an international peace enforcement operation of 60,000 troops from European countries, the United States, and even Russia.

History of the Kosovo Crisis

Most parties to the Dayton negotiations were aware that Kosovo represented another potential ethno-political battleground in the Balkans. Kosovo, a small southern province of Serbia in Yugoslavia, had a population of about 2 million in the early 1990s. Ninety percent of the population were ethnic Albanian Muslim, or Kosovars. The remaining 10 percent were Serbs, who adhere to Orthodox Christianity. The demographics of the province, however, belied the tremendous religious and historical significance of Kosovo to the Serbs. Kosovo was the site of several Serbian Orthodox shrines from the Dark and Middle Ages, and many Serbs viewed Kosovo as the heart of their centuries-old religious traditions. In 1389, southern Slavs lost a major battle with the Ottoman Empire in Kosovo at the Field of Blackbirds, opening five centuries of Turkish rule of the Balkans. The Serbs did not succeed in fully dominating Kosovo until the Balkan War of 1912, when they destroyed all vestiges of Ottoman rule and forcibly expelled tens of thousands of ethnic Albanians from the region.[10]

In the immediate aftermath of World War II, the Kosovars were ruled in "semicolonial fashion by the Serbian communists, whose discriminatory policies caused 250,000 ethnic Albanians to emigrate from Kosovo."[11] In the interest of ethnic harmony (and political stability), however, in 1974 Tito recognized limited autonomy for Kosovo and for Vojvodina as part of the new constitutional arrangement. After Tito's death in 1980, Kosovo slowly became engulfed by ethnopolitical struggles. On the surface, Yugoslavia remained a communist country with a centralized federal government in Belgrade, but behind the rhetoric of ideology, Serb officials were well aware of simmering ethnic tensions in Kosovo. Ethnic Albanians there remained largely impoverished and disempowered by the communist system, while Serbs controlled municipal governments, schools, and police forces, in spite of being a minority in the province.

In the late 1980s Milosevic decided to use Kosovo as a staging ground for his rise to power in Serbia. In a speech commemorating the 600-year anniversary of the Serbs' defeat at the Field of Blackbirds, Milosevic promised the Serb minority that he would never allow the "sacred ground" of Kosovo to be taken from Serb control.[12] In 1989 he revoked Kosovo's provincial autonomy and imposed direct rule from Belgrade. Ethnic Albanians in Kosovo were outraged and deeply resented the Serb crackdown. In September 1991, the Kosovo political assembly voted in favor of independence and established a shadow government. Groups who favored armed insurrection against Serb dominance formed the Kosovo Liberation Army (KLA) in 1996, a guerrilla force that rapidly gained support.[13]

In the early 1990s, the administration of George Bush believed that a conflict in Kosovo would have far more serious consequences for U.S. interests than had the wars in Bosnia, Croatia, or Slovenia. Bush's advisers feared that Kosovo could become a tinderbox igniting a broader war involving Bulgaria, Greece, Turkey, and the Former Yugoslav Republic of Macedonia because of its location on the Serbia-Kosovo border and the mix of ethnic groups in the region. Conse-

quently, Secretary of State Lawrence Eagleburger sent a cable to the U.S. embassy in Belgrade on Christmas Eve 1992 with instructions to read verbatim a one-sentence message to Milosevic, in person: "In the event of conflict in Kosovo caused by Serbian action, the United States will be prepared to employ military force against Serbians in Kosovo and in Serbia proper."[14] The Clinton administration reiterated the so-called Christmas Warning to Milosevic in February and July 1993, as the conflict in Bosnia worsened. After the signing of the Dayton Peace Accord in 1995, Milosevic and his allies worked to establish political footholds in Serb-dominated areas of internally divided Bosnia. In Kosovo, Serb paramilitary units and police continued to control the province with a tight fist, which Western governments chose to interpret as "compliance" with the Christmas Warning.

THE DIPLOMACY OF DELAY

Simmering tensions came to a boil on February 28, 1998, when two Serb policemen were killed by Kosovars, and Serb police units retaliated by killing dozens of Kosovars suspected of nationalist activities and their families in Drenica. A few weeks later, Serb police units rounded up suspected members of the KLA and destroyed several neighborhoods in Racak. KLA fighters were undeterred by Serb reprisals in early 1998, however, and they pressed ahead in attacks against the Serb police and paramilitary presence in the province. Milosevic responded with sweeps of key villages in the search for KLA fighters. Images of the slain were televised around the world.

President Clinton and his advisers began to consider ways to respond to what was clearly becoming another ethnic war in the Balkans. His key foreign policy advisers during the crisis included Secretary of Defense William Cohen, Secretary of State Madeleine Albright, National Security Adviser Samuel Berger, and Chairman of the Joint Chiefs of Staff General Henry Shelton, the core of the Principals Committee of the National Security Council.

The committee agreed in early 1998 that conditions in the Balkans had changed so significantly that they were no longer willing to follow through on the Christmas Warning. The rise of the KLA and its attacks on Serb police and civilians had complicated the situation. The Kosovars were no longer peaceful civilians, according to Western intelligence reports. Perhaps more important, U.S. freedom to respond militarily in Kosovo was now vastly limited by the introduction into Bosnia of troops from NATO nations as part of the Dayton Peace Accord. U.S. military action would place these peacekeepers in jeopardy from Serb retaliation.

In early 1998 Clinton's advisers disagreed on a number of issues related to Kosovo, divisions that would become apparent in subsequent high-level meetings. Secretary of State Albright was an outspoken advocate of coercive diplomacy to restore stability to the region. She compared the standoff with Milosevic to the appeasement at Munich that led to Adolf Hitler's aggression in Europe. She began describing the events unfolding in Kosovo as "ethnic cleansing" and warned that the United States had learned a hard lesson from Bosnia—diplomacy not backed by force is ineffective against tyrants like Milosevic. Albright argued that NATO should immediately threaten air strikes against Serb units and facilities in Kosovo to stop the killings. She later noted, "I felt that there was still time to do something about this, and that we should not wait as long as we did on Bosnia to have dreadful things happen; that we could get it ahead of the curve."[15] Other top administration officials disagreed with Albright, however. National Security Adviser Berger preferred diplomatic options, and Secretary Cohen and General Shelton argued against the deployment of U.S. troops.

Unfortunately, there was no sustained focus on the crisis in Kosovo in the early months of 1998 by the Principals Committee. Instead, the White House was dealing with the burgeoning Monica Lewinsky scandal, Russia's severe economic problems, and upcoming presidential trips to China and Africa. One adviser recalled, "I hardly remember Kosovo in political discussions. It was all impeachment, impeachment, impeachment. There was nothing else."[16] There was little consensus about how to deal with Kosovo throughout the spring of 1998, so U.S. officials explored diplomatic routes. Robert Gelbard, the administration's envoy to the Balkans, was sent to Belgrade to confront Milosevic about escalating violence in Kosovo, and he

hinted that NATO was considering the use of military force against Serbia.[17] Milosevic was reportedly so offended by Gelbard's harsh criticisms of Serb actions that he refused further meetings with the envoy.

Meanwhile, Albright decided to use the bully pulpit of her position as secretary of state to push for a more rapid and aggressive response to Milosevic's crackdown in Kosovo. She hoped that if she made her case persistently, she could possibly "force the administration to come along, convince the public and the American Congress to come along, and in the end give the allies no choice but to join what the United States is about to embark upon."[18] At a hastily arranged news conference on her way to a March 1998 meeting of the Contact Group in London, Albright announced without an administration consensus, "We are not going to stand by and watch the Serbian authorities do in Kosovo what they can no longer get away with doing in Bosnia. We have a broad range of options available to us."[19] At the London meeting she aggressively pushed for the West to actively resist Serbian aggression in Kosovo. Back in Washington there was much concern about the tenor of Albright's statement. The Pentagon was not supportive of issuing threats without careful consideration of U.S. willingness and ability to carry them out. Berger was also said to be concerned that U.S. credibility could be damaged by threatening actions that the president was unwilling to undertake.[20] According to close observers, the White House saw the Kosovo situation very differently from Albright. The White House believed,

> Milosevic is a man who, however odious his behavior, however wrong his policies, if you deal with him with the right kind of carrots and the right kind of sticks, you get a deal. There's a strong belief in the White House, and in other parts of the administration, that forceful rhetoric—threats without really having a policy behind it, such as those coming from the State Department—was the wrong kind of policy at the wrong time.[21]

In a May 1998 meeting at the White House, Gelbard made the case for air strikes against Serbia. Berger challenged Gelbard's proposal, saying that he had doubts about how such actions would play on the domestic front: "Are we going to bomb on Kosovo? Can I explain that to Congress? They'll kill us."[22]

Berger also argued that threats should not be made without specific actions in mind. Gelbard responded that he had already worked out some targets with NATO's supreme allied commander, General Wesley Clark. According to secondary accounts, "Berger rejected the plan and no one else in the room supported Mr. Gelbard."[23] Instead the administration turned to Richard Holbrooke, negotiator of the Dayton accord, to convince Kosovar leader Ibrahim Rugova to meet with Milosevic.[24] In return, Rugova was granted a meeting with President Clinton in the Oval Office on May 27 in which he warned that Kosovo was headed for all-out war and pleaded the case for urgent Western intervention and an increased U.S. presence to halt the escalating violence. According to reports, Clinton told him, "We will not allow another Bosnia to happen in Kosovo," but the president made no specific guarantees.[25]

NATO Military Planning

The conflict in Kosovo continued to escalate during the summer. At a NATO summit of defense ministers in June, Secretary of Defense Cohen asked allied ministers to consider developing contingency plans for intervention in Kosovo, but the Europeans were skeptical about taking any action without explicit authority from the UN Security Council. Eventually NATO defense ministers agreed to authorize the military command to begin planning options. They also agreed to present a show of force on the Yugoslavian border to send a message of resolve to Milosevic. On June 15, eighty-five NATO warplanes flew over Albania and Macedonia, but Serb generals interpreted it as a sign of NATO's *lack* of military resolve and derogatorily referred to the operation as the "Balkan Air Show." Soon thereafter, Serb forces began to retake the initiative in clashes with the KLA. By midsummer, more than 250,000 Kosovars had been made homeless by the fighting.

NATO planners considered a range of possibilities, including a massive air campaign, a peacekeeping operation, and an all-out ground war against Serbia. Alliance planning, however, was confounded by mixed political signals from NATO governments. In July, U.S. officials reportedly told NATO planners that "there is no way we are ever going to consider the deployment of ground troops, NATO or U.S., in [Kosovo]. The only thing that we are willing to do, and even to look at seriously, is the question of air strikes."[26]

In September, NATO military planners reported to President Clinton a worst-case scenario: 200,000 troops would be required to stop the killings in Kosovo and to occupy Serbia in the event of a ground war. They estimated that 75,000 troops would be needed for a more narrowly defined mission to occupy Kosovo and create safe havens for the ethnic Albanians there. For the White House, a major military invasion and occupation was out of the question. In high-level deliberations, Clinton drew parallels between such an operation and the Vietnam War and the debacle in Somalia. Key advisers expressed similar skepticism, warning that the American public knew little about the region or its problems and probably could not locate Kosovo on a map. Secretary Cohen and General Shelton argued that the operational details for ground operations were not well developed and that such a mission would be too vague and open-ended.[27] In consultation with General Clark, Secretaries Albright and Cohen began to believe that a concentrated program of air strikes might achieve the same objective as an invasion. They reasoned that the air war against Bosnian Serb positions in 1995 had brought Milosevic to the negotiating table in Dayton, so perhaps it would work a second time.

The Clinton Administration Moves to Strike

Serious fighting between Serb forces and the KLA in September—and televised images of massacres—pushed the West into action. On September 16, Serb paramilitary units attacked a village in central Kosovo, killing twenty-two civilians, and on September 29 Western media reported a massacre in Donji Obrinje.

On September 23, the Security Council had passed Resolution 1199, which called for a cease-fire, a Serb withdrawal of forces, and the return of refugees. NATO defense ministers meeting in Vilamoura, Portugal, deliberated air strikes against Serbia. NATO secretary-general Javier Solana argued that the very credibility of the alliance was at stake and that the West could not stand by and allow a gradual takeover of the province by Serb forces. He was outraged by a Serb diplomat who had joked, "A village a day keeps NATO away."[28] On September 24, 1998, with the legitimization of Resolution 1199, NATO leaders agreed to warn Milosevic that an activation order for allied air strikes might be issued in the near future.

The president convened a meeting of the Principals Committee on September 30 to evaluate the U.S. response to the crisis. Sitting on the conference table in front of the participants that morning was a copy of the day's *New York Times,* with a front-page story and pictures of the massacre in Donji Obrinje. Secretary Albright reiterated her plea for air strikes to bring Milosevic to the bargaining table. Instead of their usual debates, however, members of the committee supported her recommendations. They decided to ask NATO ministers for an activation order authorizing General Clark to put alliance aircraft on ready alert.

The committee also agreed to send Holbrooke back to Belgrade with the threat of air strikes to win Milosevic's acceptance of Resolution 1199, but he was instructed that U.S. ground troops were not to be involved in any settlement he negotiated, including peacekeeping.[29] Ideally, the administration hoped to achieve peace in Kosovo, but more pragmatically it believed that a diplomatic settlement with a moderate level of commitment would at least stabilize the crisis in the short term. Holbrooke and Albright believed that a commitment of U.S. troops was necessary for a lasting settlement, but unfortunately, strained relations between the president and Congress made such a commitment politically impossible.

The White House decided to go on a domestic political offensive to build support for a possible NATO air war against Serbia. The president outlined the plan for air strikes in a letter to leading senators in early October. Clinton wrote that the air strikes "would start out strong and progressively expand in scale and scope" if Serbian forces remained in Kosovo. "There will be no pinprick strikes," the president promised.[30] The congressional response to Clinton's appeal was swift. On October 4, Senate majority leader Trent Lott, R-Miss., warned the president that Congress would not support military action.[31] Other Republican and Democratic leaders expressed their displeasure with the White House approach as well. Critics inside and outside the government warned of the "wag the dog" scenario—a reference to the 1998 film of the same name that portrayed a fictional president's decision to

go to war against Albania to distract the public from a sex scandal in Washington.[32]

Early Attempts at Coercive Diplomacy

By mid-October, the White House recognized that there was little domestic consensus for military action in Kosovo, and the NATO alliance was also divided on the question. Furthermore, the pressures of congressional elections in November had diverted a great deal of Washington's attention inward. Clinton pinned his hopes on negotiations with Milosevic. Holbrooke and his diplomatic team traveled to Belgrade for nine days of talks. On October 15, Holbrooke announced a settlement. Milosevic agreed to withdraw the majority of Serb forces from Kosovo and ordered the end to paramilitary and police repression of Kosovars. Milosevic further agreed to permit 1,800 unarmed, international inspectors to monitor the peace in Kosovo and to allow overflights by NATO reconnaissance planes to complement verification of Serb compliance.[33] Clinton hailed the deal as a triumph of coercive diplomacy—a carrot-and-stick diplomatic approach backed by the threat of force. The president announced that Milosevic had "agreed to internationally supervised democratic elections in Kosovo, substantial self-government and a local police—in short, rights that the Kosovars have been demanding since Mr. Milosevic stripped their autonomy a decade ago."[34]

The Organization for Security and Cooperation in Europe (OSCE) sponsored the creation and deployment of the unarmed international observer force and selected veteran U.S. diplomat William Walker to head the operation. OSCE observer groups began patrolling Kosovo in November 1998. Although Americans participated as unarmed monitors, the United States refused to contribute combat troops to an extrication force stationed in Macedonia, to be mobilized if the monitors required emergency evacuation from the province.

Unfortunately, the warring factions in the region viewed the October agreement more as an opportunity to regroup and gain strategic advantage than a pledge for permanent peace. According to NATO officials, Serb forces began sending reinforcements and equipment to the region under cover of darkness in the late fall. At the same time, KLA forces took the opportunity to relocate troops and resupply. Ethnic Albanians living in other countries, including the United States, stepped up financial support of the KLA resupply effort in the winter of 1998–1999. Soon both sides were engaged in attacks and counter-attacks, but this time OSCE observers were caught in the middle. Ambassador Walker was personally threatened at one point by a drunken belligerent Serb wielding a gun and a hand grenade, and OSCE representatives began to plead to their home governments for security.

THE ROAD TO OPERATION ALLIED FORCE

In December 1998—just weeks after OSCE representatives arrived and began monitoring operations—Serbian soldiers rounded up and killed thirty-six suspected KLA rebels. The Kosovars retaliated sporadically in the northern part of the province. Observers estimated that some 2,500 ethnic Albanian Kosovars had been killed in the struggle for autonomy by the end of 1998 and about 230,000 had fled their homes in the face of the violence and fear of Serb paramilitary killings.[35]

NATO and U.S. intelligence agencies began to detect signs of increased Serbian activity around Kosovo in January 1999 and learned that the Serbs were planning a massive encircling operation against the KLA after the spring thaw. The plan was to move tanks and artillery into Kosovo to attack KLA strongholds and drive hundreds of thousands of ethnic Albanians from key areas. Intercepted messages suggested that Serbian military leaders believed that the West would tolerate the operation if they "only attacked a village a week."[36]

Despite this deteriorating situation, there was little response from the Clinton administration. The White House was distracted by brinksmanship with Iraq over United Nations inspections of suspected nuclear, chemical, and biological weapons facilities. Saddam Hussein had once again chosen to challenge the UN inspection regime, and Western allies were confronted with a dilemma over the proper course of action to force compliance. Thus after consideration of problems in the Persian Gulf, the president approved four days of isolated bombings of Iraq.

October Plus

On January 15, the Principals Committee met to discuss the deteriorating situation in Kosovo. All agreed

that Milosevic had reneged on the October agreement.[37] The most recent intelligence on Kosovo, completed in November, concluded that "the October agreement indicates that Milosevic is susceptible to outside pressure. He will eventually accept a number of outcomes, from autonomy to provisional status with final resolution to be determined, as long as he remains the undisputed leader in Belgrade." The report also concluded, however, that Milosevic would accept a change in the status of Kosovo "only when he believes his power is endangered" by "insurgents driving up the economic and military costs of holding onto the province, or the West threatening to use sustained and decisive military power against his forces."[38] Albright insisted that it was time to use threats of military intervention to force a comprehensive settlement. She argued that Milosevic "understands only the language of force."[39]

General Shelton continued to voice the Pentagon's strong opposition to using force in Kosovo.[40] First, the Joint Chiefs of Staff questioned whether the conflict in Kosovo significantly affected U.S. national interests. They doubted Albright's domino theory that the fall of Kosovo would inevitably cause the conflict to spread throughout the Balkans. It struck them as reminiscent of the flawed arguments that led to the ill-conceived U.S. participation in the Vietnam War. Second, Shelton argued that air strikes would not guarantee the political aims of the administration; they would neither inhibit the ethnic cleansing taking place on the ground nor force Milosevic to the negotiating table. Third, ground troops were out of the question, in part because the months it would take to build up the 100,000 to 200,000 troops needed to control Kosovo would provide Serbia with time to overrun the province and ethnically cleanse it. Given the lack of a clear vision for Balkan policy, the Pentagon feared that any use of ground troops would devolve into a long-term, open-ended commitment. The Pentagon therefore suggested the increased use of economic sanctions and other non-military forms of pressure, such as indicting Milosevic for war crimes in Bosnia.

Albright failed to carry the day at this meeting. Berger remained unconvinced that the threat of military intervention was a wise choice at this time. On the political front, the Senate impeachment trial of Clinton over the Lewinsky matter had just begun. There was little sense that the American public would support a military escalation in an obscure part of Europe during a political crisis at home. Furthermore, there was no allied commitment for a more aggressive stance. National Security Council analysts believed that Albright underestimated the difficulties of using military forces to support diplomacy. Cohen, too, rejected Albright's recommendations and was generally supportive of the Pentagon position. Speaking about his position in January 1999, Cohen recollected,

> I felt that military force should be the absolute last resort. Everything else has to fail before you turn to the military. And if you turn to the military, you must be very clear on what the objectives are, measuring those political objectives, and how military action can be consistent with carrying out and furthering those goals. I want to be very clear that we have domestic support before we ever commit our forces to combat. . . . Also we must have the support of the allies.[41]

Albright, Berger, and Cohen could only agree on what was called the October Plus strategy, that is, bolstering the ongoing process constructed by Holbrooke the previous fall by renewing shuttle diplomacy between the warring sides in an effort to better protect the peace monitors, train a Kosovar police force, and prepare for elections. After the meeting, Albright was furious that the White House had made no progress toward constructing a more comprehensive, effective policy. "We're just gerbils running on a wheel," she said.[42]

The policy gerbils would soon break free from their cage, however. On the day of the disappointing Principals Committee meeting, Serb forces executed forty-five unarmed villagers in Racak. The bodies were discovered by OSCE monitors, and Ambassador Walker personally called the State Department with the news. Albright realized that with swift action, Racak could be the event to galvanize U.S. and NATO policy on Kosovo. One adviser reportedly told her, "Whatever threat of force you don't get in the next two weeks you're never getting . . . at least until the next Racak."[43]

Berger reconvened the Principals Committee on the evening of January 19, a night of high drama. The Senate impeachment trial of President Clinton had begun days before, and that night the president was to deliver his State of the Union address to the very Congress that was seeking to remove him from office. It also became clear that Racak had changed the decision-making dynamics in the administration. One senior U.S. official observed, "Racak made clear that Milosevic was not going to live up to his commitments."[44] There was also growing evidence that a major escalation was planned for the spring. Above and beyond the humanitarian concern for the hundreds of thousands of refugees that would be generated by the fighting, the administration began to see the containment of this conflict as a vital interest to the United States. More decision makers seemed to accept Undersecretary of State Thomas Pickering's argument that "the conflict in Kosovo has no natural boundaries."[45] As fighting in the province intensified and huge numbers of refugees flooded across Kosovo's borders, the administration began to fear that the war would engulf large parts of southern and central Europe. A foreign policy official describing administration thinking at the time said, "In short, we're at the edge of a precipice. There's a reason why our central military alliance in the world is in Europe. It's the history of the 20th century."[46]

Albright opened the Principals meeting by once again presenting her strategy to issue an ultimatum to Milosevic and back it with the threat of NATO bombing. The ultimatum would require that Milosevic accept NATO troops in Kosovo to enforce the terms of a peace agreement and that Serbia withdraw almost all of its forces from the province and provide it with meaningful autonomy. Albright argued that the United States, in order to convince Milosevic and the allies of the seriousness of its commitment, had to be prepared to deploy ground troops as part of a peace deal. She added that after eight years of issuing ultimatums, U.S. and NATO credibility was at risk. One adviser commented at the time, "There are massive bloodbaths all over the world and we're not intervening in them . . . [but] this one's in the heart of Europe. I'd argue that the alliance itself is at risk because if it's unable to address a major threat within Europe, it really loses its reason for being."[47]

Albright knew that to gain approval of her position she had to be sensitive to other political realities. The NATO allies would only accept ground troops as a

peacekeeping operation for implementing a settlement, not as combat units invading Kosovo to impose
a settlement. An aide to Albright who helped draft her
position noted, "Our assumption was that we had to
find ways to minimize the percentage of American
troops and emphasize a 'permissive environment' if
there was any hope of getting the Pentagon and the
president and Congress to buy it."[48] Consequently, the
issue of using combat ground troops to halt ethnic
cleansing or to force Milosevic to negotiate was never
seriously discussed.[49]

Until this meeting, Berger had opposed doing anything more than supplement the October agreement.
Cohen and General Shelton had been even more
adamant in their refusal to go beyond October Plus.
Both sought to avoid strategies calling for the introduction of more U.S. troops to the Balkans in any role.[50]
Berger and Cohen also realized, however, that "the politics [were] moving in the direction that Albright wants
to go."[51] Berger therefore agreed to Albright's proposal.
In the early stages of the discussion, Cohen continued
to resist the use of ground troops even in a permissive
environment. According to one participant, a two-part
consensus evolved at the meeting: one was to make a
credible threat of military force, and the other was to
demand the attendance of Serb and Kosovar representatives for a meeting at which the basic principles of a
settlement would be decided in advance by the Contact
Group, including Russia. These basic principles would
be non-negotiable, including a NATO implementation
force.[52] The following day Berger informed President
Clinton of the new consensus. Clinton agreed with it,
though he made no formal decision about whether U.S.
troops would participate in the implementation of a
settlement.

Planning for Action

On January 21, Clinton phoned British prime minister
Tony Blair to discuss the new U.S. direction in Kosovo
strategy. Both agreed that there were two options available: reprisal bombings for Racak or a comprehensive
diplomatic agreement enforced by NATO troops.[53]
Even as the Clinton administration moved toward a
more aggressive policy on Kosovo, however, it was
troubled by the inability to agree on an analysis of
Milosevic's motivation and likely reaction to the pol-

icy options being considered. One senior administration official, looking back, noted,

> As we contemplated the use of force over the past 14
> months, we constructed four different models. One
> was that the whiff of gunpowder, just the threat of
> force would make [Milosevic] back down. Another
> was that he needed to take some hit to justify acquies-
> cence. Another was that he was a playground bully
> who would fight but back off after a punch in the nose.
> And fourth was that he would react like Saddam Hus-
> sein. On any given day people would pick one or the
> other. We thought the Saddam Hussein option was
> always the least likely, but we knew it was out there
> and now we're looking at it.[54]

High-ranking officials at the State Department
tended to view Milosevic as the schoolyard bully,
based on his concession in Bosnia after NATO air
strikes and a ground offensive by Croatian troops and
on his willingness to bargain with Holbrooke in October 1998 under the threat of additional NATO air
strikes. An Albright aide stated, "What happened in
Bosnia and in October showed that the threat of force
can work, not that it will work, and therefore it was
worth trying."[55] On the other hand, most of the Pentagon and parts of the intelligence apparatus tended to
see Milosevic as far more intransigent and dangerous.
A late January intelligence report concluded, "Confronted with a take it or leave it deal, Milosevic may
opt to risk a NATO bombing campaign rather than surrender control over Kosovo. He may assume he can
absorb a limited attack and the allies will not support a
long campaign." Another report filed just a week later
contradictorily predicted, "Milosevic will seek to give
just enough to avoid NATO bombing."[56]

Albright spent much of the rest of January negotiating the terms for NATO's threat of force. On January
30, after UN secretary-general Kofi Annan indicated
that force would be justified to bring the Serbs to the
bargaining table, the allies agreed that they had sufficient legal grounds to use force if Serbia refused to
enter into negotiations. NATO ministers approved its
second activation order in preparation for war. Clinton
and his foreign policy advisers convened on February
1 for further consideration of the plan to threaten air
strikes. Clinton recognized that because Kosovo was
probably more important to Milosevic than was

Bosnia, he "may be sorely tempted to take the first round of air strikes. I hope we don't have to bomb, but we may need to."[57] Though the administration was now committed to the use of air strikes as part of a strategy of coercive diplomacy, the Joint Chiefs of Staff continued to doubt its efficacy. Despite conflicting intelligence analyses of Milosevic's motivation and likely reaction to coercion, none of the participants at the meeting raised the issue of contingencies if the bombings failed. An administration official later observed, "Governments make the decisions that are necessary to make and they leave for another day decisions that are very hard, for eventualities that everybody hopes will never occur."[58]

Secretary of State Albright did order her department's Policy Planning director, Morton Halperin, to investigate the possible negative consequences of the threat of air strikes. Halperin later presented decision makers with a five-page memorandum titled "Surprises." The memo noted a number of problematic possibilities, including (1) that the Kosovars would renege on an agreement or initiate military operations; (2) that Milosevic would continue low-level fighting while offering a false peace; (3) that NATO would ultimately refuse to launch air strikes; or (4) that Russia would resist peace efforts, perhaps by offering military assistance to Serbia.[59] One official said that by far the most troubling possibility raised in the memo was the chance that the NATO bombings would touch off a massive offensive by the Serbs. This would leave Clinton vulnerable to charges that his air strikes had caused the very harm that they were intended to prevent. The official noted that the only solution to such an eventuality would be "to try to get the military resources" to win the war "as quickly as we could."[60] Ultimately, no serious contingency plans were made for positioning U.S. troops in the region for humanitarian purposes or for combat should the bombing strategy fail.

Defiance at Rambouillet

On February 6, an international diplomatic conference was opened at Rambouillet, France, to give Milosevic and the Kosovars one last chance to reach an agreement (and to convince the Europeans that all reasonable efforts had been taken to avoid the use of force). The United States wanted to protect ethnic Albanian Kosovars from Serbian repression but did not support independence for the province. It was thought that independence would be a destabilizing precedent calling into question the legitimacy of other multiethnic nations in central Europe, including Bosnia. The basic allied proposal at Rambouillet included a cease-fire, the removal of most Serbian security forces from Kosovo, the demilitarization of the KLA, a NATO peacekeeping force with access to all of Yugoslavia, and greater internal autonomy for Kosovo for at least three years.

Milosevic did not bother to attend the conference, and the Serb delegation refused to sign any agreement that included NATO peacekeeping troops in Kosovo. The Kosovar delegation also rejected the allied proposal, demanding instead a guarantee of complete independence for Kosovo. In late February, with both parties to the dispute obstructing agreement, the allies recessed the conference. Albright angrily announced that "if the talks crater because the Serbs do not say yes, we will have bombing. If the talks crater because the Albanians have not said yes, we will not be able to support them; and, in fact, will have to cut off whatever help they're getting from the outside."[61] After the talks reconvened in Paris on March 15, the Kosovars signed on to the proposal, but once again the Serbs refused. Albright later observed that the Kosovar's signing at Rambouillet was critical in two ways: solidifying the European allies' support for the use of force against the Serbs and selling the Albanians on the settlement.[62]

While the Rambouillet talks were stalled through much of February and March, preparations to increase the pressure on Milosevic continued in Washington. On February 13—one day after he was acquitted in his Senate impeachment trial—President Clinton announced his intention to include U.S. troops among the post-settlement implementation forces. A former NSC adviser observed, "Once the Lewinsky scandal ended, once the final political step in that torturous year-long process [was] over, the president [felt] able to commit to the deployment of ground troops. He wasn't able to commit beforehand."[63] Although in private Clinton had always agreed that U.S. troops would participate in the implementation of a Rambouillet settlement, this was the first public acknowledgment of that policy.

On March 13, Clinton and his top advisers met to assess the diplomatic situation. In two days talks would reconvene in Paris, and the Kosovars were expected to sign the agreement. Milosevic would now have to accept the terms of Rambouillet or suffer NATO air strikes. Most in the White House thought he would reluctantly acquiesce or perhaps take a few symbolic strikes from NATO before agreeing. The group contacted Ambassador Christopher Hill for his assessment of the likelihood that an accord could be reached. He answered, "Zero point zero percent."[64] One participant recalled "stunned silence in the room."[65] They now realized that Milosevic had decided to challenge NATO.

Two days later, at another White House meeting, final preparations were made for the air strikes. By this time, the Joint Chiefs of Staff had unanimously voted to support them. In spite of continuing reservations, they were swayed ultimately by the need to protect U.S. leadership in NATO and by the brewing humanitarian catastrophe in Kosovo.[66] Despite the military's acquiescence, General Shelton conveyed their fear that "[i]n the short term, military action would make things worse in Kosovo."[67] CIA director George Tenet had warned in early February that NATO air strikes might set off a wave of ethnic cleansing by the Serbs.[68] Shelton's and Tenet's assessment was supported by a March military intelligence report concluding that Milosevic intended to ethnically cleanse all 1.8 million Albanians within a week.[69] By the March 15 meeting, U.S. and NATO estimates indicated that there were now 30,000 Serbian forces in Kosovo—twice the limit allowed by the October agreement—and there were an additional 40,000 troops with 300 tanks massing on the Kosovo border.[70] The White House downplayed the prognosis of massive ethnic cleansing and assumed that if Milosevic attacked Kosovo his primary target would be the KLA, not the civilian population.

When on March 18 the Kosovars signed the Rambouillet agreement, Albright decided to send Holbrooke to Belgrade. No one was confident that he would have much success at this point; General Clark objected that a mission by Holbrooke gave Milosevic more time to deploy troops and equipment. Holbrooke and Hill met with Milosevic on March 22 to deliver the ultimatum that unless the Serbs signed the Rambouil-

let accord, NATO would begin bombing. Milosevic refused.[71] Faced with Milosevic's intransigence, Holbrooke immediately recommended to Clinton and Albright that his mission be canceled.[72] The following night, Holbrooke briefed NATO secretary-general Solana in Brussels on the collapse of the talks. Solana then gave General Clark authorization for the air campaign. On March 24, Berger met with Clinton to discuss the failure of the Holbrooke mission. Berger informed Clinton, "We're going to go, unless you say otherwise." Clinton simply replied, "Let's do it."[73]

Despite Pentagon recommendations for a massive air campaign, a more limited option was chosen. Only ninety-one approved targets, restricted to purely military facilities, were on the bombing list for the first three days. The list was a compromise to maintain unity within NATO, as a number of members were uncomfortable with any bombing. In addition, most civilians in the Clinton administration felt that a moderate air campaign would be sufficient to bring Milosevic back to the table.

Clinton Addresses the Nation

On March 24, President Clinton addressed the nation on television to announce that NATO air strikes on Yugoslavia had begun. He portrayed the U.S. intervention as part of a moral imperative to protect the Kosovars. Furthermore, he said, the bombing would protect U.S. national interests by preventing the spread of war in this historically volatile region and helping create "a Europe that is prosperous, secure, undivided and free." He then outlined the objectives of the campaign:

> Our mission is clear: to demonstrate the seriousness of NATO's purpose so that the Serbian leaders understand the imperative of reversing course. To deter an even bloodier offensive against innocent civilians in Kosovo and if necessary to seriously damage the Serbian military's capacity to harm the people of Kosovo. In short, if President Milosevic will not make peace, we will limit his ability to make war.[74]

Clinton also said that should Milosevic agree to a settlement, NATO would provide peacekeeping troops. "If NATO is invited to do so, our troops should take part in that mission to keep the peace. But I do not intend to put our troops in Kosovo to fight a war."[75]

Clinton's declaration that he had no intention of using U.S. troops to fight a war in Kosovo had been carefully prepared. Berger had included this reference in the address. The ever-cautious Berger was "a pivotal voice against moving toward the use of ground troops" in any combat role in Kosovo.[76] Berger saw a number of problems with a ground option. A U.S.-led ground war in Kosovo could split NATO, destroy U.S. relations with Russia, and devastate U.S. public support for efforts to stop Milosevic in Kosovo. In addition, Berger felt that NATO had far greater military advantages in the air compared to on the ground: "We had an advantage of 100-1, 1000-1 from the air. . . . If we were forced to go in on the ground in deep summer, it would have been maybe 3-1 or 2-1. Milosevic would have been able to be on much more equal grounds with NATO."[77] Defending the decision to explicitly rule out a ground option in Clinton's speech, Berger rationalized, "We would have been paralyzed by a debate in NATO, and paralyzed, in my judgement, by a debate in this country by what was at that point a hypothetical, distant option."[78]

President Clinton, too, had strong reservations about the use of U.S. ground troops in a combat role. Beyond his inclination to worry about his hold on public support, his advisers were also warning him of the danger of an open-ended commitment. One senior adviser said that if NATO sent troops into Kosovo, "Invade, occupy and stay there. You own this country."[79] Clinton echoed these concerns in an interview with Dan Rather in the first week of the air campaign, saying, "The thing that bothers me about introducing ground troops into a hostile situation, into Kosovo and into the Balkans, is the prospect of never being able to get them out."[80]

Clinton would later say that he was faced with "a bunch of bad options."[81] To Clinton and Berger, deploying ground troops was too dangerous—politically and militarily—while doing nothing was morally bankrupt and called into question the international credibility of the president, the United States, and NATO. With all its flaws, the choice of air strikes without ground troops seemed the only viable option.

Others in the administration saw a president torn by moral and pragmatic instincts—and his historical understanding of both. Clinton was morally unwilling to allow Serb forces to overrun and ethnically cleanse Kosovo, but he also was only willing to bear the political cost of air strikes, even though many advisers thought ground troops necessary.[82] Clinton had seen the terrible human consequences of delay and inaction in Bosnia and Rwanda and the political cost of Vietnam and Somalia. He had also witnessed the eventual success of intervention in Bosnia. Former senior adviser George Stephanopoulos observed, "You take Somalia, that's what forces you out. You take Bosnia, that's what pushes you in. It highlights how there are no good choices."[83]

The War

The Kosovo war lasted 78 days. Operation Allied Force consisted of strikes primarily targeted against Serbian military, paramilitary, and police units. Within the first ten days of the campaign, Serbian security forces took almost full control of Kosovo on the ground and pushed more than 500,000 Kosovars across the border into Albania and Macedonia, creating a massive humanitarian crisis. By the end of the war, 860,000 Kosovars had been expelled from the country and another 600,000 were internal refugees. A senior NATO military official acknowledged that the alliance always recognized that Milosevic might respond harshly to the air strikes, but he conceded, "We underestimated the ferocity and velocity of Milosevic's offensive to transform the ethnic balance in Kosovo."[84]

It soon became clear that Milosevic would not politely concede after a brief air war; the humanitarian crisis rapidly worsened. NATO leaders ordered the pace of the bombings escalated, but there were not enough aircraft in theater to sustain around-the-clock war for several more weeks. It was not until May that the augmented air campaign, Papa Bear, reached its full strength.[85] As the war dragged on, an increasing number of attacks were aimed directly at command and communications facilities and infrastructure inside Serbia, including high-profile targets in downtown Belgrade.

The United States was heavily engaged in Operation Allied Force. Its military contributed more than 725 aircraft, hundreds of artillery and multiple-launch rocket systems for theater ground attack, and about 5,500 supporting troops in the theater of operation.

U.S. Navy ships fired 450 Tomahawk cruise missiles, and the Air Force launched 90 cruise missiles.[86] Tens of thousands of soldiers were committed to the air operation at military bases worldwide. President Clinton also activated 5,000 reservists to provide logistical support. Experts estimated that U.S. participation in the war totaled some $5 billion.[87]

Eleven weeks into the campaign, the war abruptly ended after Milosevic agreed to limited provincial autonomy for Kosovo, to remove Serb security forces from the region, and to a 50,000-strong NATO peacekeeping force under UN auspices. More than 600,000 Kosovars were repatriated. Seven thousand U.S. soldiers were deployed to Kosovo as part of the peacekeeping force, with an estimated operational cost of some $3.5 billion annually.[88] Peacekeepers and nongovernmental organizations in Kosovo soon discovered that some 10,000 Albanian civilians had been killed during the conflict. The Clinton administration and NATO allies celebrated their military victory over Milosevic, but they were left to consider whether their actions in Kosovo had been a triumph of coercive diplomacy.

CONCLUSION: DEFINING THE NATIONAL INTEREST

Clinton administration decision making on the crisis in Kosovo was shaped by a number of factors. First, the complexity of the problem in Kosovo made decision making more difficult. Without cold war orientations that seemed to simplify perspectives on world events, administration officials had great difficulty defining the significance of the problem in Kosovo for U.S. national interests. Moreover, without the old bipolar forces shaping events and behavior, predicting the outbreak and pattern of conflict had become much more problematic.

Second, the administration long debated whether Kosovo was "merely" a human rights crisis or whether it had deeper implications for U.S. national security. The lack of agreement about the significance of the problem, in turn, made it less likely that a policy consensus could be achieved quickly. Secretary Albright and the State Department argued that Milosevic's actions were not only a grievous human rights viola-

tion, but also a threat to the stability of central Europe and hence vital to U.S. national interest. The Pentagon doubted that security interests were at risk. Only when the crisis boiled over during the winter of 1998–1999—with more brazen and severe acts of ethnic cleansing, a flood of refugees spilling into neighboring countries, and a growing recognition that NATO's impotence was on full display—was the administration able to agree that a policy of coherent, forceful coercive diplomacy was necessary.

Constructing that option, however, was further complicated by the inability of the administration to ascertain Milosevic's motivation and strategy in Kosovo and hence his likely response to efforts to limit his aggression. Without the cold war structural constraints to limit Milosovic's options, the Clinton administration could no more understand Milosevic in Serbia than it could Saddam Hussein in Iraq or Mohamed Farah Aideed in Somalia. The administration's efforts to agree upon the substance of a coercive diplomacy option were slowed by the inability to decide whether Milosevic was a wily international negotiator, a schoolyard bully, or a fanatical nationalist willing to fight to the end. Ultimately, its initial policy underestimated his resolve and his willingness to order horrific measures against the Kosovars.

Finally, the role of domestic politics was also significant in this case. At various times, the precarious political standing of President Clinton distracted the administration from paying sufficient attention to the burgeoning crisis in the Balkans. Even when policy makers focused on the crisis in Kosovo, the costs and benefits of policy options were often viewed through a domestic politics lens. Throughout the crisis, the White House consistently opposed the deployment of U.S. troops in a variety of roles on the basis of the domestic political costs. Concerns about congressional opposition, lack of public support, and electoral setbacks were abundant. As intervention in Kosovo was contemplated in the White House, contrasting historical analogies were raised. Clinton's desire to avoid another Rwanda—where the West passively accepted the slaughter of hundreds of thousands of innocent civilians—was more than balanced by the images of Vietnam and Somalia. Visions of the political debacles in Vietnam and Somalia consistently raised domestic red flags for intervention in Kosovo. Clinton's sensitivity to these events was no doubt heightened by the escalating partisan conflict that had plagued Washington since the mid-1980s. Ultimately the option chosen—an air war—seemed to be heavily determined by a desire to restrain Milosevic's aggression, but at the least possible domestic cost to the United States.

NOTES

1. See John G. Stoessinger, *Why Nations Go to War* (New York: St. Martin's Press, 1998), 185–195.

2. Christopher Bennett, *Yugoslavia's Bloody Collapse: Causes, Course and Consequences* (London: Hurst, 1995); see also Laura Silber and Alan Little, *The Death of Yugoslavia* (London: Penguin, 1997).

3. Stoessinger, *Why Nations Go to War,* 191.

4. Noel Malcolm, *Bosnia: A Short History* (New York: New York University Press, 1994), 54–55.

5. See Susan L. Woodward, *Balkan Tragedy: Chaos and Dissolution after the Cold War* (Washington, D.C.: Brookings Institution Press, 1995).

6. Misha Glenny, *The Fall of Yugoslavia: The Third Balkan War* (New York: Penguin, 1992), 6.

7. See Sabrina Petra Ramet, "War in the Balkans," *Foreign Affairs* 71, no. 4 (fall 1992): 174–181.

8. See Steven L. Burg and Paul S. Shoup, *The War in Bosnia-Herzegovina: Ethnic Conflict and International Intervention* (Armonk, N.Y.: M. E. Sharpe, 1999).

9. "Maßnahmen zur Absicherung des Friedensvertrages für Bosnien-Herzegowina," *Reihe Stichworte für die Öffentlichkeitsarbeit und Truppeninformation* (Bonn: Bundesministerium der Verteidigung Presse- und Informationsstab Referat Öffentlichkeitarbeit, 1995).

10. William Hagen, "Kosovo: The History behind It All," *Foreign Affairs* 78, no. 4 (July/August 1999): 57.

11. Ibid., 58.

12. Roger Cohen, "Crisis in the Balkans: Kosovo Notebook," *New York Times,* July 2, 1999, A1.

13. "Chronology of Events Relating to the Kosovo Conflict," *New York Times,* March 24, 1999, A6.

14. Barton Gellman, "The Path to Crisis: How the United States and Its Allies Went to War," *Washington Post,* April 18, 1999, A1.

15. Ibid.

16. Elaine Sciolino and Ethan Bronner, "Crisis in the Balkans: The Road to War," *New York Times,* April 18, 1999, A1.

17. Doyle McManus, "Crisis in Yugoslavia: Debate Turns to Finger-Pointing on Kosovo Policy," *Los Angeles Times,* April 11, 1999, 1.

18. WGBH, "Interview with Ivo Daalder," *Frontline: War in Europe, 2000,* http://www.pbs.org/wgbh/pages/frontline/shows/kosovo/interviews/daalder.html.

19. Gellman, "The Path to Crisis." The Contact Group was made up of diplomats from France, Germany, Great Britain, Russia, and the United States, who attempted to coordinate their responses to the Balkan crises in the 1990s.

20. Gellman, "The Path to Crisis."

21. WGBH, "Interview with Ivo Daalder."

22. John Harris, "Berger's Caution Has Shaped the Role of U.S. in War," *Washington Post,* May 16, 1999, A1.

23. Sciolino and Bronner, "Crisis in the Balkans."

24. Ibid., A6.

25. Ibid., A1.

26. WGBH "Interview with Ivo Daalder."

27. Gellman, "The Path to Crisis."

28. Ibid.

29. Accounts of the September 30 meeting are from WGBH, "Interview with Ivo Daalder."

30. Sciolino and Bronner, "Crisis in the Balkans."

31. Ibid.

32. Ibid.

33. Jane Perlez, "Yugoslav Leader Is Not Complying with Kosovo Pact," *New York Times,* October 16, 1998, A1; and Jane Perlez, "Two Exempt Army Battalians Are Deployed by Milosevic," *New York Times,* October 20, 1998, A14.

34. Sciolino and Bronner, "Crisis in the Balkans."

35. Michael Mandelbaum, "A Perfect Failure: NATO's War against Yugoslavia," *Foreign Affairs* 78, no. 5 (September/October 1999): 2.

36. Sciolino and Bronner, "Crisis in the Balkans."

37. Gellman, "The Path to Crisis."

38. Ibid.

39. Michael Hirsh and John Barry, "How We Stumbled into War," *Newsweek,* April 12, 1999, 40.

40. Bradley Graham, "Joint Chiefs Doubted Air Strategy," *Washington Post,* April 5, 1999, A1.

41. WGBH, "Interview with William Cohen," *Frontline: War in Europe, 2000,* http://www.pbs.org/wgbh/pages/frontline/shows/kosovo/interviews/cohen.html.

42. Gellman, "The Path to Crisis."

43. Ibid.

44. Barton Gellman, "U.S. Has 'Vital Interests' in Containing Conflict," *Washington Post,* February 21, 1999, A1.

45. Ibid.

46. Ibid.

47. Barton Gellman, "In the End Allies See No Credible Alternative," *Washington Post,* March 23, 1999, A12.

48. Gellman, "The Path to Crisis."

49. John Harris, "Clinton Saw No Alternative to Air Strikes," *Washington Post,* April 1, 1999, A1.

50. Sciolino and Bronner, "Crisis in the Balkans."

51. WGBH, "Interview with Ivo Daalder."

52. Gellman, "The Path to Crisis."

53. Sciolino and Bronner, "Crisis in the Balkans."

54. Thomas Lippman, "State Department Miscalculated on Kosovo," *Washington Post,* April 7, 1999, A1.

55. Ibid.

56. Sciolino and Bronner, "Crisis in the Balkans."

57. Gellman, "The Path to Crisis."

58. Ibid.

59. Ibid.

60. Ibid.

61. WGBH, *Frontline: War in Europe, 2000,* http://www.pbs.org/wgbh/pages/frontline/shows/kosovo/etc/script1.html.

62. Sciolino and Bronner, "Crisis in the Balkans."

63. WGBH, "Interview with Ivo Daalder."

64. Hirsh and Barry, "How We Stumbled into War," 38.

65. Ibid.

66. Graham, "Joint Chiefs Doubted Air Strategy."

67. Hirsh and Barry, "How We Stumbled into War," 39.

68. Lippman, "State Department Miscalculated on Kosovo."

69. Craig Whitney and Eric Schmitt, "Crisis in the Balkans: NATO Had Signs Its Strategy Would Fail Kosovars," *New York Times,* April 1, 1999, A1.

70. Ibid.

71. WGBH, "Interview with Richard Holbrooke," *Frontline: War in Europe, 2000,* http://www.pbs.org/wgbh/pages/frontline/shows/kosovo/interviews/holbrooke.html.

72. Michael Hirsh, "He Was Calm, Unyielding," *Newsweek,* April 5, 1999, 37.

73. Michael Elliott, "Mission Uncertain," *Newsweek,* April 5, 1999, 30.

74. William Clinton, "Statement by the President to the Nation," March 24, 1999, http://www2.whitehouse.gov/WH/Newhtml/19990324-2872.html.

75. Ibid.

76. Harris, "Berger's Caution Has Shaped the Role of U.S. in War."

77. WGBH, "Interview with Sandy Berger," *Frontline: War in Europe, 2000,* http://www.pbs.org/wgbh/pages/frontline/shows/kosovo/interviews/berger.html.

78. Harris, "Berger's Caution Has Shaped the Role of U.S. in War."

79. Harris, "Clinton Saw No Alternative to Air Strikes."

80. Ibid.

81. Sciolino and Bronner, "Crisis in the Balkans."

82. John Harris, "In Handling of Crisis, a Different President," *Washington Post,* June 8, 1999, A1.

83. John Harris, "Stakes Are Growing for Clinton," *Washington Post,* April 2, 1999, A1.

84. Harris, "Clinton Saw No Alternative to Air Strikes."

85. Rebecca Grant, "Air Power Made It Work," *Air Force Magazine,* November 1999, 30.

86. Tom Raum, "Cost of Kosovo Conflict Said to Be $4 Billion," *Washington Post,* June 8, 1999, A1.

87. Eric Schmitt, "The World: The Bombs Are Smart, People Are Smarter," *New York Times,* July 4, 1999, D6; see also "*Frontline: War in Europe, 2000:* Facts and Figures," http://www.pbs.org/wgbh/pages/frontline/shows/kosovo/etc/links.html.

88. Raum, "Cost of Kosovo Conflict Said to Be $4 Billion."

26

THE WAR AGAINST TERRORISM

Dan Balz and Bob Woodward

Balz and Woodward capture the sense of urgency and the tension on the National Security Council as the second Bush Administration deliberates over how to respond to the shocking terrorist attacks against the United States that occurred on September 11, 2001.

TUESDAY, SEPTEMBER 11

.... At 9 P.M., Bush met with his full National Security Council, followed roughly half an hour later by the meeting with a smaller group of key advisers who would become his war cabinet.

Powell, back in Washington from Peru, described the immediate diplomatic tasks: dealing with Afghanistan and its ruling Taliban, which harbored bin Laden, and neighboring Pakistan, which had closer ties to the Taliban regime than any other nation.

"We have to make it clear to Pakistan and Afghanistan this is showtime," Powell said.

"This is a great opportunity," Bush said, adding that the administration now had a chance to improve relations with other countries around the world, including Russia and China. It was more than flushing bin Laden out, he indicated.

Cheney raised the military problem of retaliating against al Qaeda's home base, noting that in Afghanistan, a country decimated by two decades of war, it would be hard to find anything to hit.

Bush returned to the problem of bin Laden's sanctuary in Afghanistan. Tenet said they must deny the terrorists that sanctuary by targeting the Taliban as well. Tell the Taliban we're finished with them, he urged.

Discussion turned to whether bin Laden's al Qaeda network and the Taliban were the same. Tenet said they were. Bin Laden had bought his way into Afghanistan, supplying the Taliban with tens of millions of dollars.

Rumsfeld said the problem was not just bin Laden and al Qaeda but the countries that supported terrorism—the point of the president's address that night.

"We have to force countries to choose," the president said.

11:08 P.M.

The President at the White House: 'We Think It's Bin Laden'

After the meeting had ended and Bush had returned to the residence, he and his wife were awakened by Secret Service agents. The agents rushed them downstairs to the bunker because of a report of an unidentified plane in the area. Bush was in running shorts and a T-shirt as he made his way down the stairs, through the tunnel and into the bunker. It proved to be a false alarm, and the Bushes returned to the residence for the rest of the night.

Like his father, Bush tries to keep a daily diary of his thoughts and observations. That night, he dictated:

"The Pearl Harbor of the 21st century took place today."

"We think it's Osama bin Laden."

"We think there are other targets in the United States, but I have urged the country to go back to normal."

"We cannot allow a terrorist thug to hold us hostage. My hope is that this will provide an opportunity for us to rally the world against terrorism."

From Dan Balz and Bob Woodward, "America's Chaotic Road to War," *Washington Post* (January 27, 2002), A1.

Dan Balz and Bob Woodward are reporters for the *Washington Post*.

WEDNESDAY, SEPTEMBER 12

. . . In the first hours after the terrorist attacks on Sept. 11, Bush and his top advisers had been preoccupied with the crisis at hand, assessing additional threats, grounding airplanes, moving government officials to safety, mobilizing emergency rescue crews, measuring the scope of the devastation in New York and Washington, determining who might be responsible. Now, on the day after, they began to turn their attention more systematically to the U.S. response. . . .

Just before 8 A.M., CIA Director George J. Tenet and a top aide arrived at the White House for the president's daily intelligence briefing. Vice President Cheney and national security adviser Condoleezza Rice joined them in the Oval Office.

Bush's father, the former president and former CIA director in the Ford administration, had once told him that the morning intelligence briefing was one of the most important things he would do every day as president.

As a new president without significant foreign policy experience, Bush had taken intelligence seriously from the start of his administration and invited Tenet for regular 20- to 30-minute sessions most mornings. It was a departure from the previous administration, when President Bill Clinton used to receive his briefing in writing.

Tenet's briefing for Bush this morning included a review of available intelligence tracing the attacks to bin Laden and his top associates in al Qaeda. One report out of Kandahar, the spiritual home of the Taliban, showed the attacks were "the results of two years' planning." Another report said the attacks were "the beginning of the wrath"—an ominous note. Several reports specifically identified Capitol Hill and the White House as targets on Sept. 11. One said a bin Laden associate—erroneously—"gave thanks for the explosion in the Congress building."

A key figure in the bin Laden financing organization called Wafa initially claimed "the White House has been destroyed," before having to correct himself. Another report showed that al Qaeda members in Afghanistan had said at 9:53 A.M. Sept. 11, shortly after the Pentagon was hit, that the attackers were following through with "the doctor's program." The second-ranking member of bin Laden's organization was Ayman Zawahiri, an Egyptian physician often referred to as "the doctor," as was another Chechen al Qaeda leader.

A central piece of evidence involved Abu Zubayda, identified early as the chief field commander of the October 2000 attack on the Navy destroyer USS Cole that killed 17 sailors in the Yemeni port of Aden. One of the most ruthless members of bin Laden's inner circle, Zubayda, according to a reliable report received after the terrorist attacks, had referred to "zero hour."

In addition, the CIA and the FBI had evidence of connections between at least three of the 19 hijackers, bin Laden and his training camps in Afghanistan.

For Tenet, the evidence on bin Laden was conclusive—game, set, match. He then turned to the agency's capabilities on the ground in Afghanistan.

As the president knew, the CIA had had covert relationships in Afghanistan authorized first in 1998 by Clinton and then reaffirmed later by Bush. The CIA was giving several million dollars a year in assistance to the Northern Alliance, the loose amalgam of opposition forces in the northern part of the country that had been fighting with the ruling Taliban. The CIA also had contact with tribal leaders in southern Afghanistan. And the agency had secret paramilitary teams that had been going in and out of Afghanistan without detection for years.

Over the past few months, as part of the administration's review of its policy on terrorism, Tenet, along with Rice and other officials, had been working on a plan to vastly expand covert action in Afghanistan and throughout the world. Tenet told Bush an even more expanded plan would soon be presented for approval, and it would be expensive. Tenet said CIA paramilitary teams would be able to provide indispensable assistance to any U.S. ground forces that might follow.

"Whatever it takes," the president said. . . .

9:30 A.M.
IN THE CABINET ROOM: CONFIDENCE, DETERMINATION

Bush convened his National Security Council in the Cabinet Room and declared that the time for reassuring the nation was over.

The enemy, he said, "hides in shadows and runs." The United States would use all its resources to find this enemy, but it would entail "a different kind of war than our nation has ever fought." He said he was confident that if the administration developed a logical and coherent plan, the rest of the world "will rally to our side." At the same time, he said, he was determined not to allow the threat of terrorism to alter the way Americans lived their lives. "We have to prepare the public," he said, "without alarming the public."

FBI Director Robert S. Mueller III began to describe the investigation underway to identify those responsible for hijacking the four airplanes the day before. Mueller said it was essential not to taint any evidence gathered so that if accomplices were arrested, they could be convicted.

But Attorney General John D. Ashcroft interrupted him. Let's stop the discussion right here, he said. The chief mission of U.S. law enforcement, he added, is to stop another attack and apprehend any accomplices or terrorists before they hit us again. If we can't bring them to trial, so be it.

The president had made clear to Ashcroft in an earlier conversation that he wanted to make sure an attack like the ones on the Pentagon and World Trade Center never happened again. Now, Ashcroft was saying, the focus of the FBI and the Justice Department should change from prosecution to prevention, a fundamental shift in priorities.

"It was made very clear to me" by Bush, Ashcroft said in an interview, "that we had a responsibility to do everything in our power and to find ways to do those things that we might not otherwise think there are ways to do, to curtail the likelihood, to reduce the risks, to prevent this from happening again."

"My instruction was this: We've got to think outside the box. . . . We can't think outside the Constitution, but outside the box. . . . If there's a question between protecting a source and protecting the American people, we burn the source and we protect the American people. That's just the way it has to be."

After he finished with the NSC, Bush continued meeting with a smaller group of senior administration officials—the half-dozen principals, including the vice president and the secretaries of state and defense who formed the war cabinet, without most of their deputies and aides.

Secretary of State Colin L. Powell said the State Department was ready to carry the president's message—you're either with us or you're not—to Pakistan and the Taliban.

Bush responded that he wanted a list of demands for the Taliban. "Handing over bin Laden is not enough," he told Powell. He wanted the whole al Qaeda organization handed over or kicked out.

Rumsfeld interjected. "It is critical how we define goals at the start, because that's what the coalition signs on for," he said. Other countries would want precise definitions. "Do we focus on bin Laden and al Qaeda or terrorism more broadly?" he asked rhetorically.

"The goal is terrorism in its broadest sense," Powell said, "focusing first on the organization that acted yesterday."

"To the extent we define our task broadly," Cheney said, "including those who support terrorism, then we get at states. And it's easier to find them than it is to find bin Laden."

"Start with bin Laden," Bush said, "which Americans expect. And then if we succeed, we've struck a huge blow and can move forward." He called the threat "a cancer" and added, "We don't want to define [it] too broadly for the average man to understand."

Bush pressed Rumsfeld on what the military could do immediately.

"Very little, effectively," the secretary replied.

Bush told his advisers what he had told [British Prime Minister Tony] Blair—that above all he wanted military action that would hurt the terrorists, not just make Americans feel better. He understood the need for planning and preparation but said his patience had limits. "I want to get moving," he said.

Powell drew an obvious conclusion from the president's words. "Focus is on winning the war," he scribbled on his pad.

When Bush posed the question of what military action could be taken immediately, Gen. Henry H. Shelton, chairman of the Joint Chiefs of Staff, later told others that he recalled feeling that the president might be heading down the same path that the Clinton administration had followed: Strike quickly, but with no follow-through.

Shelton, just three weeks away from retirement, knew there were two important problems in formulating a response. First was geography: The United States had no bases close to Afghanistan. Any large-scale military strike would entail multiple in-flight refuelings for helicopters or aircraft involved in an operation. The second problem was al Qaeda, a guerrilla organization whose members lived in caves, operated with mules and large sport-utility vehicles, and presented few desirable targets. Their training camps were mostly empty. Airstrikes might destroy a few buildings or tents but also send the message that the United States was looking to fight terrorism on the cheap.

Shelton was relieved as he rather quickly realized Bush was not looking for an easy or obvious response, not demanding military options on his desk by the next day.

Bush said he knew some of the generals might have had reservations about him. "I think General Shelton wasn't sure about the commander in chief at this point in time," Bush said last month. "He was a little uncertain as to whether or not we were going to create expectations for him that he couldn't live up to."

Bush said he knew the military would resist committing forces to an ill-defined mission. But he also believed he needed to push the Pentagon to think differently about how to fight this war. "They had yet to be challenged to think on how to fight a guerrilla war using conventional means," he said. "They had come out from an era of strike from afar—you know, cruise missiles into the thing."

Shelton, though he would soon be gone, was part of a national security team notable for its experience. Cheney was a former secretary of defense, White House chief of staff and leader in the House. Powell had served as national security adviser and as chairman of the Joint Chiefs of Staff and, like Cheney, was an architect of the Persian Gulf War during the administration of Bush's father. Rumsfeld had been White House chief of staff and secretary of defense in Gerald Ford's administration a quarter-century earlier. Tenet was serving as CIA director under his second president. Rice had been a Russia specialist on the NSC staff in the first Bush administration. Ashcroft was a former state attorney general, governor and senator. Mueller was a highly respected former prosecutor.

But for all the experience around the table, this was a team that had not fully lived up to expectations. Cheney had struggled, particularly early in the admin-

istration, not to appear to be overshadowing his boss. His true role—the power behind the throne or simply the sage, confidential adviser—remained a mystery to outsiders. Rumsfeld had irritated lawmakers on Capitol Hill and many of his senior military officers at the department with his brusque and sometimes secretive style of management. Powell suffered from perceptions, fair or not, that he had been pushed to the edges of the new administration, a view encapsulated by a headline on the cover of the Sept. 10 Time magazine: "Where have you gone, Colin Powell?"

Rice and Tenet had become presidential confidants but were little known to the public. Ashcroft, attacked for his conservative views, had survived a bitter confirmation battle in the Senate, while Mueller had taken over the FBI just one week before the attacks.

The biggest unknown of all was Bush himself. He had come to the presidency with little foreign policy experience, and his early actions on global climate change and national missile defense had rattled U.S. allies in Europe. America's friends feared the administration was infected with a new strain of unilateralism, a go-it-alone attitude of looking inward rather than engaging the world as the lone superpower might be expected to do. . . .

At 4 P.M., the NSC reconvened. Bush reviewed the draft statement, which now said that the goal was to "eliminate terrorism as a threat to our way of life, including terrorist organizations, networks, finances and access to weapons of mass destruction."

Bush said it was inadequate. It's not just us, he said, referring to the "our way of life" phrase, but a cause on behalf of all our friends and allies around the world. He wanted the statement to capture that idea. Others suggested making it read, "our way of life and U.S. interests."

"That still doesn't get it," Bush said.

What about "and to all nations that love freedom," he said.

Not surprisingly, the president's language was adopted.

However, the statement left unanswered some important questions, which then dominated much of the discussion during the afternoon meeting. One was how broadly to define the mission. Who or what was the real target of a war on terrorism? The second was the role of an international coalition. The country's principal reference point was the 1991 Gulf War launched by Bush's father, but the president believed—and others shared his view—that this war and, therefore, this coalition would have to be different.

As the meeting continued, Rumsfeld hammered on a point he had made before. He asked, "Are we going against terrorism more broadly than just al Qaeda? Do we want to seek a broader basis for support?"

Bush said his instinct was to start with bin Laden. If they could strike a blow against al Qaeda, everything that followed would be made easier. But Rumsfeld worried that a coalition built around the goal of taking out al Qaeda would fall apart once they succeeded in that mission, making it more difficult to continue the war on terrorism elsewhere.

Powell argued that it would be far easier initially to rally the world behind the specific target of al Qaeda. They could win approval of a broad U.N. resolution by keeping it focused on al Qaeda.

Cheney again focused on the question of state sponsorship of terrorism. To strike a blow against terrorism inevitably meant targeting the countries that nurture and export it, he said. In some ways the states were easier targets than the shadowy terrorists.

Bush worried about making their initial target too diffuse. Let's not make the target so broad that it misses the point and fails to draw support from normal Americans, he said. What Americans were feeling, he added, was that the country had suffered at the hands of al Qaeda.

As the discussion turned to the shape of the international coalition, several things became clearer. Everyone believed that a coalition would be essential, particularly to keep international opinion behind the United States. But Bush was prepared, if necessary, to go it alone. The United States had an absolute right to defend itself, he believed, no matter what others thought; although he believed that the rightness of the cause would bring other nations along.

Cheney argued that the coalition should be a means to wiping out terrorism, not an end in itself—a view that others shared. They wanted support from the rest of the world, but they did not want the coalition to tie their hands: The mission should define the coalition, not the other way around.

In that case, Rumsfeld argued, they wanted coali-

tion partners truly committed to the cause, not reluctant participants. Powell offered what a colleague later described as the "variable geometry" of coalition-building. The coalition should be as broad as possible, but the requirements for participation would vary country by country. This would entail, as Rumsfeld put it, a coalition of coalitions.

Rumsfeld then raised the question of Iraq, which he had mentioned in the morning meeting. Why shouldn't we go against Iraq, not just al Qaeda? he asked. Rumsfeld was not just speaking for himself when he raised the question. His deputy, Paul Wolfowitz, was even more committed to a policy that would make Iraq a principal target of the first round in the war on terrorism and would continue to press his case. Arrayed against the policy was the State Department, led by Powell, and among those who agreed with him was Shelton, chairman of the Joint Chiefs.

Everyone around the table believed that Iraqi President Saddam Hussein was a menace, a leader bent on acquiring and perhaps using weapons of mass destruction. Any serious, full-scale war against terrorism would have to make Iraq a target—eventually. The issue Rumsfeld raised was whether they should take advantage of the opportunity offered by the terrorist attacks to go after Hussein immediately.

Powell countered that they were focused on al Qaeda because the American people were focused on al Qaeda, and the president agreed. "Any action needs public support," Powell said. "It's not just what the international coalition supports; it's what the American people want to support. The American people want us to do something about al Qaeda."

Bush made clear it was not the time to resolve the issue. And he underscored again that his principal goal was to produce a military plan that would inflict real pain and destruction on the terrorists.

"I don't want a photo-op war," he told his advisers. He also wanted "a realistic scorecard" and "a list of thugs" who would be targeted. Everyone was thinking about the Gulf War, he said, which was the wrong analogy. "The American people want a big bang," he said. "I have to convince them that this is a war that will be fought with many steps."

Although they were moving quickly, Bush was still impatient. In the December interview, he said that he recalled the problems of Vietnam as the U.S. military fought a conventional war against a guerrilla enemy and that he "instinctively knew that we were going to have to think differently" about how to fight terrorists. "The military strategy was going to take awhile to unfold," he said. "I became frustrated. . . ."

THURSDAY, SEPTEMBER 13 2 P.M.
MAKING KEY DECISIONS:
'THIS IS WAR. DO IT.'

At the National Security Council meeting that afternoon in the Situation Room, the president said he was going to approve the CIA proposal to give paramilitary and financial support to the Northern Alliance.

"I'd like to tell you what we told the Pakistanis today," Powell said, getting out a copy of the seven demands he had presented to them. He knew the president didn't like to sit still for long readings, but he was proud of what they had done, unencumbered by a long interagency debate. So he read them aloud. When he finished, Powell reported that Musharraf had already accepted all of them.

"It looks like you got it all," the president said. He thought it was the State Department at its best, no striped-pants formality.

"Can I have a copy of that?" some of the others asked. Treasury Secretary Paul H. O'Neill reported on the effort to go after the finances of the terrorists. In early, pre-Sept. 11 deliberations about what to do with bin Laden during the spring and summer, Treasury officials had resisted efforts to go after terrorists' financial assets and there was continuing institutional resistance to imposing sanctions.

Bush noted that some bureaucrats were nervous about this new authority but dismissed concerns that the moves might be unsettling to the international financial order. "This is war, this isn't peace. Do it," he said. "He [bin Laden] needs money and we need to know whoever is giving him money and deal with them."

Shelton continued to offer a pessimistic assessment of the immediate military options. The contingency plans on the shelf were only cruise missiles against training camps. "It's just digging holes," he said.

Rumsfeld said they needed new tasks for the military if they wanted to go after states harboring bin Laden. "We've never done that before," he said.

Bush was concerned that the meetings with his national security advisers were too much on the fly, sometimes lasting 90 minutes or an hour, sometimes much less. Bush's time was being chopped into small pieces to accommodate the demands of both his private and public roles in the crisis. They had not had time to chew on the issue the way he wanted, so he asked his advisers to come to Camp David with their spouses that weekend, in the hope that a day together at the presidential retreat in Maryland would give them the setting and the time to talk at greater length and in more detail about what they wanted to do.

"This is a new world," Bush said insistently. "General Shelton should go back to the generals for new targets. Start the clock. This is an opportunity. I want a plan—costs, time. I need options on the table. I want Afghan options by Camp David. I want decisions quick."

Rumsfeld was trying to push the Pentagon, and he applauded Bush's decisiveness and sense of urgency. But he reminded the president of the embarrassments of some earlier attacks—the bombing of the Chinese Embassy in Belgrade during the 1999 Kosovo conflict or the missile attack on the Sudan chemical plant in 1998 that was part of the unsuccessful operation on bin Laden in Afghanistan.

"We owe you what can go wrong," Rumsfeld said, "things that can take wind out of our sails. For example, hitting camps with no people."

"Tell the Afghans to round up al Qaeda," Bush said. "Let's see them, or we'll hit them hard. We're going to hurt them bad so that everyone in the world sees, don't deal with bin Laden. I don't want to put a million-dollar missile on a five-dollar tent."

A note-taker at the meeting wrote down snatches of dialogue that captured the sense of urgency.

"We need new options," Rumsfeld said at one point. "This is a new mission."

The president seemed to agree. "Everything is on the table," Bush said. "Look at the options."

The president also told his military advisers that the British really wanted to participate. "Give them a role," he said.

"Time is of the essence," Bush said. "By the time we get to Camp David, we need a clear timetable for action—but I want to do something effective. . . ."

SATURDAY, SEPTEMBER 15

CIA Director George J. Tenet arrived at Camp David with a briefcase stuffed with top-secret documents and plans, in many respects the culmination of more than four years of work on Osama bin Laden, the al Qaeda network and worldwide terrorism.

The briefing packet he handed to President Bush and other members of the war cabinet carried a cover sheet entitled "Going to War." In the upper left corner was a picture of bin Laden inside a red circle. A red slash was superimposed over his face in the CIA's adaptation of the universal symbol of warning and prohibition.

Bush had assembled his advisers in Laurel Lodge at the 125-acre presidential retreat in the Catoctin Mountains of Maryland for a day of intensive discussions about how to respond to the attacks of Sept. 11. They had been conferring regularly but mostly in short meetings. This session would give them a chance to talk at length without interruption and to revisit some of the questions they had been wrestling with the past four days.

Tenet was just one of several advisers called on to offer ideas and options on a day designed more for deliberation and recommendations than presidential decision. But Tenet's 30-minute presentation, an expanded version of what he had told Bush and the war cabinet on Sept. 13, sketched the architecture of what the president was looking for: a worldwide campaign on terrorism with an opening phase focused on bin Laden, al Qaeda and the Taliban regime in Afghanistan.

Tenet brought with him a detailed master plan for covert war in Afghanistan and a top-secret "Worldwide Attack Matrix" outlining a clandestine anti-terror campaign in 80 countries around the world. What he was ready to propose represented a striking and risky departure for U.S. policy and would give the CIA the broadest and most lethal authority in its history.

Another option discussed by Bush's advisers during the week—a military campaign against Iraq—also

would be considered at Camp David. But at a key moment, when asked by Bush, four of his five top advisers would recommend that Iraq not be included in an initial round of military strikes.

Seated around a large table in the wood-paneled conference room, Bush and his advisers were informally dressed, many wearing jackets because of the chilly temperatures that morning. Bush was flanked on his right by Vice President Cheney and his left by Secretary of State Colin L. Powell, with Secretary of Defense Donald H. Rumsfeld next to Powell.

Bush had recorded his weekly radio address from the same cabin earlier in the day, and conferred with Chief of Staff Andrew H. Card Jr. and national security adviser Condoleezza Rice. At 9:19 A.M. he invited reporters into the conference room for a few questions. He was pointing toward war but deliberately circumspect about what he intended to do—and when.

"This is an administration that will not talk about how we gather intelligence, how we know what we're going to do, nor what our plans are," he said. "When we move, we will communicate with you in an appropriate manner. We're at war."

The morning agenda called for a series of presentations, with each followed by a period of freewheeling discussion—sometimes brief, sometimes lengthy, other times focused, in many cases quite unfocused. By the end of the morning, the unstructured format sometimes seemed to leave the president's team even farther from consensus.

9:30 A.M.
TENET MAKES THE CASE FOR WIDER CIA ROLE

The session began with a prayer, followed by the first presentations—from Powell and Treasury Secretary Paul H. O'Neill. Powell talked about the international coalition, with special emphasis on Pakistan. O'Neill reviewed Treasury's efforts to develop a plan to attack al Qaeda's financial assets.

Then came Tenet with his professionally packaged briefing papers. He flipped past the cover to the first page, which read, "Initial Hook: Destroying al Qaeda, Closing the safe haven." The haven was Afghanistan.

Then he went methodically, page by page, through the briefing material, providing for the president and the others the basic covert-action foundation for an unconventional war on terrorism.

It would start with a half-dozen small CIA paramilitary teams on the ground in Afghanistan. They could eventually link up with military Special Forces units, who would bring firepower and technology to aid the opposition fighters in Afghanistan. The plan called for intelligence-sharing with other nations and a full-scale attack on the financial underpinnings of the terrorist network, plus covert operations across the globe.

At the heart of the proposal was a recommendation that the president give the CIA what Tenet labeled "exceptional authorities" to attack and destroy al Qaeda in Afghanistan and the rest of the world. Tenet wanted a broad, general intelligence order that would allow the CIA to conduct the necessary covert operations without having to come back for formal approval for each specific operation. Tenet said he needed the new authority to allow the agency to operate without restraint—and he wanted encouragement from the president to take risks.

Tenet had with him a draft of a presidential intelligence order that would give the CIA power to use the full range of covert instruments, including deadly force.

For more than two decades, the CIA had simply modified previous presidential findings to obtain formally its authority for counterterrorism. Tenet's new proposal, technically called a Memorandum of Notification, was presented as a modification to the worldwide counterterrorism intelligence finding signed on May 12, 1986, by President Ronald Reagan. As if symbolically erasing the more recent past, it superseded five such memoranda signed by President Bill Clinton.

Another proposal was that the CIA increase liaison work with key foreign intelligence services. Tenet hoped to obtain the assistance of these agencies with some of the hundreds of millions of dollars in new funding he was seeking. Using such intelligence services as surrogates could triple or quadruple the CIA's effectiveness.

Like much of the world of covert activity, these kinds of arrangements carried risks: It would put the United States in league with questionable agencies, some with dreadful human rights records. Some of these intelligence services had a reputation for ruthlessness and they used torture to obtain confessions. Tenet acknowledged that these were not people you were likely to be sitting next to in church on Sunday.

Tenet also said the United States already had a "large asset base," given the work the CIA had been doing in countries near Afghanistan.

The unmanned Predator surveillance aircraft that was now armed with Hellfire missiles had been operating for more than a year out of Uzbekistan to provide real-time video of Afghanistan. It could be used to kill bin Laden and his key lieutenants from the air—a major focus of what Tenet now proposed. In addition, he said, the United States should seek to work closely with Tajikistan, Turkmenistan and Pakistan to stop the travel of al Qaeda leaders and "close all border crossings" to them. Tenet called for initiating intelligence contact with some rogue states that he said might be helpful in trying to destroy al Qaeda.

A key portion of Tenet's briefing covered operations inside Afghanistan, and here he presented in more detail how the Northern Alliance, the loose amalgam of forces that had been fighting the Taliban for years, could be used. The CIA believed the alliance was potentially a powerful force but was desperate for money, weapons and intelligence. Tenet advocated substantially stepping up "direct support of the Northern Alliance," a proposal the president had said he would approve. U.S. ground forces could then link up with the Northern Alliance fighters.

Operationally, Tenet envisioned a strategy to create "a northern front, closing the safe haven." His idea was that Afghan opposition forces, aided by the United States, would move first against the northern city of Mazar-e Sharif, try to break the Taliban's grip on that city and open up the border with Uzbekistan. From there the campaign could move to other cities in the north, he said.

The CIA director also described a role for the opposition tribes in the southern part of Afghanistan, groups hostile to the northern opposition forces but crucial to a campaign against al Qaeda and the Taliban. Tenet said the CIA had begun working with a number of tribal leaders in the south the previous year. Some would try to play on both sides, he said, but once the war began, they could be enticed by money, food, ammunition and supplies to join the U.S.-led campaign.

On the financial front, Tenet called for clandestine computer surveillance and electronic eavesdropping to locate the assets of al Qaeda and other terrorist groups, with a particular focus on the charitable groups that were a critical element in bin Laden's funding.

Tenet then turned to another top-secret document, called the "Worldwide Attack Matrix," which described covert operations in 80 countries that were either underway or that he was now recommending. The actions ranged from routine propaganda to lethal covert action in preparation for military attacks. Included were efforts to disrupt terrorist plots or attacks in countries in Asia, the Middle East and Africa. In some countries, CIA teams would break into facilities to obtain information.

Because the CIA had been working aggressively against terrorism for years, Tenet said, the agency had done extensive target development and network analysis. What it needed was money and flexibility—so the CIA could move quickly, even instantly, if it discovered terrorist targets—and broad authority.

Rumsfeld was enthusiastic about what Tenet laid out that morning, despite potential friction between the CIA and the Pentagon over roles and responsibilities in any military campaign. "I was convinced we had to get people on the ground," Rumsfeld said in an interview. "And to the extent the CIA had relationships or could develop relationships that would facilitate that, [then] that would be critically important."

"Rumsfeld understood the utility of having the CIA involved," the president said in an interview last month. "I think he quickly grasped what I grasped. . . . It was near unanimity on the immediate plan for Afghanistan, which was to mate up our assets with the Northern Alliance troops."

When the CIA director finished his presentation, Bush left no doubt what he thought of it, virtually shouting with enthusiasm: "Great job."

After a break, Bush turned to Robert S. Mueller III, who had taken over as FBI director the week before the attacks.

Mueller, a former federal prosecutor, had spent years working on the 1988 terrorist bombing of Pan Am Flight 103. He knew that the worst thing that could happen to an FBI director was to have a major domestic terrorist incident on his watch. The second thing he knew was that he had not prepared a presentation. He had been shocked that he had been invited to the Camp David war-planning session and expected to be called on somewhat later, if at all.

Not used to the company and slightly intimidated by the presence of the nation's top leadership, Mueller soon found himself giving a routine summary of the investigation into the four Sept. 11 hijackings. He told other FBI officials afterward that he was so unhappy with his own performance that he brought his remarks to an early close. At least one of the president's advisers concluded that the FBI was still too focused on prosecuting terrorists and not on preventing them from acting.

Attorney General John D. Ashcroft provided an update to the group on his efforts to develop a legislative package to expand the powers of law enforcement to fight terrorism. He outlined a two-phase strategy, aimed first at "immediate disruption and prevention of terrorism" and followed by longer-term efforts to put terrorists "off keel." Ashcroft warned that it was "important to disrupt" the terrorists now, but added, "We need to remember these are patient people," noting that eight years passed between the two attacks on the World Trade Center. The administration needed a new long-term strategy, he said, "because that's the kind of strategy they have in place."

The final presentation of the morning came from Gen. Henry H. Shelton, chairman of the Joint Chiefs of Staff, who had also brought a big briefcase to Camp David. Bush had ordered the Pentagon to come to the meeting with plenty of options, and Shelton was prepared to talk about military action against both Afghanistan and, if pressed, Iraq, although he opposed that step then. But as the day developed, he discussed only three options, all aimed at Afghanistan.

The first called for a strike with cruise missiles, a plan the military could execute quickly if speed was the president's overriding priority. The missiles could be launched by Navy ships or Air Force planes from hundreds of miles away. The targets included al Qaeda's training camps.

The problem, Shelton said, was that the camps were virtually empty and therefore the missile attacks would not be that effective. Clearly, Shelton was not enamored of this idea, nor were the others. Bush had brushed off the possibility from Day One that his response would be an antiseptic "pinprick" attack.

Option Two combined cruise missiles with manned bomber attacks. Shelton said Bush could initially choose a strike lasting three or four days or something longer, maybe up to 10 days. The targets included al Qaeda training camps and some Taliban targets, depending on whether the president wanted to go after the Taliban militarily at the start. But this too had limits. As Cheney had said the first night of the crisis, there were few high-value targets in Afghanistan, a country devastated by two decades of war. Another disadvantage was that it could reinforce perceptions that the United States wanted a largely risk-free war on terrorism.

Shelton described the third and most robust option as cruise missiles, bombers and what the planners like to call "boots on the ground." This option included all the elements of the second option along with U.S. Special Forces, the elite commandos, and possibly the Army and Marines being deployed inside Afghanistan. But he said it would take a minimum of 10 to 12 days just to get initial forces on the ground—in reality it took far longer—because bases and overflight rights would be needed for search-and-rescue teams to bring out any downed pilots.

If there was already a consensus to go to war, the discussions that followed many of the morning's presentations underscored to the participants the complexity and uncertainty of their undertaking.

Bush and his team faced a far different situation than Bush's father, George H.W. Bush, had 11 years earlier, after Iraq had invaded Kuwait in 1990. On Saturday, Aug. 4, 1990, again at Camp David and in the same lodge, Gen. Norman Schwarzkopf, then commander of the Central Command, had presented a detailed, off-the-shelf proposal for military action. It was called Operations Plan 90–1002, and it was the basic military plan that would be executed over the next seven months to oust Iraq from Kuwait.

In the case of Afghanistan, a military plan would have to be devised quickly, once the president made decisions about the shape of the war, the initial focus of the campaign and the relationship between the CIA and the Pentagon.

Based on the recollections of many of the participants and some notes taken at the meeting, the topics that morning included the politics of the region— Afghanistan and the surrounding countries; the shaping of a coalition; the need to think unconventionally about fighting the war; and whether Iraq should be included in the war's first phase.

At one point, as they discussed the inherent risks of any operation in Afghanistan, someone said this was not likely to be like the Balkans, where ethnic hatreds had occupied the Clinton administration for most of its tenure. Rice said the problems of Afghanistan and the surrounding region were so complicated, "We're going to wish this was the Balkans."

The ideal result from this campaign, the president said, would be to kick terrorists out of some places like Afghanistan and through that action persuade other countries that had supported terrorism in the past, such as Iran, to change their behavior.

Powell noted that everyone in the international coalition was ready to go after al Qaeda, but that extending the war to other terrorist groups or countries could cause some of them to drop out.

The president said he didn't want other countries dictating terms or conditions for the war on terrorism. "At some point," the president said, "we may be the only ones left. That's okay with me. We are America."

Powell didn't reply, but going it alone was precisely what he wanted to avoid if possible. In Powell's view, the president's formulation was not realistic. The United States could not launch an effective war in Afghanistan or worldwide without a coalition. He believed the president made such statements knowing they might not withstand a second analysis. The tough talk might be necessary but it was not policy.

In contrast, Cheney took the president at his word, and was convinced the president was absolutely serious when he said they would go it alone if necessary.

Rumsfeld raised another problem. Although everyone agreed that destroying al Qaeda was the first priority, singling out bin Laden, particularly by the president, would elevate bin Laden the way Iraqi President Saddam Hussein had been elevated during the Gulf War.

Rumsfeld told the others the worst thing they could do in such a situation was to misstate their objective. It would not be effective to succeed in your objective of removing or killing bin Laden or Taliban leader Mohammad Omar without solving the basic problem of terrorism. Vilification of bin Laden could rob the United States of its ability to frame this as a larger war.

Another puzzle to the group was the Taliban itself. The Taliban clearly would be pressured in hopes that it would break with al Qaeda and perhaps give up bin Laden. Few thought this was likely, but they agreed they had to make the effort. Some of Bush's advisers believed the Taliban might fracture, that some faction might break off and help in rounding up bin Laden, but there was no reliable evidence or intelligence to support this notion.

Bush noted that British Prime Minister Tony Blair had suggested giving the Taliban not just an ultimatum but also a deadline.

Several others argued against a deadline; they did not want a deadline to dictate the timing of when to start military action. As Bush had said the previous day at Washington National Cathedral, the military campaign would begin at "an hour of our choosing." During this part of the discussion, Bush said, according to notes of one participant, "I want to give the Taliban a right to turn over al Qaeda; if they don't, there have to be consequences that show the United States is serious."

Afghanistan's history nagged at the president's advisers. Its geography was forbidding and its record of rebuffing outside forces was real. Despite attractive options presented earlier in the morning, several advisers seemed worried. Bush asked his advisers: What are the worst cases out there? What are the real downside risks?

One was triggering chaos in Afghanistan that would spill over into Pakistan. This was seen as a great danger by many, particularly Rice and Cheney. Afghanistan was already a mess, Cheney noted. If Pakistan went, then you have unleashed a whole other set of demons. He was worried that Pakistan's choice to support the United States could lead to internal unrest that might bring down the government—and give Islamic fundamentalists access to Pakistan's nuclear weapons.

The discussion highlighted the critical importance of Pakistan's president, Gen. Pervez Musharraf, who,

everyone now understood, was the most important barrier between stability and a worst-case scenario. Have the Pakistanis fully thought through the risks of supporting the United States, Bush asked.

Powell said he believed they had. First, Musharraf had seen how serious the administration was about terrorism. Second, he said, the general realizes he has gradually been losing control of his country, and he may see this as an opportunity to stop the slide into extremism. Musharraf did not want Pakistan to turn into a rogue state, Powell believed. He wanted a more secular, westernized country.

President Musharraf is taking a tremendous risk, the president said. We need to make it worth his while. We should help him with a number of things, including nuclear security. Put together a package of support for Pakistan, he directed.

Another risk they faced was getting bogged down in Afghanistan. Rice knew it had been the nemesis of the British in the 19th century and the Soviets in the 20th. She wondered whether it might be the same for the United States in the 21st.

These fears were shared by others, which led to a different discussion: Should they think about launching military action elsewhere as an insurance policy in case things in Afghanistan went bad? They would need successes early in any war to maintain domestic and international support. Rice asked whether they could envision a successful military campaign beyond Afghanistan.

In this context, the issue of Iraq once again was on the table. The full sequence is not clear from the recollections and notes of several key participants. But all agree that the Iraq strategy's principal advocate in the group was Deputy Defense Secretary Paul Wolfowitz. He had been the department's third-ranking official under Cheney during the Gulf War and believed that the abrupt and incomplete end to the ground campaign, with Hussein still in power, had been a mistake.

The Bush administration had been seeking to undermine Hussein from the start, with Wolfowitz pushing efforts to aid opposition groups and Powell seeking support for a new set of sanctions. Rumsfeld and Wolfowitz had been examining military options in Iraq for months but nothing had emerged. The fear was that Hussein was still attempting to develop weapons of mass destruction, and without United Nations inspectors in the country, there was no way to know the exact nature of the threat they faced. Wolfowitz argued that the real source of all the trouble and terrorism was probably Hussein. The terrorist attacks of Sept. 11 created an opportunity to strike. Hussein was a bad guy, a dangerous leader bent on obtaining and probably using weapons of mass destruction. He also likely was culpable in the attacks of the previous Tuesday, at least indirectly, and all of them ought to acknowledge it.

Rumsfeld had helped raise the Iraq issue in previous meetings, but not as vehemently as his deputy. Now, Rumsfeld asked again: Is this the time to attack Iraq? He noted that there would be a big buildup of forces, with not that many good targets in Afghanistan. At some point, if the United States was serious about terrorism, it would have to deal with Iraq. Is this the opportunity?

Powell objected. You're going to hear from your coalition partners, he told the president. They're all with you, every one, but they will go away if you hit Iraq. If you get something pinning Sept. 11 on Iraq, great—let's put it out and kick them at the right time. But let's get Afghanistan now. If we do that, we will have increased our ability to go after Iraq—if we can prove Iraq had a role.

Bush let the discussion continue but he had strong reservations about Iraq. He was concerned about two things, which he described in an interview last month. "My theory is you've got to do something and do it well and that . . . if we could prove that we could be successful in this theater, then the rest of the task would be easier," he said. "If we tried to do too many things—two things, for example, or three things—militarily, then . . . the lack of focus would have been a huge risk."

His other concern was one that he did not express to his war cabinet but that he said later was part of his own thinking. He knew that around the table were a number of advisers—Powell, Cheney and Wolfowitz—who had been with his father during the Gulf War deliberations. "And one of the things I wasn't going to allow to happen is, that we weren't going to let their previous experience in this theater dictate a rational course for the new war," the president said.

Bush also noted that, whatever his comments were about Iraq that morning, they seemed to bring the debate to a close. "There wasn't a lot of talk about Iraq in the second [afternoon] round," he said. "The second round of discussion was focused only on Afghanistan, let me put it to you that way."

Wolfowitz had persisted in making his arguments about Iraq and other issues, and had annoyed some of his colleagues by showing up at meetings that were called for principals only—not for deputies. To Card, the president's chief of staff, it seemed as if Wolfowitz was just banging a drum, not providing additional information or new arguments.

At one point during the morning, Wolfowitz interrupted his boss, Rumsfeld, and repeated a point he had made earlier in the discussion. There was an awkward silence around the table. Rumsfeld seemed to ignore the interruption but his eyes narrowed. Some thought he might be annoyed; others thought he was just listening carefully.

Bush flashed a pointed look in Card's direction. During a break in the meeting, the chief of staff took Rumsfeld and Wolfowitz aside.

"The president will expect one person to speak for the Department of Defense," Card said.

12:45 P.M.
AFTER OPEN-ENDED MORNING, GEARING UP FOR 'ACTION SESSION'

Lunch was finally served, and Bush told his advisers that they should take some time to exercise or rest. He said: Then I want everybody back here at 4 o'clock, and I want to hear what you think we ought to do.

Rice was concerned about the apparent lack of focus during the last part of the morning. The National Security Council meetings usually were more structured, with the principals reporting on their departments or agencies, and then together they would work through the problem and come up with options. The morning meeting had started well, but then had become repetitive, unusually freewheeling. She didn't know where the morning discussion had left them.

How are we going to get a plan out of this? she wondered. Have we got anything here? She had listened carefully to the president that morning and she could tell he was heading toward action. He had remarked,

"After today, we'll have a plan of action now," and referred to the session as "an action meeting."

Rice convened the principals—Powell, Rumsfeld, Tenet, Card—without the president. She expressed her concerns to the others. We need to bring more discipline to the discussion in the afternoon, she said.

Powell went back to his cabin, where Alma, his wife, was reading a book. As he saw it, the big questions were still on the table: what to do, when to do it, and do you go after this one thing—al Qaeda and Afghanistan—that they knew was out there, or do you expand the war at this time? Back in the cabin, he sat down in a chair and closed his eyes for half an hour.

Rice went back to her cabin, returned some phone calls and went off to exercise. About 3:45 P.M., she ran into the president outside his cabin. He had worked out on the elliptical machine and lifted weights. Now he told his national security adviser he had a plan for the afternoon. "I'm going to go around the table and I'm going to ask people what they think," the president said. "What do you think about that?" "That's fine," she replied. "Do you want me just to listen?"

"I want you to listen," Bush said.

That was consistent with their usual working arrangement. Rice would listen for him and then offer assessments in private. Her principal role was to help make the decision-making process orderly, to ensure that Bush had received all the information he needed. Every morning about 7:15, she, Powell and Rumsfeld were on the phone together to share information and ideas.

4 P.M.
BACK IN LAUREL LODGE, THE ADVISERS HAVE THEIR SAY

The entire team reconvened in Laurel Lodge. The president said he wanted to hear recommendations from the principals—Powell, Rumsfeld, Tenet, Card and the vice president. Okay, who will start? He looked at Powell.

Powell expected more general discussion but plunged ahead. The focus ought to be on bin Laden and al Qaeda, he said, their camps and their infrastructure. Make them the target. All the states that supported ter-

ror, you can do at a time of your choosing. They are not going anywhere. The coalition and the energy that had been created were directed against Sept. 11.

It looked as if 6,000 people were dead from the World Trade Center and Pentagon attacks (by January, the estimate was down to 3,100). To do anything that did not focus on al Qaeda would not be understood, either by the American people, the coalition or, he argued, international opinion.

If we weren't going after Iraq prior to Sept. 11, why would we be going after them now when the current outrage is not directed at Iraq, Powell asked. Nobody could look at Iraq and say it was responsible for Sept. 11. It was important not to lose focus.

Powell also felt that the Defense Department was overestimating its ability to do two things at the same time from the same command, with the same commander and staff. Military attacks on both Afghanistan and Iraq would be under the jurisdiction of the Central Command, which is responsible for the region that included the Middle East and South Asia.

He didn't make that point, but figured it was his ace in the hole. Powell also noticed that no military plan had been presented for Iraq. No one, neither Rumsfeld nor Wolfowitz, had told the president precisely what should be done in Iraq and how it might be done. Nobody had taken it to the next step and said, This is what we're talking about. The absence of a plan was a gaping hole.

Continuing, Powell said, tell the Taliban, "You're responsible." Be firm with the Taliban's leaders. If they don't act and throw bin Laden and his terrorists out of Afghanistan, then we tell them, "We're going to hold you accountable." The focus should be on military targets. Also, a public case should be made that bin Laden was the guilty one. That was important. Evidence mattered.

Rumsfeld was next. We must not undercut our ability to act over the long term, he said, which meant they should keep thinking about what to do about terrorism in general. Patience was important. Rooting out bin Laden would take very different intelligence than they had. The doctrine of "hit, talk, hit," in which the United States would strike, pause to see the reaction, and then hit again, sounded too much like Vietnam. Rumsfeld said there was a need for unconventional approaches, especially the Special Forces information operations, in gathering intelligence on the ground.

But Rumsfeld, significantly, did not make a recommendation on Iraq.

Tenet attempted to summarize. The plan, he said, should include the elements of strike, strangle, surround and sustain. He mentioned his own plan for a global approach but basically supported the position that the initial military focus should be on Afghanistan.

Card was next. He did not have much foreign policy experience, so he began by speaking generally. "What is the definition of success?" he asked. He said it would first be proving that this was not just an effort to pound sand—as the president had repeatedly made clear. They should demonstrate to the world that the effort was directed at terrorists beyond Afghanistan.

Consideration should be given to contemporaneous actions in other parts of the world—that could be in Indonesia, the Philippines, Malaysia, Yemen or Somalia, he said. This could be covert, not overt military action, though it was important to consider a plan that would demonstrate to the world relatively quickly the worldwide nature of the problem.

Card also said he didn't think the case had been made for Iraq to be a principal target.

Cheney was last and, according to notes from that day, talked the longest and most comprehensively. We need to do everything we can to stop the next attack, he said. Are we being aggressive enough? We need a group now that's going to look at lessons learned from where we've been. And in going after bin Laden we need to consider the broader context. A week ago, before Sept. 11, we were worried about the strength of our whole position in the Middle East—where we stood with the Saudis, the Turks and others in the region. Now they all want to be part of our efforts, and that's an opportunity. We need to reach out for that opportunity.

Building a coalition to take advantage of the opportunities, he said, suggests that this may be a bad time to take on Saddam Hussein in Iraq. We would lose momentum.

Cheney thus joined Powell, Tenet and Card in opposing action on Iraq. Rumsfeld had not committed one way or the other. To anyone keeping a tally, it was 4 to 0 with Rumsfeld abstaining—a heavy body of advice against Iraq.

Still, the vice president expressed deep concern about Hussein and said he was not going to rule out going after Iraq at some point—just not now.

Earlier in the day he told the group, "We've indicted bin Laden, but now we must wage war against him." He said the CIA must push every button it could and said it was also crucial to deal with the charitable organizations that helped finance bin Laden. He recommended strengthening the Northern Alliance in Afghanistan and hitting the Taliban—but not necessarily in a massive way at first. We need to knock out their air defenses and their air power at the start, he said. We need to be ready to put boots on the ground. There are some places only special operations forces will get them, he added. And we need to ask: Do we have the right mix of forces?

Finally, he returned to the question of homeland defense. They must do everything possible to defend, prevent or disrupt the next attack on America, he said. The issue was very worrisome. He had reviewed the work of five government commissions that had recently studied terrorism. The president had assigned him the task of coming up with a homeland security plan back in May. It's not just borders and airline security, but biological and other threats that they had to think about, he said.

Cheney was the last to make any recommendations. There was some additional discussion, including the themes to strike on the Sunday morning talk shows where Cheney, Powell, Rumsfeld and Ashcroft would be appearing. At the end of the meeting, Bush went around the table and thanked everyone. No one was quite certain where things stood.

"I'm going to go think about it and I'll let you know what I've decided," Bush said. Powell and Rumsfeld left Camp David, but most of the others stayed over for dinner and the night. Bush had invited his advisers to bring their spouses, and after dinner that evening someone suggested to Ashcroft, who in the Senate had been a member of a group called the Singing Senators, that he sing some songs.

"I don't want to sing," he said, "but if you'll sing, I'll play."

He sat down at the piano and began playing a number of traditional American melodies, from "Old Man River" and "Nobody Knows the Trouble I've Seen" to "America the Beautiful" and "God Bless America." Rice, herself an accomplished pianist, was the principal vocalist. Bush was at a table nearby, joining in trying to assemble an elaborate wooden jigsaw puzzle.

MONDAY, SEPTEMBER 17

At 9:35 a.m., President Bush and his war cabinet reconvened at the White House. Some of those gathered around the conference table in the Cabinet Room did not know what to expect—perhaps more review and discussion, even more questions or analysis.

When their meeting broke up Saturday afternoon at Camp David, Bush had not made up his mind about the options presented to him that day. But after returning to the White House Sunday, he had told national security adviser Condoleezza Rice what he wanted to do. Now he shared his decision with the other advisers.

"The purpose of this meeting is to assign tasks for the first wave of the war against terrorism," the president said, sitting at the traditional center seat on the window-side. "It starts today. . . ."

PART VIII

CONTROVERSIES

> For reasons that must be left to students of psychology, every President since Kennedy seems to have trusted his White House aides more than his cabinet.
>
> —*Henry K. Kissinger*
> *White House Years,* 1979

EDITORS' INTRODUCTION

In this section of the book, we look more closely at two controversies that have arisen over the performance of the NSC system. The first is related to the ongoing competition for the president's ear between the adviser and the secretary of state—often nothing less than a pitched bureaucratic battle over who will lead America's foreign policy. The second concerns the misappropriation of the NSC staff for questionable operational purposes, manifested in the Iran–*contra* affair during the Reagan Administration. In the more than a half-century history of the NSC, no other single event has been as damaging to the reputation of the Council and its staff as this scandal, which became the object of executive and legislative investigations in 1987. If the Cuban missile crisis was the NSC's finest hour, the Iran–*contra* affair was its worst.

NSC Versus State

First, we take up the conflict between the adviser and the secretary of state. The Iran–*contra* affair is more spectacular, with shredded documents, a long-haired beauty smuggling secret papers out of NSC files, former generals covertly selling arms to terrorists, and a self-promoting Marine lieutenant colonel on the NSC staff creating a supersecret organization ("The Enterprise") to carry out a private foreign policy contrary to the laws of Congress. Nevertheless, the tensions between the adviser and the Department of State have been more enduring and, in the minds of critics, have raised serious questions about the possible ill effects on coherent national security planning of having a competing "mini State Department" within the White House.

Leslie H. Gelb, at the time a *New York Times* editor, with broad experience in the government as well (and later president of the Council on Foreign Relations), has examined the NSC–State problem following Secretary Cyrus Vance's resignation from the Carter Administration (see "Why Not the State Department?" 1980, in For Further Reading). Looking back on the intramural conflicts between Vance and Brzezinski, Gelb is dismayed by the "disarray in American foreign policy" that their disagreements had engendered. The political infighting reflected, he writes, " . . . a replay of the historical struggle between the palace guard and the king's ministers, between any personal staff and the line officers." And at a deeper level, "it was a story about presidents, their wants and needs as they see them."

Gelb notes that virtually every serious observer of the way American foreign policy is conducted ends up recommending that the Department of State should be given the leading role as presidential adviser-in-chief. Moreover, virtually every president vows to adopt this approach. "Yet," Gelb concludes, "none ever followed through and did it." He offers an explanation: ". . . presidents soon find that the State Department—with some exceptions from time to time—does a poor job of framing its proposals in terms that will elicit political support, and it does not think about potential costs to the president . . . The irrepressible ethos of the building is to look outside the United States, not inward." In contrast, the nearness of the NSC staff members to the White House staff and the president gives them a different outlook, one that is more attentive to the president's needs. Gelb continues: ". . . one is far more conscious of presidential stakes and interests when in residence in Pennsylvania Avenue. It is not a question of learning politics, but a matter of being there and knowing specifically what politicians in the White House are thinking of at a particular time."

Though being in the White House has its obvious advantages (as noted by several writers in this volume), Gelb emphasizes that sheer proximity alone is insufficient to guarantee the national security adviser preeminence. No ineluctable force automatically drives the NSC adviser and staff to the forefront, as the examples of strong secretaries of state like Acheson, Dulles, and Kissinger underscore. "The only safe prediction on organization," observes Gelb, "is that however the formal system is constructed, actual power will gravitate to the person whose policy views and style prevail with the president." The Nixon years provide a classic illustration. In his memoirs, Kissinger candidly portrays his rise to power at the expense of Secretary of State William Rogers. "In the Nixon Administration [the normal] preeminent role for the secretary of state was made impossible," Kissinger remembers, "by Nixon's distrust of the State Department bureaucracy, by his relationship with Rogers, by Rogers' inexperience and by my own strong convictions" (Kissinger, 1979: 30).

In the first selection in this part of the book, Bert A. Rockman, a political scientist at Ohio State University, captures the tension between the NSC staff and the Department of State with his emphasis on one word in the title of his selection: "America's *Departments* of State." According to him, "The United States possesses two foreign ministers within the same government, the one who heads the Department of State, and the one who is the assistant to the president for national security affairs." The Department of State is staffed chiefly by "regulars," he observes; that is, men and women—FSOs [Foreign Service Officers]—who are members of a structured career service. In contrast, the NSC staff has a strong component of "irregulars," individuals free from the routine channels of a career service (although many NSC staffers serve on loan from the departments and agencies that deal with foreign, defense, and intelligence policy).

The regulars are, in a word, bureaucrats. The irregulars are "civilians" from outside the government—often from the nation's universities and think tanks. (Fifty-nine percent of the NSC staff under Brzezinski held Ph.D. degrees, Rockman states, compared with less than 8 percent of the FSOs in the State Department at the time.) The irregulars move in and out of the government as opportunities present themselves and administrations change hands. Not surprisingly, the two groups sometimes have different perspectives. The regulars have the kind of detailed knowledge about foreign nations that comes from reading the daily cables from overseas and spending time in service abroad at American embassies. The NSC irregulars, while usually having considerable expertise themselves, also often have good ties with the White House.

Unencumbered by layers of organizational bureaucracy, NSC irregulars are able to communicate quickly with one another in an environment of relatively close-knit physical and ideological proximity. Not that the NSC staff and national security adviser always agree; but the odds favoring harmony are greater between them than between the State Department bureaucrats and the secretary of state, who is as likely to be traveling abroad as tending to internal disputes within Foggy Bottom. "No wonder presidents find their political and policy needs better served from within the White House," Rockman concludes. "From every vantage point, the departments sooner or later are perceived as representing or pursuing interests that are not those of the president. This is especially so for the State Department because it is frequently seen as representing interests of other countries."

Rogue Elephant in the White House

The final articles in this section address the Iran-*contra* affair, which involved the use of the NSC staff for operational purposes. Long before this scandal surfaced in 1986, it was clear that the Reagan Administration had come to rely on the NSC in an operational capacity. The NSC staff orchestrated the plans for several of the president's most dramatic foreign policy activities, such as the response against terrorists who hijacked the passenger ship *Achille Lauro* (this counterterrorism operation was the brainchild of Lt. Col. Oliver North, which gave him added status in the White House to pursue his Iran-*contra* schemes) and the air strike against Libyan leader Muammar Quaddafi. Boasted one NSC staff aide to a *Time* correspondent: "We're the only ones who can make things happen" (Doerner, 1986: 39). That attitude led to the ultimate disorder displayed by the Reagan NSC system: its "rogue elephant" behavior during the Iran-*contra* affair.

The affair gained national notoriety in November 1986 after publication of an article in a Middle East periodical about the covert sale of U.S. arms to Iran. The purpose of the sale was twofold: to curry favor with the regime in Iran in hopes of improving America's relations in this part of the Middle East and—the immediate objective—to solicit Iran's assistant for the release of American hostages held by terrorists in Lebanon (including the CIA's station chief there, William Buckley). Further reports indicated that, through sleight-of-hand by NSC staffer North, the profits from these sales had been diverted to the anticommunist *contras* in Nicaragua. Fragmentary news reports regarding North's relations with the *contras* from his "command post" inside the NSC had appeared as much as a year earlier in the *Christian Science Monitor* and other American newspapers.

The revelations brought sharp criticism from key lawmakers. In the first place, the operation raised serious questions about the adherence of the Reagan Administration to the 1980 Intelligence Accountability Act, as well as the Boland Amendment. Respectively, the two laws required timely reports to Congress on all important covert actions and prohibited the supply of war materiel to the *contras*. Other statutes may have been violated, too, including the Arms Export Control Act and related provisions banning the sale of weapons to terrorist groups (which Iran had been known to support). Legal questions aside, the initiative seemed foolhardy to critics. Was it sensible policy to barter for the release of hostages through the sale of weapons, or (as critics contended) would this simply encourage the taking of more hostages in the future by terrorist organizations that sought additional weaponry?

In response to the criticism, President Reagan established a presidential commission to investigate the allegations. The president selected former U.S. senator John Tower (R–Texas) to chair the blue-ribbon panel, and named as its other two members former U.S. senator and Secretary of State Edmund Muskie (D–Maine) and former NSC adviser Brent Scowcroft. Often, presidential commissions are formed merely as a tactic to appease lawmakers and dampen their ardor for conducting investigations of their own. The Tower Commission carried out a serious inquiry, however, and produced a revealing report on how the NSC had assumed an operational role far beyond its mandate. The next selection is taken from this report, published in February 1987.

"The arms transfers to Iran and the activities of the NSC staff in support of the Contras are case studies in the perils of policy pursued outside the constraints of orderly process," begins the commission in its summary of what went wrong. Side-stepping the issue of whether or not the Boland Amendment applied to the NSC staff, the commission (which refers to itself as "the Board" in this report) emphasizes the political error of the staff's involvement in activities opposed by the Congress. "Even if it could be argued that these [Boland Amendment] restrictions did not technically apply to the NSC staff, these activities presented great political risk to the President," wrote the three commissioners. "The appearance of the President's personal staff doing what Congress had forbade other agencies to do could, once disclosed, only touch off a firestorm in the Congress and threaten the Administration's whole policy on the Contras."

The commission found the NSC decision-making process for the Iran initiative far too casual. The NSC principals barely seemed to have focused on the proposal. Indeed, only the president, the vice president, national security adviser Vice Adm. John Poindexter, his staff aide (North), and White House chief of staff Donald Regan were present at a key meeting (held on January 17, 1986) to discuss the initiative. The president's approval for the arms sale was evidently given only orally, rather than in the usual written "finding," and was communicated only to one person: Poindexter. The commission members found it "difficult to conclude that his [President Reagan's] actions constituted adequate legal authority."

The secretaries of state and defense in the Reagan Administration, as well as their deputies, were kept away from information about the operation, apparently, in the commission's phrase, because of an "obsession with secrecy." The commission notes that Poindexter may even have gone so far as to mislead the secretary of state—not to mention the president, who claims never to have been informed about the diversion of profits to the *contras*. Other departments and agencies normally consulted on important foreign policy initiatives were cut out as well, as the operation quickly evolved into the private preserve of selected CIA officials and the NSC staff. One result was to exclude the usually detailed interagency staff work on a proposal. "This deprived those responsible for the initiative of considerable expertise," the commission states, "—on the situation in Iran; on the difficulties of dealing with terrorists; on the mechanics of conducting a diplomatic opening. It also kept the plan from receiving a tough, critical review." By drawing the circle of secrecy too tightly within the executive branch, the panel concludes, "important advice and counsel were lost."

The Tower Commission—with its two former lawmakers—observes further that "consultation with the Congress could have been useful to the President, for it might have given him some sense of how the public would react to the initiative." Left in the dark, Congress had no opportunity to respond. The secretaries of state and defense were at least aware of the Iranian arms sale, and the commission faults them for failing to take steps that would have reined in Lt. Col. North and the NSC staff involved in the affair.

One of the most troubling developments in the Iran-*contra* scandal was the role assumed by the NSC staff as an operations group. Cut off from other departments and agencies for reasons of secrecy and concern that the Boland Amendment clearly applied to them, the NSC staff— essentially North operating with Poindexter's authority—turned to a private network of businesspeople, wealthy financial contributions (here and abroad), former U.S. military officers, and outside mercenaries, as well as a few CIA officers, to carry out the Iran-*contra* activities. "Some of these were individuals with questionable credentials and potentially large personal financial interests in the transactions," the Tower Commission reports. "This made the transactions unnecessarily complicated and invited kickbacks and payoffs." In understatement, the commission labels this privatization of foreign policy "unprofessional." The commission found fault especially with the NSC staff for not refusing to be drawn into operational activities or to seek full legal counsel regarding its proper role (if any) in the Iran arms sale and support for the *contras*.

Though the criticism of Poindexter and North was well deserved, the Tower Commission was careful to trace the ultimate responsibility back to another individual: the chief executive of the United States. "The NSC system will not work unless the President makes it work," the commissioners emphasized. ". . . . By his actions, by his leadership, the President therefore determines the quality of its performance." They continued:

> [The President] . . . did not force his policy to undergo the most critical review of which the NSC participants and the process were capable. At no time did he insist upon accountability and performance review. Had the President chosen to drive the NSC system, the outcome could well have been different. As it was, the most powerful features of the NSC system—providing comprehensive analysis, alternatives and follow-up—were not utilized.

The president, the commission concluded, "must insist upon accountability." Scowcroft later observed: "The problem at the heart was one of people, not of process . . . It was not that the structure was faulty, but that the structure was not used."

In the wake of the Tower Commission inquiry came a joint House–Senate investigation chaired by Senator Daniel Inouye (D–Hawaii) and Lee H. Hamilton (D–Indiana)—the Inouye–Hamilton Committee, known formally as the Select Committee to Investigate Covert Arms Transactions with Iran. Its nationally televised hearings began in May of 1987 and continued through early August. The witnesses—North, Poindexter, and Secretary of State George P. Shultz among others—produced what Representative Hamilton referred to at one point as "some of the most extraordinary testimony ever given to the United States Congress." Excerpts from these hearings, which make up the final selection in this section, are included to convey a sense of how far the NSC staff had strayed during the Iran-*contra* affair beyond its expected duties.

The testimony reveals NSC staff involvement in a range of dubious undertakings: appeals to wealthy Americans and foreign leaders to finance operations that Congress had prohibited and refused to fund—nothing less than the dismissal of fundamental constitutional procedure; the shredding of classified documents taken from safes in the White House because they may have implicated the staff in improper activities; attempts to mislead other officials in the executive branch about the nature of the Iran-*contra* connection; outright lies to members of Congress. After listening to North, Poindexter, and a parade of other witnesses, Senator Warren B. Rudman (R–New Hampshire) told the press that he was disgusted by those individuals who had "wrapped themselves in the flag and go around spitting on the Constitution" (Cohen and Mitchell, 1988: 76).

The attempts to mislead government officials included, according to Poindexter, a successful effort to keep the president himself unaware of the *contra* diversion (an operation the president later said he would have opposed) so that he might maintain "plausible denial." As Poindexter stated in his testimony to the Inouye–Hamilton Committee, "If I had discussed that in the White House before I left, I think it would have made it much more difficult for the President to distance himself from the decision." Whatever Poindexter's intentions, the end result was a deeply troubling aggrandizement of authority into the hands of the national security adviser and a member of his senior staff—devoid even of presidential, let alone congressional, accountability.

As for the Congress, an institution Poindexter seems to have held in contempt while serving in the White House, the vice admiral's approach was to ignore it or try to fool its members—an approach one strong administration supporter, Representative (and later vice president) Dick Cheney (R–Wyoming), called "stupid" during the investigative hearings into the affair. " . . . it's self-defeating," Cheney went on, "because, while it may in fact allow you to prevail in the problem of the moment, eventually you destroy the President's credibility." Reacting to the obsession for secrecy and the unwillingness of executive officials to engage the American people and their representatives in debate about foreign policy objectives for fear Congress might make the "wrong" decisions (such as the Boland Amendment), Senator Rudman forcefully and eloquently reminded North and the other perpetrators of the scandal that "the American people have a constitutional right to be wrong."

Lt. Col. North testified that he had assumed that the president did know about the diversion of funds to the *contras*. He had sent Poindexter five memos on the subject, he told lawmakers (the vice admiral remembered only one), and assumed the national security adviser had been given a green light to go ahead with the operation. North testified, too, that DCI William J. Casey was fully aware of and encouraged the covert action in Nicaragua. Some believe that in fact Casey, who died in May 1987, was the mastermind behind the entire Iran-*contra* scheme.

Caught up, too, in the deceits was Secretary of State Shultz, who told Congress he had become embroiled in a "battle royal" with Casey, Poindexter, and others for the president's ear. Shultz believed that the president had been given "cooked" (biased) intelligence by the CIA to support Casey's policy and that he himself, as secretary of state had been repeatedly lied to by the NSC staff, the CIA, and other agencies so they could pursue the covert arms deal and the *contra* diversion without fear of criticism or interference from the State Department. Shultz's testimony before the Inouye–Hamilton panel made it clear that the secretary of state—supposedly the top spokesperson for the United States on foreign affairs—had often been left completely in the dark on the crucial details of the most controversial foreign policy initiatives of the Reagan Administration. "When the President hangs out his shingle and says, 'You don't have to go through the State Department, just come right into the White House,' he'll get all the business," Shultz complained to the Inouye–Hamilton Committee. ". . . . But it's wrong; you can't do it that way . . ."

Some "ship of state" the American republic had become. The NSC staff and the CIA were at the helm, with the president and the secretary of state consigned to the hold (along with, by their accounts, the vice president and the secretary of defense).

Early in the inquiry, Representative Hamilton drew three major conclusions from this "depressing story. . . . a story about remarkable confusion in the processes of government" that would hold up well throughout the investigative hearings. The first dealt with the dangers of excessive secrecy. Disturbed in particular by an admission from the assistant secretary of state for Latin America, Elliott Abrams, that he had misled Congress in November 1986 about his knowledge of the *contra* funding, Hamilton observed that the government "cannot function unless officials tell the truth."

Hamilton further concluded that the "privatization of foreign policy is a prescription for confusion and failure"—not to say, he might have added, a crippling blow to the concept of constitutional government in the United States. And, third, he lamented the absence of accountability. "The question now is," he concluded: "how can we prevent it from happening again?" This concern, along with reforms to make the NSC system work more effectively, animate the readings in Part IX.

27

AMERICA'S DEPARTMENTS OF STATE

Bert A. Rockman

Drawing on the scholarly literature on organizational behavior, political scientist Bert Rockman helps us understand why foreign policy making has become more concentrated in the White House and what this reality means with respect to the evolution of the modern NSC.

The United States possesses two foreign ministers within the same government: the one who heads the Department of State, and the one who is the assistant to the president for national security affairs. The former heads a classically contoured bureaucracy. Proximate to him are appointed officials, often with substantial foreign policy experience. At greater distance is a corps of professional foreign service officers (FSOs). Beneath the national security assistant, on the other hand, is a smaller professional staff of somewhat variable size (ranging in recent times from about three dozen to slightly over 50) whose members typically are drawn from universities, other agencies, and research institutes.

This latter group—the National Security Council staff—is the institutional embodiment of White House aspirations for imposing foreign policy coordination. Its "director," the president's assistant for national security affairs, in recent years has come to be seen as the president's personal foreign policy spokesman as well as an influential molder, and sometime executor, of his policy choices. Though, at least publicly, the overt role of the president's national security assistant has been diminished in the Reagan administration relative to the prominence it attained during the Nixon and Carter presidencies, a common perception is that, since the Kennedy administration, policy power has drifted steadily from the State Department to the pres-

ident's team of foreign policy advisers (Campbell, 1971; George, 1972a; Destler, 1972a, 1972b, 1980; Allison and Szanton, 1976). If perceptions govern, this alone may constitute sufficient evidence of such a drift. Beyond perception, however, there is unmistakable evidence of growth in the role of the national security assistant (who postdates the founding of the National Security Council itself), and in the size and character of the NSC staff. Since McGeorge Bundy's incumbency, and especially because of the Kissinger and Brzezinski periods, the assistant to the president for national security affairs has become a visible public figure in his own right (Destler, 1980, pp. 84–85). In general, his role has evolved from one of coordinating clearance across departments to one of policy adviser. Similarly, the NSC staff itself has grown greatly, boosted especially during the Nixon administration. It is less and less composed of graying and grayish anonymous career foreign service officers, and more and more composed of foreign policy intellectuals and prospective high-fliers, many of whom are drawn from America's leading universities.

I do not mean to imply that the presidential foreign policy apparatus and the State Department always or even usually clash, nor that they have wholly overlapping functions. Nonetheless, it is clear that the NSC, at least in form, is today something far beyond what it was in Truman's time or in Eisenhower's. To some

From Bert A. Rockman, "America's *Departments* of State: Irregular and Regular Syndromes of Policy Making," *American Political Science Review* 75 (December 1981): 911–27.

Professor Rockman is director of the Institute for Public Policy at Ohio State University.

degree Truman, protecting what he believed to be his prerogatives, held the then-nascent National Security Council at arm's length as an advisory forum. Eisenhower, on the other hand, employed it frequently as a collegial body, one whose statutory members and staff were also, in some measure, representatives of their departments (Hammond, 1960, pp. 905–10; Falk, 1964, pp. 424–25). Since then, the role and character of the NSC staff, and especially that of the national security assistant, have mutated. This evolution into a role not originally envisioned for the NSC or the then special assistant (executive secretary in Truman's time) has notable consequences for policy making.

Even within the constricted sphere of executive forces on policy making, the foreign policy process involves a complex of actors and not merely a bilateral relationship between the NSC and the State Department. Although the State Department's position has been most eroded by the policy role of the NSC, neither it nor the NSC is a monolithic force. The national security assistant and the NSC staff are *not* the same actors, nor necessarily of common mind. Similar cautions are even more necessary to describe relationships between the secretary of state and the foreign service professionals of the State Department. A significant difference in intraorganizational relationships, however, is that the national security assistant to some extent selects his own staff, whereas the secretary of state has a department to manage and an established subculture that exists well below the level of those whom he selects. If the NSC staff is more nearly the creation of the national security assistant, the secretary of state, unless he divorces himself from the department, is more likely to be seen as its creation. This difference provides one of these actors with considerable strategic advantages in influencing the views and decisions of presidents.

As clearly as this somewhat ambiguous distinction permits, the NSC (and the national security assistant) and the State Department (though not necessarily the secretary) have come to embody, respectively, the differing commitments given to the roles of "irregulars" (those not bound to a career service) and of "regulars" (members of a career service) in the policy process. The correlation is quite far from unity, of course. There are mixes of personnel and outlooks within each orga-

nizational setting, but there are characteristically different career lines and perspectives as well. Above all, each setting provides for different roles. The operational responsibilities of the State Department give it the advantages of detailed knowledge and experience, and the political disadvantage of lacking an integrated world view. The NSC, on the other hand, is less constrained by the existence of operational responsibilities, by distance between it and the president, or by the communications complications typical of large hierarchically structured organizations. Its sterling political assets, however, are offset in some measure by the disadvantages of removal from day-to-day detail and highly specialized expertise. The differences between these organizational settings, to be sure, are quite significant. The NSC is a fast track. In contrast, the State Department can be a ponderously slow escalator. One setting is oriented to solving problems, the other to raising them. One is more oriented to attaining a bottom line, the other to journeying down a bottomless pit. In sum, the presidential foreign policy apparatus largely exhibits the advantages and disadvantages of an organ that is staffed to some degree by irregulars, and which is not charged with line functions. The State Department, in the main, illustrates the advantages and disadvantages of a hierarchically structured organization responsible for implementation, and which, therefore, tends to have a regular's orientation.

My objectives in this article then are (1) to sketch a general explanation for the growth of both coordinative institutions and of "irregular" personnel in government; (2) to identify both general and specific reasons for this phenomenon in the United States with respect to the official foreign policy community, in particular the tendencies toward Executive Office centrism; (3) to identify, within the foreign policy context, modal characteristics of the irregular and regular syndromes of policy making, and in so doing, to discuss the conjunction between personnel and institutional base; (4) to trace the implications of these different policy syndromes; and (5) to evaluate some proposed solutions to the problem of both resolving foreign policy-making authority and of organizationally synergizing the "irregular" and "regular" syndromes in foreign policy making. Finally, I conclude by suggesting that the problem of defining foreign policy-making authority in American government is but an element of the larger problem of governance in Washington. Whatever specific palliatives emerge need to be fully grounded in these sobering facts.

THE QUEST FOR POLICY INTEGRATION

The growth of coordinative institutions in modern governments and the growth in importance of irregular staffers in government are not the same thing, but they are traceable to the same sources, namely, the need to compensate for the inadequacies of traditional ministries in absorbing the policy agendas and perspectives of the central decision-making authority within the executive. The massive expansion of policy agendas themselves—"overload," as Klein and Lewis (1977, p. 2) call this phenomenon—is the signal cause of efforts to overcome the parochialness of the ministries and their civil servants. Problems of assimilation clearly have multiplied as governments pursue more and more complex, frequently conflicting objectives (Rose, 1976a; Neustadt, 1954). The forms taken by these coordinative mechanisms have varied across both political systems and policy arenas. The extent to which they have been composed of irregulars has similarly varied.

The more feeble the gravitational pull of directional authority in government, the more necessary it becomes to institutionalize coordinative functions. In Britain, the relatively strong pull of cabinet government, and the doctrine of ministerial responsibility, means that the interface of politics and policy often takes place within the ministries themselves. There, irregulars are usually planted directly in the ministries. In the Federal Republic of Germany, the gravitational pull of cabinet government is substantially weaker, and the activism of the *Bundeskanzleramt* (the Chancellery) is greater than that of the British Cabinet Office (Dyson, 1974, pp. 361–62). In the case of the United States where the gravitational pull of political forces is exceedingly weak, mechanisms to achieve policy integration abound not only in the Executive Office of the Presidency, but even throughout Congress. The development of these mechanisms throughout the EOP is particularly intriguing in view of the fact that the American line departments are already well saturated with officials whose political pedigrees have been carefully checked out. American administration, as is well known, is laden with irregulars at some depth beneath the cabinet secretary, yet even this has often been considered insufficient to attain presidential control and integration over policy (Nathan, 1975; Heclo, 1975).

This, of course, brings us to the central issue, which is whether the quest for policy integration, defined as comprehensive control over vital policy objectives, can accommodate expertise defined in terms of specialized knowledge. The dilemma, as Paul Hammond once observed, is this (1960, p. 910):

> While the mind of one man may be the most effective instrument for devising diplomatic moves and strategic maneuvers and for infusing . . . creative purpose, its product is bound to be insufficient to meet the needs of the vast organizational structures . . . which are the instruments of foreign policy.

The growth of integrative machinery has brought to the fore officials who sometimes differ from their counterparts in the operating agencies.[1] At least as important, though, is that they are provided substantial policy-influencing opportunities without equivalent operational responsibility. To the extent that "central" staff agencies have challenged more traditional bureaucratic sources of policy, they have merely reflected the perplexing problems that nearly all modern democratic governments face in both integrating and controlling policy objectives, and in rendering them politically acceptable.

From these more general observations, I wish to take up the special case of the National Security Council and the assistant to the president for national security affairs as a remarkable example of how the facilitating function evolved into far more heady activities. This evolution also starkly illustrates the advantage of a staff agency at the expense of the traditional operating agencies. Put another way, it reflects the advantages that "irregulars" often have over "regulars."

FROM MANAGER TO COMPETING SECRETARY OF STATE

From its inception in 1947, the National Security Council was designed to be a high-level policy review committee rather than a strictly staff operation (Sapin, 1967, p. 84). As a mechanism for arriving at major policy decisions, however, a support staff quickly emerged underneath the statutory membership of the NSC. Indeed, until the Eisenhower administration came into power in 1953, there was no overall coordinator who had immediate access to the president. In 1953, however, Eisenhower appointed a special assistant to the president for national security affairs whose responsibilities, among others, entailed playing an executive director's role with the NSC staff. An indication of how far the function of the president's national security assistant, and that of the NSC staff as well, has diverged from the original coordinating and facilitating function is the fact that it takes a monumental effort to recall who these presidential assistants were.[2]

Why has the national security assistant and the NSC staff moved from this relatively modest, if necessary, role to one which frequently has vied with the secretary of state and the State Department for foreign policy-making influence? At the outset of the Carter administration, for example, a sympathetic article referred to the NSC staff as the "other cabinet" (Berry and Kyle, 1977). There are numerous answers to this question, of course. At bottom, though, the "many" reasons are made particularly compelling by the peculiar political culture of Washington politics—an inheritance in part of extravagant institutional disaggregation.

It is true, of course, that whatever clout the national security assistant has exists only at the sufferance of the president (Art, 1973; Destler, 1977). Presidents can make or break the role of their national security assistants as policy advocates. They *can* minimize the visibility of their assistant; they *can* play down the substantive functions of the NSC staff relative to the State Department, for example. There are obvious manipulables in the relationship between America's "second State Department" and the White House, but the norms that have been established now seem firm in spite of the present and perhaps momentary diminution of the NSC role in the Reagan administration. The tendency to shift from central clearance to central direction has helped give the NSC apparatus and, above all, a policy-advocating national security assistant, an unusually important role. In the Reagan administration, Richard

Allen has proclaimed his role model to be that of Eisenhower's anonymous special assistant, Gordon Gray. But Allen's own prior roles largely have been advocacy and advisory ones, rather than managerial or facilitative ones (Smith, 1981).

Overload as an Explanation

Understandably, the National Security Act of 1947 which set up the National Security Council was enacted at the beginning of America's postwar eminence as the leading Western power. The role of global power with far-reaching responsibilities produces a busy agenda, and the busier that agenda the more the management of policy and of advice becomes important. According to a relatively recent report prepared for the president, there have been at least 65 studies of the U.S. foreign policy machinery since 1951 (*National Security Policy Integration*, 1979, p. 49). This abundance of studies bears witness to the great diversity of actors with some share of the foreign policy pie, to continuing problems of coordination between them, and to their reputed lack of responsiveness to the president. How, under these circumstances, is a president to make decisions without some final filter that reduces unmanageable complexity to at least endurable perplexity?

Undoubtedly, in an age of instant communication, some of the present NSC apparatus would have had to have been invented did it not already exist. Working out statements with counterparts in the Elysée, the Chancellery, or 10 Downing Street before the principals are themselves engaged is the kind of task that may need to be located close to the head of government. However, the enhanced role of the national security assistant over the past two decades (Destler, 1980) makes it unlikely that these tasks are sufficient to satisfy policy drives created by recent organizational practices.

Institutional and Organizational Explanations

"Overload" explains the existence of coordinative mechanisms such as the NSC. It does not, however, explain the transformation of a once-anonymous role with a small staff to prominent contender for policy-making power in foreign affairs.

Because government in Washington is as un-planned as the society it governs, criticisms of the foreign policy-making machinery overwhelmingly recommend organizational reforms (Campbell, 1971; Destler, 1972b; Allison and Szanton, 1976). As with virtually all governmental activity in the United States, fragmentation also characterizes the process of foreign policy decision making. Centrifugal tendencies began at the top levels of American government, induced in part by the absence of effective mechanisms for cabinet decision making.[3] Lack of clarity at the top molds bureaucratic tendencies below. Thus, while the problems of bureaucratic politics exist everywhere, they are made more obvious by unclear boundaries of authority, by the fractionation of power centers, and by the ready availability of the press as a resource in policy struggles. Contemporary Washington epitomizes these conditions. It is not difficult, therefore, to find targets for reform.

Despite repeated calls for its resuscitation, the cabinet is to the functioning of American government what the appendix is to human physiology. It's there, but no one is quite sure why. Whatever initial presidential intentions may be, presidents soon learn that cabinet meetings are mainly for public relations benefits rather than for decision making. They also learn another lesson of particular importance in Washington, namely, that the probability of leaks to the press which may foreclose presidential options is geometrically expanded by the number of participants involved. Later I will discuss how an "information-leaky" environment, unique to Washington among world capitals, estranges presidents from their cabinet departments. For now it is useful merely to indicate that the extreme splintering of responsibilities means that presidents with innovative intentions will be desirous of centralizing in the White House that which is otherwise uncontrollable or unresponsive to them.

All leaders are apt to demand more responsiveness than they can or even ought to get. But American presidents crave responsiveness in part because so little is obviously available to them. Large organizations, and especially those that are highly professionalized, develop definable subcultures and resist intrusions from inexpert outsiders. Regardless of what it is that presidents order the first time, there is a strong ten-dency for them to be served fudge—or jelly, to employ the culinary metaphor used by President Kennedy. While this frustration is not peculiar to the foreign policy and national security agencies, foreign policy matters are often far more central to what it is a president, or a prime minister for that matter, must attend to (Rose, 1976b, pp. 255–56; 1980, pp. 35–38). Typically, too, there is less legislative direction of the foreign policy organs than of departments having primarily domestic responsibilities or impacts.

Among the agencies involved with foreign policy, moreover, the State Department largely deals with political analysis, impressionistic evidence, and judgment. Since politicians who become presidents are likely to defer to no one when it comes to making what are essentially political judgments, the vulnerability of the State Department becomes apparent. It is not only that the department moves slowly that frustrates presidents; it is often the message that it delivers that leads them to despair (Silberman, 1979).

In addition to its distance from the White House, a problem which to some extent affects all line departments, the culture and technology of the State Department are also factors in its organizational disadvantage. These factors interact with, indeed greatly exacerbate, its distance problem. The State Department is a regular organization *par excellence* with a highly developed professional subculture. The stock in trade of the regular foreign service officers, granted individual differences among them, is a large supply of cold water with which to dash ideas that emanate elsewhere or which challenge prevailing professional perspectives. In the words of one sympathetic observer:

> The most useful service that a senior State Department official can perform in a policy-making role is to douse the facile enthusiasms of administration "activists" in the cold water of reality. But most of them bring so little energy and skill to this task that they merely project an image of negativism (Maechling, 1976, pp. 11–12).

Put somewhat more generally, "Political appointees seem to want to accomplish goals quickly while careerists opt to accomplish things carefully" (Murphy et al., 1978, p. 181).

As a citadel of foreign service professionalism, the State Department is an inhospitable refuge for ideas and initiatives blown in from the cold. "It's all been tried before" is a refrain that may characterize the responses of professional bureaucrats whatever their substantive craft, but it is one that is at the heart of the department's perceived unresponsiveness.

Ironically, in this light, the professional subculture of the foreign service, as some have noted, ill prepares foreign service officers for the rough-and-tumble of bureaucratic politics (Destler, 1972b, pp. 164–66; Maechling, 1976, pp. 10–12; and even Silberman, 1979). Indeed, the recruitment of FSOs traditionally has made them America's closest facsimile of the British administrative class (Seidman, 1980, pp. 144–47). This is manifest also in operating style, a style characterized as one of "alert passivity" (Allison and Szanton, p. 126). While American bureaucrats in the domestic departments readily adopt the role of advocate to a far greater extent than their European peers (Aberbach, Putnam and Rockman, 1981, pp. 94–98), FSOs tend to be more like British bureaucrats, defusing programmatic advocacy so as to maintain the flexibility necessary to deal with the differing priorities imposed by new leaders. Unlike their colleagues in the domestic departments, officials in State lack domestic constituencies to help them weather episodic storms. In addition, the foreign service is oriented to serving abroad. The cost of this absorption is a lack of sophisticated political understanding of the policy-making machinery. In a system in which boundaries of authority are remarkably inexact, FSOs tend to lack both skills and bases for effective bureaucratic infighting— a considerable disadvantage.

As noted, the modal technology of the State Department is soft and impressionistic, and thus endlessly vulnerable. This helps to explain why the State Department is especially apt to be victimized. For as a former department official comments:

> New presidents and their staffs soon start to search for opportunities for leadership, areas in which to demonstrate that the President is on top of things and making policy. When this game is played, the loser is almost invariably the State Department and not, for example, the Pentagon. . . . To do more than scratch the surface of a few front page military issues would require a much larger White House staff than any President would want to contemplate. Foreign policy, on the

other hand, is largely a matter of words, and the President and his staffers can step in at any time and put the words together themselves (Gelb, 1980, p. 35).

Once the staff has been constructed to oversee policy proposals, the next step toward advocacy seems nearly ineluctable unless the president is fully and unequivocally committed *in combination* to the secretary of state as the principal foreign policy maker *and* the State Department institutionally as the principal source of foreign policy advice—a combination that almost necessarily eliminates skilled policy entrepreneurs such as Henry Kissinger from the role. Why this combination of conditions is first unlikely to happen, but difficult to sustain if it does, is the question that needs to be addressed. To do so requires an exploration of the Washington political culture.

The Political Culture of Washington as an Explanation

To explain the transformation of the NSC from a central clearance mechanism and a long-range policy planning one to an active center of policy making requires a focus on institutional and organizational features such as those we have just discussed. Yet the peculiar climate that pervades government in Washington helps to explain these institutional and organizational operations. For the distinguishing characteristic of government in Washington is its near-indistinguishability from politics in Washington. While politics in the capitals of all democratic states mixes together a variety of interests—partisan, pressure-group, bureaucratic, regional, and so forth—the absence of party as a solvent magnifies the importance of other interests. Above all, the overtness of the bureaucratic power struggle is likely to be in inverse proportion to the intensity and clarity of the partisan struggle.

Confronted with singular responsibility and inconstant support, presidents are often driven to managerial aspirations over "their" branch of the government. Sooner or later they sense that at best they are confronted with inertia, at worst, opposition. Rarely can they rely consistently upon their party for support, especially if they are Democrats; rarely too can they assume that their cabinets are composed of officials who are not essentially departmental emissaries. Cabinet ministers everywhere, of course, are departmental ambassadors to the cabinet. All ministers find it convenient, if not necessary, at some time to promote departmental agendas pushed from below. The late R. H. S. Crossman's assertion that "the Minister is there to present the departmental case" is universally true (1972, p. 61), yet he also observes that an American cabinet is only that—an aggregation of departmental heads (p. 67).

The basic themes of American governmental institutions are distrust and disaggregation. Together, they fuel suspicion. Presidents often come to divide the world into "us" and "them." "They" typically cannot be relied upon. "They" will be seen as torpid, bureaucratically self-interested, and often uncommitted or skeptical of presidential initiatives. Above all, "they" will be seen as an uncontrollable source of hemorrhaging to the press.

Unmediated by any tradition of, or basis for, a cabinet team, distance defines "us" and "them." There are always winners and losers in executive politics everywhere, but the more ambiguous the boundaries of authority, the less clear the adjusting mechanisms by which the winners and losers are determined, and the more pervasive the involvement of the media in policy struggles (a largely American phenomenon), the more ferocious the struggle. Under these conditions, the department heads will tend to lose ground to the White House because whatever advantages in autonomy distance permits, the more obvious are the disadvantages in accessibility.

Washington is a capital as obviously open as Moscow is obviously closed. The intimate involvement of the prestige press in internecine executive policy debates is legendary. Little remains confidential in Washington for very long, at least insofar as the exposure of confidentiality can assist any of the policy contestants. The lifelines connecting presidents to the cabinet departments are longer and perceived to be more porous than those that link presidents to the Executive Office. This perception undoubtedly is fortified by the belief that under most circumstances cabinet secretaries would as soon push their departmental perspectives or even their own special agendas than those of the White House. The secretary of state is not immune from this. Despite the "inner" role of the secretary of state (Cronin, 1975, pp. 190–92), *to the extent that he is perceived within the White House as someone who presses the interests and perspectives of the foreign service regulars, he is apt to be written off as one of "them."* The case of William Rogers is instructive in this regard, and even more so is that of Cyrus Vance who began in office with strong presidential support for his power stakes.

Although one must beware of self-serving tales that dribble *ex post facto* to the prestige American press from disgruntled ex-officials, the evidence, however partial it may be, is that leaks to the press are more likely to be blamed on the cabinet departments than on the executive office staff itself. A report in the *Washington Post*, for instance, indicates that after President Carter severely chastised noncareer and career State Department officials in early 1979 for suspected press leaks regarding policy toward Iran, Secretary Vance pressed upon him the view that the State Department was being unfairly singled out as a source of leaks that were regularly occurring everywhere, especially from within the NSC staff. The president's response, according to the report, was to meet with his national security assistant and several of his senior staff members and request them to smooth their relations with their counterparts at the State Department (Armstrong, 1980). To officials at State, the president threatened; to NSC officials, the president cajoled. "Us" versus "them," in other words, was not unique to the Nixon administration (Aberbach and Rockman, 1976).

The isolation of presidents from their cabinet departments, the absence of a common point of meaningful political aggregation—all of this within the information-leaky environment peculiar to Washington among world capitals—is a ready stimulant to the "us" versus "them" outlook that commonly develops in the White House, and in the departments as well. Distance and distrust are promoted on both ends of the tether line connecting departments to the White House. Departmental frustrations are often exacerbated by presidential distrust of bureaucratic institutions in an antibureaucratic culture. American politicians who enter through the gates of the White House have neither learned to endure the frustrations that arise through a slow and steady apprenticeship in party politics such as is found in Britain, nor to appreciate by virtue of living in their midst the skills and qualities that professional civil servants bring to government.

Because it contains memory traces from the past, bureaucracy is the enemy of novelty. Memory imposes constraint, while presidents typically want to make their mark as innovators.[4] Presidential frustrations derive, therefore, from the incapacity of large organizations to be immediately responsive to presidential wishes, and from the tendency of such organizations to protect their interests and core technologies from presidential intrusion. On the other hand, departmental frustrations arise when departments become the victims of imagined nonresponsiveness to presidents, as related in a recently revised version of the trade, proposed by the Soviets during the 1962 Cuban missile crisis, of American Jupiter missile bases in Turkey for those installed by the Soviets in Cuba.[5]

Thus far, I have outlined generally why presidents in America tend toward White House centrism—that is, why they seek to build a policy-making apparatus around them rather than relying exclusively upon the cabinet departments. I have not attempted to explain exhaustively this drive toward centrism, nor its ebbs and flows across particular administrations. My concern is with the trend line rather than the perturbations within it. Some aspects of the drive toward centrism are undoubtedly largely idiosyncratic, having to do with particular presidential styles and personalities within administrations. There are some reasons too that are probably universal, for example, the growth of technological capacity for central control, and some that are speculative, for example, hypothesized imperatives of leaders to try to exert control over policy without comprehending the mechanics—to reach, in other words, a bottom line without much concern for the algorithm. Of the reasons I explicitly cite, however, one—the increased agenda of governments—can be found in all modern democracies, and has resulted in efforts to devise coordinative machinery. The other reasons I have identified are more system-specific, and are rooted in institutional and cultural considerations. A dispersed policy universe generates needs for greater centrism. The weaker the pull of political gravity, the more the emphasis upon central staffing. Thus, according to one report, the load on central staff personnel in the EOP (at least during the Carter presi-

dency) is immense when compared with staff counterparts in other nations (Campbell, 1980, p. 22). This apparently reflects White House obsessions for detailed policy control in an environment in which such control is as elusive as it is expected.

FOREIGN POLICY BY IRREGULARS: WHITE HOUSE AND DEPARTMENTAL SETTINGS

The conditions that make American presidents turn to staff at the White House rather than bureaucrats, or even their appointees in the departments, undoubtedly characterize all policy sectors. Departmental appointees who have strong links to the career subcultures within their departments are often viewed with suspicion at the White House. They will be seen as advocates of parochial interests. Officials at the White House want presidential objectives to be "rationally" managed. Officials in the departments, on the other hand, want "rational" policies as they define them. This difference in perspective exists everywhere, and is by no means a peculiar characteristic of White House-State Department relations. What is peculiar about this particular relationship, however, is the extent to which the foreign service regulars are cut adrift from other sources of support in the political system and within their own department. Unlike their counterparts in the domestic agencies, they have no statutory-based standards to apply, only their judgments and knowledge to rely on. Unlike analysts in the domestic agencies, and in other national security agencies such as the Defense Department and CIA, their "data" are contained in imprints rather than print-outs.

Thus, at least since Dean Acheson's stewardship, most secretaries of state who wielded great influence (Dulles, Rusk under Johnson, and Kissinger) traveled light—in other words, without much departmental baggage. Strong secretaries often have been strong precisely because they ignored the department. When secretaries of state are perceived as representing departmental perspectives, they become especially vulnerable to competing sources of influence—most particularly from within the White House. Why?

One must begin with the fact that foreign policy is a *high-priority* item. By its importance, its capacity to push other items on the agenda to a lesser place, foreign policy, though not equally appetizing to all presidents, becomes the main course of the presidential meal. The extent to which foreign policy is a focal point of attention, of course, depends on the extent to which any nation is deeply involved and committed as an actor in world affairs. And that, understandably, is related to a nation's capacities for such involvement.

Crises especially lend themselves to central direction. Foreign policy is often nothing but crises—either reacting to them or creating them. Filled with crisis and presumed to be of first-order importance, foreign affairs are, in fact, glamorous. Much more than apparently intractable or technically complex domestic problems, foreign affairs often seem to be contests of will—games against other players rather than games against nature.

In such games, regular bureaucrats are unlikely to be key players. Their instincts are to think small, to think incrementally, and to see the world in not highly manipulable terms. The glitter that presidents often see in foreign policy is at odds with the cautious instincts of the professional service entrusted to deal with it. Unattached to specific operational responsibilities and accessible to the White House, the NSC can take on the qualities of a think-tank unencumbered by the more limited visions that flow from the State Department itself. Moreover, the NSC, like any staff organization, is far more readily adapted to the changing foreign policy themes of presidents than a line bureaucracy such as the State Department. State is, of course, highly adaptable to modulated swings in policy, but not to strong oscillations. Organizational memory and bureaucratic inertia preclude it from reinventing the world every four years.

This particular difference in settings—White House staff versus line bureaucracy—also implies a difference in styles of policy analysis. One setting is accessible to power, the other more remote. One is especially attractive to the ambitious and purposive, the other to the cautious and balanced. One setting is tailored for "in-and-outers" and "high-fliers" borrowed from other agencies, while the other is meant for "long-haulers." One effect of this difference in settings is that even though the NSC staff is not overwhelmingly composed of academic figures, more NSC staffers are apt to be academics than their counterparts

at state. For example, a study of senior foreign service officers indicates that fewer than 8 percent are Ph.D.s (Mennis, 1971, p. 71), while 58 percent of the NSC staff with which Zbigniew Brzezinski began were holders of the Ph.D. degree,[6] as are 43 percent of the present staff. Such differences do not reflect merely ephemeral circumstance. The Reagan NSC also represents a mixture of scholars and government career officers with Washington experience (Smith, 1981). And as Destler describes the NSC staff under Presidents Kennedy and Nixon: "The typical staff members were not too different from the Kennedy period—relatively young, mobile, aggressive men, combining substantial background in the substance of foreign affairs with primary allegiance to the White House" (1972b, p. 123).

In other words, there is a correlation between background and organizational setting even though it is quite far from perfect. Backgrounds, of course, are only frail indicators of differences in syndromes of policy thought, and such differences need not imply substantive disagreement. Nonetheless, the correlation implies that the White House miniature of the State Department is more innovative than the real one at Foggy Bottom, more aggressive, and also more enthusiastic for White House policy directions.

The NSC staff and the national security assistant, of course, may conflict (as may the regulars in the State Department and their noncareer superiors). There have been notable clashes in the past, especially in the immediate aftermath of the American incursion into Cambodia in 1970 during the Vietnam engagement. The national security assistant and the NSC staff are not necessarily in agreement upon substance, but their *forma mentis* are likely to differ from those of their State Department counterparts. If presidents are served amorphous goo from the State Department bureaucracy (which they often see as representing other nations' interests to Washington), they may be provided with clear-headed principles from their in-house foreign policy advisers. Concerned with direction and results, presidents are usually predisposed to cut through the rigidities of complex bureaucratic systems and the cautions of the foreign policy regulars. In this, of course, lies the potential for isolating policy advice from implementation. Going through the bureaucracy often means spinning wheels, but ignoring the bureaucracy poses the prospect of personalizing policy rather than institutionalizing it. In this latter course, there is, to be sure, less wheel-spinning but there is, at least in the long run, also more spinning of castles in the air.

Finally, the soft technology of foreign relations means that it is just precisely the kind of thing that politicians think they are better qualified for than anyone else (Merton, 1968, p. 265). A former noncareer ambassador writes, for instance: "The average American has a sounder instinctive grasp of the basic dynamics of foreign policy than he does of domestic macroeconomics. . . . Common sense—the sum of personal experience—will take one further in the realm of foreign policy than in macro-economics" (Silberman, 1979, pp. 879–80). Because little seems mystical or technical about foreign policy to presidents, reliance upon cumbersome bureaucratic machinery seems unnecessary. In most instances, presidents like to be directly engaged with foreign policy because it is more glamorous and central to their historical ambitions, less dependent upon congressional approval, and because it activates their "head of state" role (and in the event of possible military involvement, their "commander-in-chief" one also). In contrast to the trench warfare and haggling involved with domestic policy formulation, foreign policy making tends to promote self-esteem and presidential prestige. With all of these possibilities, it is improbable, therefore, that presidents want the powers of foreign policy making to be distant from them. Usually, they want it close to them. Presidents need to legitimate White House centrism, then, by investing it in a flexible staff operation headed by an unattached foreign policy "expert." These specific reasons, encapsulated within the more general determinants already discussed, have led the White House Department of State to loom as a contender for policy-making influence with the "cabinet" Department of State.

IRREGULAR AND REGULAR SYNDROMES

In spite of the alluring differences implied by the personnel distinction between irregulars and regulars, neither end of this distinction is a monolith nor is it always generalizable in the same ways across policy sectors and political systems. One reason for this is that bureaucratic cultures reflect the character of the host political culture, as those who have contrasted British and American administrative styles have observed (Sayre, 1964). Both British senior civil servants and their American counterparts, for instance, are bureaucratic regulars, yet they differ substantially in the manner in which they confront their roles—a difference that results from the political ambience surrounding them. Especially in administrative systems where there is little tradition of rotating officials across departments, there may be sharp differences in the characteristics of regulars across various departments. In the United States where these departmental subcultures are quite firmly implanted (McGregor, 1974, pp. 24–26; Seidman, 1980, pp. 133–73; Aberbach and Rockman, 1976, pp. 466–67), there is a stylistic gap between the entrepreneurial subcultures often found in social and regulatory agencies and the foreign service subculture of neutral competence.

Similar differences exist amongst irregular personnel as well, and as previously noted, American administration is permeated with irregulars. American elite civil servants' responsibilities began at a level of authority significantly below that of their British counterparts. Indeed, as defined earlier, the distinction between "irregular" and "regular" within departmental settings *must be* hierarchically related. Still, the appointed irregulars in the departments often have had prior experience in that department, 35 to 40 percent according to one estimate (Stanley et al., 1967, p. 41). The professional perspectives of their departments often have been assimilated by these officials, and at least in this respect it is possible to distinguish them from the corps of presidential policy advisers.

Precise comparisons of administrative structures such as those of Britain and the United States are always perilous, but it would not be stretching matters excessively to say that Executive Office irregulars are somewhat akin to the high-fliers of the British civil service without the latter's attachments to the civil service system. Typically, they have less experience in government than their senior line counterparts. With the growth of the institutional presidency, however, the American system has displayed a penchant for mismatching titles of formal authority and possibilities for

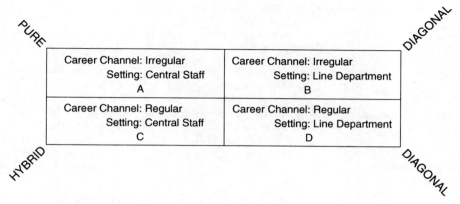

Figure 27.1 Career channel and organizational setting matrix

influencing policy. The high-fliers, therefore, often are better positioned to exert more policy influence in the American system than are the senior officials in the line departments. In the American system, proximity breeds possibilities.

Two very broad distinctions need to be made. One is that between personnel and their relation to career service channels. The other is between organizational settings—central staff versus line department. Further differentiations, of course, can be made within each of these categories. Table 1 illustrates the possible intersection of personnel career channels and their organizational settings. Although I have no measure of the relative influence of setting and career channel on policy thinking and behavior, it is likely that departmental appointees (cell B of Fig. 27.1) will be subject, with varying degrees of susceptibility, to the magnetic pull of their departments. Similarly, central staff officials with career backgrounds (cell C of Fig. 27.1), also with varying susceptibility, may be inclined to retain their career perspectives and be sensitive to their promotion opportunities—in short, to maximize their departmental interests even while serving in integrative staff structures. This problem reportedly plagued the NSC to some extent under Eisenhower (Falk, 1964, pp. 424–25). The distinction between cells A and D is obviously the purest. I assume here the probability of interactive effects between structure and personnel.

Beginning with a broad distinction between irregular staff and regular bureaucratic settings, Table 27.1

sketches some of the important respects in which these settings differ. These differences point to modal variations in function, in vantage point, in personnel, and in orientations to policy. In the analysis that follows, however, I start with differences between personnel, work back to settings, and then to forms of policy thinking.

How do irregulars differ from regulars? First, irregulars are more likely to be charged with coordinating functions (policy planning, for instance) than are regulars even when they are each engaged in departmental responsibilities. These functions provide the irregular with greater breadth and the capacity to see a more integrated policy picture, but one limited in depth. On the other hand, the regular is located so as to see detail but is less able or likely to see beyond it. These structural features also lead to different interpretations of rationality. The irregular is apt to define rationality as coherence from the vantage point of policy management. The regular, however, is apt to see rationality in terms of informed policy making.

Free of operational responsibilities, irregulars are apt to be conceptualizing and deductive (more "theoretical" or "ideological") in policy thinking than are foreign policy regulars. Intimate detailed knowledge possessed by the regular tends to induce skepticism toward ideas that are abstract and aesthetically interesting. As the regular sees him, the irregular is a simplifier with tendencies toward an excess of imagination and a scarcity of discriminating judgment. Irregulars

Table 27.1 Differences between Irregular Central Staff Settings and Regular Bureaucratic Settings in Foreign Policy Making

	Irregular Staff Settings	**Regular Bureaucratic Settings**
Typical Responsibilities	Coordinating functions which provide breadth and integrative perspectives, and foster coherence	Implementing functions which provide detailed knowledge and particularistic perspectives, and foster local rationality
Location Relative to Decisional Authority	Proximate to political authority, therefore perceived as "Us"	Distant from political authority, therefore perceived as "Them"
Type of Personnel	Irregulars and regular "floaters" with few organizational commitments	A mix of irregulars and regulars toward the top, with regulars with long-term organizational commitments at the core
Typical Policy-Making Styles	Activists	Skeptics
	Theorists	Specialists
	Conceptualizers	Inductivists
	Deductivists	"Complexifiers"
	"Simplifiers"	
Dominant Policy Implications	Directive and thematic, initiatory and bold	Cautious and nonthematic, incrementalist and narrow-gauged
Resulting Policy Problems	Superficiality	Particularism

are rarely lacking in expertise; but their possibilities for thought are distanced from the immediacy of operational problems. Whether by role difference, by recruitment path, or by their interactive effects, the irregular is more disposed to theoretical thought than the regular. Theories are the precursors of activism for they simplify reality sufficiently to permit general, though not necessarily operational, plans of action. The inductivism that is more characteristic of the regulars leads them often toward perceiving complication; it leads them frequently to be skeptical about generalized schemes of action; often it leads them into paralysis. It is both the virtue and the liability of the regular's "hands-on" involvement that he will be predisposed to illustrate the invalidity of proposals and the assumptions they are based on than to advance alternative solutions. After all, it is normally the regular who has to live with the consequences of "rashness."

Ideas and skepticism, while polar intellectual traits, are nonetheless each valuable ones. Large bureaucracies are the wellspring of skepticism and the depressant of ideas. This bureaucratic characteristic flows from the inertia associated with established routines as well as from the concreteness of the regular official's world. Met daily, concreteness and detail induce awareness of complexity. It is this awareness of complexity that ironically is at the heart of the State Department's self-perception as a protector of real long-term interests (Gelb, 1980, p. 34).

Given their natural proclivities, regular bureaucrats are apt to be oriented to the long term within their specialized realms, and likely to be skeptical of overarching themes. This characteristic is not especially attractive to presidents whose "common-sense" approaches to foreign policy often coincide with what is also politically supportable. Being policy generalists, presidents tend to be impatient with "can't-doers," failing to understand or appreciate the skepticism of the foreign policy regulars. From the presidential vantage point, sober thoughts are mere fudge, and skepticism rarely accords with presidents' political needs. Unattached foreign policy "experts" on the other hand, can articulate ideas and push proposals unencumbered by bureaucratic constraints or operational responsibilities. This gives them an obvious advantage over those representing the particularizers in the foreign policy bureaucracy. As for the secretary of state, his advisory and policy-making roles will likely be as large as his distance from the department is great.

There are dangers in the detachment of policy advice and policy influence from operational responsibilities. The triumph of theory over fact is obviously troubling. If regulars, by their skepticism (and probably also their convenience) tend toward incrementalist thinking, it is also true that, at least in the short run, no one ever died of incrementalism. Still, the failure to produce and institutionalize policy integration can be a long-term carcinogenic agent. For politics contoured only by those with operational attachments are likely to suffer from deficiencies of imagination.

PROPOSED SOLUTIONS TO THE INTEGRATION PROBLEM

The problems of generating integrated and informed policy are obviously apt to receive attention in inverse proportion to the power of the political tools for achieving it. By this standard, America's foreign policy machinery is beset with continuing difficulties. Proposals, official and unofficial, to remedy the foreign policy machinery of the United States abound. They tend to fall into three broad classifications: (1) those emphasizing the role of a strong State Department with a powerful secretarial and presidential direction; (2) those emphasizing the importance of multiple streams of information with a national security assistant playing the more traditional role of traffic manager rather than the one of advocate acquired over the last two decades; and (3) those emphasizing strengthened cabinet-level coordination and the interchange of officials beneath this level. My intent here is to highlight their particular perspectives and their uncertainties.

1. Strengthening the Secretary of State

This is not only a common proposal, but also one that seems most obviously apt to connect political strength to institutional capabilities. As Destler has put it:

> The issue is not whether the Secretary or the President has primacy. Rather it is who—the Secretary or the National Security Assistant—should be the central foreign affairs official short of the President and acting

as his "agent of coordination." If the President is known to rely primarily on the Secretary of State for leadership in foreign policy-making across the board, he should prove far more formidable than a "mere cabinet officer" (1972b, p. 359).

A strengthened secretary of state, however, must have the confidence of the president, and this, in turn, requires a strengthened State Department which means, in Destler's view, a lessened diplomatic role for the secretary and a more forceful policy advocate and organizational management role. What Destler has in mind by the latter, however, is essentially a State Department so transformed that it would be a more coherent tool of presidential direction. In other words, an important element of Destler's proposed reforms is to do unto the State Department that which often has been tried in domestic departments: politicize it. Again, in his words:

> There will remain an inevitable tension between the interests and predispositions of Foreign Service officers and those of Presidents. So no Secretary of State who did not build a strong "political" component into the State Department could hope to satisfy a President bent on controlling the foreign affairs bureaucracy (1972b, p. 288).

Although it does not do full justice to Destler's arguments to say that coherence from the president's standpoint is the exclusive value with which he is concerned, his prescriptions move in the direction of making it the primary one. The potential trap, as Alexander George has noted, is that managerial rationality would come to displace substantive rationality, a likely probability if the State Department is to be politicized, if in essence it is to become a larger, deeper NSC (1972b, pp. 2811–83).

In this guise, a strengthened secretary of state necessitates a weaker national security assistant, indeed, a virtual elimination of the position. A strong secretary of state with a close relationship to the chief executive, Destler claims, has been the best check on the role of the national security assistant as a central policy advocate. But, as he also notes, the very existence of the assistant in the White House makes it difficult to generate that close relationship (1980, pp. 86–87).

The responsiveness of the State Department, of course, is also dependent upon a president knowing his own mind. Presidents differ in this regard, but it is not immediately clear how consistent they can be concerning policy directions to what, after all, are mostly reactive opportunities and necessities. Thematic agreement may be conducive to operational agreement, but it can be no more than that. Alternatively, overarching clarity in foreign policy may simply be dogmatism.

A more likely possibility, one that may be symbolized by personalities such as Alexander Haig and Henry Kissinger, is that of the entrepreneurial secretary of state who cuts a demanding figure in his own right. The entrepreneurship, however, may well come at the cost of organizational debilitation. While the relationship between Alexander Haig, the State Department, and the White House remains to be developed as of this writing, Kissinger, as secretary of state, was both a policy advocate and presidential spokesman, but in spirit he never left the White House in these roles. Nor, in fact, had he physically left it until late 1975. A secretary who draws nourishment from the Department's professional foreign service roots, however, is apt to find himself, sooner or later, designated as one of "them." This, at least since Dean Acheson, has largely been the case.

In any event, the problem lingers of generating political coherence (organizational rationality) in such manner as to effectively utilize substantive rationality (derived from specialized sub-units). A politicized State Department, one suspects, would be more coherent and responsive. But could it then effectively contribute to informed policy making?

2. Encouraging Multiple Advocacy

As proposed by Alexander George (1972a), the organizational strategy of multiple advocacy assumes the virtues of local rationality. In spirit, it is to foreign policy formulation an application of Chairman Mao's "Hundred Flowers Bloom" campaign. It makes a virtue of what is a necessary vice, the multiplicity of perspectives generated by the division of labor which bureaucratic sprawl leaves in its wake. George's interesting suggestion is to return to the basic concept of the old special assistant's role as a managerial custodian, a facilitator of varying perspectives so that the president may avail himself of the full play of diversity surrounding him. In its new form, the assistant would be constrained from playing the role of policy advocate, or from presenting foreign policy views to the public. His facilitating role would be greatly expanded, and in that presumably would lie his status. To some extent, this super-custodian presumably would be something akin to the director of the Office of Management and Budget, but without the capacity to pass judgment upon departmental requests—in other words, largely powerless. I am not the first to point out that in Washington those with status but without power quickly become worked around rather than through.

We may question, too, the assumption that presidents, or leaders of other large organizations, for that matter, are thirsting for information, diversity, and knowledge. Mao, after all, quickly came to disown the "Hundred Flowers Bloom" campaign. Facts, information, knowledge are great legitimizers of action. Not surprisingly, leaders often find it best to screen them selectively. A reasonable hypothesis is that the longer presidents (leaders in general) have been in power and thus the more prior commitments they have established and defenses they have constructed around them, the more likely it is that their tolerance for diversity declines. Even if at first presidents are predisposed to hunt facts, in the end facts are more likely to haunt presidents. Removed from electoral concerns, presidential interests in policy, per se, are often suspect (recall Nixon's response to Haldeman's request for policy direction on propping up the Italian lira), but whatever interests they do have also are apt to diminish as their term wears on and as more decisions become responses rather than initiatives. None of this perhaps would be so important were it not for the fact that George insists that presidents must assume a magistrate's role; otherwise, diversity becomes hyperpluralist babble. For without this particular role assumption, the rich flow of information and analysis likely would reinforce local rationality. Coherence and direction would famish.

The assumption that foreign policy contestants ought essentially to emulate lawyers in an American litigation proceeding by pressing their "interested" rendition of the "facts" before a disinterested presidential magistrate is curious. Being that presidents are neither disinterested themselves, nor unlimited in their attention spans, it is more likely that the chief magistrate will be the president's national security assistant. There is, in short, little incentive for the president to cope with detailed arguments, and none for the assistant to shy away from policy advocacy. As interesting as they are, proposals for functional changes that do not account for the costs to, and incentives of, the actors involved are more nearly prayers.

3. Strengthening the Cabinet and Rotating Officials

In *Presidential Power*, Richard Neustadt quotes a White House aide to President Eisenhower as saying, "If some of these Cabinet members would just take time out to stop and ask themselves, 'What would I want if I were President?', they wouldn't give him all the trouble he's been having" (1980, p. 31). The reasons for this estrangement are well known. And the underlying assumption about it, namely, that role alteration diminishes parochialism, is taken as the point of origin for its alleviation. To alleviate this condition, a two-pronged strategy has been advanced (Allison and Szanton, 1976, pp. 78–80; Allison, 1980). The strategy requires a dash of something a bit new and something old.

What is somewhat new is the recommendation that NSC staffers be continually rotated between the agencies and the White House so as to mold together agency and White House perspectives among individuals. The model for this suggestion is that of the British civil service generalist. As matters stand, of course, a substantial portion of the NSC staff previously served in another agency (State, Defense, and CIA, in that order) either indirectly or directly before arriving at the NSC. Estimates from the 1977 list show that nearly 40 percent had such experience (as compiled [by] Berry and Kyle, 1977), and to define things more narrowly, Destler (1972b, p. 249) indicates that as of April 1971 almost half of the NSC staff had some prior experience either in the State Department or the military services. Thus it is not that many of these officials are lacking experience in the agencies (though it should be kept in mind that over 60 percent of the 1977 staff had no prior agency experience), but rather that for most of them, present roles are likely to be especially compelling.[7] Recombinant socialization does

not necessarily mean intellectual integration. In the face of a highly centrifugal structure of government, knowing how it looks from "there" may be merely a tactical advantage in the struggle to influence policy rather than a basis for policy integration. For such proposals to work, structures that provide for collectively responsible points of decision making are essential.

Thus, the other part of this recommended strategy is to create an Executive Committee of Cabinet Officials (ExCab) to provide ongoing high-level policy review. "A body like ExCab," Graham Allison claims, "would yield most of the advantages of the collegial participation of major department heads while avoiding the unwieldiness of the full cabinet" (1980, p. 46). ExCab, however, as even its promoter willingly admits, is not an altogether new idea. The Nixon administration after all, had proposed a set of "super cabinet"departments and, failing congressional approval, then created by executive fiat an informal set of "super-secretaries." Though Nixon's political demise brought this operation into formal disrepair, it is unfair to pass judgment upon it, since its creation only shortly preceded Nixon's calamitous, if protracted, fall from grace. To be sure, there are a number of operational problems that this approach does not automatically avoid. There is first the question of who is in and who is out. Only in a cabinet of nonentities of the sort Nixon tried to create for his second administration is it likely that department secretaries would accede to more powerful presences. Secondly, while the ExCab proposal potentially permits diversity to flow with decisional responsibility, many of the difficulties presidents have in dealing with the full cabinet also arise even with a reduced foreign policy-focused cabinet. It is not merely the presence of diversity within the executive that distresses presidents, for that evidently is a condition affecting top leaders everywhere to some degree. Rather, it is the ease with which opposition or losing forces within the executive can go to Capitol Hill or the press, usually reaching the former by means of the latter. It is difficult for collegial government, however reduced the number of relevant actors, to flourish under such conditions. Any proposal to reform the organizational apparatus of American foreign policy making needs to be sensitive to this problem. Though the possible, but as yet unknown, impact of organizational reforms should not be disconnected, these neither alter fundamentally the institutional framework of largely antagonist forces in Washington nor the culture of openness that both sustains and reinforces this adversarial framework.

CONCLUSION

Presidents ultimately determine foreign policy. Whatever system of advice and decision making exists can exist only with the president's approval. It is within the range of presidential discretion to permit the national security assistant to become a leading contestant for foreign policy influence. Similarly, it is within the scope of presidential judgment to permit the national security assistant to appear as the chief foreign policy representative for their administrations. Nixon and Carter did permit these things; indeed, they encouraged them, though for different reasons. Thus far, the Reagan model (if there is one) has resulted in decreased visibility for the national security assistant. The NSC professional staff, however, is no smaller than it was during the Carter administration, and at least one report indicates a more direct White House staff involvement monitoring operations through the NSC machinery (Evans and Novak, 1981). Additionally, somewhat reminiscent of Nixon's "administrative presidency" model, a loyal operative has been slipped into the deputy secretary's role at State. In the last 14 months of the Ford administration, the role of the national security assistant and, to a modest degree, that of the NSC veered closer to the Eisenhower model of a dominant secretary of state and a "neutral competent" national security assistant (Brent Scowcroft). The reason for this, however, now seems clear. Ford's secretary of state, Henry Kissinger, was his leading foreign policy spokesman and leading foreign policy maker, yet not really his foreign minister. To be both, foreign minister (representing departmental perspectives) and leading foreign policy maker has within it increasingly the seeds of an insoluble role conflict.

Presidents vary, of course, in their ideas as to how foreign policy making ought to be organized, what they want from it, and how much weight is given at least at the outset to the values of harmony and diversity. The difficulty lies in isolating which aspects of their variability will lead to a heightened emphasis upon staff irregulars, and how they will be used. Similar results, as the disparate cases of Nixon and Carter indicate, may flow from different organizational modes. While each held widely different models of the policy-shaping process in foreign affairs, each also further enlarged the role of the NSC as a policy mechanism. Early on, Nixon seemed to prefer policy to be shaped at the White House, and as much as possible to skirt around the bureaucracy. Carter's organization, on the other hand, seemed to exaggerate Alexander George's ideal of multiple advocacy except, quite importantly, that Zbigniew Brzezinski was meant to be an advocate and not just a mediator. Different intentions seem to have produced fairly similar results—a highly visible national security assistant and a "competing" State Department.

The variability of presidents notwithstanding, the overall thrust since Eisenhower seems fairly clear: more White House centrism in foreign policy making, and an enlarged NSC role. Presidential variability tells us a lot about form—the particular uses made of the NSC mechanism and of the national security assistant—but it does not tell us why the NSC today looks so different from the NSC of 25 years ago, nor does it tell us why the national security assistant has so often been a primary policy maker. While the water has both risen and receded, the watermark is a good bit higher now than it was then.

To explain this trend toward centrism, and thus the importance of policy irregulars, my analysis focuses upon a theory of government—a theme somewhat broader than its specific target. The proposals for reconstituting America's foreign policy mechanisms that have been examined here certainly represent a more precise approach. Yet, government and politics in Washington, and the open culture that surrounds it, represent the limits against which these various proposals bump. From the hyperpoliticized ambience of American government the role needs of foreign policy contestants are shaped. Institutional fragmentation and weak parties not only beget one another, they also promote a level of bureaucratic politics of unusual intensity—grist for the mill of a highly inquisitive press.

No wonder presidents find their political and policy needs better served from within the White House. From this vantage point, the departments sooner or later are perceived as representing or pursuing interests that are not those of the president. This is especially so for the State Department because it is frequently seen as representing interests of other countries. With virtually no domestic constituencies and reflecting a subculture that, much like the British civil service, emphasizes "neutral competence" and balance, the foreign service regulars in the State Department are singularly disadvantaged. The steamy adversarial climate of Washington's executive politics does not nourish such values. The White House (and often department heads) are anxious for "movement," and unreceptive to "let's wait a moment." In the long run, the danger in any such setting is that the tools of central clearance will metamorphose into mechanisms for central dominance.

In sum, the reasons why America has a competing State Department turn out to be both excruciatingly complex and yet remarkably simple. Its simplicity lies in the structure of antagonistic forces given form by the American Constitution. Its complexities lie in the conditions—the importance of foreign policy, the role of the media, the burgeoning of policy intellectuals— that have since ripened.

The problem of reconciling "the persistent dilemmas of unity and diversity" (Fenno, 1975, p. 339) remains to be solved as much in the foreign policy sphere as in the domestic one, especially as the distinction between these arenas erodes. In unity lies strategic direction and clarity, but also the dangers of a monocled vision. In diversity lies sensitivity to implementation and to nuance, but also the dangers of producing least common denominators. Ironically, during the Eisenhower presidency when the NSC performed most nearly like a cabinet committee producing consensus from diversity, it was criticized for the ambiguities remaining in its products (Destler, 1977, pp. 152–53). If not a fudge factory, it was at least a fudge shop.

Each president to some extent will develop mechanisms that suit him best. Among other things, the policy system established will reflect the idiosyncracies of interpersonal chemistry. Each, though, has inherited an in-house foreign policy apparatus defined in the last 20 years more by how it has been used than by its original statutory rationale. How that apparatus will evolve cannot be foretold with preciseness. But how and why it has evolved from its inception to its present state is a saga that should be of as much interest to students of American government as to those of foreign policy.

NOTES

1. Campbell and Szablowski (1979) note, for instance, that senior officials in the Canadian central coordinating agencies differ from the main-line civil servants in the traditional line ministries in that they are more likely to have entered laterally rather than to have moved through the civil service system.

2. From earliest to latest in the Eisenhower administration, they were Robert Cutler, Dillon Anderson, and Gordon Gray. During the Truman administration there were two executive secretaries of the NSC. Each, Sidney Souers and James Lay, reflected the "neutral competence" ideal.

3. This, of course, is a by-product of the presidential system. Ironically, the Eberstadt Report, which set forth the rationale for the National Security Act and, thus, the NSC, apparently was motivated by a desire to create a high level British type cabinet committee. As Hammond notes (1960, p. 899): "The Eberstadt Report assumed that the proposed National Security Council could be a kind of war cabinet in which the responsibilities of the President could be vested. . . . The premise arose . . . out of an inclination to modify the Presidency as an institution."

4. A recent study of organizational memory development among three EOP agencies, for example, finds that the NSC consistently has the least cross-administration continuity as measured by several indicators (Covington, 1981). The author of this report concludes that organizational continuity reflects presidential detachment, whereas lack of memory reflects intense presidential interest.

5. As Barton J. Bernstein (1980, p. 103 n.) observes from his study of recently declassified materials regarding this episode:

> A chief executive may often express preferences (not orders) for policies, and that he may sincerely reinterpret them as *orders* when his own inaction leaves him woefully unprepared in a crisis. In this way, a president can place blame on a subordinate, and other aides who listen to his charges tend to believe that the president actually issued an order, and not simply stated a wish or a hope.

For a general review of this incident, see Bernstein (1980), and also Hafner (1977).

6. Compiled from data in Berry and Kyle (1977).

7. The Carter NSC figures are essentially reversed under Reagan. Among the present NSC staff, roughly 60 percent have had prior government experience, and 40 percent have not.

REFERENCES

Aberbach, Joel D., Robert D. Putnam, and Bert A. Rockman (1981). *Bureaucrats and Politicians in Western Democracies.* Cambridge, Mass.: Harvard University Press.

Aberbach, Joel D. and Bert A. Rockman (1976). "Clashing Beliefs within the Executive Branch: The Nixon Administration Bureaucracy." *American Political Science Review* 70: 456–68.

Allison, Graham (1980). "An Executive Cabinet." *Society:* 17, July/August, 41–47.

———, and Peter Szanton (1976). *Remaking Foreign Policy.* New York: Basic Books.

Armstrong, Scott (1980). "Carter Given Oaths on 'Leaks.'" *The Washington Post,* 16 July 1980, pp. A1, A4.

Art, Robert J. (1973). "Bureaucratic Politics and American Foreign Policy: A Critique." *Policy Sciences* 4: 467–90.

Bernstein, Barton J. (1980). "The Cuban Missile Crisis: Trading the Jupiters in Turkey?" *Political Science Quarterly* 95: 97–126.

Berry, F. Clifton, Jr., and Deborah Kyle (1977). "The 'Other Cabinet': The National Security Council Staff." *Armed Forces Journal* 114 (July): 12–20.

Campbell, Colin (1980). "The President's Advisory System under Carter: From Spokes in a Wheel to Wagons in a Circle." Presented at the annual meeting of the American Political Science Association, Washington, D.C.

———, and George J. Szablowski (1979). *The Superbureaucrats: Structure and Behaviour in Central Agencies.* Toronto: Macmillan of Canada.

Campbell, John Franklin (1971). *The Foreign Affairs Fudge Factory.* New York: Basic Books.

Covington, Cary R. (1981). "Presidential Memory Development in Three Presidential Agencies." Presented at the annual meeting of the Midwest Political Science Association, Cincinnati.

Cronin, Thomas E. (1975). *The State of the Presidency.* Boston: Little, Brown.

Crossman, R. H. S. (1972). *The Myths of Cabinet Government.* Cambridge, Mass.: Harvard University Press.

Destler, I. M. (1980). "A Job That Doesn't Work." *Foreign Policy* 38:80–88.

——— (1977). "National Security Advice to U.S. Presidents: Some Lessons From Thirty Years." *World Politics* 29: 143–76.

——— (1972a). "Making Foreign Policy: Comment." *American Political Science Review* 66: 786–90.

——— (1972b). *Presidents, Bureaucrats, and Foreign Policy: The Politics of Organizational Reform.* Princeton, N.J.: Princeton University Press.

Dyson, K. H. F. (1974). "Planning and the Federal Chancellor's Office in the West German Federal Government." *Political Studies* 21: 348–62.

Evans, Rowland, and Robert Novak (1981). "The Education of Al Haig." *Washington Post,* 1 May 1981, p. A19.

Falk, Stanley L. (1964). "The National Security Council under Truman, Eisenhower, and Kennedy." *Political Science Quarterly* 79: 403–34.

Fenno, Richard F., Jr. (1975). "The President's Cabinet." In Aaron Wildavsky (ed.), *Perspectives on the Presidency.* Boston: Little, Brown.

Gelb, Leslie H. (1980). "Muskie and Brzezinski: The Struggle over Foreign Policy." *New York Times Magazine,* 20 July 1980, pp. 26–40.

George, Alexander L. (1972a). "The Case for Multiple Advocacy in Making Foreign Policy." *American Political Science Review* 66: 751–85.

——— (1972b). "Making Foreign Policy: Rejoinder." *American Political Science Review* 66: 791–95.

Hafner, Donald L. (1977). "Bureaucratic Politics and 'Those Frigging Missiles': JFK, Cuba and U.S. Missiles in Turkey," *Orbis* 21: 307–32.

Hammond, Paul Y. (1960). "The National Security Council as a Device for Interdepartmental Coordination: An Interpretation and Appraisal." *American Political Science Review* 54: 899–910.

Heclo, Hugh (1975). "OMB and the Presidency: The Problem of 'Neutral Competence.'" *The Public Interest* 38 (Winter): 80–98.

Klein, Rudolf, and Janet Lewis (1977). "Advice and Dissent in British Government: The Case of the Special Advisers." *Policy and Politics* 6: 1–25.

Maechling, Charles, Jr. (1976). "Foreign Policy-Makers: The Weakest Link?" *Virginia Quarterly Review* 52: 1–23.

McGregor, Eugene B., Jr. (1974). "Politics and the Career Mobility of Bureaucrats." *American Political Science Review* 68: 18–26.

Mennis, Bernard (1971). *American Foreign Policy Officials: Who They Are and What They Believe Regarding International Politics.* Columbus: Ohio State University Press.

Merton, Robert K. (1968). "Role of the Intellectual in Public Bureaucracy." In R. K. Merton, *Social Theory and Social Structure.* New York: The Free Press.

Murphy, Thomas P., Donald E. Nuechterlein, and Ronald J. Stupak (1978). *Inside the Bureaucracy: The View from the Assistant Secretary's Desk.* Boulder, Colo.: Westview.

Nathan, Richard P. (1975). *The Plot that Failed: Nixon and the Administrative Presidency.* New York: John Wiley.

National Security Policy Integration (1979). Report of a Study Requested by the president under the Auspices of the President's Reorganization Project. Washington, D.C.: Government Printing Office.

Neustadt, Richard E. (1954). "Presidency and Legislation: The Growth of Central Clearance." *American Political Science Review* 48: 641–71.

——— (1980). *Presidential Power: The Politics of Leadership from FDR to Carter.* New York: John Wiley.

Rose, Richard (1976a). *Managing Presidential Objectives.* New York: Free Press.

——— (1976b). "On the Priorities of Government: A Developmental Analysis of Public Policies." *European Journal of Political Research* 4: 247–89.

——— (1980). "Government against Sub-governments: A European Perspective on Washington." In Richard Rose and

Ezra Suleiman (eds.), *Presidents and Prime Ministers: Giving Direction to Government.* Washington, D.C.: American Enterprise Institute.

Sapin, Burton M. (1967). *The Making of United States Foreign Policy.* New York: Praeger.

Sayre, Wallace S. (1964). "Bureaucracies: Some Contrasts in Systems." *Indian Journal of Public Administration* 10: 219–29.

Seidman, Harold (1980). *Politics, Position, and Power: The Dynamics of Federal Organization.* New York: Oxford University Press.

Silberman, Laurence H. (1979). "Toward Presidential Control of the State Department." *Foreign Affairs* 57: 72–93.

Smith, Hedrick (1981). "A Scaled-down Version of Security Adviser's Task." *New York Times,* 4 March 1981, p. A2.

Stanley, David T., Dean E. Mann, and Jameson W. Doig (1967). *Men Who Govern: A Biographical Profile of American Federal Executives.* Washington, D.C.: Brookings Institution.

28

The NSC Staff as Rogue Elephant

Tower Commission

In the aftermath of the Iran-*contra* scandal involving questionable arms sales to Iran and the funneling of the profits to the *contras* for a covert war in Nicaragua, President Ronald Reagan established a blue-ribbon panel to investigate the affair. The president selected a former U.S. senator, Republican John Tower of Texas, to head up the inquiry. This selection summarizes the commission's findings, which were highly critical of both the president and the NSC staff.

What was Wrong

The arms transfers to Iran and the activities of the NSC staff in support of the Contras are case studies in the perils of policy pursued outside the constraints of orderly process.

The Iran initiative ran directly counter to the Administration's own policies on terrorism, the Iran/Iraq war, and military support to Iran. This inconsistency was never resolved, nor were the consequences of this inconsistency fully considered and provided for. The result taken as a whole was a U.S. policy that worked against itself.

The Board believes that failure to deal adequately with these contradictions resulted in large part from the flaws in the manner in which decisions were made. Established procedures for making national security decisions were ignored. Reviews of the initiative by all the NSC principals were too infrequent. The initiatives were not adequately vetted below the cabinet level. Intelligence resources were underutilized. Applicable legal constraints were not adequately addressed. The whole matter was handled too informally, without adequate written records of what had been considered, discussed, and decided.

This pattern persisted in the implementation of the Iran initiative. The NSC staff assumed direct operational control. The initiative fell within the traditional jurisdictions of the Departments of State, Defense, and CIA. Yet these agencies were largely ignored. Great reliance was placed on a network of private operators and intermediaries. How the initiative was to be carried out never received adequate attention from the NSC principals or a tough working-level review. No periodic evaluation of the progress of the initiative was ever conducted. The result was an unprofessional and, in substantial part, unsatisfactory operation.

In all of this process, Congress was never notified. . . .

A. A Flawed Process

1. Contradictory Policies Were Pursued

The arms sales to Iran and the NSC support for the Contras demonstrate the risks involved when highly controversial initiatives are pursued covertly.

Arms Transfers to Iran. The initiative to Iran was a covert operation directly at odds with important and well-publicized policies of the Executive Branch.

From *Report of the President's Special Review Board* (Tower Commission), Washington, D.C. (February 26, 1987), pp. IV 1–13.

The Tower Commission members included the chair, John Tower (R–Texas); Edmund Muskie, former Democratic senator from Maine and secretary of state in the Carter Administration; and Brent Scowcroft, national security adviser in the Ford and first Bush administrations.

But the initiative itself embodied a fundamental contradiction. Two objectives were apparent from the outset: a strategic opening to Iran, and release of the U.S. citizens held hostage in Lebanon. The sale of arms to Iran appeared to provide a means to achieve both these objectives. It also played into the hands of those who had other interests—some of them personal financial gain—in engaging the United States in an arms deal with Iran.

In fact, the sale of arms was not equally appropriate for achieving both these objectives. Arms were what Iran wanted. If all the United States sought was to free the hostages, then an arms-for-hostages deal could achieve the immediate objectives of both sides. But if the U.S. objective was a broader strategic relationship, then the sale of arms should have been contingent upon first putting into place the elements of that relationship. An arms-for-hostages deal in this context could become counter-productive to achieving this broader strategic objective. In addition, release of the hostages would require exerting influence with Hizballah, which could involve the most radical elements of the Iranian regime. The kind of strategic opening sought by the United States, however, involved what were regarded as more moderate elements.

The U.S. officials involved in the initiative appeared to have held three distinct views. For some, the principal motivation seemed consistently a strategic opening to Iran. For others, the strategic opening became a rationale for using arms sales to obtain the release of the hostages. For still others, the initiative appeared clearly as an arms-for-hostages deal from first to last.

Whatever the intent, almost from the beginning the initiative became in fact a series of arms-for-hostages deals. . . .

While the United States was seeking the release of the hostages in this way, it was vigorously pursuing policies that were dramatically opposed to such efforts. The Reagan Administration in particular had come into office declaring a firm stand against terrorism, which it continued to maintain. In December of 1985, the Administration completed a major study under the chairmanship of the Vice President. It resulted in a vigorous reaffirmation of U.S. opposition to terrorism in all its forms and a vow of total war on terrorism whatever its source. The Administration continued to pressure U.S. allies not to sell arms to Iran and not to make concessions to terrorists.

No serious effort was made to reconcile the inconsistency between these policies and the Iran initiative. No effort was made systematically to address the consequences of this inconsistency—the effect on U.S. policy when, as it inevitably would, the Iran initiative became known. . . .

NSC STAFF SUPPORT FOR THE CONTRAS. The activities of the NSC staff in support of the Contras sought to achieve an important objective of the Administration's foreign policy. The President had publicly and emphatically declared his support for the Nicaragua resistance. That brought his policy in direct conflict with that of the Congress, at least during the period that direct or indirect support of military operations in Nicaragua was barred.

Although the evidence before the Board is limited, no serious effort appears to have been made to come to grips with the risks to the President of direct NSC support for the Contras in the face of these Congressional restrictions. Even if it could be argued that these restrictions did not technically apply to the NSC staff, these activities presented great political risk to the President. The appearance of the President's personal staff doing what Congress had forbade other agencies to do could, once disclosed, only touch off a firestorm in the Congress and threaten the Administration's whole policy on the Contras.

2. The Decision-making Process Was Flawed

Because the arms sales to Iran and the NSC support for the Contras occurred in settings of such controversy, one would expect that the decisions to undertake these activities would have been made only after intense and thorough consideration. In fact, a far different picture emerges.

ARMS TRANSFERS TO IRAN. The Iran initiative was handled almost casually and through informal channels, always apparently with an expectation that the process would end with the next arms-for-hostages exchange. It was subjected neither to the general procedures for interagency consideration and review of policy issues nor the more restrictive procedures set out in NSDD 159 for handling covert operations. This had a number of consequences.

(i) The opportunity for a full hearing before the President was inadequate. In the last half of 1985, the Israelis made three separate proposals to the United States with respect to the Iran initiative (two in July and one in August). In addition, Israel made three separate deliveries of arms to Iran, one each in August, September, and November. Yet prior to December 7, 1985, there was at most one meeting of the NSC principals, a meeting which several participants recall taking place on August 6. There is no dispute that full meetings of the principals did occur on December 7, 1985, and on January 7, 1986. But the proposal to shift to direct U.S. arms sales to Iran appears not to have been discussed until later. It was considered by the President at a meeting on January 17 which only the Vice President, Mr. Regan, Mr. Fortier, and VADM Poindexter attended. Thereafter, the only senior-level review the Iran initiative received was during one or another of the President's daily national security briefings. These were routinely attended only by the President, the Vice President, Mr. Regan, and VADM Poindexter. There was no subsequent collective consideration of the Iran initiative by the NSC principals before it became public 11 months later.

This was not sufficient for a matter as important and consequential as the Iran initiative. Two or three cabinet-level reviews in a period of 17 months was not enough. The meeting on December 7 came late in the day, after the pattern of arms-for-hostages exchanges had become well established. The January 7 meeting had earmarks of a meeting held after a decision had already been made. Indeed, a draft Covert Action Finding authorizing the initiative had been signed by the President, though perhaps inadvertently, the previous day.

At each significant step in the Iran initiative, deliberations among the NSC principals in the presence of the President should have been virtually automatic. This was not and should not have been a formal requirement, something prescribed by statute. Rather, it should have been something the NSC principals desired as a means of ensuring an optimal environment for Presidential judgment. The meetings should have been preceded by consideration by the NSC principals

of staff papers prepared according to the procedures applicable to covert actions. These should have reviewed the history of the initiative, analyzed the issues then presented, developed a range of realistic options, presented the odds of success and the costs of failure, and addressed questions of implementation and execution. Had this been done, the objectives of the Iran initiative might have been clarified and alternatives to the sale of arms might have been identified.

(ii) The initiative was never subjected to a rigorous review below the cabinet level. Because of the obsession with secrecy, interagency consideration of the initiative was limited to the cabinet level. With the exception of the NSC staff and, after January 17, 1986, a handful of CIA officials, the rest of the executive departments and agencies were largely excluded.

As a consequence, the initiative was never vetted at the staff level. This deprived those responsible for the initiative of considerable expertise—on the situation in Iran; on the difficulties of dealing with terrorists; on the mechanics of conducting a diplomatic opening. It also kept the plan from receiving a tough, critical review.

Moreover, the initiative did not receive a policy review below cabinet level. Careful consideration at the Deputy/Under Secretary level might have exposed the confusion in U.S. objectives and clarified the risks of using arms as an instrument of policy in this instance.

The vetting process would also have ensured better use of U.S. intelligence. As it was, the intelligence input into the decision process was clearly inadequate. First, no independent evaluation of other Israeli proposals offered in July and August appears to have been sought or offered by U.S. intelligence agencies. The Israelis represented that they for some time had had contacts with elements in Iran. The prospects for an opening to Iran depended heavily on these contacts, yet no systematic assessment appears to have been made by U.S. intelligence agencies of the reliability and motivations of these contacts, and the identity and objectives of the elements in Iran that the opening was supposed to reach. Neither was any systematic assessment made of the motivation of the Israelis.

Second, neither Mr. Ghorbanifar nor the second channel seem to have been subjected to a systematic intelligence vetting before they were engaged as intermediaries. Mr. Ghorbanifar had been known to the CIA for some time and the agency had substantial doubts as to his reliability and truthfulness. Yet the agency did not volunteer that information or inquire about the identity of the intermediary if his name was unknown. Conversely, no early request for a name check was made of the CIA, and it was not until January 11, 1986, that the agency gave Mr. Ghorbanifar a new polygraph, which he failed. Notwithstanding this situation, with the signing of the January 17 Finding, the United States took control of the initiative and became even more directly involved with Mr. Ghorbanifar. The issues raised by the polygraph results do not appear to have been systematically addressed. In similar fashion, no prior intelligence check appears to have been made on the second channel.

Third, although the President recalled being assured that the arms sales to Iran would not alter the military balance with Iran, the Board could find no evidence that the President was ever briefed on this subject. The question of the impact of any intelligence shared with the Iranians does not appear to have been brought to the President's attention.

A thorough vetting would have included consideration of the legal implications of the initiative. There appeared to be little effort to face squarely the legal restrictions and notification requirements applicable to the operation. At several points, other agencies raised questions about violations of law or regulations. These concerns were dismissed without, it appears, investigating them with the benefit of legal counsel.

Finally, insufficient attention was given to the implications of implementation. The implementation of the initiative raised a number of issues: should the NSC staff rather than the CIA have had operational control; what were the implications of Israeli involvement; how reliable were the Iranian and various other private intermediaries; what were the implications of the use of Mr. Secord's private network of operatives; what were the implications for the military balance in the region; was operational security adequate. Nowhere do these issues appear to have been sufficiently addressed.

The concern for preserving the secrecy of the initiative provided an excuse for abandoning sound

process. Yet the initiative was known to a variety of persons with diverse interests and ambitions—Israelis, Iranians, various arms dealers and business intermediaries, and Lt. Col. North's network of private operatives. While concern for secrecy would have justified limiting the circle of persons knowledgeable about the initiative, in this case it was drawn too tightly. As a consequence, important advice and counsel were lost.

In January of 1985, the President had adopted procedures for striking the proper balance between secrecy and the need for consultation on sensitive programs. These covered the institution, implementation, and review of covert operations. In the case of the Iran initiative, these procedures were almost totally ignored.

The only staff work the President apparently reviewed in connection with the Iran initiative was prepared by NSC staff members, under the direction of the National Security Advisor. These were, of course, the principal proponents of the initiative. A portion of this staff work was reviewed by the Board. It was frequently striking in its failure to present the record of past efforts—particularly past failures. Alternative ways of achieving U.S. objectives—other than yet another arms-for-hostages deal—were not discussed. Frequently it neither adequately presented the risks involved in pursuing the initiative nor the full force of the dissenting views of other NSC principals. On balance, it did not serve the President well.

(iii) The process was too informal. The whole decision process was too informal. Even when meetings among NSC principals did occur, often there was no prior notice of the agenda. No formal written minutes seem to have been kept. Decisions subsequently taken by the President were not formally recorded. An exception was the January 17 Finding, but even this was apparently not circulated or shown to key U.S. officials.

The effect of this informality was that the initiative lacked a formal institutional record. This precluded the participants from undertaking the more informed analysis and reflection that is afforded by a written record, as opposed to mere recollection. It made it difficult to determine where the initiative stood, and to learn lessons from the record that could guide future action. This lack of an institutional record permitted specific proposals for arms-for-hostages exchanges to be presented in a vacuum, without reference to the results of past proposals. Had a searching and thorough review of the Iran initiative been undertaken at any stage in the process, it would have been extremely difficult to conduct. The Board can attest first hand to the problem of conducting a review in the absence of such records. Indeed, the exposition in the wake of public revelation suffered the most.

NSC STAFF SUPPORT FOR THE CONTRAS.   It is not clear how Lt. Col. North first became involved in activities in direct support of the Contras during the period of the Congressional ban. The Board did not have before it much evidence on this point. In the evidence that the Board did have, there is no suggestion at any point of any discussion of Lt. Col. North's activities with the President in any forum. There also does not appear to have been any interagency review of Lt. Col. North's activities at any level.

This latter point is not surprising given the Congressional restrictions under which the other relevant agencies were operating. But the NSC staff apparently did not compensate for the lack of any interagency review with its own internal vetting of these activities. Lt. Col. North apparently worked largely in isolation, keeping first Mr. McFarlane and then VADM Poindexter informed.

The lack of adequate vetting is particularly evident on the question of the legality of Lt. Col. North's activities. The Board did not make a judgment on the legal issues raised by his activities in support of the Contras. Nevertheless, some things can be said.

If these activities were illegal, obviously they should not have been conducted. If there was any doubt on the matter, systematic legal advice should have been obtained. The political cost to the President of illegal action by the NSC staff was particularly high, both because the NSC staff is the personal staff of the President and because of the history of serious conflict with the Congress over the issue of Contra support. For these reasons, the President should have been kept apprised of any review of the legality of Lt. Col. North's activities.

Legal advice was apparently obtained from the President's Intelligence Oversight Board. Without passing on the quality of that advice, it is an odd source. It would be one thing for the Intelligence Oversight Board to review the legal advice provided by some other agency. It is another for the Intelligence Oversight Board to be originating legal advice of its own. That is a function more appropriate for the NSC staff's own legal counsel.

3. Implementation Was Unprofessional
The manner in which the Iran initiative was implemented and Lt. Col. North undertook to support the Contras are very similar. This is in large part because the same cast of characters was involved. In both cases the operations were unprofessional, although the Board has much less evidence with respect to Lt. Col. North's Contra activities.

ARMS TRANSFERS TO IRAN.   With the signing of the January 17 Finding, the Iran initiative became a U.S. operation run by the NSC staff. Lt. Col. North made most of the significant operational decisions. He conducted the operation through Mr. Secord and his associates, a network of private individuals already involved in the Contra resupply operation. To this was added a handful of selected individuals from the CIA.

But the CIA support was limited. Two CIA officials, though often at meetings, had a relatively limited role. One served as the point man for Lt. Col. North in providing logistics and financial arrangements. The other (Mr. Allen) served as a contact between Lt. Col. North and the intelligence community. By contrast, George Cave actually played a significant and expanding role. However, Clair George, Deputy Director for Operations at CIA, told the Board: "George was paid by me and on the paper was working for me. But I think in the heat of the battle, . . . George was working for Oliver North."

Because so few people from the departments and agencies were told of the initiative, Lt. Col. North cut himself off from resources and expertise from within the government. He relied instead on a number of private intermediaries, businessmen and other financial brokers, private operators, and Iranians hostile to the United States. Some of these were individuals with questionable credentials and potentially large personal financial interests in the transactions. This made the transactions unnecessarily complicated and invited kickbacks and payoffs. This arrangement also dramatically increased the risks that the initiative would leak.

Yet no provision was made for such an eventuality. Further, the use of Mr. Secord's private network in the Iran initiative linked those operators with the resupply of the Contras, threatening exposure of both operations if either became public.

The result was a very unprofessional operation. . . .

The implementation of the initiative was never subjected to a rigorous review. Lt. Col. North appears to have kept VADM Poindexter fully informed of his activities. In addition, VADM Poindexter, Lt. Col. North, and the CIA officials involved apparently apprised Director Casey of many of the operational details. But Lt. Col. North and his operation functioned largely outside the orbit of the U.S. Government. Their activities were not subject to critical reviews of any kind.

After the initial hostage release in September, 1985, it was over 10 months before another hostage was released. This despite recurring promises of the release of all the hostages and four intervening arms shipments. Beginning with the November shipment, the United States increasingly took over the operation of the initiative. In January, 1986, it decided to transfer arms directly to Iran.

Any of these developments could have served as a useful occasion for a systematic reconsideration of the initiative. Indeed, at least one of the schemes contained a provision for reconsideration if the initial assumptions proved to be invalid. They did, but the reconsideration never took place. It was the responsibility of the National Security Advisor and the responsible officers on the NSC staff to call for such a review. But they were too involved in the initiative both as advocates and as implementors. This made it less likely that they would initiate the kind of review and reconsideration that should have been undertaken.

NSC STAFF SUPPORT FOR THE CONTRAS. As already noted, the NSC activities in support of the Contras and its role in the Iran initiative were of a piece. In the former, there was an added element of Lt. Col. North's intervention in the customs investigation of the crash of the SAT aircraft. Here, too, selected CIA officials reported directly to Lt. Col. North. The limited evidence before the Board suggested that the activities in support of the Contras involved unprofessionalism much like that in the Iran operation.

iv. Congress was never notified. Congress was not apprised either of the Iran initiative or of the NSC staff's activities in support of the Contras.

In the case of Iran, because release of the hostages was expected within a short time after the delivery of equipment, and because public disclosure could have destroyed the operation and perhaps endangered the hostages, it could be argued that it was justifiable to defer notification of Congress prior to the first shipment of arms to Iran. The plan apparently was to inform Congress immediately after the hostages were safely in U.S. hands. But after the first delivery failed to release all the hostages, and as one hostage release plan was replaced by another, Congress certainly should have been informed. This could have been done during a period when no specific hostage release plan was in execution. Consultation with Congress could have been useful to the President, for it might have given him some sense of how the public would react to the initiative. It also might have influenced his decision to continue to pursue it. . . .

B. Failure of Responsibility

The NSC system will not work unless the President makes it work. After all, this system was created to serve the President of the United States in ways of his choosing. By his actions, by his leadership, the President therefore determines the quality of its performance.

By his own account, as evidenced in his diary notes, and as conveyed to the Board by his principal advisors, President Reagan was deeply committed to securing the release of the hostages. It was this intense compassion for the hostages that appeared to motivate his steadfast support of the Iran initiative, even in the face of opposition from his Secretaries of State and Defense.

In his obvious commitment, the President appears to have proceeded with a concept of the initiative that was not accurately reflected in the reality of the operation. The President did not seem to be aware of the way in which the operation was implemented and the full consequences of U.S. participation.

The President's expressed concern for the safety of both the hostages and the Iranians who could have been at risk may have been conveyed in a manner so as to inhibit the full functioning of the system.

The President's management style is to put the principal responsibility for policy review and implementation on the shoulders of his advisors. Nevertheless, with such a complex, high-risk operation and so much at stake, the President should have ensured that the NSC system did not fail him. He did not force his policy to undergo the most critical review of which the NSC participants and the process were capable. At no time did he insist upon accountability and performance review. Had the President chosen to drive the NSC system, the outcome could well have been different. As it was, the most powerful features of the NSC system—providing comprehensive analysis, alternatives and follow-up—were not utilized.

The Board found a strong consensus among NSC participants that the President's priority in the Iran initiative was the release of U.S. hostages. But setting priorities is not enough when it comes to sensitive and risky initiatives that directly affect U.S. national security. He must ensure that the content and tactics of an initiative match his priorities and objectives. He must insist upon accountability. For it is the President who must take responsibility for the NSC system and deal with the consequences.

Beyond the President, the other NSC principals and the National Security Advisor must share in the responsibility for the NSC system.

President Reagan's personal management style places an especially heavy responsibility on his key advisors. Knowing his style, they should have been particularly mindful of the need for special attention to the manner in which this arms sale initiative developed and proceeded. On this score, neither the National Security Advisor nor the other NSC principals deserve high marks.

It is their obligation as members and advisors to the Council to ensure that the President is adequately served. The principal subordinates to the President must not be deterred from urging the President not to proceed on a highly questionable course of action even in the face of his strong conviction to the contrary.

In the case of the Iran initiative, the NSC process did not fail, it simply was largely ignored. The National Security Advisor and the NSC principals all had a duty to raise this issue and insist that orderly process be imposed. None of them did so.

All had the opportunity. While the National Security Advisor had the responsibility to see that an orderly process was observed, his failure to do so does not excuse the other NSC principals. It does not appear that any of the NSC principals called for more frequent consideration of the Iran initiative by the NSC principals in the presence of the President. None of the principals called for a serious vetting of the initiative by even a restricted group of disinterested individuals. The intelligence questions do not appear to have been raised, and legal considerations, while raised, were not pressed. No one seemed to have complained about the informality of the process. No one called for a thorough reexamination once the initiative did not meet expectations or the manner of execution changed. While one or another of the NSC principals suspected that something was amiss, none vigorously pursued the issue.

Mr. Regan also shares in this responsibility. More than almost any Chief of Staff of recent memory, he asserted personal control over the White House staff and sought to extend this control to the National Security Advisor. He was personally active in national security affairs and attended almost all of the relevant meetings regarding the Iran initiative. He, as much as anyone, should have insisted that an orderly process be observed. In addition, he especially should have ensured that plans were made for handling any public disclosure of the initiative. He must bear primary responsibility for the chaos that descended upon the White House when such disclosure did occur.

Mr. McFarlane appeared caught between a President who supported the initiative and the cabinet officers who strongly opposed it. While he made efforts to keep these cabinet officers informed, the Board heard complaints from some that he was not always successful. VADM Poindexter on several occasions apparently sought to exclude NSC principals other than the President from knowledge of the initiative. Indeed, on one or more occasions Secretary Shultz may have been actively misled by VADM Poindexter.

VADM Poindexter also failed grievously on the matter of Contra diversion. Evidence indicates that VADM Poindexter knew that a diversion occurred, yet he did not take the steps that were required given the gravity of that prospect. He apparently failed to appreciate or ignored the serious legal and political risks presented. His clear obligation was either to investigate the matter or take it to the President—or both. He did neither. Director Casey shared a similar responsibility. Evidence suggests that he received information about the possible diversion of funds to the Contras almost a month before the story broke. He, too, did not move promptly to raise the matter with the President. Yet his responsibility to do so was clear.

The NSC principals other than the President may be somewhat excused by the insufficient attention on the part of the National Security Advisor to the need to keep all the principals fully informed. Given the importance of the issue and the sharp policy divergences involved, however, Secretary Shultz and Secretary Weinberger in particular distanced themselves from the march of events. Secretary Shultz specifically requested to be informed only as necessary to perform his job. Secretary Weinberger had access through intelligence to details about the operation. Their obligation was to give the President their full support and continued advice with respect to the program or, if they could not in conscience do that, to so inform the President. Instead, they simply distanced themselves from the program. They protected the record as to their own positions on this issue. They were not energetic in attempting to protect the President from the consequences of his personal commitment to freeing the hostages.

Director Casey appears to have been informed in considerable detail about the specifics of the Iranian operation. He appears to have acquiesced in and to have encouraged North's exercise of direct operational control over the operation. Because of the NSC staff's proximity to and close identification with the President, this increased the risks to the President if the initiative became public or the operation failed.

There is no evidence, however, that Director Casey explained this risk to the President or made clear to the President that Lt. Col. North, rather than the CIA, was running the operation. The President does not recall ever being informed of this fact. Indeed, Director Casey should have gone further and pressed for operational responsibility to be transferred to the CIA.

Director Casey should have taken the lead in vetting the assumptions presented by the Israelis on which the program was based and in pressing for an early examination of the reliance upon Mr. Ghorbanifar and the second channel as intermediaries. He should also have assumed responsibility for checking out the other intermediaries involved in the operation. Finally, because Congressional restrictions on covert actions are both largely directed at and familiar to the CIA, Director Casey should have taken the lead in keeping the question of Congressional notification active.

Finally, Director Casey, and, to a lesser extent, Secretary Weinberger, should have taken it upon themselves to assess the effect of the transfer of arms and intelligence to Iran on the Iran/Iraq military balance, and to transmit that information to the President. . . .

29

CONGRESS AND THE NSC

Inouye–Hamilton Committee

In response to the Iran-*contra* scandal, the Congress created an investigative panel to examine what had happened. The House–Senate Joint Committee heard from twenty-eight witnesses in public hearings, including Lieut. Col. Oliver L. North, Vice Admiral John N. Poindexter (President Reagan's national security adviser at the time), and Secretary of State George P. Shultz. Their testimony, excerpted in this selection, takes us behind the scenes of the Iran-*contra* affair, disclosing many of the intrigues that occurred inside the NSC during this period, as well as the systematic attempts by several key NSC officials to conceal them from lawmakers.

THE COMMITTEE HEARD FROM LIEUT. COL. OLIVER L. NORTH IN JULY OF 1987

July 7, 1987

John W. Nields Jr., chief counsel for the House.

Q The American people were told by this Government that our Government had nothing to do with the Hasenfus airplane [a secret CIA military-supply flight which crashed in Nicaragua in 1986], and that was false. And it is a principal purpose of these hearings to replace secrecy and deception with disclosure and truth. And that's one of the reasons we have called you here, sir. And one question the American people would like to know the answer to is what did the President know about the diversion of the proceeds of Iranian arms sales to the contras. Can you tell us what you know about that, sir?

A You just took a long leap from Mr. Hasenfus's airplane.

As I told this committee several days ago—and if you will indulge me, counsel, in a brief summary of what I said: I never personally discussed the use of the residuals or profits from the sale of U.S. weapons to Iran for the purpose of supporting the Nicaraguan resistance with the President. I never raised it with him and he never raised it with me during my entire tenure with the National Security Council staff.

Throughout the conduct of my entire tenure at the National Security Council, I assumed that the President was aware of what I was doing and had, through my superiors, approved it. I sought approval of my superiors for every one of my actions, and it is well documented.

I assumed, when I had approval to proceed from either Judge Clark, Bud McFarlane or Admiral Poindexter, that they had indeed solicited and obtained the approval of the President. To my recollection, Admiral Poindexter never told me that he met with the President on the issue of using residuals from the Iranian sales to support the Nicaraguan resistance. Or that he discussed the residuals or profits for use by the contras with the President. Or that he got the President's specific approval.

Nor did he tell me that the President had approved such a transaction.

But again, I wish to reiterate throughout I believed that the President had indeed authorized such activity.

From witness testimony, Select Committee on Secret Military Assistance to Iran and the Nicaraguan Opposition, the Inouye–Hamilton Joint Committee, co-chaired by Senator Daniel K. Inouye (D–Hawaii) and Representative Lee Hamilton (D–Indiana) (July and August 1987).

The testimony presented here is from national security adviser Vice Admiral John M. Poindexter and NSC staff aide Lieut. Col. Oliver L. North, as well as Secretary of State George P. Shultz.

No other person with whom I was in contact with during my tenure at the White House told me that he or she ever discussed the issue of the residuals or profits with the President.

In late November, two other things occurred which relate to this issue. On or about Friday, Nov. 21, [1986] I asked Admiral Poindexter directly: Does the President know? He told me he did not. And on Nov. 25, the day I was reassigned back to the United States Marine Corps for service, the President of the United States called me. In the course of that call, the President said to me words to the effect that: I just didn't know.

Those are the facts as I know them, Mr. Nields. I was glad that . . . you said that you wanted to hear the truth. I came here to tell you the truth, the good, the bad and the ugly. I am here to tell it all, pleasant and unpleasant. And I am here to accept responsibility for that which I did. I will not accept responsibility for that which I did not do. . . .

Q I'm not asking you about words now, Colonel. I am asking you whether you didn't continue to send memoranda seeking approval of diversions or residuals—whatever the word—for the benefit of the contras up to the President for approval?

A I did not send them to the President, Mr. Nields. This memorandum went to the National Security Adviser, seeking that he obtain the President's approval. There is a big difference. This is not a memorandum to the President.

Q And my question to you is: Didn't—isn't it true that you continued to send them up to the National Security Adviser, seeking the President's approval?

A Is it my recollection that I did, yes sir.

Q And Admiral Poindexter never told you: Stop sending those memoranda?

A I do not recall the admiral saying that. It is entirely possible, Mr. Nields, that that did happen.

Q Well if it had happened, then you would have stopped sending them, isn't that true?

A Yes.

Q But you didn't stop sending them. You've just testified you sent them on five different occasions.

A I testified that to my recollection there were about five times when we thought we had an arrangement that would result in the release of American hostages and the opening of a dialogue with Iran. And that we

thought the deal was sufficiently framed that we could proceed with it. And that I thought—because I don't have those records before me—that I had sent memoranda forward, as I always did, seeking approval.

That's what I think and that's what I recall.

Q And was there ever a time when Admiral Poindexter said: Don't send them up for the President's approval; just send them up for my approval?

A Again, I don't recall such a conversation.

Q Well in fact, isn't it true that it was Admiral Poindexter that wanted you to send these memoranda up for the President to approve?

A I don't recall Admiral Poindexter instructing me to do that, either. . . .

Q So far from telling you to stop sending memoranda up for the President's approval, Admiral Poindexter was specifically asking you to send memoranda up for the President's approval?

A Well, again, in this particular case that's true, Mr. Nields. And I don't believe that I have said that Admiral Poindexter told me to stop. Did I?

Q Where are these memoranda?

A Which memoranda?

Q The memoranda that you sent up to Admiral Poindexter, seeking the President's approval?

A Well, they're probably in these books to my left that I haven't even looked through yet. And if I try to guess, I'm going to be wrong. But I think I shredded most of that. Did I get them all. I'm not trying to be flippant, I'm just——

Q Well, that was going to be my very next question, Colonel North. Isn't it true that you shredded them?

A I believe I did. . . .

Q Well, that's the whole reason for shredding documents, isn't it, Colonel North—so that you can later say you don't remember whether you had them and you don't remember what's in them?

A No, Mr. Nields. The reason for shredding documents and the reason the Government of the United States gave me a shredder—I mean, I didn't buy it myself—was to destroy documents that were no longer relevant; that did not apply or that should not be divulged.

And again, I want to go back to the whole intent of a covert operation. Part of a covert operation is to offer plausible deniability of the association of the

Government of the United States with the activity. Part of it is to deceive our adversaries. Part of it is to insure that those people who are at great peril carrying out those activities are not further endangered.

All of those are good and sufficient reasons to destroy documents. And that's why the Government buys [and] gives them to people running [a] covert operation. Not so that they can have convenient memories. I came here to tell you the truth; to tell you and this committee and the American people the truth. And I'm trying to do that, Mr. Nields. And I don't like the insinuation that I'm up here having a convenient memory lapse like perhaps some others have had. . . .

Q   Is it correct to say that following the enactment of the Boland Amendment, our support for the war in Nicaragua did not end and that you were the person in the United States Government who managed it?

A   Starting in the spring of 1984, well before the Boland proscription of no appropriated funds made available to the D.O.D. and the C.I.A., etc., I was already engaged in supporting the Nicaraguan resistance and the democratic outcome in Nicaragua.

I did so as part of a covert operation. It was carried out starting as early as the spring of '84, when we ran out of money and people started to look in Nicaragua, in Honduras and Guatemala, El Salvador and Costa Rica for some sign of what the Americans were really going to do, and that that help began much earlier than the most rigorous of the Boland proscriptions. And yes, it was carried out covertly, and it was carried out in such a way as to insure that the heads of state and the political leadership in Nicaragua—in Central America—recognized the United States was going to meet the commitments of the President's foreign policy.

And the President's foreign policy was that we are going to achieve a democratic outcome in Nicaragua and that our support for the Nicaraguan freedom fighters was going to continue, and that I was given the job of holding them together in body and soul. And it slowly transitioned into a more difficult task as time went on and as the C.I.A. had to withdraw further and further from that support, until finally we got to the point in October when I was the only person left talking to them. . . .

Q   Well maybe it would be most useful to get into specifics of the areas of your support. I take it one area of your support was to endeavor to raise money from sources other than the U.S. Treasury?

A   That's correct. Boland proscriptions do not allow us to do so, and so we sought a means of complying with those Boland proscriptions by going elsewhere for those monies.

Q   And you went to foreign countries?

A   I did not physically go to those foreign countries.

Q   Representatives of—

A   Representatives of foreign countries and I had discussions about those matters, yes.

Q   And you asked them for money for the contras?

A   I want to be a little bit more specific about that. I don't recall going hat in hand to anybody asking for money. I do recall sitting and talking about how grateful this country would be if the issue that they had discussed with others were indeed brought to fruition. For example, a representative of Country 3 and I met and we talked about an issue that had been raised with him beforehand by others outside the Government, and I told him that I thought that was a dandy idea. And I told him where he could send the money. And he did so. . . .

Q   Now, my next question is you've indicated that the national security advisers, for whom you worked, authorized you to seek support from foreign countries, both financial and operational?

A   Yes.

Q   Was your—were your activities, in that respect, known to others in the White House, other than the national security advisers?

A   Well, I want to go back to something I said at the very beginning of all of this, Mr. Nields. I assumed that those matters which required the attention and decision of the President of the United States did indeed get them.

I assumed that. I never asked that. I never walked up to the President and said, oh by the way Mr. President, yesterday I met with so-and-so from Country 4. Nor did he ever say, I'm glad you had a meeting with Country 4 and it went well.

Q   Do you know whether or not the President was aware of your activities seeking funds and operational support for the contras, from third countries?

A   I do not know.

Q   Were you ever——

A   I assumed that he did.

Q Were you ev—what was the basis of your assumption?

A Just that there was a lot going on and it was very obvious that the Nicaraguan resistance survived—I sent forward innumerable documents, some of which you've just shown us as exhibits, that demonstrated that I was keeping my superiors fully informed, as to what was going on. . . .

Q Mr. McFarlane has testified that he gave you instructions not to solicit money from foreign countries or private sources. Did he give you those instructions?

A I never carried out a single act—not one, Mr. Nields—in which I did not have authority from my superiors. I haven't, in the 23 years that I have been in the uniformed services of the United States of America ever violated an order—not one.

Q But that wasn't the question. The question was—

A That *is* the answer to your question.

Q No, the question was did Mr. McFarlane give you such instructions?

A No. I never heard those instructions.

Q And I take it that it was your understanding, from what you've just said, that quite to the contrary, you were authorized to seek money from foreign countries?

A I was authorized to do everything that I did.

Q Well, again, that isn't the question.

A I was authorized to have a meeting, in this particular case by Mr. McFarlane, for the purpose of talking to the man about a suggestion that had been made to him by others, and to encourage that process along. And I did so. I had already provided to Mr. McFarlane a card with the address of an account, an offshore account which would support the Nicaraguan resistance. And thank God, somebody put money into that account and the Nicaraguan resistance didn't die—as perhaps others intended. Certainly the Sandinistas and Moscow and Cuba intended that. And they didn't die, they grew in strength and numbers and effectiveness as a consequence. And I think that is a good thing. . . .

I get the sense that somehow or another we've tried to create the impression that Oliver North picked up his hat and wandered around Washington and foreign capitals begging for money, and I didn't do that. I didn't have to do it because others were more willing to put up the money than the Congress because they saw well what was happening to us in Central America, and the devastating consequences of a contra wipeout and an American walkaway and write-off; to what was going to happen to this country and to democracy elsewhere in the world.

I didn't have to wander around and beg. There were other countries in the world, and other people in this country, who were more willing to help the Nicaraguan resistance survive, and cause democracy to prosper in Central America, than this body here. And that is an important factor in all of what you do, counsel, and in what this committee is going to do. It's got to be part of your assessment, as to why is it that other countries in the world were willing to step up and help in a desperate cause when we were not willing to do so ourselves.

That has got to be something that is debated not just by pulling people before this group and hammering at them and haranguing them and reducing it to pettiness. It has got to be something that the American people come to understand, how desperately important it was not just to us, not just to Ollie North and not just to President Ronald Reagan. It was important to these other people who put forth that money. And I didn't beg them, they offered. And that's important, sir. . . .

July 8, 1987

Q You testified about Admiral Poindexter and the President. Who else, if anyone—and I don't mean to imply anything in the question. But leaving those two people aside, who else in the Government was aware of either the plan or the fact of using proceeds of arms sales to Iran for the contras?

A Well I, if I may clarify what I testified to yesterday, it is my assumption the President knew and then I subsequently testified that I was told he did not know. I know that Admiral Poindexter knew. I know that Mr. McFarlane knew at a point in time when he was no longer in the Government. And [CIA] Director [William J.] Casey knew.

Aside from that, I can't speak with certainty as to who else, inside the government, knew for sure. . . . But the only ones that I know for sure, who I confirmed it with, were those three. . . .

Q When did Director Casey first learn of it?

A Actually, I—my recollection is Director Casey learned about it before the fact. Since I'm confessing to things, I may have raised it with him before I raised it with Admiral Poindexter. Probably when I returned from the February—from the January discussions.

Q You're referring now to the discussions, the trip, during which you had the discussion with Mr. [Nanucher] Ghorbanifar [a go-between in the Iranian arms deal] in the bathroom?

A Yes, I don't recall raising the bathroom [discussion], specifically, with the Director, but I do recall talking with the Director and I don't remember whether it was before or after I talked to Admiral Poindexter about it. But I—I was not the only one who was enthusiastic about this idea. And I—Director Casey used several words to describe how he felt about it, all of which were effusive.

He referred to it as the ultimate irony, the ultimate covert operation kind of thing, and was very enthusiastic about it. He also recognized that there were potential liabilities. And that there was risk involved. . . .

Q What kinds of risks did he identify to you?

A This very political risk that we see being portrayed out here now; that it could indeed be dangerous, or not dangerous so much as politically damaging.

Q Do you have any reason to believe that Director Casey, given the political risk, ever discussed the matter with the President?

A I have no reason to believe that he did because he never addressed that to me. I never, as I indicated yesterday, no one ever told me that they had discussed it with the President. . . .

Q And there came a time, did there not, when you had an interview with members of the House Intelligence Committee?

A I did. . . .

Q And they were interested in finding out the answers to the questions raised by the resolution of inquiry?

A Exactly.

Q Your fund-raising activities, military support for the contras?

A That's right. . . .

Q But I take it you did considerably more which you did not tell the committee about?

A I have admitted that here before you today. . . . I will tell you right now, counsel, and all the members here gathered, that I misled the Congress. . . .

Q You made false statements to them about your activities in support of the contras?

A I did. Furthermore, I did so with a purpose. And I did so with the purpose of hopefully avoiding the very kind of thing that we have before us now, and avoiding a shut-off of help for the Nicaraguan resistance, and avoiding an elimination of the resistance facilities in three Central American countries, wherein we had promised those heads of state on my specific orders—on specific orders to me I had gone down there and assured them of our absolute and total discretion.

And I am admitting to you that I participated in the preparation of documents to the Congress that were erroneous, misleading, evasive and wrong. And I did it again here when I appeared before that committee convened in the White House Situation Room. And I make no excuses for what I did. I will tell you now that I am under oath and I was not then.

Q We do live in a democracy, don't we?

A We do sir, thank God.

Q In which it is the people not one marine lieutenant colonel that get to decide the important policy decisions for the nation?

A Yes, and I would point out that part of that answer is that this marine lieutenant colonel was not making all of those decisions on his own. As I indicated yesterday in my testimony, Mr. Nields, I sought approval for everything that I did.

Q But you denied Congress the facts?

A I did.

Q You denied the elected representatives of our people the facts, upon which, which they needed—

A I did.

Q —to make a very important decision for this nation?

A I did, because of what I have just described to you as our concerns. And I did it because we have had incredible leaks from discussions with closed committees of the Congress.

THE CONGRESSIONAL COMMITTEE HEARD FROM REAR ADM. JOHN M. POINDEXTER. HERE ARE EXCERPTS FROM HIS TESTIMONY, AS RECORDED BY THE NEW YORK TIMES
July 15, 1987

Arthur L. Liman, chief counsel to the Senate committee. Now let's turn to the Iran initiative. Were you advised sometime in August of 1985 by Mr. McFarlane that the President had approved some Israeli transactions with Iran?

Admiral Poindexter   Mr. Liman, that is a very fuzzy time period for me. . . . The period of time you're asking about, August of 1985, I was the deputy, and I did not have primary responsibility on this issue. . . .

Q   But you did become aware that there was an Iran initiative?

A   Yes, I did.

Q   And you became aware of that from a conversation with Mr. McFarlane?

A   I did. . . .

Q   Now, admiral, did there come a time in connection with this transaction, when the C.I.A. sent over to you a proposed finding for the President to sign?

A   Yes, Mr. Liman. That is the finding that I discussed with you earlier on the second of May.

Q   Did you receive the letter of Nov. 26, 1985, from William Casey addressed to you which says, pursuant to our conversation, this should go to the President for his signature and should not be passed around in any hands below our level?

A   I did receive that.

Q   And you received the finding with it. Is that correct?

A   Well, I must say that I don't actually remember getting it, but I'm sure that I did. I'm sure they came together.

Q   Now, Admiral, when you saw the finding, am I correct that the finding itself was essentially a straight arms-for-hostage finding?

A   That is correct. It had been prepared essentially by the C.I.A. as a what we call a C.Y.A. effort.

Q   Did the President of the United States sign that finding?

A   As I've testified before, he did, on or about the 5th of December. I'm vague on the date. . . .

Q   Do you recall who was present when the President signed the finding?

A   No, I don't. One of the reasons that I think my recollection is very poor on the circumstances of the President's actually signing this is that, recall that, that was a day or so after Mr. McFarlane had resigned and the President had just—I guess we had announced it on the fourth. Mr. McFarlane actually resigned, I think, on the 30th of November, we announced it on the fourth of December, and my recollection is that he

signed this the following day on the fifth. My recollection now is that the C.I.A., especially the Deputy Director, John McMahon, was very anxious to get this signed. I frankly was never happy with it, because it was not fully staffed, and I frankly can't recall when I showed it to the President who was there or exactly what the discussion was or even what I recommended to him at this point. I simply can't remember that.

Q   But you do recall that whatever you recommended, the President read it and he signed it.

A   Yes, he did. He did sign it.

Q   And there was, in fact, the recommendation from Bill Casey that he sign it, and Bill Casey was a person whose advice the President valued.

A   He did.

Q   Now what happened to that finding?

A   As I said earlier, I destroyed that by tearing it up on the 21st of November because I thought it was a significant political embarrassment to the President. And I wanted to protect him from possible disclosure of this. To get into the details of exactly how it happened, which I assume you're interested in—

Q   Yes. When you say the 21st of November, you're talking about the 21st of November 1986.

A   1986. That's correct.

Q   Now, would you tell the panel the circumstances of your destroying this finding because you thought it would be a significant political embarrassment to the President?

A   I will. The finding, the existence of the finding I had completely forgotten in early November 1986. As I said before, the finding initially was prepared by the C.I.A. for the reason that I stated. I can recall in my time at the White House one or possibly two other findings that had a retroactive nature to them. I frankly was always uncomfortable with that because I thought it didn't particularly make a lot of sense.

The finding was very narrow. It was prepared before there had been thorough discussion of the issue. As I said earlier, I came into the issue in a full, responsible way in early December of 1985. Prior to that time, Mr. McFarlane had handled it. I felt that it was important that we improve on this finding so that we clearly lay out what the objectives were in the Iranian . . . After this finding was signed, it was retained in my immediate office and at some point after it was signed I had apparently given it to Commander Thompson, my military assistant, to put in an envelope in his safe to keep.

I had, as I said, completely forgotten about it. On November the 21st, when Ed Meese [the Attorney General] called me and said—well, to go back a step, we'd run into a problem in November of what had actually happened in 1985. It was very dim in people's memories. We didn't think we had much in writing.

As I think you've heard Colonel North testify, we frankly did not realize the old PROF notes [the White House electronic message system] existed. My policy was to erase them, and I apparently did it the right way, and I don't think Colonel North did it the right way. So we didn't have the benefit that these committees have in going back over these old PROF notes, or we didn't realize that we had that opportunity.

But Ed Meese and I talked many times during the month of November, and when it became clear that there was a disagreement between Cabinet-level officials as to what had happened in November of 1985, he indicated that he wanted to come over and ask the President to have a fact-finding session primarily with the Cabinet-level officials involved to try to sort out what had happened, actually happened in November of 1985. And he called me early in the morning on the 21st of November and told me this, and he said he had an appointment to see the President at 11:30, and he wanted me and Don Regan [the White House chief of staff] to go with him, which we did at 11:30.

He told the President about the controversy, not really controversy, the different recollections as to what had happened in November. And he said he thought it would be useful if he would have a couple of his people that were close to him look into the matter to see if they could piece together what had happened. The President readily agreed. . . .

So Ed called me after lunch, . . . and he asked if I would have the appropriate documents pulled together so they could take a look at them. I said I would do that. After he called, I called Commander Thompson, my military assistant, and asked him to take charge of pulling these documents together.

And then I called Colonel North and told him of my conversation with Mr. Meese and asked him to cooperate with Commander Thompson and Mr. Meese's people. . . .

Later in the afternoon or early evening, Commander Thompson brought into my office the envelopes that I had given him earlier containing the material we had on the Iranian project in the immediate office, which was essentially the various findings. And he

pulled out this November finding—it was actually signed in December. And my recollection is that he said something to the effect that they'll have a field day with this, or something to that effect. . . . The import of his comment was that up until that time in November of 1986, the President was being beaten about the head and shoulders, that this was, the whole Iranian project, was just an arms-for-hostage deal.

Well, this finding, unfortunately, gave that same impression. And I, frankly, didn't see any need for it at the time. I thought it was politically embarrassing, and so I decided to tear it up. And I tore it up, put it in the burn basket behind my desk.

I can't recall, but I believe that Colonel North was there in the office, but I'm a little fuzzy on that point.

Q Was Commander Thompson there when you tore it up?

A I believe he was, but I can't swear to it. I know he brought it in, and I can recall his comment, but exactly how long it took me, because I—when he made his comment he said, I said, well let me see the finding. And he pulled it out and gave it to me, and I read it and at some point after that I tore it up, but it was within a short period of time.

Q Admiral, you talked about the fact that the President was being beaten around the head and shoulders by the media for sanctioning an arms-for-hostage deal and that this finding seemed to corroborate it, and you therefore destroyed it in order to prevent significant political embarrassment. Did you regard one of the responsibilities of the national security adviser to protect the President from political embarrassment?

A I think that it's always the responsibility of a staff to protect their leader and certainly in this case where the leader is the Commander in Chief. I feel very strongly that that's one of the roles. And I don't mean that in any sense of covering up, but one has to always put things in the President's perspective and to make sure that he's not put in a position that can be politically embarrassing.

Q Now, Admiral, a finding represents a decision of the President of the United States, correct?

A A finding, I don't believe, is discussed in any statute. It is discussed in various Presidential directives. It is an artifact of what the statute calls a Presidential determination.

Q And the President, when he signed this finding, was making a determination?

A That's correct, but it's important to point out that the finding, that early finding was designed for a very specific purpose, and was not fully staffed and did not in any way ever represent the total thinking on the subject.

Q The President didn't authorize you to destroy the finding, correct?

A He certainly did not. . . .

Meeting of the N.S.C.

Q Let's go to the—on Dec. 7, 1985, after the finding had been signed by the President, there was a meeting, was there not, between the principals of the National Security Council?

A Yes, there was.

Q And you recall Mr. Weinberger was there, and Secretary Shultz was there, Don Regan was there, Mr. McMahon of the C.I.A. was there, do you recall that?

A Yes, I do.

Q . . . At this meeting, there was a discussion again, or there was a discussion of the Iran initiative? Is that so? . . .

A Yes, yes, there was. . . .

Q And the subject on the table was an Israeli initiative, under which the Israelis would ship arms to the Iranians and we would replenish the arms. Hopefully there would be better relations with Iran. And as a token of good faith, the American hostages would be released. Is that a fair summary?

A Well, I think it's a partial summary.

Q Well, why don't you complete it?

A We had been concerned, in the National Security Council, for some period of time, with the situation in Iran. Unfortunately, we have very poor intelligence on what's happening in Iran. The National Security Council staff had prepared a draft finding, earlier in 1985, to try to get the Government focused on what we saw as a very significant, looming problem in Iran, as Ayatollah Khomeini eventually passed from the scene and there was some sort of succession.

We didn't want a repeat of the 1970's, when things were happening in Iran that we weren't aware of, and eventually went out of our control, and out of control of the Government there.

. . . We felt that we needed to take an initiative to get closer to people in the Iranian Government, so that we could find out what's happening and hopefully have some influence in the future or, at least, have information on which to base the United States policy.

Q Admiral, see if this part is correct: that the currency for trying to get that influence that was being demanded, as reported by the Israelis, involved arms?

A That is often the currency of any sort of business in the Middle East.

Q And in this case that was the currency being demanded?

A Yes, that is correct.

Q And it is also true that we did not want to authorize arms shipments to the Iranians, unless we were assured of getting our hostages back, is that so?

A As I was trying to lay out a moment ago, what our concerns were, what our major objective was, the President was clearly also concerned about the hostages. The President is a very sensitive person, and he is concerned about individuals when they're in difficulty. And so he, just as a human being, was concerned about the hostages.

I don't think that the President is overly concerned about them, but he recognized that we did have an opportunity here to try to get the hostages back. And there was no way that we could carry on discussions with Iranian officials about broader objectives, until we got over the first obstacle. And the first obstacle was to get the hostages back. And the President felt that, that it was worth taking some risks here.

Q Now, did the Secretary of State and the Secretary of Defense express objections?

A They expressed, as opposed to some reports, very strong, vociferous objection and clearly laid out for the President the other side of the issue.

Q And without going into undue detail, could you just tick off the points they made?

A Well, there are the obvious points that have been made since this all has become public. Secretary Shultz was concerned about our operation to staunch the flow of arms into Iran, which is one of the methods that we are using to try to stop the war between Iran and Iraq. . . .

But in its simplest terms, what was being proposed here was not in accordance with that particular method that we were using. He was concerned that if the European countries found out about it, that it would lessen their willingness to cooperate. In reality though, in my opinion, we've never had good cooperation from anybody on Operation Staunch. The European countries continue to send military equipment and supplies into Iran. Iran's been able to carry on the war for six, going on seven, years now, I guess.

Other objections were that of it was contrary to the Arms Export Control Act. Secretary Weinberger had slightly different reasons, but they're generally along the same lines.

Q   And there's no doubt in your mind that the President listened to, and understood, those objections?

A   ... The President listened to all of this very carefully. And at the end of the discussion, at least the first round, he sat back and he said something to the effect—and I, this is not a direct quote—but it was something to the effect that, I don't feel that we can leave any stone unturned in trying to get the hostages back. We clearly have a situation here where there are larger strategic interests. But it's also an opportunity to get the hostages back. And I think that we ought to at least take the next step. ...

Q   Now, one other question which just has been handed to me, that Colonel North apparently testified that Secretary Shultz and Secretary Weinberger's opposition was not vigorously expressed in this January period. I take it that it was vigorously expressed at the January 7th meeting, and it was expressed by the Secretary of State at that January 16th meeting and that no one had any doubt about where both of them stood.

A   That's true of the earlier meetings. On the 16th of January, I think it was pretty clear to George [Shultz] that the President wanted to go ahead with this at that point, and so although he voiced objection, I wouldn't say that, and this is probably why Colonel North's recollection is as it was. In fact, I think probably the 16 January meeting may have been the only meeting that Colonel North was in attendance where he may have heard the other Cabinet officers give their views. But it is accurate that both George Shultz and Cap Weinberger vigorously made this case as to why we should not do this.

Legality and Approval

Q   Right. Now, admiral, is it correct that in the discussions that you had leading up to the January 17th finding, there was no discussion with the President of the United States about the possibility of using proceeds of the sale to support the contras?

A   There was none.

Q   And there was none with you.

A   There was none with me.

Q   Now, would you tell us, and I'm going to break this into different questions, when was the first time that you were told by Colonel North about this possibility?

A   My best recollection is that this took place sometime in February of 1986.

Q   And would you tell us what Colonel North said to you?

A   My recollection is that he had just come back from a meeting in London, and he was giving me a general update on the situation as he saw it. And he was reviewing the status of the work that was in progress at C.I.A. and Defense in addition to the results of his meeting in London. And near the end of the conversation, my recollection is that he said something to the effect that, Admiral, I think we can, I have found a way that we can legally provide some funds to the democratic resistance or as they have been called here—and I frankly agree with Congressman [Henry J.] Hyde [R.-Illinois] that I have no problem with calling them contras—through funds that will accrue from the arms sales to the Iranians.

Q   Did he use the word legally?

A   My best recollection is that he did, but of course I know that Colonel North is not a lawyer, and so I was taking that in a layman's sense that that was his conclusion.

Q   Do you recall in reciting this in your deposition you didn't use the word legally?

A   I don't recall that, that I didn't. I believe that he did, he may not have.

Q   Now, did he tell you what the method would be for doing this?

A   This was a very general discussion, but this was clearly a new aspect that I had not thought about before. To make a long story short, in the end I thought it was a very good idea at the end of this conversation, and I personally approved it.

Q   Did he ask you for your approval?

A   I don't recall how he phrased his request, but he was clearly looking for a signal from me whether or not to proceed ahead along this line.

Q   And you gave it.

A   And I gave it to him. . . .

In order to put this in perspective, and I think it's important to understand my state of mind at the time and what things were of concern to us. The President's policy with regard to support for the contras had not changed since 1981. The various versions of the Boland Amendment came and went. But the President was steadfast in his support for the contras. . . . So I was absolutely convinced as to what the President's policy was with regard to support for the contras.

I was aware that the President was aware of third-country support, that the President was aware of private support. And the way Colonel North described this to me at the time, it was obvious to me that this fell in exactly the same category that these funds could either be characterized as private funds because of the way that we had, that Director Casey and I had agreed to carry out the finding. They could be characterized as private funds or they could be characterized as third-country funds. In my view, it was a matter of implementation of the President's policy, with regard to support for the contras.

We were in the process of working on our legislative plan to get $100 million from Congress for essentially unrestricted support to the contras. . . .

The President was bound and determined and still is, that he will not sit still for the consolidation of a Communist government on the mainland of America. And in order to prevent that, he feels that the most effective way, with which I also agree, is to keep pressure on the Communist Sandinista Government. And the most effective way to do that, given all of the factors considered and because we don't want to send U.S. soldiers to Nicaragua, is to provide support to the contras and keep them alive until we can get the $100 million. . . .

And so after weighing all of these matters—and I also felt that I had the authority to approve it because I had a commission from the President which was in very broad terms. My role was to make sure that his policies were implemented. In this case, the policy was very clear, and that was to support the contras. After working with the President for five and a half years, the last three of which were very close and probably closer than any other officer in the White House except the chief of staff, I was convinced that I understood the President's thinking on this and that if I had taken it to him that he would have approved it.

Now I was not so naïve as to believe that it was not a politically volatile issue; it clearly was because of the divisions that existed within the Congress on the issue of support for the contras. And it was clear that there would be a lot of people that would disagree, that would make accusations that indeed have been made. So although I was convinced that we could properly do it and that the President would approve if asked, I made a very deliberate decision not to ask the President so that I could insulate him from the decision and provide some future deniability for the President if it ever leaked out. Of course, our hope was that it would not leak out.

Q   When you say deniability, are you saying that your decision was not to tell the President so that he would be able to deny that he knew of it?

A   That's correct.

Q   And did you at any time prior to the Attorney General's finding this on November 22d tell the President of the United States of the fact that proceeds from the Iranian arms sale were being used to support the contras?

A   I don't—I did not. I want to make this very clear because I understand it's an important issue. I did not talk to anybody else except Colonel North about this decision until, to my knowledge, my best recollection—and I don't want to quibble here over times in late November 1986—but my recollection is the first mention that I made to anybody besides Colonel North was on November 24, 1986, to Ed Meese.

Q   And so that the answer is you did not tell the President of the United States.

A   I did not.

Q   And that for a period of whatever it is, nine months, you kept it from the President of the United States, for the reasons you've given.

A   Mr. Liman, this clearly was an important decision but it was also an implementation of very clear policy. If the President had asked me, I very likely would have told him about it. But he didn't. And I think—you know, an important point here is that on this whole issue, you know, the buck stops here with me. I made the decision; I felt that I had the authority to do it. I thought it was a good idea. I was convinced that the President would in the end think it was a good idea. But I did not want him to be associated with the decision. . . .

Q   Were there any other examples during your term as national security adviser where you withheld a decision from the President that you had made in order to give him deniability?

A Well, this again—this decision, in my view, was a matter of implementation, and there were many details of implementation that were not discussed with the President. This particular detail was the only one of its kind in terms of the disagreements and the controversy that existed over the issue.

Q Were there any other decisions that you withheld from the President that you had made because they were politically explosive?

A I don't recall anything else that fell in that same category, although there were lots—I want to make a distinction here between what I felt my authority was and why I didn't discuss it with the President. Number one, I felt that it was within my authority because it was an implementation of a policy that was well understood, that the President felt very strongly about. It was not a secret foreign policy, the President's policy with regard to the contras was clearly understood by every member of the Congress and the American people. So it wasn't matter of going out and making a secret foreign policy. . . .

    You know, frankly, as Colonel North has testified, I thought it was a neat idea, too. And I'm sure the President would have enjoyed knowing about it. But on the other hand, because it would be controversial—and I must say that I don't believe that I estimated how controversial it would be accurately—but I knew very well that it would be controversial, and I wanted the President to have some deniability so that he would be protected and at the same time we'd be able to carry out his policy and provide the opposition to the Sandinista Government. . . .

Aiding the Contras

Q Now as I understand your testimony, you genuinely believed that in approving the diversion, that it was consistent with the policies of the President, in terms of third-country support. You've already testified to that. And I'd like to ask you some questions about that. Is it a fact that the Administration had gone to Congress in 1985 and gotten permission from Congress to solicit third-country support?

A Yes, we worked with members of Congress to get that provision.

Q And is it a fact that that provision for obtaining third-country support was limited to humanitarian aid?

A Since leaving the White House and going back over this material, that is correct. I can't say that during the discussions, that I can recall in the White House, there was great distinction made between humanitarian aid or any other kind of aid, at that particular time. There was with respect to the $27 million. But I just simply don't recall great distinctions being made.

Q Well, are you saying that when Congress worked out the legislation with the Administration that authorized solicitation for humanitarian aid, the Administration interpreted that as meaning that it could solicit for lethal aid?

A No, I'm not saying that at all. I'm just giving you my recollection of the time.

Q Now, and you also understood that that bill provided that it was only the State Department that could do the solicitation, do you recall that, sir?

A Yes, I recall that.

Q Now, was the money that you were getting from the Ayatollah, or [Gen. Richard] Secord [another go-between], however you viewed it, was that money to be limited to being disbursed for humanitarian aid?

A In no way. You see the distinction here is that—and this is contrary to what you have heard before, from other witnesses. But I never believed, and I don't believe today, that the Boland Amendment ever applied to the National Security Council staff or the President's personal staff. But the problem was that the Boland Amendment did apply to the State Department. It did apply to C.I.A. And it did apply to the Defense Department.

    We had been running this operation, on our own, for a long period of time because there was no other alternative, in order to keep the contras alive. And we wanted help. We wanted also a more public recognition of the fact that the U.S. was supporting the contras in some way.

    I frankly, I personally still wanted that to be done in—the public support to be done in such way that we could slowly turn back to a covert program, run by the C.I.A. But it was important to me, and to others, that we get the State Department back into the game.

Q I understand you. Did you ever discuss, with the President of the United States, that the N.S.C. was raising money for lethal aid?

A Mr. Liman does—are you, if I may ask to clarify the question—are you saying that raising money is soliciting money?

Q I don't want to get into a semantic debate about solicitation. I mean every day in the newspapers, in the financial sections, they have announcements of offerings, and they say this is not a solicitation. So please do not get me into that semantic debate. Let's talk about raising money, obtaining money, for lethal aid. That the N.S.C. was obtaining money for lethal aid?

A The President was aware that we were encouraging, I guess would be a fair way to describe it, third countries to contribute to the cause of the contras in Central America, in their fight against the Communist Sandinistas. And, of course, we were doing that primarily by pointing out to them the dangers that we saw. And, as Colonel North has testified, it wasn't very difficult. They clearly understood the problem. The Central American countries understood, the neighboring countries. The other countries that are on your list, that I've heard you talk about up here....

Financing Covert Projects

Q Colonel North testified that in addition to the use of the proceeds of the Iranian arms sale for the contras, it was to be used for a series of other covert projects. Do you remember that testimony of his?

A I heard that testimony.

Q Was that the first time you ever heard about that?

A It's the first time that I heard it discussed in that depth. I must say there was, as far as I was concerned, no such plan. I don't at all doubt that Colonel North and Director Casey may have discussed that. Frankly, it's an idea that has some attractive features in my mind, but there was no plan that was brought to me or that I took to the President to proceed in that kind of direction. That would have required substantial discussion....

Q You testified this morning that if the President had asked you about what countries were helping, you probably would have told him about this. Do you recall that?

A That would have been a difficult situation, and I don't—

Q But you wouldn't lie to the President?

A I wouldn't lie to the President, and if he had outright asked me about it, I would have told him. He didn't.

Q Are you saying that with the interest the President had in the contra movement and his concern about the dire straits it was in financially that he never asked you which countries were helping?

A That's correct. The President is—as I've said—is not

a man for great detail. He—and I don't mean that in any sort of funny way—I don't think a President ought to get involved in details—he has to maintain a strategic perspective, and he's got enough to worry about. I think by and large the President has the same sort of management philosophy that I do, and that is that he picks good people for the job and gives them a lot of authority to carry out that job, and he wanted the contras supported. We were reporting to him on the status of the contras, in general terms, and he knew that they were surviving and that was the thing that was important to him.

AT THE CONCLUSION OF POINDEXTER'S APPEARANCE, REPRESENTATIVE LEE H. HAMILTON, DEMOCRAT OF INDIANA, THE CHAIRMAN OF THE HOUSE COMMITTEE, ADDRESSED HIM ABOUT HIS TESTIMONY DURING THE HEARINGS:
July 21, 1987

Representative Hamilton.... Admiral Poindexter, I want to say that we have indeed appreciated your testimony.... None of us, I think, can know all of the circumstances that you confronted as the national security adviser to the President.

... It is, however, ... our job to examine your role in the decision-making process....

Now, your comments about secrecy in government ... concerned me ... a great deal. You have testified that you intentionally withheld information from the President, denied him the opportunity to make, probably, the most fateful decision of his Presidency—whether to divert the funds from the Iranian arms sales to aid the contras.

You said your objective was to withhold information from the Congress. And apparently, so far as I understood the testimony, without direction or authority to do so. As many have mentioned, you destroyed the Dec. 5, '85, finding. You apparently intended to have original documents, relating to the contras, either altered or removed. You were unwilling to speak candidly with senior Justice and C.I.A. officials about the Hawk missile shipments to Iran. And you kept the ... Secretaries of State and Defense, uninformed....

All of us who work with our system of government sometimes feel impatient with its painstaking procedures. . . . Yet, your comment about Congress, and I quote it directly: I simply did not want any outside interference, reflects an attitude which makes, in my judgment at least, our constitutional system of checks and balances unworkable.

Instead of bringing each agency dealing with foreign policy into the process, you cut those agencies out of the process. You told the committees, I firmly believe in very tight compartmentation. You compartmentalized not only the President's senior advisers, but in effect, you locked the President himself out of the process.

You began your testimony by saying that the function of a national security adviser is to present options and to advise the President. Yet, you told the committees the buck stops here with me. That is not where the buck is supposed to stop.

You wanted to deflect blame from the President but that is another way of saying you wanted to deflect responsibility from the President. And that should not be done in our system of government.

You testified that diverting funds to the contras was a detail, a matter of implementation of the President's policies. And you felt that you had the authority to approve it. Yet, this was a major foreign policy initiative, as subsequent events have shown, with very far-reaching ramifications. And this member, at least, wonders what else could be done in the President's name, if this is mere implementation of policy. . . .

Probably more important, secrecy contributed to disarray in the Oval Office. The President apparently did not know that you were making some of the most important foreign policy decisions of his Presidency. You've testified, I was convinced that the President would, in the end, think the diversion was a good idea. Yet, the President has stated that he would not've approved the diversion.

Excessive secrecy placed the President in an untenable position and caused him to make false and contradictory public statements. Let me cite some of them:

On Nov. 6, 1986, the President said, the speculation, the commenting and all, on a story that came out of the Middle East has no foundation.

A week later, the President said, we did not, repeat, we did not, trade weapons, or anything else, for hostages.

But on March 4, the President said: A few months ago, I told the American people I did not trade arms for hostages. My heart and my best intentions still tell me that's true but the facts and the evidence tell me it is not.

Turning to the solicitation of private aid for the contras, the President said, on May 5, I don't know how that money was to be used. And I have no knowledge that there was ever any solicitation by our people with these people.

But on May 15, the President altered his view. He said: As a matter of fact, I was definitely involved in the decisions about support to the freedom fighters. It was my idea to begin with.

May I suggest that the President was unaware of some important actions taken by his staff and, therefore, he misspoke. Because he lacked information, the President inflicted serious and repeated political wounds upon himself. Polls continue to indicate that a majority of the American people still feels that the President, despite his statements to the contrary, did know that money from the Iran arms sales was channeled to the contras. . . .

POINDEXTER   I just have one brief comment.

HAMILTON   Yes, indeed.

POINDEXTER   Mr. Chairman, with regard to your closing statement I would just simply say that we'll have to agree, you and I, to disagree on your interpretation of many of the events. And finally, I leave this hearing with my head held high that I have done my very best to promote the long-term national security interests of the United States. Thank you.

FOLLOWING ARE EXCERPTS FROM SECRETARY OF STATE GEORGE P. SHULTZ'S TESTIMONY:
July 24, 1987

Representative Lee H. Hamilton, chairman of the House committee. Mr. Secretary, do you have an opening statement?

MR. SHULTZ   No, I don't. But with your permission, Mr. Chairman, I'd like to make a few remarks.

Q   Please proceed.

A   . . . I have on numerous occasions—including, I think, before your committee right here, Chairman [Dante B.] Fascell [D.-Florida, chairman of the House Foreign Affairs Committee]—been asked about what advice I gave the President on this, that or the other, subject. And I have always taken a position, in 10 and a half years as a member of the Cabinet, that those conversations are privileged and I would not discuss them. This is an exception, and I have made this material available on the President's instruction. But I mention it because if I'm testifying before you on some other subject sometime and you try to use this as a precedent, I won't buy it. I'm just putting you on notice right now.

Thank you, Mr. Chairman.

Q   Thank you, Mr. Secretary. We'll begin the questions this morning with Mr. Belnick. . . .

Mark A. Belnick, executive assistant to the chief counsel of the Senate committee. Mr. Secretary, I'd like to begin this morning by reviewing certain key events that the panel has been considering in order to establish when the Secretary of State was first informed of those events. . . .

Let me begin by this question. Mr. Secretary, when were you first informed that the President of the United States had signed a covert action finding authorizing the sale of U.S. arms to Iran?

A   On November the 10th, 1986, at a meeting in the Oval Office, with the President's principal advisers, during a briefing by Admiral Poindexter on what had transpired over the past year or so. . . .

Q   Mr. Secretary, when were you first informed that this nation had sold weapons directly to Iran?

A   . . . This all started to break in very early November 1986. . . .

Q   Prior to then, . . . had any member of the United States Government informed you that the United States had sold weapons directly . . . to Iran?

A   No.

Q   Mr. Secretary, when were you first informed of the McFarlane mission to Teheran?

A   It was after the mission, but I think shortly after it was completed.

Q   And were you given the details of the mission at that time?

A   I was told that it had fizzled, . . . that the whole project had been told to stand down.

Q   Were you told at that time that Mr. McFarlane had brought U.S. weapons with him to Teheran?

A   No. . . .

Q   Mr. Secretary, when were you first informed that United States negotiations with the second channel in

the early autumn of 1986 had produced agreement on a so-called nine-point agenda which provided for additional arms sales to Iran in exchange for hostages and which contained provision also with respect to actions directed at the Government of Iraq?

A   On December 13th of 1986. But if I may interrupt your questioning, I'd like to expand on that.

Q   Please.

A   In the course of the effort to come to grips with what was taking place, the President put the management of Iran matters into my hands by that time—we're talking in December—sort of at first a little bit but then for sure. And I discovered that the C.I.A. had a meeting scheduled with an Iranian for that date. And so we considered what to do. And we decided that we should go ahead with that meeting, that the C.I.A. representative who was scheduled to be the representative there, Mr. Cave, should go. But we would have accompanying him Mr. Charles Dunbar, who is a Foreign Service officer and Farsi speaker. And we would have instructions carefully written, designed to use the meeting as a means to tell that channel that there would be no more arms sales discussed in that channel or anywhere else. . . .

At the meeting, the message was delivered, but also as our representative listened, there was back and forth discussion about this agenda, nine-point agenda. And so gradually then, and in discussion with Mr. Cave, Mr. Dunbar got a reasonable idea of what was on this agenda. And then he called that back on Dec. 13, which was a Saturday, to the department. And I saw it on Saturday afternoon. And it was astonishing.

So I called the President, or I called the White House to get an appointment with the President. And there was a lot of back and forth, what did I want to see him about and so on. And I didn't seem to be getting an appointment right away, so I picked up the phone Sunday morning and I called the President. I said, "Mr. President, I have something I should bring over here and tell you about right now." So he said, 'Fine, come over.' He happened to be in Washington.

I went up to the family quarters, and Al Keel, who was then acting national security adviser, went with me, at my request. And I told the President the items on this agenda, including such things as doing something about the Dawa prisoners, which made me sick to my stomach that anybody would talk about that as something we would consider doing.

And the President was astonished. And I have never seen him so mad. He's a very genial, pleasant man and doesn't—very easy-going. But his jaw set, and his eyes flashed, and both of us, I think, felt the same way about it. And I think in that meeting I finally felt that the President deeply understands that something is radically wrong here. . . .

Q . . . In particular, Admiral Poindexter testified that he did not withhold anything from you that you did not want withheld from you. . . . Mr. Secretary, . . . let me ask you first whether you ever told Admiral Poindexter or any other member of the Administration that you did not want to be kept informed of the Iran initiative?

A I never made such a statement. What I did say to Admiral Poindexter was that I wanted to be informed of the things I needed to know to do my job as Secretary of State, but he didn't need to keep me posted on the details, the operational details of what he was doing. That's what I told him. . . . The reason for that was that there had been a great amount of discussion of leaks in the Administration, and justifiably so. And we were all very concerned about it. And there had been in connection with what to do about it, discussion of the idea of giving very large numbers of people who were—who had access to classified information, lie detector tests on a regular or random basis, which I opposed.

While I was on a trip abroad in the latter part of 1985, a directive encompassing that idea was signed. So I didn't comment on it while I was abroad, but when I got back here I did comment on it, registered my opposition, talked to the President about it. And it got changed. Now that, I recognized, put me at odds with the intelligence and national security community, to put it mildly. So . . . in terms of particulars, like who is going to go someplace to meet somebody and so forth, . . . it seemed to me in the light of the suspicions cast on me as a result, and the hostility, that I would not know that. So I felt it would probably leak, and then it wouldn't be my leak. . . .

But that doesn't mean that I just bowed out insofar as major things having to do with our foreign policy are concerned. . . . To consider that that statement would mean that I shouldn't be informed of things like that is ridiculous. . . .

Q Do you recall what you told Admiral Poindexter about your views concerning the Iran initiative, as he described it to you in that briefing?

A Well, I told him that I thought it was a very bad idea, that I was opposed to it. . . . I was in favor of doing things that had any potential for rear-ranging the behavior of Iran and our relationship with Iran. But I was very much opposed to arms sales in connection with that.

Q Did you tell him at that time that in your view, the proposed policy amounted to paying for hostages and had to be stopped?

A Yes.

Q In that same conversation, sir, on Dec. 5, . . . did he tell you that on the very same day, the President had signed a covert action finding authorizing an arms shipment to Iran?

A No. . . .

Q Now do you recall another briefing, listed on the chronology by Admiral Poindexter a month later, on Feb. 28, in which he discussed the hostage situation and advised you then of a possible high-level meeting between Bud McFarlane and certain Iranian representatives?

A Yes, I do. He told me that as a result of the discussions they had been having, that the Iranians had said they wanted a high-level meeting and if there were a proper high-level meeting, discussing our future possible relationships, that would be the occasion in which hostages . . . would be released. I said, 'Well, that sounds almost too good to be true. But anyway, if that's the case, I'm in favor of it.' . . .

Q Did Admiral Poindexter tell you that the agenda for any meeting between Mr. McFarlane and Iranian representatives would include current deliveries of U.S. arms?

A No. . . . This negotiation had been taking place in a manner consistent with what I thought was proper, and I thought, well, maybe I won the argument after all, with the President.

Q In that light, did Admiral Poindexter tell you on Feb. 28 that only one day before, that was on Feb. 27, the United States had shipped 500 TOW's, TOW missiles, to Iran, and that about 10 days earlier the United States had also shipped 500 TOW missiles to Iran?

A No, he did not. . . .

Q In May 1986, . . . you were advised . . . of an approach to a British entrepreneur by Mr. Nir about . . . an arms deal to Iran . . . which supposedly had White House approval which had John Poindexter as the point man and which included participants such as Mr. Adnan Khashoggi and Mr. Ghorbanifar?

A Yes. . . . I received a cable from the Under Secretary of State, Mr. Armacost, . . . in Tokyo. . . .

Q Once you received this information, you spoke to Don Regan . . . and Admiral Poindexter. Am I correct?

A That's correct.

Q I understand that in those conversations you objected strongly to any such deal, to the United States being involved, insisted that if there was such an operation it be called off and warned that the President was seriously exposed and at risk. . . . Is that a fair summary?

A Yes. . . . You can imagine how I felt when I read this cable. . . . I said more or less what you said. Don Regan seemed to me to be very upset about it. He said he would take it up with the President when he saw him. . . . He later told me that the President was upset and this was not anything he knew about. And Admiral Poindexter told me . . . we are not dealing with these people, this is not our deal. . . .

Q Well, when Admiral Poindexter told you that this was not our deal, . . . did he inform you that our deal involved an upcoming mission . . . to Teheran, which would be led by Bud McFarlane, which would include a shipment of Hawk spare parts to Iran?

A No. . . .

Q Also, Mr. Secretary, if I could, let me ask you to turn to exhibit 24. That exhibit, sir, is a PROF note dated May 17, 1986, . . . from Oliver North to Admiral Poindexter about the McFarlane mission to Teheran. . . . Colonel North suggests to Admiral Poindexter that there be a quiet meeting with Bud McFarlane and the President prior to the departure of the mission, and he queries whether the participants . . . ought to include you and the Secretary of Defense and the D.C.I. [Director, Central Intelligence: William J. Casey]. Do you see that?

A Yes, I see that.

Q If you turn, then, please, to the next exhibit, . . . you'll see Admiral Poindexter's reply to that suggestion, . . . and I quote, 'I don't want a meeting with R.R., Shultz and Weinberger.' . . . I take it you were unaware of this exchange, as well?

A Obviously. . . .

Q Mr. Secretary, you testified earlier, . . . that you had told Admiral Poindexter that while you didn't need to be informed of what you called operational details,

you did want and need to be kept informed of those facts which you needed in order to do your job—correct?

A Correct.

Q Sir, in order to do your job as the nation's chief diplomat, and as a statutory member of the National Security Council, and at a time when, through Operation Staunch, you were in charge of attempting to persuade our allies and other nations throughout the world not to sell arms to Iran, did you need to know that the United States itself was selling arms to Iran, that the President had signed covert action findings authorizing those sales, and that the President's former national security adviser was in Teheran on a diplomatic mission, bringing with him the first installment on the delivery of U.S. Hawk parts? Did you need to know those facts?

A Certainly. One of the many arguments that I used, and Secretary Weinberger used, in opposing having an arms sale dimension to the Iran initiative, one of the arguments, was that we felt that one way of getting the Iran-Iraq war to come to an end was to do everything we could to deny weapons to the country that was refusing to come to an end, and so we had a rather vigorous program, called Operation Staunch.

Q Sir, did you ever express the view that Colonel North was a loose cannon?

A No, I didn't. What I said—I think what you're referring to is an incident . . . in which I told Elliott Abrams [Assistant Secretary of State for Latin America]—the question was where, where are the freedom fighters getting their arms. . . . And Elliott said he didn't know. And I said, well, you're our pointman here, you should find out, or something like that.

Q As I understand, that conversation took place on Sept. 4, 1985. Secretary Abrams has described that conversation here, based on a note that he took, in which he said you told him to 'monitor Ollie.' Is that your recollection? . . .

A . . . No reason why Elliott shouldn't have taken it that way, because Colonel North was commonly seen as a principal contact with the freedom fighters.

Q Did you have a view at that time that Colonel North, because of any information that you had about him, was someone who had to be watched closely or that Elliott ought to monitor?

A There was talk around about erratic behavior on his part, but I had no particular knowledge about it and didn't want to pass judgment. . . . I can't get myself in the position of supervising people down the line working for others.

Q But you did expect, based on what you told Secretary Abrams Sept. 4, 1985, that he would keep himself informed about . . . how the contras were getting supplied with arms, and not simply shut his eyes to that?

A Yes.

Q All right, sir, in light of what you now know, . . . regarding, for example, the role of Colonel North and other N.S.C. staff members in assisting the contras during the period of the Boland restrictions, the involvement in the Hasenfus flight, the involvement of at least one of our own ambassadors, Mr. Tams, in negotiations for an airstrip to be used in Central America for contra resupply and in helping, as he testified to this panel, on instructions from Colonel North, to open a southern military front against Nicaragua, during the period of the Boland restrictions, . . . is it your view that Secretary Abrams carried out your instruction to keep himself, and you, informed?

A What has been brought out, in these hearings about all of the activities you mentioned, has surprised a lot of people. It surprised me. It must have been a surprise to Chairman Hamilton, who looked into this a couple of times and had assurances. So I imagine it has surprised the President. So things have come out that we didn't know about. . . .

Senator Daniel K. Inouye, chairman of the Senate Committee. Mr. Secretary, at the outset of these hearings, which began about two months ago, I made a sad prediction that when the story began to unfold, the American people will have the right to ask, how did this ever happen here? Or, how could this ever happen in the United States? And I think, at the same time, Americans would have the right to demand that it never happen again.

The story we have heard over the past 10 weeks of testimony, to some has been sad and depressing and distressing, and to many of us on this panel, many of us old-timers and a bit sophisticated, but we found it shocking and at times frightening.

And I believe that made the question that the Americans will ask, and the expectations they have, a bit more compelling.

Mr. Secretary, you and I have lived through the agony and the nightmare of Watergate. And we saw it ruin a President, ruin his senior advisers, demoralize

the country and cause the American people to lose faith in their political leaders.

And therefore, it's especially troubling to me, and I'm sure it's to you, to see this nation once again faced with this breakdown of trust, between the important branches of Government, and more importantly, between the Government and the American people. . . .

My question is a very general one, Mr. Secretary, but with your background in public service and being at the helm of the State Department, I hope you can give us a response. How did this happen again? And how did life-long public servants, and patriotic Americans, like Admiral Poindexter, Bud McFarlane and Bill Casey and Oliver North, find themselves in a position where they misled you, kept information away from the Secretary of State, from the Secretary of Defense, lied to the Congress, withheld information from the President of the United States, destroyed . . . Government documents to hide or cover up their activities, and involved rather shady characters—and that's an understatement, I think—in participating in the formulation of foreign policy, and the implementation of such, while, at the same time, skirting around the people who should be doing that work, to wit, the Secretary of State and the ambassadors.

And more importantly, Mr. Secretary, if you could also touch upon and advise us as to how we can prevent this from happening again. . . .

A I would say with respect to the revelations that were brought out this morning, . . . that's not the way life is in Government as I have experienced it. . . .

Public service is a very rewarding and honorable thing, and nobody has to think they need to lie and cheat in order to be a public servant or to work in foreign policy. Quite to the contrary. If you are really going to be effective, . . . you have to be straightforward, and you have to conduct yourself in a basically honest way. . . .

I think there are a lot of things to be learned myself reflecting on these events, if not from these events, that seem to me . . . worth mentioning. . . . One that I think was most vivid in response to Senator [Sam] Nunn's [D.-Georgia] question, and that is I think the importance of separating the function of gathering and analyzing intelligence from the function of developing and carrying out policy. If the two things are mixed in together, it is too tempting to have your analysis and the selection of information that's presented favor the policy that you're advocating.

I believe that one of the reasons the President was given what I regard as wrong information, for example, about Iran and terrorism was that the agency, or the people in the C.I.A., were too involved in this. So that's one point. And I feel very clear in my mind about this point.

And I know that long before this all emerged, I had come to have grave doubts about the objectivity and reliability of some of the intelligence I was getting. . . .

Mark A. Belnick, executive assistant to the chief counsel of the Senate committee. And did you begin developing the view, particularly as of Nov. 10, . . . that the President's advisers were misleading him and not giving him the facts concerning what had actually transpired in the Iran initiative?

A I developed a very clear opinion that the President was not being given accurate information, and I was very alarmed about it, and it became the preoccupying thing that I was working on through this period. And I felt that it was tremendously important for the President to get accurate information. . . . His judgment is excellent when he's given the right information, and he was not being given the right information.

And I felt as this went on that the people who were giving him the information . . . had a conflict of interest with the President. And they were trying to use his undoubted skills as a communicator to have him give a speech and give a press conference and say these things, and in doing so he would bail them out. . . . I don't want to try to attribute motives to other people too much, although I realize I am, but that's the way it shaped up to me. So I was in a battle to try to get what I saw as the facts to the President and get—and see that he understood them.

Now this was a very traumatic period for me because everybody was saying I'm disloyal to the President. I'm not speaking up for the policy. And I'm battling away here, and I could see people were calling for me to resign if I can't be loyal to the President, even including some of my friends and people who had held high office and should know that maybe there's more involved than they're seeing. And I frankly felt that I was the one who was loyal to the President, because I was the one who was trying to get him the facts so he could make a decision. And I must say, as he absorbed this, he did; he made the decision that we must get all these facts out. But it was a—it was a battle royal.

Q Mr. Secretary, in that battle royal to get out the facts, which you waged and which the record reflects that you waged, who was on the other side?

A Well, I can't say for sure, I—I feel that Admiral Poindexter was certainly on the other side of it. I felt that Director Casey was on the other side of it. And I don't know who all else, but they were the principals. . . .

Senator Inouye. Mr. Secretary, I have another question. And I ask this with great reluctance because I realize it is rather personal in nature, but I think it is relevant. . . . I've been advised that in August of 1986 you tendered a letter of resignation to the President of the United States. Is that true? And if so, can you tell us something about it?

A . . . That is true. And I have asked the President to let me leave this office on a couple of other occasions, earlier. . . .

Q Was that in any way related to the Iran-contra affair?

A Well, in August of 1986 I thought that it was over. . . . I didn't know anything about the contra side of it anyway. But on the effort with Iran, I thought it was basically on a proper track.

But it was because I felt a sense of estrangement. I knew the White House was very uncomfortable with me. I was very uncomfortable with what I was getting from the intelligence community, and I knew they were very uncomfortable with me—perhaps going back to the lie-detector test business. I could feel it.

What I have learned about the various things that were being done, I suppose explains why I was not in good odor with the N.S.C. staff and some of the others in the White House. I had a terrible time. There was a kind of guerrilla warfare going on, on all kinds of little things. For example, as you know, the Congress doesn't treat the State Department very well when it comes to appropriated funds. And not only have we historically taken a beating but we've been cut brutally . . . and I think in a manner that is not in the interests of the United States. . . .

But anyway, one of the conventions that's grown up—because we have no travel money to speak of . . . —the Air Force runs a White House Presidential Wing and when the Secretary of State has a mission, that gets approved and then I get an airplane and the airplane, it is paid for out of this budget. If I had to pay for that airplane, I couldn't travel. So you have me grounded unless I can get approved.

Now it's not a problem; the system works all right

and it's just assumed that that's the way it's supposed to be. But I started having trouble because some people on the White House staff decided that they were going to make my life unhappy and they stopped approving these airplane things. And we fought about it and so on. And finally, I—I hated to do this. I went to the President and I gave him little memorandums to check off—yes, no. And that's no business for the Secretary of State to be taking up with the President of the United States.

But I found out there was a character in the White House that was in charge of doing this. His name was Jonathan Miller, and you've seen him here, and he was . . . trying to knock me out of trips. . . . But this was an atmosphere that I found—I felt that I was no longer on the wavelength that I should be on. And so I told the President, "I'd like to leave and here's my letter." And he stuck it in his drawer and he said, "You're tired. It's about time to go on vacation and let's talk about it after you get back from vacation." So I said, "O.K.," and I guess everybody knows what happened. In early—beginning early September last year, it was a tremendous stretch of activity and so nothing ever happened on that. . . .

At an earlier time, in the middle of 1983, I resigned. And that was because I discovered that Bud McFarlane, who was then the deputy national security adviser, was sent on a secret trip to the Middle East . . . without my knowledge, while we're busy negotiating out there. And also I found some things happened with respect to actions on Central America that I didn't know about beforehand.

So I went to the President and I said, "Mr. Presi-dent, you don't need a guy like me for Secretary of State if this is the way things are going to be done, because when you send somebody out like that McFarlane trip, I'm done." In the labor relations business—I used to be Secretary of Labor and there used to be a lot of intervention in labor disputes and we used to say, "When the President hangs out his shingle, he'll get all the business." When—when the President hangs out his shingle and says, "You don't have to go through the State Department, just come right into the White House," he'll get all the business.

That's a big signal to countries out there about how to deal with the U.S. Government. And it may have had had something to do with how events transpired, for all I know. But it's wrong; you can't do it that way. . . .

So the other time I resigned was after my big lie-detector test flap, and again I could see that I was on the outs with everybody and so I said, "Mr. President, why don't you let me go home. I like it in California." . . . And again, he wouldn't let that happen. And that was in late 1985. Mr. McFarlane had resigned, and Mr. McFarlane and I, I think, worked very effectively together in . . . our efforts with the U.S.S.R. and . . . in the end I didn't feel, with Mr. McFarlane having left, that it was fair to the President or the country for me to leave at the same time, so I didn't.

But I do think that in jobs like the job I have, where it is a real privilege to serve in this kind of job, or the others that you recounted, that you can't do the job well if you want it too much. You have to be willing to say goodbye, and I am.

Q   I thank you very much, Mr. Secretary.

PART IX

REFORMS

The President bears a special responsibility for the effective performance of the NSC system.

The Tower Commission
February 1987

EDITORS' INTRODUCTION

Part V of the Tower Commission's report on the Iran-*contra* affair, the first selection in the final section of this book, sets out "Recommendations on Organizing for National Security." The report includes several specific injunctions, including ones relating to NSC involvement in covert actions, which are designed to prevent a recurrence of the rogue operations conducted by the NSC staff during the Reagan Administration. But Part V of the commission's report does more than that.

Harry Truman immortalized a saying with a sign he had on his White House desk: "The Buck Stops Here." The Tower Commission, based not only on its inquiry into President Reagan's mishandling of the Iran-*contra* activities but also on its review of NSC operations over the past forty years, arrived at the same conclusion. "The President bears a special responsibility," said the commission, "for the effective performance of the NSC system." Moreover, the commission added: "A President must at the outset provide guidelines to the members of the National Security Council, his National Security Advisor, and the National Security Council staff. These guidelines, to be effective, must include how they will relate to one another, what procedures will be followed, what the President expects of them. If his advisors are not performing as he likes, only the President can intervene."

With that statement, the Tower Commission's report transcended the Iran-*contra* affair. It placed the responsibility for the NSC advisory system squarely on the shoulders of the president. The Commission did not search for surrogates to be held responsible for the disorders that have afflicted the NSC over the years, including the battles that have been fought between secretaries of state and national security advisers or other cabinet secretaries, with the NSC adviser often caught in the crossfire. Yes, said the commission, "If the system is to operate well, the national security adviser must promote cooperation rather than competition among himself and the other NSC principals." "But," the commission concluded, "the President is ultimately responsible for the operation of this system. If rancorous infighting develops among his principal national security functionaries, only he can deal with them . . . It is the President's responsibility to ensure that it does not take place."

As a conclusion to its report, the Tower Commission offered eight recommendations, the first of which returns this book to its starting point—the origins of the NSC and, specifically, the National Security Act of 1947. Stated the commission:

> The flaws of procedures and failures of responsibility revealed by our study do not suggest any inadequacies of the National Security Act of 1947 that deal with the structure and operation of the NSC system. Forty years of experience under the Act demonstrates to the Board that it remains a fundamentally sound framework for national security decision-making. It strikes a balance between formal structure and flexibility adequate to permit each President to tailor the system to fit his needs.

The President's Needs

"To fit his needs"—it is the common thread that runs through the history of the National Security Council, from its beginnings in 1947 to the present. It explains, in large measure, why President Truman initially ignored the Council (to avoid being "captured" by its statutory advisers and decisions), why President Eisenhower "institutionalized" the NSC system ("the old soldier is accustomed to well-staffed work"), why President Kennedy turned increasingly to his national security adviser for policy advice and management (State spoke with "too many voices and too little vigor"), why President Nixon placed Henry Kissinger in charge of his national security decision-making apparatus ("He was determined to run foreign policy from the White House"), and why President George W. Bush immediately convened a meeting of his full National Security Council upon his return to Washington and the White House on the evening of 9/11.

Whereas presidential needs have varied since the NSC first met in September 1947—reflecting the style, personality, and idiosyncrasies of the Oval Office occupant—a president's national security advisory requirements have not. Several lists of the most important of these advisory functions have been offered and, not surprisingly, they share many similarities, including:

- First, the identification of key issues requiring presidential attention (and the sorting out of those issues that do not);
- Second, the consideration of all available intelligence, information, and analysis relating to the issue under examination;
- Third, the presentation of a wide range of options for the president to consider (along with a thorough assessment of the expected consequences of each);
- Fourth, an articulation of the means for effectively implementing the president's decision;
- And, finally, an evaluation of that decision once its results can be assessed (in other words, assisting the president in assuring performance, or revising policy if necessary).

But how are these advisory functions best performed? By formal meetings of the full NSC or through smaller, more intimate presidential meetings with key advisers, such as the first President Bush's "core group" gatherings in the Oval Office? Should a president give primacy to his secretary of state for his foreign policy-making system, or centralize control of that system in the White House? And how involved should the president become in searching for information and policy options and overseeing the execution of his decisions—reaching out into the bureaucracy as Kennedy sometimes did or preferring, like Reagan, to remain aloof from the details, focusing instead on the "big picture?"

These are questions a president must answer. They are also questions that observers of the NSC—including former members of the Council and staff, members of Congress, academicians, and journalists—have addressed, offering proposals to improve the functioning of the NSC system and remedies for the kinds of disorders the NSC has experienced during its sometimes turbulent history.

In this section we will survey several of those proposals and suggested reforms—but first a cautionary note. As the Tower Commission stated in its report on the Iran-*contra* affair: "There is no magic formula which can be applied to the NSC structure and process to produce an optimal system." Still, that is not to say that the lessons of over half a century of experience with the NSC cannot be distilled into prescriptions for a more effective and efficient Council as it meets the challenges of the future. Or, as William Bundy—the brother of McGeorge Bundy and himself a high-ranking State Department official—once put it: "Surely the experiences of eight presidents ought by now to have thrown up a few hints of what to avoid and what to seek."

MANAGING INSTITUTIONAL TENSIONS   The title of a *New York Times* opinion piece toward the end of the Reagan Administration captured Richard C. Holbrooke's strong views on the subject: "Stop the Ruinous Turf Wars Over Foreign Policy." Holbrooke, then a New York investment banker and later President Clinton's ambassador to the United Nations, summed up the problem this way:

> Rogers and Kissinger. Vance and Brzezinski. Muskie and Brzezinski. Haig and Allen. Haig and Clark. Shultz and McFarlane. Shultz and Poindexter.
> Five Secretaries of State, six so-called national security advisers, four administrations.
> Policies that ranged across the ideological spectrum. Widely differing personalities and styles.
> Yet, one constant: friction between the two top advisers to the President on foreign policy—friction that, in most cases, adversely affected not only the conduct but also the content and coherence of foreign policy, and in at least two Administrations—Jimmy Carter's and Ronald Reagan's—led directly to large-scale political problems and erosion of public confidence in the President's ability to govern.

Clearly, dealing with the institutional tensions between the national security adviser and the secretary of state has been a recurrent problem throughout much of the NSC's recent history. The question is whether that institutional tension can be effectively and constructively managed or whether, by its bureaucratic nature, it is inherently disruptive to the president's policy and advisory process. Leslie H. Gelb captured this dilemma in what he has called the two "iron laws" governing relations between the White House and the departments of State and Defense: first, that things won't work well with a strong national security adviser to the president and, second, that without a strong adviser, things won't work at all (Gelb, January 7, 1982: A 20). Madeleine Albright appeared to confirm that "iron law" when she was asked to comment on a report stating that Sandy Berger had assumed some of the duties of secretary of state. "As far as I am concerned," she told *New York Times* reporter Jane Perlez, "a strong national security adviser is very important for a strong secretary of state." (Perlez, December 14, 1999: A1).

In the second selection in Part IX, Theodore C. Sorensen, former special counsel to President Kennedy and one of his closest aides, addresses the issue of institutional tension from a slightly different perspective—that of the appropriate relationship between (as his article is entitled) "The President and the Secretary of State." Sorensen argues that the debate over who should run foreign policy—the White House or the State Department—is, in effect, OBE ("overtaken by events"). In Sorensen's words: ". . . . the principal reason for the increasing concentration of foreign policy responsibility in the White House is our increasingly dangerous world." Moreover, Sorensen writes, "No president is willing to entrust the nation's security and survival (and his own political effectiveness and survival) wholly to professional diplomats or to a secretary of state necessarily lacking his perspective."

That said, Sorensen makes the case that future administrations would be ill-advised to limit the secretary and the Department of State to a "housekeeping, clerk, and messenger role," and he offers seven basic principles to guide the State–White House relationship. First among these is a clear statement by the president that he "genuinely wishes the secretary of state to be not his sole but his principal adviser, spokesman, negotiator and agent in foreign affairs—not his coordinator or decision-maker . . ." As for his national security adviser, the president should fill that post "with a skilled and trusted deputy possessing a personal style and outlook compatible with both his own *and the secretary's*" (emphasis added). Sorensen also underscores (as do virtually all observers of the NSC) the central role the president must play in making this work: "Finally, the president himself must be in command of his own forces . . . Ultimately he will determine the quality of his principal foreign policy advisers and their advice."

Improving the NSC System

Determining the quality of his advisers and their counsel is up to the president, and so too is the responsibility for ensuring that the NSC system is run as effectively and efficiently as possible. It is to that subject that the co-directors of the The National Security Project—Ivo Daalder of the Brookings Institution and I.M. Destler of the Center for International and Security Studies at the University of Maryland—turn their attention in the third selection of this chapter. Their "Policy Brief," entitled "A New NSC for a New Administration," appeared in November 2000, on the eve of the change of administrations from Bill Clinton to George W. Bush.

Daalder and Destler assert that, as the NSC has grown in size, it "has become more like an agency than a presidential staff. It is immersed in policy detail and focuses predominantly on the short term. It does not give sufficient attention to the critical task that it alone can perform: coordinating the policy process so that, simultaneously, agencies get a full and fair hearing and the president can make clear foreign policy choices in a timely manner." The challenge, say the authors, is to refocus the NSC on its "primary, critical role," and it is the president who "must ensure that this key function is restored."

To accomplish this, the authors identify eight features of an effective NSC for managing the policy-making process. Their "Back to Basics" prescriptions include cutting the NSC's size, simplifying its structure, and enhancing its seniority. Daalder and Destler are advocates of a strong NSC—"The national security adviser and key aides must be tough enough to coordinate policy, pull agencies and officials together, ensure presidential decisions are implemented, and give the president substantive advice." But they also argue for a "subdued" NSC: "The adviser and staff must keep a low profile, limit press contacts, eschew operations, and work principally within the executive branch." Only by doing so, they contend, can the NSC do what it was established to do, namely, focus on "the policy issues and choices that are (or should be) the president's business—nothing less, but also nothing more."

Meeting the Challenges of the Twenty-first Century

There is broad recognition today that the United States has moved into a new national security era—one no longer defined by the threat of a single adversary, but one with multiple challenges from many sources, including the proliferation of weapons of mass destruction and their means of delivery, the potential for catastrophic terrorism, and conflict with so-called "rogue nations," such as Iraq and North Korea. "The president's business," to use the phrase cited above from

Daalder and Destler, has expanded. This reality also dictates that our institutions, including the NSC, be adjusted to meet these new threats. Organizational coherence in national security decision making can and will make a difference in meeting the challenges the United States will face in the twenty-first century.

The final selection in Part IX focuses on this changing security environment and how America should respond. The U.S. Commission on National Security/21st Century was established in 1999 by the Department of Defense to undertake the most comprehensive examination of U.S. national security requirements and organization since a similar effort was made in 1947 (resulting in the National Security Act and the creation of the NSC). The commission's co-chairs—selected by the secretary of defense in consultation with the secretary of state and the national security adviser—were former U.S. senators Gary Hart (D–Colorado) and Warren Rudman (R–New Hampshire). They were chosen, according to the commission's charter, "for their national recognition and significant depth of experience and public service."

The commission concluded Phase I of its work with the publication of its first report in September 1999. Entitled "New World Coming: American Security in the 21st Century," the report stressed that mass-casualty terrorism directed against the U.S. homeland was of serious and growing concern. A year-and-a-half later, in March 2001, the commission issued its Phase III report, "Road Map for National Security: Imperative for Change." The commission reiterated its earlier warning: "The combination of unconventional weapons proliferation with the persistence of international terrorism will end the relative invulnerability of the U.S. homeland to catastrophic attack. A direct attack against American citizens on American soil is likely over the next quarter century." As we would tragically learn, that attack would come much earlier—it was just six months away.

Phase III of the commission's work focused on reforming the national security apparatus to meet the challenges and threats it identified. The centerpiece of its recommendations was the creation of a National Homeland Security Agency to unite the Coast Guard, Customs Service, Federal Emergency Management Agency, and the Border Patrol into a new institution whose director would have cabinet status. A new Department of Homeland Security would later become the centerpiece of President Bush's organizational response to the attacks of September 11.

"Beyond the pressing matter of organizing homeland security," the Phase III report states, "this Commission recommends significant organizational redesign for the Executive Branch," including several measures affecting the structure and operation of the National Security Council. That portion of the commission's report is included as the last selection of this volume.

Of greatest concern to the commission in its review of the Council was what it referred to as the expansion of the role of the NSC staff. "In many ways," said the commission, "the NSC staff has become more like a government agency than a Presidential staff." The commission therefore recommended that the National Security Adviser and NSC staff should return to their more "traditional and unique roles, namely coordinating the policy making process, so that all those with stakes are involved, and all realistic policy options are considered and analyzed." At the same time, the commission argued that the role of the NSC in the interagency process should be strengthened to include, as stated in one of the commission's key recommendations, "coordinating the multiplicity of national security activities, broadly defined to include economic and domestic law enforcement activities as well as the traditional national security agenda."

The Hart–Rudman Commission went on to call for the NSC adviser and staff to "forego operational control of any aspect of U.S. policy" (echoing the earlier Tower Commission) and for the adviser to "keep a low public profile." But in one respect the commission urges the president to add to the national security adviser's responsibilities: in the critical area of strategic planning. It is the commission's view that the strategic planning function is largely absent within the U.S. government—that there is no "overarching strategic framework guiding U.S. national security policy making and resource allocation." To establish "clear goals and priorities" for national security, including the threat posed by international terrorism, the commission urged the president to "personally guide a top-down strategic planning process and delegate authority to the National Security Advisor to coordinate that process."

Policy integration and coordination: the Hart–Rudman Commission saw this as the NSC's primary and "unique" role, as did the Tower Commission, the Jackson Subcommittee, and the Eberstadt report before that. That latter report, issued in September 1945, stated: "The National Security Council would be the keystone of our organizational structure for national security." The September 2001 terrorist attacks on the United States reaffirmed the preeminent role the NSC continues to have in the making of American foreign and security policy and can be expected to have well into the future.

30

RECOMMENDATIONS ON ORGANIZING FOR NATIONAL SECURITY

Tower Commission

In selection 28 (found in Part VIII of this text), weaknesses in the NSC as discovered by the Tower Commission were laid out. Presented here are the commission's recommendations for reform.

RECOMMENDATIONS

"Not only . . . is the Federal power over external affairs in origin and essential character different from that over internal affairs, but participation in the exercise of the power is significantly limited. In this vast external realm, with its important, complicated, delicate and manifold problems, the President alone has the power to speak or listen as a representative of the nation."

—*United States v. Curtiss-Wright Export Corp., 299 U.S. 304, 319 (1936).*

Whereas the ultimate power to formulate domestic policy resides in the Congress, the primary responsibility for the formulation and implementation of national security policy falls on the President.

It is the President who is the usual source of innovation and responsiveness in this field. The departments and agencies—the Defense Department, State Department, and CIA bureaucracies—tend to resist policy change. Each has its own perspective based on long experience. The challenge for the President is to bring his perspective to bear on these bureaucracies for they are his instruments for executing national security policy, and he must work through them. His task is to provide them leadership and direction.

The National Security Act of 1947 and the system that has grown up under it affords the President special tools for carrying out this important role. These tools are the National Security Council, the National Security Advisor, and the NSC staff. These are the means through which the creative impulses of the President are brought to bear on the permanent government. The National Security Act, and custom and practice, rightly give the President wide latitude in fashioning exactly how these means are used.

There is no magic formula which can be applied to the NSC structure and process to produce an optimal system. Because the system is the vehicle through which the President formulates and implements his national security policy, it must adapt to each individual President's style and management philosophy. This means that NSC structures and processes must be flexible, not rigid. Overprescription would . . . either destroy the system or render it ineffective.

Nevertheless, this does not mean there can be no guidelines or recommendations that might improve the operation of the system, whatever the particular style of the incumbent President. We have reviewed the operation of the system over the past 40 years, through good times and bad. We have listened carefully to the views of all the living former Presidents as well as those of most of the participants in their own national security systems. With the strong caveat that flexibility and adaptability must be at the core, it is our judgment that the national security system seems to have worked best when it has in general operated along the lines set forth below.

Reprinted from Report of the President's Special Review Board (the Tower Commission), Washington, D.C., February 26, 1987, pp. V-1–V-7.

Organizing for National Security Because of the wide latitude in the National Security Act, the President bears a special responsibility for the effective performance of the NSC system. A President must at the outset provide guidelines to the members of the National Security Council, his National Security Advisor, and the National Security Council staff. These guidelines, to be effective, must include how they will relate to one another, what procedures will be followed, what the President expects of them. If his advisors are not performing as he likes, only the President can intervene.

The National Security Council principals other than the President participate on the Council in a unique capacity.[1] Although holding a seat by virtue of their official positions in the Administration, when they sit as members of the Council they sit not as cabinet secretaries or department heads but as advisors to the President. They are there not simply to advance or defend the particular positions of the departments or agencies they head but to give their best advice to the President. Their job—and their challenge—is to see the issue from this perspective, not from the narrower interests of their respective bureaucracies.

The National Security Council is only advisory. It is the President alone who decides. When the NSC principals receive those decisions, they do so as heads of the appropriate departments or agencies. They are then responsible to see that the President's decisions are carried out by those organizations accurately and effectively.

This is an important point. The policy innovation and creativity of the President encounters a natural resistance from the executing departments. While this resistance is a source of frustration to every President, it is inherent in the design of the government. It is up to the politically appointed agency heads to ensure that the President's goals, designs, and policies are brought to bear on this permanent structure. Circumventing the departments, perhaps by using the National Security Advisor or the NSC staff to execute policy, robs the President of the experience and capacity resident in the departments. The President must act largely through them, but the agency heads must ensure that they execute the President's policies in an expeditious and effective manner. It is not just the obligation of the

National Security Advisor to see that the national security process is used. All of the NSC principals—and particularly the President—have that obligation.

This tension between the President and the Executive Departments is worked out through the national security process described in the opening sections of this report. It is through this process that the nation obtains both the best of the creativity of the President and the learning and expertise of the national security departments and agencies.

This process is extremely important to the President. His decisions will benefit from the advice and perspective of all the concerned departments and agencies. History offers numerous examples of this truth. President Kennedy, for example, did not have adequate consultation before entering upon the Bay of Pigs invasion, one of his greatest failures. He remedied this in time for the Cuban missile crisis, one of his greatest successes. Process will not always produce brilliant ideas, but history suggests it can at least help prevent bad ideas from becoming Presidential policy.

The National Security Advisor It is the National Security Advisor who is primarily responsible for managing this process on a daily basis. The job requires skill, sensitivity, and integrity. It is his responsibility to ensure that matters submitted for consideration by the Council cover the full range of issues on which review is required; that those issues are fully analyzed; that a full range of options is considered; that the prospects and risks of each are examined; that all relevant intelligence and other information is available to the principals; that legal considerations are addressed; that difficulties in implementation are confronted. Usually, this can best be accomplished through interagency participation in the analysis of the issue and a preparatory policy review at the Deputy or Under Secretary level.

The National Security Advisor assumes these responsibilities not only with respect to the President but with respect to all the NSC principals. He must keep them informed of the President's thinking and decisions. They should have adequate notice and an agenda for all meetings. Decision papers should, if at all possible, be provided in advance.

The National Security Advisor must also ensure that adequate records are kept of NSC consultations and Presidential decisions. This is essential to avoid confusion among Presidential advisors and departmental staffs about what was actually decided and what is wanted. Those records are also essential for conducting a periodic review of a policy or initiative, and to learn from the past.

It is the responsibility of the National Security Advisor to monitor policy implementation and to ensure that policies are executed in conformity with the intent of the President's decision. Monitoring includes initiating periodic reassessments of a policy or operation, especially when changed circumstances suggest that the policy or operation no longer serves U.S. interests.

But the National Security Advisor does not simply manage the national security process. He is himself an important source of advice on national security matters to the President. He is not the President's only source of advice, but he is perhaps the one most able to see things from the President's perspective. He is unburdened by departmental responsibilities. The President is his only master. His advice is confidential. He is not subject to Senate confirmation and traditionally does not formally appear before Congressional committees.

To serve the President well, the National Security Advisor should present his own views, but he must at the same time represent the views of others fully and faithfully to the President. The system will not work well if the National Security Advisor does not have the trust of the NSC principals. He, therefore, must not use his proximity to the President to manipulate the process so as to produce his own position. He should not interpose himself between the President and the NSC principals. He should not seek to exclude the NSC principals from the decision process. Performing both these roles well is an essential, if not easy, task.

In order for the National Security Advisor to serve the President adequately, he must have direct access to the President. Unless he knows first hand the views of the President and is known to reflect them in his management of the NSC system, he will be ineffective. He should not report to the President through some other official. While the Chief of Staff or others can usefully interject domestic political considerations into national security deliberations, they should do so as additional advisors to the President.

Ideally, the National Security Advisor should not have a high public profile. He should not try to compete with the Secretary of State or the Secretary of Defense as the articulator of public policy. They, along with the President, should be the spokesmen for the policies of the Administration. While a "passion for anonymity" is perhaps too strong a term, the National Security Advisor should generally operate offstage.

The NSC principals of course must have direct access to the President, with whatever frequency the President feels is appropriate. But these individual meetings should not be used by the principal to seek decisions or otherwise circumvent the system in the absence of the other principals. In the same way, the National Security Advisor should not use his scheduled intelligence or other daily briefings of the President as an opportunity to seek Presidential decision on significant issues.

If the system is to operate well, the National Security Advisor must promote cooperation rather than competition among himself and the other NSC principals. But the President is ultimately responsible for the operation of this system. If rancorous infighting develops among his principal national security functionaries, only he can deal with them. Public dispute over external policy by senior officials undermines the process of decision-making and narrows his options. It is the President's responsibility to ensure that it does not take place.

Finally, the National Security Advisor should focus on advice and management, not implementation and execution. Implementation is the responsibility and the strength of the departments and agencies. The National Security Advisor and the NSC staff generally do not have the depth of resources for the conduct of operations. In addition, when they take on implementation responsibilities, they risk compromising their objectivity. They can no longer act as impartial overseers of the implementation, ensuring that Presidential guidance is followed, that policies are kept under review, and that the results are serving the President's policy and the national interest.

The NSC Staff   The NSC staff should be small, highly competent, and experienced in the making of public policy. Staff members should be drawn both from within and from outside government. Those from within government should come from the several departments and agencies concerned with national security matters. No particular department or agency should have a predominate role. A proper balance must be maintained between people from within and outside the government. Staff members should generally rotate with a stay of more than four years viewed as the exception.

A large number of staff action officers organized along essentially horizontal lines enhances the possibilities for poorly supervised and monitored activities by individual staff members. Such a system is made to order for energetic self-starters to take unauthorized initiatives. Clear vertical lines of control and authority, responsibility and accountability, are essential to good management.

One problem affecting the NSC staff is lack of institutional memory. This results from the understandable desire of a President to replace the staff in order to be sure it is responsive to him. Departments provide continuity that can help the Council, but the Council as an institution also needs some means to assure adequate records and memory. This was identified to the Board as a problem by many witnesses.

We recognize the problem and have identified a range of possibilities that a President might consider on this subject. One would be to create a small permanent executive secretariat. Another would be to have one person, the Executive Secretary, as a permanent position. Finally, a pattern of limited tenure and overlapping rotation could be used. Any of these would help reduce the problem of loss of institutional memory; none would be practical unless each succeeding President subscribed to it.

The guidelines for the role of the National Security Advisor also apply generally to the NSC staff. They should protect the process and thereby the President. Departments and agencies should not be excluded from participation in that process. The staff should not be implementors or operators and staff should keep a low profile with the press.

Principal Recommendation

The model we have outlined above for the National Security Council system constitutes our first and most important recommendation. It includes guidelines that address virtually all of the deficiencies in procedure and practice that the Board encountered in the Iran/Contra affair as well as in other case studies of this and previous administrations.

We believe this model can enhance the performance of a President and his administration in the area of national security. It responds directly to President Reagan's mandate to describe the NSC system as it ought to be.

The Board recommends that the proposed model be used by Presidents in their management of the national security system.

Specific Recommendations

In addition to its principal recommendation regarding the organization and functioning of the NSC system and roles to be played by the participants, the Board has a number of specific recommendations.

1. The National Security Act of 1947   The flaws of procedure and failures of responsibility revealed by our study do not suggest any inadequacies in the provisions of the National Security Act of 1947 that deal with the structure and operation of the NSC system. Forty years of experience under that Act demonstrate to the Board that it remains a fundamentally sound framework for national security decision-making. It strikes a balance between formal structure and flexibility adequate to permit each President to tailor the system to fit his needs.

As a general matter, the NSC staff should not engage in the implementation of policy or the conduct of operations. This compromises their oversight role and usurps the responsibilities of the departments and agencies. But the inflexibility of a legislative restriction should be avoided. Terms such as "operation" and "implementation" are difficult to define, and a legislative proscription might preclude some future President from making a very constructive use of the NSC staff.

Predisposition on sizing of the staff should be toward fewer rather than more. But a legislative restriction cannot foresee the requirements of future Presidents. Size is best left to the discretion of the President, with the admonition that the role of the NSC staff is to review, not to duplicate or replace, the work of the departments and agencies.

We recommend that no substantive change be made in the provisions of the National Security Act dealing with the structure and operation of the NSC system.

2. Senate Confirmation of the National Security Advisor It has been suggested that the job of the National Security Advisor has become so important that its holder should be screened by the process of confirmation, and that once confirmed he should return frequently for questioning by the Congress. It is argued that this would improve the accountability of the National Security Advisor.

We hold a different view. The National Security Advisor does, and should continue, to serve only one master, and that is the President. Further, confirmation is inconsistent with the role the National Security Advisor should play. He should not decide, only advise. He should not engage in policy implementation or operations. He should serve the President, with no collateral and potentially diverting loyalties.

Confirmation would tend to institutionalize the natural tension that exists between the Secretary of State and the National Security Advisor. Questions would increasingly arise about who really speaks for the President in national security matters. Foreign governments could be confused or would be encouraged to engage in "forum shopping."

Only one of the former government officials interviewed favored Senate confirmation of the National Security Advisor. While consultation with Congress received wide support, confirmation and formal questioning were opposed. Several suggested that if the National Security Advisor were to become a position subject to confirmation, it could induce the President to turn to other internal staff or to people outside government to play that role.

We urge the Congress not to require Senate confirmation of the National Security Advisor.

3. The Interagency Process It is the National Security Advisor who has the greatest interest in making the national security process work, for it is this process by which the President obtains the information, background, and analysis he requires to make decisions and build support for his program. Most Presidents have set up interagency committees at both a staff and pol-

icy level to surface issues, develop options, and clarify choices. There has typically been a struggle for the chairmanships of these groups between the National Security Advisor and the NSC staff on the one hand, and the cabinet secretaries and department officials on the other.

Our review of the operation of the present system and that of other administrations where committee chairmen came from the departments has led us to the conclusion that the system generally operates better when the committees are chaired by the individual with the greatest stake in making the NSC system work.

We recommend that the National Security Advisor chair the senior-level committees of the NSC system.

4. Covert Actions Policy formulation and implementation are usually managed by a team of experts led by policymaking generalists. Covert action requirements are no different, but there is a need to limit, sometimes severely, the number of individuals involved. The lives of many people may be at stake, as was the case in the attempt to rescue the hostages in Tehran. Premature disclosure might kill the idea in embryo, as could have been the case in the opening of relations with China. In such cases, there is a tendency to limit those involved to a small number of top officials. This practice tends to limit severely the expertise brought to bear on the problem and should be used very sparingly indeed.

The obsession with secrecy and preoccupation with leaks threaten to paralyze the government in its handling of covert operations. Unfortunately, the concern is not misplaced. The selective leak has become a principal means of waging bureaucratic warfare. Opponents of an operation kill it with a leak; supporters seek to build support through the same means.

We have witnessed over the past years a significant deterioration in the integrity of process. Rather than a means to obtain results more satisfactory than the position of any of the individual departments, it has frequently become something to be manipulated to reach a specific outcome. The leak becomes a primary instrument in that process.

This practice is destructive of orderly governance. It can only be reversed if the most senior officials take the lead. If senior decision-makers set a clear example and demand compliance, subordinates are more likely to conform.

Most recent administrations have had carefully drawn procedures for the consideration of covert activities. The Reagan Administration established such procedures in January, 1985, then promptly ignored them in their consideration of the Iran initiative.

We recommend that each administration formulate precise procedures for restricted consideration of covert action and that, once formulated, those procedures be strictly adhered to.

5. The Role of the CIA   Some aspects of the Iran arms sales raised broader questions in the minds of members of the Board regarding the role of the CIA. The first deals with intelligence.

The NSC staff was actively involved in the preparation of the May 20, 1985, update to the Special National Intelligence Estimate on Iran. It is a matter for concern if this involvement and the strong views of NSC staff members were allowed to influence the intelligence judgments contained in the update. It is also of concern that the update contained the hint that the United States should change its existing policy and encourage its allies to provide arms to Iran. It is critical that the line between intelligence and advocacy of a particular policy be preserved if intelligence is to retain its integrity and perform its proper function. In this instance, the CIA came close enough to the line to warrant concern.

We emphasize to both the intelligence community and policymakers the importance of maintaining the integrity and objectivity of the intelligence process.

6. Legal Counsel   From time to time issues with important legal ramifications will come before the National Security Council. The Attorney General is currently a member of the Council by invitation and should be in a position to provide legal advice to the Council and the President. It is important that the Attorney General and his department be available to interagency deliberations.

The Justice Department, however, should not replace the role of counsel in the other departments. As the principal counsel on foreign affairs, the Legal Adviser to the Secretary of State should also be available to all the NSC participants.

Of all the NSC participants, it is the Assistant for National Security Affairs who seems to have had the least access to expert counsel familiar with his activities.

The Board recommends that the position of Legal Adviser to the NSC be enhanced in stature and in its role within the NSC staff.

7. Secrecy and Congress   There is a natural tension between the desire for secrecy and the need to consult Congress on covert operations. Presidents seem to become increasingly concerned about leaks of classified information as their administrations progress. They blame Congress disproportionately. Various cabinet officials from prior administrations indicated to the Board that they believe Congress bears no more blame than the Executive Branch.

However, the number of Members and staff involved in reviewing covert activities is large; it provides cause for concern and a convenient excuse for Presidents to avoid Congressional consultation.

We recommend that Congress consider replacing the existing Intelligence Committees of the respective Houses with a new joint committee with a restricted staff to oversee the intelligence community, patterned after the Joint Committee on Atomic Energy that existed until the mid-1970s.

8. Privatizing National Security Policy   Careful and limited use of people outside the U.S. Government may be very helpful in some unique cases. But this practice raises substantial questions. It can create conflict of interest problems. Private or foreign sources may have different policy interests or personal motives and may exploit their association with a U.S. government effort. Such involvement gives private and foreign sources potentially powerful leverage in the form of demands for return favors or even blackmail.

The U.S. has enormous resources invested in agencies and departments in order to conduct the government's business. In all but a very few cases, these can perform the functions needed. If not, then inquiry is required to find out why.

We recommend against having implementation and policy oversight dominated by intermediaries.

We do not recommend barring limited use of private individuals to assist in United States diplomatic initiatives or in covert activities. We caution against use of such people except in very limited ways and under close observation and supervision.

Epilogue

If but one of the major policy mistakes we examined had been avoided, the nation's history would bear one less scar, one less embarrassment, one less opportunity for opponents to reverse the principles this nation seeks to preserve and advance in the world.

As a collection, these recommendations are offered to those who will find themselves in situations similar to the ones we reviewed: under stress, with high stakes, given little time, using incomplete information, and troubled by premature disclosure. In such a state, modest improvements may yield surprising gains. This is our hope.

NOTE

1. As discussed in more detail in Part II [not reprinted in this text] the statutory members of the National Security Council are the President, Vice President. Secretary of State, and Secretary of Defense. By the phrase "National Security Council principals" or "NSC principals," the Board generally means those four statutory members plus the Director of Central Intelligence and the Chairman of the Joint Chiefs of Staff.

31

THE PRESIDENT AND THE SECRETARY OF STATE

Theodore C. Sorensen

In this selection, a former top aide to President Kennedy and a keen observer of national security policy offers thoughtful insights on the tension between the NSC directors and the secretary of state, along with six recommendations to improve the White House–State Department relationship.

The next president, regardless of party, must restore mutual respect between the White House and Department of State.

Although the Iran-*contra* hearings focused on the executive-legislative imbalance, they also revealed a pattern of White House disdain for the Department of State so pervasive that Secretary George Shultz's own blunt testimony, while preserving his personal reputation, confirmed his department's emasculation. Never informed by the president of key foreign policy decisions, deliberately deceived by what senators termed a White House "junta" utilizing "rather shady characters" to carry out U.S. foreign policy, the secretary testified to "a sense of estrangement," of not being "in good odor" with the White House staff.

This was no attack of Foggy Bottom paranoia. National Security Adviser John Poindexter had placed the State Department on the list of those "who didn't need to know" certain overseas actions. His assistant, Oliver North, gave the department the code name "Wimp." Poindexter's predecessor Robert McFarlane once said North should be secretary of state. Both McFarlane and Poindexter traveled secretly abroad without informing the department. Still other White House aides vetoed Shultz's trips and suggested anonymously to the press that he resign.

II

Although the House and Senate committees investigating the Iran-*contra* affair were assured that new personnel and procedures would halt such conflicts, this was neither the first nor the last time Mr. Shultz was shut out or shot down by the White House. Nor was he the first secretary of state to encounter this treatment.

Indeed, his appointment followed Reagan's "acceptance" of a resignation frequently threatened, but never tendered, by Alexander Haig. Despite repeated presidential assurances that "you are my foreign policy guy," Secretary Haig found his policy pronouncements publicly disputed by White House assistants (who reciprocated his ill will), his procedural requests unanswered, and his authority over personnel and crisis management—even his place on Air Force One and in presidential receiving lines—downgraded. Like Shultz, Haig at one point felt obliged to acknowledge that he could not speak for the Administration.

Ironically, candidate Reagan had denounced White House-State Department feuding under President Carter, just as candidate Carter four years earlier had pledged that there would be no Kissinger-like "Lone Ranger" in his administration. But Carter's secretary of state, Cyrus Vance, soon found National Security Adviser Zbigniew Brzezinski cabling ambassadors,

Reprinted by permission from Theodore C. Sorensen. "The President and the Secretary of State," *Foreign Affairs*, 66 (Winter 1987/88). 231–248. Copyright 1987 by the Council of Foreign Relations, Inc.

Theodore C. Sorensen, who served as Special Counsel to President John F. Kennedy, now practices international law in New York City.

initiating negotiations, briefing the press, pronouncing policy and giving the president inaccurate summaries of their discussions. Carter thought he could balance Vance and Brzezinski and ride both horses simultaneously, even incorporating inconsistent paragraphs from each in a speech. But the ultimate result was delay and ineffectiveness.

Some say perfect harmony between the secretary of state and national security adviser (more accurately, the assistant to the president for national security affairs) prevailed only when Henry Kissinger briefly held both jobs. But when Kissinger wore his White House hat only, he substantially increased the national security adviser's visibility and staff, and sought, in his words, to bypass "as much as possible" Secretary of State William P. Rogers, selected by President Nixon specifically for his "ignorance of foreign policy." One senator remarked that Washington was laughing at Rogers, with Kissinger "secretary of state in everything but title." Another said: "They let Rogers handle Norway and Malagasy, and Kissinger would handle Russia and China and everything else he was interested in."

Kissinger's dominant role—recognized by the press and foreign governments despite White House claims to the contrary—reflected not merely his intragovernmental maneuvering but also the specific preference of a president knowledgeable in foreign affairs, who once remarked he "would have to wait 20 years for a new idea from the State Department."

Even as secretary, Kissinger neglected most of the rest of the State Department, relying largely upon a small coterie much as John Foster Dulles had done two decades earlier. Dulles, though he personally enjoyed unchallenged authority as President Eisenhower's secretary of state, not only ignored most of the Foreign Service but also permitted it to be gutted by Senator Joe McCarthy and others.

Paradoxically it was Eisenhower—who would not even send his brother or the vice president abroad without checking with Dulles—who expanded the National Security Council staff and its responsibilities and created the position of special assistant to the president for national security affairs (first filled by Robert Cutler). During the Kennedy Administration Cutler's successor in that office, McGeorge Bundy, assumed an increasingly important role; the NSC staff, described by Cutler as "scrupulously non-policy making" and nonpartisan, became an active part of the president's own staff, with an increased proportion of non-career officers. Secretary of State Dean Rusk—who, unlike Rogers and Haig, had unlimited access to his president—avoided feuding with Bundy and others whom Kennedy involved in foreign policy, including the president's brother, the attorney general; but he did not always welcome their participation. (Kennedy once quipped that, even when they were alone, Rusk would whisper to him that there were still too many present.) For his part, Kennedy both admired the State Department's talent and regarded it as a "bowl of jelly," a vast paperwork machine producing too few innovations and too many delays.

Although Rusk was closer to Kennedy's successor, Lyndon Johnson, and Bundy's successor, Walt Rostow, the concentration of foreign policy authority in the White House escalated along with the Vietnam War. Johnson, more than most presidents, reached outside both State and the White House for emissaries and advice, once tossing a draft U.N. speech onto the White House dinner table and asking assorted guests for revisions.

In the Truman-Marshall-Acheson era, now regarded as the State Department's Golden Age, two successive secretaries enjoyed true preeminence, coordinating policy and strengthening the Foreign Service with no interference from the newly formed NSC's technical staff. Nevertheless, even President Truman, who had not tolerated James Byrnes' failure as secretary to clear a national radio address, occasionally overrode George Marshall and Dean Acheson, for example, reinserting the "Point Four" program in his 1948 inaugural speech after the department had deleted it and taking the Palestine issue largely out of the department's hands. Long before there was a national security adviser, Secretary Marshall bristled at White House Counsel Clark Clifford's involvement in Palestine policy.

But Truman's overall approach contrasted sharply with that of Franklin Roosevelt. Bored by Secretary Cordell Hull, a political appointee, and distrustful of what he termed a "horse and buggy" State Department, F.D.R. inserted his own men to run the department

(Summer Welles, Raymond Moley, Adolph Berle), refused to take the secretary to wartime Allied summit meetings, did not inform him of key diplomatic decisions (or the atomic bomb), created a host of new wartime agencies, and utilized the devoted Harry Hopkins as his coordinator, emissary and principal adviser. Hull, who retained the title and trappings of office, found himself, in his own words, "relied upon in public and ignored in private."

Hull was not the first secretary to find his turf invaded. Woodrow Wilson typed his own diplomatic messages, induced the resignation of both William Jennings Bryan and Robert Lansing (with whom he did not consult about declaring war on Germany), and conducted foreign relations largely through his personal envoy, Colonel Edward House. Theodore Roosevelt often ignored Secretary John Hay, corresponded directly with other heads of state, and personally made all key decisions on Panama. William McKinley initiated war against Spain without consulting Secretary of State William Day. Even our first secretary of state, Thomas Jefferson, found his jurisdiction challenged by Treasury Secretary Alexander Hamilton, who regarded himself as George Washington's prime minister.

III

Must the next secretary of state face similar treatment? Presidents Kennedy, Johnson, Nixon, Carter and Reagan all assured their nominees to that office, publicly or privately, that the secretary would be the president's principal adviser, administrator, formulator and spokesman on foreign policy. No doubt most of those statements, like each new president's promise of the cabinet's collective importance (delivered at its only important meeting, when it gathers for its first group photograph), were sincerely intended. But each time hope was followed by frustration.

Why? F.D.R. threatened to be not only his own secretary of state but also his own secretary of war and navy. Yet, with a few notable exceptions, secretaries of defense have more successfully resisted White House direction than their colleagues at State. Indeed, the Defense Department's (and the CIA's) increasingly active role in foreign affairs has further aggravated

State's decline. Military matters somehow look less intriguing to a president than diplomacy, more complex and expensive to tinker with, less politically promising.

No president would dream, for example, of anointing a campaign contributor or crony as a military theater commander. But making him an ambassador, and permitting him to bypass the secretary of state, is commonplace. A practice harking back to Benjamin Franklin and Charles Francis Adams is not all that new; a practice utilizing Averell Harriman, David Bruce, Ellsworth Bunker and Mike Mansfield is not all that bad. If "political" ambassadors could be kept below 25 percent of the total (as in the Carter Administration) and dispatched largely to countries more scenic than sensitive, the secretary might tolerate the chagrin of senior officers passed over by unprepared and ineffective amateurs. After all a non-career ambassador with the president's ear may more easily control those representing other agencies on the embassy staff and more willingly take on the State Department's critics. But the current postwar peak, with 40 percent of appointees being non-career diplomats, many of them placed in key capitals and even in mid-level Washington posts previously reserved for career specialists, can only accelerate the department's decline.

A more important reason for that decline is the distrust that stems from each new president's determination to make new policy, announce his own "doctrine" (four in the last two decades), and change his predecessor's policies. In the State Department the president all too often encounters an emphasis on caution and continuity from career personnel who served that predecessor. From the Defense Department and CIA, seemingly less bogged down in endless paper, inflexible procedures and multiple clearances, he obtains—sometimes—quicker answers, crisper memoranda and the promise of clearer results.

Thus Kissinger deplored the State Department's "mushy compromises," Poindexter its "fear of failure" and Arthur Schlesinger its "intellectual exhaustion." White House advisers, Dean Rusk said recently, do not like to hear that the world is too intractable for their proposals "and, not liking the message . . . are inclined to shoot the messenger." But Kennedy, despite his respect for Rusk, occasionally expressed another view of the department: "They never have any ideas over there, never come up with anything new."

In addition to this traditional presidential impatience Kennedy's more populist successors harbored antiestablishment suspicions of all professional bureaucrats, particularly diplomats. Brzezinski thought Vance represented a soft elite. Poindexter (himself a product of the military bureaucracy) dismissed both State and Defense career services as "not willing to take risks." White House aides for decades have briefed the press and public, confident that they can represent the president's views better than the State Department.

But the principal reason for the increasing concentration of foreign policy responsibility in the White House is our increasingly dangerous world. Since the days when Dean Acheson could serve as both secretary of state and Truman's personal adviser and coordinator, the overlap between national and international issues, the number and speed of thermonuclear missiles, and the foreign policy pressures from Congress, the press and public, have all mounted to a point where no president can conscientiously delegate to anyone his constitutional responsibilities in foreign affairs.

No president is willing to entrust the nation's security and survival (and his own political effectiveness and survival) wholly to professional diplomats or to a secretary of state necessarily lacking his perspective. No president, as Kennedy observed, is now willing to become as dependent on one man's advice as Truman was on Acheson's.

Alexander Haig, having closely observed Kenedy's hands-on control of the Cuban missile crisis and Johnson's personal direction of Vietnam War tactics, should not have been surprised at President Reagan's insistence that crisis management be based in the White House where greater speed, precision and secrecy are assured. Reagan's counterparts in Moscow and other capitals are increasingly conducting foreign policy out of their offices and paying less attention to their foreign ministries. It is absurd to accuse the White House of "meddling" in the prerogatives of a department established by Congress in 1789 to fulfill such duties as the president should from time to time instruct.

The modern president's personal foreign policy needs are threefold. First, to assist him in his public and private consideration and discussions of international issues, he needs someone to organize the flow of information inundating his desk from countless sources, and to relate each issue to his overall foreign and domestic priorities and politics. Second, to help *him* resolve (not to resolve without him) conflicting or overlapping recommendations from the State and Defense Departments, the CIA and some 40 other agencies responsible for international finance, trade, transportation, communications and other functions, the president needs someone to identify all the problems, options and issues, to define their respective risks and consequences, to monitor the implementation of his decisions, and to act as a catalyst for government action, a clearinghouse for cabinet statements, and a presidential emissary to foreign and domestic leaders. Finally, a strong president needs independent advice and analysis, alternative evaluations of recommendations from the State Department and elsewhere, and new long-term proposals to supplement those of his departments.

These coordinating and other roles are best handled by the national security adviser (and his staff), who can fulfill the president's need for someone in the White House who, to the maximum extent possible, speaks his language, sees the whole government through his eyes, and understands his political needs. The secretary of state can neither assume that role nor assign one of his people to it (as Reagan's former chief of staff Donald Regan believed Shultz hoped to do). No secretary of defense, treasury, agriculture, commerce or other department will accept as either fair or final the secretary of state's decision on their internationally related matters, just as he would not accept their decision on his. No White House will accept as objective the secretary of state's evaluation of his own department's proposal, or permit a secretary of state to hog whatever acclaim may flow from a foreign policy success. (The Marshall Plan was so dubbed by Truman only when it faced tough sledding in the Republican-controlled Congress as elections neared.)

George Shultz, like Dulles, believed that the secretary could think "presidentially" by occupying an office adjacent to the White House. But this confuses proximity with perspective. Shultz testified that he already had unlimited access to President Reagan but used that privilege sparingly "because he's a busy person." (Any secretary of state, with unavoidable administrative, congressional, travel and other commitments, is also a busy person—too busy to fulfill the role of assistant to the president.) An auxiliary office next door to the White House would be convenient for those occasions when his presence is required for a prolonged period; but substituting such an office for his present quarters a few blocks away would not significantly increase the influence in the Oval Office of a secretary highly esteemed by the president, much less one who is not.

More important, Shultz's proposal confuses the president's need for staff support in the performance of specific White House duties with his need for a strong professional department fulfilling a broader institutional role. Separating the secretary from his department, either physically or philosophically, would diminish both. Leaving White House duties to the White House staff serves the secretary's long-run interests as well as the president's.

IV

But the next president would be ill advised to limit the secretary and Department of State to a housekeeping, clerk and messenger role. The caution, continuity and constant consultations for which the department is chided reflect in large part the reality of a dangerous world that does not change merely because we change presidents. The department's institutional memory, in-depth planning and orderly procedures can protect an eager president from his errors as well as his enemies. The experienced eye and pragmatic perspective of career specialists—unlikely to view Iranian weapons buyers as "moderates" to be wooed with a Bible, cake and concessions—are needed to balance White House pressures for quick and dramatic solutions that conform with campaign slogans or popular sentiment.

Many on the McFarlane-Poindexter team at NSC had formerly served at the State Department, where, said a colleague, nine out of ten of their unrealistic proposals had failed; but "now suddenly there was no filter between them and the ability to act." A president's aides, relatively unrestrained by statute and unaccountable to Congress, may please him more often

than career officers loyal to the department as well as the presidency. ("Sycophants," wrote Haig, "are knee-deep around the White House.") But they also serve who only stand and say no.

Thus, despite his complaints about the State Department, J.F.K. recognized its strengths, directly telephoning or summoning assistant secretaries, ambassadors and desk officers (including some sub-cabinet officers he had injudiciously named before selecting and consulting Secretary Rusk). Kennedy's Cuban missile crisis decisions were notably informed by the participation of career experts, particularly Llewellyn Thompson.

In the department described by Brzezinski as the most "turf-conscious" in Washington, productivity is directly proportional to participation. Foreign Service morale was high when Truman looked primarily to his secretary of state to run foreign policy. Its morale is low after years of budget cuts at home and terrorist attacks abroad, investigations from the outside and ideological purges within. The next president, seeking a more supportive department, must offer more support to it.

If he has read recent history as well as the Constitution, he will also know that he needs the support of Congress; and a foreign policy lacking the full participation of the secretary of state is less likely to be trusted and supported by Congress. Unlike the national security adviser and other White House aides governed by the doctrine of executive privilege, the secretary of state is accountable not only to the president but also to the Congress that confirms his appointment (Senate only), provides his funds and statutory authority, and hears his testimony.

A successful secretary of state seeks mutual respect with legislators from both parties, even when resisting their micro-management or criticism. They do not want him, their primary channel of information and influence on foreign affairs, shut out of key decisions. Kissinger, when national security adviser, occasionally provided private informal briefings to Senate Foreign Relations Committee members, sometimes at the home of the chairman, William Fulbright. But congressmen resented the fact that taking testimony from Secretary Rogers was "a rather empty exercise," and further resented Kissinger's appearing before the press but not the Congress to answer questions. To the extent the secretary of state feels excluded from foreign affairs decisions, Congress feels excluded; and that is ultimately unhealthy for the president.

Moreover, unless the NSC staff becomes as large as the State Department—in which case it would suffer many of the same ills and more—no White House has time to make and implement the myriad foreign policy decisions that a superpower makes daily. The president, with the secretary's help, will make the choices that affect his place in the headlines or history books. But every single day more than 1,000 cables are sent from the department over the secretary's signature; the department's representatives are participating in more than a dozen international conferences; and foreign ministers and ambassadors from more than eight score countries, in Washington, the United Nations and their home capitals—to say nothing of Congress and the news media—are seeking the department's position on countless issues.

In Dean Acheson's apt metaphor, the president is head gardener in foreign policy, trying to shape forces he cannot totally control: "If he tries to do it all himself—to be his own secretary of state . . . he will soon become too exhausted and immersed in manure and weed-killer to direct anything wisely." An ancient adage of the legal profession holds that a lawyer trying to represent himself has a fool for a client. A president trying to be his own secretary of state is in much the same position.

Nor can the president be his own chief negotiator. There is glory at the summit. But there is also peril and pressure. A subordinate negotiator from State can better delay a response, risk an offense, repudiate a mistake, provide a buffer and protect the president's prestige. But as Secretary Shultz testified: "When the president hangs out his shingle and says 'you don't have to go through the State Department, just come right into the White House,' he'll get all the business."

Finally, a president who overrules or undercuts his secretary of state risks a resignation potentially harmful to the country or Congress. F.D.R. reportedly took pains to avoid driving Hull to the point of resignation. Although Wilson induced Robert Lansing's resignation, confident that it would be at most "another two-day wonder," he had been less sanguine in 1915 about

Bryan's more stormy departure blasting "pro-war" policies. Bryan, however, neither respected nor effective as secretary, found his resignation assailed by some as too tardy to be an expression of conscience and by others as too helpful to the kaiser to be an expression of patriotism. He could not even be chosen delegate to the 1916 Democratic Convention.

Unlike the British cabinet member who can return to Parliament to combat the policy that triggered his exit, the American secretary of state contemplating resignation realizes that, like Bryan, he will no longer influence that policy from either inside or outside the government. To resign with a blast stirs debate; but most secretaries will regard that course as disloyal and unprofessional.

Yet resignations in protest are not un-American. "My duty will be to support . . . the President's Administration," John Quincy Adams wrote to his mother when appointed secretary of state. "If I can't, my duty is to withdraw from public service." Cyrus Vance decided "as a matter of principle"—after President Carter approved the Iranian hostage operation over his opposition—that he "could not honorably remain as secretary of state when I so strongly disagreed with a presidential decision that went against my judgment as to what was best for the country."

That sums up the valid grounds for resignation. Not fatigue or frustration, not a fit of pique or prima donna demands, not losing an internal debate or a seat on Air Force One, but the hypocrisy of publicly supporting a major presidential policy that the secretary cannot conscientiously implement. "You can't do the job well if you want it too much," Secretary Shultz wisely observed. "You have to be willing to say 'goodbye.'"

Despite being "deliberately deceived" in a "systematic way" by the White House about actions directly contrary to his assurances to other foreign ministers, despite presidential approval of policies he deemed "crazy" and "pathetic," Shultz never said goodbye. His resignation, he believed, would not have reversed the president's course on Iran but merely denied him Shultz's help on other issues.

Although others who have resigned in protest may have drawn a different line, presidents rarely do reverse course as the result of a cabinet resignation.

Indeed, the threat of resignation may be more effective than the act, assuming the threat is both infrequent and believed. But presidents grow weary of those constantly threatening to submit their resignation and—as Secretary Haig discovered—may ultimately "accept" it whether or not submitted.

V

Note that Bryan and Vance did not resign because the State Department's "primacy" had been lost to House and Brzezinski (although Acheson, asked later what he would have done had a powerful national security adviser been installed, quickly replied: "I'd resign"). In fact, "primacy"—the focus of so many studies on State Department authority—can be a misleading term. Haig may have described his battle to become Reagan's foreign policy "vicar" as a "struggle for primacy between the president's close aides and myself"; but, in terms of actual decision-making, both reality and the Constitution permit only the president, not the secretary or the White House staff, to be "prime" in the executive branch.

Only the president has ultimate power. If he consistently upholds his secretary of state—as Truman and Eisenhower did—he will bestow a de facto primacy among his *advisers*. But controversial foreign policy initiatives will still face interminable bureaucratic infighting at the third and fourth levels of government unless they are known to have been decided personally by the president, whoever may have advised him. The NSC staff can monitor and coordinate the implementation of presidential decisions at those levels without usurping whatever advisory primacy the president may have bestowed upon the secretary of state. Thus Mr. Shultz erred in quarreling with the conclusion of the Tower Commission, appointed by President Reagan to determine whether structural changes were needed in the foreign-policy-making apparatus, that coordination by the NSC staff was necessarily at the heart of a decisionmaking process that needed no substantive revamping.

Decades of earlier studies by high-level commissions and commentators had similarly focused on structure and process. Some had even proposed new offices: a second vice president for foreign affairs, a super-cabinet secretary of foreign affairs above the secretary of state, a first secretary of the government. Other studies, in the best tradition of the Maginot Line mentality, reflected the perceived shortcomings of the previous administration's machinery. Indeed, the NSC system itself—which has aggravated State's sense of isolation for nearly 20 years—began as an organizational reform reflecting criticism of State's mistreatment under Franklin Roosevelt.

But formal, obligatory structures and procedures are neither the problem nor the solution. Alexander Haig may have blamed his difficulties largely on the White House's refusal to approve the organizational plan he presented to the president on Inauguration Day. But each president will consult whom he wishes to consult. Who gets to write the final options paper, and who gets to read it and when, can influence the president's choice; but he will often make that choice on the basis of unrecorded and uncontrollable conversations, including those with his spouse, personal secretary or barber. No table of organization can offset human chemistry, incompetence or excessive zeal. No theoretical model can effectively impose on a president a decision-making system unsuited to his needs, interests and experience.

Kennedy was not comfortable with Eisenhower's approach, and Kennedy's worked less well for Johnson. In the 1961 Berlin crisis Kennedy preferred not to convene the NSC, which included the director of the Office of Emergency Preparedness. In the 1962 Cuban missile crisis he convened only the dozen or so individuals whose judgment he valued, later formally titling the group the NSC "Executive Committee." Johnson, Carter and Reagan, contrary to today's recurrent proposal that still more individuals (from Congress or the Joint Chiefs of Staff, for example) be added to every NSC meeting, all devised smaller groups to make the real decisions. Even Truman looked not to the NSC he founded but to individuals—such as Marshall, Acheson, Lovett and Harriman—in making his decisions.

Thus, what matters most is not whether the foreign policy interagency groups or senior interagency groups are chaired by the national security adviser, as urged by the Tower Commission, or by a State or Defense Department representative, as urged by

Shultz. Nor is the test whether an advance assurance of unfiltered access is given by the president to his secretary of state (as it was to Vance) or denied him (as it was to Rogers). What matters is whose advice, written or unwritten, the president ultimately values the most on any given issue. No structure can predetermine that.

Nor can any statute, as the Tower Commission wisely concluded. The passage of new laws is not a remedy for the violation of existing laws, and legislative "reforms"—as those statutes seeking to curb the president's war powers and intelligence activities demonstrate—are not always effective. Congress could no doubt prohibit the national security adviser and his staff from engaging in covert and other operations, or limit the size of that staff. But any attempt to mandate how the NSC should function—in effect, instructing the president whom he must and must not hear—would be both unwise and unworkable. To hear is not to heed. To meet is not to decide. No president should be required to convene a formal body, whose views he does not seek, to reach a decision he prefers to reach elsewhere.

Another legislative proposal—subjecting the national security adviser to Senate confirmation and congressional testimony—would only make matters worse. Either the president would rely on some other foreign policy aide serving under a different title, or the national security adviser and secretary of state would have virtually indistinguishable roles. If his operational functions are returned to the departments where they belong, the national security adviser's principal function is to give the president confidential advice, for which he should not be—and under the Constitution cannot be—accountable to a separate branch of government.

One advocate of change has asserted that confirmation hearings for John Poindexter might have "smoked out" the qualities that led him into trouble. But what are the qualities that foretell trouble in this post, and what qualities guarantee success? In contrast with the highly visible Brzezinski, Admiral Poindexter was all but invisible, rarely speaking to the public or press. That did not help Shultz. Poindexter's predecessors under Reagan—Richard Allen, William Clark and Robert McFarlane—were not of the assertive Kissinger mold; but they still clashed with Shultz and

Haig (although, as Allen remarked, "Mother Teresa could have been national security adviser and . . . had conflict with Al Haig"). Unlike Nixon, Carter encouraged his national security adviser and secretary of state to argue out their differences in front of him. State still lost ground.

Over the years, some national security advisers have been academics, lawyers or businessmen, others have had a military background. Some have been strategic thinkers, some coordinators, others presidential confidants. In each case, the State Department's authority receded, usually because the president—not the national security adviser—so ordained, and usually without much resistance from the department.

VI

A foreign policy dominated by a strong national security adviser is not necessarily lacking in initiative and imagination, as Henry Kissinger demonstrated; and a foreign policy dominated by an unchallenged secretary of state is not necessarily one of strength and wisdom, as Secretaries Dulles and Charles Evans Hughes demonstrated. Nor is tension between two Washington officials, a familiar occurrence in a city founded on checks and balances, invariably unhelpful to a president who thrives on competition in creative thinking. Any candidate who promises total consistency in his future administration's foreign policy statements is unfamiliar with the real world of Washington.

But the "guerrilla warfare" of which Secretary Shultz spoke need not be the inevitable result of this creative tension. The next president, before he takes office, without shortchanging Defense and other departments outside the scope of this article, should reach an explicit understanding with each of his State Department and White House nominees on certain basic principles and practices.

First, the president should select a strong-minded secretary of state who shares his view of the world but possesses independent stature (not, however, presidential ambitions), and then make clear not merely to the secretary but to his cabinet, NSC staff, the departmental bureaucracies and the public that he genuinely wishes the secretary of state to be not his sole but his principal adviser, spokesman, negotiator and agent in foreign affairs—not his coordinator or decision-maker—until such time as he proves unable to fulfill the president's requirements in that role, at which time his resignation will be accepted. The president should make equally clear that he will respect the following prerogatives: the secretary's authority over all other State Department personnel, including noncareer ambassadors; the department's authority over the separate overseas information, development and arms control agencies; and each ambassador's authority over embassy staff members reporting to Defense, the CIA and other departments.

Second, the president should meet with the secretary, with only the national security adviser present, at least several times a week when they are both in Washington and confer by telephone when they are not. Each such discussion should be a candid and confidential exploration of each other's views (not merely a briefing by the secretary or instructions from the president) on issues large and small, on personalities foreign and domestic. No recommendation from the national security adviser or other presidential aide, and no White House activity in the foreign policy area, should be withheld from the secretary; no recommendation of the secretary should be unheard by the president; and no subsequent rejection of that advice on a major issue should occur without advance notice to the secretary. They need not be chums (Dean Rusk has remarked he thought it appropriate that he was the only cabinet member whom President Kennedy did not address by his first name); but between them loyalty, confidence and respect must flow both ways. Each must recognize the other's very different role and responsibilities.

Third, the secretary of state must fully exercise the responsibility thus given him, personally participate (like Acheson) in drafting the president's speeches, deliver the bad news along with the good, and inside the Oval Office question his chief's views, and the national security adviser's, whenever he feels they are wrong. But he must also accept the fact that the modern White House—not only the president—inevitably exercises some of the authority once lodged in his department. (Even Marshall and Acheson succeeded in part by making clear their deference to presidential power.) The secretary cannot accommodate every critic or shy away from every controversy, but he should avoid those battles on which he has not yet checked with the president or knows the president must overrule him (not, however, distancing himself, as Shultz did, from a matter on which he has been overruled). He must understand U.S. domestic politics and its impact on both the president and foreign affairs; take blame for all failures while letting the president take credit for all successes; exercise both diplomacy and salesmanship in representing the president with Congress and the press as well as with foreign leaders; make it a high priority to respond to White House requests for new options in both the time frame and the style preferred by the president; and maintain close and candid relations with his cabinet colleagues and particularly the national security adviser. Should he ever conclude that he cannot in good conscience help implement some major presidential decision, then he should not threaten his resignation, but irrevocably submit it.

Fourth, the secretary must truly lead and manage the department (few do), adopt the president's program and politics as his own, convey them to the department's professionals, win their cooperation and respect for those policies, and utilize their talents in senior policymaking posts without subjecting them to any ideological test, without regard to who served his predecessor, and without confining all major tasks to a small inner circle. But—again like Marshall and Acheson—he must not hesitate to prod and prune the Foreign Service, reduce its paperwork and procedural delays, and broaden its base.

Fifth, the president—spurning those who insist that he look for strength in either his secretary of state or his national security adviser but not both—should fill the latter post with a skilled and trusted deputy possessing a personal style and outlook compatible with both his own and the secretary's. In performing the advisory and coordinating functions summarized above, within the limitations prescribed by the president, drawing upon the useful model contained in the Tower Commission report, and mindful of the secretary's primary role as outlined above, the national security adviser should present his own views to the president without concealing them from the secretary, and convey the views of the secretary and others accurately, taking pains not to permit his own advocacy to diminish theirs, not to forfeit their trust and respect, and not to represent his own thinking as the president's without knowing his chief's express wishes. Coordination of process must not again become control of policy. On whatever issues the president wants the national security adviser to cover, he should review, but not duplicate, the cable flow and other work of the State Department as an adviser outside the line of command between the president and secretary. No important matter should be decided at his desk. The "buck" does not stop there.

Sixth, the national security adviser should maintain low visibility, if not the unrealistic standard of "a passion for anonymity": few speeches, still fewer on-the-record press conferences, and even fewer public missions abroad. His meetings with foreign officials should be reported to the secretary. The presidential instructions he relays to U.S. ambassadors should be cleared and transmitted through the secretary. His confidential foreign travels should be coordinated with the secretary. He should appreciate congressional and domestic politics and the talents of a Foreign Service that has, in McGeorge Bundy's words, an "almost instinctive desire to turn toward the sunlight of presidential leadership." His professional staff should be substantially smaller than the present one (Kennedy and Bundy successfully relied on only a dozen), and selected—without political clearance—from among both specialists outside the government and career ser-

vants within. Whether or not the president has a chief of staff or other senior policy adviser, the assistant for national security affairs should report directly to the president as often each day as necessary. He should keep the chief of staff and presidential press secretary informed, but also urge the president to keep the number of White House aides involved in foreign policy meetings and missions to a minimum.

Finally, the president himself must be in command of his own forces, attentive and decisive on international issues, permitting no policy vacuum or power struggle, melding diverse views into one voice, building an atmosphere of team loyalty that minimizes leaks and backbiting, stimulating the thinking of others without suppressing his own. He will not strengthen the Department of State by stifling its creativity. He will not win the confidence of Congress by transferring power to his own unaccountable staff. He must dismiss any White House aides overstepping their bounds. He must devise a suitable system for making decisions but, more importantly, he must make them.

None of these recommendations should be imposed by Congress or adopted wholesale by the president. He must personally tailor the cloth to fit his own frame. Indeed, all of the above boils down to the strength and judgment of our next president. Ultimately he will determine the quality of his principal foreign policy advisers and their advice. We—all of us—will determine the quality of that next president.

32

A New NSC for a New Administration

Ivo H. Daalder
I.M. Destler

In this policy brief, two veteran NSC watchers offer their views on how to avoid past NSC pitfalls. They identify eight "back to basics" features of an effective NSC, and argue that it is necessary to refocus the NSC on its most critical function: coordination of the policy process.

One of the most important choices any president-elect must make is how to organize and staff the National Security Council (NSC). Chief executives from John Fitzgerald Kennedy to William Jefferson Clinton have found their foreign policy held hostage to the management choices they made between election and inauguration.

Today's challenge is to refocus the organization on its primary, critical role. For as it has grown in size, the NSC has become more like an agency than a presidential staff. It is immersed in policy detail and focuses predominantly on the short term. It does not give sufficient attention to the critical task that it alone can perform: coordinating the policy process so that, simultaneously, agencies get a full and fair hearing and the president can make clear foreign policy choices in a timely manner.

The new president must ensure that this key function is restored. To do so, he must cut the NSC's size, simplify its structure, and enhance its seniority.

BACKGROUND

The NSC was established in 1947 to integrate U.S. foreign and defense policy. By law, the Council is the United States government's most exalted official committee, composed of just four members: the president, vice president, secretary of state, and secretary of defense. In practice, the NSC has become a presidential staff of foreign policy experts headed by the assistant to the president for national security affairs, who has been a key foreign policy player in every administration since John F. Kennedy's.

Over the years, the NSC has expanded from a small, presidential staff of about ten policy people in the early 1960s to what is today a fully ensconced, agency-like organization of 225 people, including about 100 substantive professionals. This organization has its own perspective on the myriad of national security issues confronting the government. It has become less like a staff and more like an operating agency. With its own press, legislative, communication, and speechmaking offices, the NSC today conducts ongoing relations with the media, Congress, the American public, and foreign governments.

There are compelling reasons why the NSC has evolved in this way. But this evolution has created serious problems. As the NSC has become more like an agency, it has become less flexible and less adaptable, and its procedures more rigid and bureaucratic. Moreover, with its immersion in policy detail, the predominant focus of its work has become short term, with the

Reprinted with permission from the Brookings Institution.

Ivo H. Daalder is a senior fellow at the Brookings Institution and a former NSC staff member under President Clinton. I.M. Destler is a professor at the School of Public Affairs at the University of Maryland.

immediate crowding out the important. Finally, with its bureaucratization there is an increasing risk that the NSC will ignore the few critical tasks for which it is uniquely suited, including:

- Managing the president's daily foreign policy activity, including his communication with foreign leaders and the preparation and conduct of his trips overseas:
- Coordinating the process by which policy on major foreign and national security issues is made by ensuring that those with strong stakes in the issue are involved in the process, and that all realistic policy options have been considered and fully analyzed—including options not favored by any agency—before they reach the president and his senior advisers for decision:
- Driving the policymaking process to make real choices, in a timely manner:
- Monitoring implementation of the decisions made by the president and his advisers.

The president-elect faces a critical decision on how to staff and organize his foreign policy team. Not all his predecessors chose wisely. Jimmy Carter mortgaged his future by choosing a national security adviser who was incompatible, in substantive views and operating style, with his secretary of state. Ronald Reagan first downgraded the NSC, then did nothing to end the conflict between the State Department, the Pentagon, and CIA, that he guaranteed by appointing bitter adversaries to head each of them.

As these examples suggest, the president needs to choose capable, compatible people to head the major foreign policy and national security departments and agencies. But their ability to function as a team ultimately depends on how he decides to staff and structure the NSC. The path of least resistance would be to replicate the current structure. But that would be a mistake. Before he makes any decision on the NSC, the president-elect needs to understand both why power has gravitated to the NSC and how this has imposed real costs on the foreign policies of his predecessors. It is against that backdrop that we offer our recommendations for a smaller, smarter, and more senior NSC staff—one that focuses first and foremost on effective management of the policy process. . . .

Avoiding Past Pitfalls

As the size and scope of the NSC continues to grow, there is an increasing risk that the staff and its operations will fall victim to one or more of the following pitfalls that have beset past administrations. Not all of these have characterized operations under Clinton. But any or all are likely to recur if present trends continue:

An Operational NSC

If a small NSC coterie conducts foreign policy operations on a particular issue in secret and without involvement of other agencies, they are immune from effective staff review. And public trust is undercut when cabinet officials, responsible for informing Congress, are "out of the loop." Iran-Contra demonstrated the extreme destructiveness of such an operational NSC system. And Henry Kissinger's penchant to use backchannels with Moscow and Beijing, while effective in the short run, undermined the president in the long run as those who had been excluded worked to reverse the "détente" policy Nixon and Kissinger had put into place vis-á-vis the Soviet Union.

Of course, not all operational activities are deleterious to the process. Sometimes, direct involvement of the national security adviser provides the best way to communicate presidential interest and commitment. But such activities should be exceptional rather than routine and conducted with the full knowledge of the other key players (especially the secretary of state). For example, when Anthony Lake and his staff engineered a fundamental shift in America's Bosnia policy in summer 1995—including travel to Europe to sell the policy to our NATO allies—he did so openly and with the full participation of all the president's senior advisers.

The NSC as a Government Agency

Once the NSC begins to act as a government agency—taking formal policy positions and conducting ongoing relations with the Congress, media, American public, and foreign governments—it loses its flexibility and its capacity to focus on the president's business. And as it competes with other agencies in these functions, it loses their trust in its ability to represent their views fairly to the president. Order breaks down, as all scramble for the president's ear. The NSC can do a few key things well—but its ability to do them depends on avoiding responsibilities best left to the departments. That means leaving many functions to others in the executive branch, and eschewing a formal White House/NSC view during the policy formulation stage (while still responding to the president's need for private advice).

The NSC as Daily Business Manager

An NSC encumbered by second-order foreign policy business will not be able to do its primary job. Anyone responding to congressional inquiries, acceding to requests for press comment, forging a public relations strategy to deal with the issue in the headlines, clearing the routine communications between Washington and overseas posts, and keeping up with current developments while staffing the president's short-term needs, will never get to what counts the most. Left behind will be the critical business—analyzing foreign trends, anticipating problems before they become too large, coordinating the activities of senior officials, developing options for dealing with important issues, creating strategies for garnering support at home and abroad, and overseeing policy implementation. For anyone enmeshed in the daily business of foreign affairs, the urgent will always crowd out the important.

The NSC as Consensus-Seeker

In all large organizations, there is a natural tendency to decide most issues through consensus among senior officials. Such a process can be efficient, and it certainly minimizes friction among the individuals and institutions involved. In both the Eisenhower and Clinton NSCs, this emphasis has pervaded decision-making on issues of presidential consequence. In the 1950s, consensus was the goal of a highly formalized process. Now, the search for consensus is driven by the president's desire to focus on domestic issues, and it is reinforced by the fear that any divisions within the administration can be politically exploited by the opposition.

But reaching agreement at the lowest possible level can carry a hefty price. It often leads to the lowest common denominator policy, lacking boldness or even clear direction. It can also delay final decisions while disagreements are resolved—enhancing the prospect for ad-hoc and reactive policymaking and needlessly limiting the options that could logically be considered if decisions were made at an earlier stage. Finally, a consensus process increases the likelihood that mistakes will go uncorrected—as the need for maintaining bureaucratic comity outweighs the requirement to reexamine policy.

The National Security Adviser as "outside leader"

The conduct of negotiations, exposition of administration policy, announcement of major policy initiatives, and public defense of policy positions are tasks best left to the president and his appointed heads of executive departments. Once the assistant for national security affairs takes on these public roles, he either displaces those, like the secretary of state, who are nominally responsible for outside leadership functions (as did Kissinger and, to a lesser extent, Sandy Berger), or feeds unhealthy competition among top officials (as was the case between Brzezinski and Vance). Of course, the growing politicization of foreign policy and the almost insatiable media demand for official commentary can at times require the public involvement of the adviser or even some on his staff. But such activity should be the exception, not the rule.

The National Security Adviser as "odd man out"

The president will be best served if his principal national security officials work well together as a team. The adviser needs to be a part of that team. He should not be the dominant player (like Kissinger), or a weak player (like Reagan's first four advisers, who could not enforce discipline in the policy process), or a player in competition with other team members (as Brzezinski was). Like Scowcroft under Bush and Lake and Berger under Clinton, the adviser can and must be a peer, balancing his role as honest broker with that of intimate presidential adviser. Any incumbent who abuses his advisory role (for example, by cutting out critical perspectives or convening meetings without key officials being present) undermines his ability to manage the policy process effectively.

BACK TO BASICS: EIGHT FEATURES OF AN EFFECTIVE MSC

As a staff that is located in the White House and reports directly to the president, the National Security Council is uniquely situated to undertake the essential tasks—enumerated earlier in this brief—for managing an effective policymaking process.

To do this, the NSC staff must be both aggressive and fair, driving the policy process forward yet representing other agencies' views fully. The national security adviser must be simultaneously strong and collegial, able to enforce discipline across the government, yet engage senior officials and their agencies rather than exclude them.

The NSC must interact comfortably with its counterpart White House policy staffs: the National Economic Council on international trade and finance, for example, and the Domestic Policy Council on issues where jurisdictions overlap. It must accept boundaries to its jurisdiction as well as joint staffing arrangements for gray areas. To serve these goals and avoid repeating prior mistakes, we need an NSC with eight distinct attributes:

Strong

The national security adviser and key aides must be tough enough to coordinate policy, pull agencies and officials together, ensure presidential decisions are implemented, and give the president substantive advice. To this end, NSC officials should generally chair interagency groups—including the principals committee of cabinet secretaries, the deputies committee, and the interagency working groups that bring together assistant secretaries. No policy proposals within its sphere should go to the president without the NSC's knowledge.

Straight

The adviser must operate "on top of the table," meaning he can be trusted by senior colleagues to fairly represent their views. NSC communications and its (rare) operational involvement must be undertaken with the knowledge of other principals. The model is Scowcroft's trip to China in 1989—which, though secret, included a senior official from the State Department—not Kissinger's in 1971, which was conducted without the secretary of state's knowledge.

Sharing

The NSC must establish a modus operandi of inclusion, building strong informal relationships with counterparts from the departments and agencies to get the work done, assuring a seat at the table for all with a substantial stake in an issue. The national security adviser and the secretaries of state and defense should be chosen with an eye to their working as a team (as was the case during the Bush and Clinton administrations).

Subdued

The NSC must be self-consciously constrained. The adviser and staff must keep a low profile, limit press contacts, eschew operations, and work principally within the executive branch. Policy implementation should fall to the departments or, if a presidential connection is judged particularly important, be coordinated and led by presidential issue managers operating outside the NSC.

Senior

The bulk of the staff should be men and women tested by prior government experience, knowledgeable in their issues, and able to work well with senior and upper-middle level officials: under secretaries, assistant secretaries, and their deputies. The staff should be leavened with a few young thinker-operators, but senior staff should set the tone. To ensure staff continuity throughout an administration, sufficient budgetary resources must be made available to pay staff and travel with White House rather than agency funds.

Small

The staff must be limited in size to about 40–45 substantive professionals, less than half the current number. Many routine activities, such as congressional correspondence, should be assigned to the State Department or other relevant agencies. Key support functions—including communication, legislative affairs, press, and speechwriting—should return to the White

House proper or to the departments. The NSC should not have a public or legislative voice that is distinct from the White House or other parts of the executive branch.

Slim

The number of subdivisions or directorates within the NSC should be limited: no more than five regional offices and five functional ones, as proposed in detail below. Each directorate should normally have a maximum of four substantive officials. Any subunits that grow larger and more operational (e.g., the current directorate dealing with transnational threats) should be moved outside the NSC—elsewhere in the Executive Office of the President if necessary, to a department or agency if possible.

Self-disciplined

The national security adviser and staff must exercise an uncommon degree of professional restraint—by resisting the natural temptation to take on new tasks, to broaden the focus of their work, and, as a result, to grow in size. Such growth is the default position for any NSC—especially when, as time passes, the initial focus on formulating new policies gives way to ensuring that presidential decisions are implemented in the way originally envisaged. The adviser must be aware that growth of staff and broadening of scope is what will assuredly happen unless she/he is determined to prevent it.

AN NSC FOR THE NEW ADMINISTRATION

With these eight characteristics as a guide, what should the NSC look like in the new administration? In our view, the next president will be best served by a NSC structure and staff that is akin to the late Reagan, Bush, and early Clinton administrations, with a new emphasis on functional competence. The basic structure should consist of a national security adviser, supported by two deputies, and ten directorates: five regional and five functional. The overall size of the NSC should be no larger than 40–45 substantive professionals. The intent is to create an NSC that is small in size, senior and expert in competence, and adaptable to the multitude of requirements that will be placed upon it.

We propose making one major change to past practice: adding a second deputy with powers equal to those of the first. This second person, an economic specialist, would be dual-hatted: reporting both to the national security adviser and the head of the National Economic Council. She/he would have overall responsibility for international economic affairs and serve as the government's sherpa to the G-8 economic summits. This person would also oversee the NSC's multilateral portfolio as well as the transnational and economic issues that flow through the regional directorates, chairing all deputies' committee meetings dealing with these issues. The other deputy would retain primary responsibility for security issues—including nonproliferation, defense, and transnational threats—as well as for traditional bilateral and regional relations.

Moving to the overall staff structure, the five regional directorates would remain similar to the past, except that Russia and all other European states would be handled by a single European Affairs unit. Although the division of labor within directorates is bound to evolve over time, the European Affairs directorate might have, under the senior director, three directors responsible for Russia, EU/NATO, and the rest of Europe respectively. Directors in Asian Affairs might deal with China, Japan/Korea, and Southeast Asia, while those in Near East/South Asian Affairs might divide their responsibilities between the Persian Gulf, Arab–Israeli issues, and South Asia.

More of the NSC staff, however, should work in the five functional directorates, in view of the growing importance of these issues. The nonproliferation and defense directorates could be combined, with much of this new unit's future work focusing on nonproliferation (of which arms control should be an integral part) rather than on defense—an area where the NSC's impact has been marginal. Directors should focus their work on weapons of mass destruction, missiles and advanced conventional weapons proliferation, export controls, and broad defense policy. A multilateral affairs directorate would address such issues as U.S. relations with the United Nations, humanitarian and refugee policy, democracy and human rights, and environmental and health policy, thus combining responsibilities that are currently spread over a number of different directorates. A much smaller transnational

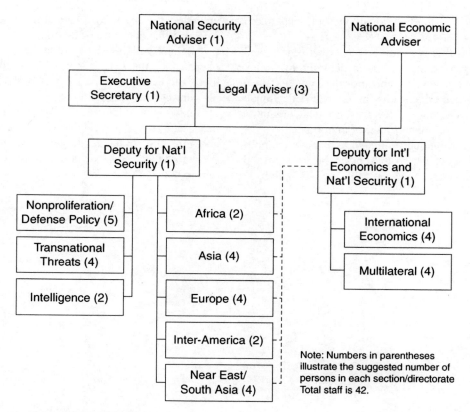

Figure 32.1 Proposed National Security Council

threats directorate should be responsible for coordinating policy on drugs and international crime, counterterrorism, and cyber security. The International Economic Affairs staff should remain dual-hatted with the National Economic Council, as is presently the case, and report directly to the similarly dual-hatted deputy for national security and international economic affairs. Finally, a small Intelligence Programs directorate remains necessary to coordinate activities in this realm, especially to ensure presidential control over any covert activities.

Any operational responsibilities on substantive issues should be assigned to departments or other agencies. And as emphasized above, support and liaison staffs—for press, communications, congressional relations, etc.—should return to the White House

proper, where a deputy in each of these offices should coordinate work on international issues.

We advance these specific prescriptions for NSC staffing and structuring not with an eye to their adoption, in their entirety, by the next administration, but to suggest how the NSC can cover a broad range of issues yet be small enough to retain flexibility and responsiveness. The primary focus of the NSC, of its staff and its work, should be the policy issues and choices that are (or should be) the president's business—nothing less, but also nothing more.

The NSC has survived peaks (Nixon's first term) and valleys (Reagan's first year) of influence. It has survived blatant misuse of power. It has survived presidential neglect. It has survived abuse of the national security adviser role. It has survived mismanagement at the top. It is a good bet to survive to its hundredth anniversary in 2047.

But survival is not the same as effectiveness, and effective organization matters in determining policy outcomes. While good organization does not guarantee good policy, bad organization makes bad policy much more likely. Getting top-level government organization right is therefore enormously important.

The NSC is uniquely situated to manage the policymaking process in ways that ensure the president and his senior advisers know the full range of options—including the advantages and drawbacks of each—when making decisions. If left to the departments, policy options will invariably reflect their bureaucratic interests, or the least common denominator among them. But unless properly structured, the NSC will not play this crucial role.

Only the president has the power to make this happen. That is why the decisions the new president makes about the NSC in the next few weeks will do much to determine the success or failure of his foreign policy during the next four years.

33

ROAD MAP FOR NATIONAL SECURITY
Imperative for Change

Hart–Rudman Report

Envisioned as the most sweeping review of U.S. national security requirements and organization since the enactment of the 1947 National Security Act, a commission co-chaired by former U.S. senators Gary Hart and Warren Rudman warned of grave new threats facing the nation, including international terrorism and the proliferation of weapons of mass destruction. As part of its "institutional redesign" of the U.S. government the commission made several recommendations on the proper role of the NSC to address these new threats.

III. INSTITUTIONAL REDESIGN

Beyond the pressing matter of organizing homeland security, and of recapitalizing core U.S. domestic strengths in science and education, this Commission recommends significant organizational redesign for the Executive Branch. This redesign has been conceived with one overriding purpose in mind: to permit the U.S. government to *integrate* more effectively the many diverse strands of policy that underpin U.S. national security in a new era—not only the traditional agenda of defense, diplomacy, and intelligence, but also economics, counter-terrorism, combating organized crime, protecting the environment, fighting pandemic diseases, and promoting human rights worldwide.

The key component of any Executive Branch organizational design is the President. As one of only two elected members of the Executive Branch, the President is responsible for ensuring that U.S. strategies are designed to seize opportunities and not just to respond to crises. He must find ways to obtain significantly more resources for foreign affairs, and in particular those resources needed for anticipating threats and preventing the emergence of dangers. Without a major increase in resources, the United States will not be able to conduct its national security policies effectively in the 21st century.

To that end, the nation must redesign not just individual departments and agencies but its national security apparatus as a whole. Serious deficiencies exist that cannot be solved by a piecemeal approach.

• Most critically, no overarching strategic framework guides U.S. national security policymaking or resource allocation. Budgets are still prepared and appropriated as they were during the Cold War.

• The power to determine national security policy has migrated toward the National Security Council (NSC) staff. The staff now assumes policymaking and operational roles, with the result that its ability to act as an honest broker and policy coordinator has suffered.

• Difficulties persist in ensuring that international political and security perspectives are considered in the making of global economic policy, and that economic goals are given proper attention in national security policymaking.

The U.S. Commission on National Security/21st Century was established by the Defense Department in 1999 and cochaired by former U.S. senators Gary Hart (D–Colo.) and Warren Rudman (R–N.H.). It released its final report, "Road Map for National Security: Imperative for Change" on March 15, 2001.

Gary Hart is an attorney and author on public and international affairs living in Colorado. Warren B. Rudman, cofounder of the Concord Coalition, practices law in Washington, D.C.

• The Department of State is a crippled institution that is starved for resources by Congress because of its inadequacies and is thereby weakened further. The department suffers in particular from an ineffective organizational structure in which regional and functional goals compete, and in which sound management, accountability, and leadership are lacking.

• America's overseas presence has not been adjusted to the new economic, social, political, and security realities of the 21st century. The broad statutory authority of U.S. Ambassadors is undermined in practice by their lack of control over resources and personnel.

• The Department of Defense has serious organizational deficiencies. The growth in staff and staff activities creates confusion and delay. The failure to outsource or privatize many defense support activities wastes huge sums of money. The programming and budgeting process is not guided by effective strategic planning. The weapons acquisition process is so hobbled by excessive laws, regulations, and oversight strictures that it can neither recognize nor seize opportunities for major innovation, and it stifles a defense industry already in financial crisis. Finally, the force structure development process is not currently aligned with the needs of today's global security environment.

• National security policymaking does not manage space policy in a serious and integrated way.

• The U.S. intelligence community is adjusting only slowly to the changed circumstances of the post-Cold War era. While the economic and political components of statecraft have assumed greater prominence, military imperatives still largely drive the collection and analysis of intelligence.

We offer recommendations in several areas: strategic planning and budgeting; the National Security Council; the Department of State; the Department of Defense; space policy; and the intelligence community. We take these areas in turn.

A. Strategic Planning and Budgeting

Strategic planning is largely absent within the U.S. government. The planning that does occur is *ad hoc* and specific to Executive departments and agencies. No overarching strategic framework guides U.S. national security policy or the allocation of resources.

Each national security department and agency currently prepares its own budget. No effort is made to define an overall national security budget or to show how the allocation of resources in the individual budgets serves the nation's overall national security goals. The Office of Management and Budget (OMB) does on occasion consider tradeoffs in the allocation of resources among the various national security departments and agencies, but this is not done systematically. Nor are department budgets presented in a way that Congress can make these tradeoffs as it fulfills its responsibilities in the budgeting process.

There is an increasing awareness of this deficiency throughout the national security community but, so far, only very preliminary steps have been taken to produce crosscutting budgets. These preliminary steps have been limited to special transnational issues such as counter-terrorism. At present, therefore, neither the Congress nor the American people can assess the relative value of various national security programs over the full range of Executive Branch activities in this area.

To remedy these problems, the Commission's initial recommendation is that strategy should once again drive the design and implementation of U.S. national security policies:

14 The President should personally guide a top-down strategic planning process and delegate authority to the National Security Advisor to coordinate that process.

Such a top-down process is critical to designing a coherent and effective U.S. national security policy. In carrying out his strategic planning responsibilities on the President's behalf, the National Security Advisor must enlist the active participation of the members and advisors of the National Security Council. This group should translate the President's overall vision into a set of strategic goals and priorities, and then provide specific guidance on the most important national security policies. Their product would become the basis for the writing of the annual, legislatively mandated U.S. National Security Strategy.

Carrying out this guidance would rest with the senior-level deputies in the departments and agencies, facilitated by the NSC staff. They would be specifically responsible for designing preventive strategies, overseeing how the departments carry forward the President's strategic goals, and reviewing contingency planning for critical military and humanitarian operations.

The Commission believes that overall strategic goals and priorities should also guide the allocation of national security resources, and therefore recommends the following:

15 The President should prepare and present to the Congress an overall national security budget to serve the critical goals that emerge from the NSC strategic planning process. Separately, the President should continue to submit budgets for the individual national security departments and agencies for Congressional review and appropriation.

The OMB, with the support of the NSC staff, should undertake the task of formulating this national security budget. Initially, it should focus on a few of the nation's most critical strategic goals, involving only some programs in the departmental budgets. Over time, however, it could evolve into a more comprehensive document. Homeland security, counter-terrorism, nonproliferation, nuclear threat reduction, and science and technology should be included in the initial national security budget. This process should also serve as a basis for defining the funds to be allocated for preventive strategies.

Such goal-oriented budgets would help both the administration and Congress identify the total level of government effort as well as its composition. Gaps and duplication could be more readily identified. Such budgets would also enable the Congress to prioritize the most critical national security goals when they appropriate funds to departments and agencies.

To modernize the nation's strategic planning and budgeting process, greater coordination and connectivity is required among all executive departments and agencies. For this purpose, *the President should call for the creation of a national security affairs network analogous to the Secret Internet Protocol Router Network (SIPRNET) of the Department of Defense.*

The President would be able to implement these recommendations on his own authority as they involve White House staff activities. As far as the budgetary implications go, this reform would not cost money but, by rationalizing the strategy and budgeting process, go far toward assuring that money is spent more efficiently and wisely.

B. The National Security Council

In exercising his Constitutional power, the President's personal style and managerial preferences will be critical in how he relates to his Cabinet secretaries and in how he structures his White House staff. But the organization and the characteristics of the national security apparatus will importantly affect the policies that emerge.

The National Security Council was created as part of the 1947 National Security Act to advise the President on the integration of domestic, foreign, and military policies, and to help coordinate the activities of the national security departments and agencies. Its statutory members currently include the Vice President, the Secretary of State, and the Secretary of Defense. The Director of Central Intelligence and the Chairman of the Joint Chiefs of Staff are statutory advisers. The NSC staff authorized by the 1947 Act has evolved over time into a major instrument of Presidential governance, wielded by the Assistant to the President for National Security Affairs (the National Security Advisor or NSC Advisor), *not specified in any statute,* who has become increasingly powerful.

Obviously, this evolution has been affected by the degree of Presidential involvement in foreign and national security policy as well as by their various personalities and leadership styles. Over the past decade, Presidents have increasingly centralized power with the NSC staff for the making and execution of national security policy. In many ways, the NSC staff has become more like a government agency than a Presidential staff. It has its own views and perspectives on the myriad of national security issues confronting the government. It has its own press, legislative, communication, and speechmaking "shops" to enable it to conduct ongoing relations with the media, Congress, the American public, and foreign governments. Aside from staffing the President, the NSC staff's primary focus has become the day-to-day management of the nation's foreign and national security policy.

Why has this centralization of power occurred? First, with the end of the Cold War, national security issues now involve even more policy dimensions—financial and trade issues, environmental issues, international legal issues, for example—and each dimension has proponents within the Executive Branch. It has become harder, therefore, to assign any one department as the leading actor for a given policy area. The traditional dividing lines between foreign and domestic policy have also blurred further. Of all the players, only the NSC staff, in the name of the President, is in a position to coordinate these disparate interests effectively.

Second, foreign policy is also now very politicized. Few, if any, issues are easily separated from domestic political debate: not military intervention, not diplomatic relations, and certainly not trade and economic interactions with the outside world. Political oversight of these policies naturally falls to the White House, with the NSC staff acting as its foreign policy arm.

Finally and most importantly, the State Department over the past few decades has been seriously weakened and its resources significantly reduced. Foreign aid programs, as well as representational responsibilities, are now dispersed throughout the government. It therefore has fallen to the NSC staff to manage the conduct of America's foreign policy that was once the prerogative of the Department of State.

This description of the origin of the problem clearly illustrates a key principle in any attempt to set it aright; namely, that the redirection of the NSC Advisor and staff cannot be expected to succeed in the longer run unless the Department of State is also set aright.

The Commission views with alarm the expansion of the role of the NSC staff and recommends the following:

16 The National Security Council (NSC) should be responsible for advising the President and for coordinating the multiplicity of national security activities, broadly defined to include economic and domestic law enforcement activities as well as the traditional national security agenda. The NSC Advisor and staff should resist the temptation to assume a central policymaking and operational role.

The National Security Advisor and NSC staff should give priority to their traditional and unique roles, namely coordinating the policymaking process, so that all those with stakes are involved, and all realistic policy options are considered and analyzed.[1] The NSC Advisor and staff should provide advice privately to the President and oversee the implementation of Presidential decisions. They should also assume those roles that are unique to the President's staff, such as preparations for overseas trips and communications with foreign leaders.

At the same time, the NSC advisor and staff should resist pressures toward the centralization of power, avoid duplicating the responsibilities of the departments, and forego operational control of any aspect of U.S. policy. *Assuming a central policymaking role seriously detracts from the NSC staff's primary roles of honest broker and policy coordinator.*

The National Security Advisor should also keep a low public profile. Legislative, press, communications, and speech writing functions should reside in the White House staff. These functions should not be duplicated separately in the NSC staff as they are today.

The President, not his personal staff or advisors, is publicly accountable to the American people. To the degree that the role of the National Security Advisor continues to be one of public spokesman, policymaker, and operator, the Commission wishes the President to understand that pressure is growing in the Congress for making the National Security Advisor accountable to the American people through Senate confirmation and through formal and public appearances before Congressional committees. Returning to a lower-profile National Security Advisor will be difficult, but such an approach will produce the best policy results and deflate this pressure.

Every President in the last thirty years has devised some organizational approach to integrating international economic policies with both domestic economic policies and national security considerations. Many methods have been tried. Most recently, in 1993 the Clinton Administration created the National Economic Council (NEC) as a parallel coordinating institution to the NSC.

The NEC experiment has been a disappointment. The Treasury Department dominates global financial policy, and its decisions have often neglected broader national security considerations—most critically, for example, in the early stages of the recent Asian economic crisis. Meanwhile, the United States Trade Representative (USTR)—and not the NEC—retains responsibility for coordinating trade policies and negotiations. The small NEC staff, as well, finds itself bureaucratically weaker than the NSC staff and (even when the staffers are dual-hatted) the NSC perspective has predominated.

The policy process should ensure that the coordination of national security activities reflects the new centrality of economics. This Commission therefore offers the following two recommendations:

17 The President should propose to the Congress that the Secretary of the Treasury be made a statutory member of the National Security Council.

Consistent with our strong preference for Cabinet government, this Commission believes the Secretary of the Treasury should be the President's right arm for international economic policy. But the Treasury's actions should be coordinated within the National Security Council process. In the NSC system of supporting sub-committees, Treasury should chair an interagency working group that manages international economic and financial policies (including managing financial crises), but it is a Presidential interest that decisions be fully coordinated with other relevant national security agencies. We understand that Secretaries of the Treasury have been routinely invited to National Security Council meetings. But designation as a statutory member of the NSC would signify the importance of truly integrating economic policy into national security policy.

18 The President should abolish the National Economic Council, distributing its domestic economic policy responsibilities to the Domestic Policy Council and its international economic responsibilities to the National Security Council.

The NSC staff should assume the same coordinating role for international economic policy as for other national security policies. *To emphasize its importance, the Commission recommends the appointment of a Deputy National Security Advisor with responsibility for international economics.* We also believe that to integrate properly the economic component of statecraft in the NSC staff system, more experts in international economics need to be recruited and placed in offices throughout the NSC staff. To ensure the integration of domestic and international economic policies, the staffs of the Domestic Policy Council, the Council of Economic Advisers, and the NSC will need to work together very closely. . . .

NOTE

1. These recommendations parallel those of the Tower Commission. See *Report of the Tower Commission* (Washington, DC: February 1987), pp. 90–93.

FOR FURTHER READING

Acheson, Dean. *Present at the Creation: My Years at the State Department*. New York: Norton, 1969.

———. "The Eclipse of the State Department." *Foreign Affairs* 49 (July 1971): 593–607.

Albright, Madeleine K. *Madam Secretary: A Memoir*. New York: Miramax, 2003.

Andrianopoulos, Argyis G. *Kissinger and Brzezinski: the NSC and the Struggle for Control of U.S. National Security Policy*. London: Macmillan, 1991.

Baker, James A. III. *The Politics of Diplomacy: Revolution, War, and Peace, 1989–1992*. New York: G.P. Putnam's Sons, 1995.

Bamford, James. "Carlucci and the NSC," *New York Times Magazine*, January 18, 1987, pp. 16ff.

Barrett, David M. "The Mythology Surrounding Lyndon Johnson, His Advisers, and the 1965 Decision to Escalate the Vietnam War." *Political Science Quarterly* 103 (Winter 1988–1989): 637–663.

———. *Uncertain Warriors: Lyndon Johnson and His Vietnam Advisers*. Lawrence: University of Kansas Press, 1993.

Best, Richard A. *The National Security Council: An Organizational Assessment*. Huntington, NY: Novinka Books, 2001.

Bloomfield, Lincoln P. "Planning Foreign Policy: Can It Be Done?" *Political Science Quarterly* 93 (Autumn 1978): 369–391.

Bock, Joseph G. and Duncan L. Clarke. "The National Security Assistant and the White House Staff: National Security Policy Decisionmaking and Domestic Political Considerations, 1947–84." *Presidential Studies Quarterly* 16 (Spring 1986): 258–279.

Bohn, Michael K. *Nerve Center: Inside the White House Situation Room*. Washington, D.C.: Brassey's, Inc., 2003.

Brzezinski, Zbigniew. "Deciding Who Makes Foreign Policy," *New York Times Magazine*, September 18, 1983, 56ff.

———. *Power and Principle: Memoirs of the National Security Adviser, 1977–1981*. New York: Farrar, Straus and Giroux, 1983.

———. "NSC's Midlife Crisis." *Foreign Policy* 69 (Winter 1987–88): 80–99.

Bundy, William. "The National Security Process: *Plus Ça Change*." *International Security* 7 (Winter 1982–83): 94–109.

Burke, John P. *The Institutional Presidency: Organizing and Managing the White House from FDR to Clinton*, 2nd ed. Baltimore: Johns Hopkins University Press, 2000.

Bush, George and Brent Scowcroft. *A World Transformed*. New York: Alfred A Knopf, 1998.

Cambone, Stephen A. *A New Structure for National Security Policy Planning*. Washington D.C.: Center for Strategic and International Studies, 1998.

Carter, Jimmy. *Keeping Faith: Memoirs of a President*. New York: Bantam, 1982.

Center for International and Security Studies at Maryland and The Brookings Institution, *"The National Security Council Project."* College Park, MD: CISS, 2001.

Oral History Roundtables include:
The Nixon Administration National Security Council (December 8, 1998)
International Economic Policymaking and the National Security Council (February 11, 1999)
The Bush Administration National Security Council (April 29, 1999)
The Role of the National Security Adviser (October 25, 1999)
China Policy and the National Security Council (November 4, 1999)
Arms Control and the National Security Council (March 23, 2000)
The Clinton Administration National Security Council (September 27, 2000)

Christopher, Warren. *American Hostages in Iran: The Conduct of a Crisis*. New Haven, CT: Yale University Press, 1985.

Clark, Keith C., and Laurence J. Legere, eds. *The President and the Management of National Security*. New York: Praeger, 1969.

Cohen, William S., and George J. Mitchell. *Men of Zeal: A Candid Inside Story of the Iran-Contra Hearings*. New York: Penguin, 1988.

Cooper, Phillip J. *By Order of the President: The Use and Abuse of Executive Direct Action*. Lawrence: University of Kansas Press, 2002.

Crabb, Cecil V. and Kevin Mulcahy. "The National Security Council and the Shaping of U.S. Foreign Policy." *International Journal of Intelligence and Counterintelligence* 3 (Summer 1989): 153–168.

———. *American National Security: A Presidential Perspective*. Pacific Grove, CA: Brooks/Cole, 1991.

Culter, Robert. "The Development of the National Security Council." *Foreign Affairs* 34 (1956): 441–458.

Destler, I. M. *Presidents, Bureaucrats and Foreign Policy: The Politics of Organization*. Princeton, NJ: Princeton University Press, 1972.

———. "National Security Advice to U.S. Presidents: Some Lessons from Thirty Years." *World Politics* 29 (January 1977): 143–176.

———. "A Job That Doesn't Work." *Foreign Policy* 38 (Spring 1980): 80–88.

———. "The Rise of the National Security Assistant, 1961–1981." In *Perspectives on American Foreign Policy,* edited by Charles W. Kegley, Jr., and Eugene R. Wittkopf. New York: St. Martins, 1983, 260–281.

———. *The National Economic Council: A Work in Progress.* Washington D.C.: Institute for International Economics, November 1996.

Destler, I.M., Leslie H. Gelb, and Anthony Lake. *Our Own Worst Enemy: The Unmaking of American Foreign Policy.* New York: Simon and Schuster, 1984.

Deutch, John, Arnold Kanter, and Brent Scowcroft. "Strengthening the National Security Interagency Process." In *Keeping the Edge: Managing Defense for the Future,* edited by Ashton B. Carter and John P. White. Cambridge. MA: MIT Press, 2001.

Doerner, William R. "The Can-Do Agency." *Time* (December 8, 1986): 39.

Drew, Elizabeth. "A Reporter at Large: Brzezinski." *The New Yorker* (July 1, 1978): 90–112.

Eisenhower, Dwight D. *The White House Years: Mandate for Change, 1953–1956.* Garden City, NY: Doubleday, 1963.

———. *The White House Years: Waging Peace, 1956–1961.* Garden City, NY: Doubleday, 1963.

Ford, Gerald. *A Time to Heal.* New York: Harper & Row, 1979.

Franck, Thomas, "The Constitutional and Legal Position of the National Security Adviser and Deputy Adviser." *American Journal of International Law* 74 (July 1980): 634–639.

Franke, Volker C., ed. *Security in a Changing World: Case Studies in U.S. National Security Management.* Westport, CT: Praeger, 2002.

Fursenko, Aleksandr and Timothy Naftali. *One Hell of a Gamble: Khrushchev, Castro, and Kennedy, 1958–1964.* New York: W.W. Norton and Co., 1997.

Gaddis, John Lewis. *We Now Know: Rethinking Cold War History.* New York: Oxford University Press, 1997.

Gelb, Leslie H. "Why Not the State Department?" *The Washington Quarterly* (Autumn 1980): 25–40.

———. "2 Laws Concerning the National Security Adviser," *New York Times* (January 7, 1982), A20.

George, Alexander L. "The Case for Multiple Advocacy in Making Foreign Policy." *American Political Science Review* 66 (September 1972): 751–795.

———. *Presidential Decisionmaking in Foreign Policy: The Effective Use of Information and Advice.* Boulder, CO: Westview Press, 1990.

Geyelin, Philip. "The Workings of the National Security System: Past, Present, and Future." An interview with Clark M. Clifford in *SAIS Review* (Winter–Spring 1988): 19–28.

Greenstein, Fred I. and John P. Burke. "The Dynamics of Presidential Reality Testing: Evidence from Two Vietnam Decisions." *Political Science Quarterly* 104 (Winter 1989–1990): 557–580.

Haig, Alexander M. "Talking Paper" (January 6, 1981), reprinted in "The Document that Sewed the Seed of Haig's Demise," *Washington Post,* July 11, 1982: C1, C5.

———. *Caveat: Realism, Reagan, and Foreign Policy.* New York: Macmillan, 1984.

Halberstam, David. *The Best and the Brightest.* New York: Random House, 1972.

Hall, David K. *The 'Custodian-Manager' of the Policy-Making Process.* Report prepared for the Commission on the Organization of the Government for the Conduct of Foreign Policy Murphy Commission, Vol. 2 (June 1975): 100–122.

Hammond, Paul Y. "The National Security Council as a Device for Interdepartmental Coordination: An Interpretation and Appraisal." *American Political Science Review* 54 (1960): 899–910.

Haney, Patrick Jude. *Organizing for Foreign Policy Crises: Presidents, Advisers, and the Management of Decision Making.* Ann Arbor: University of Michigan Press, 1997.

Harris, John F. "Berger's Caution Has Shaped Role of U.S. in War," *Washington Post,* May 16, 1999, A1.

Heilbrunn, Jacob. "Condoleezza Rice: George W.'s Realist." *World Policy Journal* 16 (1999–2000): 49–54.

Hunter, Robert E. "Presidential Control of Foreign Policy: Management or Mishap?" *The Washington Papers, No. 91.* New York: Praeger, 1982.

Inouye–Hamilton Report (Report of the Congressional Committees Investigating the Iran-contra Affair), S. Rept. No. 100–216 and H. Rept. No. 100–433, U.S. Congress Washington, D.C.: U.S. Government Printing Office, November 1987.

Jackson, Henry M., ed. *The National Security Council: Jackson Subcommittee Papers on Policy-Making at the Presidential Level.* New York: Praeger, 1965.

Janis, Irving L. *Groupthink.* Boston: Houghton Mifflin, 1972.

Johnson, Loch K. *America's Secret Power: The CIA in a Democratic Society.* New York: Oxford University Press, 1989.

Johnson, Lyndon Baines. *The Vantage Point: Perspectives on the Presidency, 1963–1969.* New York: Holt, Rinehart, & Winston, 1971.

Johnson, Robert H. "The National Security Council: The Relevance of Its Past to Its Future." *Orbis* 13 (Fall 1969): 709–735.

Jordon, Amos A., and William J. Taylor, Jr. *American National Security: Policy and Process.* Baltimore, MD: Johns Hopkins University Press, 1984.

Keller, Bill. "The World According to Powell," *New York Times Magazine,* November 25, 2001, 61ff.

Kirschten, Dirk. "Competent Manager (Carlucci)." *National Journal* 19 (February 28, 1987): 468–479.

Kissinger, Henry A. *White House Years.* Boston: Little, Brown, 1979.

———. *Years of Upheaval.* Boston: Little, Brown, 1982.

Kolodziej, Edward A. "The National Security Council: Innovations and Implications." *Public Administration Review* 29 (November/December 1969): 573–585.

Lake, Anthony. *Six Nightmares: Real Threats in a Dangerous World and How America Can Meet Them.* Boston: Little, Brown, 2000.

Lay, James S., Jr. "National Security Council's Role in the U.S. Security and Peace Program." *World Affairs* 115 (Summer 1952): 37–39.

Lemann, Nicholas. "Without a Doubt" [a profile of Condoleezza Rice]. *New Yorker* (October 14 and 21, 2002): 164–179.

Lippman, Thomas W. *Madeleine Albright and the New American Diplomacy.* Boulder, CO: Westview Press, 2000.

Lord, Carnes. *The Presidency and the Management of National Security.* New York: Free Press, 1988.

———. "NSC Reform for the Post-Cold War Era." *Orbis* 44 (Summer 2000): 433–450.

May, Ernest R. and Philip D. Zelikow. *The Kennedy Tapes: Inside the White House During the Cuban Missile Crisis.* Cambridge, MA: Harvard University Press, 1997.

McLellan, David. *Cyrus Vance.* Totowa, NJ: Rowman & Allanheld, 1985.

McNamara, Robert S., with Brian VanDeMark. *In Retrospect: The Tragedy and Lessons of Vietnam.* New York: Random House, 1995.

Menges, Constantine Christopher. *Inside the National Security Council: The True Story of the Making and Unmaking of Reagan's Foreign Policy.* New York: Simon and Schuster, 1988.

Milbank, Dana and Mike Allen. "Iraq Flap Shakes Rice's Image." *The Washington Post* (July 27, 2003): A1.

Mulcahy, Kevin V. "The Secretary of State and the National Security Adviser: Foreign Policy Making in the Carter and Reagan Administrations." *Presidential Studies Quarterly* 16 (Spring 1986): 280–299.

———. "Re-thinking Groupthink: Walt Rostow and the National Security Advisory Process in the Johnson Administration." *Presidential Studies Quarterly* 25 (Spring 1995): 237–250.

Murphy Commission (Commission on the Organization of the Government for the Conduct of Foreign Policy). *Report.* Washington, D.C.: U.S. Government Printing Office, 1975.

Nixon, Richard M. *RN: The Memoirs of Richard Nixon.* New York: Grosset & Dunlop, 1978.

Odeen, Philip A. "The Role of the National Security Council in Coordinating and Integrating U.S. Defense and Foreign Policy." In *Public Policy and Political Institutions,* Vol. 5, edited by Duncan L. Clarke. Greenwich, CT: JAI, 1985, 19–41.

Painton, Priscilla. "Brent Scowcroft: Mr. Behind-the-Scenes." *Time* 138 (October 7, 1991): 24–26.

Patterson, Bradley H., Jr. *The White House Staff: Inside the West Wing and Beyond.* Washington, D.C.: Brookings Institution Press, 2000.

Perlez, Jane. "With Berger in the Catbird Seat, Albright's Star Dims." *New York Times,* December 14, 1999, A14.

———. "Rice on Front Line in Foreign Policy Role." *New York Times,* August 19, 2001, A1.

Powell, Colin, with Joseph E. Persico. *My American Journey: An Autobiography.* New York: Random House, 1995.

Prados, John. *Keepers of the Keys: A History of the National Security Council from Truman to Bush.* New York: Morrow, 1991.

Rice, Condoleezza. "National Security Challenges for the New Administration." In *Peaceworks.* Washington D.C.: U.S. Institute of Peace, January 17, 2001: 57–62.

Ripley, Randall B. and James M. Lindsay, eds. *U.S. Foreign Policy After the Cold War.* Pittsburgh, PA: University of Pittsburgh Press, 1997.

Roberts, Chalmers M. "The Day We Didn't Go to War." *The Reporter* 11 (September 14, 1954): 31–35.

Rostow, Walt W. *The Diffusion of Power.* New York: Macmillan, 1972.

Russakoff, Dale. "Lessons of Might and Right" [a profile of Condoleezza Rice], *Washington Post Magazine,* September 9, 2001, W23 ff.

"Samuel R. (Sandy) Berger." *National Journal* (June 14, 1997): 1175–76.

Sander, Alfred D. "Truman and the National Security Council: 1945–1947." *Journal of American History* 59 (September 1972): 369–388.

Sarkesian, Sam Charles. *U.S. National Security: Policymakers, Processes, and Politics.* Boulder, CO: Lynne Rienner, 2002.

Schlesinger, Arthur Jr. "Effective National Security Advising: A Most Dubious Precedent." *Political Science Quarterly* 115 (Fall 2000): 347–351.

Schneider, Keith. "Poindexter at the Security Council: A Quick Rise and a Troubled Reign." *New York Times,* (January 12, 1987), A6.

Sciolino, Elaine. "Compulsion to Achieve—Condoleezza Rice." *New York Times,* December 18, 2000, A1.

Scowcroft, Brent and George H.W. Bush. *A World Transformed.* New York: Knopf, 1998.

Shoemaker, Christopher C. *The NSC Staff: Counseling the Council.* Boulder, CO: Westview Press, 1991.

Shultz, George P. *Turmoil and Triumph: My Years as Secretary of State.* New York: Simon & Schuster, 1993.

Smith. Hedrick. *The Power Game: How Washington Works.* New York: Random House, 1988.

Sorensen, Theodore C. *Kennedy.* New York: Harper & Row, 1965.

Souers, Sidney W. "Policy Formulation for National Security." *American Political Science Review* 43 (June 1949): 534–543.

Strong, Robert A. *Decisions and Dilemmas: Case Studies in Presidential Foreign Policy Making.* Englewood Cliffs, N.J.: Prentice Hall, 1998.

Szanton, Peter. "Two Jobs, Not One." *Foreign Policy* 38 (Spring 1980): 89–91.

Tower Commission (President's Special Review Board). *Tower Commission Report.* New York: Bantam/Time, 1987.

Truman, Harry S. *Memoirs: Years of Trial and Hope.* Garden City, NY: Doubleday, 1956.

U.S. Department of State. *History of the National Security Council 1947–1997.* Office of the Historian, Bureau of Public Affairs. Washington, D.C.: U.S. Government Printing Office, 1997.

U.S. Congress, Senate Committee on Foreign Relations. *Hearings on the National Security Adviser: Role and Accountability.* April 17, 1980, 96th Cong., 2nd Sess.

Vance, Cyrus. *Hard Choices: Critical Years in America's Foreign Policy.* New York: Simon & Schuster, 1983.

Wise, David. "Scholars of the Nuclear Age." In *The Kennedy Circle,* edited by Lester Tangler. Washington, D.C.: Robert B. Luce, 1961, 29–57.

Woodward, Bob. *Bush At War.* New York: Simon & Schuster, 2002.

INDEX

CPSIA information can be obtained at www.ICGtesting.com
Printed in the USA
BVOW04s0614050515

398979BV00004B/10/P